Gary Cornell

# The Visual Basic 3 for
# Windows Handbook

**Osborne McGraw-Hill**

Berkeley  New York  St. Louis  San Francisco  Auckland  Bogotá  Hamburg  London  Madrid  Mexico City
Milan  Montreal  New Delhi  Panama City  Paris  São Paulo  Singapore  Sydney  Tokyo  Toronto

**ACQUISITIONS EDITOR**
William Pollock

**ASSOCIATE EDITOR**
Emily Rader

**TECHNICAL EDITOR**
Keith Pleas

**PROJECT EDITORS**
Cindy Brown
Claire Splan

**COPY EDITORS**
Garry Morris
Kim Torgerson

**PROOFREADERS**
Lindy Clinton
Pat Mannion

**COMPUTER DESIGNER**
Helen Worsley

**SERIES DESIGN**
Seventeenth Street Studios

**COVER DESIGN**
Compass Marketing

Osborne **McGraw-Hill**
2600 Tenth Street
Berkeley, California 94710
U.S.A.

For information on software, translations, or book distributors outside of the U.S.A., please write to Osborne **McGraw-Hill** at the above address.

The Visual Basic 3 for Windows Handbook

7890 DOC 9987654

ISBN 0-07-881986-5

This book is printed on acid-free paper.

*For my parents*

# Contents

# Acknowledgments

One of the best parts of writing a book is when the author gets to thank those who have helped him or her, for rarely (and certainly not in this case) is a book by one author truly produced alone. First and foremost, I have to thank the team at Osborne/McGraw-Hill. Their patience, dedication, help, cheerfulness—you name it—went way beyond the call of duty. To Bill Pollock, Emily Rader, Cindy Brown, Claire Splan, Lydia Puller, Gary Morris, Kim Torgerson, Lindy Clinton, Pat Mannion, Helen Worsley: Thanks!

Next, I have to thank those people at Microsoft (whose names I unfortunately don't know) who created Visual Basic and have now made it even better in version 3. It's a great product. Dee Dee Walsh handles Visual Basic's publicity. Her patience with strange requests and her general all-around helpfulness also went way beyond the call of duty. Tricia Bull at Waggener-Edstrom has been incredibly helpful in getting me the Microsoft products and information I needed to get this book out on time.

Fred Mosher and David Schneider read earlier versions of this book carefully and patiently pointed out many ways to make this book better. John Tralka helped me check the hundreds of program listings. Keith Pleas went far beyond what an author can expect (or hope) to have from a tech reviewer. I'm really grateful to him!

Finally, thanks to all my friends who put up with my strange ways and my occasionally short temper for lo, so many months. In particular, thanks to Fran for her special friendship and support.

# About the Author

Gary Cornell, who holds a Ph.D. in mathematics from Brown University, is a computer programmer and professor of mathematics at the University of Connecticut. He has written or coauthored several acclaimed books on BASIC, including **Visual Basic for DOS Inside & Out** and **Visual Basic 2 for Windows Inside & Out**.

# Introduction

When Visual Basic 1.0 was released, Bill Gates, Chairman and CEO of Microsoft, described it as "awesome." Steve Gibson in *Infoworld* said Visual Basic is a "stunning new miracle" and will "dramatically change the way people feel about and use [Microsoft] Windows." Stewart Alsop was quoted in the *New York Times* as saying Visual Basic is "the perfect programming environment for the 1990s."

So what is all the hype about? Exactly what is Visual Basic and what can it do for you? Well, Bill Gates describes Visual Basic as an "easy yet powerful tool for developing Windows applications in Basic." This may not seem like enough to justify all the hoopla until you realize that Microsoft Windows is used by millions of people and that developing a Microsoft Windows application used to require an expert C programmer supplied with about 20 pounds worth of documentation and at least 20 (and more likely 30) megabytes of hard disk space for the needed C compiler and the essential add-ons. As Charles Petzold (author of one of the standard books on Windows programming in C) put it in the *New York Times:* "For those of us who make our living explaining the complexities of Windows programming to programmers, Visual Basic poses a real threat to our livelihood."

Visual Basic 2.0 was faster, more powerful and even easier to use than Visual Basic 1.0. Visual Basic 3 adds a simple way to control the most powerful databases available. It also adds support for common dialog boxes to the standard edition and makes it easier to communicate with other Windows applications.

So welcome to the latest and best version of Visual Basic, the programming tool of the 1990s!

## About This Book

This tutorial is a comprehensive, hands-on guide to all the ins and outs of Visual Basic 3 programming which doesn't assume that you've programmed before. (However, people familiar with QuickBASIC or another structured programming language will, of course, have an easier time.) You'll start at the beginning and quickly move along the road to mastery. Soon you'll be writing sophisticated Windows programs that take full advantage of Visual Basic's exciting and powerful event-driven nature. Finish this book and you will have mastered Visual Basic!

I've tried hard to stress the new ways of thinking needed to master Visual Basic programming, so even experts in more traditional programming languages can benefit from this book. I've taken this approach because trying to force Visual Basic into the framework of older programming languages is ultimately self-defeating—you can't take advantage of its power if you continue to think within an older paradigm.

To make this book even more useful there are extensive discussions of important topics left out of most other introductory books. There's a whole chapter on recursion. There are methods of keeping file information secret and ways to add protection to programs you may want to distribute. It also includes an extensive discussion of sorting and searching techniques and lots of tips and tricks. My goal was not only to introduce a topic but to take you the one step further that leads you to mastery.

Finally, the main body of this book ends with a professional quality check-book management program. This was chosen because, in my opinion, nothing shows off the power of Visual Basic better then a program like this. This program took less than a week to design and implement. It is easy to imagine an entire finance program capable of generating millions of dollars in sales written in only a few weeks using Visual Basic. (This is not simply my imagining what could happen—Microsoft's highly successful accounting package "Profit" was written in record time because it was done almost entirely using Visual Basic.)

## How This Book Is Organized

This book can be used in a variety of ways depending on your background and needs. People familiar with structured programming techniques can skim the complete discussions of the programming constructs such as loops and Sub and Function procedures that Visual Basic inherited from QuickBASIC 4.5; these appear in Chapters 5 through 9. Beginners will want to work through this material more carefully.

Here are short descriptions of the chapters:

Chapters 1 and 2 show you how to install Visual Basic and help you become familiar with the Visual Basic environment.

Chapters 3 and 4 start you right off with the notion of a customizable window (called a form) that is the heart of every Microsoft Windows (and, thus, Visual

Basic) application. You'll see how to add the basic controls—such as command buttons, text boxes, lines, shapes, and labels—to your forms.

Chapters 5 through 9 discuss the core programming techniques needed to release Visual Basic's powers. You'll see how to take full advantage of Visual Basic 3's variants and its many built-in functions. You also learn how to add your own functions to Visual Basic 3. You'll see how to sort and search through data, use the grid control, and use modular programming techniques to make your programs more flexible, powerful, and easier to debug.

Chapter 10 shows you how to finish the user interface. It takes you through most of the rest of the controls you can add to your forms. You'll see how to add list boxes, radio (option) buttons, check boxes, scroll bars, and all the other controls that Microsoft Windows users expect in their Windows applications—and that make Windows applications so much easier to use than their counterparts running under DOS.

Chapter 11 shows you the powerful debugging tools in Visual Basic 3. You'll learn how to isolate bugs (programming errors) and then eradicate them.

Chapter 12 introduces you to the world of graphics. Since Microsoft Windows is a graphically based environment, the powers of Visual Basic in this arena are pretty spectacular.

Chapter 13 shows you how to analyze the way a user is manipulating his or her mouse.

Chapter 14 shows you how to handle files in Visual Basic, including sophisticated methods for encrypting (that is, keeping the contents of files safe from casual probes).

Chapter 15 introduces you to the world of dynamic data exchange (DDE) and object linking and embedding (OLE). DDE lets you automate the transfer of information between Windows applications—and you'll be able to have Visual Basic coordinate the transfers! OLE lets you embed other Windows applications within a Visual Basic application so users can take full advantage of many of their other Windows applications.

Chapter 16 is an extensive treatment of *recursion*. Recursion is one of the most powerful programming tools available, and it's too often slighted in introductory books. In addition to powerful methods for sorting data, this chapter gives you a short introduction to recursive graphics, or fractals. Fractals are one of the most powerful tools in graphics—for example, they were used in the Genesis sequence in *Star Trek II: The Wrath of Khan*.

Chapter 17 is an introduction to the Data manager and other data access features added to Visual Basic 3. You'll see how to control the most powerful PC databases with only a few lines of code using the new data control.

Chapter 18 is the checkbook manager. It's a long program, but by this stage nothing in it will be foreign to you.

Appendix A introduces the Visual Basic Professional Edition, emphasizing how to use the Help compiler to build in sophisticated Help systems and the Setup kit to automate the distribution of your programs to other people. It also provides an overview of the other features of this important upgrade to Visual Basic so you can make an informed decision regarding whether to upgrade your Visual Basic system to include the Professional Edition's capabilities.

Appendix B shows you how to use the new Setup Wizard that makes distributing your files a breeze.

Appendix C quickly surveys the differences between QuickBASIC and Visual Basic.

Appendix D opens up to you the exciting world of third-party tools and resources.

Appendix E contains, courtesy of Microsoft, answers to what they regard as the most frequently asked questions about Visual Basic. We added this appendix in the hope that it will save you hours of waiting on the line for Microsoft's support services to help you.

## Conventions Used in This Book

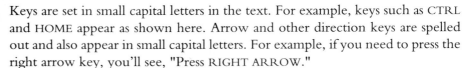

Keys are set in small capital letters in the text. For example, keys such as CTRL and HOME appear as shown here. Arrow and other direction keys are spelled out and also appear in small capital letters. For example, if you need to press the right arrow key, you'll see, "Press RIGHT ARROW."

When you need to use a combination of keys to activate a menu item, the first two keys will be separated by a plus sign and the entire key combination will appear in small capital letters. For example, "Press CTRL+A, B" indicates that you should hold down the key marked "Ctrl" on your keyboard while pressing first an "A" and then a "B." On the other hand ALT+F+P means press the "Alt" key, then the "F" key, and then the "P" key—you don't have to hold down the "Alt" key.

DOS commands, filenames, and file extensions appear in full capital letters: COMMAND.COM, .TXT, and so on. Microsoft Windows is referred to just as Windows most of the time. Keywords in Visual Basic appear with the first letter of each word capitalized: for example, Print, DeBug, FontSize, and so on.

The syntax for a command in Visual Basic is set in ordinary type except that items the programmer can change appear in italics. For example, the Name command used to rename a file would appear as

Name *OldFileName As NewFileName*

Finally, programs are set in a monospaced font, as shown here:

```
Sub Form_Click()
  Print "Hello world!"
End Sub
```

and lines of code that should appear on one line when you program, but which for typographic reasons need to be on more than line in this book, will be outdented or an underscore will be used as follows:

```
    Print "This line is much too long to fit on one line
but is outdented to indicate it should be entered on one line"

    M$ = "This line is also too long to fit but it " + _
"has underscores to indicate it should be entered on" _
"one line"
```

# Disk Order Form

The companion disk contains all the programs in *Visual Basic 3 for Windows Handbook* that have more than two lines of code. In addition, the disk contains around 50 bonus procedures with full source code. The disk also includes the commented source code for both the version of the checkbook manager given in the text and one that adds even more features. Here's a sample of what else this disk has to offer:

*Procedures for working with arrays*

*Business procedures for...*

◆ Calculating internal rate of return

◆ Analyzing a loan or annuity

◆ Determining straight-line, sum-of-digits, or double-declining balance depreciations

*Mathematics procedures for...*

◆ Numerical integration

◆ Working with vectors

◆ Matrix algebra

To order your disk, send your name, address, and the disk size you require (5 1/4 inch or 3 1/2 inch) along with a check or money order for **$25.00** payable to Gary Cornell: Books on Science (CT residents add sales tax) to

Gary Cornell
128 Moulton Road
Storrs, CT 06268

. . . . . . . . . . . . . . . . . . . . . . . . . . . . . . (cut here) . . . . . . . . . . . . . . . . . . . . . . . . . . . .

Please rush one companion disk for *Visual Basic 3 for Windows Handbook* to

Name _____

Address _____

City _____ State _____ ZIP _____

Disk Size:      3.5 _____                    5.25 _____

We offer a 30-day, money-back guarantee.

This is solely the offering of the author. Osborne/McGraw-Hill takes no responsibility for the fulfillment of this offer.

# Chapter 1

# Getting Started

*t*his chapter gives you an overview of what Visual Basic is all about. It tells you what equipment you need to run Visual Basic, how to set it up, and how to use the built–in tutorial. Although you don't need to be an expert user of Microsoft Windows, you do need to know the basics before you can master Visual Basic—that is, you need to be comfortable with manipulating a mouse, and you need to know how to manipulate a window and how to use the File Manager or Program Manager built in to Microsoft Windows.

However, there is no better way to master Microsoft Windows than to write applications for it—and that is what Visual Basic is all about.

**note:** *This chapter assumes you are using the standard edition of Visual Basic. See Appendix A for information on the Visual Basic Professional Edition.*

## Why Windows and Why Visual Basic?

Graphical user interfaces, or *GUIs* (pronounced "gooies"), have revolutionized the microcomputer industry. They demonstrate that the proverb "a picture is worth a thousand words" hasn't lost its truth. Instead of the cryptic C:> prompt that DOS users have long seen (and that some have long feared), users are presented with a desktop filled with icons. This provides a visual image of what the computer has to offer. The screen in Figure 1-1 shows a typical example of a Windows desktop.

Perhaps even more important in the long run than the look of Microsoft Windows applications is the *feel* that applications developed for it have. Windows applications generally have a consistent user interface. This means that users can spend more time mastering the application and less time worrying about which keystrokes do what within menus and dialog boxes.

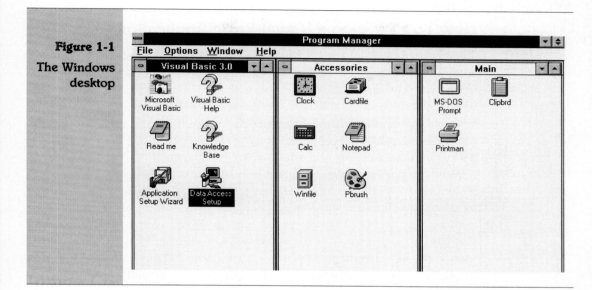

**Figure 1-1**

**The Windows desktop**

All this comes at a price, though; before Visual Basic, developing Windows applications was much harder than developing DOS applications. Programmers had to worry about too much, such as what the mouse was doing, where the user was inside a menu, and whether he or she was clicking or double-clicking at a given place. Developing a Windows application required expert C programmers, and even they had trouble. (The Microsoft Windows software development kit that was required in addition to a C compiler weighed in at nine and a half pounds.)

Visual Basic has changed this situation. Sophisticated Windows applications can now be developed in a fraction of the time previously needed. Programming errors (bugs) don't happen as often—and if they do, they're a lot easier to detect and fix. Programming for Windows has become fun (at least most of the time).

You don't have to pay much of a performance penalty: applications developed under Visual Basic run quickly. This is not to say that you can eliminate C or assembly language programming for Windows; extending Visual Basic still requires tools that, at present, are available only in these languages. See Appendix A for more on extending Visual Basic using the Visual Basic Professional Edition.

## How You Develop a Visual Basic Application

The first step in developing a Visual Basic application is to plan what the user sees—in other words, to design the screens. What menus do you want? How large a window should the application use? How many windows should there be? Should the user be able to resize the windows? Where will you place the *command buttons,* the "buttons" the user clicks to activate the applications? Will the applications have places to enter text (*text boxes*)? In Visual Basic, the objects a program designer places on windows are called *controls.*

What makes Visual Basic different from almost any other programming tool is the ease with which you can design the screen. You literally draw the user interface, much like using a paint program. In addition, when you're done drawing the interface, the command buttons, text boxes, and other controls that you have placed in a blank window will automatically recognize user actions such as mouse movements and button clicks. Visual Basic 3 also comes with a menu design feature that makes creating both ordinary and pop-up menus a snap.

Only after you design the interface does anything like traditional programming occur. Objects in Visual Basic *will* recognize events like mouse clicks; how the objects respond to them depends on the code you write. You will always need to write code in order to make controls respond to events. This makes Visual Basic programming fundamentally different from conventional programming.

Programs in conventional programming languages run from the top, down. For older programming languages, execution starts from the first line and moves with the flow of the program to different parts as needed. A Visual Basic program works completely differently. The core of a Visual Basic program is a set of independent pieces of code that are *activated* by, and so respond to, only the events they have been told to recognize. This is a fundamental shift. Now instead of designing a program to do what the programmer thinks should happen, the user is in control.

Much of the programming code in Visual Basic that tells your program how to respond to events like mouse clicks occurs in what Visual Basic calls *event procedures.* Essentially, everything executable in a Visual Basic program is either in an event procedure or is used by an event procedure to help the procedure carry out its job. In fact, to stress that Visual Basic is fundamentally different from ordinary programming languages, the documentation uses the term *project,* rather than *program,* to refer to the combination of programming code and user interface that goes into making a Visual Basic application possible.

Here is a summary of the steps you take to design a Visual Basic application:

1. Customize the windows that the user sees.

2. Decide what events the controls on the window should recognize.

3. Write the event procedures for those events.

4. Write any procedures that the event procedures need for their job.

Here is what happens when the application is running:

1. Visual Basic monitors the windows and the controls in each window for *all* the events that each control can recognize (mouse movements, clicks, keystrokes, and so on).

2. When Visual Basic detects an event, it examines the application to see if you've written an event procedure for that event.

3. If you have written an event procedure, Visual Basic executes the code that makes up that event procedure and goes back to step 1.

4. If you have not written an event procedure, Visual Basic waits for the next event and goes back to step 1.

These steps cycle continuously until the application ends. Usually, an event *must* happen before Visual Basic will do anything. Event-driven programs are *reactive* more than *active*—and that makes them more user-friendly.

## THE FEATURES OF VISUAL BASIC 3

Visual Basic lets you add menus, text boxes, command buttons, option buttons (for making exclusive choices), check boxes (for non-exclusive choices), list boxes, scroll bars, and file and directory boxes to blank windows. You can use grids to handle tabular data, communicate with other Windows applications, and access data bases.

You can have multiple windows on a screen. These windows have full access to the clipboard and to the information in most other Windows applications running at the same time.

The programming language built into Visual Basic (an extension of the one available in QBasic or QuickBASIC) has easy-to-use graphics statements, powerful built-in functions for mathematics and string manipulations, and sophisticated file-handling capabilities.

Moreover, Visual Basic makes it easy to build large programs by allowing modern *modular programming techniques*. This means you can break a program into easier-to-handle, and therefore less error-prone, modules. (A *module* is a manageable, relatively small piece of programming code.) Modules ideally accomplish one task and have a well-defined interface with the rest of the program so that they can be coded and tested independently. This way you can concentrate on how each module does its job and how the pieces of the program communicate with each other inside your application.

Visual Basic also provides sophisticated error handling for the all-too-common task of preventing new users from bombing an application. (*Bombing* is computer jargon for ending a program abruptly and abnormally. *Bugs* is the jargon for the programming errors that usually cause bombing.) Visual Basic has an intelligent interpreter/editor that often detects, and can even suggest, the changes needed to correct routine programming and typographical errors that are common when you begin building an application. It has an extensive online help system for quick reference while you're developing an application.

## WHAT YOU NEED TO RUN VISUAL BASIC

Visual Basic is a sophisticated program. The standard edition requires an IBM-compatible computer at least as powerful as an AT—that is, a chip compatible with and at least as powerful as an Intel 80286 chip, but realistically speaking you should have a fast 386-class or better processor.

For the full Visual Basic system, you'll need the following:

◆ A hard disk with at least 13 megabytes free (a minimal system without icons, data access, the tutorial, or sample applications needs 3.5MB)

◆ A mouse or other pointing device compatible with a mouse

◆ A graphics monitor and card with EGA resolution (higher resolution is best)

◆ MS- or PC-DOS version 3.1 or higher

◆ Microsoft Windows 3.0 or higher, running in standard or enhanced mode (3.1 is best)

◆ At least 2MB of RAM (4MB is better)

Regardless of the formal requirements, it's much easier to work with Windows, and especially Visual Basic, when you have a lot of memory and a chip at least as powerful as an Intel 33 MHz 386. Microsoft Windows is power-hungry: the more memory and speed your computer has, the better.

# Setting Up Visual Basic

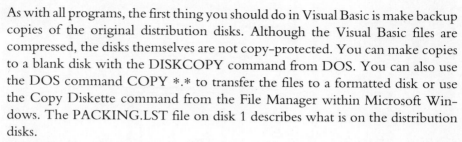

As with all programs, the first thing you should do in Visual Basic is make backup copies of the original distribution disks. Although the Visual Basic files are compressed, the disks themselves are not copy-protected. You can make copies to a blank disk with the DISKCOPY command from DOS. You can also use the DOS command COPY *.* to transfer the files to a formatted disk or use the Copy Diskette command from the File Manager within Microsoft Windows. The PACKING.LST file on disk 1 describes what is on the distribution disks.

Send in the registration card. It's true that you'll get a certain amount of junk mail as a result, but it also will be easier to get support and notices of upgrades from Microsoft.

## Running the Setup Program

The disks for Visual Basic contain an automated Setup program to install Visual Basic. Windows must be running for the Setup program to work. You can run the Setup program as many times as you want, which means you are not tied into the options you choose the first time. (It's a good idea for first-time users to use the default options.) The first time you set up Visual Basic, the Setup program asks for your name or the name of the company that bought the copy of Visual Basic. It keeps track of this information and uses it to remind you to whom the program is licensed—every time you start Visual Basic.

If Microsoft Windows is running, follow these steps to install it from the A drive. (You can install Visual Basic from any floppy drive by substituting the name of the drive you're using in the instructions below.)

1. Place disk 1 in the A drive.

2. Open the File Manager or Program Manager and choose Run.

3. Type **A:SETUP**.

Your screen will look something like the one in Figure 1-2 if you used the Run option from the Program Manager. Make sure that the Run Minimized button is not checked. (This option shrinks any Microsoft Windows application to an icon when it starts.)

4. Press ENTER.

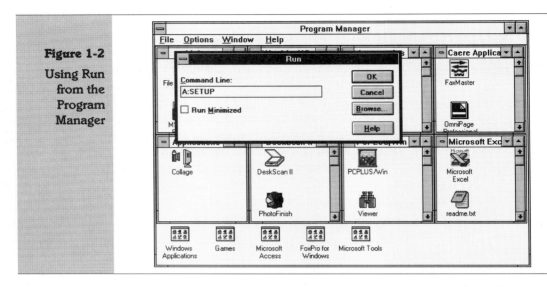

**Figure 1-2**

Using Run
from the
Program
Manager

After a short delay, during which you are told that the program is initializing itself, you are presented with a dialog box like the one shown in Figure 1-3. Click the Continue button to move on with the installation procedure.

Next, a dialog box appears asking for your name and company name. This information is copied to the disk you use to install Visual Basic. Another dialog box then asks you to confirm this information.

The next dialog box, shown here, indicates that the Setup program will install Visual Basic in a new directory called C:\VB. If you are not satisfied with this,

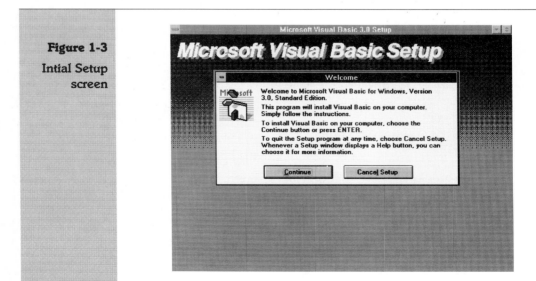

**Figure 1-3**

Intial Setup
screen

make any changes in the box and then click the Continue button (or just press ENTER). If you want to leave the Setup program, click the Cancel Setup button.

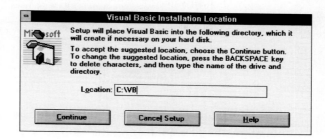

Suppose you accept the defaults and click the Continue button. Visual Basic then checks whether the directory exists. If the directory doesn't exist, you are asked whether you want to create it with the dialog box shown here:

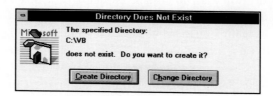

**note:**

*Visual Basic 3 by default installs itself in the same directory as older versions of Visual Basic. Since Visual Basic 3 can run programs written using Visual Basic 1.0 and 2.0 with at most minor modifications, this is not usually a problem. If you need to save an earlier version of Visual Basic, install Visual Basic 3 in a different directory.*

Click the Create Directory button. You are next shown a dialog box like the one in Figure 1-4. Clicking the Complete Installation button lets you install all of Visual Basic. The amount of space needed for a complete installation is approximately 13 megabytes and some of that will need to be in the drive that holds Windows itself. To install only part of Visual Basic, choose the Custom Installation button.

If you choose the Custom Installation button, you'll see a screen like the one in Figure 1-5. The amount of space needed for each of the different parts of Visual Basic is given. This dialog box also tells you how much space you have left on your hard disk. For example, Figure 1-5 shows that there is more than enough room for the full system.

**Figure 1-4**

Installation
options

If you need to save space, you can choose not to install the Icon library, the tutorial, or the files containing the sample programs—or any combination of the three. This can save you almost 6MB of disk space. The Drivers button shown in Figure 1-5 is used for adding the libraries needed for accessing databases (see Chapter 17).

To unselect an item, use the mouse or arrow keys to move to the item you do not want to install. Notice that a box encloses the item. Now press the SPACEBAR or click the mouse. Check boxes in Windows (and in Visual Basic as well) are *toggles*; you switch them between on and off with the SPACEBAR or with a mouse click.

Once you've selected the items you want to install, click the Install button. The Setup program (which was written in Visual Basic, by the way) starts running. Setting up Visual Basic takes a fair amount of time—around ten minutes on a 386 machine. This is because of the decompression needed to reverse Microsoft's shrinking more than 12MB onto so few disks. As the Setup program copies the file, you can see—both visually via a gauge and explicitly via a message—what percentage of the job is done. For example, when the Setup program finishes with the first disk, you will see a screen like Figure 1-6.

**Figure 1-5**

Custom
installation
options

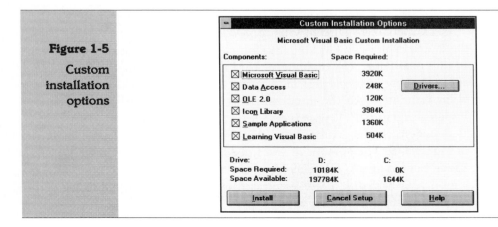

Place the disk the dialog box asks for in the appropriate drive (B in Figure 1-6) and press ENTER. When the Setup program finishes its job, you'll need to insert the first disk once more the first time you set up Visual Basic. After Visual Basic Personalizes your copy of the program, you're presented with a message box that looks like this:

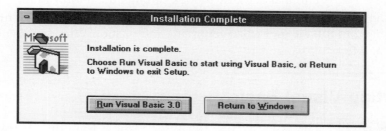

After you've completed the installation procedure, Visual Basic is installed in its own program group. You can use the Program Manager or the Windows Setup program to move Visual Basic to another program group. Consult the documentation that came with your Windows package or a book such as *Windows 3.1 Made Easy* by Tom Sheldon (Berkeley, CA: Osborne/McGraw-Hill, 1992) to see how to do this.

**Figure 1-6**

After the Setup program finishes with the first disk

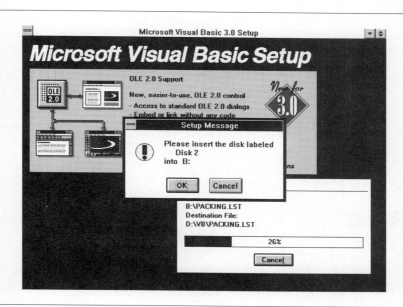

If there are any corrections or additions to the documentation, you'll find them in a file called README.TXT. If this file was on the distribution disks, the Setup program automatically copies this file and places an icon to represent it on the Windows desktop in the Visual Basic program group. If you double-click on this icon, Microsoft Windows loads the file into the NotePad. This makes it easy to look through the information.

Finally, you don't have to explicitly set up a printer for Visual Basic. Visual Basic uses whatever printer information Windows is currently using.

## Starting Visual Basic

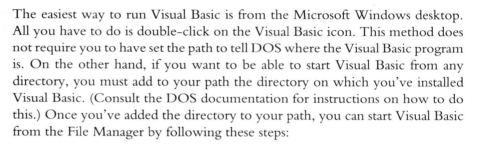

The easiest way to run Visual Basic is from the Microsoft Windows desktop. All you have to do is double-click on the Visual Basic icon. This method does not require you to have set the path to tell DOS where the Visual Basic program is. On the other hand, if you want to be able to start Visual Basic from any directory, you must add to your path the directory on which you've installed Visual Basic. (Consult the DOS documentation for instructions on how to do this.) Once you've added the directory to your path, you can start Visual Basic from the File Manager by following these steps:

1. Choose Run from the File Manager. (Press ALT+F+R as a shortcut.)

2. Type **VB** and press ENTER.

Again, assuming you've added the directory containing Visual Basic to your path, you can have Visual Basic start up when you load Windows. For this, type **WIN VB** at the DOS prompt.

You can also start a specific Visual Basic project by double-clicking on the associated icon or double-clicking in the File Manager at the project name.

## The Tutorial

When you start up Visual Basic, you see a copyright screen telling you to whom the copy of Visual Basic is licensed. After that you see a screen like the one in Figure 1-7.

The next chapter explains all the parts of this screen. For now, though, you might want to work through the online tutorial. Doing this will complement and reinforce the information presented in the next chapter. (The tutorial was also written in Visual Basic, by the way.)

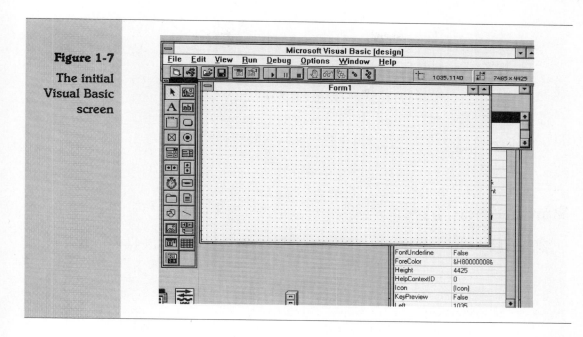

**Figure 1-7**

**The initial Visual Basic screen**

The shortcut for starting the tutorial is to first press ALT+H. This opens the Help menu. Now press L to select the tutorial. Another way to get to the tutorial is by using the mouse. Click the Help item on the main menu bar and then click the item marked Learning Microsoft Visual Basic. The following illustration shows the main menu bar with the Help menu pulled down:

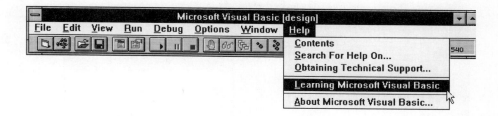

Assuming you've installed the tutorial, selecting these items will usually take you directly to the tutorial. The main screen for the tutorial is shown in Figure 1-8.

Don't be alarmed if you are instead presented with a message box like the one in Figure 1-9. You may see a screen like this if you do something—a mouse click in the wrong place, for example—that Visual Basic interprets as the start

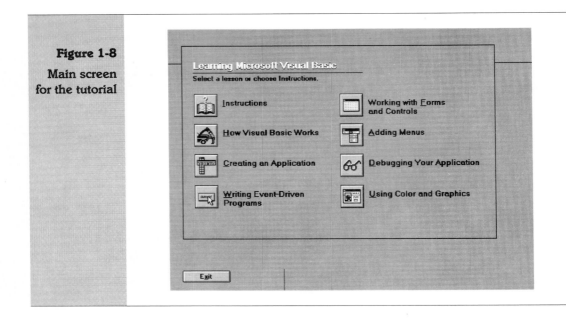

**Figure 1-8**

Main screen for the tutorial

of developing an application. Since Visual Basic never loads a new application without trying to save the current one, you have to clear this dialog box. To

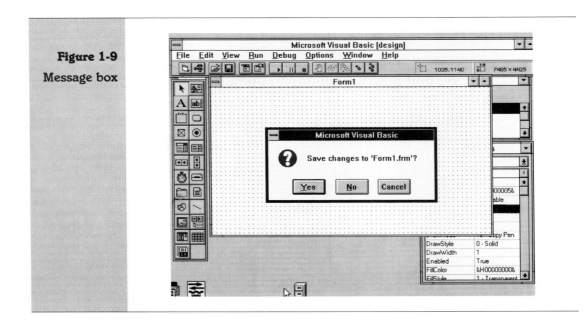

**Figure 1-9**

Message box

do this, do *not* press ENTER (which would tell Visual Basic to save your work). Instead, press ALT+N or click the No button. (You may have to do this twice before the tutorial starts.)

The tutorial is very easy to use. Before you begin, you might want to click the Instructions button. This gives you a screen like the one in Figure 1-10. Here you will find instructions for using the Visual Basic tutorial. When you are done with this screen, click the Close Instructions button.

The tutorial takes control of the keyboard and mouse so that you can't really go far wrong. You don't have to cover the lessons in any order, and you can return to them as often as you want. Once installed, the tutorial is always available to you.

Each lesson covers various topics that you may or may not be interested in; you can skip around. You double-click on a heading or topic to open it, and the easiest way to move from screen to screen is to press the SPACEBAR. You can also click the button marked ">". If you want to go back to a previous screen, click the button marked "<". To go back to the main screen and choose a different lesson, click the Options button and choose the Menu option. (As in all Windows applications, underlined letters in command buttons, like the letter *M* in Menu, are shortcut keys. You need only press the letter to choose the option. Only the Options menu in the tutorial has shortcut keys.)

**Figure 1-10**

**Instructions for the Visual Basic tutorial**

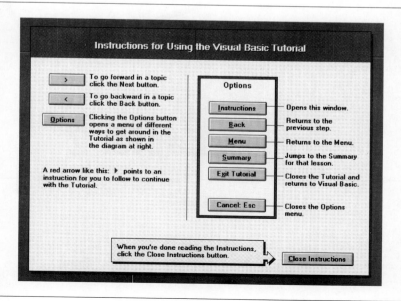

# Chapter 2

# The Visual Basic Environment

tHIS chapter shows you how to use the menus and windows that make up the Visual Basic standard edition environment. When you're finished, you'll be comfortable with the online help, the editing tools, and the file-handling utilities built into the standard edition of Visual Basic. (See Appendix A for information on the Visual Basic Professional Edition.)

If you are not completely comfortable with the look and feel of Microsoft Windows applications, then this chapter will help. After all, Visual Basic is itself a well-designed Microsoft Windows application, and the way its menus and windows respond is typical of Windows programs. Experienced Microsoft Windows users may want to skim much of this material. Remember, though, that until you are familiar with how a Windows application should look and feel, you can't take full advantage of the power of Visual Basic.

If you are developing an application with Visual Basic for your personal use, then conforming to the Windows standard is not essential. However, if others will be using your application, following the Windows standard essentially eliminates the learning curve for using your application. For example, Windows users expect a single click with a mouse to select an item and a double click to activate the item. (The most complete guidelines for a Windows application can be found in Microsoft's publication *The Windows Interface: An Application Design Guide* (Part# 28921—contact Microsoft for price and availability).

The default settings built into the design process of a Visual Basic application make it easy to conform to the Microsoft Windows guidelines. Windows default to the proper shape and can be moved and resized as users expect. Similarly, menus respond the way users are accustomed to. Of course, Visual Basic doesn't lock you into these defaults, but it is not a good idea to make changes casually.

**note:**  *The online tutorial discussed in Chapter 1 is a good complement to the material presented in this chapter.*

Given the power of Visual Basic, with its richness of tools and detailed menus, it's easy to be overwhelmed at first. To help reduce any confusion, this chapter gives you a detailed description of what the environment has to offer.

## An Overview of the Main Screen

As mentioned in Chapter 1, when you start up Visual Basic, you are presented with a copyright screen indicating to whom the copy of Visual Basic is licensed. After a short delay, you are automatically dropped into the Visual Basic environment, as shown in Figure 2-1.

**note:** *Visual Basic remembers how you arranged the screens the previous time and reuses that arrangement. For this reason, your screen may look different from Figure 2-1.*

The screen is certainly crowded. You can see the six parts in the standard Visual Basic environment, although two windows are partially obscured. One

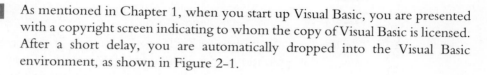

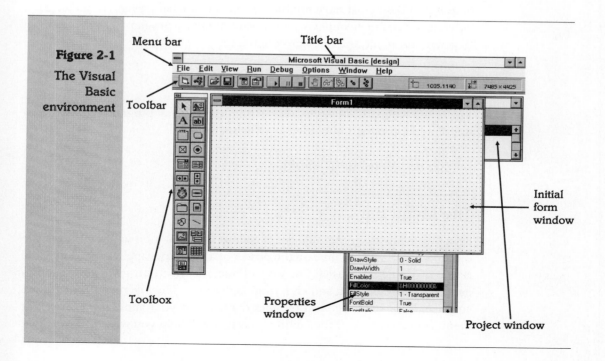

**Figure 2-1**
The Visual Basic environment

Menu bar

Title bar

Toolbar

Toolbox

Properties window

Initial form window

Project window

other window is also available. The Properties window is used when customizing a form or control and is discussed at length in Chapters 3 and 4. Another window, called the Immediate window, shows up when you are running or debugging a program; see Chapter 11.

Following is a description of the other parts of the main screen. Subsequent sections of this chapter cover the most commonly used parts of the menus.

## Title Bar

The *title bar* is the horizontal bar located at the top of the screen; it gives the name of the application and is common to all Microsoft Windows applications. Interactions between the user and the title bar are handled by Windows, not by the application. Everything below the title and menu bar in a Windows application is called the *client area*. Your application is completely responsible for the look, feel, and response of the objects you place in this area.

For Visual Basic, the title bar starts out by displaying

Microsoft Visual Basic [design]

This is typical of Microsoft Windows applications: in sophisticated programs (like Visual Basic) that have multiple states, the title bar changes to indicate the different states. For example, when you are running a program within the Visual Basic environment, the title bar switches to

Microsoft Visual Basic [run]

and when you are *debugging* (correcting errors in a program), temporarily stopping the program, the title bar switches to

Microsoft Visual Basic [break]

## The Menu Bar

Selecting items from the pull-down menus listed on a *menu bar* is one of the most common ways to unleash the power of a Windows application. The same is true of Visual Basic itself. For Visual Basic, the menu bar gives you the tools needed to develop, test, and save your application. The File menu contains the commands for working with the files that go into your application. The Edit menu contains many of the editing tools that will help you write the code that activates the interface you design for your application, including the search-and-replace editing tools. The View menu gives you fast access to the different parts of your program. The Run menu lets you test out your application while developing it. The Debug menu gives you access to the tools used to correct (debug) problems (*bugs* in computer jargon; Chapter 11 offers a detailed discussion of debugging techniques).

The Options menu lets you control the Visual Basic environment. The Window menu gives you quick access to the different windows that make up the Visual Basic environment. You also use it to design your own menus. It lets you control the colors used while you are designing your applications. Finally, you use the Help menu to gain access to the very detailed online help system provided with Visual Basic.

Notice that all the menus have one letter underlined. Pressing ALT and the underlined letter opens up that menu. Another way to access the menu is to press ALT alone to activate the menu bar. When you do, notice that the File menu item is highlighted. You can now use the arrow keys to move around the menu bar. Press ENTER or DOWN ARROW to open the menu. Once a menu is open, all you need is a single key, called an *accelerator key* (also called an *access* or *hot key*), to select a menu option. For example, if the Help menu is open, pressing L brings up the tutorial. Accelerator keys are not case-sensitive.

Some menu items have *shortcut keys*. A shortcut key is usually a combination of keys the user can press to perform an action without opening a menu. For example, as is common in Windows applications, pressing ALT+F4 exits Visual Basic without going through the File menu.

## The Toolbar

The *toolbar* shown in Figure 2-2 is immediately below the menu bar and was added in Visual Basic 2.0. As is becoming more common in Windows applications, Microsoft added toolbar icons to let you activate common tasks

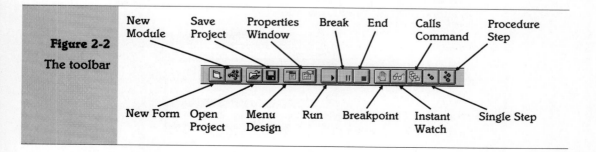

**Figure 2-2**

**The toolbar**

New Module    Save Project    Properties Window    Break    End    Calls Command    Procedure Step

New Form    Open Project    Menu Design    Run    Breakpoint    Instant Watch    Single Step

without using the menus. Since every item on the toolbar has a keyboard equivalent for the same task, which you choose is a matter of taste.

Reading from left to right, here is what the tools on the toolbar do:

***New Form*** This button lets you add a new form (customizable window) to a project. Same as New Form on the File menu (ALT+F+F). See Chapter 5 for information on using multiple forms in your applications.

***New Module*** This button lets you open a new module for specialized program-ming code. You'll see how to use them in Chapter 8. This is the same item as New Module on the File menu (ALT+F+M).

***Open Project*** This button let's you save an existing Visual Basic project (see the section "Loading and Running Programs" in this chapter). Same as ALT+F+O on the File menu.

***Save Project*** Lets you save your Visual Basic project (see Chapter 3). Same As ALT+F+V on the File menu.

***Menu Design*** Used to design menus (see Chapter 10). Same as ALT+W+M on the Window menu or using the shortcut key combination of CTRL+M.

***Activate Properties Window*** The Properties window is at the bottom right of Figure 2-1. You use this to modify the default size, shape, and color of your Visual Basic objects (see Chapters 3 and 4). This is the same as pressing the F4 shortcut or choosing Properties on the Window menu (ALT+W+O). Here's an example of the Properties window.

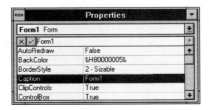

**Run** This lets you run the application. After you design an application, this is the same as choosing Run from the Run menu (F5 is the shortcut).

**Break** Pauses a running program. (Programs can usually be continued by using the Run tool or SHIFT+F5.) Same as the Break item on the Run menu or using the CTRL+BREAK combination.

**End** Ends the running program. Same as the End item on the Run menu.

**Breakpoint** A debugging tool; see Chapter 11. This places a temporary stop sign at a specific place in your program. Available from the Debug menu; the shortcut is F9.

**Instant Watch** Also a debugging tool discussed in Chapter 11. This lets you take a snapshot of what is happening to various parts of your program. Also available from the Debug menu; the shortcut is SHIFT+F9.

**Calls Command** Shows a list of current procedure calls. A debugging tool. See Chapters 11 and 16.

**Single Step** Moves through your program one line at a time. Also a debugging tool, discussed in Chapter 11. Available from the Debug menu or with the F8 shortcut.

**Procedure Step** Used when your program has grown more sophisticated by breaking down specific tasks into different procedures (see Chapter 8). Also moves through your program one line at a time, but treats a procedure as a single step. Also a debugging tool, discussed in Chapter 11. Available from the Debug menu; the shortcut is SHIFT+F8.

## The Toolbox

Located at the left of the screen in Figure 2-1, just below the toolbar, the *toolbox* contains the 22 basic tools for developing your application.

You use the toolbox to place command buttons, text buttons, and the other controls in your application. (See Chapters 3, 4, 9, 10, 14, and 17 for more details on the toolbox. See Appendix A for information on how Visual Basic Professional Edition gives you an even more powerful toolbox. See Appendix D for information on how outside vendors also can give you an even more powerful toolbox.)

## The Initial Form Window

The initial *Form window* takes up much of the center of the screen. This is where you customize the window that users will see. The Visual Basic documentation uses the term *form* for a customizable window. (See Chapter 3 for more details on the initial Form window.)

**note:**   *Since the Visual Basic manuals use the term "form" to describe a customizable window together with objects like command buttons that you can add to it, this book follows that convention.*

## The Project Window

Since it is quite common for Visual Basic applications to share code or previously customized forms, Visual Basic organizes applications into what it calls *projects*. Each project can have multiple forms, and the code that activates the controls on a form is stored with the form in separate files. General programming code shared by all the forms in your application can be divided into different modules, which are also stored separately. Located at the far right of the screen and partially obscured by the initial Form window, the *Project window* contains a list of all the customizable forms and general code (modules) that make up your application. Here's what the initial Project window looks like (it was obscured in Figure 2-1):

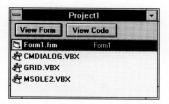

Notice that four items are already listed in the Project window. The first is the initial form on which you will build the application. The other three items contain the files needed to add the Grid control (see Chapter 9), Common dialog boxes (Chapter 10), and the OLE 2.0 control (see Chapter 15).

Although Visual Basic stores separately all the files that go into making up the project, it does keep track of where they are. It creates a file, called the *project make file*, that tells it (and you, if you look at the file) where the individual files that make up a project are located. Visual Basic creates the Make file whenever you choose Save Project from the File menu (or equivalently, the Save Project tool from the toolbar) and creates a different Make file whenever you choose Save Project As. Make files have a .MAK extension in their filename.

# The Help System

The Setup program that installs Visual Basic automatically installs the more than 1MB of help information that comes with it. The online help system contains essentially all of the information in the *Language Reference* that comes with Visual Basic. In addition, there are hundreds of example programs and dozens of useful tables.

The online help system contains a very useful feature: it is context-sensitive for help. This means that you can press F1 at the appropriate time and you bypass the help menus to go directly to the needed information. You can get information about any keyword in the Visual Basic programming language, about an error message, or about the parts of the Visual Basic environment.

For example, the screen in Figure 2-3 shows you what happens when you press F1 after entering the keyword *Print*, which is used to display text. The screen in Figure 2-4 shows what you would see if you pressed F1 when you were in the Form window.

Once you start up the help system, you can move the help window anywhere you want. You can resize it or shrink it to an icon as necessary.

**Figure 2-3**

Help Screen
for Print

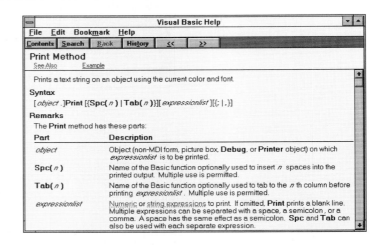

## The Help Menu

Following is a description of each of the items on the Help menu.

**Figure 2-4**

Help Screen
for Form
Window

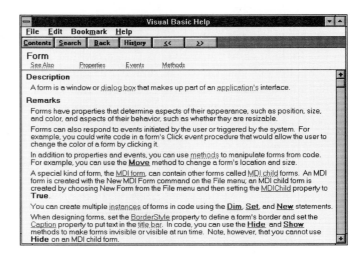

**Contents**  The Contents option, activated by pressing ALT+H+C (or C alone if the Help menu is open), tells you how the Visual Basic help system is organized.

**Search**  The Search option, activated by pressing ALT+H+S (or S alone if the Help menu is open), lets you search for help on a specific topic.

**Obtaining Technical Support**  Tells you how to get help from Microsoft. (ALT+H+O is the access key combination if the Help menu isn't open; press O if it is.) This option also contains hints on advanced topics.

tip:

*If you are a member of CompuServe, Microsoft is very efficient about giving answers to the questions posted by users in its MSBASIC forum. Other users monitor the questions and often provide helpful advice as well. (For instance, the author of this book frequently logs on to this forum and is one of the people who will, on occasion, provide advice there.)*

**Learning Microsoft Visual Basic**  You've already seen how choosing this option starts the online tutorial. (ALT+H+L is the access key combination if the Help menu isn't open; press L if it is.)

**About**  The About option gives you the copyright notice and serial number of your copy, tells you to whom the copy of Visual Basic is licensed, and shows you the amount of memory your system has available. (ALT+H+A is the access key combination if the Help menu isn't open; press A if it is.)

## Getting into the Help System

Although you can always use the context-sensitive help feature built into Visual Basic to get into the help system, selecting Contents from the Help menu is more common. This leads you to the initial help screen, shown in Figure 2-5. This is an independent window with a title bar containing a control box and minimize and maximize buttons. This lets you move, maximize, shrink to an icon, or close the window as you see fit. The help window also has scroll bars that let you move easily through the information.

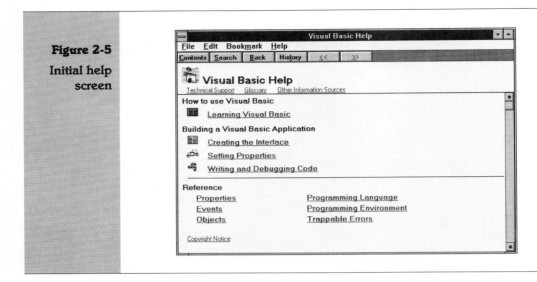

**Figure 2-5**

**Initial help screen**

The help system in Visual Basic is tied together by icons or links that are indicated by an underline. (They also are highlighted in green on color monitors.) These are called *jumps* in the Visual Basic manuals and are similar to the hyperlinks in QuickBASIC. The idea is that you use these as gateways to new information. If you move the mouse pointer to a jump (the pointer icon changes to a little hand) or an icon and click the left mouse button, you are immediately taken to the topic indicated. You can also use the TAB key to move forward between jumps and press SHIFT+TAB to move back. If you use the TAB key, the jump you moved to is highlighted. Press ENTER to choose the highlighted topic.

When you jump around via these links, Visual Basic keeps track of where you were. You can press ALT+B or click the Back button to move back to where you were.

If a word or phrase in the help system is marked with a dotted underline (also green on color monitors), you can get a short definition of the term by using the mouse; move to the item and hold down the left mouse button. The help system displays a short definition in a window until you release the mouse button.

The help system contains lots of examples of code that can illustrate how to use commands. (Chapter 5 shows you how to run this code.)

## THE HELP BUTTONS

You use the six buttons located below the menu bar in the help window to navigate through the help system. If an option makes no sense—for example, you can't move backward from the initial screen—then the icon for the option is dimmed.

***The Contents Button*** The Contents button takes you back to the original Contents help screen available from the Help menu. As the screen in Figure 2-5 indicated, there are many jumps for moving through the help system quickly.

***The Search Button*** Click on the Search button for a complete, alphabetical index of topics in the system. Clicking the Search button or pressing ALT+S opens the Search dialog box, shown in Figure 2-6, which lets you search through an alphabetical list of all the keywords in the help system.

Once you've opened the Search dialog box, enter the first letter of the keyword, and the index shifts to topics beginning with that letter. As you enter additional letters, you narrow the search more. You can also use the scroll bars to move through the list. If you press ENTER or click the Search button, the help system finds all the topics that pertain to that keyword. For example, as

**Figure 2-6**
**Search box**

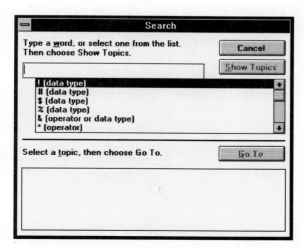

**Figure 2-7**

Search dialog box for keywords "Form window"

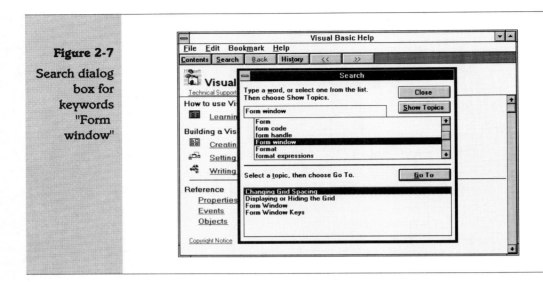

the screen in Figure 2-7 shows, there are many topics relating to the keywords "Form window."

If more than one topic is found by the help system, you can move through the topics with the UP ARROW and DOWN ARROW keys or the scroll bars. Once you've decided on a topic you want to look at, click the Go To button or press ALT+G. To close the Search box, press ESC or click the Cancel button.

**The Back Button**  The Back button, activated by pressing ALT+B, takes you to the topic you last looked at. The help system keeps a record of all the topics you've looked at, but it erases this record if you close or shrink the help window.

**The History Button**  This opens up a little window that gives you the chain of topics within the help system that you've just worked through. Here's an example of what the History window looks like:

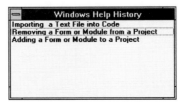

If you move through this window and press ENTER, you'll immediately be taken back to that specific topic.

**The Forward and Backward Buttons**  These buttons take you either to the next topic alphabetically in the help system or to the previous topic. They let you browse through the system.

## THE HELP WINDOW MENU BAR

The menu bar for the help system is common to many Microsoft Windows applications. The available menus are described in the following sections.

**The Help Window File Menu**  The File menu in the help window lets you open another help file for a different application by choosing Open. You can also print a topic by choosing Print Topic; however, you cannot print part of a topic except by copying that part, using the Help Edit menu, to another Windows application or to Visual Basic itself. The File menu also lets you change your printer by choosing the Printer Setup option, or you can leave help by choosing Exit.

**Help Window Edit Menu**  The Edit menu in the help window lets you copy part or all of a topic to the Windows clipboard. Once you have done so, you can copy the information to your Visual Basic application or to any other Windows application, such as the NotePad, by using the Paste command on the application's Edit menu. If you choose Copy, you get a dialog box containing all the text for that topic in a text box. It looks like this:

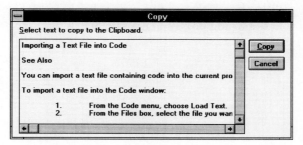

You can use the ordinary Windows SHIFT+arrow keys convention to select the region you want to copy. Then click the Copy button to place the material in the Windows clipboard for future pasting.

The Annotate option lets you add your own notes on the information contained in a topic. This information remains tied to the help file until you delete it. Windows places a little paper clip icon at the beginning of the topic to show that you've added an annotation.

If you select the Annotate option, Windows opens up a dialog box where you type the information you want to add. This box has automatic word wrap, and you can press the arrow keys and DEL to edit the text. (It does not have an overstrike/insert toggle.) If you want to end a line before the text wraps, press CTRL+ENTER. Use the TAB key to move around the dialog box and the three command buttons. Pressing ENTER chooses the button currently selected.

To delete an annotation, move to the paper clip icon that marks the annotation by using the mouse or by pressing SHIFT+TAB. Click the left mouse button, and choose the Delete option in the box.

---

*Help Window Bookmark Menu* Choose the Bookmark menu in the help window to mark specific topics in the help system that you may want to return to quickly. Once you choose Define from this menu, Windows opens up a dialog box for the name of the bookmark. The default is to use the name of the topic. Each time you add a bookmark, the Bookmark menu grows to incorporate the name. You then can open the menu and select the item from the list of bookmarks to quickly move to the topic. If there are more than nine bookmarks, Windows adds an option called More to this menu. Choosing this option then displays a dialog box that lists all the bookmarks. You move through this dialog box in the same way as you would any Windows list box.

To delete a bookmark, choose Define from the menu. This again opens a dialog box listing all the current bookmarks. Select the item from the list given in the dialog box and click the Delete button.

---

*The Help Menu in the Help System* This gives you a detailed guide on how to use the help system.

**Figure 2-8**

**The File menu**

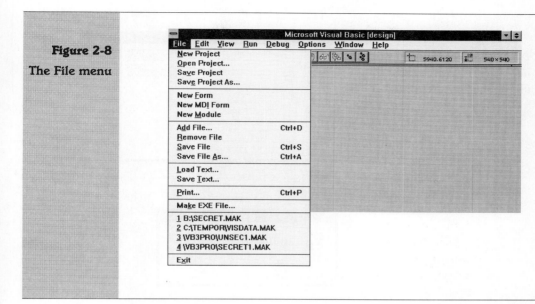

# More on the File Menu

You will need the main File menu to work with the files that make up your project. This menu includes commands for saving, loading, and printing files. We cover them briefly here and you'll see more about them in Chapter 3. The File menu also lets you exit Visual Basic. (As you've seen, the other way to exit Visual Basic is to use ALT+F4 when the focus is on the main menu bar, and like any Windows application you can also open up the Control box on the menu bar and choose Close.) The File menu is shown in Figure 2-8.

Most of the items on the main File menu are useful only when you've started developing your own applications, as discussed in the later chapters of this book. What follows is a brief discussion of each of the items, which should help you orient yourself.

*New Project* The New Project option unloads the current project. If you've made any changes to a project since you've last saved it, a dialog box like the following pops up, asking you if you want to save your work:

**Figure 2-9**

**Open Project dialog box**

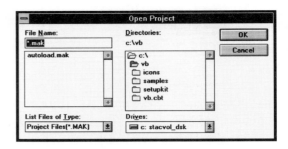

If you answer Yes by pressing ENTER or ALT+Y, you are led to another dialog box for saving files. (See Chapter 3 for details on how to use this dialog box.) To select the New Project option when the File menu is open, press N; if the File menu is not open, press ALT+F+N.

*Open Project* The Open Project option lets you work with an existing Visual Basic application. Since the "O" is underlined, the quick way to select this option is to press "O" when the File menu is open or to press the access keys ALT+F+O when it is not. As the ellipses after the item indicate, choosing this option opens a dialog box. The Open Project dialog box is shown in Figure 2-9. For more details on how to use this dialog box, see the section "Loading and Running Programs" later in this chapter.

*Save Project* The Save Project item saves all the files in the current project and creates the initial Make file. (Recall that a Make file is a list of all the files used in the project plus some other information used by Visual Basic.) The first time you choose this option, a dialog box identical to the one for the Save Project As option opens up. Press V when the File menu is open; if it is not open, press ALT+F+V.

The forms that make up your application are usually stored in a binary format that is not readable by other applications. You can also have them and the code in your application stored in ASCII format, which is readable by most word processors. (Files saved in ASCII format are often called *text-only files* or simply text files.)

**Save Project As**  The Save Project As option pops up a dialog box that lets you save all the files that make up the current project with a new name. It does this by creating a new Make file and saving the files with their current names. (For details on how to use this dialog box, see Chapter 3.) You can also use this option to keep backup copies of the project on a different disk or to save different versions of the project. To select this option when the File menu is open, press E; if the File menu is not open, press ALT+F+E.

**New Form**  You use the New Form item to add multiple windows to your application. (See Chapter 5 for more on this option.) To select this option, press F when the File menu is open; press ALT+F+F when it is not.

**New MDI Form**  An MDI (multiple document interface) form is used to have windows act as child windows to a main window. This is discussed in Chapter 10.

**New Module**  You use the New Module option to add programming code that you'll want to share among all the parts of the application you develop. In Visual Basic, code is attached to a specific window (form) unless you place it in a module. Press M to select this option when the File menu is open; when the File menu is not open, press ALT+F+M.

**Add File**  The Add File option opens a dialog box that lets you incorporate into your application work previously done. You can add already finished forms, general-purpose code (modules), or even files that add new capabilities to Visual Basic. These are called *custom control files*. (See Appendix A for more information.) To select this option, press D when the File menu is open; press ALT+F+D or use the CTRL+D shortcut when it is not.

**Remove File**   Use the Remove File option to delete the part of your Visual Basic application you're currently working with from the application. This option does not delete the file from the disk where it was stored. For that you'll need to use the File Manager built into Windows or ordinary DOS commands. To select the Remove File option, press R if the File menu is open; press ALT+F+R when it is not. You can remove any of the three custom controls from Visual Basic from a specific project by using this option.

**Save File**   The Save File option saves the active form or module (general-purpose code) to disk. The first time you choose this option, Visual Basic opens a dialog box identical to the one for the Save File As option. To select this option, press S when the File menu is open; when it is not, press ALT+F+S or use the CTRL+S shortcut.

**Save File As**   The Save File As option pops up a dialog box that lets you save the active form or module (general-purpose code) to disk, possibly with a new name. Use this option to keep backup copies of a specific piece of a project on a different disk or to save different versions. You also use this option when part of your current application will be useful in other projects. (In this case, you would use the Add File option to add the file to a different project.) To select Save File As, press A when the File menu is open; press ALT+F+A when it is not.

**Load Text**   Use the Load Text option to bring code that was written in another language or with another editor into Visual Basic. You can either replace or merge the text. (See Appendix C for the changes you'll need to make to QuickBASIC code before you can successfully incorporate it into a Visual Basic project.)

**Save Text**   The Save Text option saves the code from the current form or module in text (ASCII) format. This keeps it readable by other word processors or programming languages. As the ellipses indicate, selecting this option opens up a dialog box in which you give the filename under which you want the code saved.

***Print***  Choosing the Print option opens the following dialog box:

This lets you print either the current form, code in the form, module (code) that you are working with, or all forms and modules in your application. To select the Print option, press P when the File menu is open; press ALT+F+P when it is not.

As with all dialog boxes, you can use the TAB key or the mouse to move the focus around the box. As the focus moves, you'll see a little box enclose the label or caption of the item.

The Print dialog box contains two command buttons. Click the OK button if you are satisfied with the options; click the Cancel button if you decide not to print anything. You can press ENTER if one of the buttons is selected, and you can always press ESC to cancel printing.

The two option (radio) buttons (Current and All) determine whether you'll be printing from the part of the application you're currently working with or printing the entire application. As with all radio buttons, the choices are mutually exclusive, and you switch between them with a mouse click or by pressing the SPACEBAR.

The three check boxes (Form, Form Text, and Code) determine whether you print the forms that make up all or part of the application (what the user sees) or the code that activates the interface. As with any check box, the choices are not mutually exclusive, and you toggle them on and off with a mouse click or by pressing the SPACEBAR when the focus is at the box.

***Make EXE File***  The Make EXE File option opens a dialog box that lets you make Visual Basic applications that can run in the Windows environment, independent of Visual Basic. Stand-alone Visual Basic applications require a file called a *dynamic link library* (DLL for short) that you can distribute freely. The DLL for Visual Basic contains the necessary support routines for running a stand-alone Visual Basic program under Microsoft Windows. The current version of this file that comes with Visual Basic 3 is called VBRUN300.DLL.

(See Chapter 3 for details on how to use this option.) To select this option, press K when the File menu is open; press ALT+F+K when it is not.

***The Most Recently Used (MRU) List*** This keeps track of the four most recently opened Visual Basic projects. If you click on one of the files listed here, Visual Basic automatically loads the project. This makes returning to work in progress easy.

***Exit*** Choosing the Exit option is the usual way to leave Visual Basic. If you've made any changes to the current project, Visual Basic asks you if you want to save them before ending the session. You'll see the same dialog boxes as for the New Project option discussed earlier. To select the Exit option, press X when the File menu is open; press ALT+F+X when it is not. ALT+F4 is the shortcut.

**tip:**    *Any Visual Basic application that handles files should have a File menu. Also, an important convention for Windows applications is that the last item on this menu should be the Exit command with an ALT+F4 shortcut.*

See Chapter 10 for how to create a menu and Chapter 14 for how to work with files.

# Editing

Visual Basic comes with a full-screen editor similar to the one used in the NotePad or Windows Write programs that come with Microsoft Windows. However, since it is a programming editor, it lacks features like word wrap and print formatting that even a primitive word processor like Write has. On the other hand, it does add features like syntax checking that can spot certain common programming typos. The Visual Basic program editor also color codes the various parts of your code. For example, Visual Basic commands can be one color, comments another. The colors used are customizable via the Environment item on the Options menu. The Visual Basic program editor is activated whenever you are writing or viewing code.

A bar (the cursor) marks where you are in the file (the insertion point). You move the insertion point around with the arrow keys or by moving the mouse pointer to the new location and clicking. What you type appears where the insertion point was.

As with any editor, you have two choices when typing: you can be in either insert mode or overstrike mode. When you are in insert mode (the default), any text you type pushes the text that follows to the right. In overstrike mode, the text replaces the old text one character at a time. You switch between these modes by pressing INS. The cursor changes to a block when you're in overstrike mode. In both modes, you have two ways of deleting a character: BACKSPACE deletes the character to the left of the cursor, and DEL deletes the character at the cursor.

When you want to work with a block of text, whether to move it, duplicate it, or just delete it, you have to select the text. To select text, first move the cursor to the start or end of the text you want to select. Then press SHIFT and an arrow key to select the text. You can also hold down the left mouse button and drag to select text.

For example, as you hold down the LEFT ARROW key, the selection grows (or shrinks) by one character to the left. Once you've selected text, you can delete it completely by pressing DEL. More common, however, is to cut (or copy) the selected text to the Windows clipboard. The clipboard can hold only one piece of text.

Once text is in the clipboard, you can paste it repeatedly to different parts of your program. To cut text, press SHIFT+DEL or open the Edit menu and choose Cut by pressing ALT+E+T. To place a copy of the text in the clipboard, press CTRL+INS or choose Copy from the Edit menu by pressing ALT+E+C.

To paste text, move the insertion point to where you want the text to be and press SHIFT+INS. (A copy remains in the clipboard until you place new text there.)

If you've cut, pasted, or deleted selected text, you can undo the action. To do this, choose Undo from the Edit menu. To select this option when the Edit menu is open, press U; press ALT+BACKSPACE when it is not. This command will be grayed if there is nothing that can be undone.

## The Edit Menu

The Edit menu contains 14 items. Here are brief descriptions of each of them.

***Undo, Redo*** Undo reverses the last edit you made. Redo reverses the last editing action. The shortcut for Undo is CTRL+Z.

***Cut, Copy, Paste*** You use Cut, Copy, and Paste after you select text. Cut places the text in the Windows clipboard, Copy places a copy of it there, and Paste takes whatever is in the clipboard and pastes it into your Visual Basic application. In particular, you can use this item to exchange information (text or graphics) between another Windows application and Visual Basic.

***Paste Link*** Paste Link is used in exchanging information dynamically between Windows applications; see Chapter 15.

***Delete*** The Delete command removes the selected information but does not place a copy in the clipboard.

***Find*** Choosing the Find option displays a dialog box in which you enter the text (string) you want Visual Basic to search for. Visual Basic searches the entire project for the string. The shortcut is CTRL+F.

***Find Next*** The Find Next option repeats the previous search. Another way to select this option is to press F3.

***Find Previous*** Choose Find Previous to search backward through the project for the text specified in the previous use of the Find dialog box. Another way to select this option is to press SHIFT+F3.

***Replace*** The Replace option opens a dialog box with two text boxes. The first is for the text to be found, and the second is for what should replace it. CTRL +R is the shortcut.

***Bring to Front, Send to Back*** The Bring to Front option brings the selected object in front of all other objects; the Send to Back option moves the object back when you are developing the project. (See Chapter 10 for more on this.)

*Align to Grid* Align to Grid is used to accurately position objects on your forms. See Chapter 4 for more on how to use the grid.

# The Options Menu

The Options menu contains two items. The second one, Project, opens up a dialog box for three items you'll need to set in the course of developing an application. These are discussed in Chapters 14 and 17. Choosing the Environment option opens up a dialog box that looks like this:

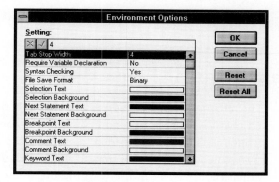

By choosing the different items, you can change the colors, set tab stops, or more generally set certain options that will be useful in programming. For example, you can change the default way Visual Basic saves files from a binary format to a text format. As an example of how to change an option in this dialog box, let's change the default tab stops from 4 to 2. To do this:

1. Click on the item marked Tab Stop Width.

2. Type **2** and press ENTER.

Other items give you a fixed list of choices to choose from. For example, the Syntax Checking item can only be toggled on and off. When you've selected it (or any other option with a fixed list of choices to make), the arrow to the right is darkened. If you click on the arrow, you'll see the two possibilities as shown here:

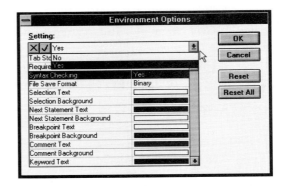

The syntax checker looks at each line of code after you press ENTER. Visual Basic then tells you immediately if there is a misspelled keyword or separator.

## Loading and Running Programs

This chapter ends by leading you through the procedures needed to run an existing Visual Basic program. Visual Basic comes with many interesting sample programs. The one described in this section is the Icon Editor. This program gives you a tool you will turn to more and more frequently as you work with Visual Basic. You can use it to modify one of the hundreds of icons supplied with Visual Basic or to start building one from scratch.

If you choose the Open Project option on the File menu or click on the Open Project tool (the third tool), you are presented with the dialog box shown in Figure 2-10. As in any Windows dialog box, you move around either with the mouse or by pressing TAB (SHIFT+TAB to move backward). You can also move directly to any location that has an access key (the underlined letter) by

**Figure 2-10**

Open Project dialog box with \VB subdirectories

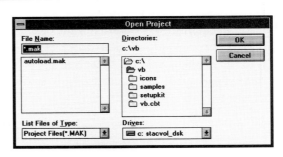

holding down the ALT key and pressing the letter. You can close the Open Project dialog box by clicking the Cancel button or by pressing ESC.

Notice in Figure 2-10 that only one file is shown. This is because Visual Basic keeps track of the files that make up a project in a file with a .MAK extension (for the "Make file"), and there is only one in the \VB directory. Of course, you can change the default for the file name extension Visual Basic uses to search by moving to the File Name list box (press ALT+N) and typing the new file pattern.

Click the item marked *samples* in the Directories list box (or press ALT+D+S and press ENTER) and then move through the subdirectories of the samples directory until you get to the one marked *iconwrks*. Double-click on it and you are placed in the ICONWRKS subdirectory. The Files box now lists the ICONWRKS.MAK file, which contains the names and locations of the files that make up the ICONWRKS project. When you now double-click on this, Visual Basic loads the ICONWRKS project, which lets you modify icons (or build them from scratch). You can also select this item by using an arrow key to move to it and then pressing ENTER.

After a short delay (possibly interrupted by a dialog box asking you if you want to save your current work), Visual Basic loads the IconWorks Editor project. Since this program (written completely in Visual Basic) dramatically shows off the power that will soon be at your fingertips, you might want to press F5 to run it. The initial screen looks like Figure 2-11. The program comes with an extensive help system, so nothing prevents you from starting now to build your own library of customized icons.

**Figure 2-11**

The IconWorks Editor

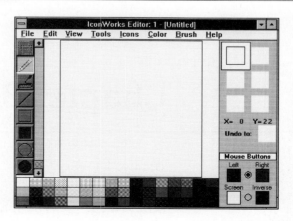

# Chapter 3

# Customizing a Form

VISUAL Basic makes it easy to build an application with all the features that a sophisticated Windows program demands. Using list boxes, dialog boxes, message boxes, and command buttons will become routine. Nonetheless, it's best first to become comfortable using Visual Basic to customize a blank form. (Remember that *form* is the term Visual Basic uses for a customizeable window.) This chapter shows you how to design forms with a given size, shape, or location. You'll learn how to print text in a form and how to print an image of a form on your printer.

Most important, you'll see how to make a form respond to events such as a mouse click or double-click in the form. (As mentioned in Chapter 1, the event-driven nature of Visual Basic is the primary reason it is both extraordinarily powerful and easy to use.)

## Starting a New Project

Whenever you want to start a new *project* (the name Visual Basic uses for an application that is being developed), you need only open the File menu and click the New Project item. You can also start Visual Basic by opening an existing project (which you can do from the File menu, the toolbar, as you saw in Chapter 2, or from the File Manager by double-clicking the name of the project file). Visual Basic 3 keeps a list of the most recently used projects on the File menu. You can click that item to work on that project.

For now, this book assumes that you've set the Program or File Manager in Windows to *minimize on use*—that is, they will be icons when you start an application. When you start Visual Basic, after a short delay your screen will look something like the one in Figure 3-1. Note the blank window in the center of the screen, which has a grid of dots. This is the *form* that you will customize. You use the grid to align objects such as command buttons and list boxes on the screen. (You'll learn more about the grid in Chapter 4.) At the top of the

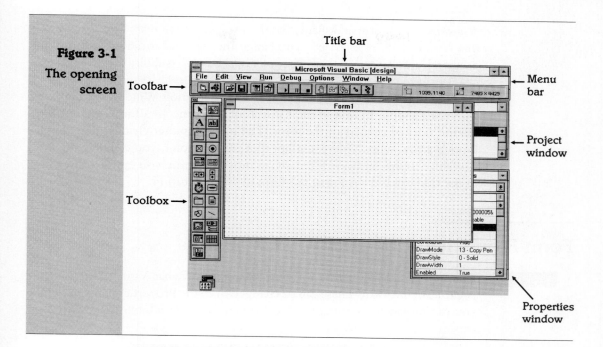

**Figure 3-1**

The opening screen

blank form is the title bar with its caption. *Caption* is the Visual Basic term for what appears in the title bar of the form. You'll see how to customize the caption shortly so you can give meaningful titles to your forms. Currently, this form is called Form1. Form1 is the default name that Visual Basic gives to a form when you start working on a new project.

To the left of the Form1 window is the toolbox. (If it is not available, use ALT+W+T to reveal it.) The toolbox is what you use to place command buttons, text boxes, and other controls needed to customize a form. (The toolbox is discussed extensively in Chapters 4, 9, 10, and 14 of this book.) Partially covered at the right of the screen is the Project window (discussed in Chapter 4). Also partially hidden is the Properties window (see "Form Properties" later in this chapter).

## Altering a Form

For now, concentrate on the form named Form1 in the center of your screen. You should be completely comfortable with the methods for changing the size and location of this form before you move on. In many Visual Basic applications, the size and location of the form at the time you finish the design (usually called *design time*) is the size and shape that the user sees at *run time*. This is not to say that Visual Basic doesn't let you change the size and location of forms as a program runs. An essential property of Visual Basic is its ability to make dynamic changes in response to user events.

One way to resize a form is common to all Microsoft Windows applications: Move the mouse to one of the *hot spots* of the form. In a form, the hot spots are the sides or corners of the form. The mouse pointer changes to a double-headed arrow when you're at a hot spot. At this point, you can drag the form to change its size or shape. Similarly, to move the form, you can click anywhere in the title bar and then drag the form to a new location.

## Form Properties

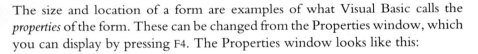

The size and location of a form are examples of what Visual Basic calls the *properties* of the form. These can be changed from the Properties window, which you can display by pressing F4. The Properties window looks like this:

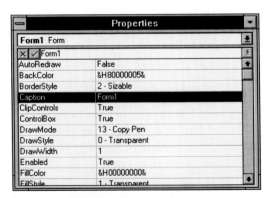

Notice that right below the title bar is a line that says "Form1 Form." This line tells you the name of the object you are working with and what type of object it is. In this case, the name is the default name, Form1. (When you have other controls on your forms, click the down arrow at the far right of this line to see a list of the controls, as discussed in Chapter 4). Next notice the highlighted line that says "Caption" in the first column and "Form1" in the second column. The word *Form1* below the line "Form1 Form" at the top of the box is the caption of the form. This text box indicates the current *setting* of the Caption property. As you move through the Properties window with the arrow keys or mouse, the text in this box changes to reflect the property in whatever line is highlighted.

If the caption line is highlighted, then whatever you enter in the text box immediately becomes the new caption for the form. This text box is called the *Settings box* for the Properties window. For example, type **First Window App** in the Settings box for the caption. Notice that as you do, the caption on the form changes instantly to reflect what you've typed.

However, if you didn't proceed exactly in the order suggested, or if you inadvertently clicked where you shouldn't have, this method might not work. It is easier to get used to a more general method for choosing and changing properties using the Properties window, described in the next section.

## The Properties Window

There are two ways to change a setting for a property, but first you must move through the Properties window until you get to the property you want to change. (The various lines are highlighted as you move through the Properties window.) Now whatever you type replaces the setting that was originally there. Another method is to move the mouse until the mouse pointer is in the Settings box inside the Properties window, click, and insert the text you want. Note that this method inserts text; it doesn't replace the text originally there. To replace text, you first have to select the text you want to replace. (Remember that you select text by holding down the mouse button and dragging the pointer across the text or by using a SHIFT+ARROW key combination.)

Use the arrow keys or the mouse to scroll through the box. As you can see, you can set a large number of properties (over 40) for a form. Although you won't learn about them all in this chapter, the next few sections discuss the most useful ones.

As with any Windows list box, you can scroll through the Properties window by repeatedly clicking an arrow in the scroll bars. However, the standard Microsoft Windows shortcut for moving through a list box doesn't work here. You can't press the first letter of the item you want to change to move to the item because anything you type goes into the Settings box.

**tip:**

*To quickly move through the properties in the Properties window, use SHIFT+CTRL+letter key. This moves you to the first property that begins with that letter. Subsequent uses of this combination move to succeeding properties that begin with the letter.*

## AN EXAMPLE

Move through the Properties window to the item marked MaxButton (for example by pressing SHIFT+CTRL+M once). Notice that the word *MaxButton* replaces the word *Caption* in the Settings box, and that the word *True* is located in the Settings box in the middle of the property box, as shown here:

```
┌──────────────────── Properties ──────────────────────┐
│ ─                                                    ▼ │
├───────────────────────────────────────────────────────┤
│ Form1  Form                                          ± │
├───────────────────────────────────────────────────────┤
│ X │ ✓ │ True                                         ± │
├───────────────────────────────────────────────────────┤
│ FontTransparent        True                         ↑ │
│ FontUnderline          False                          │
│ ForeColor              &H80000008&                    │
│ Height                 4425                           │
│ HelpContextID          0                             │
│ Icon                   (Icon)                        │
│ KeyPreview             False                         │
│ Left                   1035                          │
│ LinkMode               0 - None                      │
│ LinkTopic              Form1                         │
│ MaxButton              True                          │
│ MDIChild               False                        ↓ │
└───────────────────────────────────────────────────────┘
```

The True setting means that the form you are designing will have a maximize button. (Remember that a maximize button appears at the top-right corner of a window and lets you maximize the window by clicking the mouse there once.)

As an experiment, for your first application change this property to False. There are two ways to do this. The simplest is just to press F and then press ENTER. The property changes from True to False. The second is to click the arrow immediately to the right of the Settings box where the word *True* appears. A list box drops down with the two options, True and False, as shown here:

```
┌──────────────────── Properties ──────────────────────┐
│ ─                                                    ▼ │
├───────────────────────────────────────────────────────┤
│ Form1  Form                                          ± │
├───────────────────────────────────────────────────────┤
│ X │ ✓ │ True                                         ± │
├───────────────────────────────────────────────────────┤
│ FontTr│ True                                          │
│ FontU │ False                                         │
│ ForeColor              &H80000008&                    │
│ Height                 4425                           │
│ HelpContextID          0                             │
│ Icon                   (Icon)                        │
│ KeyPreview             False                         │
│ Left                   1035                          │
│ LinkMode               0 - None                      │
│ LinkTopic              Form1                         │
│ MaxButton              True                          │
│ MDIChild               False                        ↓ │
└───────────────────────────────────────────────────────┘
```

Select the False option by pressing the DOWN ARROW and then pressing ENTER. A general feature in Visual Basic is that whenever a property has only a fixed number of options, the arrow to the right of the settings box is black rather than gray.

Now change the MinButton property to False. (Return to the Properties window and then move to the MinButton property and change its value to False.)

With both of these properties set to False, run this application and see what happens. There are three ways to run a Visual Basic application:

♦ Select the Start option from the toolbar by clicking the forward arrow (the seventh tool).

♦ Select the Start option from the Run menu by using the mouse or by pressing ALT+R+S.

♦ Press F5 as a shortcut.

After a short delay, the form will pop up looking like the one in Figure 3-2. Notice that this form has neither a minimize nor a maximize button. Notice also that, unlike when you changed the caption, these changes show up only at run time (that is, when you ran the application).

To return to developing an application, move the mouse to the Run menu and click the End option or use the stop tool (the tool that looks like a stop button on a cassette recorder). This brings you back to the application you've just developed.

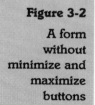

**Figure 3-2**

A form without minimize and maximize buttons

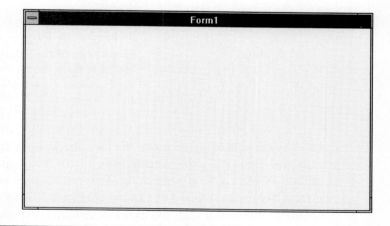

Form1

Designing a form that lacks both minimize and maximize buttons may not seem like much, but it does illustrate the absolutely essential process of changing the properties of a Visual Basic object.

## A SUMMARY OF HOW TO WORK WITH THE PROPERTIES WINDOW

Here is a summary of the general method for changing the properties of a Visual Basic form:

1. Display the Properties window by pressing F4.

2. Move to the Properties window and select an item from the properties in the list box.

3. Enter the new setting for the property.

4. Press ENTER to accept the new setting.

Following is a table containing the keyboard shortcuts for manipulating the properties window when it has the focus.

| Key | Action |
| --- | --- |
| SHIFT+CTRL+letter key | Moves to the first item beginning with that letter |
| RIGHT ARROW/ DOWN ARROW | Moves to the next item in the Properties list box |
| LEFT ARROW/UP ARROW | Moves to the previous item in the Properties list box |
| PGDN/END | Moves to the last item displayed in the Properties list box or to the last item |
| PGUP/HOME | Moves to the first item displayed in the Properties list box or to the first item |
| F4 | Brings up the Properties window (you can also use the Window menu) |

After you enter a new setting, press ENTER, click the mouse, or press TAB to accept the changes and move the focus back to the list of properties.

If the focus is in the Settings box in the Properties window, the usual Windows editing keys will work: ALT+BACKSPACE undoes the last action, CTRL+INS copies selected text to the clipboard, and so on.

Sometimes you'll want to change your mind after you've changed a setting. If you haven't moved away from the Settings box, you can go back to the previous setting by clicking the cross (Cancel box) to the far left of the Settings box. To accept the setting you've just typed, instead of pressing ENTER, you can click the check box (Enter box) next to the Cancel box. (As usual, both are gray when disabled and black when they can be used in the usual way.)

When Visual Basic can display a complete list of the settings for a specific property, you can click the down arrow button to see the list (the down arrow will be darkened). If the Settings box itself has the focus, then the same keys or key combinations work on the Settings list as worked for the Properties list box: F4 to open or close, PGDN to move to the last item shown, and so on.

## The Most Common Properties of a Form

Following is a list of some of the most common properties of forms. You may need to set these in the early stages of mastering Visual Basic. The next two sections discuss other form properties.

You will use these properties time and time again. As you'll see in later chapters, a single property can pertain to many different objects. For example, you will want to set the font properties for text boxes, command buttons, and the like.

*BorderStyle* BorderStyle is an example of a property that offers only a small number of choices. Because of this, the arrow to the right of the location for this property setting is enabled (darkened). You can choose among four values for this property. The default value, 2, allows the user to size and shape the form via the hot spots located on the boundary of the form.

Change this setting to 1 (called *fixed single*), and the user will no longer be able to resize the window. All the user will be able to do is minimize or maximize the window (unless, of course, you turn off those options as well when you design the application).

Set this value to 0, and the application will show no border whatsoever and therefore no minimize, maximize, or control box buttons. Because of this, a form created without a border cannot be moved, resized, or reshaped. This setting is useful when you want your forms to be inviolate.

The fourth setting, 3 (called *fixed double*) is not often used for ordinary forms, but it is commonly used for dialog boxes. It gives a nonsizeable (it has no hot spots) border that is twice as thick as normal.

▬▬

***Caption*** As you've already seen, the Caption property sets the title of the form. The caption is also the title that Microsoft Windows uses for the application icon when the user minimizes the application.

▬▬

***ControlBox*** ControlBox is another property that goes into effect only when a user runs the application. As in any Microsoft Windows application, control boxes are located in the far-left corner of the title bar. Clicking the box displays a list of common window tasks such as window minimizing, maximizing, and closing, along with keyboard equivalents when they exist.

You have only two choices: You can either have a control box or not. Therefore, there are only two possible settings, so the list box to the right of the settings area is enabled. Note that if your application doesn't have a control box, a user without a mouse is in trouble. He or she won't be able to minimize, maximize, or close the application. Control boxes are generally not a good thing to remove.

▬▬

***Enabled*** Enabled is another property you do not want to change casually. Set Enabled to False, and the form cannot respond to any events. Usually you toggle this property back and forth in response to some event. To make your forms respond dynamically, you must write code. The Properties window is most often used for setting the static properties of your objects.

▬▬

***FontName*** The FontName property is another example of a setting with a finite number of choices. The pull-down list shows the fonts available. (This list depends on the fonts Windows knows about.) The font you choose is used when you display information on the form; the font does not affect the form caption.

▬▬

***FontSize*** The FontSize property determines the size of the text displayed on the form. The sizes you can choose are determined by the font you select via the FontName property.

▬▬

***FontBold, FontItalic, FontStrikethru, FontUnderline, Font Transparent*** Just as with FontName, the other font properties affect what is displayed in the form. These properties are either True or False and can usually be combined at will.

For example, you can have bold, italic script that uses strike-through. The Font Transparent property determines if the background shows through or not. Often, you switch among these properties in response to events. Like any responsive activity in Visual Basic, switching requires writing code.

■■■

***Height, Width*** Height and Width are interesting properties—and not only because they can be set two ways. They are examples of properties that use the Microsoft Windows *twips* scale to measure the sizes of the objects involved. There are 1440 *twips* to an inch (567 to a centimeter). The term actually stands for *one twentieth of a point*. (Points are a common measure for printers; this book is set in 11-point type.) Move to the properties bar and choose the Height property. Notice that the current value is 4425 twips (which means the default size of a form when printed is slightly more than 3 inches, or slightly less than 8 centimeters).

**caution:**

*Twips measure how large the object would be if it were printed; they do not correspond exactly to the size of the object on your screen. For example, on a 15-inch diagonal monitor, the default size of a form is approximately 4.5 inches. (See the section, "An Example: The Screen Object and Available Fonts," in Chapter 6 for a discussion of how to adjust your Visual Basic projects for different-size monitors.)*

Look at the far right of the toolbar.

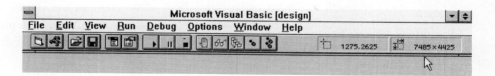

Notice the last box has the value 7485 × 4425. (The numbers you will see depend on your screen resolution.) This tells you the current value in twips for the width and height of the form. Now drag the form to change the width and height. Notice that when you change the size of the form by dragging, the value at the far left of the toolbar changes to reflect the new size. If you look in the Properties window, you'll see that the values for these properties change as well.

Of course, using the mouse and dragging to set the height and width is a less precise procedure than you may need. Luckily, since Height and Width are properties, their values can be changed directly via the Properties window. You just have to enter the value you want in the Settings box. For example, if you change the width to 3743 twips, you will cut the window in half (at least as close to half as the screen can display it).

Like the Caption property, any changes you make to the height and width of the form go into effect immediately—they do not wait until the application runs.

**note:** *Unless you disable the border by changing the Border Style property, a user can size and reshape the various forms in the application regardless of how you set them at design time.*

*Left, Top* The Left and Top settings determine the distance between the left or top of the form and the screen. Set the value of the Top property to 0, and the form you're designing is flush with the top. Set the value of the Left property to 0, and it will be flush with the left side of the screen.

These settings work in much the same way as the Height and Width properties. You change them in the same two ways. They are also measured in twips, and changes go into effect when you reset the values, not when the user runs the application.

*MousePointer* MousePointer is an amusing (and occasionally useful) property that sets the shape of the mouse pointer. The default value is 0, but as the pull-down list indicates, there are 12 other values. A setting of 4, for example, turns the mouse pointer into a rather pretty square within a square. The setting you will use most often is 11. This value changes the mouse pointer to an hourglass and, as in other Microsoft Windows applications, it is useful for telling a user that he or she has to wait until the computer finishes what it is doing.

*Visible* Visible is another property that is dangerous to change by mistake. Set the value of this property to False, and the form will no longer be visible (and, therefore, it will be difficult for the user to manipulate!). You usually will want to make a form invisible only when you are designing an application with multiple forms. Then you will often want to hide one or more of the forms by using the Visible property. Often, you will reset this property by using code and not at the time you design the application.

*WindowState*  The WindowState property determines how the form will look at run time. There are three possible settings. A setting of 1 reduces the form to an icon, and a setting of 2 maximizes the form. A setting of 0 is the normal default setting. This property is most often changed in code.

## The Scale Properties

You will often need to accurately position objects or text in a form. Some people are not comfortable thinking in terms of twips. To help you, Visual Basic provides five properties that affect the scale used in a form. (For more information on the scale properties, see Chapter 12.)

*ScaleMode*  The ScaleMode property allows you to change the units used in the forms's internal coordinate system. Tired of twips? There are seven other possibilities. You can create your own units (the value of this setting is 0), keep the default twips (this value is 1), or use one of the six remaining choices. An interesting setting—especially for graphics—is 3. This uses one *pixel* (a picture element—the smallest unit of resolution on your monitor) as the scale. And of course, if you are more comfortable with them, you can choose inches (5), millimeters (6), or centimeters (7).

*ScaleHeight, ScaleWidth*  Use the ScaleHeight and ScaleWidth properties when you set up your own scale for the height and width of the form. Resetting these properties has the side effect of setting the value of the ScaleMode property back to 0. For example, if you set the value of each of these properties to 100, then the form uses a scale that has point 50,50 as its center. You will probably reset the values of these properties only when you are writing an application that uses graphics. (See Chapter 12 for more information on these properties.)

*ScaleLeft, ScaleTop*  The ScaleLeft and ScaleTop properties describe what value Visual Basic uses for the left or top corner of the form. The original (default) value for each of these properties is 0. Like ScaleHeight and Scale-Width, these properties are most useful when you are working with graphics.

For example, if you are writing a program that works with a graph, you rarely want the top-left corner to be at point 0,0.

## Icons

The Icon property is one you will use frequently. This property determines the icon your application will display when it is minimized or turned into a stand-alone application on the Windows desktop. Visual Basic comes with a large library of icons that you can use freely. Pictures of them appear in Appendix B of the *Visual Basic Programmer's Guide*. In addition, as you saw in Chapter 2, the IconWrks sample program lets you design custom icons easily.

To see how to choose an icon for your application, go to the Properties window and select the Icon property. The Settings box looks like this:

| Properties | |
|---|---|
| **Form1** Form | |
| ☒ ✓ (Icon) | ... |
| ForeColor | &H80000008& |
| Height | 4425 |
| HelpContextID | 0 |
| Icon | (Icon) |
| KeyPreview | False |
| Left | 1275 |
| LinkMode | 0 - None |
| LinkTopic | Form1 |
| MaxButton | True |
| MDIChild | False |
| MinButton | True |
| MousePointer | 0 - Default |

Note that to the right of the Settings box is a box with three dots. As in all Windows applications, these three dots (usually called an ellipsis) indicate that a dialog box is available to help you select the value of the property. Click the box containing the three dots, and the following dialog box appears:

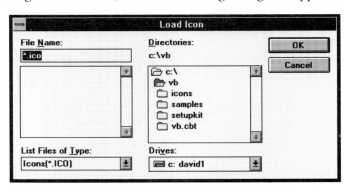

Assuming that you have installed Visual Basic in the ordinary way, the icons supplied with Visual Basic are found in the subdirectories of the ICONS directory that is under the directory where Visual Basic is installed. As always, there are many ways to get to this subdirectory; probably the fastest is to move the mouse pointer to the icons subdirectory in the dialog box and double-click. Of course, you can type the full path name of the file in the File Name text box or move the focus to the Directories list and select the name by keystrokes alone.

To see an example of how to set the Icon property, go to the ICONS subdirectory and move through the list of its subdirectories until you get to the one marked [misc]; double-click this name. The Files list box now shows the more than 70 icon files in this directory. To choose the FACE03 icon, either move the focus to the File Name text box and type the name of the icon or move through the list until you can select FACE03. Press ENTER to accept this choice. To be sure that you really have changed the icon for the Form1 application, click the application's minimize button.

# Color Properties

The colors you use in an application can have a dramatic effect on how easy and pleasurable the application is to use and, as a result, how well it is received. You can specify the background color (BackColor) and the foreground color (ForeColor) for text and graphics in the window. Visual Basic has many ways to change the colors of an application dynamically by using code. See Chapter 12 for more information on using code to achieve this effect.

## Accessing BackColor and ForeColor via the Color Palette

Suppose you try to set the BackColor property. If you open the Properties window and select BackColor, you'll see the following:

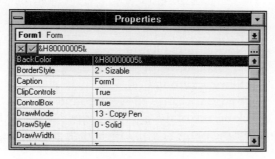

The setting is &H80000005&, which is rather cryptic to say the least. In fact, Visual Basic describes color codes by using a hexadecimal code (base 16), as described later in the section, "Colors and Counting in Base 16." In theory, using hexadecimal code allows you to set up to 16,777,216 different colors—usually finer control than one really needs. The most common way to set colors is to choose one of the color properties and click the ellipsis to the right of the Settings box. A box filled with small colored boxes opens up as shown here. (Although you cannot see the colors here, you can get an idea of what the color palette looks like.)

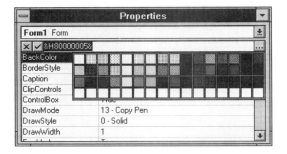

Click whatever color you like, and the color code for that color is placed in the Settings box.

## WORKING WITH THE COLOR PALETTE

You can also create your own colors by working with the color palette directly. Open up the color palette by going to the Window menu and choosing the Color palette (ALT+W+C). Here's what you see:

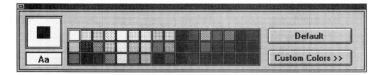

Notice, to the left of the palette, a dark box enclosed in a lighter box. The inner box displays the current foreground color, and the outer box displays the current background color.

You can change the foreground color by clicking the inner box and then clicking any of the colored boxes displayed. To change the background color, click the outer box and then click any of the colored boxes displayed.

The text box in the bottom-left corner of the color palette displays the foreground and background colors for any text in the form or control you've selected. To go back to the default colors specified in the Windows control panel, click the Default command button at the right.

You can also create your own colors for the color palette. To do this, follow these steps:

1. Click the Custom Colors button on the color palette. Visual Basic adds a line of blank boxes at the bottom of the palette. Each of these boxes represents a possible custom color.

2. Click one of these blank boxes and then click the Define Colors command button (which is now enabled). This opens the Define Color dialog box, shown here:

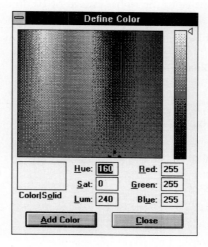

3. Now you can change the amount of red, green, or blue; color; hue; saturation; or luminosity of your form to suit your needs by adjusting the controls in the dialog box.

4. Press the Add Color button to create the custom color or the Close button to cancel.

## Colors and Counting in Base 16

To set colors directly from the Properties window, you'll need to know a bit about counting in binary (base 2) and hexadecimal (base 16) formats. (This information is also useful in various other contexts in Visual Basic; although you may want to skip this section now, you will probably want to return to it later.)

A computer is ultimately a giant collection of on-off switches, and a disk is a collection of particles that can either be magnetized or not. Think of each memory location in your PC as being made up of eight on-off switches. This affects the internal representation of numbers inside a PC. For example, when you write 255, you ordinarily think two hundreds, five tens, and five ones. The digits are arranged in *decimal notation,* or base-10 notation, with each position holding numbers 10 times as large as the position to the right. However, your computer thinks in *binary notation* (base-2 notation) and stores the number 255 in a single-memory location as 11111111, meaning one 128, one 64, one 32, one 16, one 8, one 4, one 2, and one 1. Each of the eight switches mentioned above represents a *bit* (for binary digit). When a switch stores a 1, the bit is said to be on, and the value stored in that position is twice the value of the digit in the place to the right (instead of 10 times the value, as in decimal notation). Eight bits form a *byte* (which is one memory location), and half a byte forms a *nibble.*

The following table shows you how to count to 15 in binary notation.

| Binary | Decimal |
| --- | --- |
| 0 | 0 |
| 1 | 1 |
| 10 | 2 |
| 11 | 3 |
| 100 | 4 |
| 101 | 5 |
| 110 | 6 |
| 111 | 7 |
| 1000 | 8 |
| 1001 | 9 |
| 1010 | 10 |
| 1011 | 11 |
| 1100 | 12 |
| 1101 | 13 |
| 1110 | 14 |
| 1111 | 15 |

Fifteen is the largest number that can be stored in a single nibble, and 255 is the largest number that can be stored in a byte. Bits are numbered with the leftmost bit called the *most significant* and the rightmost (or zero) bit called the *least significant.*

Binary numbers are difficult for most people to handle. Hexadecimal numbers (base 16) are much easier. Each place in a hexadecimal numbering scheme is 16 times the previous place. So instead of saying "1's place, 10's place, 100's place," as you learned in grade school (for decimal notation), in hexadecimal (hex) notation you say, "1's place, 16's place, 256's place," and so on. For example, hexadecimal 10 is decimal 16. Hexadecimal notation uses A for decimal 10, B for decimal 11, C for decimal 12, D for decimal 13, E for decimal 14, and F for decimal 15. In Visual Basic programs, you prefix a number with &H to indicate that it is a hexadecimal number. Thus, you would write decimal 49 as &H31. Each hexadecimal digit represents four binary digits, or one nibble.

To convert binary numbers to hexidecimal format, group the digits from right to left in groups of four and convert. For example, 11010111 (1101 0111, in two groups of four) is hexadecimal D7: 1101 is 13 in decimal format and D in hexadecimal format, and 0111 is 7 in both decimal and hexadecimal formats.

## HOW COLOR WORKS IN VISUAL BASIC

The settings for the color properties are indicated by hexadecimal coding. Every color code in Visual Basic is made up of six hexadecimal digits, from &H000000& (0) to &HFFFFFF& (16,777,215). This might seem awkward, but the code actually is fairly simple to use—if you understand hexadecimal notation.

Finally, it's a good idea to get into the habit of adding another ampersand to the end of a color code—for example: &HFFFFFF&. This tells Visual Basic to treat the color code as a long integer. *Long integers* are integers greater than 32,767 or less than −32,768, and color codes are usually outside these limits. Forgetting the identifier doesn't usually cause problems, but it's best not to take chances. (For more information on long integers and the other types of numbers in Visual Basic, see Chapter 5.)

To understand the code, think of *RGB* (red, green, and blue) *color monitors* as being told to send out a specific amount of redness, greenness, and blueness. The combination of these primary colors gives you all the remaining ones. In the coding used by Visual Basic, the last two hexadecimal digits give you the amount of redness, the middle two give you the amount of greenness, and the first two, the most significant, give you the amount of blueness. Here are a few examples of hexadecimal color codes and the colors they produce:

| Hex Color Code | Color |
| --- | --- |
| &H0000FF& | Maximum red (no green or blue) |
| &H00FF00& | Maximum green (no red or blue) |
| &HFF0000& | Maximum blue (no red or green) |

| Hex Color Code | Color |
| --- | --- |
| &H000000& | Black (no color) |
| &HFFFFFF& | White (all colors) |
| &H00FFFF& | Yellow (red and green) |
| &H808080& | Gray (equal mixtures of all colors) |

The reason why &H808080& is an equal mixture of all colors is that half of &HFF& is about &H80&, because half of 255 is about 128; 128 is equal to 8 × 16, which is equal to &H80&.

Some people find it convenient to think of the color code as &HBBGGRR& (B for blue, G for green, and R for red).

In the preceding section, you saw how to set the background and foreground colors of the window by using the color palette. To change these settings directly, move to the Properties window, select BackColor or ForeColor, decide how much red, green, or blue you want, and type the appropriate hexadecimal code.

The ForeColor property determines the color used for both text and graphics in the window. The foreground color should be sufficiently different from the background color to allow some contrast.

## Making a Form Responsive

By this point, you should be comfortable with designing Visual Basic forms. The essence of a Microsoft Windows program (and, therefore, of Visual Basic) is to make your forms responsive to user actions. Visual Basic objects can recognize many different events. (Forms recognize more than 20.) For example, if a user clicks an area on the screen, you may want a message displayed; if the user clicks a command button, you may want an action performed. To effect these actions, you write programs in Visual Basic's structured programming language.

Although Visual Basic objects can recognize many different events, the objects will sit there totally inert unless you've written code to tell them what to do when an event occurs. Thus, for any event to which you want a Visual Basic object to respond, you must write an event procedure telling Visual Basic what to do. Event procedures are nothing more than the lines of programming code that tell Visual Basic how to respond to a given event.

## The Code Window

Here, you will design your form so that it responds to a mouse click. Double-click in any blank part of Form1 (your form may have a different name). A new window opens up, and your screen looks something like the one in Figure 3-3. Double-clicking the form opens the *Code window*. This is where you enter the code to tell Visual Basic how to respond to the event.

Notice the two text boxes in the top screen, marked Object and Proc. If you click the arrow next to the Object list box, you pull down the *Object list box,* shown here:

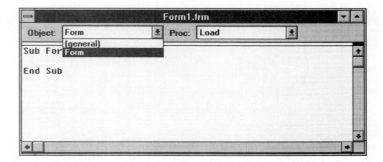

This box lists all objects in your form. You have yet to put any text boxes, command buttons, or other controls on this form, so no objects except the form

**Figure 3-3**

Starting to code: initial screen

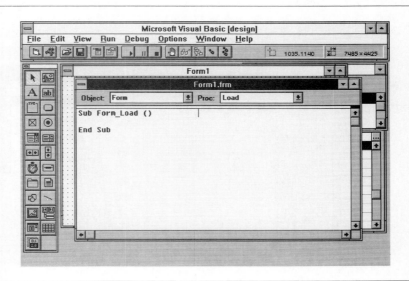

itself (and an object called "general," discussed in Chapter 5) are listed in this box. If you pull down the *Procedure list box* (the one abbreviated Proc:) at the right, you see a list of all the events that the Visual Basic object named in the Object box can recognize. A form can recognize more than 20 events; the Procedure list box has 23 items in it.

In Figure 3-3, below the Object and Procedure list boxes, you see the following code:

```
Sub Form_Load ()

End Sub
```

This code is an example of an *event procedure template*. Like any template, it gives you a framework in which to work. The Form_Load event is invoked whenever Visual Basic brings up a form. It is used to set initial properties of forms via code; you'll learn more about it in Chapters 4 and 5. (The chapters that follow discuss in detail how to write code for Visual Basic, so don't worry if you are a novice programmer. If you are an experienced programmer, you can move through these chapters quickly.)

For now, we want to enter the code that tells Visual Basic how to respond to a click here. To do this we have to bring up the template for the Form_Click procedure. Move to the Proc (procedure) list box and click the down arrow. As in any list box, you can quickly go to an item by pressing the first letter of the item. Press C. The screen will look like Figure 3-4. Now press ESC to close the list box. The cursor moves to the blank line between "Sub" and "End Sub."

**Figure 3-4**

Code window
for Click
procedure

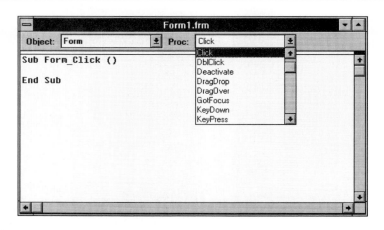

## A SIMPLE EVENT PROCEDURE

Suppose you want to write the code necessary for Visual Basic to respond to a mouse click with a message. You can use all the normal Windows editing keys to enter code. For example, you can switch between insert and overstrike modes when you type. You can select text and copy or cut it.

If the cursor is not at the blank line between Sub and End Sub, move it there by clicking the blank line. Press the SPACEBAR twice (this indentation will improve readability) and type **Print "You clicked the mouse once."** Your Code window will look like this:

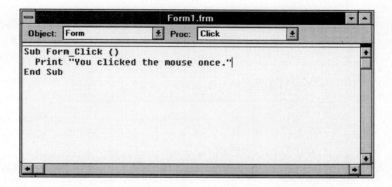

Now press F5 to run the application. As soon as the form pops up, move the mouse until the pointer is inside the form and click once. You'll see something like this:

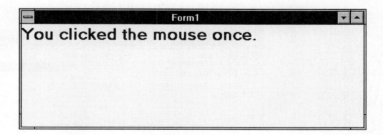

As you've probably guessed, the Print command sends the exact text found between the quotation marks directly to the screen. (In the preceding illustration, the FontSize property for the form was set to 18 points to make a larger splash; the default size is 8.25 points.) The default position for text is the top-left corner of the screen, but you'll soon see how to change this.

## MORE GENERAL EVENT PROCEDURES

In general, no matter what event you want the form to respond to, the code for an event procedure for a form in Visual Basic begins with something that looks like this:

Sub Form_*NameOfTheEvent* ( )

The following table gives some examples.

| Event Procedure | Tells the Form |
|---|---|
| Sub Form_DblClick ( ) | To respond to a double click |
| Sub Form_GotFocus ( ) | To respond when it receives the focus |
| Sub Form_LostFocus ( ) | To respond when it loses the focus |

## MONITORING MULTIPLE EVENTS

Visual Basic is always monitoring your application screen for events, but unless you write code for the event, nothing happens. For example, you can add more code to monitor (and print) something when the user double-clicks.

To do this, end the previous program by going to the Run menu and clicking End (or click the end tool—the one that looks like the stop button on a cassette recorder). Now open the Code window (if it is not already open) by double-clicking a blank part of the form. Notice that Visual Basic now displays the code for the click event. Suppose you want to write code for the double-click event. Move the mouse to the arrow that drops down the list box for procedures and click. Your Code window should look something like this:

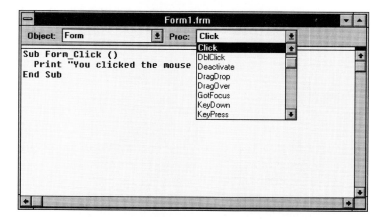

Select the double-click event by pressing D. Notice that the Click event procedure is now in bold—this is how Visual Basic indicates that an event procedure already exists for a particular event.

A new event template for the double click opens. Just as before, you can type between the beginning and ending lines of this event template. For example, type **Print "I said to click once, not twice!"** The Code window will look like this:

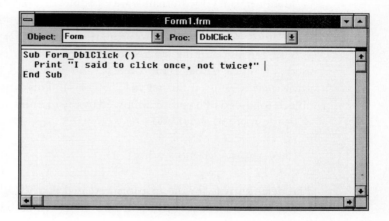

Now run the application and double-click. What you'll see will look something like this:

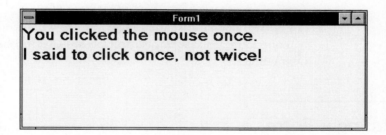

Notice that both lines of text appear on the screen. This is because in monitoring for a double click, Visual Basic also detected the single click and activated the code for that event as well.

If all you want to do is clear the screen before displaying the second message, you need only make the first line of the double-click procedure the Cls command, which clears any text and graphics in the form. The double-click event procedure now looks like this:

```
Sub Form_DblClick ()
  Cls
  Print "I said to click once, not twice!"
End Sub
```

The Print and Cls commands are examples of what Visual Basic calls methods. Roughly speaking, *methods* are Visual Basic statements that affect what Visual Basic objects *do* (as opposed to properties, which affect what they *are*).

You can use another syntax for the Print or Cls command. This syntax is used for other Visual Basic objects, and it follows the general format *Object.Method* (discussed further in Chapter 4). This syntax uses the name of the object, followed by a period, followed by the method, followed by (if applicable) what the method should do:

ObjectName.Method WhatToDo

The default name for the first form created in a Visual Basic project is Form1, so the double-click procedure in this syntax would be written as follows:

```
Sub Form_DblClick ()
  Form1.Cls
  Form1.Print "I said to click once, not twice!"
End Sub
```

You will need to use the longer version when your projects involve more than one form, because this version lets Visual Basic know which form to apply the method to.

## Printing a Form

 Visual Basic relies on the underlying Windows program to handle its printing needs. For this reason you should make sure you have configured Windows with the name of your printer when you set up Windows. Most of the time you won't need to get involved with the Windows Print Manager; Visual Basic takes care of the interface pretty well. It uses whatever printer information is contained in the Microsoft Windows environment control panel.

To dump the entire contents of a form to the printer in Visual Basic requires only a single command: PrintForm. Since this also affects what the form does, as opposed to what it is, it is another example of a Visual Basic method. PrintForm tries to send to your printer a dot-for-dot image of the entire form—including even those parts of the form that are hidden.

## Typos

Nobody types completely accurately all the time. Visual Basic can point out many typing errors when you enter a line—even before you try to run your program.

Suppose you made a typo when you were writing the Click event procedure presented earlier and misspelled the command word "Print" by typing "Printf" instead. Your Code window would look like this:

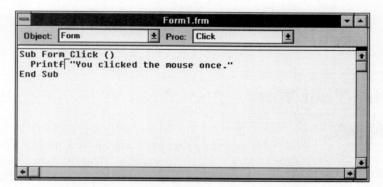

If you try to run the program, Visual Basic will immediately respond with an error message box, and your screen will look something like Figure 3-5. Notice that the offending word is highlighted and the message box tells you that you made a syntax error—that what you entered doesn't conform to the grammar of a Visual Basic program. If you press ENTER or click the OK command button, the offending word remains highlighted, and you can either type the correct replacement or move the mouse pointer to the "f" and press DEL. After you make the correction, the program will run as before.

If you need some help determining what is causing the error, press F1 for context-sensitive help when the error message is on the screen. Visual Basic opens the help window and gives you some general information on the error. For example, if you activate the help window while the misspelled word "Printf" is highlighted, it will offer the explanation shown in Figure 3-6.

Visual Basic can even find some syntax errors before you run your program. To make sure this feature is on (or to turn it on if it is off), press ALT+O+E to

**Figure 3-5**

Syntax error
message box

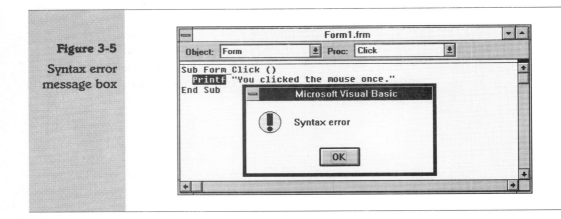

open up the Environment options dialog box. Move to the item marked Syntax Checking and make sure that it is listed as on.

## Saving Your Work

You should get into the habit of saving your work frequently. Visual Basic will not let you exit the program or start a new project without asking you if you

**Figure 3-6**

Help screen
for syntax
error

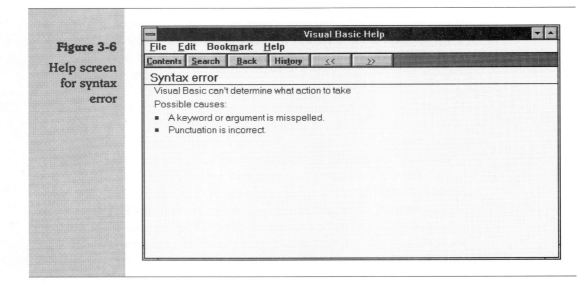

want to save your work. In fact, Visual Basic 3 lets you automatically save your work before a project runs. This is a useful preventative from the dire effects of system crashes, because you can't save a project while it is running or you are in break mode. To do this, change the "Save Project before Run" option to yes in the Environment Options dialog box (ALT+O+E). Most of the ways of saving your work are listed on the File menu. Because much of a Visual Basic application is made up of graphical files, the usual method of saving work stores information in a special binary form that is accessible only to Visual Basic.

**note:** *The binary format used in Visual Basic 3 is incompatible with earlier versions of Visual Basic. Because the binary formats are incompatible, you will almost always be better off saving files in text format.*

## Saving from the File Menu

The following sections describe the five save methods that are listed on the File menu.

*Save Project* Save Project saves the entire project. To select this option, press ALT+F+V. When you first try to save a project by clicking this option, Visual Basic opens a dialog box (see Figure 3-7) with a suggested name—the name you gave the primary form plus an .FRM extension. If you press ENTER, Visual Basic saves all the information on your form and all the code you've attached to it in binary (compressed) format. You can check the Save As Text option to save the form in ASCII format (see Chapter 4).

After Visual Basic saves the form, it pops up another dialog box that asks you for the name of a .MAK file. The .MAK file (sometimes called a make file or project file) is a housekeeping file that Visual Basic uses to determine the location of the various files that make up your application. When you create a stand-alone application, Visual Basic combines all the files (looking for them where the .MAK file tells it to) into one.

If you use the Save Project option to save revised versions of the same project during the course of developing and improving it, Visual Basic no longer provides you with a dialog box; it assumes you want to use the same names every time.

**Figure 3-7**

Saving a file when saving a project

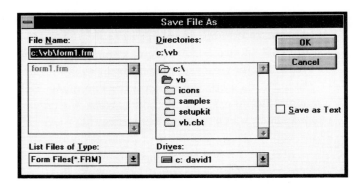

**note:** *When you save a form by using the Save Project option, Visual Basic does not keep a backup copy of the previous version. For this reason, you may prefer to use another method to save your projects.*

**Save Project As** The Save Project As option provides the same sort of dialog box as when you first use the Save Project option, but it asks only for the new name of the .MAK file, unless you've changed the form. If you have, then it opens up a dialog box that looks like this:

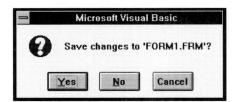

Note that if you click the Yes button, the changes to the Form are saved to a file with the same name as before. This means you will have lost the information contained in the original .FRM file.

**caution:** *Save Project As does not make a backup copy of the unchanged files in the project. It saves a new .MAK file with the current file names.*

To make a backup of the other files in your project or store a copy of one of them on another disk, or under a different name, use the Save File As option described next.

**Save File As** The Save File As option opens up a dialog box that looks like Figure 3-7. This box allows you to rename the current form (.FRM) file *and is the only way to make a backup copy or store a copy of the current form on another disk.* To select this option, press ALT+F+A. The next time you save the project, Visual Basic will update the .MAK file to reflect the new name.

**tip:** *To save a backup copy of a project, do the following:*
*1. Save each of the files on the project with a new name.*
*2. Choose the Save Project As option and give the project file (.MAK) a new (path) name.*
*(You can also use the File Manager to copy these files while still in Visual Basic.)*

**Save File** Use Save File when you start writing a program with multiple forms. This option lets you save only the current form or module. To select this option, press ALT+F+S. The first time you choose this option, Visual Basic pops up a dialog box like the one for Save File As. Subsequent uses do not pop up a dialog box—the saving occurs almost without your being aware of it.

## Saving Code Only

There is one more method for saving some of the information in your project. This is the Save Text option (ALT+F+T). The ellipsis after this menu option tells you that choosing the option leads to a dialog box, which looks like Figure 3-8. This dialog box lets you save the code for the current project in normal text (ASCII) format. The default name for the text version of code is always the name of the project with a .TXT extension—in this case, FORM1.TXT.

As your projects become more sophisticated, you will find yourself reusing code fragments more and more. To effectively do this, you need to save the code in ordinary text (ASCII) format. If you choose to save the form information in text format, then as you'll see in the next chapter, Visual Basic saves both the code and a text description of the form. When you save the code using the Save Text option, Visual Basic creates an ordinary file containing only the code for the event procedures that are attached to the form. Since this is ordinary

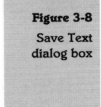

**Figure 3-8**

Save Text dialog box

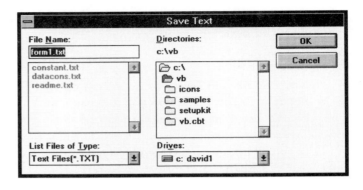

text, you can use any Windows text editor (such as NotePad) or word processor (such as Windows Write) to look at this file.

**tip:**

*If the word processor or text editor is running in another Windows session simultaneously, you can cut and paste into Visual Basic to make reusing code fragments easier.*

## Creating Stand-Alone Windows Programs

One of the most exciting features of Visual Basic is the capability that lets you change your projects into stand–alone Microsoft Windows programs. To do this, simply go to the File menu and choose the Make EXE File option (ALT+F+K). This opens a dialog box that looks like Figure 3-9. The default name for the .EXE version of your file is the project name (the name of the .MAK file with an .EXE extension). For the stand-alone program, the Windows desktop uses the same icon that Visual Basic uses for the project, and as you can see in Figure 3-9, this icon appears in the dialog box at the far right. If you have set a custom icon for one of the forms in your project, Visual Basic lets you choose which one to use (see the section "Icons" earlier in this chapter). If you haven't set the icon, Visual Basic uses the default Visual Basic icon.

When you distribute a Visual Basic 3 program, it is also necessary to supply a *dynamic link library,* called VBRUN300.DLL, to the user. VBRUN300.DLL is a file that comes with Visual Basic. No matter how many different stand-alone Visual Basic applications users have, they need only one copy of this file in a

**Figure 3-9**
**Make EXE File**
**dialog box**

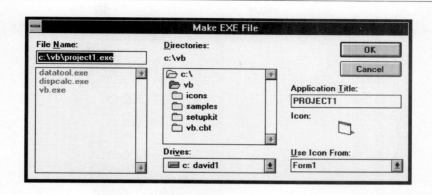

Windows directory accessible to Windows. They also need only one copy of any custom control files used by the Visual Basic applications. (The directory containing the system files for Windows itself is the usual choice.) This file contains various support routines that a Visual Basic program needs to handle the screens, numbers, and other parts of the application. Microsoft freely allows you to distribute the VBRUN300.DLL file, as stated in the Visual Basic programmer's guide: "No additional license or payment to Microsoft is necessary to distribute copies of the run-time library."

**note:** *In most cases, VBRUN300.DLL will be able to run .EXE programs created with Visual Basic 1.0 and Visual Basic 3.*

Visual Basic 3 comes with a setup wizard that makes distributing your programs easy. See Appendix B for more information.

# Chapter 4

# Building the User Interface

CHAPTER 3 showed you how to customize a blank form. You saw how to use the Properties window to make a form more visually appealing, as well as how to write simple event procedures to make them responsive to a user. This chapter shows you how to use the toolbox to add controls to a form.

You'll see several controls in this chapter: command buttons to initiate actions, text boxes to accept or display data, labels to identify controls and data, and image controls to display pictures. The line and shape controls make creating lines and shapes easy.

The techniques for using the Properties window that you saw in Chapter 3 will appear again; it's a good idea to make sure you are completely comfortable with the techniques for setting properties before you continue. Just as with forms, controls remain inert until you write event procedures to tell them how to respond, and the techniques for writing event procedures for controls are similar to those you use for writing a form. For example, to have clicking a command button initiate an action requires writing an event procedure almost identical to the one that made a blank form respond to a click.

Finally, you'll see how message boxes can make applications more friendly by, for example, warning users of irreversible steps they may be taking.

## The Toolbox

As the name suggests, the toolbox is a set of tools you use to embellish a blank form with the controls needed for sophisticated Windows programs. The standard edition of Visual Basic comes with 22 different tools. One of the more exciting features of Visual Basic is its extendability. For example, Appendix A of this book describes the custom controls available with the Visual Basic Professional Edition. You can also buy custom tools from third-party developers that can extend Visual Basic in even more dramatic ways. The standard edition of Visual Basic comes with three custom controls: a grid control for handling tabular data (see Chapter 9), one for adding standard ("common") dialog boxes (see Chapter 10), and an OLE (object linking and embedding) control (see Chapter 15) for communicating with other Windows applications.

Once you install a custom control, it becomes just as much a part of your version of Visual Basic as the tools supplied by Microsoft with the standard version of Visual Basic. In fact, if you click on the Project window to bring it to the front of the desktop, then, as you can see here,

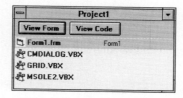

Visual Basic automatically adds the three custom controls supplied with the standard edition of Visual Basic to every project. Files holding custom controls always have the .VBX extension.

**tip:**

*A custom control is added automatically to Visual Basic if you add to the AUTOLOAD.MAK file in the Visual Basic directory a line naming the .VBX file. Thus, you can force or prevent any custom control from loading automatically by changing the AUTOLOAD.MAK file.*

Figure 4-1 shows the toolbox supplied with the standard version of Visual Basic, including the custom controls loaded automatically. The toolbox is usually located on the far left of the Visual Basic screen, but it need not be visible at all times. If the toolbox isn't visible, you must make it visible in order to work with controls. To open up the toolbox, go to the Window menu on the main menu bar by pressing ALT+W+T. You can move the toolbox using ordinary Windows techniques. Here are brief descriptions of the tools covered in this chapter.

**Command Buttons** Command buttons are sometimes called push buttons. The idea is that when the user moves the mouse to the command button and clicks, something interesting should happen (and will, once you write the event procedure that tells Visual Basic how to respond to the mouse click). When you click a command button, it gives the illusion of being pressed. This optical

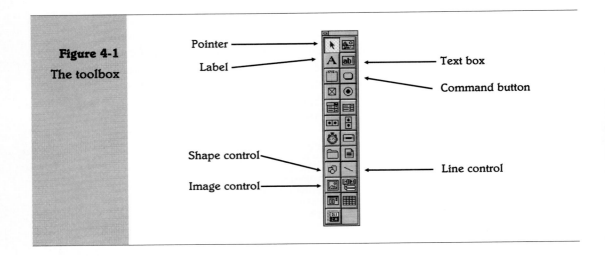

**Figure 4-1**

**The toolbox**

Pointer

Label

Text box

Command button

Shape control

Image control

Line control

illusion comes from the shading used by Visual Basic for command buttons and is inherited from Microsoft Windows.

---

**Image Controls** This control is one of the two controls that can be used to display pictures. This control uses the fewest Windows resources for displaying images. (Picture boxes—see Chapter 10—can do more but use more resources.) Since image controls also recognize the click event, you can use them to replace command buttons. However, unlike command buttons, image controls do not give the user any feedback when they've been pressed unless you program them to do so in the project.

---

**Text Boxes** Text boxes are sometimes called edit fields. You use text boxes to display text or to accept user input. Most of the code you write for text boxes is for processing the information users enter into them. All the ordinary Windows editing tools, such as cutting and pasting, are available when you enter information in a text box. Text boxes can allow word wrap and may have scroll bars for moving through the text. The latter is occasionally vital because text boxes can accept large amounts of text. The usual limit for a text box is approximately 32,000 characters.

***Labels*** Labels are for information that users can't change. They identify objects and occasionally are used to display output. You have almost complete control over how the label displays information—whether the text is boldfaced, what size it appears, and so forth. Although labels do respond to 12 events, usually they are used passively—for display purposes only.

***The Line and Shape Controls*** These are the fastest ways to draw lines and certain shapes such as circles and rectangles. They are similar to labels in that these are passive controls used for display purposes only. They do not respond to any events and so cannot be made responsive to the user.

***The Pointer*** The first item on the toolbox is not a control but is used to manipulate controls after you create them. Click the pointer when you want to select, resize, or move an existing control. It is automatically activated after you place a control on a form.

# Creating Controls

Most of the methods for using the toolbox are similar to those used in a paint program like the Microsoft Paintbrush program, which comes with Windows. You use a combination of pointing, clicking, and dragging to manipulate the toolbox. For example, to draw an item from the toolbox on a form:

1. Move the mouse pointer to the tool you want to use and click. The tool changes color (shade) to indicate that you've selected it.

2. Move the mouse pointer to the form. Think of this as the paint area in which you will draw the control. Notice that the mouse pointer has changed from an arrow to a cross-hair shape.

3. Hold the mouse button down and drag the mouse to create the object. As you drag the mouse pointer, an outline of the control appears on the form.

One corner of the control is determined by where you pressed the mouse button in step 3, and the other is determined by where you release the button.

Notice as well that when you release the mouse button, the control has eight little boxes, called *sizing handles,* jutting out. (Line controls are one-dimensional and have only two sizing handles.) You will use these to move and resize a control after you've created it. The pointer control is automatically highlighted when you release the left mouse button as well.

Notice that as you manipulate the control, it seems to move or enlarge in fits and starts, not smoothly. As the old computer joke goes, this is not a bug in Visual Basic, it really is a feature. The position of controls on a form in Visual Basic default so that they are located only at grid points. If you are willing to have a control appear off the grid, you can smooth out the motion of the controls. However, doing this makes it more difficult to align the control on a form. If you want to do this, the section called "The Grid" at the end of this chapter shows you how. That section also shows you how to make the grid even finer, which is often preferable to removing the grid completely.

**tip:**

*The dotted grid can help you accurately locate the control.*

There are two reasons why the feature of locating controls only at grid points—called *aligning to the grid* or *snapping to the grid*—makes positioning controls in Visual Basic a snap. First, the corners and sides of any control will always end up on a grid mark. Second, you have a small amount of leeway when you move the cross hair. Only when the vertical line of the cross hair hits a grid mark does the object move left or right. Similarly, only when the horizontal line of the cross hair hits a grid mark does the object move up or down.

In theory you can have 255 objects on a single form, but you will rarely use this many. For example, Excel never has more than 7 controls on a screen at any given time. One reason to limit the number of controls on a form is that Microsoft Windows is limited in the number of controls and windows it can handle at any one time. If you start adding too many controls or menus to a form, your program will slow down dramatically. As Windows gets closer to its limits, it is possible that Visual Basic will crash and need to be terminated by Windows.

## Working with an Existing Control

Let's suppose you've used the techniques described in the previous section to create a command button on a blank form. (When you create a command button, the command button appears with a centered caption: Command1, Command2, and so on. As you'll soon see, you can easily change these captions via the Properties window.)

The techniques in the last section let you create a control and place it anywhere you like on a form. In Visual Basic you are never forced to keep a control at its original size or at its original location. The techniques needed for moving or resizing controls are the same for all Visual Basic controls. You can also cut and paste controls by cutting out the control and using the Copy item on the Edit menu. (Chapter 9 describes the effect of copying an existing control.)

To work with an existing control you must first select it. This is done by moving the mouse pointer until it is inside the control and clicking. (Or you may just use the tab key until the focus is at the control. You can tell where the focus is by looking at the sizing handles.)

## RESIZING AN EXISTING CONTROL

Suppose you've created a command button but aren't happy with its size. To change the size of an existing command button, you need to use the sizing handles mentioned earlier. Figure 4-2 shows you a command button with a pointer at one of its eight sizing handles on an otherwise blank form.

If the sizing handles no longer appear, you can make them reappear by moving the mouse pointer to the control and clicking once. When the sizing handles are visible, you know the control is selected. The four corner handles let you change the height and width at the same time. The mouse pointer changes to a double-sided diagonal arrow when you move the pointer to one

**Figure 4-2**

Command button with sizing handles

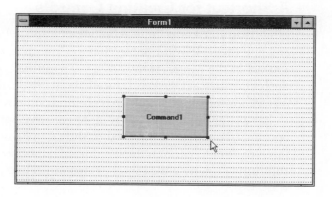

of the corner sizing handles. The four side handles let you change the size in one direction only. At these handles, the mouse pointer changes to a straight double-sided arrow.

To actually resize a control:

1. Move the mouse pointer to a sizing handle and click and hold down the left mouse button.

2. Drag the mouse until the control is the size you want.

For example, if you want to shrink a control button in from the left side while keeping the right side fixed, move the mouse pointer to the sizing handle in the center of the left side, click, and drag the mouse over to the right. You also can get feedback on the size and position of the control by looking at the far right of the toolbar.

### MOVING AN EXISTING CONTROL

In order to move an existing control, the focus must be at that control. Notice that when you move the mouse so that the mouse pointer is inside the form, its shape returns to the form of an arrow. The cross-hair pointer shows up only when you are creating a new control. Now, to move an existing control:

1. Move the pointer anywhere inside the control, click the left mouse button, and hold it down.

2. Drag the mouse until the control is at the location you want it to be and then release the left button.

## A Shortcut for Creating Controls

Now that you know how to move controls, you may prefer a shortcut for creating them. If you double-click on any of the toolbox icons, that control appears in the center of the screen. The more controls you double-click on, the higher they get stacked. You then can use the techniques from the previous section for moving controls to reposition and resize the controls on the stack.

For example, suppose you want to create an application with five command buttons symmetrically dispersed, as shown in Figure 4-3. The easiest way to do this is to double-click on the Command button icon five times. This stacks five command buttons in the center of the form. Then you can easily use the method

**Figure 4-3**

Form with multiple command buttons

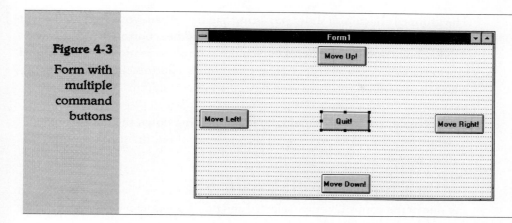

given in the previous section to move the buttons to the locations shown in Figure 4-3.

You may have noticed that the captions are more informative than the usual Command1, Command2, and so on. You change the captions by adjusting the Caption property of the command buttons via the Properties window. You will see how to do this in the section "Properties of Command Buttons" later in this chapter.

## Working with Multiple Controls

Occasionally you'll want to move a group of controls in the same direction. For example, you may have three command buttons lined up and want to keep them aligned but move them up a couple of grid marks. To work with multiple controls as a single unit, you must first tell Visual Basic that you wish them to be temporarily treated as a unit. There are two ways to do this. The easiest was new to Visual Basic 2.0 and works much like the method used to select an area in Windows Paintbrush:

1. Imagine a rectangle that hits only those controls you want to select. Move to one corner of this imagined rectangle and click the left mouse button.

2. Hold the left mouse button down and drag the dotted rectangle until it hits all (and only) the controls you want to select. Then release the mouse button.

The grouped controls all show *gray* sizing handles. When you select any one of the controls and move it, Visual Basic moves the other controls in a similar way.

The above method only works when the controls to be moved can be placed in a rectangular "lasso" that excludes any other controls. If the controls are widely scattered on the form, you'll need another method:

Select each control by moving to it and holding down the left mouse key while pressing CTRL. (From the second control on, the sizing handles turn gray.)

Regardless of what method you choose, if you move the mouse pointer to any one of the controls you've selected and drag it to its new location, the other controls move along with it.

To undo the selection process for multiple controls, move the mouse pointer outside the selected controls and click.

## Deleting Controls

You may end up with too many controls on your form—especially if you use the double-click method a lot. To delete a control:

1. Move the mouse pointer until it is inside the control and click the left mouse button to select it.

2. Press DEL or open the Edit menu and choose the Delete option by pressing ALT+E+D.

The methods for selecting multiple controls so you can move them as a unit, discussed in the previous section, are also used when you want to delete many controls at once. Once you've told Visual Basic that you want the controls considered as a unit, the DEL key or Delete menu option works on all the controls in the group. You can also use the ordinary windows editing shortcut keys such as CTRL+INS to paste.

# Properties of Command Buttons

Just as you use the Properties window to customize the size and shape of blank forms, you can use it to customize controls. For example, if you don't like the default values for a control's property, you can open the Properties window and change it.

The next few sections take you through what are the most useful properties of command buttons. But you also may want to scroll through the list of properties and use the online help for any property that has a name that intrigues you, even if that property is not covered in this chapter.

## The Caption Property

The Caption property of a form determines the name that shows in the title bar. Similarly, the Caption property on a command button determines the message the user sees. Any text you use for the caption on a command button is automatically centered within the button. However, command buttons aren't resized to fit the caption you choose—you have to do that yourself.

Command buttons always start out with captions like Command1, Command2, and so on. The number indicates the order in which the buttons were created. Let's create a simple command button like the one shown in Figure 4-4. This message will not fit inside the default size of a command button. Luckily, you can create a caption first via the Properties window and then resize the control to fit it. More of the message shows up as you enlarge the control, so it's easy to judge when to stop.

Double-click on the command button icon to create the button in the center of the screen. The Properties window should be visible. If the Properties

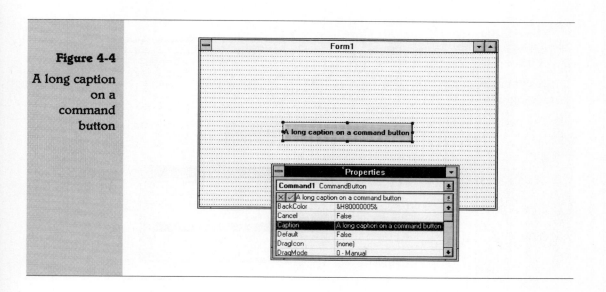

**Figure 4-4**

**A long caption on a command button**

window is not visible, use the F4 shortcut to make it appear.

Let's suppose that you want to change the Caption property of the command button. If for some reason the Caption property isn't showing up on the Properties window for the command button, the method to get to it is similar to the one you learned in the last chapter:

1. Move to the Properties window.

2. Go to the Caption property by using the mouse or the UP ARROW and DOWN ARROW keys.

Now you can type the new setting for the Caption property. If you need to replace the old setting (or part of it), hold down the left mouse button and drag it until all the text you want to use is highlighted. Overwrite the old setting or fill in the blank area by typing the phrase **A long caption on a command button**.

The results are shown in Figure 4-5. Now you can resize the command button to fit the new caption.

**tip:**    *The* SHIFT+CTRL+*letter combination you saw for moving through the Properties window of a form works for controls as well.*

**Figure 4-5**

**Designing a long caption**

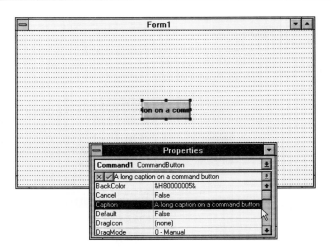

# The Name (Control Name) Property

The Name property (CtlName in Visual Basic 1.0) is very important when you start writing event procedures for controls. This property determines the name Visual Basic uses for the event procedures you write to make a control respond to the user. Picking meaningful names for controls goes a long way toward making the inevitable debugging process for developing an application easier. For example, suppose you are writing the code to make clicking a command button move a form to the left, as you did with the Move Left command button in the form in Figure 4-3. When you have five command buttons in an application, writing code that looks like this

```
Sub Command4_Click ()

End Sub
```

to make a form move left is a lot more confusing than writing it like this:

```
Sub LeftButton_Click ()

End Sub
```

Don't go overboard; the setting you use for a control's name should be meaningful but not ridiculous; the names of controls *do* enlarge the size of the file created by Visual Basic when you've finished programming the project. The limits on a control name in Visual Basic are as follows:

◆ A control name must begin with a letter. (After that, you can use any combination of letters, numbers, and underscores.)

◆ The name cannot be longer than 40 characters.

Microsoft's convention is to use an abbreviation for the type of control followed by the meaningful part. An example would be using the name btnHelp rather than HelpButton. This approach offers the advantage of grouping the objects in the Properties window, but the disadvantage of being a bit harder to read. This book does not use this convention. Whatever you do, however, follow some convention or else your code may be unreadable soon after you've written it!

## Other Useful Properties for Command Buttons

There are 28 properties you can control for a command button. Many of them are similar to the ones you saw for a form in Chapter 3. For example, command buttons have BackColor, Height, and Width properties. What follows is a short discussion of the most basic ones.

*BackColor*   As with forms, the BackColor property sets the background color for the button, but really only changes the colors of the four corners. Because of this, the BackColor property is rarely changed. To set it directly from the Properties window requires the hexadecimal coding you saw in Chapter 3. Otherwise you can set the background color by using the methods described in Chapter 3 to access the color palette. Command buttons do not have a ForeColor property, so you must accept the default color for this. This property is rarely changed.

*Height, Width*   The Height and Width properties measure the height and width of the command button. Note that the units used are the ones set by the scale properties for the surrounding *container*. Usually the container is the form, but as you'll see in Chapter 10, you can block out regions within a form by using frames or picture boxes. This means the default measurement for the height and width of a command button is expressed in *twips* (1/20 of a printer's point, or 1/1440 of an inch). On the other hand, if you set the ScaleMode property of the surrounding form to 4 (inches), the Height and Width properties for command buttons will also be measured in inches. You can change the settings for these properties directly from the Properties window or by using the sizing handles. As with a form, the current values for the size of the command button are displayed at the far right of the Properties window for the command button.

*Left, Top*   The Left and Top properties determine the distance between the command button and the left edge and top of the container (again, usually the form), respectively. As with the Height and Width properties, these properties use the scale determined by the surrounding form. You can also change them by dragging and, as with forms, the values are displayed to the right of the settings box on the Properties window.

■

*Visible* The Visible property determines whether the command button is visible or not. It's quite common to have your code alternately make a command button visible and invisible, depending on the situation. Like the Visible property for forms, this property can only be set to True or False.

■

*Enabled* The Enabled property determines if the button can respond to any event whatsoever. If you set this property to False, Visual Basic will not respond to any event concerning that button. Unlike the Visible property, the button remains on the form but is inert. The Enabled property is more often temporarily toggled on or off via code in order to maintain flexibility in your program. Changing this property also changes the appearance of an item, usually by graying out the text.

■

*MousePointer* Setting the mouse pointer to something different than the usual arrow is a good way to give a user feedback that he or she has moved the focus to the command button. (Recall that "having the focus" is the standard phrase in Microsoft Windows to describe that a control is primed to receive input.) The same 13 settings that are available for the MousePointer on a form are available for a command button.

■

*Font Properties* All the font properties—FontBold, FontItalic, FontName, FontSize, FontStrikeThru, and FontUnderline—can be set independently for each command button. These properties allow you to control how the caption appears within the button.

## Shortcuts for Setting Properties

Suppose you want to set the Caption property for all the command buttons on your form. If you set it once and immediately select another command button, the Caption property for the new control is the one that appears on the Properties window. In general then, Visual Basic remembers the property just set for a control and, if possible, brings up the same property for the next control you select on the Properties window. (But you still have to change the property.)

Similarly, if you select a group of controls, the Properties window will show only the common properties that the controls in the group share. Change one of them and all of them change.

**tip:**

*The easiest way to work with the different controls on a form is to click the down arrow to the right of the first line of the Properties window. This gives you a list of all the objects on the form. Here's an example of what you'll see:*

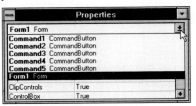

# Simple Event Procedures for Command Buttons

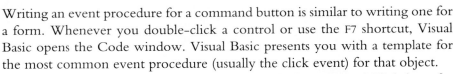

Writing an event procedure for a command button is similar to writing one for a form. Whenever you double-click a control or use the F7 shortcut, Visual Basic opens the Code window. Visual Basic presents you with a template for the most common event procedure (usually the click event) for that object.

Suppose you set up a command button with the caption "Click here for HELP!" Moreover, suppose you set the control name (the Name property) for this control to the more meaningful HelpButton. Figure 4-6 shows what you will see in the Code window. Notice that the event procedure template has a similar form to the ones you saw in Chapter 3. The only difference is that the control name for the object is used, followed by an underscore, followed by the name of the event. This is the general form for the event procedure template for controls:

    Sub ControlName_EventName ( )

    End Sub

Click the down arrow to the right of HelpButton. Your code window should look like the one in Figure 4-7. Notice that the list of objects in the Object list box has grown to include one named HelpButton. Visual Basic always keeps track of all the objects in your project, and you can write event procedures for

**Figure 4-6**

Event
template for
the click event

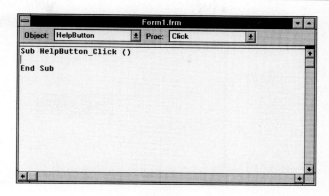

any of them by opening the Code window, moving through the Object list box, and selecting the object that interests you.

Suppose we add a simple Print statement to this event procedure, as shown here:

```
Sub HelpButton_Click ()
    Print "No Help is yet available. Sorry."
End Sub
```

Now if you run this program (by pressing F5) and click the form, you should see something like what is shown in Figure 4-8.

In general, you have to be aware of the problems of using Print statements with a form that has controls on it already. If a control is located where the text

**Figure 4-7**

Pull-down list
box showing
objects in a
project

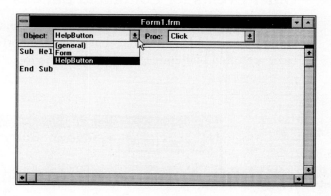

**Figure 4-8**

**Results of clicking on the Help button**

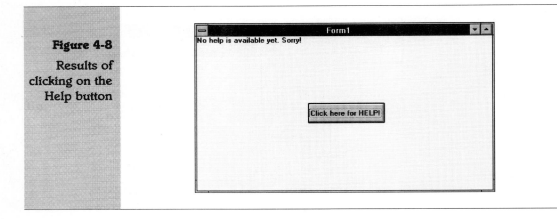

is supposed to appear, the information printed to the form appears behind the control. Figure 4-9 shows an example of this.

The usual way to handle help information (or any other information you don't want obscured) is to use a separate form for it, or occasionally a Message Box. You might then have the user close the window when he or she has digested the information. (Chapter 5 shows you how to do this.) Also, you should be aware that if you iconize a window or move another window so that it temporarily covers a form with text on it, the text will disappear. You can overcome this by setting the AutoRedraw property of the form to True. (See the section in this chapter on this important property.) Another possibility is to rewrite the text as needed. The Paint event procedure is the usual place to do this. This is because Visual Basic generates the Paint event whenever a form is moved, enlarged, or uncovered when AutoRedraw is false.

## Other Events for Command Buttons

Command buttons can respond to eight events, but clicking is by far the most common. Two others you may find useful are GotFocus and LostFocus. Naive users are often inattentive to just where the focus is and may get confused if

**Figure 4-9**

**Text obscured by existing control**

what they type or click seems to be having no effect. Controls in Visual Basic can monitor whether the person has inadvertently moved the focus. You can then remind users that they've moved the focus and ask if they really want to do that. An event procedure that looks like this

```
Sub CommandButton_LostFocus

End Sub
```

lets you write the code to respond to users moving the focus away from that button—for example, by asking them if they really want to.

Similarly, code like this

```
Sub CommandButton_GotFocus

End Sub
```

might include code to generate help about that command button.

Command buttons can also respond to a user's pressing specific keys (see Chapter 6) and to mouse events (see Chapter 13).

## Some Final Points on Command Buttons

Usually, the user of the application you develop chooses a command button by moving the mouse pointer to the button and clicking. However, sometimes you will want more flexibility. One other method for activating a command button is common to all Microsoft Windows applications: move the focus by pressing TAB, and then press the SPACEBAR when the focus is where you want it to be. The user knows a button has received the focus when it gives the appearance of being three-dimensional. What actually happens is Visual Basic draws a thinly dashed box around the text in the button and a fine rectangle around the button itself. Both of these methods generate the click event for that button. In other words, Visual Basic activates the click event procedure in either case if one is available for that control. As you'll see in Chapter 5, you can also activate a quick event via code.

In addition, sometimes you want to give people an escape button for an action. This button cancels an action or otherwise extricates the user from some sort of situation he or she doesn't want to be in. You activate this command button (one to a form) by pressing ESC on the keyboard. A command button that does this is called a *cancel button* in the Visual Basic manuals.

You usually use the Properties window to make a command button the cancel button, although you can use code as well. If you have scrolled through the list of properties available for a command button, you may have noticed the Cancel property. If you set the Cancel property to True, you ensure that pressing ESC generates the click event for this button, regardless of where the user has moved the focus. Setting the Cancel property to True for one button automatically sets it to False for all the other command buttons on the form.

Another possibility—but one that has its problems for novice users—is to set up a default command button for the form. This generates the Click procedure for the chosen (default) button whenever someone presses ENTER. This can be a problem because unsophisticated users are apt to press ENTER at the strangest times. (This is mostly because it's natural to think that if the focus is at a command button, pressing ENTER will work. Pressing the SPACEBAR is not something Windows neophytes are apt to remember.) In any case, if you want to use this option, set the Default property of the button to True. Also, you can have at most one default command button to a form.

**tip:** *You can combine the default and cancel buttons into a default cancel button. This feature is especially useful if you are about to take an irreversible action.*

# Access Keys

Many Windows applications allow pressing ALT and one other key, the *access key,* to quickly activate a control or a menu item—Visual Basic itself, for example. These access letters are underlined in the caption of the control or name of the menu item.

Visual Basic makes it easy to set up an access key for any object that has a caption property. When you set the caption, all you have to do is place an ampersand (&) in front of the letter you want to be the access key. For example, look at Figure 4-10. Notice that the *C* in the Caption property is underlined. When the application is running, you can activate this button either by pressing the ALT+C combination or by clicking on the button.

While it is possible to have the same access key for more than one control on a form, doing so is unusual. What happens in this situation is that the focus moves to the next control with an access key, but the control is not activated until you click the mouse or press the SPACEBAR.

**Figure 4-10**

Caption
allowing
access key for
control

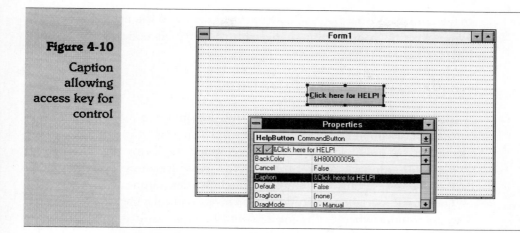

## Image Controls

Image controls hold pictures. They can also be used to create toolboxes (see Chapter 10). The toolbox icon for an image control is the sun over a mountain (see Figure 4-1). Image controls can be used to display icons or pictures created with a program like Windows Paintbrush. They can also hold Windows metafiles. Here are typical examples of image controls:

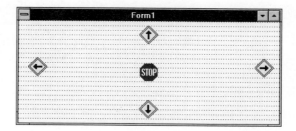

Since image controls respond to the click event, you can use these images (taken from the TRAFFIC icon directory) to substitute for the command buttons in Figure 4-3.

You load a picture into an image control by resetting the value of the Picture property. If you choose the Picture property for the image control, this opens up a dialog box that lets you choose what image file to load.

You can also reset the Picture property directly by copying an image from a graphics program like Windows Paintbrush to the Windows clipboard and then using the Copy command on the Edit menu to paste the image into the image control. Visual Basic will attach the graphic to the project when you save it. Finally, you can also change this property via code, as you'll see in Chapter 12.

### PROPERTIES OF IMAGE CONTROLS

Many of the properties of image controls are similar to those for command buttons. For example, you can set the Left and Top properties to control where the image control is located. However, unlike for forms, the BorderStyle property for an image control has only two possible settings: you can either have no border (setting = 0) or a fixed single border (setting = 1).

The most important new property of an image control is the Stretch property. This determines whether the image control adjusts to fit the picture or the picture adjusts to fit the control. If the stretch property is left at the default value of False, the control resizes itself to fit the picture. If you change it to True, the picture resizes (as best it can) to fit the control. As a general rule, only Windows metafiles—which essentially store directions for drawing pictures rather than actual bitmaps—can be enlarged without great loss of detail. To see this, start up a new project and place two large image controls on the form. Set the Stretch property to True for one of them and leave it as the default for the other. Load the TRFFC07 "slippery road" icon. Here's what you'll see:

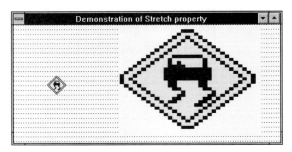

Notice that the detail in the enlarged image is greatly reduced (Stretch property = True).

# The Line and Shape Controls

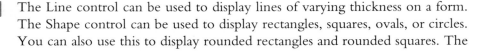

The Line control can be used to display lines of varying thickness on a form. The Shape control can be used to display rectangles, squares, ovals, or circles. You can also use this to display rounded rectangles and rounded squares. The icon for the Line control on the toolbox is a diagonal line and the icon for the Shape control is three overlapping shapes. Figure 4-11 shows the various possibilities for lines and shapes.

## The Shape Control

The Shape control has 18 properties. Usually, you change them dynamically with code while the application is running. The most important properties for the Shape control at design time are described in the following sections.

**The Shape Property** This determines the type of shape you get. There are six possible settings (shown in the following order in Figure 4-11):

| Setting of Shape Property | Effect |
| --- | --- |
| 0 | Rectangle (default) |
| 1 | Square |
| 2 | Oval |
| 3 | Circle |
| 4 | Rounded rectangle |
| 5 | Rounded square |

**The BackStyle Property** This property determines whether the background of the shape is transparent or not. The default value is 1, which gives you an opaque border; BackColor fills the shape and obscures what is behind it. Set it to 0 (Transparent) and you can see through the shape to what is behind it.

**Figure 4-11**

**The Line and Shape controls**

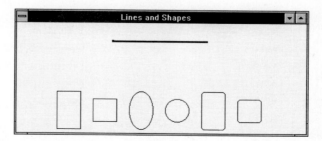

**BorderWidth** BorderWidth determines the thickness of the line. It is measured in pixels and can range from 0 to 8192 (too large to display on most forms).

**BorderStyle** Unlike image controls, the BorderStyle has six possible settings, shown here. Only five are really useful. Having no border prevents the control from being visible unless you modify the FillStyle and FillColor properties.

| Value of BorderStyle Property | Effect |
| --- | --- |
| 0 | No border shown |
| 1 | Solid (default) |
| 2 | A dashed line |
| 3 | A dotted line |
| 4 | A dash–dot line |
| 5 | A dash–dot–dot line |

**note:**  *If you set the BorderWidth property to greater than 1, then resetting the BorderStyle property has no effect.*

**FillColor, FillStyle** The FillColor property determines the color used to fill the shape in the manner set by the FillStyle property. You can set the FillColor property in the same way as setting any color property, either directly via a hexadecimal code or by using the color palette.

The FillStyle property has eight possible settings:

| Setting For FillStyle Property | Effect |
| --- | --- |
| 0 | Solid |
| 1 | Transparent (default) |
| 2 | Horizontal line |
| 3 | Vertical line |
| 4 | Upward diagonal |
| 5 | Downward diagonal |
| 6 | Cross |
| 7 | Diagonal cross |

## The Line Control

The Line control has ten properties. Usually, you change them dynamically with code while the application is running. The most important properties for the Line control at design time are the BorderWidth property and the Border-Style property. BorderWidth determines the thickness of the line. It is measured in pixels and can range from 0 to 8192 (too large to display on most forms). Like the Shape control, the BorderStyle property has six possible settings, but as before, only the last five are really useful.

# Text Boxes and Labels

Text boxes are the primary method for accepting input and displaying output in Visual Basic. In fact, printing too many lines of text to a form will often lead to a run-time error and, in any case, you can't scroll back through the form for lines that may have slipped off the top. (The icon in the toolbox for a text box shows the letters *ab,* as shown in Figure 4-1.)

tip:    *Use a text box for all but the simplest text displays.*

Text boxes never treat what a user types in as a number; this means that getting numeric information to a Visual Basic program requires transforming a string of digits into a number by using a built-in function or Visual Basic 3's built-in automatic conversions (see Chapter 5).

Use labels to display information you don't want the user to be able to change. Probably the most common use for labels is to identify a text box or other control by describing its contents. Another common use is to display help information. The icon for a label is the bold, capital letter *A.*

## Standard Properties of Text Boxes

There are 40 properties for text boxes. Many of them should be familiar to you. As before, the Name property is used only for the code you write; the user never sees it. The six font properties (FontBold, FontItalic, and so on) work in the same way as before: they control how text appears in the box. The only difference is that, since users can move the focus to a text box and type information there, the font properties also affect what the user places inside the text box. As with command buttons, the Height, Width, Left, and Top properties use the scale determined by the surrounding container.

Unlike command buttons (but like forms), you can set both the BackColor and ForeColor properties for a text box. The ForeColor property affects the color of the text that is displayed. BackColor affects the rest of the text box. Both of these can be set independently of the surrounding container. To set them from the Properties window also requires using the hexadecimal &HBBGGRR coding that you've seen before. As before, you may find it easier to use the color palette.

As with command buttons, the Enabled property affects whether the text box will respond to events. In particular, if a text box is disabled, the user cannot enter text inside it. When a text box is disabled, it is grayed.

Also as before, it is quite common to toggle the Visible property between True and False with code in order to make a text box appear and disappear.

The MousePointer property has the same 13 possible settings as for forms; you often change this property to dramatize that the focus is now within the control.

## Some Special Properties for Text Boxes

There are three properties you have not seen before and one property that works differently for text boxes than for forms. The three new properties are Text, MultiLine, and ScrollBars, and they are very important for mastering text boxes. The BorderStyle property works differently for text boxes than for forms.

*Text* The Text property is the analog of the Caption property for a command button or a form. The Text property controls the text the user sees. When you create a text box, the default value for this property is set to the default value for the Name property for that control—Text1, Text2, and so on. Because text boxes do not have a Caption property, you will need a trick to give the user an access key for them. You'll see how to do this shortly. If you want a text box to be empty when the application starts up, select the Text property and blank out the original setting.

*ScrollBars* The ScrollBars property determines if a text box has horizontal or vertical scroll bars. These are useful because Visual Basic allows you to accept long or multiple lines of data from a single text box; roughly 32,000 characters is the usual limit. Without scroll bars, it becomes much harder for the user to move through the data contained in the text box, thus making editing the information that much more difficult.

There are four possible settings for the ScrollBars property:

| Value | Meaning |
| --- | --- |
| 0 | This is the default value. The text box lacks both vertical and horizontal scroll bars |
| 1 | The text box has horizontal scroll bars only (limits text to 255 characters) |
| 2 | The text box has vertical bars only |
| 3 | The text box has both horizontal and vertical bars |

**MultiLine** The MultiLine property determines if a text box can accept more than one line of text when the user runs the application and is usually combined with resetting the value of the ScrollBars property. In any case, if you set this to True, a user can always use the standard methods in Microsoft Windows to move through the text box: the arrow keys, HOME, CTRL+HOME, END, and CTRL+END.

Visual Basic automatically word wraps when a user types more than one line of information into a text box—unless you've added horizontal scroll bars to the text box. Also, users can use the ENTER key to separate lines unless you've added a default command button to the form (yet another reason to be careful of this). If you have a default command button, the user has to press CTRL+EN-TER to break lines.

Since forms are limited in the amount of text they can display and do not scroll, MultiLine text boxes are the usual method for displaying large amounts of text in Visual Basic. The limit for a MultiLine text box is approximately 32,000 characters.

**BorderStyle** As with the Image control, there are only two possible settings for the BorderStyle property for a text box. The default value is 1, which gives you a single-width border, called a *fixed single*. If you change the value of this property to 0, the border disappears.

**MaxLength** This property determines the maximum number of characters the text box will accept. The default value is 0 which (somewhat counter-intuitively) means there is no maximum other than the (roughly) 32,000–character limit for multi-line text boxes. Any setting other than zero will limit the user's ability to enter data into that text box to that number of characters.

■

*PasswordChar* As you might expect from the name, this lets you limit what the text box displays (although all characters are accepted and stored). The convention is to use an asterisk (*) for the password character. Once you set this property all the user sees is a row of asterisks. This property is often combined with the MaxLength property to add a password feature to your programs.

## Event Procedures for Text Boxes

Text boxes can recognize 12 events. Events like GotFocus and LostFocus work exactly as before. Three others—KeyDown, KeyUp, and KeyPress—are for monitoring exactly what the user types. For example, you would use these events to write a program that allows someone to use dollar signs when entering amounts that ultimately need to be treated as numbers. This type of data processing requires a fair amount of code, which you'll see in Chapter 6.

Although the Change event lacks the flexibility of the key events you'll see in Chapter 6, you may find it very useful. Visual Basic monitors the text box and calls this event procedure whenever a user makes any changes in the text box. No matter what the user types, Visual Basic will detect it. One of the most common uses of this event procedure is to warn people that they should not be entering data in a specific text box, blanking out what they typed.

## Labels

There are 31 properties for labels. Most of them overlap with the properties for text boxes and forms, and many of them should be familiar to you by now. Like forms (but unlike text boxes), labels have a Caption property that determines what they display. This property is originally set to be Label1 for the first label on your form, Label2 for the second, and so on. At design time you can have at most one line of text as the caption for a label. With code (see Chapter 5) you can add blank lines of text to a caption.

As before, the Name property is used only for the code you write; the user never sees it. The six font properties (FontBold, FontItalic, and so on) work in the same way as before: they control how text appears in the label. As with command buttons, the Height, Width, Left, and Top properties use the scale determined by the surrounding container.

As with text boxes, you can set the BackColor and ForeColor properties for a label. The ForeColor property affects the color of the text that is displayed. BackColor affects the rest of the label. Both of these can be set independently of the surrounding container. Setting them from the Properties window also requires using the hexadecimal &HBBGGRR coding that you've seen before; using the color palette is often easier.

The Enabled property is not often used for labels. Its primary role is to determine if the user can move the focus to the control which follows the label in tab order (see the section following called Access Keys for Text Boxes). As before, it is quite common to toggle the Visible property between True and False to make a label appear and disappear.

The MousePointer property uses the same 13 possible settings. This is rarely changed for labels, but one possibility is to change the icon when the user moves from the label to the control that is being labeled.

## Useful Properties for Labels

There are five especially useful properties for labels, two of which you have not seen before: Alignment and AutoSize. The third, WordWrap, works slightly differently than it did for text boxes. For example, WordWrap can be used only when you set AutoSize to be true. Also, the BorderStyle property has one neat use that can give more polish to your applications.

*Alignment* The Alignment property has three possible settings. The usual (default) value is 0, which means the text in the label is left-justified (flush left). Set the value of this property to 1, and the text inside the label will be right-justified; set the value to 2, and the text is centered.

*BorderStyle, BackStyle* The BorderStyle property has the same two possible values as text boxes do. The difference is that the default value is 0, so labels do not start out with a border. Set the value to 1, and the label resembles a text box. This is occasionally useful when your program displays results. Using labels with a border property value of 1 for displaying output avoids the problem of text boxes being changed by the user. Your form will have a control that looks like a text box, but it will not be responsive to the user. As with Shapes, BackStyle determines whether the label is transparent or opaque.

*AutoSize, WordWrap* Unlike command buttons, labels can be made to automatically grow horizontally to encompass the text you place in them; this is a function of the AutoSize property. The default value for this property, though, is set to False, and you need to change it to True to take advantage of it. If you also set the WordWrap property to be True, then the label will grow in the vertical direction to encompass its contents, but the horizontal size will stay the same. In addition, the words will be wrapped so that they are never broken as indicated here:

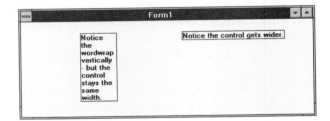

The labels in this example have the BorderStyle set to 1 so that you can see them more easily, and each started out at the same width.

## Event Procedures for Labels

Labels respond to 12 events. For example, they can respond to clicking, double-clicking, or the Change event. The most common event procedures for a label are mouse events (see Chapter 13). You can use a click of the right mouse button to provide context-sensitive help or pop up a menu, for example. One problem is that labels do not respond to key events or detect whether the user has shifted the focus. This dramatically restricts the use of event procedures for labels. Labels in Visual Basic remain primarily descriptive and not responsive.

# Navigating Between Controls

Using the mouse is the most common way to move from control to control in a Windows application, but your applications have to allow for using the TAB key as well. *Tab order* is the term used in a Windows application for the sequence of controls that pressing TAB moves you through. In a Visual Basic application, the order in which you create the controls is the order used for the tab order. The first control you create at design time is the one that receives the focus when the application starts up. If you press TAB once when the application is running, you move to the second control you created at design time, and so on. If you press TAB when the focus is at the last control you've created, the focus moves back to the first one. (Disabled controls are skipped.)

It's possible to change the setting for the tab order via the Properties window or by writing code. The property you need to set is the TabIndex property. If you set this value to 0 for a control, this control automatically becomes the first control in tab order, and all the other controls move upward in tab order. What used to be the first control in tab order is now the second, the second is now the third, and so on. If you change a control with a higher tab index, then only controls with tab indexes larger than it are affected. If you create a control and set the TabIndex property at design time, the settings for the TabIndex property are moved higher to make way for the new control. You can also change the TabIndex via code (see Chapter 5).

## Access Keys for Text Boxes

Text boxes lack a Caption property, so you need a trick to allow users to quickly move the focus to them via an access key. The trick works like this: labels have captions so you can set an access key for them by using the ampersand (&) in front of the letter you want to make the access key. However, labels do not respond to the GotFocus or LostFocus events. So what happens when you use the access key? If you press the access key for a control that does not respond to focus events, the focus moves to the next control in tab order that will accept it.

This makes it easy to give an access key for a text box. You create a label for the text box, set up the access key for the label, and then create the text box. (Doing this ensures that the text box follows the label in tab order.)

# Message Boxes

Message boxes display information in a dialog box superimposed on the form. They wait for the user to choose a button before returning to the application. Users cannot switch to another form in your application as long as Visual Basic is displaying a message box. Message boxes should be used for short messages or to give transient feedback. For example, you would not generally use them to provide a help screen. A good example of where an application might display a message box is when the user moves the focus away from a text box before placing information inside it. The simplest form of the message box command looks like this:

MsgBox("The message goes in quotes")

Message boxes can hold a maximum of 1024 characters, and Visual Basic automatically breaks them at the right of the dialog box. You can set line breaks yourself, as you will see in Chapter 5. For example, suppose you wrote an application and thought the user needed to be reminded that nothing would happen until he or she clicked a command button. You might add a LostFocus event procedure that looks something like this:

```
Sub Command1_LostFocus ()
    MsgBox "You have to click the button for anything to happen"
End Sub
```

When you run this application and move the focus away from the command button, you will see a screen like the one shown in Figure 4-12. Notice in Figure 4-12 that the title bar for the message box isn't particularly informative. You can add your own, more informative, title to a message box. For this you have to use the full form of the message box statement by adding two options to it. This is the complete syntax for the MsgBox command:

MsgBox *MessageInBox, TypeOf Box, TitleOfBox*

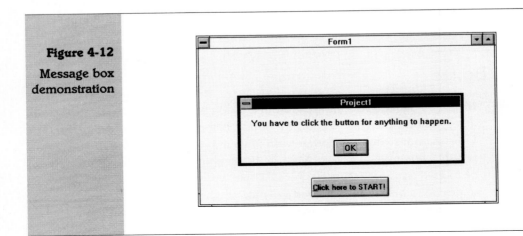

**Figure 4-12**

**Message box demonstration**

You have already seen the item called *MessageInBox*—this gives the text in the box. You combine three different groups of numbers to specify the kind of message box. The three groups of numbers control what kind of buttons appear, what kind of icons appear, and, finally, which button is the default button for the box. The following tables summarize this information.

| Value | Meaning |
|---|---|
| 0 | Displays an OK button only |
| 1 | Displays OK and Cancel buttons (pressing ESC works like clicking it) |
| 2 | Displays Abort, Retry, and Ignore buttons |
| 3 | Displays Yes, No, and Cancel buttons |
| 4 | Displays Yes and No buttons only |
| 5 | Displays Retry and Cancel buttons |

Here is the group of numbers for the icons that appear in the box:

| Value | Icon That Appears |
|---|---|
| 16 | Displays a stop sign icon |
| 32 | Displays a question mark icon |
| 48 | Displays an exclamation point |
| 64 | Displays an *i* (the information message icon) |

These numbers determine the default buttons (pressing ENTER clicks them):

| Value | Default Button |
|---|---|
| 0 | First button |
| 256 | Second button |
| 512 | Third button |

You can combine these options by adding the values together. For example, the statement

```
MsgBox "Example of buttons", 2+48+256, "Test"
```

displays a message box that looks like this:

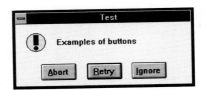

This box contains an exclamation point with Abort, Retry, and Ignore buttons, and the second button, Retry, would be the default button for this form. (You can also do the addition yourself.)

**note:** *You can arrange for a message box to stop all Windows applications until it is closed by temporarily adding 4096 to the value. This should not be done casually!*

Although message boxes do not have event procedures associated with them, it is possible to determine which button was pressed by assigning the value of the MsgBox to a variable and reading off the value, as you will see in Chapter 6.

# The Grid

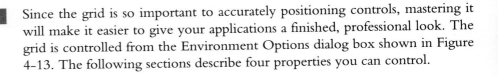

Since the grid is so important to accurately positioning controls, mastering it will make it easier to give your applications a finished, professional look. The grid is controlled from the Environment Options dialog box shown in Figure 4-13. The following sections describe four properties you can control.

*Grid Width, Grid Height* This property controls the width (in twips) between grid marks. The default is 120 twips. Change these both to 60, as shown in Figure 4-13, and the grid becomes twice as fine.

*Show Grid* You can turn the grid on or off by changing this setting. The default setting is on. There is usually little reason to turn the grid off.

*Align to Grid* The Align to Grid option determines whether controls automatically move to the next grid mark or whether they can be placed between

**Figure 4-13**

Grid setting
via
Environment
Options dialog
box

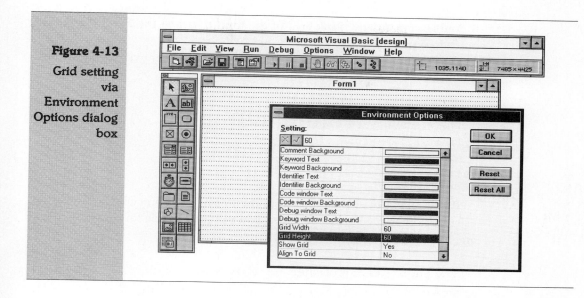

grid marks. Usually you are better off changing the grid spacing to match your design requirements than turning this option off.

It's possible to align an item to the grid even if you've chosen to turn this option off. To do this, select the control by clicking it once (the sizing handles show up) and choosing the Align to Grid option from the Edit menu by pressing ALT+E+A.

# What Happens When a Visual Basic Application Runs

When the user runs an application developed with Visual Basic, he or she usually sees the initial form that you've designed. However, much more than that is going on in the background. When Visual Basic loads a form, it checks whether you've written an event procedure for initializing the form. This event procedure is called the Form_Load procedure. The most common use of this procedure is to initialize form level variables (see Chapter 5) and change the default settings for controls. Some people even prefer to use the Form_Load procedure to set the properties for a form rather than using the Properties window. In fact, it is often easier to set properties this way (see the section in Chapter 5 on resetting properties for more information). Since the Form_Load procedure is the default event procedure for a form, all you usually have to do is double-click in any blank area of the form to get to the Form_Load event procedure template.

Exceptions can only occur when you've written other event procedures for the form.

```
Sub Form_Load ()
   'Initialize form level variables
   'Initialize properties
   ' etc
End Sub
```

Right after Visual Basic processes the Form_Load procedure, Visual Basic calls four other event procedures—if you've written code for them. Here they are, in the order they are called:

The Form_Resize procedure

The Form_Activate procedure

The Form_GotFocus procedure

The Form_Paint procedure (only if the AutoRedraw property, discussed in the next section, is False)

Generally speaking, initial information you want printed to the form should be done by placing Print statements in one of the other event procedures rather than in the Form_Load procedure. Unless you first use the Show method or set the AutoRedraw property to True, nothing will show up!

Visual Basic generates the Form_Resize event whenever the user resizes a form or minimizes and then restores the form. For this reason, the most common use of this event procedure is to recalculate (and rescale if necessary) the size and position of any objects on your form. For example, suppose you spent a lot of time positioning controls symmetrically on a form. Without repositioning them in the Form_Resize procedure, a user can, all too easily, spoil your hard work!

Visual Basic calls the Form_Activate event procedure whenever a form becomes active (that is, when the user moves the focus to it). However, if you move to a different application running under Microsoft Windows and then return to the form, Visual Basic does not call the Form_Activate event procedure again. For this reason the Form_Activate event procedure is usually used only in multiple form applications.

The Form_Paint procedure is where you put Print methods when the AutoRedraw property is set to False. Visual Basic calls this event whenever the form is moved, enlarged, or newly uncovered. You then use this event procedure to redraw the information on the form. However, when the AutoRedraw property is set to True, this event is *not* called and you'll need to use the Refresh method directly (see the section on this method later in this chapter).

After Visual Basic processes any statement that affects the display, it calls on Windows to do the work. Windows in turn tells the display adapter how to display the image. When you install Windows, the installation program checks (or you tell it) what hardware and software you have. Then the installation program installs the necessary screen and print drivers.

Since Windows is a graphical environment, all this means that what you can do with Visual Basic depends on the driver programs that Windows uses for controlling the screen and printer, but using these driver programs is automatic. You do not have to worry about all the possible combinations of hardware a user may have. This is different from what MS-DOS programmers are used to. For programming graphics under DOS, you needed to have part of the program check what kind of graphics board was installed (or even if there was a graphics board at all) and adjust itself accordingly.

Nothing comes for free, however. Windows has to do a lot to manage a graphics environment, and this forces trade-offs. For example, the Visual Basic default is that when you move a form or temporarily hide it, or when one form covers another and moves away, the original text and graphics will probably disappear. This will happen even if the window that covers your form comes from a completely different Windows application. You can arrange for Visual Basic to have *persistent graphics,* but the cost is that Visual Basic must keep a pixel-by-pixel copy of the object in memory. This is called a *bitmap of the screen.* Since many machines will not have enough available memory to store more than a couple of screens, Windows may use your hard disk for temporary storage, but this slows down reaction time dramatically.

# The AutoRedraw Property for Forms

As you'd expect, persistent graphics are determined by a Boolean (true or false) property of forms and picture boxes. Like most properties, you can set this at design or run time. Set the AutoRedraw property to True and Visual Basic saves a copy of the object in memory. Set it to False and you will have to manage the redrawing of graphics yourself.

For a resizeable form, Visual Basic saves a screen representation of the window. In particular, this means that when you enlarge the form or when it is covered by another form, no text displayed on the form (and no graphics information—see Chapter 12) is lost. This requires by far the most memory.

There is one other problem you must be aware of when you set AutoRedraw to True. When AutoRedraw is True, Visual Basic draws the complete image to memory before displaying it on the screen. Only when the bitmap is complete and Visual Basic is in *idle time* (not responding to a specific event—see Chapter 8) will the image finally show up on your screen. On the other hand, you can use the Refresh method to display the image at different stages. However, each time Visual Basic processes a Refresh statement, it redraws every dot in the image from scratch. This can be painfully slow.

Visual Basic activates the Paint event each time a part of the form is newly exposed. This often happens when the user moves or enlarges the form. You can write the necessary code in the Paint procedure whenever you want to redraw part of a form (or picture box—see Chapter 12). Therefore, the least memory-intensive way to handle the problem of text or graphics disappearing because a user covered a form is to redraw the form or picture box. This again shows the constant trade-off in programming between memory-intensive and CPU-intensive activities. Set AutoRedraw to True and you use up memory (if you have it), so this potentially can speed up the program. Using the Paint event procedure (or the hard disk, if you don't have enough memory) uses up time. You have to choose what's best for the application. At the extremes, the choice is easy: if the amount of drawing to be done is minimal, using the Paint event procedure is better. In any case, Visual Basic calls the Paint procedure for the object only if the AutoRedraw property of the object is set to False.

**caution:** *Do not put any statements that move or resize the object inside the Paint procedure. This is because Visual Basic will just call the Paint procedure again and again, and you'd be stuck in an infinite regression.*

## The Refresh Method

The other method you need to get started with Visual Basic programming is the Refresh method. This method applies to forms and controls; it forces an immediate refresh of the form or control and, as mentioned previously, will let you see an image develop even when AutoRedraw is True. If you use the Refresh method, Visual Basic will also call any Paint event procedure you have written for the object. It is quite common to use this method inside the Form_ReSize procedure in order to redisplay any graphics that are calculated in the Paint event procedure. Also, while Visual Basic handles refreshing the screen during idle time, occasionally you will want to take control of this yourself. Whenever Visual Basic processes an *Object*.Refresh statement, it will redraw the object immediately and generate the Paint event if the object supports this.

# The ASCII Representation of Forms

One of the most exciting innovations in Visual Basic 2.0 was the possibility of getting an ASCII representation of a form. The ASCII representation of a form is an extremely useful debugging tool. Using it, you can easily check that the properties of the various controls and forms are exactly what you want. To see what the ASCII representation of a form looks like, do the following:

1. Start up a new project.

2. Add a form and set the caption to "ASCII".

3. Add a command button in the default size, in the default location, and using the default name of Command1 by double-clicking.

4. Add a Click procedure to the command button with the single line of code: Print "You clicked me!"

5. Save the project. When the Save File As dialog box pops up, choose the Save As Text option.

6. Choose the name ASCII.TXT.

Now, if you examine the file in another word processor like Windows Write or in a text editor like Windows Notepad, here's what you would see. (Don't be intimidated by the length of the following listing; we will go over the pieces step by step.)

```
VERSION 3.00
Begin Form Form1
   Caption        =    "ASCII"
```

```
ClientHeight     =    4020
ClientLeft       =    1095
ClientTop        =    1485
ClientWidth      =    7365
Height           =    4425
Left             =    1035
LinkTopic        =    "Form1"
ScaleHeight      =    4020
ScaleWidth       =    7365
Top              =    1140
Width            =    7485
Begin CommandButton Command1
    Caption          =    "Command1"
    Height           =    495
    Left             =    3120
    TabIndex         =    0
    Top              =    1800
    Width            =    1215
End
End
Sub Command1_Click ()
  Print "You clicked me!"
End Sub
```

The idea of the ASCII form representation is simple: It contains a textual description of the form's properties. The listing begins with the version of Visual Basic used, followed by the name of the form. Then comes the current settings of all the properties associated with the form. For example, the new caption is reflected by the line of code that looks like this

```
Caption     = "ASCII"
```

because this is what we reset the Caption property to be. The Client properties describe the form's position *vis-a-vis* the desktop.

After the properties of the form come the various controls on the forms in the same format, indented slightly for readability. The ASCII format for a control starts like the following:

Begin *ControlType ControlName*

In our example this is

```
Begin CommandButton Command1
```

Then come the properties of the control. For example, since we didn't change the control name or any of the other properties, the above listing shows the default values for a command button. Finally, whatever code is attached to the form is listed after all the controls are described.

**tip:**

*You can use a word processor to modify the ASCII representation of the form; then reload the project into Visual Basic and see the changes you've made.*

# Chapter 5

# First Steps in Programming

B Y now you have a feel for what a Visual Basic application looks like. You've seen how to customize forms by adding controls, and you've started writing the event procedures that are the backbone of a Visual Basic application. But as you've probably realized, the event procedures you've seen didn't do much. To do more, you must become comfortable with the sophisticated programming language built into Visual Basic.

If you are familiar with QuickBASIC, Pascal, C, or even QBASIC, you'll have an easier time of it, and the next four chapters will go pretty quickly. If you are familiar only with the older interpreted BASIC found on PCs (GW-BASIC, BASICA), you'll want to read these chapters much more carefully. In any case, there are subtle differences between Visual Basic programming and conventional programming that can trip up even experienced programmers, so you probably don't want to skip these chapters.

## The Anatomy of a Visual Basic Program

It can't be stressed enough that the key to Visual Basic programming is recognizing that Visual Basic generally processes code only in response to events. If you think of a Visual Basic program as a set of independent pieces that "wake up" only in response to events they have been told to recognize, you won't go far wrong, but if you think of the program as having a starting line and an ending line and moving from top to bottom, you will. In fact, unlike many programming languages, executable lines in a Visual Basic program must be inside procedures or functions. Isolated executable lines of code don't work. For illustration purposes, this book may show you fragments of a program, but they are not meant to (nor can they) work independently.

Basically, even if you know a more conventional programming language very well, you shouldn't try to force your Visual Basic programs into its framework. If you impose programming habits learned from older programming languages on your Visual Basic programs, you're likely to run into problems.

# The Code Window

You always write code in the Code window. Figure 5-1 shows the Code window with the Object list box pulled down for the calculator application that comes with Visual Basic. As you have seen, this window opens whenever you double-click a control or form. You can also click View Code from the Project window or View menu or press F7 to open the Code window.

The Code window has a caption that lists the form (the CALC.FRM in Figure 5-1), two list boxes, and an area for editing your code. All the usual Windows editing techniques are available when you enter code (as discussed in Chapter 2). The left list box, called the *Object box,* lists all the controls on the form, plus an object called general that holds common code that can be used by all the procedures attached to the form. You'll see more about this kind of code in Chapter 8 and in the sections in this chapter titled "Changing the Defaults for Types" and "Constants."

The right-hand list box, named *Proc,* is the Procedure list box. As you have seen, this list box gives all the events recognized by the object selected in the Object list box. If you have already written an event procedure, it shows up in bold in the Procedure list box.

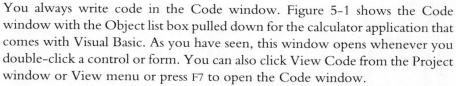

**Figure 5-1**

Object list box for calculator project

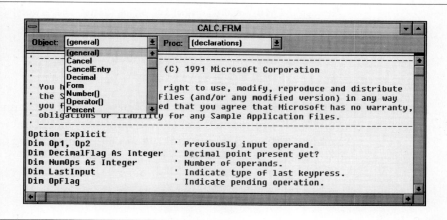

# Statements in Visual Basic

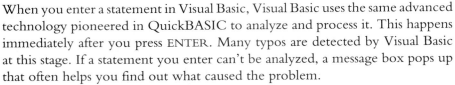

When you enter a statement in Visual Basic, Visual Basic uses the same advanced technology pioneered in QuickBASIC to analyze and process it. This happens immediately after you press ENTER. Many typos are detected by Visual Basic at this stage. If a statement you enter can't be analyzed, a message box pops up that often helps you find out what caused the problem.

Except within quotation marks, case and spacing are ignored by Visual Basic. Nonetheless, Visual Basic does try to impose its own conventions. It capitalizes the first letter of command words and often adds extra spaces for readability. For example, no matter how you capitalize the command word Print—PRint, Print, print, and so on—pressing ENTER will change it to Print. It's a good idea to stick to a standard method of spacing and capitalization in your code.

Statements in Visual Basic rarely use line numbers, and each statement generally occurs on its own line. You can combine statements on one line by placing a colon (:) between the statements. Lines are limited to 255 characters and can't be extended to the next line. If you use a line with more characters than can fit in the window, Visual Basic scrolls the window toward the right as needed.

Sometimes in this book you'll see lines that easily fit this limit but are longer than can fit on one line of a printed page. When this happens, either you will be explicitly told that the statements are meant to be on one line, or the succeeding line will be "outdented" and the double quotation marks or parentheses will be closed on that succeeding line. Another common convention in this book is the use of an underscore as the line continuation character. Here are some examples of these conventions:

```
Print "This is an example of a line that won't fit on a
single line of the page."

MsgBox "You have to click a button for anything to happen" _
306, "Test Button"
```

If you were entering this line in Visual Basic, in the first example you'd continue typing until you reached the closing quotation mark, and in the second, you would omit the underscore and continue until you reached the quotation mark after *Button*.

## Remark Statements

Remark (or Rem) statements are put into programs to explain what code does. It's easy to question why comments are important—until you try to modify (or fix) a program someone else wrote or even a program you wrote months ago. Remark statements are neither executed nor processed by Visual Basic. As a result, they do not take up any room in the compiled code.

There are two ways to indicate a remark statement. The first is to use the Rem keyword:

```
Sub Command1_Click ()
   Rem    Comments describing the procedure would go here
   Rem

End Sub
```

As usual, the programming lines are indented to improve readability. The second method to indicate a Remark statement is to use a single quotation mark ('), which is not the apostrophe found below the tilde (~) but the one usually found below the double quotation mark ("):

```
Sub Command1_Click ()
   'A comment describing the procedure would go here
   '

End Sub
```

You can also add comments to the ends of lines. In this case it is easier to use the single quotation mark because the Rem form requires a colon before it. For example:

```
PrintForm   'Dump the current window
```

or

```
PrintForm   :Rem A bit more cumbersome
```

Everything on a line following a Rem statement is ignored, regardless of whether it is an executable Visual Basic statement or not. Commenting out executable statements is a common technique to help debug your programs.

## The End Statement

When Visual Basic processes an End statement, the program stops. If you are developing a program, you are dumped back into the development environment. The effect is exactly the same as choosing the End option on the Run menu. In a stand-alone program, after the End statement, all windows opened by the program are closed and the program is cleared from memory.

You can have as many End statements within a Visual Basic program as you want, but it is good programming practice to restrict the number of events that end a program.

# Assignment and Property Setting

Giving values to variables and resetting properties are two of the most common tasks in Visual Basic code. Visual Basic uses an equal sign for both these operations; for example,

```
InterestRate = .05
```

You can also use the optional keyword Let that was common in earlier versions of BASIC:

Let *Variable*Name = *value*

The variable name always appears on the left, and the value always appears on the right. Visual Basic *must* be able to obtain a value from the right side of an assignment statement. It will do any processing needed to make this happen. You can consider an assignment statement as a way for a Visual Basic variable to get a (new) value or as a means of copying information from a source to a destination.

## Assigning to Properties

If you want to change a property setting for a Visual Basic object, place the object's name followed by a period and then the name of the property on the left side of the equal sign, and put the new value on the right-hand side:

object.*property* = *value*

For example, suppose you have a text button (control name of Text1) and want to blank it out in code rather than use the properties bar. You need only have a line like this in an event procedure:

```
Text1.Text = ""
```

Since there is nothing between the quotation marks, the text assigned to this property is blank. Similarly, a line like

```
Text1.Text = "This is the new text."
```

in an event procedure changes the setting for the text property to the text in the quotation marks.

You can change the setting of a property via code as often as you need to. For example, if you wanted to change the caption on a command button called Command1, you would place a line like this in an event procedure:

```
Command1.Caption = "Put new caption here."
```

Similarly, if you wanted to make a button called Command5 the first button in Tab order, you would add a line like this to an event procedure:

```
Command5.TabIndex = 0
```

Now suppose you want a form called Form1 to move around when various command buttons are clicked. Here is an example of one of the event procedures you would need:

```
Sub LeftButton_Click ()
  Form1.Left = Form1.Left - 75
End Sub
```

Look at the key line "Form1.Left = Form1.Left – 75." On the left-hand side of the assignment statement is the property that gets the value, but it seems that the property occurs on the right-hand side as well. What happens is that Visual Basic first analyzes the right-hand side of any assignment to extract a value from it. In this case it looks at the current position of the left side of the form and calculates the number of twips it is from the left. It then subtracts 75 from this number. Only after it has done this does it look to the left side. Visual Basic now changes the old value of the "Left" property to a new one.

All this can be a little confusing. Some people find it helpful to remember that right-hand sides of assignment statements are there only for the values they yield, and only the left-hand side gets changed.

Every Visual Basic object has a default property (for example, text boxes have the Text property). When referring to the default property, you don't need to use the property name. For example, you can enter

```
Text1 = "This is new text"
```

However, this approach can lead to less readable code and requires you to remember what the default property of the control is. Thus, in spite of the very small gain in speed this approach yields, this book doesn't use this feature of Visual Basic 3.

## BOOLEAN PROPERTIES

Properties that take only the value True or False are called *Boolean properties,* after the English logician George Boole. We've discussed many Boolean properties already. Boolean properties specify whether a command button is visible, is enabled, or is the default cancel or command button. Visual Basic 3 has built-in constants for these important property values. A statement such as

```
Command1.Visible = False
```

in an event procedure hides the command button. The control stays hidden until Visual Basic processes the statement

```
Command1.Visible = True
```

If you want the TAB key to skip over a control while a program is running, change the TabStop property to False:

```
Control.TabStop = False
```

Internally, Visual Basic uses the values 0 for False and −1 for True for property settings (actually, any nonzero value will work for True). The usual way to toggle between Boolean properties is with the Not operator. Suppose you have a statement such as

```
Command1.Visible = Not(Command1.Visible)
```

in an event procedure. This statement works as follows: Visual Basic finds the current value of Command1.Visible and then the Not operator reverses this value; that is, if the value was True, it changes to False, and vice versa.

**note:** *For the Not operator to work properly in toggling a Boolean property between on and off, you must use the built-in True constant or a value of −1 for True.*

(For additional information on the Not operator, see "Bit Twiddling" in Chapter 7.)

**tip:** *Another example of a Boolean property is the Value property of command buttons. Setting this property to True in code has the same effect as the user clicking the button. This feature is useful for self-running demonstrations when combined with the SetFocus method to move the focus to the correct control.*

# Variables

Variables in Visual Basic hold information (values). Whenever you use a variable, Visual Basic sets up an area in the computer's memory to store the information. Variable names in Visual Basic can be up to 40 characters long and, provided the first character is a letter, can include any combination of letters, numbers, and underscores. The case of the letters in the variable name is irrelevant. The following table lists some possible variable names and indicates whether they are acceptable.

| | |
|---|---|
| Base1_Ball | Acceptable |
| 1Base_Ball | Not acceptable—first character is not a letter |
| Base.1 | Not acceptable—uses a period |
| ThisIsLongButOK | Acceptable—only 15 characters long |

All characters in a variable name are significant, but case is irrelevant. BASE is the same variable as base. On the other hand, Base is a different variable from Base1, and both are different from Base_1. However, Visual Basic always changes the form of the names of your variables to reflect the capitalization pattern you last used. If you use Mortgageinterest, mortgageinterest, and MortgageInterest successively as variable names, then when you move off the line Visual Basic will automatically change all occurrences to MortgageInterest because this was the last one you used.

**tip:** *This feature is often useful in detecting typos in variable names. If you think a misspelled variable name is causing a problem, change one occurrence to all caps, move off the line, and scan the program to see if all the occurrences of the variable name have been changed. If you find one that wasn't changed, you will know that that variable name contains a typo. Correct the error and then change the variable name back to the form you want; all occurrences of the name will change again as well. For another way to help detect typos and variable names, see the section, "Requiring Declaration of Variables" later in this chapter.*

Choosing meaningful variable names helps document your program and makes the inevitable debugging process easier. Meaningful variable names are an excellent way to clarify the point of many kinds of program statements.

You can't use names reserved by Visual Basic for variable names: for example, Print is not acceptable as a variable name. However, you can embed reserved words within a variable's name. For example, PrintIt is a perfectly acceptable variable name. Visual Basic will present an error message if you try to use a reserved word as a variable name, usually immediately after you press ENTER.

The most common convention for variable names is to use capitals only at the beginning of the words that make up the parts of it (for example, MortgageInterest, not Mortgageinterest). This convention is called *mixed case variable names*. This is the convention used in this book, as most people find it much more readable. Some people add underscores as well (for example, Mortgage_Interest)—this style is not used in this book because it wastes space and occasionally causes problems in debugging.

## Variable Types

Visual Basic handles seven standard types of variables. It is also possible to define your own variable types, as you will see in Chapter 9. There are two other variable types that you will see in Chapters 8 and 17. The seven standard variable types are described here.

### STRING

String variables hold characters. One method to identify variables of this type is to place a dollar sign ($) at the end of the variable name: AStringVariable$.

String variables can theoretically hold up to 65,535 characters, although a specific machine may hold less due to memory constraints, overhead requirements for Windows, or the number of strings used in the form.

One of the most common uses of string variables is to pick up the information contained in a text box. For example, if you have a text box named Text1, then

```
ContentOfText1$ = Text1.Text
```

assigns the string contained in the text box to the variable named on the left-hand side.

### INTEGERS

Integer variables hold relatively small integer values (between −32,768 and +32,767). Integer arithmetic is very fast but is restricted to these ranges. The identifier used is the percent sign (%):

```
AnIntegerVariable% = 3
```

### LONG INTEGERS

The *long integer variable* is a type that was introduced in QuickBASIC. It holds integers between −2,147,483,648 and +2,147,483,647. The identifier used is the ampersand (&). Long integer arithmetic is also fast, and there is very little performance penalty on 386DX and 486DX machines for using long integers rather than ordinary integers.

```
ALongIntegerVariable& = 123456789
```

### SINGLE-PRECISION

For single-precision numbers, the identifier is an exclamation point (!). These variables hold numbers that are approximations. They can be fractions, but you can be sure of the accuracy of only seven digits. This means that if an answer comes out as 12,345,678.97, the 8.97 may or may not be accurate. The answer could just as well be 12,345,670.01. Although the accuracy is limited, the size (range) of these numbers is up to 38 digits. Calculations will always be approximate for these types of variables. Moreover, arithmetic with these numbers is slower than with integer or long integer variables.

## DOUBLE-PRECISION

Double-precision variables hold numbers with 16 places of accuracy and allow more than 300 digits. The identifier used is a pound sign (#). Calculations are also approximate for these variables. You can rely only on the first 16 digits. Calculations are relatively slow with double-precision numbers. Double-precision variables are mainly used in scientific calculations in Visual Basic—because of the data type described next.

## CURRENCY

Currency variables are a type that will be new to GW-BASIC and Quick-BASIC users. They are designed to avoid certain problems inherent in switching from binary fractions to decimal fractions. (It's impossible to make 1/10 out of combinations of 1/2, 1/4, 1/8, 1/16, and so on.) The currency type can have 4 digits to the right of the decimal place and up to 14 to the left of the decimal point. Arithmetic will be exact within this range. The identifier is an "at" sign (@)—*not* the dollar sign, which identifies strings. While calculations other than addition and subtraction are about as slow as for double-precision numbers, this is the preferred type for financial calculations of reasonable size. (For those who are interested, this type uses 19-digit integers, which are then scaled by a factor of 10,000. This gives you 15 places to the left of the decimal point and 4 places to the right.)

## THE VARIANT TYPE

The variant type was new to Visual Basic 2.0. The variant data type is designed to store all the different possible Visual Basic data received in one place. It doesn't matter whether the information is numeric, date/time, or string; the variant type can hold it all. Visual Basic automatically performs any necessary conversions so you don't (usually) have to worry about what type of data is being stored in the variant data type. On the other hand, as you'll see in the next chapter, you can use a built-in function to determine whether data stored in the variant type is numeric, date/time, or string. This function lets you easily check user entries to see whether they match the format you want. Using variants rather than the specific type is a little slower because of the conversions needed, and some programmers feel relying on automatic type conversions leads to sloppy programming.

## Fine Points of Variables

Unlike many other versions of BASIC, in Visual Basic you cannot use variables like A% and A!, which differ only in the type identifier, in the same program. Using them produces a duplicate definition error when you try to run your program.

The first time you use a variable, Visual Basic temporarily assigns it a default value of "empty" and gives it the variant type. The "empty" value disappears the moment you assign a value to the variable.

Every other type of variable also has a default value. For string variables, this is the null (empty) string—the one you get by assigning "" to a string variable. For numeric variables, the default value is zero. You should only rely on the default values if this is documented (by a Remark statement, for example) in your program. Otherwise, you risk creating a breeding ground for hard-to-find bugs. It is therefore quite common to use the first statements in an event procedure to initialize the variables.

### SWAPPING

A common task within a procedure is *swapping,* or interchanging the values of two variables. Surprisingly enough, the designers of Visual Basic left out the command Swap that QuickBASIC has for this. You have to write the code yourself.

Suppose you have two variables, $x$ and $y,$ and you try the following to swap variables within an event procedure:

```
x = y
y = x
```

This doesn't work, and it is important that you understand why. What goes wrong is that the first assignment gives the current value of $y$ to the variable $x,$ but it wipes out the previous value of $x.$ The result is that the second statement merely copies the original value of $y,$ which is what it was already anyway. The solution is to use a temporary variable:

```
temp = x      ' copy old value of x to temp
x =  y        ' x now has old value of y
y = temp      ' retrieve original value of x, give to y
```

## The Dim Statement for Types

Many people prefer not to use the identifiers to specify the type of a variable. Instead they use the Dim statement. Here are some examples:

```
Dim I As Integer
Dim TextBox As String
Dim Interest As Currency
```

The technical term for these statements is *declarations*. You can combine multiple declarations on a single line:

```
Dim Year as Integer, Rate As Currency, Name as String
```

Declaring the types of variables used in an event procedure before using them—and commenting as needed, of course—is a good programming habit. It can make your programs more readable since it is easy to skip over the single-character identifiers. Most people prefer the following to using the variables Years%, Rate@, and Currency@:

```
Sub Calculate_Click
   ' This procedure calculates mortgage interest
   Dim Years As Integer
   Dim Rate As Currency
   Dim Amount As Currency
   .
End Sub
```

You can also say: Dim Years%, Rate@, and so on if you prefer using a type identifier.

**note:** *If a variable is declared in a Dim statement, then trying to use variables with the same name but a different type identifier at the end of the variable will cause a "Duplicate definition" error when the program is run.*

For example, if you use the statement Dim Count As Integer to declare the integer variable Count, then the variables Count\$, Count!, Count#, and Count@ may not be used. Count% may be used, however, and is recognized by Visual Basic as just another way of denoting the variable Count.

Finally, to give a variable the variant data type, just use the Dim statement without any As clause or identifier:

```
Dim Foo      'makes Foo have the variant data type
```

You can also use

```
Dim Foo As Variant
```

## Changing the Default for Types

Sometimes you know a program will only (or primarily) use integer variables. In this case it is convenient to change the defaults built into Visual Basic. (Recall that undeclared variables are assumed to be variants.) You change the defaults with what is called a DefType statement. Here are some examples:

| Def Type Statement | What It Does |
| --- | --- |
| DefInt A–Z | Changes the default—all variables are assumed to be integers |
| DefInt I | All variables beginning with I are assumed to be integers |
| DefStr S–Z | All variables beginning with the letters S through Z are assumed to hold strings |

The general forms of the various DefType statements are

DefInt *letter range* (for integers)
DefLng *letter range* (for long integers)
DefSng *letter range* (for single precision)
DefDbl *letter range* (for double precision)
DefCur *letter range* (for currency)
DefStr *letter range* (for strings)
DefVar *letter range* (for variants)

The letters in the ranges need not be caps: DefStr s–Z and DefStr S–Z work equally well. You can always override the default settings by using an identifier or a Dim statement for a specific variable.

These are the first examples of statements that are not found within event procedures. A good way to remember why this must be so is that you use definers to change defaults. You would not bother doing this unless you wanted the change to be true for more than one event procedure.

Any information that you want to be usable by all the event procedures attached to a form is placed in the general section of the form. To put definers in the (general) section, follow these steps:

1. Open the Code window.

2. Select the (general) object from the list of objects presented in the left-hand (Object) list box.

3. Select (declarations) from the Proc (Procedure) list box.

4. Type the definers.

You will often need form-level declarations when you experiment with the example code found in the Help system. You can use the Copy button in the example code combined with the Edit menu to paste in the declarations needed for the example code to run.

**tip:**

*Many programmers put a DefInt A-Z as a form level declaration in order to insure that all variables default to integers. This is done because integer variables are handled fastest. Since you can override any form level declarations, this technique is occasionally useful.*

## Requiring Declaration of Variables

One of the most common bugs in programs is the misspelled variable name. Most versions of BASIC (and Visual Basic itself) allow you to create variables "on the fly" by merely using the variable name in your program. However, when you use this feature, you can easily misspell a variable name, and a misspelled variable name will almost certainly yield a default value that causes your program to behave incorrectly. Such an error is among the most difficult to eradicate—because you need to find the misspelled variable name.

One way to avoid this problem is to force all variables to be declared. Then you will be notified if a variable name is spelled incorrectly in a procedure. The designers of Visual Basic give you this option, but do not force you to use it.

To turn on this option, add the command Option Explicit in the declaration section for the form. After Visual Basic processes this command, it will no longer allow you to use a variable unless you declare it first. If you try to use a variable without declaring it, an error message will appear, as shown here:

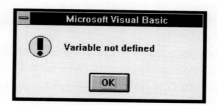

**note:**   *You can also use the Environment Window on the Options menu to require variable declaration.*

## Scope of Variables

Programmers refer to the *scope* of variables when they want to talk about the availability of a variable used in one part of a program to the other parts of a program. In older programming languages, where *all* variables were available to *all* parts of the program, keeping variable names straight was always a problem. If, in a complicated program, you had two variables named Total, the values could (and would) contaminate each other. The solution in modern programming languages like Visual Basic is to isolate variables within procedures. Unless you specifically arrange it, changing the value of a variable named Total in one procedure will not affect another variable with the same name in another procedure. The technical explanation for this is that variables are *local* to procedures unless specified otherwise. In particular, an event procedure will not normally have access to the value of a variable in another event procedure.

As always, it is not a good programming practice to rely on defaults. If you want to be sure a variable is local within an event procedure, use the Dim statement inside the event procedure.

# Sharing Values Across Procedures

Of course, occasionally you will want to share the values of variables across event procedures. For example, if an application is designed to perform a calculation involving one interest rate at a time, that rate should be available to all the procedures in a form. Variables that allow such sharing are called *form-level*

*variables.* Figure 5-2 shows the scope of variables for a Visual Basic project with a single form.

Just as with the DefType statements, you put the Dim statements for form-level variables in the Declarations section. For example, if you open the Code window, select (declarations) for the (general) object, and enter

```
Dim InterestRate As Currency
```

then the following is true:

◆ The value of the variable named InterestRate will be visible to all the procedures attached to the form.

◆ Any changes made to this variable in one event procedure will persist.

Obviously, the last point means you have to be careful when assigning values to form-level variables. Any information passed between event procedures is a breeding ground for programming bugs. Moreover, these errors are often hard to pinpoint.

Although most programmers don't think it is a good idea, you can use the same variable name as both a local and a form-level variable. Any Dim

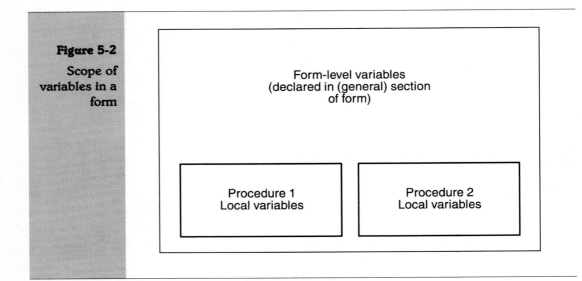

**Figure 5-2**

Scope of variables in a form

Form-level variables
(declared in (general) section
of form)

Procedure 1
Local variables

Procedure 2
Local variables

statements contained in a procedure take precedence over form-level declarations—they force a variable to be local. Therefore, you lose the ability to use the information contained in the form-level variable. Duplicating the names makes the form-level variable invisible to the procedure. Visual Basic doesn't tell you whether a form-level variable has been defined with the same name as a local variable. This is one more reason to make sure that variables you want to be local really are local by dimensioning them inside the procedure. This forces the variable to be local to that procedure.

**tip:**

*Some programmers like to prefix form level variables with the letter "f" (for example, fInterest) and global variables with the letter "g" (for example, gInterest). This makes it easier to tell at a glance what are form level variables and what are global variables. See Chapter 8 for more on global variables.*

## Having Values Persist

When Visual Basic invokes an event procedure, the old values of local variables are wiped out. They go back to their default values. (As mentioned before, you are often better off if they are reinitialized.) Such variables are called *dynamic variables*. However, such variables are not enough for all programming situations. For example, suppose you need to keep track of how many times a command button has been clicked. If the counter is always set back to zero, you're in trouble. You *could* have the values persist by using a form-level variable, but it is generally a good idea to reserve form-level variables only for sharing information. Most programmers choose this method only if other event procedures needed the count.

The solution is to use *static variables*. These variables are not reinitialized each time Visual Basic invokes a procedure. Besides being ideal for counters, they are ideal for making controls alternately visible or invisible (or for switching between any Boolean properties, for that matter) and as a debugging tool.

To make a variable static within a procedure, replace the keyword Dim with the keyword Static:

```
Static Counter As Integer, IsVisible As Integer
```

Here is an example of an event procedure for a command button that counts the clicks and displays the number:

```
Sub Command1_Click()
   'This procedure uses a static variable to count clicks
   Static Counter As Integer      ' Counter starts at 0
   Counter = Counter + 1
   Print Counter
End Sub
```

The first time you click, the counter starts out with its default value of zero. Visual Basic then adds 1 to it and prints the result. Notice that by placing the Print statement after the addition, you are not off by 1 in the count.

Occasionally, you want all local variables within a procedure to be static. To do this, add the keyword Static before the word "Sub" that starts any procedure:

```
Static Sub Command1_Click()
```

## Strings

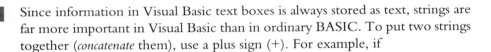

Since information in Visual Basic text boxes is always stored as text, strings are far more important in Visual Basic than in ordinary BASIC. To put two strings together (*concatenate* them), use a plus sign (+). For example, if

```
Title$ = "Queen "
Name$ = "Elizabeth "
Numeral$ = "I"
```

then

    Title\$ + Name\$ + Numeral\$ = "Queen Elizabeth I"
    Title\$ + Name\$ + Numeral\$ + Numeral\$ = "Queen Elizabeth II"

The + joins strings in the order in which you present them. Thus, unlike when you add numbers together, order is important when you use the + sign to join two strings together. You can use the + sign to join together two strings before Visual Basic will make the assignment statement. Here is an example using the variables defined above:

```
CurrentQueen$ = Title$ + Name$ + Numeral$ + Numeral$
```

**tip:** *If you need to concatenate other Visual Basic data use an ampersand (&) in place of the +. For example, C=A% & B$ concatenates an integer variable and a string variable by changing them both to variants.*

## ASCII/ANSI Code

A computer doesn't have one kind of memory for text and another for numbers. Anything stored in a computer's memory is changed into a number (actually, a binary representation of a number). The program keeps track of whether the memory patterns are codes for text or not. Usually, the code for translating text to numbers is called the ASCII code (American Standard Code for Information Interchange). The ASCII code associates with each number from 0 through 255 a displayable or control character, although Windows cannot display all 255 ASCII characters, and uses a more limited set of characters called the ANSI character set. The control characters, and such special keys as TAB and line feed, have numbers less than 32. The value of the function Chr$(n) is the string consisting of the character of ASCII value *n*. The statement

```
Print Chr$(n)
```

either displays the character numbered *n* in the ANSI sequence or produces the specified effect that the control code will have on your screen—or both. For instance, the statement

```
Print Chr$(227)
```

prints the Greek letter pi (π) on the screen.

The following code uses the ASCII/ANSI value for the quotation mark, 34, to display a sentence surrounded with quotation marks.

```
Print Chr$(34);
Print "Quoth the raven, nevermore.";
Print Chr$(34)
```

The output of this command looks like this:

```
"Quoth the raven, nevermore."
```

The preceding output also can be produced by the statement

```
Print """Quoth the raven, nevermore.""";
```

since Visual Basic 3—unlike many other forms of DOS BASIC—treats """ as the literal quotation mark inside Print statements.

Visual Basic has a function that takes a string expression and returns the ASCII/ANSI value of the first character: it is Asc. If the string is empty (the null string), using this function generates a run-time error.

As you'll see in Chapter 6, ASCII/ANSI order is what Visual Basic uses by default to compare strings when you use relational operators like < or >. The most important use of the ASCII/ANSI codes is for the KeyPress event procedure, which also is covered in Chapter 6.

## THE NEWLINE CODE

One of the most important uses of the Chr$ function is to set up a newline code for use in your programs. If you want to place separate lines in a multiline text box or add breaks in a message box, you'll need this code.

As in an old-fashioned typewriter, new lines are made up of two parts: a carriage return to bring the cursor to the first column and the line feed to move it to the next line. To set up a newline code, first define NewLine as a form-level string variable, and then define

```
NewLine = Chr$(13) + Chr$(10)
```

in the Form_Load procedure. (Chr$(13) is the carriage return and Chr$(10) is the line feed.)

Once you have created the newline character, you can add line breaks in message boxes or multiline text boxes by using the NewLine character. The fastest way to do this is to first set up a string variable that includes the newline character:

```
TextString$ = "Visual Basic For Windows" + NewLine
TextString$ = TextString$ + "Osborne McGraw-Hill" + NewLine
TextString$ = TextString$ + "Berkeley, CA"
Text1.Text = TextString$
```

Similarly, you can force a break in a message box by setting up the message string using the NewLine (combination of Chr$(13) + Chr$(10)) as needed.

**tip:** *It is much faster to build up the string first and then change the Text property once than to change the Text property repeatedly.*

## Fixed-Length Strings

A fixed-length string is a special type of string that plays an important role in later chapters (Chapters 9 and 14). These variables are created with a Dim statement. Here is an example:

```
Dim ShortString As String * 10
```

This sets up a string variable (in spite of not using the identifier). However, this variable will always hold strings of length 10. If you assign a longer string to ShortString, as shown here,

```
ShortString = "antidisestablishment"
```

what you get is the same thing as

```
ShortString = "antidisest"
```

As you can see, the contents of the variable are changed because the right part of the string is cut off. Similarly, if you assign a shorter string to ShortString, like this:

```
ShortString = "a"
```

then you still get a string of length 10. Only this time the variable is padded on the right so that the string is really stored in the same way as

```
ShortString = "a          "
```

Thus, fixed-length strings are "right padded" if necessary.

Chapter 14 explains how fixed-length strings are used with random-access files. People whose only experience is with the clumsy method of handling random-access files in interpreted BASIC are in for a very pleasant surprise.

# Numbers

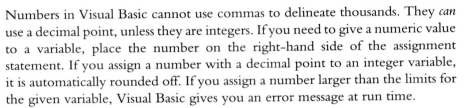

Numbers in Visual Basic cannot use commas to delineate thousands. They *can* use a decimal point, unless they are integers. If you need to give a numeric value to a variable, place the number on the right-hand side of the assignment statement. If you assign a number with a decimal point to an integer variable, it is automatically rounded off. If you assign a number larger than the limits for the given variable, Visual Basic gives you an error message at run time.

Here are some examples:

| Number | Acceptable Variable Type |
|--------|--------------------------|
| 3001 | Okay for all numeric variables |
| 3000001 | Okay for all but short integer variables |
| 30000.01 | Okay for all but integer variables (rounded off for them and long integer variables) |
| 3,001 | Illegal because it uses a comma |

To change a string of digits to a number, use the built-in function Val:

Val("3001") = 3001

You will find the Val function essential in all your Visual Basic applications, because all input received from text boxes is in the form of strings (text). Unlike other forms of BASIC, Visual Basic does not provide a way to enter numbers directly.

The Val function reads through the string until it encounters a nonnumeric character (or a second period). The number you get from it is determined by where it stopped searching:

Val ("30Something") = 30

Similarly, you will have to change a number back to a string of digits when you want to display it in a text box. There are many ways to do this, depending on the form you want the number to take. The function Str$ is the simplest. It converts a number to a string but doesn't clean it up in any way. It also leaves a space in front of positive numbers:

```
Str$(123)          = "123"
Str$(123.4567)     = "123.4567"
Str$(–987654321)   = "–987654321"
```

To polish the display, the Str$ function is often replaced by the Format$ function. (See the section "The Format$ Command" later in this chapter.) The Format$ function is very versatile. Among its many features, this function lets you cut off extraneous digits and display a (large) number with commas or a leading dollar sign.

Another possibility that was introduced in Visual Basic 2.0 is storing information in the variant data type. If you assign a variable that holds numeric information currently stored in the variant data type to a numeric variable, then Visual Basic will perform the conversion automatically. However (unlike when you use the Val command, for example), you must be careful that the variable of the variant data type holds something with no extraneous characters or extra periods beyond the one allowed. Otherwise, an error message will appear. Visual Basic has built-in functions to check the variable; see the section "What Is It?" in Chapter 6.

## Operations on Numbers

The following table gives you the symbols for the five fundamental arithmetic operations:

| Operator | Operation |
| --- | --- |
| + | Addition |
| – | Subtraction (and to denote negative numbers) |
| / | Division |
| * | Multiplication |
| ^ | Exponentiation |

For integers and long integers, there is one symbol and one keyword for the arithmetic operations unique to numbers of these types:

| Operator | Operation |
| --- | --- |
| \ | Integer division (this symbol is a backslash) |
| Mod | The remainder after integer division |

The ordinary division symbol (/) gives you a value that is a single-precision, double-precision, or currency answer, depending on the objects involved. The backslash (\), on the other hand, throws away the remainder in order to give you an integer. For example, 7\3 = 2. Since a / gives either a single- or double-precision answer, use a \ or the Mod operator if you really want to work with integers or long integers.

The Mod operator is the other half of integer division. This operator gives you the remainder after integer division. For example, 7 Mod 3 = 1. When one integer perfectly divides another, there is no remainder, so the Mod operator gives zero: 8 Mod 4 = 0.

The usual term for a combination of numbers, variables, and operators from which Visual Basic can extract a value is a *numeric expression*.

## PARENTHESES AND PRECEDENCE

When you do calculations, you have two ways to indicate the order in which you want operations to occur. The first way is by using parentheses, and you may well prefer this method. Parentheses let you easily specify the order in which operations occur. Something like 3 + (4 * 5) gives 23 because Visual Basic does the operation within the parentheses (4 times 5) first and only then adds the 3. On the other hand, (3 + 4) * 5 gives 35 because Visual Basic adds the 4 and the 3 first to get 7 and only then multiplies by 5.

Here's another example:

((6 * 5) + 4) * 3

The innermost parentheses give 30, the second set of parentheses tells Visual Basic to add 4 to get 34, and then Visual Basic multiplies 34 by 3 to get 102.

Visual Basic allows you to avoid parentheses, provided you carefully follow rules that determine the precedence of the mathematical operations. For example, multiplication has higher precedence than addition. This means 3 + 4 * 5 is 23 rather than 35 because the multiplication (4 * 5) is done before the addition.

The following list gives the order (hierarchy) of operations:

exponentiation (^)
negation (making a number negative)
multiplication and division
integer division

the remainder (Mod) function
addition and subtraction

For example, −4 ^ 2 gives −16 because Visual Basic first does the exponentiation (4 ^ 2 = 4 * 4 = 16) and only then makes the number negative.

Think of these as being levels. Operations on the same level are done from left to right, so 96 / 4 * 2 is 48. Because division and multiplication are on the same level, first the division is done, giving 24, and then the multiplication is done. On the other hand, 96 / 4 ^ 2 is 6. This is because the exponentiation is done first, yielding 16, and only then is the division done.

To show you how obscure using the hierarchy of operations can make your programs, try to figure out what Visual Basic would do with this:

    4 * 2 + 16 / 8 + 2 ^ 3 ^ 4

Here's what happens: first the exponentials (level 1) are computed left to right (2 ^ 3 = 8, 8 ^ 4 = 8 * 8 * 8 * 8 = 4096), then the multiplication and division from left to right (4 * 2 = 8, 16 / 8 = 2), and then the addition (8 + 2 + 4096 = 4106).

Examples like this one should convince you that a judicious use of parentheses will make your programs clearer and your life easier as a result.

## More on Numbers in Visual Basic

If you've tried any calculations involving large numbers in Visual Basic, you've probably discovered that Visual Basic often doesn't bother printing out large numbers. Instead, it uses a variant on *scientific notation*. For example, if you ask Visual Basic to print a 1 followed by 25 zeros using a statement like Print 10 ^ 25, what you see is 1E+25.

If you are not familiar with this notation, think of the E+ as meaning: move the decimal place to the right, adding zeros if necessary. The number of places is exactly the number following the "E." If a negative number follows the "E," move the decimal point to the left. For example, 2.1E−5 gives you .000021. You can enter a number using the E notation if it's convenient; Visual Basic doesn't care whether you enter 1000, 1E3, or 1E+3. To make a number double precision, use a "D" instead of an "E."

If you assign the value of a single-precision variable to a double-precision variable, you do not suddenly increase its accuracy. The number may have more (or even different) digits, but only the first six or seven can be trusted. When you assign a value of one type to a variable of a different type, Visual Basic does a type conversion if it can. If it cannot figure out a way to do this that makes sense, it generates an error at run time.

When you use numbers in your program and do not assign them to a variable of the variant type, Visual Basic assumes the following:

◆   If a number has no decimal point and is in the range −32768 to 32767, it's an integer.

◆   If a number has no decimal point and is in the range for a long integer (−2,147,483,648 to 2,147,483,647), it's a long integer.

◆   If a number has a decimal point and is in the range for a single-precision number, it is assumed to be single precision.

◆   If a number has a decimal point and is outside the range for a single-precision number, it is assumed to be double precision.

These built-in assumptions occasionally lead to problems. This is because the realm in which an answer lives is determined by where the questions live. If you start out with two integers, Visual Basic assumes the answer is also an integer. For example, a statement like

```
Print 12345*6789
```

starts with two integers, so the answer is assumed to also be an integer. But the answer is too large for an integer, so you would get an overflow error. The solution is to add the appropriate identifier to at least one of the numbers. Use the statement

```
Print 12345&*6789
```

and Visual Basic treats both 12345 and the answer as long integers.

You can also use a built-in function to force a type conversion.

| Conversion Function | What It Does |
| --- | --- |
| CInt | Makes a numeric expression an integer by rounding |
| CLng | Makes a numeric expression a long integer by rounding |
| CSng | Makes a numeric expression single precision |
| CDbl | Makes a numeric expression double precision |
| CCur | Makes a numeric expression of the currency type |

| Conversion Function | What It Does |
|---|---|
| CStr | Makes *any* expression a string |
| CVar | Makes *any* expression a variant |

Numeric conversions will be performed only if the numbers you're trying to convert are in the range of the new type; otherwise Visual Basic generates an error message. Using the numeric conversion functions has the same effect as assigning the numeric expression to a variable of the type specified.

# An Example Program: A Mortgage Calculator

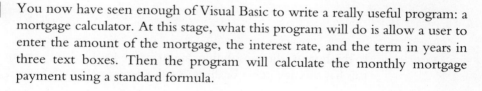

You now have seen enough of Visual Basic to write a really useful program: a mortgage calculator. At this stage, what this program will do is allow a user to enter the amount of the mortgage, the interest rate, and the term in years in three text boxes. Then the program will calculate the monthly mortgage payment using a standard formula.

**note:** *Visual Basic 3 actually has many financial functions available. These functions are discussed in Chapter 7. In particular, there's a function for doing calculations that are even more sophisticated than mortgage analysis.*

The first thing to do is design the form. Figure 5-3 shows the form with the caption not yet changed. This form has two command buttons, four labels, and four text boxes. It uses the default sizes for all the controls. This lets you use the double-click method for generating them. You then need to move the controls around by using the sizing handles until you are happy with the locations. Table 5-1 lists the controls in this project, following the Tab order.

As you can see in Figure 5-3 or by looking at the ampersands in Table 5-1, this form has many access keys for the controls. There are even access keys for the labels. As you saw in Chapter 4, this gives quick access to the text boxes. For this to work, though, the text box must follow the label in Tab order. The TabStop property for the MortgagePayment text box has been changed to False since there is no reason in this application to allow the user to move the focus

**Figure 5-3**

Form for mortgage example

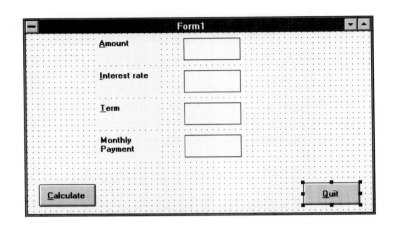

to this box. (Other possibilities are to set the Enabled property to False, although this has the side effect of dimming the box, or to use a bordered label.)

| Control | Control Name | Caption (or Text) |
|---|---|---|
| Form | | Mortgage Calculator |
| 1st label | Label1 | &Amount |
| 1st text box | MortgageAmount | |
| 2nd label | Label2 | &Interest Rate |
| 2nd text box | InterestRate | |
| 3rd label | Label3 | &Term |
| 3rd text box | MortgageTerm | |
| 4th label | Label4 | &Monthly Payment |
| 4th text box | MortgagePayment | |
| Left command button | Calculate | &Calculate |
| Right command button | Quit | &Quit |

**Table 5-1**
**The Controls for the Mortgage Calculator Program in Tab Order**

Let's go over one way to code this application. All the code is attached to the two command buttons. The code for the Quit button is simple:

```
Sub Quit_Click ()
   End
End Sub
```

The code to actually calculate the mortgage payment is a little more complicated. First, you need a formula for mortgage payments. The formula for monthly mortgage payments is

$$Principal*MonthInt/(1-(1/(1+MonthInt))^{\wedge}(Years*12))$$

where *MonthInt* is the annual interest rate divided by 12. Here's the code that activates the calculation. The program assumes the interest rate is given as a percent.

```
Sub Calculate_Click ()
   'This calculates the mortgage
   'Using the formula
   'Principal*MonthInt/(1-(1/(1+MonthInt))^(Years*12))

   Dim Years As Integer, Payment As Currency
   Dim MonthInt As Single, Amount As Currency
   Dim Percent As Single, Principal As Currency
   ' Get info
   Years = Val(MortgageTerm.Text)
   Principal = Val(MortgageAmount.Text)
   Percent = Val(InterestRate.Text) / 100
   MonthInt = Percent/12

   Payment = Principal * MonthInt / (1 - (1 / (1 + MonthInt))^ _
(Years * 12))    ' this and preceding line are one line
   MortgagePayment.Text = Str$(Payment)
End Sub
```

For more accuracy, this program keeps the years in an integer variable, the interest rate and percent as a single-precision number, and all the others as currency variables. The program will run a little more quickly if it uses single-precision variables instead of currency variables. The next point to remember is that text boxes do not give numbers; it is good programming to convert the data inside them by using the Val command instead of relying on

Variants. This program assumes that the user enters the interest rate as a percent. Because the Val function stops when it encounters a nonnumeric character, the user may use a percent sign at the end of what he or she types. (Converting a percent to a decimal means dividing by 100.) To make the logic of the program clearer, there is a separate calculation for the monthly interest.

Finally, the program converts the data back to a string in order to assign it to the text property of the MortgagePayment text box instead of using the automatic conversion provided by Variants.

## Improvements to the Mortgage Calculator

There are lots of ways the mortgage calculator program can be improved. Probably the most important would be to make the program more "bullet–proof." Inexperienced users often enter information in the wrong form or use the wrong kind of information. For example, they might use commas or dollar signs for the mortgage amounts. In the next chapter you'll see how to write the code to either allow or prevent this as you see fit.

For now, though, suppose you wanted to add two command buttons that either increase or decrease the interest rate (say by 1/8% = .00125) and then redo the calculations. Here's a simple way to write the code for a button to increase the interest rate:

```
Sub Increase_Click()
   Dim NewRate As Single

   Percent = Val(InterestRate.Text) / 100
   NewRate = (Percent + .00125)*100
   InterestRate.Text = Str$(NewRate)
   Calculate_Click
End Sub
```

Before getting to the question of why this program may not be the best solution, take a look at the key statement, *Calculate_Click*. This is the first example you've seen of one event procedure using (the technical term is *calling*) another event procedure. As your programs get more sophisticated, event procedures become more and more interrelated. Chapter 8 discusses this in depth. What happens here is that when Visual Basic calls the Click procedure, it uses the current contents of the text boxes. Because the line

```
InterestRate.Text = Str$(NewRate)
```

changes the contents of the text box directly, the Click procedure has new data to work with.

Now why would some people think this version of the mortgage program is not the most efficient programming solution? The offending line is

```
Percent = Val(InterestRate.Text) / 100
```

What this line does is recalculate something that has been calculated once already. While not a mistake, it is inefficient. In a more complicated program, these inefficiencies might grow until they really put a drag on the performance of your application. They also might become a breeding ground for bugs. A better solution is to make all the numeric information gotten from the text boxes the values of form-level variables. Add the following to the (declarations) section of the form and remove the corresponding declarations from the event procedures.

```
Dim Principal As Single, Percent as Single
Dim Years As Integer, Payment As Currency
```

Inefficiencies are common when you modify an old program for new uses. You end up forcing the original program into a frame in which it was never supposed to appear. You're likely to introduce bugs as well. Often you're better off rewriting the program from scratch.

Debugging a program will always be necessary, but it will never be fun. Programs rarely run perfectly the first time. One way to cut down on debugging time is to get into the habit of "thinking first and coding later" (sometimes described as "the sooner you start coding, the longer it takes"). If you think through the possibilities carefully first—for example, deciding which variables should be global and which should be local—you'll go a long way towards "bug proofing" your programs.

# Constants

A program is easiest to debug when it's readable. Try to prevent the MEGO ("my eyes glaze over") syndrome that is all too common when a program has lots of mysterious numbers sprinkled about. It's a lot easier to read a line of code like

```
Calculate.Visible = True
```

than one like

```
Calculate.Visible = -1
```

As mentioned before, Visual Basic 3 has two constants built-in for True and False to let you do this.

More generally, Visual Basic's *named constant* feature allows you to use mnemonic names for values that never change. Constants are declared just like variables, and the rules for their names are also the same: 40 characters, first character a letter, and then any combination of letters, underscores, and numerals. The convention is to use all capitals for constants.

If you have only one form or want the constants visible to the event procedures for only one form, put them in the (declarations) section for the (general) object, just as you did with the definers that change Visual Basic's default types. You can also define a constant within a procedure, but this is less common, and only that procedure would have access to the constant.

You set up a constant by using the keyword Const followed by the name of the constant, an equal sign, and then the value:

```
Const PIE = 3.14159
```

You can set up string constants:

```
Const USERNAME = "Bill Smith"
Const LANGUAGE = "Visual Basic Version 2.0"
```

You can even use numeric expressions for constants—or define new constants in terms of previously defined constants:

```
Const PIEOVER2 = PIE/2
```

---

 **caution:** *True and False are now reserved words. Visual Basic 1.0 code that made them user-defined constants will need to be changed so that these offending lines are removed.*

---

What you can't do is define a constant in terms of Visual Basic's built-in functions or the exponentiation operator. If you need the square root of ten in a program, you need to calculate it before you can write

```
Const SQUAREROOTOFTEN = 3.16227766
```

Visual Basic uses the simplest type it can for a constant, but you can override this by adding a type identifier to a constant. For example,

```
Const THISWILLBEALONGINTEGER& = 37
```

forces Visual Basic to treat the constant 37 as a long integer instead of an ordinary integer. (Constants are not affected by any definers you set up.) Even if you use a type identifier at the end of the constant when you define it, you don't need to use the identifier in the program. Using the preceding example, all subsequent occurrences of this constant can be

```
THISWILLBEALONGINTEGER
```

As mentioned, the convention is to use all caps for constants, but this is not required. Moreover, references to constants don't depend on the case.

## The Supplied Constant File

Visual Basic comes with a four-page file of predefined global constants you can incorporate into your programs. The file is named CONSTANT.TXT and must be in what is called a code module. (You'll learn more about code modules in Chapter 8.) Each section is headed by a comment that explains what the constants are. Here are some excerpts of what the file contains.

The file contains property values (so you don't constantly have to go to the help files):

```
'=================='
'                  '
' Property values  '
'                  '
'=================='

' Alignment (label)
Global Const LEFT_JUSTIFY = 0          ' 0 - Left Justify
Global Const RIGHT_JUSTIFY = 1         ' 1 - Right Justify
Global Const CENTER = 2                ' 2 - Center
```

The file contains color codes (so you don't have to think of how the primary colors blend together):

```
' BackColor, ForeColor, FillColor (standard RGB colors):

Global Const BLACK = &H0&
Global Const RED = &HFF&
Global Const GREEN = &HFF00&
Global Const YELLOW = &HFFFF&
Global Const BLUE = &HFF0000
Global Const MAGENTA = &HFF00FF
Global Const CYAN = &HFFFF00
Global Const WHITE = &HFFFFFF
```

The file contains mouse pointer codes (so you know what they are):

```
' MousePointer (form, controls)
Global Const DEFAULT = 0           ' 0 - Default
Global Const ARROW = 1             ' 1 - Arrow
Global Const CROSSHAIR = 2         ' 2 - Cross
Global Const IBEAM = 3             ' 3 - I-Beam
Global Const ICON_POINTER = 4      ' 4 - Icon
Global Const SIZE_POINTER = 5      ' 5 - Size
Global Const SIZE_NE_SW = 6        ' 6 - Size NE SW
Global Const SIZE_N_S = 7          ' 7 - Size N S
Global Const SIZE_NW_SE = 8        ' 8 - Size NW SE
Global Const SIZE_W_E = 9          ' 9 - Size W E
Global Const UP_ARROW = 10         ' 10 - Up Arrow
Global Const HOURGLASS = 11        ' 11 - Hourglass
Global Const NO_DROP = 120
```

The file also contains many other constants that become more useful as you write more sophisticated procedures.

To incorporate the CONSTANT.TXT file into your program:

1. Add a new code module. You do this by going to the File menu and choosing Module (ALT+F+M).

2. Open the File menu again and choose Load Text by pressing ALT+C+L.

3. Select the file named CONSTANT.TXT, which is stored in the same directory as Visual Basic itself.

Since the constants are defined by using the Global keyword, you would need to make extensive changes if you put them in the general section of a form.

<br /><br />

**note:**

*Many of the examples in the help files require you to incorporate the CONSTANT.TXT file into a code module before you can run the example. You may prefer to use the Windows Notepad to copy only those constants you need into your project. This saves a little space in the .EXE file.*

# Projects with Multiple Forms

As your applications grow more complicated, you won't want to restrict yourself to applications that are contained in only a single form. Multiple forms will add flexibility and power to your applications. This is over and above solving the problems you've already seen with controls blocking out text that you've printed to a form. To add additional forms to an application you're designing, open the File menu and choose New Form by pressing ALT+F+F.

The Project window lists all the forms by name with an .FRM extension. Visual Basic stores each form as a separate file and uses the .MAK file to keep track of where they are stored. The following shows you the Project window with an application that has three forms:

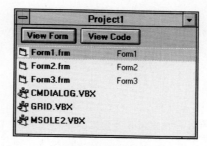

The new form is placed by default in the center of the screen—usually blocking out the original form. As you can imagine, when you are customizing more than one form at design time, the screen begins to get cluttered.

**tip:**

*The easiest way to bring a form to the foreground so you can work with it is to open the Project window and double-click the form name or select the form by name and click the View Form button.*

## Writing Code for Multiple Forms

Although forms do not have a control name that you use for writing code for event procedures, they do have a FormName property that you can use to refer to other properties of the form. Setting this property to something meaningful via the properties bar makes it easier to refer to the different properties or apply a method to the form. The default value for this property starts at Form1 for the first form, Form2 for the second form, and so on. Using the default value means you have to refer to properties when you code, like this:

```
Form3.Height = Screen.Height/2     'cut the default height in 2
```

If Form3 was your "Help Form," for example, the code will be a lot easier to read if you set the form name to HelpForm and write

```
HelpForm.Height = Screen.Height/2  'set HelpForm height to
                                   'half normal
```

Form names are used only in code to refer to properties and methods; they are not used for event procedures. For example, to apply the Cls (clear screen method) to the preceding form, you would write

```
HelpForm.Cls
```

On the other hand, regardless of how you name a form, the Click procedure template for the form itself will always look like this in the Code window:

```
Sub Form_Click ()

End Sub
```

This will rarely cause problems since event procedures for a form are attached to the form.

Although you do not need the form name to refer to properties of the current form, using the form name sometimes makes your code cleaner. This is because code for one form can affect controls on another form. Suppose your HelpForm had a Quit button you wanted to disable via code within an event procedure attached to a different form. It is safer (and clearer) to write

```
HelpForm!Quit.Enabled = False
```

even in event procedures attached to the HelpForm, than to use

```
Quit.Enabled = False
```

although both have the same effect. The general syntax is

FormName!ControlName.Property = Value

where an exclamation point separates the form name from the control. (You can also use the period that was used in Visual Basic 1.0, although Microsoft discourages this because it may not be allowed in future versions of Visual Basic.)

Finally, global constants are available to all the code attached to the project. (You can also use *global variables,* which are variables visible to the entire project. For more on these important objects, see the section on global variables in Chapter 8.)

## How to Handle Multiple Forms at Run Time

Visual Basic displays at most one form when an application starts running. This is called the *startup form.* Any other forms in your application must be explicitly loaded and displayed via code. The startup form is usually the initial form that appears when you begin a new project. If you want to change this, select the Project option on the Options menu by pressing ALT+O+P. Choosing this option gives you the following dialog box:

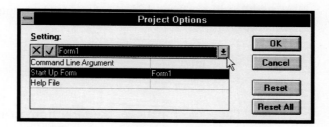

All you need to do now is select the form (by name) that you want to be the startup form by clicking on the down arrow (indicated by the pointer) and choosing the form you want.

The four keywords to handle forms are described here.

**Show**   The Show keyword shows the form on the screen. To do this, Visual Basic first checks that the form is loaded into memory. If it is not, then it loads the form first. The basic syntax for the Show method is

FormName.Show

The Show method also moves the form to the top of the desktop if it was covered by another form. Show can also be used in the FormLoad event of any form to display information without needing to set Auto Redraw to True.

**Load**  The Load keyword places the form into memory but does not display it. Visual Basic also loads the form into memory whenever you refer to its properties or controls in code. Because of this, the main reason to load a form prior to showing it is to speed up response time. The trade-off is that you use up more memory. Its syntax is

Load *FormName*

When Visual Basic loads a form it sets all the properties of the form to the ones you initially made at design time and invokes the Form_Load event procedure.

**Hide**  The Hide keyword removes the form from the screen but doesn't unload it from memory. The controls are not available to the user, but you can still refer to them in code. The values of the form-level variables do not disappear. As with loading a form, hiding a form trades response time for memory. The syntax is

FormName.Hide

**Unload**  The Unload removes the form from memory. All information contained in its form-level variables is lost. The syntax for this command is

Unload *Formname*

**tip:**  *When a form is unloaded, Visual Basic generates the QueryUnload event. This event procedure is a good place to put code you want to be activated at the end of the useful life of the form, for example, when the user chooses Close from the control box or the ALT+F4 combination.*

## An Example Using Multiple Forms

To see an example of an application with multiple forms, create a project with two forms and add a command button to each form. The command button on the first form will move the second form to the left and bring it to the forefront. The command button on the second form will bring the first form back to the top without moving it from its original place. For illustration purposes, the default names for all the objects are left unchanged.

The command button for the first form needs the following code:

```
Sub Command1_Click ()
  ' Moves the second form around and displays it
  Form2.Show
  Form2.Left = Form2.Left - 75
End Sub
```

Because the control name was deliberately not set to be more meaningful, the event procedure for the second command button would start off just like the first:

```
Sub Command1_Click ()
  ' Show original form
  Form1.Show
End Sub
```

The control names were left unchanged here to make the point that this is sloppy programming. Although Visual Basic will know which Command1_Click procedure belonged where, in a more sophisticated program, this sloppiness would be an obvious breeding ground for confusion. Even if the form names seem clear enough, it is better to use control names such as Form2Shift (or Microsoft's convention cmdForm2Shift) for the first command button and Form1ToTop for the second. (You will probably also want to set the caption properties to explain what actions the buttons perform.)

## Keeping the Focus in a Form (Modality)

Message boxes require that users close them before they can work with a form. This property is often useful for a form as well. For example, you may want to make sure a user has digested the information contained in a form before he or she shifts the focus to another form in the application. (Users can switch to a completely different application within the Windows environment, unless you are using a system modal message box. See Chapter 4 for more details.) This property is called *modality* in the Microsoft Windows documentation. You make a form modal by adding an option to the Show method that displays the form. If you have a line of code in a procedure that reads

```
FormName.Show 1
```

then Visual Basic displays the form rigidly. No user input to any other form in the application will be accepted until the modal form is hidden or unloaded. Once a form is shown by using the modal setting, a user cannot move the focus to any other form until the modal form is hidden or unloaded. In particular, neither mouse clicks nor keypresses will register in any other form. Usually you have a default command or cancel button on a modal form.

**tip:**

*A dialog box is usually a modal form with a fixed double border.*

Forms default to be nonmodal, but you can also use the following code to force them to be nonmodal:

```
FormName.Show 0
```

## Input Boxes

Text boxes are the normal way for a Visual Basic application to accept data. (For those who know ordinary BASIC, there is no direct analog of the Input statement.) There is one other method that is occasionally useful. The Input-Box$ function displays a modal dialog box on the screen. This is the principal advantage of input boxes; it is sometimes necessary to insist that a user supply some necessary data before letting him or her move on in the application. The disadvantages are that the dimensions of the input box are fixed beforehand and that you lose the flexibility that text boxes provide. Here is an example of an input box:

As you can see, input boxes have a title bar and four components, three of which are controls. The first is the prompt, "Please enter your name." There are always two command buttons labeled OK and Cancel. Finally, there is a text box at the bottom. Visual Basic always places the focus here when it processes a statement containing an InputBox$ function. The simplest syntax for the InputBox$ function is

StringVariable = InputBox$( prompt$)

where the prompt is a string or string variable. This gives a dialog box that is roughly centered horizontally and one-third of the way down the screen.

Now the user types whatever he or she wants in the text box. Pressing ENTER or clicking the OK button causes whatever is in the text box to become the value of the string variable. Pressing ESC or clicking the Cancel box causes Visual Basic to assign the null string to the variable. The full syntax for the InputBox$ function is

InputBox$(prompt$ [, *title$*, *default$*, *xpos%*, *ypos%*])

Here are short descriptions of these items.

___

***prompt$***  prompt$ is a string or string variable whose value Visual Basic displays in the dialog box. It is limited to roughly 255 characters. The prompt doesn't wrap, and you have to explicitly add line separators. (See Chapter 6 for how to do this.)

*title$* title$ is optional and gives the caption used in the title bar. There is no default value; if you leave this out, nothing is displayed in the title bar.

*default$* default$ is also optional. It lets you display default text in the Edit box where the user will be entering information.

*xpos%,ypos%* Also optional, both *xpos%* and *ypos%* are integral numeric expressions. *xpos%* is the distance in twips between the left edge of the input box and the left edge of the screen. *ypos%* gives the distance in twips between the top of the box and the top of the screen.

The notation just presented may seem cryptic at first, but it is a good idea to get used to it. It is the notation used in both the manual and the online documentation. With this notation, anything in square brackets is optional. In this case, the parentheses are outside the square brackets, so they are required. The commas separate the optional elements (the *arguments*) in this function. If you skip one of the arguments, you still have to use a comma as a separator. (How else would Visual Basic know which argument belongs where?) For example,

InputBox$("Example", , *default$*, *xpos%*, *ypos%*)

leaves out the title of the dialog box.

**note:** *You can also use InputBox(prompt$, default, xpos%, ypos%), which returns a variant rather than a string.*

## Printing on Forms

Since you now know how to add other blank forms to your applications, you are in a better position to display information in an application. This is because, as you've already seen, controls on a form can obscure any information Visual Basic displays by using the Print method. The general syntax for the Print method applied to a form is

FormName.Print *expressions to print*

Where Visual Basic displays the information depends on the current value of two properties of a form, called CurrentX and CurrentY. CurrentX refers to the horizontal position where Visual Basic will display information, and CurrentY refers to the vertical position where it will display information. The units used are determined by the scale set up with the various scale methods you saw in Chapter 3.

Whenever you use the Cls method to clear a form, Visual Basic resets the CurrentX and CurrentY values to zero. Using the default setting for the various scale properties would mean that the next Print statement puts information in the top left-hand corner. If you have changed the scale (for example, by using the ScaleLeft and ScaleTop properties), Visual Basic will use whatever location on the form now represented 0,0. (For more information on the scale properties, see Chapter 12.)

You set CurrentX and CurrentY the same way you'd set any property:

FormName.*CurrentX* = *Value*
FormName.*CurrentY* = *Value*

The value may be any numeric expression from which Visual Basic can extract a single-precision value.

**note:**

*Many Visual Basic programmers prefer to use text boxes or labels instead of printing directly to a form, except when they need to mix fonts.*

## An Example: Centering Text Inside a Form

Suppose you wanted to display a message in the exact center of a form. This turns out to be not as easy as it sounds. As a first approximation, here is an outline of what you need to do to find the coordinates of the exact center of the form:

1. Find the current value of the ScaleHeight and ScaleWidth properties. This tells you how large the internal area of the form (without the borders and title bar) is.

2. Divide these values in half.

3. Find the values of the ScaleLeft and ScaleTop properties for the form.

4. Add the results from step 2 to the values from step 3. This gives you the coordinates of the exact center of the form.

The problem is that this doesn't quite finish the job. If you reset the values CurrentX and CurrentY to the results from step 4 of this outline, you would start printing at the center of the screen, but the message wouldn't be centered. What you also need to do is take into account the font size and the length of the message and then shift over and up by half the length and width of the message. The key to doing this is two built-in methods: TextWidth and TextHeight. The syntax for the TextWidth method is

FormName.TextWidth(*string*)

After processing this statement, Visual Basic returns the value for the width of the string inside the parentheses, using the current font and coordinate system.

5. Use the TextWidth method on the string you want to center. Now subtract one-half the value Visual Basic obtains from this method from the value in step 4, and make this the value of CurrentX.

Similarly, the syntax for the TextHeight method is

FormName.TextHeight(*string*)

and it gives the width of the string inside the parentheses. Subtracting half this number from the value of CurrentY obtained in step 4 gives you the location where you should start printing the message.

In general, TextHeight is used to determine the amount of vertical space and TextWidth the amount of horizontal space you need to display a string.

Here is another example in which these methods are useful. Suppose you want to display information at the beginning of the tenth line of text as it would appear in the ordinary coordinate system (0,0 as the top left). Use the following fragment:

```
CurrentY = FormName.TextHeight("string") * 9
CurrentX = 0
```

You have to multiply by 9 rather than 10 to take into account that Visual Basic starts with 0,0 for the top-left corner.

## The Font Properties in Code

Which fonts and font sizes you can use depend on what kind of hardware is available to the system in which you run the application. Visual Basic lets you find out this information; Chapter 6 will show you how.

To assign a font name in code, place the name in quotation marks on the right-hand side of an assignment statement:

```
ObjectName.FontName = "Modern"
Object.FontName = "Helv"                    'Helvetica
```

All objects that display text let you set these properties. These include forms, command buttons, labels, and text boxes. Of these, only forms (and picture boxes—see Chapter 10) let you combine different fonts. If you change these properties at run time for any other control, all the old text switches to the new font as well. The rule is that if text is specified by a property (like the Caption property for command buttons), changing a font changes the previous text. On the other hand, if you display text by using the Print method, the changes are not retroactive and therefore go into effect only for subsequent Print statements.

You can change all the font properties via code. Except for FontSize, they are all Boolean properties (True or False). As with FontName, any control that displays text lets you set the following:

```
ObjectName.FontSize = 18                    '18 point type
ObjectName.FontBold = True
ObjectName.FontItalic = True
ObjectName.FontStrikethru = False
ObjectName.FontUnderline = False
```

As with changing fonts, only forms (and picture boxes) let you mix these font properties.

Forms (and picture boxes) have one other font property you may occasionally find useful: FontTransparent. If you set this to True (−1), background graphics and background text will show through the text displayed in the transparent font.

These properties can be combined in almost any way you want. If your hardware and software support it, you can have 18-point bold italic script type in a control if that seems appropriate.

## Tables

Although the CurrentX and CurrentY properties give you absolute control over the placement of text in a form, this is often too cumbersome a method to use. When you want to display a table on a blank form, or just have lots of text in one font size, you are often better off using the built-in *print zones* on a form. Print zones are always set 14 columns apart, and Visual Basic recalculates this distance depending on the font characteristics in effect.

Each column is the width of the average character in the font. Many fonts in Windows applications are *proportional*. (This means that a wide character, such as an "m," takes up more space than a narrow character, such as an "i". Proportional spacing gives a more polished look to the screen.)

Each time you use a comma in a Print method (statement), Visual Basic displays the data to the next print zone. For example, a statement like

```
Form1.Print FirstName$, MiddleInit$, LastName$
```

tries to have the value of the string variable FirstName$ printed in the first zone, the value of the variable MiddleInit$ at the beginning of the second zone, and the value of the variable LastName$ printed at the beginning of the third zone. However, if a previous expression runs over into the next print zone, Visual Basic moves to the beginning of the next zone for the next Print statement.

### THE TAB AND SPC COMMANDS AND SEMICOLONS

Normally, after Visual Basic processes a statement involving the Print method, it moves to the next line. You also use an empty Print statement to add a blank line. If you want to suppress the automatic carriage return, place a semicolon at the end of the statement. For example:

```
Sub Form_Click ()
  ' demonstrates the difference between using a ; and not
  Form1.Print "This is a test"
  Form1.Print "of the Print method"
  Form1.Print                      'blank line

  Form1.Print "This is a test";
  Form1.Print "of the Print method"
  Form1.Print                      'blank line
End Sub
```

The Tab function lets you move to a specific column and start printing there. The Tab function also uses the average size of a character in the current font to determine where the columns are. Its syntax is

Print Tab(ColumnNumber%);

ColumnNumber% is an integral expression. If the current column position is greater than its value, TAB skips to this column on the next line. If the value is less than 1, Visual Basic moves to the first column. In theory, you can have values as large as 32,767 for the column. But since Visual Basic doesn't wrap around to the next line, you wouldn't really want to do this.

The Spc function has a similar syntax to the Tab function:

Spc(*Integer%*)

This function inserts the specified number of spaces into a line starting at the current print position. The value inside the parentheses can't be negative.

**note:** *To position text inside a multiline text box, you need to insert spaces and newline characters. Text boxes do not support direct positioning of text.*

# The Printer

Visual Basic uses the printer you set up when you installed Microsoft Windows. Visual Basic makes it easy to use whatever resolution, font properties, and so on, that Windows can coax from the printer.

You've already seen one method for sending information to a printer: the PrintForm command sends a screen dump of a form to the printer. If your application has more than one form, you have to use the form name in this command:

FormName.PrintForm

Because this command does a bit-by-bit dump of the whole form (including captions and borders), it lacks flexibility. Moreover, most printers have higher resolution than the screen.

Most of the printer commands in Visual Basic are *page oriented*. This means that Visual Basic calculates all the characters (actually dots) that will appear on a page before it sends the information to the printer. This allows you to have complete control over the appearance of the printed page.

The usual way to send information to a printer is the Print method, which also sends information to a form. Since Visual Basic methods only send to *objects* in Visual Basic, you need a built-in Visual Basic object for printing. The object for printing is called, naturally enough, the Printer object. There are essentially no differences between how you use the Print method for a form and how you use it for a printer. For example, because the Print method is page oriented, you can set the CurrentX and CurrentY properties to precisely position text or even dots on a page. (See Chapter 12 to learn how to do this.)

The syntax used to send text to the printer is similar:

Printer.Print *text*

Semicolons and commas also work the same way they did for forms. The semicolon suppresses the automatic carriage return; the comma moves to the next free print zone (still 14 columns apart). The TAB and Spc functions do not work differently either.

You control the font properties in the same fashion. For example:

```
Printer.FontName = "Script"          'Use script font
Printer.FontBold = True
Printer.FontSize = 18                '18 point type
```

As with printing to forms, font changes are not retroactive. They affect only text printed after Visual Basic processes the change.

## Useful Properties and Methods for the Printer

If you check the online help, you'll see there are 28 properties and 9 methods for the Printer object. Most of the ones that are unfamiliar to you, such as DrawMode and FillStyle, are covered in Chapter 12. The vast majority, however, should be familiar to you since you've seen them for forms. What follows are short descriptions of some printer properties and methods you will use most often.

*Height, Width* The Height and Width properties give you the height and width of the paper in the printer as reported by Windows. This is measured in twips, regardless of how you set the scale properties. You obviously can't change these at run time; they are *read-only* properties. One example of how you might use these properties is to make sure that someone has switched to wider paper before printing something that would not fit on the usual 8 1/2 by 11-inch paper. (For 8 1/2 by 11-inch paper, Visual Basic reports an available width of 12,288 twips and an available height of 15,744 twips.)

*EndDoc* You use the EndDoc method to tell Windows that a document is finished. The syntax is

    Printer.EndDoc

This releases whatever information there is about the page or pages still in memory and sends it to the Microsoft Windows print manager for printing.

*NewPage* The NewPage method ends the current page and tells the printer to move to the next page. The syntax is

    Printer.NewPage

*Page* The Page property keeps track of the number of pages printed in the current document. The counter starts over at 1 after Visual Basic processes a statement with EndDoc. It increases by 1 every time you use the NewPage method or when the information you send to the printer with the Print method didn't fit on the previous page. A common use of this property is to print a header at the top of each page:

```
Printer.NewPage       'start new page
Printer.Print "You are on page";Printer.Page
```

# The Format$ Command

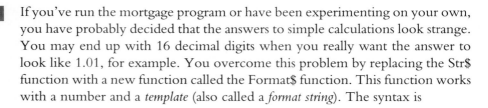 If you've run the mortgage program or have been experimenting on your own, you have probably decided that the answers to simple calculations look strange. You may end up with 16 decimal digits when you really want the answer to look like 1.01, for example. You overcome this problem by replacing the Str$ function with a new function called the Format$ function. This function works with a number and a *template* (also called a *format string*). The syntax is

    Format$(*NumericExpression*, *FormatString$*)

For example,

```
Print Format$(123.456789,"####.##")
```

yields 123.46. Visual Basic rounds the number off so as to have only two digits after the decimal point.

The Format$ function, unlike the Str$ function, does not leave room for an implied + sign. This means that in a statement like

```
Print "The interest rate is ";Format$(Payment,"#####.##")
```

the extra space after the word "is" is essential.

In general, a # is the placeholder for a digit, except that leading and trailing zeros are ignored. For example,

```
Print Format$(123.450,"####.####")
```

yields 123.45. Visual Basic users, unlike QuickBASIC users, won't have to worry about having too few #'s before the decimal point in the format string. Visual Basic will print all the digits to the left of the decimal point. This way you can concentrate on deciding the number of decimals you want displayed and adjust the format string accordingly.

If you want to have Visual Basic display leading and trailing zeros, you use a zero in place of the # in the format string. For example,

```
Print Format$(123.450,"000.000")
```

yields 123.450.

You may want to display numbers with commas every three digits. For this, place a comma between any two-digit placeholders:

```
Print Format$(123456789.991,"#,#.##")
```

This yields 123,456,789.99.

One subtle point about the comma: if you place the comma immediately to the left of the decimal point (or use two commas), Visual Basic interprets this to mean it should skip the three digits that fall between the comma and the decimal point (or between the two commas). This is occasionally useful in scaling numbers. If your program was dealing with Japanese yen and you needed to display one hundred million yen, you might want to write 100 million yen rather than 100,000,000 yen. To do this, you use the following statement:

```
Print Format$(100000000,"#00,,");" million yen"
```

Combining the # with the zero in the format string ensures that trailing zeros aren't suppressed.

If you want to express a number as a percentage, place a percent sign at the end of the format string. Visual Basic will automatically multiply the expression by 100 before converting. For example,

```
Print Format$(1.234,"###.##%")
```

yields 123.4%.

If you need to display a −, +, $, (, ), or spaces, you use them in the format string exactly in the place you want them to occur. For example, if you want to have a dollar sign in front of a value, use this:

```
Print Format$(Amount,"$###.##")
```

The Format$ is important, but because the number of options is so large, you have seen only a sample of the possibilities in this section. You will find yourself frequently turning to the online help for this function.

One final point about the Format$ function: it is often useful to set up string constants for the various format strings. Especially when you have to repeatedly format values, it's worth first setting up a constant like

```
Const MONEY = "###,###.##"
```

From that point on you can write

```
Format$(Amount, MONEY)
```

which is far more readable and less prone to typos and will be easier to modify in the future.

**note:** *You can also use Format (without the $) to work with Variants.*

## Calendar Information

Visual Basic has many built-in functions you can use to read the information contained in the systems clock about the time, day, and year. If you combine this with built-in functions for converting dates to numbers, financial calculations become much easier.

### The Date$ Function

The Date$ function returns a string of the form *Month–Day–Year (mm–dd–yyyy)*. The month and day always use two digits; the year uses four (for example, 01-01-1992 for 1 January 1992). You can also use this function as a statement to reset the current date in the system. The least ambiguous way to do this is by assigning a string to Date$ in one of the following forms:

```
Date$ = "mm-dd-yyyy"
Date$ = "mm/dd/yyyy"
```

where *mm* are numerals between 01 and 12, *dd* are days between 01 and 31, and *yyyy* are years between 1980 and 2099.

If you try to reset the date to an illegal date like 31 February, you get an "Illegal Function call" message box when you run the program. You can also use a two-digit year, but this is not practical for forward-looking programs; Visual Basic assumes you mean 20th-century and not 21st-century dates when there is ambiguity.

One point to remember: if your computer has a built-in clock calendar, to permanently reset the clock you may have to use the setup program that came with the computer. The changes made by Date$ may remain only until you reboot your computer.

You can also read the time in the system clock or temporarily (see the preceding paragraph) reset it with the Time$ function. The Time$ function returns an eight–character string of the form *hh:mm:ss* using a 24–hour clock. To reset it, assign a string of the correct form to Time$:

| Example of Time Command | Effect |
| --- | --- |
| Time$ ="hh" | Sets the hour; minutes, seconds are set to 0 |
| Time$ ="hh:mm" | Sets the hour, minutes; seconds are set to 0 |
| Time$ ="hh:mm:ss" | Sets the hour, minutes, seconds |

The hours range between 00 for midnight and 23 for 11:00 P.M.

## The Numeric Calendar Functions

To do financial calculations accurately, your programs have to be able to calculate the number of days that have passed between two dates—taking leap years into account, if possible! Visual Basic usually stores this information in the form of a variant that looks like a double-precision number where the digits to the left of the decimal point represent the date and the digits to the right of the decimal point represent the time. It turns out that midnight on December 30, 1899, would be 0.000000. Midnight on December 31, 1899, would be 1.000000, and midnight on January 1, 1900, would be 2.000000. Midnight on January 1, 2000, would be 36526.000000 because 36,526 days have passed since December 30, 1899. In the Visual Basic documentation, numbers of this form are called *serial numbers*. Visual Basic makes the adjustment necessary for leap years when it does this calculation.

The most important function for applications that use this information is DateValue(*String*). This function yields a variant representing the date defined by the string expression inside the parentheses. Besides accepting strings in the expected form of *mm-dd-yyyy*, this function can also accept the name of the month or any unambiguous abbreviation for the month. For example, all of the following return the value zero:

```
DateValue("12-30-1899")
DateValue("December 30, 1899")
DateValue("Dec 30, 1899")
DateValue("30 December 1899")
DateValue("30-Dec-1899")
```

You cannot use this function if the date doesn't make sense. For example,

```
DateValue("2-30-1992")
```

gives an "Illegal function call" message at run time.

Of course, you will usually need to know what serial number represents the current day and time. For this, Visual Basic has the built-in Now function, as shown here:

```
Print "The serial number for today is ";Now
```

This returns the information about the date and time in the system clock.

You will occasionally need the DateSerial function. Its syntax is

DateSerial(*Year%,Month%,Day%*)

Year% is an integer between 1753 and 2078 inclusive (or an integral expression that Visual Basic can reduce to this form). *Month%* is an integer (or integral expression) with a value between 1 and 12, and *Day%* must be between 1 and 31. You also can use this function only if the date makes sense. For example,

```
DateSerial(1992,2,30)
```

will also give an "Illegal function call" message at run time.

You can apply the Format$ function to any serial number to display the information contained in the number. For example, if it is now 10:01 P.M. on January 1, 1992, the results are as follows:

| Form | Display |
| --- | --- |
| Format$(Now,"m/d-yy") | 1/1/92 |
| Format$(Now,"hh:mm") | 22:01 |
| Format$(Now,"hh:mm AM/PM") | 10:01 PM |
| Format$(Now,"hh:mm AM/PM mm/dd/yy") | 10:01 PM 01/01/92 |

There are many other possibilities for format strings attached to serial numbers. The online documentation is very useful if you need some special form.

**Figure 5-4**

**Form for days alive demo**

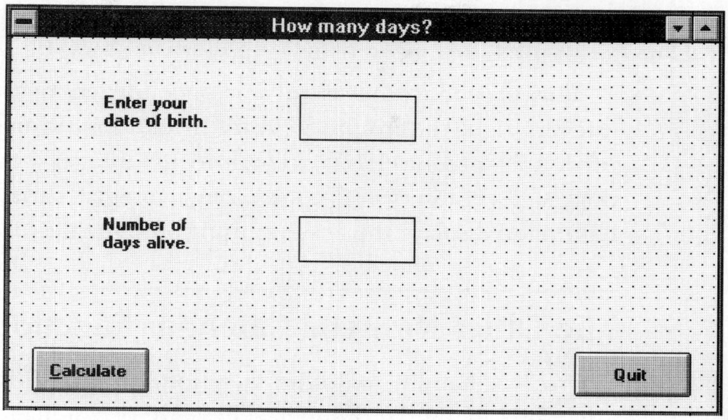

## An Example of the Date Functions

Suppose you want to write an application that will tell the user how many days he or she has been alive. The screen for that application might look like the one shown in Figure 5-4, which, as you can see, has two labels, two text boxes, and two command buttons. The following table describes the properties of these controls:

| Control | Control Name | Caption (Text) |
| --- | --- | --- |
| Top text box | Birthdate | — |
| Bottom text box | Answer | — |
| Left button | Calculate | &Calculate |
| Right button | Quit | Quit |

Notice that because of the ampersand in front of the "C" on the caption for the command button, a user can use the ALT+C combination as an access key to do the calculation. On the other hand, the Quit button must be clicked.

Besides the simple End statement for the Quit button event procedure that ends the application, all the code for this application is in the Calculate_Click event procedure:

```
Sub Calculate_Click ()
  Dim NumberOfDays As Long
  NumberOfDays = Now - DateValue(BirthDate.Text)
```

```
Answer.Text = Format$(NumberOfDays,"###,###")
End Sub
```

This procedure needs to use long integers because the limit on ordinary integers would be around 89 years. In addition, Visual Basic does the subtraction in double precision but rounds to an integer because you are assigning a double-precision value to a (long) integer variable. Finally, the Format$ command displays the answer, using a comma.

## The Other Numeric Calendar Functions

There is a handful of other functions that let you analyze the information contained in a serial number. These are occasionally useful when you need to write applications that work on a day-to-day or even a minute-to-minute basis.

▬

***Day(SerialNumber)*** The Day(*SerialNumber*) function returns an integer between 1 and 31 that is the day of the month represented by the serial number inside the parentheses.

▬

***Hour(SerialNumber)*** The Hour(*SerialNumber*) function gives an integer between 0 and 23 for the hour of the day (military time).

▬

***Minute(SerialNumber)*** The Minute(*SerialNumber*) function gives an integer between zero and 59 for the number of minutes represented in the serial number.

▬

***Month(SerialNumber)*** The Month(*SerialNumber*) function gives an integer between 1 and 12 for the month.

▬

***Second(SerialNumber)*** The Second(*Serial Number*) function gives you the number of seconds between zero and 59.

▬

***Weekday(SerialNumber)*** The Weekday(*SerialNumber*) function gives you an integer between 1 (Sunday) and 7 (Saturday) for the day.

*Year(SerialNumber)*  The Year(*SerialNumber*) function gives an integer between 1753 and 2078 for the year determined by the serial number.

*TimeValue(string expression)*  The TimeValue(*string expression*) function returns the time represented by the string expression.

*TimeSerial(hour,minute,second)*  The TimeSerial(*hour,minute,second*) function returns a serial number corresponding to the time.

# Chapter 6

# Controlling Program Flow

HIS chapter shows you how to make a program repeat operations (loops) or check if a condition is True or False (conditionals). The parts of a programming language that let you do this are called *control structures*. (This term has nothing to do with the controls you place on forms in Visual Basic.) The control structures in Visual Basic are essentially the same ones that are in QuickBASIC; users familiar with QuickBASIC may need only to skim this chapter. If you are familiar only with GW-BASIC, you're in for a pleasant surprise. The control structures in Visual Basic are far richer and allow you far more flexibility than the ones in older, interpreted BASICs.

## Repeating Operations

Suppose you need to repeat an operation. In programming (as in real life), you may want to repeat the operation a fixed number of times, continue until you reach a predetermined specific goal, or continue until certain initial conditions have finally changed. In programming, the first situation is called a *determinate loop* and the latter two are called *indeterminate loops*. Visual Basic allows all three kinds of loops, so there are three different control structures in Visual Basic for repeating operations.

### Determinate Loops

Suppose you want to print the numbers 1 to 10 on the current form inside an event procedure. The simplest way to do this is to place the following lines of code inside the procedure:

```
For I% = 1 To 10
  Print I%
Next I%
```

In the preceding example, the line with the For and To keywords is shorthand for "for every value of I% from 1 to 10." You can think of a For-Next loop as winding up a wheel inside the computer so the wheel will spin a fixed number of times. You can tell the computer what you want it to do during each spin of the wheel.

For and Next are keywords that must be used together. The statements between the For and the Next are usually called the *body* of the loop, and the whole control structure is called, naturally enough, a *For-Next loop*.

The keyword For sets up a counter variable. In the preceding example, the counter is an integer variable: I%. In this example, the starting value for the counter is set to 1. The ending value is set to 10. Visual Basic first sets the counter variable to the starting value. Then it checks whether the value for the counter is less than the ending value. If the value is greater than the ending value, nothing is done. If the starting value is less than the ending value, Visual Basic processes subsequent statements until it comes to the keyword Next. At that point it adds 1 to the counter variable and starts the process again. This process continues until the counter variable is larger than the ending value. At that point, the loop is finished, and Visual Basic moves past it. Figure 6-1 shows a flow diagram for the For-Next loop.

**tip:** *Whenever possible, choose integer variables for the counter in a For-Next loop. This allows Visual Basic to spend as little time as possible on the arithmetic needed to change the counter and so speeds up the loop.*

Finally, you may have noticed that the body of the For-Next loop is indented. As always, the purpose of the spacing in a program is to make the program more readable and therefore easier to debug. The designers of Visual Basic made it easy to consistently indent code. The Visual Basic editor remembers the indentation of the previous line, and every time you press ENTER, the cursor returns to the spot directly below where the previous line started. To move the cursor back, you can use the LEFT ARROW key. Or if you get into the habit of using the TAB key to start each level of indentation, you can use the SHIFT+TAB combination to move backward one tab stop. (If you've used the TAB key, you can undo the indentation pattern for a block that you've used by selecting the block of text and then pressing SHIFT+TAB.) Each tab stop is set four spaces in from the previous one, although as you saw in Chapter 2, you can change this setting from the Options menu.

**Figure 6-1**

Flow diagram
for For-Next
loop

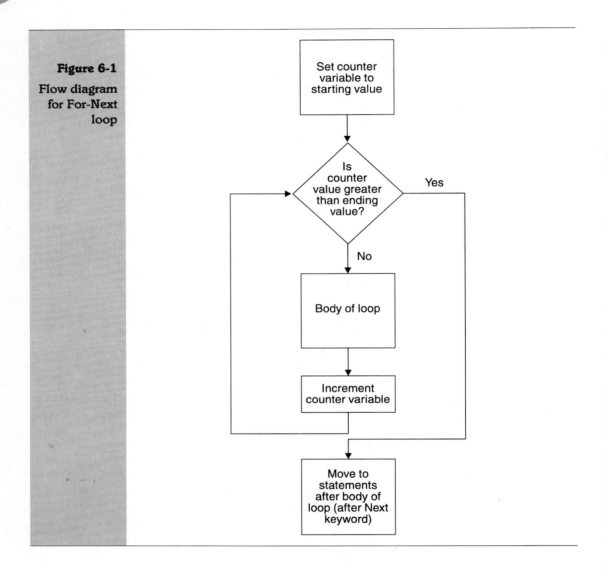

The most common type of error in using loops is the *off-by-one error.* When this error occurs, instead of performing an operation, say, 500 times as you had planned, the program seems to perform it 499 or 501 times. If your program suffers from this problem, the debugging techniques in Chapter 11 can help you pinpoint the fault in the loop that is causing the off-by-one error. Obviously, it's best to avoid off-by-one errors in the first place. One way to do this is to keep in mind that the loop terminates only when the counter exceeds (not equals) the test value.

## AN EXAMPLE: A RETIREMENT CALCULATOR

With a For–Next loop, you can compute many financial quantities without knowing a formula. For example, suppose you wanted to write a program that would allow users to enter the following:

◆ The fixed amount of money they think they can put away for retirement each year

◆ The interest rate they expect to get each year

◆ The number of years until retirement

The program would then tell them how much money they will have when they retire. There are sophisticated formulas involving geometric progressions for this sort of calculation, but common sense (and a very simple For–Next loop) suffices. What happens is that each year you get interest on the previous amount, and you add the new amount to it.

Assume that the interest is compounded annually. Then this program will need four text boxes, four labels, and two command buttons. The screen in Figure 6-2 shows the form.

The control names for the text controls in the program should be self-documenting: AmountPerYear, InterestRate, NumberOfYears, and NestEgg. The command buttons should be named Calculate and Quit.

**Figure 6-2**

Form for retirement calculator

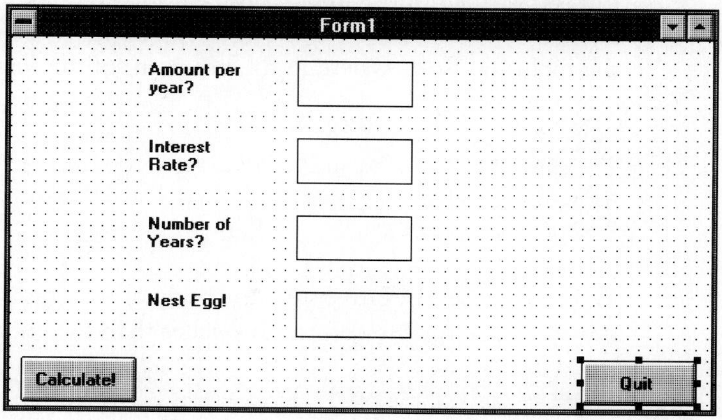

Here is the Calculate_Click procedure that does everything:

```
Sub Calculate_Click()
  'Calculate retirement value assuming fixed
  'deposit and fixed interest rate

  Dim Amount As Currency, Total As Currency
  Dim Interest As Single
  Dim Years As Integer, I As Integer

  Total = 0
  Amount = Val(AmountPerYear.Text)
  Interest = Val(InterestRate.Text)/100
  Years = Val(NumberOfYears.Text)
  For I = 1 To Years
    Total = Amount + Total + (Total*Interest)
  Next I
  NestEgg.Text = Format$(Total,"###,###.##")
End Sub
```

The new total is gotten from the previous year by adding the interest earned to the previous total amount.

## MORE ON FOR-NEXT LOOPS

You don't always count by ones. Sometimes it's necessary to count by twos, by fractions, or backward. You do this by adding the Step keyword to a For-Next loop. The Step keyword tells Visual Basic to change the counter by the specified amount rather than by 1, as was done previously.

For example, a space simulation program would not be complete without the inclusion, somewhere in the program, of the fragment

```
For I% = 10 To 1 Step -1
  Print "It's t minus"; I%; "and counting."
Next I%
Print "Blastoff!"
```

When you use a negative step, the body of the For-Next loop is bypassed if the starting value for the counter is smaller than the ending value.

**caution:** *Loops with fractional Step values will run more slowly than loops with integer Step values.*

**Figure 6-3**

**Form for mortgage table**

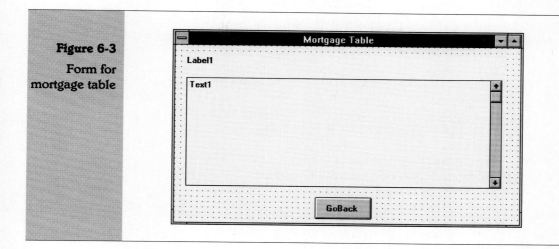

## AN EXAMPLE: IMPROVING THE MORTGAGE CALCULATOR

Here's a more serious example. Let's modify the mortgage program to add another form showing a table with various interest rates. You can add another button to the original form to bring up a form with a multiline text box showing the mortgage payments for a rate 1 percent above and below the rate initially selected.

This new form (see Figure 6–3) will contain a labeled, multiline text box with vertical scroll bars added at design time. Let's call the new form FormTabel and the text box on it MortgageTabel. We'll call the label TableLabel and place it right above the multiline text box. We will use this label to describe what the user will see. We will also add a command button for returning to the original form.

All the work is done in the ShowTabel_Click procedure attached to the added command button on the original form. The code for this example may seem long, but most of the complications relate to formatting the display nicely. Essentially, what we need to do is enclose the original formula in a For–Next loop with a step of 1/8% = 1/800 = .00125. Here's the code:

```
Sub ShowTabel_Click ()
   'Calculates a mortgage table using original amounts
   'but having the interest rate move up by 1/8%
   'local variables and constants
   Dim NewLine As String, SpaceChar As String, T$
   Dim Years As Integer, Payment As Currency
   Dim MonthInt As Single, Principal As Currency
```

```
Dim Percent As Single, Interest  As Single
Dim StartInterest As Single, EndInterest As Single
Const DAMOUNT = "###.00"
Const IRATE = "00.00%"
NewLine = Chr$(13) + Chr$(10)   'for multiline text box
                                'above could be form level
                                'constants

'Get info
 Years = Val(MortgageTerm.Text)
 Principal = Val(MortgageAmount.Text)
 Percent = Val(InterestRate.Text) / 100
 StartInterest = Percent - .01              '1% change
 EndInterest = Percent + .01

 'Make new form visible
 Hide
 FormTabel.Show

 FormTabel!TabelLabel.Caption = "Interest Rate" + Space$(18) +_
"Payment"
 For Interest = StartInterest To EndInterest Step .00125
   MonthInt = Interest / 12
   Payment = Principal * MonthInt / (1 - (1 / (1 + MonthInt))_
^ (Years * 12))
   T$ = T$ + Format$(Interest, IRate) + Space$(25) +_
Format$(Payment, DAmount) + NewLine
 Next Interest
 FormTabel!MortgageTable.Text = T$
End Sub
```

The program starts with the Dim statements that define the variables. Next come the string constants for the Format$ command; for example, the IRATE constant displays the interest rate as a two-place decimal percent. The NewLine character is needed for the multiline text box. Next comes the code for extracting the information from the text boxes on the original form and for hiding the original form and showing the form named FormTabel used for displaying the table. Next comes the ! character, which refers to a control on the FormTabel form within code attached to the original form.

Finally comes the For-Next loop that does all the work. Because it is much faster to build a string up rather than to repeatedly change the text property of a text box, the code inside the For-Next loop adds to the string T$. After the

For-Next loop finishes, the text property of the multiline text box is changed to T$.

## NESTED FOR-NEXT LOOPS

Suppose you want to allow not only a range of interest rates in the mortgage table but also a range of dollar amounts—say with horizontal scroll bars to move through the information. For each dollar amount, you want to run through an entire range of interest rates. This is a typical situation: You have an inner loop that does something interesting in a particular case, and you want to alter the situation to address a slightly different case. Placing one loop inside another is called *nesting* loops.

You'll see how to solve the mortgage problem a little later in this section. For now though, let's look at a simpler example of a multiplication table. A fragment such as

```
For I% = 2 To 12
  Print 2*I%
Next I%
```

gives you the "twos table." To get an entire multiplication table, you need to enclose this loop with another one that changes the 2 to a 3, the 3 to a 4, and so on. The loop looks like this:

```
For J% = 2 To 12
  For I% = 2 To 12
    Print I%*J%,
  Next I%
  Print
Next J%
```

Here's what is happening: The value of J% starts out at 2, and then Visual Basic enters the inner loop. The value of I% starts out at 2 as well. Now Visual Basic makes 11 passes through the loop before it finishes. Once it does this, it processes the extra Print statement before it processes the Next J% statement. At this point Visual Basic changes the value of J% to 3 and starts the process all over again.

Sometimes it's helpful to think of the inner loop in a nested For-Next loop as really doing one thing—that is, as a statement in Visual Basic a bit more complicated than the usual ones. If you keep in mind the idea of the inner loop of a nested For-Next loop as accomplishing one task, then an outline for the nested loops to modify the mortgage program given in the previous section is easy. Here it is:

For *Principal* = *StartingAmount* To *EndingAmount* Step 1000
    The original loop with new display statements & principal modified
Next *Principal*

Nested loops have a reputation for being hard to program, hard to understand, and a breeding ground for bugs. This need not be true. If you are careful about outlining the loops, they won't be hard to program. If you are careful about your indentation pattern, they won't be hard to understand (or, therefore, to debug).

The rule for nesting For–Next loops is simple: the inner loop must be completed before the Next statement for the outer loop is encountered. You can have triply nested loops, quadruply nested loops, or even more. You are limited only by how well you understand the logic of the program, not by Visual Basic.

### AN EXAMPLE: THE SCREEN OBJECT AND AVAILABLE FONTS

Another good example of a For–Next loop gives you a list of the fonts available to Windows. You can do this by using a simple For–Next loop to analyze a property of the *Screen object*. The Screen object is one that you will use frequently within Visual Basic. For example it will let you manipulate forms by their placement on the screen. For our example you need two properties of the Screen object. The first is the FontCount property, which gives you the number of available fonts that the printer or screen has available:

```
NumberOfScreenFonts = Screen.FontCount
NumberOfPrinterFonts = Printer.FontCount
```

The second is the Fonts property. Screen.Fonts(0) is the first font for your display, Screen.Fonts(1) is the second, and so on, up to Screen .Fonts(FontCount−1), which is the last. All this information is determined by how Microsoft Windows was set up and by the hardware and software you have.

To run this program, create a new project with a blank form. Add the Click procedure given here, press F5, and then click anywhere in the form.

```
Sub Form_Click()
  Dim I As Integer
```

```
  Print "Here is a list of the fonts for your display."
  For I = 1 To Screen.FontCount - 1
    FontName = Screen.Fonts(I)
    Print "This is displayed in ";Screen.Fonts(I)
  Next I
End Sub
```

To report on the fonts that Windows can pull out of your printer, change the keyword Screen to the keyword Printer.

The screen object also supports the Height and Width properties. These give you the height and width of the physical screen, in twips, as reported by Windows. You can use these properties to adjust the size of a window to fit the screen on which it is running. For example, use the following code if you want to have the Form_Load( ) procedure initialize the size of the form that Visual Basic is loading to be 50 percent of the full screen:

```
Sub Form_Load()
  Width = Screen.Width/2
  Height = Screen.Height/2
End Sub
```

## Indeterminate Loops

Let's go back to the retirement problem we discussed earlier. Instead of asking how much money a person will have at the end of a specified number of years, let's ask how long until the person has $1,000,000—again assuming that the same amount of money is put in each year and that the interest rate doesn't change. You could use the previous program and try trial and error, but you can use a more direct approach. You'll soon see how to resolve this and many similar problems.

The modified retirement program offers a good example of a task that comes up repeatedly in programming. Loops need to either keep on repeating an operation or not, depending on the results obtained within the loop. Such loops are indeterminate—that is, not executed a fixed number of times—by their very nature. You use the following pattern when you write this type of loop in Visual Basic:

Do
   *Visual Basic statements*
Until *condition is met*

Figure 6-4 shows what Visual Basic does in a Do loop.

A simple example of this is a password fragment in a Form_Load procedure that starts an application. If you compiled a project to a stand-alone program with a Form_Load procedure that looks like this:

```
Sub Form_Load()
'Password protection

  Do
    X$ = InputBox$("Password please?")
  Loop Until X$ = "Vanilla Orange"
End Sub
```

it would be more difficult for anyone who didn't know the password to use this program. (It would not be impossible, however; a very experienced programmer could find the password by carefully examining the .EXE file, but it wouldn't be easy.)

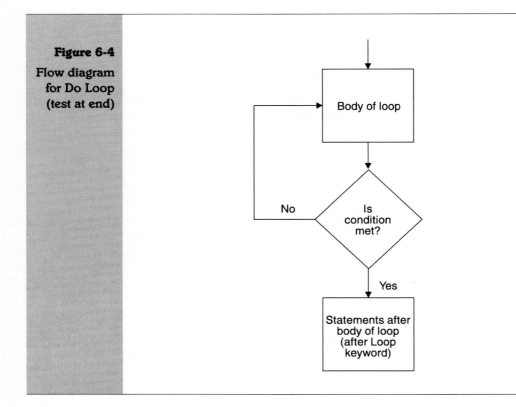

**Figure 6-4**

Flow diagram
for Do Loop
(test at end)

It's important to remember that the test for equality is strict: typing **VA-NILLA ORANGE** would not work, nor would **Vanilla orange**. Another point worth keeping in mind is that the test is done only at the end of the loop, when Visual Basic processes the Until statement. If you change the fragment to

```
Sub Form_Load()
 Do
   X$ = "Vanilla Orange"
   X$ = InputBox$("Password please?")
 Loop Until X$ = "Vanilla Orange"
End Sub
```

then whether you break out of the loop still depends on what the user types in the input box. Initializing the variable to the correct value is irrelevant.

When you write an indeterminate loop, something must change; otherwise the test will always fail and you'll be stuck in an infinite loop. To stop an infinite loop, you can use the CTRL+BREAK combination or choose End from the Run menu or use the toolbar. The CTRL+BREAK combination also works when the program is run away from the Visual Basic development environment, provided you have BREAK = ON in your CONFIG.SYS file. You can also close the application, of course.

## THE RELATIONAL OPERATORS

In more sophisticated programs, you need ways to check for something besides equality. You do this by means of the *relational operators*. The relational operators are listed here.

| Symbol | Checks (Tests For) |
| --- | --- |
| < > | Not equal to |
| < | Less than |
| <= | Less than or equal to |
| > | Greater than |
| >= | Greater than or equal to |

For strings, these operators test for ANSI order. This means that "A" comes before "B," but "B" comes before "a" (and a space comes before any typewriter character). The string "aBCD" comes after the string "CDE" because uppercase letters come before lowercase letters. (The online help contains a complete ANSI table that you can find by using the Search button and looking for the

ANSI character set.) The ANSI codes from 0 to 31 are for control combinations and include the BACKSPACE and ENTER keys.

**note:** *You can make all comparisons in the code attached to a form insensitive to case by putting the statement*

```
Option Compare Text
```

*in the Declarations section of the form. Use Option Compare Binary to return to the default method of comparing strings by ANSI order.*

The Option Compare Text uses an order determined by the country set when you install Windows.

As another example, suppose you wanted to prevent a "Divide by zero" error when a user enters data in a text box. Use a fragment like this:

```
Do
   N$ = InputBox$("Non-zero number? Please!")
   Number = Val(N$)
Loop Until Number <> 0
```

Or, to test that the first character of a string in a text box was not a space or a control code, use this:

```
Do
   Text$ = Text1.Text
Loop Until Text$ > Chr$(32)
```

These kinds of loops are the first steps for stopping a user from entering the wrong kind of data. Testing input data is one way to begin to bulletproof a program. In fact, a large part of bulletproofing programs (the jargon is "making them robust") requires making them tolerant of input errors. Instead of blowing up because of a typo, they check that the data entered is usable. If not, they warn the user. The more robust a program is, the less likely it is to behave strangely for an inexperienced user. (The section on "What Is It?" in this chapter has more on checking input.)

You can even monitor keystrokes as they are made inside any control that accepts input. For this, see the section "An Example: The KeyPress Procedure" later in this chapter.

You now can write the program mentioned in the beginning of this chapter. Here is the Calculate_Click procedure that will determine how long it takes to accumulate $1,000,000:

```
Sub Calculate_Click()
   '  Calculate retirement value assuming fixed
   ' deposit and fixed interest rate

   Dim Amount As Currency, Total As Currency
   Dim Interest as Single
   Dim Years As Integer, I as Integer

   Amount = Val(AmountPerYear.Text)
   Interest = Val(InterestRate.Text)/100
   Do
      Total = Amount + Total + (Total*Interest)
      Years = Years + 1
   Loop Until Total >= 1000000
   NumberOfYears.Text = Str$(Years)
End Sub
```

The body of the loop is much like the one in the retirement program from the first section—figure the yearly change and add it to the previous total to get a new total. This time, however, another counter (Years) keeps track of the number of years. Finally, the loop continues as long as the value of the variable Total is less than 1,000,000. The moment the total equals or exceeds this target, the loop ends and Visual Basic reports the results.

You should be aware of a problem that frequently occurs with these new kinds of loops. Consider this fragment:

```
Total = 0
PassNumber = 0
Do
  Total = Total + .1
  PassNumber = PassNumber + 1
  Print PassNumber, Total
Loop Until Total = 1
```

You might think this program would end after 10 passes through the loop, but it doesn't. In fact, this fragment results in an infinite loop, and you need to press the CTRL+BREAK combination or use the toolbar to stop it. This infinite loop occurred for a subtle but important reason. In this fragment, by default, all the numbers are converted from variants to single-precision variables, and as discussed in Chapter 5, these numbers are only approximations. Visual Basic's internal characterization of .1 is off by a little in, say, the seventh place. As Visual Basic adds .1 to the total, tiny errors accumulate, and the resulting total, although it comes very close to 1, never exactly equals 1. Thus, in loops, check only integer and long integer variables for equality.

This program should be rewritten to allow for a tiny error by changing the test to read

```
Loop Until Total > .99999999
```

or, to be sure that the number is at least 1,

```
Loop Until Total >= 1
```

Changing the test to either case ensures that the program really will stop after ten passes through the loop. Single, double, and currency variables can be checked only to see if they are close (within a certain tolerance).

## SOPHISTICATED INDETERMINATE LOOPS

A common task is reading in a list of names until the last one is encountered, keeping count all the while. Suppose you are looking through the dictionary and happen to notice that the last entry is the name of an insect: the zyzzyva. You decide you want to add up the number of different types of insects that occur in North America. You take out your entomology book and start running the following code:

```
InsectCount = 0
  Do
    InsectName$ = InputBox("The next insect name")
    InsectCount = InsectCount + 1
  Loop Until InsectName$ = "zyzzyva"
Print "The number of different types of insects is_
 ";InsectCount
```

Although this fragment may seem like a prototype for code that reads in a list of items until the last one is encountered, you won't always know what the last entry of the list is. It's only a coincidence that the last word in most dictionaries is the name of an American insect. In general, you won't know the last entry, so you're likely to use a group of strange characters (like **"ZZZ"**) to act as a flag. Instead of testing for a zyzzyva, you test for a flag. (Another possibility is using a command button to stop the count.)

It's easy to modify the "InsectCount" fragment to test for a flag. Here is a program that does this (but beware that it has a subtle bug):

```
NameCount = 0
Do
   Entry$ = InputBox$("Name - type ZZZ when done")
   NameCount = NameCount + 1
Loop Until Entry$ = "ZZZ"
Print "The total number of names is ";NameCount
```

The problem with this fragment is that it suffers from an off-by-one error. Imagine that the list consists of only one name besides the flag. What happens? Let's work through this program by hand. The user types the first name and the count increases to 1. Next the user types **ZZZ**. However, because the test is only done at the end of the loop, the count increases to 2 before the test is done. Therefore, when the loop ends, the count is 2 when it ought to be 1. One possible cure is to subtract 1 from the count once the loop ends. The trouble with this type of ad hoc solution (in the jargon, a "kludge"—pronounced "klooge") is that the programmer ends up having to constantly figure out how far off the results of the loops are when they finish in order to move backward.

Moving backward is a bit silly when Visual Basic makes the cure for this so easy: move the test to the top. Consider this:

```
NameCount = 0
Entry$ = InputBox$("Name - ZZZ to end")
Do Until Entry$ = "ZZZ"
   NameCount = NameCount + 1
   Entry$ = InputBox$("Name - ZZZ to end")
Loop
```

Now the user types the first name before the loop starts. Once this is done, the program does an initial test. The loop is entered and 1 starts being added to the counter only if this test fails. (Notice that this kind of loop also works if there is nothing in the list except the flag.) Figure 6-5 shows a picture of what Visual Basic does for this type of loop.

**Figure 6-5**

Flow diagram
for Do loop
(test at
beginning)

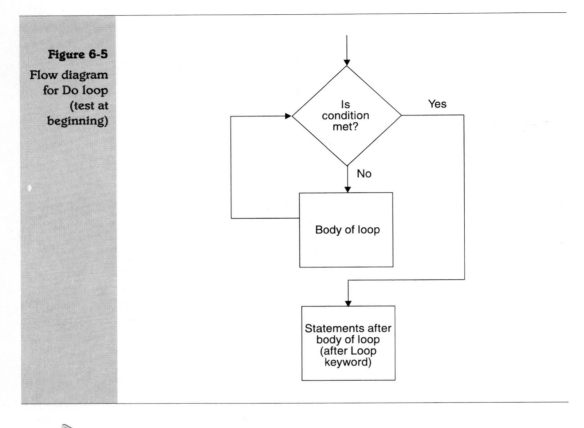

**tip:**

*A good rule of thumb is that if you are going to use the flag, put the test at the end; if not, put it at the beginning.*

With the test at the end, the loop is always executed at least once; with the test at the beginning, the loop may not be executed at all. Also remember that when the test is at the top, you obviously have to have something to test. Therefore, when the test is done at the beginning, initialize all variables to be tested before the loop starts. Finally, don't forget that you usually have to have two assignment statements when the test is at the top—the first before the test and the second (to keep the process going) inside the loop.

You must follow a similar rule, when nesting Do loops together or when nesting them with For-Next loops, to those you follow for nesting For-Next loops alone: inner loops must be finished before the outer loops are tested. Choose a reasonable indenting pattern and you will not have any problems.

Keep in mind that Visual Basic is always asking a True–False question in a Do loop; it's just hidden sometimes. Luckily, all arithmetic operators are done first (they have higher precedence than the relational operators). Visual Basic has no trouble interpreting

```
Loop Until Number*5 > 10
```

as meaning first do the calculation and then do the test (but as always, parentheses make things clearer).

## THE DO WHILE LOOP

Visual Basic has other kinds of loops. These loops consist of replacing the keyword Until with the keyword While. This new loop may seem superfluous since you can always change a Do Until into a Do While by reversing the relational operator. For example,

```
Do
Loop Until X$ <>""
```

is the same as

```
Do
Loop While X$ = ""
```

and

```
Do
Loop Until Number > 5
```

is the same as

```
Do
Loop While Number <= 5
```

Given this, why bother learning this new type of loop? There are two reasons why the While loop isn't superfluous. The first is that, as much as possible, you want to write a program conforming to the way your mind works. Sometimes you will think of an operation as going on *until* something happens, while other times you think of it as continuing *while,* as the saying goes, "the status is quo." The richness of Visual Basic's programming language makes the fit better between your thought patterns and the computer program you're trying to write. In fact, psychologists have found that tests with positive conditions are easier to understand. Do While Number = 0 is easier to process for most people than its counterpart, Do Until Number <> 0.

## DO LOOPS WITH AND, OR, NOT

The previous section gave you one reason to use both Do Until and Do While loops but this is not the only reason. Probably the best reason to use both kinds of loops comes when you have to combine conditions. This is most commonly done with the Or, Not, and And keywords. These three keywords work just like they do in English. You can continue a process as long as both conditions are True or stop it when one turns False. However, it becomes increasingly confusing to try to force combination of the And, Or, and Not operators into loops that they don't seem to fit. For example, suppose you want to continue a process while a number is greater than zero and a text box is empty. It is much easier to say

```
Do While Number > 0 And Text1.Text = ""
```

than to say

```
Do Until Number <=0 Or Text1.Text <> ""
```

although they both mean the same thing.

## THE WHILE/WEND LOOP

There is one other loop possible in Visual Basic. To preserve compatibility with interpreted BASIC, Visual Basic allows a variant on the Do While loop (that is, the test at the top). Instead of saying

```
Do While X = 0

Loop
```

you can say

```
While X = 0

Wend
```

# Making Decisions

At this point, all your programs can do is to decide whether to repeat a group of statements or not. They can't, as yet, change which statements are processed depending on what the program has already done or what it has just encountered. The next few sections take care of this. All the commands in these sections deal with turning an outline containing a phrase like

If *condition* Then *Do something else...*

into Visual Basic code. Visual Basic uses the If–Then in much the same way that you do in normal English. For example, to warn a user that a number must be positive, use a line like this:

```
If X < 0 Then MsgBox "Number must be positive!"
```

More generally, when Visual Basic encounters an If–Then statement, it checks the first clause (called, naturally enough, the If clause) and checks whether it's True. If that clause is True, the computer does whatever follows (called the Then clause). If the test fails, processing skips to the next statement.

The If–Then is also used to determine which button was pressed in a message box. To do this, assign the value of the MsgBox function to a variable and then use an If–Then to check the value. For example,

```
X% = MsgBox ("Yes/No?",4)
If X% = 6 Then Print "Yes button clicked."
```

Notice that you need to use parentheses when using MsgBox in this way. The online help gives the values needed to check for the other kinds of buttons.

Just as in the loops from the previous sections, you can use the If–Then to compare numbers or strings. For example, a statement like

```
If A$ < B$  Then Print A$;" comes before ";B$;"
```

tests for ANSI order (unless an Option Compare Text statement has been processed) and

```
If A <= B  Then Print A; " is no more than "; B
```

tests for numerical order.

Suppose you need to write a Social Security calculator. The way this tax works is that you pay (in 1992) 6.20 percent of the amount you make up to $53,400. After that, whether you make $55,000 or $5,550,000 per year, you pay no more social security tax. To write code that would activate this type of calculator, you need to write

```
If Wages < 53400 Then STax=.062*Wages Else STax=53400*.062
```

When Visual Basic processes an If-Then-Else, if the test succeeds, Visual Basic processes the statement that follows the keyword Then (the Then clause). If the test fails, Visual Basic processes the statement that follows the keyword Else (called the Else clause). Figure 6-6 shows you what Visual Basic does with an If-Then-Else in flow-diagram style.

You can also use the keywords And, Or, and Not in an If-Then. These let you check two conditions at once. For example, suppose you have to check if a number is between zero and 9:

```
If Digit >=0 And Digit <= 9 Then Print "Ok"
```

The ways of using the And operator should be pretty clear by now, but one word of caution. In both speaking and writing, we sometimes say, "If my average is greater than 80 and less than 90, then ...." Translating this sentence construction directly into code won't work. You must repeat the variable each time you want to test something. To do the translation from English to Visual Basic, say, "If my average is greater than 80 and my average is less than 90, then ...."

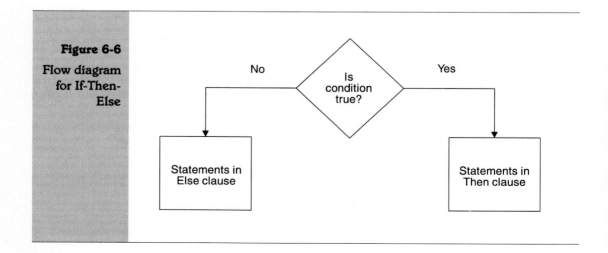

**Figure 6-6**

Flow diagram for If-Then-Else

A final note on And: you do not have to use the same variable. A statement like

```
If (Grade4>Grade3) And Average >60 Then Print "Improving!"
```

is a perfectly good Visual Basic statement. (The parentheses are there only to improve readability; they are not needed. As you saw earlier, Visual Basic calculates relational operators before worrying about the logical connectors like And.)

Using the keyword Or in an If-Then is similar. The test is successful if either one of the conditions is True. Suppose you had to test if at least one of two numbers was nonzero:

```
If A <> 0 Or B <> 0 Then ...
```

There are other, somewhat less common ways of combining tests. For example, you can use the Eqv (equivalence) operator. This test asks whether two conditions are both true or both false. For example,

If (X = True And Y = True) or (X = False And Y = False) ...

is the same as

If X Eqv Y ...

Another useful operator (especially for graphics programs and file security programs) is the Xor (exclusive Or). This corresponds to the English "If A or B but not both." (See Chapters 12 and 14 for more on this operator.)

Similarly, there's the Not that you've already seen. Choosing to use this depends a lot on personal taste (a lot like deciding between Do While and Do Until). Most people find it easier just to change the relational operators. For example,

```
If Not (A$ = "Big Blue")
```

is harder to write than

```
If A$ <> "Big Blue"
```

Similarly,

```
If Not (A > 50)
```

is exactly the same as

```
If A <= 50
```

If you prefer to use the Not, you'll need parentheses; without them your program is apt to be unreadable.

Since Visual Basic is really testing for a Boolean (True-False) relation in the If clause, you can actually have any Boolean property. For example, in the statement

```
If Text1.Enabled Then ...
```

Visual Basic processes the Then clause only when the Text1 box is enabled.

## The Block If-Then

More often than not, you will want to process multiple statements if a condition is True or False. For this you need the most powerful form of the If-Then-Else, called the block If-Then. This lets you process as many statements as you like in response to a True condition, as in this example:

> If I win the lottery Then
>   I'm happy
>   My family is happy
>   And, the tax man is happy.

Here, there are three statements in response to something being True. To write this statement in Visual Basic, you use a slightly different format from the usual If-Then. The block If-Then looks like this:

> If *thing to test* Then
>   *lots of statements*
> Else
>   *more statements*
> End If

Now, you do not put anything on the line following the keyword Then; press ENTER immediately after typing it. This bare "Then" is how Visual Basic knows it's beginning a block. The Else is optional; putting it there (again alone on a line) means that another block will follow, to be processed only if the If clause is False. However, whether the Else is there or not, the block If must end with the keywords End If.

For an example of this, let's modify the original mortgage program in Chapter 5 so the program checks whether the user wants to calculate the payment or the maximum he or she can borrow *depending on which text box is empty*. The comments in the following program give the formula you need for this. (You have to do a little algebra on the original formula.)

```
Sub Calculate_Click ()
  ' This calculates the mortgage
  ' Using the formula, Payment =
  ' Principal*MonthInt/(1-(1/(1+MonthInt))^(Years*12))
  ' Principal =
  ' Payment * (MonthInt / (1 - (1 / (1 + MonthInt))^
  ' (Years * 12)))-1

  Dim Years As Integer, Payment As Currency
  Dim MonthInt As Single, Amount As Currency
  Dim Percent as Single

  ' Get info
  Years = Val(MortgageTerm.Text)
  Principal = Val(MortgageAmount.Text)
  Payment = Val(MortgagePayment.Text)
  Percent = Val(InterestRate.Text) / 100
  MonthInt = Percent/12
  If Payment = 0 Then
    Payment = Principal * MonthInt / (1 - (1 / (1 + _
MonthInt))^ (Years * 12))
    MortgagePayment.Text = Format$(Payment,"###,###.##")
  Else
    Principal = Payment * (MonthInt / (1 - (1 / (1 + _
MonthInt))^ (Years * 12)))^-1
    MortgageAmount.Text = Format$(Principal,"###,###.##")
  End If
End Sub
```

Again, as usual, the indentation is there to make the program more readable; Visual Basic doesn't care.

## What Is It?

You can easily use If-Then to determine whether the user has entered a string in the form of a date or a number. The procedure depends on the variant data type combined with two new Boolean functions (functions that return either True or False). For example, the built-in function IsDate tells you whether an expression can be converted to a date. Consider the following code that checks whether the contents of a text box are in the right form to be used as a date:

```
Dim DT      ' DT is a variant
DT = Text1.Text
If IsDate(DT) Then
   ' do whatever you want with the date
Else
   MsgBox "Please enter the text in the form of a date!"
End If
```

Similarly, you can use the IsNumeric function to determine whether a variable can be converted to a number. This gives you a quick way of checking for extraneous characters in a string of digits:

```
Dim NT      'NT is a variant
NT = Text1.Text
If IsNumeric(NT) Then
   ' do whatever you want with the number
Else
   MsgBox "Please enter the data in the box as a number!"
End If
```

Similarly, you can use the Like operator in an If-Then to do pattern matching (see Chapter 7 for an example of this).

## An Example: The Dir$ Command

Another good example of where you'll need an If-Then-Else is when, during a program, you have to find out if a file or files exist with a specific extension. (You can also use a file list box—see Chapter 14.) The function needed is

Dir$(*filespec*)

where *filespec* is a string expression that contains the filename or file pattern. It is not case sensitive. You can use the two DOS wildcards ( ? for a single character match and * to allow more characters). You can also include path name information. Each time Visual Basic encounters a Dir$ command with a filespec, it returns the first filename it finds that matches the pattern. When no filenames match, Visual Basic returns the empty string. To continue searching for the same pattern, you call the Dir$ function with no pattern.

Here is a program fragment that checks if the current directory contains any .TXT files:

```
Dir$("*.TXT")
If X$ = ""   Then
  Print "No text files found"
Else
 Print "First file found is "; X$
End If
```

To find all the files with a .TXT extension, use this:

```
Dir$("*.TXT")
Do While X$ <> ""
   Print "Text File found is "; X$
   X$ = Dir$                      'Don't reuse the file spec
Loop
```

## Combining the If-Then with Loops

Suppose you need to check that there is exactly one file with a .TXT extension in the current directory. To do this, you have to use the Dir$ function, but you need to allow two ways to leave the loop. Here is a fragment that does this:

```
NameOfFile$ = Dir$("*.TXT")
NumberOfFiles = 0
Do Until NameOfFile$ = "" Or NumberOfFiles > 1
  NumberOfFiles = NumberOfFiles + 1
  NameOfFile$ = Dir$
Loop
If NumberOfFiles = 0 Then Print "No Files Found"
If NumberOfFiles > 1 Then Print "Too Many Files"
```

Notice that Visual Basic enters the loop only if it finds an example of the file. You have to allow for the loop never being entered at all. Once the loop is entered, you have Visual Basic add 1 to the file count.

These kinds of loops are so common that computer scientists gave them a special name, *Eureka loops,* after Archimedes' famous bathtub experience. You set up a loop to end if either one of two situations prevails. Then you follow the loop by a test for what actually took place.

Another example of this type of loop would occur if you modified the program that calculated how long it would take to build up a $1,000,000 nest egg to end either if the number of years until you retired was exceeded or you reached the $1,000,000 goal.

You can use the If-Then to give you a way to write a loop that "tests in the middle." For this, you combine the If-Then with a new command: the Exit Do. Whenever Visual Basic processes the Exit Do statement, it pops you out of the loop, directly to the statement following the keyword Loop.

More generally, Visual Basic allows you to set up a potentially infinite loop at any time; just leave off the tests in a Do loop (an unadorned Do at the top and an equally unadorned Loop at the bottom). Once you've done this, the loop will end only when Visual Basic processes an Exit Do statement. (During program development, you can always end the program prematurely from the Run menu, and you can also use the toolbar or CTRL+BREAK combination, of course.) There is a version of the Exit command for leaving a For–Next loop as well; in this case, it takes the form Exit For.

Visual Basic places no restriction on the number of Exit statements you place inside a loop, but loops that have 37 different ways to end are awfully hard to debug. As a general rule, most programmers aim for programs that have only "single entry/single exit" loops. They also find it easier to debug programs that have the loop test at the beginning or end of the loop. Most programmers use the Exit Do (or Exit For) only for abnormal exits from loops, such as when a program is about to divide by zero and leave the loop rather than generate a "Divide by zero" error.

## Select Case

Suppose you were designing a program to compute grades based on the average of four exams. If the average was 90 or higher, the person should get an A, 80 to 89, a B, and so on. This is such a common situation that Visual Basic has another control structure designed exactly for it. It's called the Select Case. To use this command, you start with something you want to test. For example, suppose you want to test if a character is a vowel. You could write

```
If Char$ = "A" Or Char$ ="a" Then Print "Vowel"
If Char$ = "I" Or Char$ ="i" Then Print "Vowel"
```

and so on.

Using the Select Case control structure (combined with the UCase$ command to turn the letter into uppercase), you can write

```
Select Case  UCase$(Char$)
  Case  "A"
    Print "Vowel"
  Case  "E"
    Print "Vowel"
  Case  "I"
    Print "Vowel"
  Case  "O"
    Print "Vowel"
  Case  "U"
    Print "Vowel"
  Case  "Y"
    Print "Y is a problem - sorry"
End Select
```

The Select Case command makes it clear that a program has reached a point with many branches; multiple If-Thens do not. (And the clearer a program is, the easier it is to debug.)

What follows the keywords Select Case is a variable or expression, and what Visual Basic is going to do depends on the value of the variable or expression. The keyword Case is shorthand for "In the case that the variable (expression) is," and you usually follow it by a relational operator. For example, to begin to check that the value of the variable Char$ is a letter, you can add the Is keyword:

```
Case Is < "A"
  Print "Character is not a letter."
  Print "Meaningless question"
```

To eliminate all possible nonletter values, you have to consult, for example, the ANSI chart available online via the Help menu. By looking at that, you can see that you also need to eliminate those characters whose ANSI codes are between 91 and 95. You do this as follows:

```
Case Chr$(91) To Chr$(95)
  Print "Character is not a letter."
  Print "Meaningless question"
```

Here, the keyword To allows you to give a range of values. Therefore, this statement is shorthand for, "In the case that the variable is in the range from Chr$(91) to Chr$(95) inclusive, do the following."

Having eliminated the case when the character was not a letter, you may want to print out the message that it is a consonant. You do this with the Case Else, which is shorthand for "Do this case if none of the other situations hold." (You could, of course, have used the LCase$ function instead, which converts letters to lowercase.)

Finally, the Select Case control structure allows you to combine many tests for equality on one line. You could write

```
Case "A", "E", "I", "O", "U"
  Print "is a vowel"
```

instead of the five tests given previously.

## Finishing Up with the If-Then

The Select Case command allows you multiple branches but allows you to test only one expression—ultimately one number or string. Suppose you have two numbers, A and B, and your outline looks like this:

```
If A=B  Do ....
If A>B  Do ....
If A<B  Do ....
```

One way to program this is to set up a variable:

```
Difference = A - B
```

and then select whether the value of Difference was zero (when A = B), greater than zero (in which case A > B), or less than zero (A < B). But now suppose someone throws in one or two extra conditions:

```
If A > B And A < 2*B
If A > 2*B
```

Now it's no longer obvious how to use the Select Case command. You could write four block If-Thens corresponding to each of the different conditions in the outline, and most of the time this wouldn't cause any problems. Problems may happen if (as in the preceding example) you have to do something to A or B in one of the blocks. From that point on you're in trouble. All further tests are off. More precisely, suppose the outline was to do one of the following:

> If A = B
>   Print A
> If A < B
>   Print A and add two to A
> If A > B
>   Print B and add two to B

Here is a translation of this outline:

```
If A = B Then Print A
If A < B Then
  Print A
  A = A + 2
End If
If A > B Then
  Print B
  B = B + 2
End If
```

Suppose the value of A was 4 and the value of B was 5. Then the second option is taken, and the program prints out 4 and makes A = 6. But now the third option is activated—contrary to the outline, which says do only one of the possibilities.

This situation is similar to when you first used the Else command. You need to continue testing within the confines of the original If-Then. This is done with the keywords

> ElseIf-Then

Here is the correct translation of the outline:

```
If A = B Then
   Print A
ElseIf A < B Then
   Print A
   A = A + 2
ElseIf A > B Then
   Print B
   B = B + 2
End If
```

Now everything is tied together. And just like in the If-Then-Else or the Select command, Visual Basic activates, at most, one clause. In particular, if A < B, then Visual Basic processes only the second clause. And when Visual Basic is done doing that, it bypasses any other ElseIfs that may be contained in the block; it goes immediately to the statement following the End If. (By the way, you could replace the final ElseIf with a simple Else; you've eliminated all the other possibilities.)

A block If-Then can have as many ElseIfs as you like but only one Else (as the last clause). The limits are determined by how much you can process rather then what Visual Basic can do. (That's why it's often preferable to use Select Case. Although any Select Case can be transformed into an If-Then-ElseIf, the latter can be much harder to read and hence to debug.)

The final point worth noting is that the block If-Then is extremely flexible. You can put any Visual Basic statement following the keyword Then—in particular, another If-Then-Else. Consider the following, which a teacher might use if he or she regarded the final exam as being not all important:

```
If FinalExam < 65 Then
   Print "You failed the final exam."
   If Average > 70 Then
      Print "You pass because your average is"
      Print "high enough to overcome failing the final"
   Else
      Print "I'm sorry failing the final and a marginal ";
      Print " passing average means failing the course"
   End If
End If
```

Is it clear (forgetting the indentation pattern for a moment) that the Else belongs to the inner If-Then? The way to see this is to "play computer." For the Else to belong to the outer If–Then, the inner If–Then must have already finished. But it hasn't because, to that point, no End If has shown up. Therefore, the first End If finishes the inner If–Then and the second finishes the outer one, and so the Else must belong to the inner If–Then. Of course, you should, as in the preceding example, use a consistent indentation pattern to make it obvious at a glance where nested If–Thens belong.

## An Example: The KeyPress Procedure

Almost all Visual Basic objects will recognize when a user presses and then releases a key. If the key that was pressed generates an ordinary ASCII/ANSI code, it triggers the KeyPress event procedure. Not only can this procedure detect what the user types, but you can also use it to change or restrict what the control will accept.

The syntax for this event procedure is a little different from all the event procedures you've seen up to now. The template for the KeyPress event procedure looks like this:

```
Sub ControlName_KeyPress(KeyAscii As Integer)

End Sub
```

Inside the parentheses is the first example of a *parameter*—the formal name for a placeholder. When Visual Basic detects the user pressing an ASCII key inside a control that recognizes this event, you get a call to this event procedure. Visual Basic replaces the parameter with the ASCII/ANSI code of the key that generated the event.

For example, a form can detect the KeyPress event if all the controls on it are disabled or invisible, or if the form's KeyPreview property is set to True. If you start a new project with a blank form and attach the following event procedure to it:

```
Sub Form_KeyPress(KeyAscii As Integer)
  Print "The ASCII code of the key you pressed is";KeyAscii
  Print "The character itself is ";Chr$(KeyAscii)
End Sub
```

you'll be able to explore the ASCII/ANSI codes for characters until you end the program.

On the other hand, if you want to cancel a keystroke, you need only reassign the parameter KeyAscii to be zero. For example, use the following to force the user to type a digit between zero and 9 into a text block:

```
Sub Text1_KeyPress(KeyAscii As Integer)
   If KeyAscii < Asc("0") Or KeyAscii > Asc("9") Then
      Beep
      KeyAscii = 0
   EndIf
End Sub
```

This event procedure absolutely prevents the user from typing anything but a digit inside the text box. The procedure blanks out any other character the user may have typed.

Since you can detect whether a user has typed a comma or more than one decimal point, you can use the KeyPress event procedure to check what he or she types in a text box. The next chapter shows you how to write a procedure that accepts a number but disregards commas, extraneous decimal points, and nonnumeric characters.

# Chapter 7

# The Built-in Functions

HIS chapter covers Visual Basic's built-in functions. These commands transform raw data into the form you need. For example, there are functions that take strings apart as well as ones that put them together. You'll also see how the pseudo-random number generator lets you build an element of indeterminacy (chance) into your programs, a necessary tool for programming games of chance or simulations.

As always, be prepared to check the on-line help about specific functions. The examples given there complement the ones given in this chapter.

## String Functions

Because information in Visual Basic text boxes is usually kept as text or variants, string functions are far more important in Visual Basic than in ordinary BASIC languages. (Relying on implicit conversions from the variant data type can occasionally lead to problems and in all cases is slower.) In Chapter 5 you saw how two strings can be joined together (concatenated) using the plus sign (+) or ampersand (&). In this section you'll see the functions available in Visual Basic that let you examine the characters in a string, take strings apart, place one string inside another, and put strings together.

For example, suppose you need a string variable that contains the lowercase alphabet. Just combine the + with a For-Next loop:

```
Lowercase$=""
For I% = Asc("a") To Asc("z")
  Lowercase$ = Lowercase$ + Chr$(I%)
Next I%
```

You can also look up the ASCII/ANSI codes for "a" (97) and "z" (122) in the help files.

You will often use two built-in functions when building up strings. The function

Space$(*NumberOfSpaces*)

yields a string consisting of only spaces, with the number of spaces determined by the value inside the parentheses. The function

String$(*Number, StringExpression$*)

yields a string of repeated characters. The character repeated is the first character of the string expression in the second position of the function, and the number of times the characters are repeated is determined by the value in the first position. You can also use the extended ASCII code in the second position. The following examples all yield the same string of 10 z's:

```
X$=String$(10,"z")
X$=String$(10,"zyzzavaa")          'only first character is used
X$=String$(10,122)                 '   122 = Asc("z")
```

## Analyzing Strings

Suppose you want to examine an expression character by character. For example, you might want to check how many periods (decimal points) are in a string expression before you convert it to a number with the Val function rather than using the IsNumeric function you saw in the last chapter. The code for this calls for a For-Next loop with the ending value set to the length of the string. In Visual Basic, the function that does this is Len( ), where the parentheses following the function hold a string expression. Unlike the TextWidth function, this function counts all spaces and nonprinting characters that appear in the string.

Next, you need a function that lets you extract a copy of individual letters or larger chunks out of a string. The most important of these functions is the Mid$ function. The syntax for this function is

Mid$(*StringExpression, Start [,length]*)

or

Mid$(*StringExpression*, *Start*)

The first entry holds the string (or string expression) you want to cut up. Next comes the starting position of the characters you want cut out of the string. The optional last position specifies the number of characters you want to pull out. These last two options can be either integers or long integers or an expression that Visual Basic can round off to lie in this range. Here are some examples of this function:

```
Mid$("VisualBasic", 1, 5) = "Visua"
Mid$("VisualBasic", 1, 6) = "Visual"
Mid$("VisualBasic", 7, 5) = "Basic"
```

If you leave out the last entry (the one telling how many letters to pull out), as shown here,

```
Mid$("VisualBasic", 7, 5) = Mid$("VisualBasic", 7)= "Basic"
```

Visual Basic retrieves a copy of the rest of the string—starting, of course, from the position determined by the second entry. You also get a copy of the rest of the string if the third entry is too large (greater than the number of characters remaining).

Programmers say that Mid$ is a function of three (or occasionally two) parameters, or arguments. Both terms are borrowed from mathematics. Think of them as meaning "the number of pieces of information to be massaged." In a function, each argument is separated from the next by commas. The Mid$ function usually uses three pieces of information: a string in the first position and integers or long integers in the remaining two positions. (Of course, you can use expressions that evaluate to these as well.)

For example, a fragment that would count the number of periods in a string expression might look like this:

```
PeriodCount% = 0
Length% = Len(StringExpression$)
For I% = 1 To Length%
  If Mid$(StringExpression$, I%, 1) = "." Then
     PeriodCount% = PeriodCount% + 1
  End If
Next I%
```

On each pass through the loop, the position (the value of I%) where the Mid$ function starts working increases. The number of characters pulled out remains the same (one).

The Mid$ function has two cousins that are occasionally useful: Left$ and Right$. As the names suggest, Left$ makes a copy of characters from the beginning of a word and Right$ picks them out from the end. Of the two, Right$ is the more common. It avoids a subtraction inside the Mid$ function and can work a bit faster as a result. For example, the following lines,

```
Mid$(A$, Len(A$) − 3, 4)
Mid$(A$, Len(A$) − 3)
Right$(A$, 4)
```

all have the same effect.

Left$ works the same way but only saves you from putting a 1 in the second position in the Mid$ function. If you want the first five characters in a string, use one of the following:

```
Mid$(A$, 1, 5)
Left$(A$, 5)
```

Mid$ has one other useful feature. You can use it as a statement to make changes inside a string. For example, if

```
BestBasic$ = "PowerBasic"
```

then the statement

```
Mid$(BestBasic$, 1, 5) = "Quick"
```

gives the string variable BestBasic$ the value "QuickBasic". When you use Mid$ this way, the second position controls where the change will start and the third position controls how many letters to pull out from the string on the right-hand side. These are the letters that will be switched into the original string. For example,

```
Mid$(BestBasic$, 1, 5) = "QuickBasic by Microsoft"
```

gives the same result as before. If the right-hand side has fewer characters than the number given in the third position of the left-hand side demands, Visual Basic changes as many characters as occur on the right-hand side. Therefore,

```
Mid$(BestBasic$, 1, 5) = "VB"
```

gives the original value of BestBasic$ the value "VBwerBasic".

## MORE ON THE MID$ STATEMENT

The Mid$ statement makes changes within a string but never changes the length of the original string. If the number in the third position is too large relative to the number in the second position—that is, greater than the remaining number of characters—then only the characters remaining can change. Finally, just as with the Mid$ function, you can leave out the last position. For example,

```
Mid$("In the beginning ",8) = "middle was"
```

changes the string to

```
"In the middle was"
```

In this case, there's just enough room to fit the string on the right-hand side into the string on the left, starting at the eighth position. Counting from the eighth position, there are ten characters left in the phrase "In the beginning ". (The space counts as a character.)

If you want to change the size of a string, the Mid$ statement is of little use. Instead, you need to follow a procedure that's a bit like splicing tape. For example, suppose you want to change the string

```
"QuickBASIC is the best programming language."
```

to read

```
"Visual Basic is the best programming language."
```

Since the string "QuickBASIC" has 10 letters and the string "Visual Basic" has 12 (counting the space), you cannot use the Mid$ statement. Instead, you must follow the splicing analogy:

1. Cut out the phrase "QuickBASIC".

2. Hold the phrase "is the best programming language".

3. Splice in the phrase "Visual Basic" and reassemble.

Here's the fragment:

```
Phrase$ = "QuickBASIC is the best programming language"
Begin$ = "Visual Basic"
EndPhrase$ = Mid$(Phrase$, 11)
Phrase$ = Begin$ + EndPhrase$
```

Programming this kind of change can be a bit painful if you always have to go in and count characters in order to find the position where a character was located. As usual, this task is simplified by one of Visual Basic's built-in functions. Like the Mid$ function, Instr also works with three (and occasionally two) pieces of information; that is, it's a function of three (occasionally two) arguments.

Instr tells you whether a string is part of another string (the jargon is "is a substring of"). And if it is, Instr tells you the position at which the substring starts. Using the same variable, Phrase$, as in the beginning of the last example, in the line of code

```
X% = Instr(1, Phrase$, "BASIC")
```

the value of X% is 6 because the string "BASIC" occurs in the phrase "QuickBASIC is the best programming language", starting at the sixth position.

In this case, Visual Basic searches the string starting from the first position until it finds the substring. If it doesn't find the string, it gives back a value of zero. Therefore, if

```
X% =Instr(1, Phrase$, "basic")
```

then the value of X% is zero because "basic" isn't a substring of the phrase "QuickBASIC is the best programming language". Remember that case is important inside quotes; the Instr function is case-sensitive.

The general form of the Instr function is

Instr(*[where to start,] string to search, string to find*)

In this case, the optional first position specifies from which position to start the search. If you leave this entry out, the search automatically starts from the first position.

**tip:**

*By using the previous value obtained by Instr you can search for repeated occurrences of a string.*

Notice as well the comma within the brackets. As usual, this means that if you put something here, you need to include the comma. If the bracket had fallen before the comma, it would indicate that the comma is always needed.

Since the Instr function returns the value zero (that is, False) when Visual Basic doesn't find a character or a nonzero value (True) when it does, you will often find yourself writing If–Then or Do loops using the Instr function to do the test. For example, you can write an If–Then

```
If Instr(Expression$,".") Then
    Print "Decimal point found."
Else
    Print "No decimal point found."
End If
```

rather than

```
If Instr(Expression$,".") <> 0 Then
    Print "Decimal point found."
Else
    Print "No decimal point found."
End If
```

and the first version will run a little faster as well.

### PARSING A STRING

Another good example of how to use the Instr command is a program that *parses* a string, which means to take it apart into logical pieces and examine the components—for example, to break a name into its component parts. Suppose you had a string made up of individual words, each separated from the next by a single space. Here is a simple outline for pulling out the individual words:

1. Find the first occurrence of a space. Everything up to the first space is a word.

2. Find the second space. Everything between these two spaces is a word.

3. Find the third space. Everything between the second and third spaces is a word.

4. Continue until there are no more spaces.

Now everything between the last space and the end of the word is the last word.

Here is a fragment that implements this outline for the contents of a text box with a control name of Text1:

```
' This fragment uses Instr to parse a phrase
' by searching for a space as the separator

Dim LenPhrase As Integer, BeforeSpace As Integer
Dim AfterSpace As Integer, SizeOfWord As Integer

Phrase$ = Text1.Text
LenPhrase = Len(Phrase$)
If LenPhrase = 0 Then
   MsgBox("No string entered!")
Else
   Separate$ = Chr$(32)                    '= space
   BeforeSpace = 0
   AfterSpace = Instr(BeforeSpace + 1, Phrase$, Separate$)
   Do Until AfterSpace = 0
     SizeOfWord = AfterSpace - BeforeSpace - 1
     NextWord$ = Mid$(Phrase$, BeforeSpace + 1, SizeOfWord)
     Print NextWord$
     BeforeSpace = AfterSpace
     AfterSpace = Instr(BeforeSpace + 1, Phrase$, Separate$)
   Loop
End If
Print Mid$(Phrase$, BeforeSpace + 1)
```

This fragment of code would usually be inside an event procedure or a general procedure (see Chapter 8). The initialization makes it easy to start the process. Without this, the fragment would have to treat the first word separately.

The next space is found starting one position in from the previous space. At the beginning of the process, this must be the first position because the If–Then–Else ends if the string is not empty.

The Do loop stops when no more spaces are left. By testing at the top of the loop, you take care of the case when there is only a single word. If you are puzzled by why the size of the word is given by one less than the value of AfterSpace – BeforeSpace, it is easy to work out an example. Suppose spaces are at the fifth and ninth positions; this means the actual word takes up positions 6, 7, and 8 (that is, it is three characters long). Setting up a variable for the size of the word makes the Mid$ statement cleaner. There's rarely a need to combine many statements into one.

Next, the program sets the new value of BeforeSpace to be the old value of AfterSpace, which moves you along to the position of the next space. This sets Visual Basic up to look for the next space. If it finds a space, the cycle continues; if not, Visual Basic moves to whatever is left since there are no more spaces. The rest of the string must be a word.

The program assumes that there is no period or other stop at the end. Another problem with this program is that it doesn't handle multiple spaces within the phrase. The problem as usual stems from the outline, which assumed that a word is bounded by no more than one space. How can you take care of the quite common possibility of a double space or even more? You need to change the outline for the previous program. The second step in the previous outline assumed that a word was always located between two spaces, one on either side of it. What you need to do is find the next space as you did before, but what is between these two spaces is a word *only if it is not empty space.*

But what really happens if there are two consecutive spaces? As always, an example helps. Suppose the string Phrase$ was given by the following line of code:

```
Phrase$ = "This" + Space$(2) + "is" + Space$(3) + "a test"
```

This puts two spaces between the first and second words in the phrase, three spaces between the second and third words in the phrase, and one space between the third and fourth words.

Let's "play computer." Especially when dealing with loops, this is often best done by setting up a little chart detailing the values the important variables are supposed to have on each pass, as shown here:

| Pass Number | Value of (Key) Variables |
|---|---|
| 0 (Before entering loop) | BeforeSpace = 0 |
|  | AfterSpace = 5 |
| (start of) 1st pass through loop | SizeOfWord = 4 |
| (end of) 1st pass through loop | BeforeSpace = 5 |
|  | AfterSpace = 6 |
| (start of) 2nd pass through loop | SizeOfWord = 0 |
| (end of) 2nd pass through loop | BeforeSpace = 6 |
|  | AfterSpace = 9 |

| Pass Number | Value of (Key) Variables |
| --- | --- |
| (start of) 3rd pass through loop | SizeOfWord = 2 |
| (end of) 3rd pass through loop | BeforeSpace = 9 |
| | AfterSpace = 10 |
| (start of) 4th pass through loop | SizeOfWord = 0 |

You will often use a table like this when you debug a program. Watch the values of the variables in the Debug window (see Chapter 11) and then check the values Visual Basic displays against your table. Examining the values of variables is of little use unless you know what the values are supposed to be.

As you can see, the table indicates that whenever you have two spaces together, the variable SizeOfWord has the value zero. Does this always have to be true? Yes, it does, because if you have two consecutive spaces, the value of AfterSpace is always one more than the value of BeforeSpace. And so the value of

$$AfterSpace - BeforeSpace - 1 = SizeOfWord$$

must be zero.

Knowing this makes it easy to modify the program. (Change the Print statements to read "If SizeOf Word > 0 Then...".) A version of this program that takes this into account and also checks for other word separators, like commas, periods, and question marks, can be found in Chapter 8.

As another example, suppose you need to decide on the number of digits before the decimal point in a number. This is easy to do if you combine the Str$ command with the Instr command. Here's an outline for this:

1. Change the number to a string.

2. Find the decimal point using Instr.

3. If the value from the previous step is zero, there's no decimal point and the number of digits is one less than the length of the converted number (because of the extra space that Str$ adds).

4. Otherwise, the number of digits in front of the decimal point is two less (because of the extra space that Str$ sticks on for the sign and the decimal point) than the value given by the Instr function.

Here's the Visual Basic fragment:

```
' find the number of digits
Dim Numeral$, Digits As Integer
```

```
Numeral$ = Str$(Number)
Digits = Instr(Numeral$, ".")
If Digits = 0 Then
    NumOfDigits = Len(Numeral$) - 1
Else
  NumOfDigits = Digits - 2
End If
```

## AN EXAMPLE: CHECKING INPUT

Probably the most important way to bulletproof a program is to check user input. This task was discussed to some extent in Chapter 6, but now you have the tools to go much further. Check what the user enters before you start processing the data; don't wait until it's too late. This section shows you how to write the code that will accept a number but disregard commas, extraneous decimal points, and so on. Exactly what is extraneous is determined by the international number setting when you set up Windows. The general procedure for writing this code is as follows:

1. Examine a character.

2. If the character is a digit, place it on the right.

3. If the character is the first decimal point, accept that too and also place it on the right. Otherwise, disregard the character.

4. All other characters are canceled.

As you saw in Chapter 6, the KeyPress event lets you examine characters as they are entered, wiping out the extraneous characters.

The main issue you have to decide is how to store the information. The two most common possibilities are

◆ Set up a form-level or global variable (see Chapter 8) for the number.

◆ Leave the text as the (variant) contents of the control and convert the contents of the box to a number inside whatever procedures need it.

The advantage of the first option is that you don't have to cancel out commas, which users might prefer. The advantage of the second is that you may not need to do the extra analysis at all.

The following fragment stores the information as the contents of a form-level variable called Numeral$

```
Sub Text1_KeyPress(KeyAscii As Integer)
  ' This fragment accepts only a number
  Static DecimalPointUsed As Integer

  Select Case KeyAscii
    Case Asc("0") To Asc("9")
      Numeral$ = Numeral$ + Chr$(KeyAscii)
    Case Asc(".")
      If DecimalPointUsed Then
        KeyAscii = 0
        Beep
      Else
        DecimalPointUsed = True
        Numeral$ = Numeral$ + Chr$(KeyAscii)
      End If
    Case Asc(",")
      ' Comma - do nothing to Numeral$
    Case Else
      KeyAscii = 0
      Beep
  End Select
End Sub
```

Since DecimalPointUsed was set up as a static variable, this information is preserved by Visual Basic during each subsequent call to the KeyPress event procedure. On the other hand, if you wanted to allow more than one number to be entered in the control, the situation would be a bit more complicated. You could make this a form or global variable and reset it back to False each time you wanted to reuse the information, or you could leave it as a static variable and set it to False whenever the text box starts out blank.

If a character is in the range from 0 to 9, then it's a digit. Therefore, it's concatenated at the right of the global variable Numeral$. Next, the fragment moves to the case that accepts a single decimal point in the number. However, entering a decimal point flips the DecimalPointUsed flag to True.

The fragment leaves the commas intact in the display but, of course, doesn't add them to the Numeral$ variable, which will be turned into a number. Any other characters are canceled and the computer beeps to provide some feedback. You might also use a message box here.

## THE LIKE OPERATOR AND FUZZY SEARCHING

The Like operator lets you compare strings using ordinary DOS wild cards but goes far beyond that. For example, it can tell you if any digits are inside a string or even if a group of characters is not inside a string. For non-null strings this operator returns True if there is a match and False if not. The case sensitivity of the Like operator depends on the current setting of Option Compare in the form or module. (Of course, you could program all these features using the Instr function but the Like operator is faster and, of course, saves you programming time.)

As with DOS a question mark (?) matches one character only and an asterisk (*) allows matches with zero, one, or more characters. For example, you could have an If–Then like this:

```
If "QuickBasic" Like "*Basic" Then
    Print "a Basic language"
Else
    Print "not a Basic language"
End If
```

will print "a Basic language.", but change the If clause to:

```
If "QuickBasic" Like "?Basic" Then
```

and you'll see "not a Basic language."

The following table summarizes the possible patterns:

| Pattern Character | What it matches |
| --- | --- |
| ? | Any single character |
| * | Zero or more characters |
| # | Any single digit |
| [list of characters] | Any single character in the list |
| [!list of characters] | Any single character not in the list |

For example, if X = ("###" Like "123"), Then X is True; but if X = ("[ABC]" Like "123"), then X is False. (But X = ("[!ABC]" Like "123") is True!)

You can also use a hyphen inside the brackets to show an ascending range. For example, "If "[0-9]" Like A$" would tell you whether a digit occurred inside A$.

**note:**

*To match a left bracket ([), question mark (?), number sign (#), or asterisk (\*), enclose them in brackets. For example: "\*[?]" would check for the occurrence of a question mark.*

## OTHER STRING FUNCTIONS

Visual Basic has quite a few functions for handling strings. This section goes through the most important remaining ones.

*LCase$ (LCase), UCase$ (UCase)* As you might expect from the name, the LCase$ function forces all the characters in a string to be lowercase (LCase without the $ switches the characters in a variant). Similarly, UCase$ switches all the characters in a string to uppercase and UCase works with the variants. These functions are used when you want to disregard the case inside a string.

*StrComp* This function can be used instead of the relational operators (such as < or >) to compare strings. Unlike the relational operators this returns a value and so you usually use it together with an assignment statement. For example, if you set X = StrComp(A$, B$), then the value of X is -1 if A$ is less than B$, 0 if A$ equals B$, and 1 if A$ is greater than B$. It is the reserved constant NULL if one of the strings is empty.

By adding a third option to StrComp you can control case sensitivity of the comparison. For StrComp(A$, B$, 1) then the comparison is not case-sensitive. For StrComp(A$, B$, 0) it is. Using StrComp this way is sometimes preferable to using the Option Compare Text feature that globally controls comparisons.

*Trim$ (Trim), LTrim$ (LTrim), RTrim$ (RTrim)* Although, as you saw earlier in this chapter, you have to work a little bit to pull out extra spaces from inside a string, you don't have to do much for spaces at the beginning or end of a string. Trim$ (Trim to work with variants) removes spaces from both the left and right of a string. For example, if:

```
A$ = "   This has far too many spaces.      "
Trim$(A$) = "This has far too many spaces."
```

Similarly, LTrim$ (LTrim) removes spaces from the left and RTrim$ (RTrim) removes spaces from the right.

**note:** *None of the Visual Basic string functions except the Mid$ statement ever change the string. They all make a copy of the string and modify that copy.*

## The Rnd Function

The Solitaire program provided with Microsoft Windows shuffles a deck of cards whenever you ask it to. In card games and most other games, the play is unpredictable. This is exactly what is meant by a game of chance. On the other hand, computers are machines, and the behavior of machines should be predictable. To write a program in Visual Basic that allows you, for example, to simulate the throwing of a die, you need a function that makes the behavior of the computer seem random. You do this by means of the function Rnd. For example, run the following Form_Click procedure on a blank form:

```
Sub Form_Click()
  Cls
  For I = 1 To 5
    Print Rnd
  Next I
End Sub
```

What you'll see will look something like the screen in Figure 7-1. As you can see, five numbers between zero and 1, each having 15 digits, roll down the screen. These numbers seem to follow no pattern: that's what is usually meant by random. They'll also have many but not all of the sophisticated statistical properties that scientists expect of random numbers. Without some changes,

**Figure 7-1**

Demonstration of the random number generator

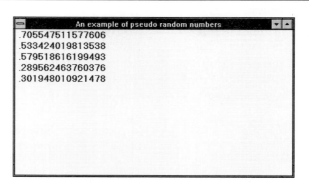

for example, they would not be very useful in simulation programs. See Chapter 9 for how to modify the built-in random number generator for simulations.

Each time the computer processes a line containing the statement "Print Rnd", a different number between zero and 1 pops out. In theory, the number can be zero but can't ever be 1. (You can also use the Rnd(1) version that is necessary in QuickBASIC.)

It's natural to wonder what a number with so many decimal places is good for. Suppose, for example, you wanted to write a program that simulated a coin toss. There are three possibilities: it could be heads, it could be tails—or it could stand on edge (don't wait up for this to happen). A fragment to simulate a coin toss might look like this:

```
' A coin toss simulator
CoinToss = Rnd
Select Case CoinToss
   Case Is < .5
     Print "Heads"
   Case .5
     Print "Stood on edge!!!!"
   Case Else
     Print "Tails"
End Select
```

Suppose you incorporate this fragment into a Form_Click procedure:

```
Sub Form_Click ()
  ' A multiple coin toss simulator
  Dim Trials As Integer, NumOfHeads As Integer
  Dim NumOfTails As Integer, I As Integer
  Dim CoinToss As Single

  Trials = Val(InputBox$("How many trials?"))
  NumOfHeads = 0
  NumOfTails = 0
  Unbelievable = 0

  For I = 1 To Trials
    CoinToss = Rnd
    Select Case CoinToss
      Case Is < .5
```

```
                 NumOfHeads = NumOfHeads + 1
             Case .5
               Print "Stood on edge!!!!"      'maybe in a couple of
                                              'years

               Beep: Beep
               Unbelievable = Unbelievable + 1
             Case Else
               NumOfTails = NumOfTails + 1
           End Select
        Next I
        Cls
        Print "Number of heads was"; NumOfHeads
        Print "Number of tails was"; NumOfTails
        If Unbelievable > 0 Then
           Print "The coin stood on edge!"
        End If
End Sub
```

Try this program with a different number of trials. You should get roughly the same number of heads as tails and no "standing on edges." (For a large number of trials, it would be very unlikely that you'd get equal numbers of heads and tails.) Now end the program and run it again, using the same number of trials as before. If you do, you'll notice that you will get exactly the same number of heads and tails as you did before. This would certainly be unusual behavior for an honest coin. What is happening?

In fact, the numbers you get using the Rnd function are only *pseudo-random*. *Pseudo* generally means false, and you've just seen one of the problems of pseudo-random numbers. Every time you start a program that uses pseudo-random numbers, you will get the same sequence of pseudo-random numbers. The program operates as if the computer's memory contains a book of these numbers, and after each program is over the book gets turned back to page 1. The book always starts at the same place and the numbers are always in the same order, so therefore the results are fixed. You need a way to shuffle the pages each time the program starts. You can do this in many ways, but the easiest way is to add a parameter to the Rnd function.

First, suppose you issue a Rnd(0). Then you get the last pseudo-random number generated. This is useful when trying to debug a program. Rnd(0) gives you a way of checking which pseudo-random number the machine just used. (Imagine trying to debug a program if an important number changes each time and you have no way of knowing its value.)

Suppose next there is a negative number inside the parentheses. (The number inside the parenthesis is usually called the *seed*.) Each time you give the command

Rnd(*negative number*)

you get the same pseudo-random number. This is another important debugging tool. It lets you rerun a program keeping the pseudo-random numbers temporarily stable. A good way to think about what a negative seed does is to imagine that there is a different list of pseudo-random numbers, each one corresponding to a different negative seed. You can think of the seed as the number from which the random numbers grow. This is done by transforming the seed using the *linear congruential method,* which transforms the number using the Mod function. The easiest way to understand what Visual Basic is doing for its random number generator is to imagine you are working only with integers. The random number generator would then use the built-in Mod function to generate the next pseudo-random number roughly as follows:

NextNumber = (A*PreviousNumber + B) mod M

Here, A, B, and M are fixed integers and the PreviousNumber starts from the seed. This method is very fast. But because A, B, and M are fixed by Visual Basic designers, this method can be unreliable if you need many random numbers for a simulation program. If you need thousands of random numbers for a program, see Chapter 9, which gives you one way of improving the built-in random number generator. The cost is that the program will run slightly more slowly and need slightly more memory.

**note:** *From this point on, this book will stop using the term "pseudo-random" and refer to the numbers coming from the Rnd function as being "random"; this follows the usual terminology in programming.*

The best way to not stack the cards at the outset is to use the exact time of the system clock to reseed the random number generator. (Since the clock is accurate to around a tenth of a second, it's quite unlikely that a program will start at exactly the same moment each time it is run.) You do this by using a new command: Randomize.

The Randomize statement can also be a useful debugging tool. This is because you can use any numeric expression in the Randomize statement. After a Randomize *Number* command, your program will always be using the same set of random numbers.

Numbers between zero and 1 may (with a little work) be good for imitating a coin toss, but the method used earlier would be cumbersome for, say, a dice simulation. The outline would be something like this:

◆ If the random number is less than 1/6, make it a 1.

◆ If more than 1/6 but less than 2/6 (= 1/3), make it a 2.

◆ If more than 2/6 but less than 3/6 (= 1/2), make it a 3, and so on.

Thinking about this outline leads to a simple trick called *scaling* that more or less automates this process. Suppose you take a number between zero and 1 and multiply it by 6. If it was less than 1/6 to start with, it will now be less than 1; if it was between 1/6 and 2/6 (1/3), it will now be between 1 and 2; and so on. All you need to do then is multiply the number by 6 and move up to the next integer. In general, if the number was between zero and 1 (but never quite getting to 1), the result of multiplying by 6 goes from zero not quite up to 6.

Unfortunately, there's no command in Visual Basic to move up to the next integer. Instead, the Fix function throws away the decimal part of a number. For example:

Fix(3.456) = 3     Fix(−7.9998) = −7     Fix(8) = 8

However, by adding 1 to the result of "fixing" a positive number, you will, in effect, move to the next highest positive integer. For example, look at the following fragment:

```
' A dice simulation using Fix

Randomize
Cls
Die% = Fix(6 * Rnd) + 1
Print "I rolled a"; Die%
```

The key to the fragment is that the number inside the parentheses—6*Rnd—is always between zero and 6, but it can't be 6 because Rnd is never 1. Applying the Fix function gives you an integer between zero and 5 (that is, 0, 1, 2, 3, 4, or 5), and now you only have to add 1 to make it a proper-looking die.

There's another function that works much the same way as Fix: Int. Int gives the *floor* of a number—the first integer that's smaller than or equal to the number. It's usually called the greatest integer function. However, thinking of it as the floor function makes it easy to remember what happens for negative numbers. With negative numbers, you move down. For example, Int(–3.5) is –4, Int(–4.1) is –5, and so on. You can see that Fix and Int work the same way for positive numbers but are different for negative ones. Using Int and adding 1 always moves to the next largest integer.

The Int and Fix functions have other uses. For example, the post office charges for first-class mail are 29 cents for the first ounce and 23 cents for each additional ounce (or fraction thereof). Suppose an item weighed 3.4 ounces. Then the cost would be 29 cents for the first ounce and 69 (3*23) for the additional ounces, counting the fraction. The cost is

.29 + Int(3.4)*.23

In general, it's given by the following fragment:

```
If Int(WeightOfObject) = WeightOfObject Then
  Cost = .29 + .23*(WeightOfObject - 1)
Else
  Cost = .29 + .23*(Int(WeightOfObject))
EndIf
```

## AN EXAMPLE USING THE RANDOM NUMBER GENERATOR

Suppose you wanted to write a "jumble" program. This would take a string and shuffle the letters around. It's a prototype for many other types of operations—for example, shuffling a deck of cards. Here's an outline for one way to do it:

1. Start at the first character.

2. Swap it with a randomly chosen character.

3. Do the same for the second character until there are no more characters left.

The swapping can be done with the Mid$ statement since you are never changing the size of the string. The screen in Figure 7-2 shows what the form might look like. Suppose the command button is given a control name of

**Figure 7-2**

**Form a jumble program**

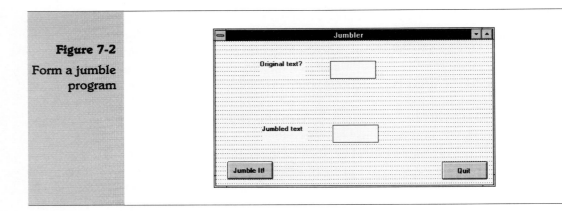

JumbleIt, the top text box is called OriginalText, and the destination text box is called JumbledText. Then the click procedure looks like this:

```
Sub JumbleIt_Click ()
   ' a Jumble program demonstrates Mid$ as a statement
   ' and the Rnd function

   Dim Phrase$, HoldChar$, I As Integer
   Dim LenPhrase As Integer, INum As Integer

   Randomize
   Phrase$ = OriginalText.Text
   LenPhrase = Len(Phrase$)
   For I = 1 To LenPhrase
    INum = Int(LenPhrase * Rnd) + 1
    HoldChar$ = Mid$(Phrase$, I, 1)
    Mid$(Phrase$, I, 1) = Mid$(Phrase, INum, 1)
    Mid$(Phrase$, INum, 1) = HoldChar$
   Next I
   JumbledText.Text = Phrase$
End Sub
```

Since values inside the string commands start at 1 and range up to the length of the string, you need to add 1 to Int(LenPhrase*Rnd). Using this value gives you a random position within the string. Once you have the random character, you swap it with the current character in the string, as determined by the counter in the For-Next loop.

Since there is no Swap statement like this,

SWAP Mid$(*Phrase$,INum, 1*), Mid$(*Phrase$,I, 1*)

you need to remember both the old and new characters in order to program the interchange.

To make this program into a card shuffler, all you need to do is give Phrase$ the right value. You can do this by using the Chr$ command. You'll see how to do this in Chapter 8.

Up to this point, all the random integers you've used have started from zero or 1. Sometimes it's convenient to have random integers that span a range. For example, take a random four-letter combination; how likely is it to be a word in English? To try this out, you need to generate four random letters and string them together. An obvious way to do this is to apply the Chr$ command to a random integer between 65 and 90 (the range of ASCII/ANSI codes for the uppercase alphabet). To get a random integer in this range:

1. Generate a random integer between 0 and 25.

2. Add it to 65 to get the ASCII/ANSI value of a lowercase letter.

Here is a translation of this into code:

```
CharNum = Int(26*Rnd) + 65
```

And here is a fragment that uses this code to continuously generate random four-letter combinations:

```
' Random 4 letter 'words'
' demonstrates Rnd for a range
Dim I As Integer, CharNum As Integer
Randomize
Cls
Do
  Word$ = ""
  For I = 1 To 4
    CharNum = Int(26 * Rnd) + 65
    Word$ = Word$ + Chr$(CharNum)
  Next I
  Print Word$
Loop
```

The key, as explained in the outline for this program given previously, is the statement defining the value of CharNum that gives you a random integer in the right range. The next statement turns it into a random uppercase letter. As usual, these two statements could have been combined into one:

```
Word$ + Chr$(Int(26*Rnd) + 65)
```

However, this code is clearly less readable than the preceding code.

Finally, this fragment creates an infinite loop because no way to end it was programmed. You can use the CTRL+BREAK combination to end it, but a way more in keeping with the spirit of Visual Basic is to use a Form_Click procedure to start the process and a Form_DblClick procedure or command button to end it (and possibly to use a multiline text box to display the "words").

## Bit Twiddling

Bit twiddling refers to looking at the individual bits that make up a number and possibly resetting them if needed. You need to do this in order to use the KeyUp and KeyDown event procedures that let you detect the non-ASCII coded keys, like the function and arrow keys. Knowing how the logical operators work on the bit level also makes it easy to program powerful systems for encrypting your data (see Chapter 14). This section builds on the section in Chapter 3 where you saw how binary arithmetic worked. (Recall that this was needed to set the background and foreground colors via the properties box.)

First, Visual Basic has built-in functions to convert a number to a string of hexadecimal (base 16) or octal (base 8) digits. They are

Hex$ for hexadecimal
Oct$ for octal

Surprisingly, Visual Basic does not have a built-in function for converting a number to binary. There are many ways to write such a program. As usual, it's best to take an example and work through it step by step. The easiest examples are, of course, zero and 1, which are the same in decimal and binary. What about 3? This is 11 in binary (1 * 2 + 1). In general, the rightmost (least significant) binary digit is given by checking whether the number is even or odd. The built-in Mod function tells this. For example, the last binary digit is the number Mod 2.

To move to the next binary digit, you have to divide by 2 and throw away the remainder (which you just took into account by using the Mod function). You continue this process until there's nothing left to divide.

As a more serious example, suppose you want to convert a number like 43 to binary:

Last Binary Digit = 43 Mod 2 = 1

Now you divide by 2, using the integer division function (the backslash) and continue the process:

Next binary digit = (43 \ 2) Mod 2 = 21 Mod 2 = 1

and then you continue this process:

Next binary digit = (21 \ 2)  Mod 2 = 10 Mod 2 = 0
Next binary digit = (10 \ 2)  Mod 2 = 5  Mod 2 = 1
Next binary digit = ( 5 \ 2)  Mod 2 = 2  Mod 2 = 0
Next binary digit = ( 2 \ 2)  Mod 2 = 1  Mod 2 = 1

Since 1 \ 2 is zero, you stop here. Stringing these digits together from bottom to top gives you 101011 (which is 43 in binary).

Here's a program that implements this outline attached to a ConvertToBinary_Click event procedure. The program assumes there are two text boxes, Text1 for the number and Text2 for the string of binary digits.

```
Sub ConvertToBinary_Click ()
  Dim Number As Integer
  Dim BinaryForm As String

  Number = Val(Text1.Text)
  BinaryForm = ""
  Do
   Digit = Number Mod 2
     If Digit = 0 Then
        BinaryForm = "0" + BinaryForm
     Else
        BinaryForm = "1" + BinaryForm
     End If
   Number = Number \ 2
  Loop Until Number = 0
```

```
      Text2.Text = BinaryForm
End Sub
```

If the number to be converted was zero, you don't want to start the loop. On the other hand, you do want to give the representation of zero in binary, as "0". The real work in this procedure is done in the Else clause. You could use a Select Case statement inside the procedure, but with two options this seems like overkill. Finally, as the example shows, when integer division gives you zero, you stop.

The next section shows you another way to write a binary conversion routine.

## The Logical Operators at the Bit Level

You may have thought that Visual Basic's using zero for False made sense, but why −1 for True? To understand this, you have to know that all the logical operators (Not, And, Or, and so on) are really functions that work on the bit (binary digit) level. Suppose you are given two integers, X and Y. Then X And Y makes a binary digit 1 only if both binary digits are 1; otherwise, it is zero. For example, if

| | |
|---|---|
| X = 7 in decimal | = 0111 in binary |
| Y = 12 in decimal | = 1100 in binary |

then X And Y = 0100 in binary (4 in decimal) because only in the third position are both bits 1. Because And gives a 1 only if both digits are 1, Anding with a number whose binary digit is a single 1 and whose remaining digits are all zero lets you isolate the binary digits of any integer. For example:

| | |
|---|---|
| X And 1 | Tells you whether the least significant (rightmost) binary digit is on. You get a zero if it is not on. |
| X And 2 | Since 2 in decimal is 10 in binary, a zero tells you that the next significant (second from the right) binary digit is off. |
| X And 4 | Since 4 in decimal is 100 in binary, this tells you whether the next significant (third from the right) binary digit is on. |

This process is called *masking* and is the key to using the KeyUp, KeyDown event procedures described in the next section. You can also easily adapt this process to write another binary conversion routine:

```
Sub ConvertToBinary_Click ()
  Dim BitPattern As Integer, Number As Integer
  Dim BinaryForm As String
```

```
      Number = Val(Text1.Text)
      BinaryForm = ""
      BitPattern = 1
      Do
        Digit = Number And BitPattern          '
        If Digit = 0 Then
          BinaryForm = "0" + BinaryForm
        Else
          BinaryForm = "1" + BinaryForm
        End If
        BitPattern = BitPattern * 2     'next bit
      Loop Until BitPattern > Number
      Text2.Text = BinaryForm
End Sub
```

The Or operator, as opposed to the And operator, gives a 1 if either or both of the binary digits are 1. Therefore,

7 Or 12 = 15 (=0111 Or 1100 = 1111 in binary)

Use Or to make sure specific bits are one (the on state). For example, X Or 4 makes sure that the third bit is on, X Or 64, the seventh bit, and so on.

One of the most interesting operators on the bit level is Xor (exclusive Or—X or Y but not both). This gives a 1 in a specific position if exactly one of the bits is on. Here's an example:

7 Xor 12 = 11 (= 0111 Xor 1100 = 1011 in binary)

Xoring has the useful property that Xoring twice with the same number does nothing. For example,

(7 Xor 12) Xor 12 = 11 Xor 12 = 7

or, on the bit level,

0111 Xor 1100 = 1011
1011 Xor 1100 = 0111

That the Xor command brings you back to where you started from if you use it twice is the key to a popular animation technique. This is because you can restore the previous display exactly as it was before (see Chapter 12). This property of the Xor operator is also the key to a popular method of encrypting information (see Chapter 14).

There are three other logical operators, Imp and Eqv and Not. X Imp Y gives 1 except when X is 1 and Y is zero. X Eqv Y is 1 only when both bits are the same—both 1 or both zero. The Not operator, on the other hand, works on a number by reversing the bits—a 1 becomes a zero and a zero becomes a 1.

Finally, for those who are curious, here's the answer to the question posed at the beginning of the section as to why −1 is True in Visual Basic. Each integer takes 16 bits. Not 0 is then

Not (0000 0000 0000 0000) = 1111 1111 1111 1111

You might expect this to be the largest integer representable in 16 bits (65,535 in decimal), but Visual Basic uses the leftmost bit for the sign. A 1 there means the number is negative. However, Visual Basic uses what is called *two's-complement notation* for negative numbers. In two's-complement notation, to represent a negative number you do the following:

1. Apply Not to the 15 bits that represent the number.

2. Set the leftmost bit to 1.

3. Add 1 to the result.

Therefore, for −1, take the bit pattern for 1:

000 0000 0000 0001

Apply Not:

111 1111 1111 1110

Add the leftmost bit as a 1:

1111 1111 1111 1110

Now add 1:

1111 1111 1111 1111

The result is that Not(0) is −1!

For an explanation of why this system really is useful consult any book on microcomputer architecture.

## KEYUP AND KEYDOWN

The KeyPress event reports on which ASCII-coded key a user pressed. The two events described in this section report much lower level information. They will tell exactly what the user did to the keyboard. If you need to determine whether he or she pressed CTRL, a function key, or the like, these are the event procedures to use. For example, if you want your application to supply context-sensitive help when the user presses F1, these are the event procedures to use.

However, these event procedures are a bit more complicated to use because you must distinguish, for example, between lowercase and uppercase letters. The syntax for both of these event procedures is the same:

Sub Control_KeyUp(*KeyCode As Integer, Shift As Integer*)
Sub Control_KeyDown(*KeyCode As Integer, Shift As Integer*)

Only the control that has the focus can respond to keyboard events. The active form has the focus if no control on the form does, unless you set the KeyPreview property to True. In this case, the form's keyboard events take precedence.

First, you have to use bit masking on the Shift parameter to determine whether the SHIFT key, the CTRL key, or the ALT key (or some combination of the three) was pressed:

```
If Shift And 1 = 1 Then Print "Shift key pressed"
If Shift And 2 = 2 Then Print "Ctrl key pressed"
If Shift And 4 = 4 Then Print "Alt key pressed"
```

This means there are eight possibilities. For example, set up a blank form and add the following event procedure:

```
Sub Form_KeyDown(KeyCode As Integer, Shift As Integer)
  Select Case Shift
    Case 0
      Print "Neither Ctrl nor Alt nor Shift key pressed"
    Case 1
```

```
        Print "Only Shift key pressed"
     Case 2
        Print "Only Ctrl key pressed"
     Case 3
        Print "Shift + Ctrl key pressed"
     Case 4
        Print "Only Alt key pressed"
     Case 5
        Print "Alt + Shift key pressed"
     Case 6
        Print "Alt + Ctrl key pressed"
     Case 7
        Print "Alt, Shift, and Ctrl keys pressed"
  End Select
End Sub
```

This procedure assumes that only the first three bits of the Shift parameter are used. Since Microsoft reserves the right to use the higher order bits, it may be preferable to start by setting the following:

```
LowerThreeBits = Shift And 7        '7 = 0111 in binary
```

and using this new variable in the Select Case statement.

The KeyCode integer parameter tells you what physical key was pressed. The code does not distinguish between the key and its shifted sibling. "A" and "a," "1" and "!" have the same codes. The codes for these integers follow the ASCII codes only for A through Z, and hence a through z, and 0 through 9 on the keyboard, and hence ! through (. All the remaining codes, whether for the arrow keys, the function keys, or the numeric keypad, are in the CONSTANT.TXT file. (If you intend to use these event procedures, you'll first want to incorporate this file into your project; see Chapter 5 for how to do this.)

For example, suppose you want to detect if a user presses F1. The code for this turns out to be &H70. After including this file into your program, a statement inside a KeyDown event procedure like

```
If KeyCode = Key_F1 Then        'easier the &H70!
    ' perhaps put a msg box with help information here
    ' or show a form until the F1 key was released
    ' check this with KeyUp!
End If
```

would be all that it takes. (You could use this to start context-sensitive help, for example.)

Here are some other sample codes taken from the CONSTANT.TXT file:

```
Global Const KEY_END = &H23
Global Const KEY_HOME = &H24
Global Const KEY_LEFT = &H25
Global Const KEY_UP = &H26
Global Const KEY_RIGHT = &H27
Global Const KEY_DOWN = &H28

Global Const KEY_NUMPAD0 = &H60
Global Const KEY_NUMPAD1 = &H61
Global Const KEY_NUMPAD2 = &H62
Global Const KEY_NUMPAD3 = &H63
Global Const KEY_NUMPAD4 = &H64
Global Const KEY_NUMPAD5 = &H65
Global Const KEY_NUMPAD6 = &H66
Global Const KEY_NUMPAD7 = &H67
Global Const KEY_NUMPAD8 = &H68
Global Const KEY_NUMPAD9 = &H69

Global Const KEY_F1 = &H70
Global Const KEY_F2 = &H71
Global Const KEY_F3 = &H72
Global Const KEY_F4 = &H73
Global Const KEY_F5 = &H74
Global Const KEY_F6 = &H75
Global Const KEY_F7 = &H76
Global Const KEY_F8 = &H77
Global Const KEY_F9 = &H78
Global Const KEY_F10 = &H79
Global Const KEY_F11 = &H7A
Global Const KEY_F12 = &H7B
```

# Financial Functions

Visual Basic 3 comes with a library of financial functions for handling standard calculations that everyone will occasionally need to do. (In fact, some of the financial example programs in Chapters 5 and 6 could have fewer lines of code and run faster if you use these functions.) Source code, however, is not supplied for these functions, which are installed in compiled form in a file called MSAFINX.DLL in your Windows \SYSTEM by the Visual Basic setup program. If you distribute a program containing these functions, you'll need to install this file for the user. The Setup Wizard (Appendix B) makes this easy.

Since the terminology in the help files may be obscure to people with no accounting or economics training, this section describes the functions most often used and the terms used in the help files to describe them.

Let's start with the function that would let you do a mortgage calculation. First off, if you look in the Help file for financial functions, all you see is a list as follows:

DDB Function
FV Function
IPmt Function
IRR Function
MIRR Function
NPer Function
NPV Function
Pmt Function
PPmt Function
PV Function
Rate Function
SLN Function
SYD Function

None of these would seem to have anything to do with a mortgage calculation. It turns out that the function you need is the Pmt function. It is described in the Visual Basic manual as follows.

"Returns the payment for an annuity based on periodic, constant payments and a constant interest rate."

Now the key word here (in fact the key word for most of the financial functions) is "annuity". An annuity is a fancy term for a series of payments made up over time. For example, when you have a mortgage, you start out with a (large) amount, make (many) payments over time, and end up with a 0 balance. (There are also balloon mortgages where the balance isn't 0.) In the retirement calculator from Chapter 6, you made periodic deposits over time and thereby ended up with a (large) amount of money at the end.

The syntax for the Pmt function is best explained as:

Pmt(*RatePerPeriod, NumPeriods, WhatYouStartWith, WhatYouEndUpWith, WhenDoYouPay*)

For example, to calculate a 30-year $100,000 mortgage at 8%, use

```
MortagePayment = Pmt(.08/12, 30*12, 100000, 0, 1)
```

**note:** *In all the entries (and the result as well), monies paid out are represented by negative numbers; monies received are represented by positive numbers.*

Here's a description of what the parameters in the Pmt function stand for

■ *RatePerPeriod* Usually the interest rate is quoted per year but you pay every month. This entry needs the interest rate per payment rate. You can ask Visual Basic to do the calculation. So if the yearly rate for the mortgage was 8% the RatePerPeriod would be .08/12 and you would use this in the first position.

■ *NumPeriods* This is the number of periods. For example, for a 30-year mortgage this would be 30 * 12. For a 20-year bi-weekly mortgage, this would be 20 * 26.

■ *WhatYouStartWith* In a mortgage, this would start out as the balance. If you were saving money for college, it would be what your initial balance was.

■ *WhatYouEndUpWith* In a mortgage, this would be 0. (In a balloon mortgage, this would be the "balloon payment.") For a savings plan, this would be the amount you wanted to end up with for retirement or college.

■ *WhenDoYouPay* Do you pay at the beginning of the period or at the end? Use a 0 for the end of the month and a 1 for the beginning. (For a $100,000 mortgage at 8%, it costs about $5 more per month to pay at the end of the month. Not that many banks allow you do to this, though.)

**note:**

*In the help files, this function is described as:*

Pmt(*rate, nper, pv, fv, due*)

*Microsoft's notation does not stress enough that the units you use for the various entries must be the same. For example, if* rate *is calculated using months,* nper *must also be calculated using months.*

## The Other Financial Functions

Now that you know the key terms and how one of these functions works, here are short descriptions of the other financial functions.

---

***FV Function*** This is the function used, for example, for a retirement calculation because it gives you the future value of an annuity based on periodic payments (or withdrawals) and a constant interest rate.

The syntax is:

FV(*InteresRatePerPeriod, NumPer, PaymentPerPeriod, StartAmount, WhenDue*)

Again, the first two arguments must be expressed using the same units. And for all arguments, monies paid out are given by negative numbers; monies received are given by positive numbers.

---

***IPmt Function*** This gives the interest paid over a given period of an annuity based on periodic, equal payments and a constant interest rate. For example, you could use this to check that your mortgage company's computers are reporting to the IRS the interest paid in a given year.

The syntax (using Microsoft's notation this time) is:

IPmt(*rate, per, nper, pv, fv, due*)

Where *rate* is the interest rate per period, and *per* is the period in the range 1 through the number of periods (*nper*). For example, the interest paid in the first month of the third year of a 30-year $100,000 mortgage at 8% is:

IPmt(*.08/12, 25, 360, 100000, 0, 1*)

(So you would use this in a loop to calculate the interest over a given year.)

**NPer Function** This function tells you how long (the number of periodic deposits/withdrawals) it will take to accumulate (disburse) an annuity. The syntax is

NPer(*rate, pmt, pv, fv, due*)

For example, suppose you are getting 5% on your money and you have $100,000 in the bank. To calculate how long it would take to spend the $100,000 that you have saved up if you withdraw the money at a rate of $1000 a month, use

NPer(.05/12, –1000, 100000, 0, 1)

**PV** This is the functional equivalent of "A bird in the hand is worth two in the bush." Getting $1000 10 years from now is not the same as getting $1000 now. How bad it is depends on the interest rates prevailing. So what this function does is tell you how much periodic payments made over the future are worth *now*. (The technical term for this is *present value*.)
    The syntax is

PV(*rate, nper, pmt, fv, due*)

The *rate* is, as usual, the interest rate per period, *nper* is the total number of payments made, *pmt* are the payments made each period. The *fv* entry is the future value or cash balance you want after you've received (made) the final payment. For example, if someone agrees to pay you $1000 a month for 10 years and the assumed prevailing interest rate is 6%, then this deal is worth:

PV( .06/12, 120, –1000, 0, 1)

to you now. (This is why lotteries can advertise big prizes but pay out so little. A $10,000,000 prize paid out over 20 years if the prevailing interest rate is 6% is worth about 6 million.)

*NPV Function* This is the net present value function. This function is used, for example, if you start by paying out money as startup costs but then get money in succeeding years. The syntax is

NPV(RatePerPeriod, ArrayOf( ))

You have to fill the array with the appropriate values in the correct order. For example, the first entry could be a negative number representing startup costs and the remaining entries a positive number representing value received. At least one entry must be positive and one entry must be negative. This function is more general than the PV function because using an array allows the amounts received or disbursed to change over time.

*Rate* This function gives the interest rate per period for an annuity. So you would use this to check on the interest rate you would really be paying if you actually responded to the standard advertising come on of "Only $49.95 a month for three years will buy you this gadget." (Use the cost today for the *pv* parameter.)
    The syntax is

Rate(*nper, pmt, pv, fv, due, guess*)

    The only entry you haven't seen is *guess*. This function uses an iterative procedure to arrive at the true interest rate. You can usually just guess .01 and let Visual Basic do the rest. What happens is the answer Rate is calculated by iteration. Visual Basic starts with the value of *guess* and repeats the calculation until the result is accurate to within 0.00001 percent. If, after 20 tries, it can't find a result, the function fails. If the function fails, try a different value for *guess*.

### THE REMAINING FINANCIAL FUNCTIONS

    The remaining financial functions are mostly used by business. Explaining them would take us too far afield.

*SLN and DDB Functions* These functions return the straight line and double declining balance depreciation of an asset over a given period. The syntaxes are:

SLN(*Cost, SalvageValue, LifeExpectancy*)

and

DDB(*Cost, SalvageValue, LifeExpectency, PeriodOfCalculation*)

**IRR, MIRR**  These give versions of the internal rate of return for a series of payments and receipts. IRR gives the ordinary internal rate of return and MIRR gives the modified rate where you allow payments and receipts to have different interest rates. The syntax for the IRR function is

IRR(*valuearray( ), guess*)

As with the NPV function, the *valuearray( )* contains the receipts and disbursements and must contain at least one negative value (a payment) and one positive value (a receipt). Also, as before, the value of *guess* is your best estimate for the value returned by IRR. In most cases, start with a guess of 1% (.01)

The MIRR function has the syntax

MIRR(*ValueArray( ), FinanceRate, ReinvestRate*)**

---

# The Numeric Functions

If you don't do a lot of scientific work, you'll be unlikely to use the information in this section very much. (One surprising use of the numeric functions is to draw curves. Chapter 12 shows you how to do this.)

**Sgn( )**  The Sgn function gives you a +1 if what is inside the parentheses is positive, −1 if negative, and a zero if it's zero. One non-obvious use of this for integers or long integers is a For-Next loop in this form:

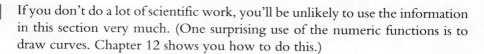

```
For I = A To B Step Sgn(A - B)
```

which, as long as A <> B, runs through the For-Next loop the correct number of times, regardless of whether A was greater than B or not.

▬▬▬

***Abs( )*** The Abs function gives the absolute value of whatever is inside the parentheses. All this function does is remove minus signs:

```
Abs(-1) = 1 = Abs(1)
```

One common use of the absolute value function is Abs(B–A). This gives the distance between the numbers A and B. For example, suppose

3 and B = 4

Then,

```
Abs(A-B) = Abs(B-A) = 1
```

because 3 and 4 are one unit apart. As another example,

```
Abs(ASC(A$) - ASC(B$))
```

gives the "distance" between the first two characters of the strings A$ and B$. You often use the Abs function to set up a tolerance test in a Do loop.

▬▬▬

***Sqr( )*** The Sqr function returns the square root of the numeric expression inside the parentheses, which must be nonnegative, or a run-time error follows.

▬▬▬

***Exp( )*** The Exp function gives $e$ ($e$ is roughly 2.7182) to the power $x$ where $e$ is the base for natural logarithms. The answer is single precision if $x$ is an integer or is itself a single-precision number; otherwise, the answer is a double-precision number.

▬▬▬

***Log( )*** The Log function gives the natural logarithm of a number. To find the common log (log to base 10) use

```
Log10(x)=Log(x)/Log(10)
```

which gives the common logarithm of the value (which must be positive) inside the parentheses. Another way to find the number of digits in a number is to use, for a number greater than 1,

$$\text{Int}(\text{Log10}(x)) + 1$$

For example, Log10(197) is between 2 and 3 because Log10(100) is 2 and Log10(1000) is 3.

As with the Exp function, the answer is single precision if $x$ is an integer or is itself a single-precision number; otherwise, the answer is a double-precision number.

**■■**

***Trig Functions*** Also for those who need them, Visual Basic has the built-in trigonometric functions Sin (sine), Cos (cosine), and Tan (tangent). The only problem is that Visual Basic expects the angle inside the parentheses following the functions to be in radian measure. To convert from degrees to radians, you need the value of $\pi$. The formula is

radians = *degrees* \* $\pi$ / 180

**tip:**

*The easiest way to find the value of $\pi$ is, early on in your program, to set up a global variable PI# using the Atn (arctangent) function in the form.*

```
Pi = 4 * Atn(1#)
```

This procedure works because the arctangent of 1 is $\pi/4$. You can also use the Atn function to find all the other inverse trigonometric functions.

The following table summarizes the inverse trigonometric functions as well as some other useful functions you may want to build from the built-in ones.

| Function | Gives |
| --- | --- |
| pi = 4\*Atn(1#) | Value of $\pi$ in double precision |
| e = Exp(1#) | Value of e in double precision |
| degrees to radians | Radians = degree \* 180/$\pi$ |
| radians to degrees | Degrees = radians \* $\pi$/180 |
| Sec (x) | 1/Cos (x) |
| Csc (x) | 1/Sin (x) |
| Cot (x) | 1/Tan (x) |
| ArcCos (x) | Atn (x/Sqr($-$x \* x + 1)) + $\pi$/2 |
| ArcSin (x) | Atn (x/Sqr($-$x \* x + 1)) |
| ArcCot(x) | Atn(x) + $\pi$/2 |
| Cosh (x) | (Exp(x) + Exp($-$x))/2 |
| Sinh(x) | (Exp(x) $-$ Exp($-$x))/2 |
| Log $_{10}$(x) | Log(x)/Log(10) |
| Log $_a$(x) | Log(x)/Log(a) |

# Chapter 8

# Procedures and Error Trapping

YOU'VE already seen how to use many of Visual Basic's event procedures. Event procedures are the core of Visual Basic programming, but they shouldn't be made too complicated. If an event procedure is much longer than one page—or even one screen length—it may be too long to easily debug. Consider doing some of the work in one or more of Visual Basic's general procedures. There are two kinds of general procedures in Visual Basic. The first type, *Function procedures*, lets you create new functions, thus extending the built-in Visual Basic functions that you saw in Chapter 7. *Sub procedures,* on the other hand, are smaller "helper programs" that are used (*called*, in the jargon) as needed. Sub and Function procedures help break down large tasks into smaller ones or automate repeated operations.

## Function Procedures

Start thinking about defining your own functions when you use a complicated expression more than once in a project. For example, suppose you need a random integer between 1 and 10. You could write

    Int((10 * Rnd) + 1)

each time you needed it, but this would eventually grow tiresome. Now suppose that the same program needs a random integer between 1 and 40, between 1 and 100, and so on. The statements needed for these are so similar to the preceding statement that you would want to automate the process—that is, to have Visual Basic do some of the work. Suppose you want to attach this function to the current form. To do this, open the Code window by double-clicking anywhere in the form or by pressing F7. Now choose New Procedure from the View menu (ALT+V+N) and the New Procedure dialog box will pop up, as shown here:

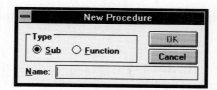

Now click the Function radio button (or use the ALT+F shortcut) and type a name. (The example uses RandomRange.) Click on OK, and a function template for the form shown in Figure 8-1 pops up in the code window. (You can also start a new procedure by typing the key word **Function** or the key word **Sub** followed by the name of the procedure anywhere in the code window and pressing the DOWN ARROW.)

tip:

*Right below these two list boxes, on top of the vertical scroll bar, is the split bar. When you are writing general procedures, being able to look at different parts of your code is very handy. As you drag the split bar with the mouse, the screen splits into two parts. The size of the parts depends on how far you've dragged the mouse. You can then use the CTRL+DOWN ARROW or CTRL+DOWN ARROW combinations to cycle independently through all the procedures attached to a specific form or module.*

The whole function will look like this:

```
Function RandomRange(X%) As Integer
   RandomRange = Int(X% * Rnd) + 1
End Function
```

**Figure 8-1**

Function template for the RandomRange function

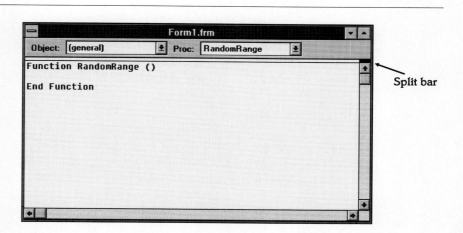

Split bar

Notice that the function template left out the $X\%$ inside the parentheses—you'll need to enter that as well.

Now you can use RandomRange just like a built-in function in any procedure attached to the current form. If you need to print a random integer between 1 and 10, you can write

```
Print RandomRange(10)
```

When naming the function (in this case, RandomRange), you must follow the same rules as you would for naming variables in Visual Basic. If you prefer, you can add a type identifier at the end of the name of a function or use the As identifier. For example, you could have written

```
Function RandomRange% ( X% )
Function RandomRange ( X% ) As Integer
```

In both cases, Visual Basic knows that the function returns integer values. The key to this function's smooth operation is the $X\%$. It's called a *formal parameter,* but it is easiest to think of it as a placeholder. You have seen parameters in various Key event procedures, such as KeyUp. To use (or call) this random integer function, you replace the formal parameter (the placeholder) with a numeric expression (a variable, number, or calculation) called an *argument.* Visual Basic then replaces all occurrences of the placeholder in the definition of the function with the value of the argument. In particular, Visual Basic does any necessary calculations and conversions to make the expression into an integar. Therefore, if

A = 3 and B = 2

then

```
N% = RandomRange(A * B + 37)
```

has the same effect as

```
N% = RandomRange(43)
```

which in turn is the same as writing

```
N% = Int(43 * Rnd) + 1
```

The value you send the function is sometimes called the *actual parameter*.

**caution:** *You shouldn't expect to get too large a random integer out of the RandomRange function. This is because RandomRange, like any integer expression, can't be larger than 32,767.*

The $X\%$ used as a parameter (placeholder) in the definition of the function has no independent existence. If you used $X\%$ as a variable somewhere earlier—even as a global variable—no assignment to its value ever affects the value of the function.

## Functions with More Than One Parameter

The function RandomRange works with one piece of information; that is, it's a function of one variable (or one argument). You frequently want the value of a function to depend on more than one piece of information. For example, suppose you want a range of random integers between $X$ and $Y$. You can modify RandomRange as follows:

```
Function RandomRangeXToY (X, Y) As Integer
   RandomRangeXToY = Int((Y - X + 1) * Rnd) + X
End Function
```

This may seem a little tricky. If so, try to see what happens with numbers like $X = 5$ and $Y = 37$. Multiplying Rnd by $Y - X + 1$ (33) and using Int gives a range between 0 and 32 (= $Y - X$). Finally, add $X$ to get the desired range (5 through 37).

If you want to make sure that the function uses only integer values, rewrite it as follows:

```
Function RandomRangeXToY (X As Integer, Y As Integer) As_
Integer
   RandomRangeXToY = Int((Y - X + 1) * Rnd) + X
End Function
```

Now the placeholders can only have integer values. If you set

```
Number% = RandomRangeXToY (2.7, 39.2)
```

then 2.7 is rounded up to 3 and 39.2 is rounded down to 39 when Visual Basic substitutes their values into the function definition. If you wrote

```
Number% = RandomRangeXToY(3, 300000)
```

you'd get an overflow error.

### AN EXAMPLE

The following program calculates the cost of mailing a letter:

```
Function Postage% (Weight As Single)
  'Calculate the cost, in cents, of mailing
  'a first-class letter of a given weight in ounces

  Postage% = 29 - 23 * (Int(-Weight) + 1)
End Function
```

(We use a trick to take into account the fact that if a letter weighs, for example, 3 1/4 ounces, you have to pay for 4 ounces. This means that in situations like this, we need to move to the next largest integer. Now imagine that you apply the Int function to −3.25. The result is −4. So we need to add one and flip the sign again to make it positive. This trick is the basis of the previous program.)
   Now, executing

```
Sub Form_Click ()
  'local variables:
  Dim WeightOfLetter As Single

  WeightOfLetter = Val(Inputbox$("Enter the weight in_
ounces:"))
  Print "The cost is"; Postage%(WeightOfLetter); "cents."
End Sub
```

and responding to the input prompt by entering 4.7 will produce this output:

   The cost is 121 cents.

To make the program robust, you need to check the information you send a function before you call the function. Otherwise, you risk a meaningless result.

With the Postage function, you need to check if the weight is a positive number. The following fragment does this:

```
If WeightOfLetter > 0 Then
   Print Postage%(WeightOfLetter)
Else
   Beep
   Msgbox "A letter must have positive weight."
End If
```

# Advanced Uses of Functions

Since the name of a function follows the same rules as the names of variables, choose meaningful function names; they will certainly make your program more readable as well as easier to debug. Keep in mind that unless you give it an explicit type identifier, the type of the function and its parameters defaults to the Variant data type (or to whatever DefType statement is currently in effect).

The general form of a Function definition is as follows:

Function *FunctionName* (*parameter1, parameter2, ...*)
   *statements*
   *FunctionName* = *expression*
End Function

where *parameter1, parameter2*, and so on are variables. These variables are referred to as the *parameters* of the function. The types of the parameters can be specified by type-declaration tags or with phrases of the form As type. Function names must begin with a letter and can consist of up to 40 characters, including letters, numbers, and decimal points.

If FunctionName (argument1, argument2, ...) appears in a Visual Basic statement, then the value of argument1 is assigned to parameter1, the value of argument2 is assigned to parameter2, and so on. After this, Visual Basic executes the statements in the function definition; the last value assigned to Function-Name inside the body of the function definition is the one used for the statement involving the FunctionName (argument1, argument2, ...). The argument entries argument1, argument2, and so on can be either constants, variables, or expressions.

A Visual Basic statement using (some people say *accessing*) a function is said to call the function and to pass the arguments to the parameters. The function is said to return its value. For instance, in the example in the previous section, the statement

```
Print "The cost is"; Postage(WeightOfLetter); "cents."
```

calls the function Postage, passes the argument WeightOfLetter to the parameter Weight. The function returns the value 121. You can even have a statement like:

```
Print "The cost is"; Postage(Weight); "cents."
```

only this time, Visual Basic looks for the variable named Weight and substitutes it for the parameter Weight. (Remember, parameters are placeholders—they have no real existence outside of that role.)

The type of value returned by the function is specified with a type-declaration tag (%, !, &, #, or $) appended to the function name, an As clause at the end of the Function line, or a DefType statement appearing above the Function definition.

Lines in your programs cannot simply use a form such as

```
FunctionName (arg1, arg2, arg3)
```

The call to a function *must* be part of an expression or statement. (It is most often placed in an assignment statement.)

You can only call a function when you use the same number of arguments as there are parameters in the function definition. Each variable argument can have the same name or a different name from its corresponding parameter, but must be of the exact same type (integer, long integer, and so on). If an argument is not a variable, its value must be of a type that can be converted to that of its corresponding parameter. For instance, an integer variable argument can be passed to an integer parameter, but not to a long integer parameter. However, an integer constant can be passed to a long integer parameter.

Nothing prevents a function from calling another function. You'll find yourself doing this frequently in order to increase the power of your Function procedures. Visual Basic allows you to call as many functions as you want from within a given function, but you can't nest function definitions. Only one function can be defined at any one time. However, functions can call themselves. This is called *recursion*; the subject is so fascinating and useful that Chapter 16 is devoted to it.

At this point, your functions in Visual Basic are manipulating the values of variables assigned to parameters; they haven't changed the values. As you saw in the KeyPress event, it's possible to change the values of variables assigned to parameters. This is because by default, in Visual Basic, the memory locations for the variables assigned to parameters are passed to the function. This lets Visual Basic make changes to the values of the variables. (See the section "Advanced Uses of Procedures and Functions: Passing by Reference/Passing by Value" later in this chapter for more on the subject.) In practice, however, you should rarely have to change the value of a parameter in a Function procedure. Generally, a function should simply manipulate existing values and return a new value.

As in event procedures, you can set up your own local variables inside Function procedures and have them be static or not, depending on the application. You can make all the variables in a Function procedure static by putting the keyword Static before the name of the function:

Static *FunctionName* (*parameter list*)

Form-level variables are visible to all the functions attached to that module or form. The purpose of using local variables is to avoid inadvertent side effects. A *side effect* means that something done in the procedure affects the rest of the program. If you use the Cls method in a function attached to a form, then every time the function is used, the form will clear; this is an obvious side effect. Any time you change the value of a parameter or a global, module, or form-level variable, you cause side effects.

There's certainly nothing wrong with controlled side effects. The key, though, is the word "controlled." You must know exactly when they're going to happen and what the fallout will be for the rest of the project.

## Leaving Functions Prematurely

You don't have to give every function an explicit value. Sometimes you are forced to exit a function prematurely.

```
Function BailOut (X) As Single
  If X < 0 Then
   Exit Function
  Else
.

.
```

```
      End If
End Function
```

This function bails out if a negative value is sent to it. Now calling the function with a negative value gives the function the value 0—the default value of any numeric variable. In general, a function that you bail out of has the default value associated to its type. A string function that you bail out of returns the null string "" as its value, for example.

You should rarely find yourself needing the Exit Function statement, and you probably wouldn't use it as in the preceding example. Check out the information you want to send to a function before you call the function (possibly by another function). The Exit Function statement should only be used if it makes the program clearer, or in emergencies. For example, some people would rewrite the FindSeparator function from Chapter 7 using an Exit Function because they felt it made the program easier to follow.

## Some Example String Functions

Suppose you want to write a function that would allow you to chop out any substring. You saw how to do this in Chapter 7; you use Instr to find out where the string is and then use Right$, Left$, and Mid$ to do the cutting. Here's the function:

```
Function CutSmall$ (Big$, Small$)
  'local variables
  Dim Place As Integer, Length As Integer

  Place = Instr(Big$, Small$)
  Length = Len(Small$)
  If Place = 0 Then
    CutSmall$ = Big$
  Else
    CutSmall$ = Left$(Big$, Place-1)+Mid$(Big$, Place+Length)
  End If
End Function
```

The local variables Place and Length defined here will, of course, have no effect on any other variable named Place or Length that might occur elsewhere within the program. Once you've finished defining a function, you can also use the Immediate window to test it if the form (module) to which it is attached is active.

As another example, suppose you want to write a function that counts the number of times a character appears in a string. This would be a function of two string variables, and it should return an integer. Let's call it CharCount%:

```
Function CharCount% (X$, Y$)
  'This function counts the number of times
  'the character Y$ is inside the string X$
  'If Y$ is not a character or Y$ does not occur in
  'X$ then this function returns zero
  'local variables: I, Count

  Dim Count As Integer, I As Integer

  Count = 0
  For I = 1 To Len(X$)
    If Mid$(X$, I%, 1) = Y$ Then Count = Count + 1
  Next I
  CharCount% = Count
End Function
```

First, notice the extended remark section. In defining a complicated function, you're best off explaining what's supposed to happen. Explain what kind of information the function expects to deal with, which local variables it uses, and what it is supposed to send out. (If users know what the function expects, they're more likely to check what they send it before the program blows up.) Most of the example programs in this book have, up to this point, been sparsely commented, mostly because the surrounding text explained it. However, when you are hired to write a program, this is the way you would be expected to comment it. In fact, you might explain what the local variables are doing as well.

The CharCount% function uses two local integer variables: Count and I. As you've seen, it's a good programming practice to Dim the local variables before going on to the main business of the function. Being local variables, they have no connection with any variables that might share the same name elsewhere in the program. The advantages this gives over the older Def FN in interpreted BASICs can't be stressed enough. (A complicated string-handling program might have 17 different functions with 17 different variables named I or Count, and you wouldn't want their values contaminating each other.)

Next, notice that the function initialized the Count variable to 0. This was done for the same reason that you would initialize a variable in the main part of a program: relying on default values is sloppy and occasionally dangerous unless you make it clear by a remark statement that you are doing so deliberately.

The For-Next loop runs through the string character by character, checking for a match and adding 1 to the value of the Count variable if it finds one. Finally, the value of the local variable Count is what this function will return. In this case, the body of the function ends with the assignment that defines the function. Using a variable like Count to accumulate information as a function works is quite common. When you're done, you use the "accumulator" that determines the value of the function in the final assignment.

As another example, let's return to the "find the next word program" from Chapter 7. Suppose you want to modify this program so it gives the next word, no matter what separator you use. Using a user-defined function makes this easy. All you have to do is replace the statement

```
AfterSpace = Instr(BeforeSpace+1, Phrase$, Separate$)
```

with a function that finds the next separator.

Before you look at an outline for this function, think about the information this function needs to *massage* (manipulate). Is it clear that it will work much like Instr except that the separators will be built into the function? Once you convince yourself of this, you will be able to understand the following outline for the function:

◆ The function works with a string and a position number.

◆ The function should search starting at the position after the position number and look character by character until it finds a separator.

◆ If successful, the function should return its position number.

◆ If not successful, the function should return 0.

Here's a function definition that follows this outline:

```
Function FindSeparator% (Phrase$, Position%)
   'local variables
   Dim Afterspace%, Answer%, LenString%, NxtChar$

   AfterSpace% = Position% + 1
   Answer% = 0
```

```
    LenString% = Len(Phrase$)
    Do Until (Answer% < > 0) Or (AfterSpace% > LenString%)
      NxtChar$ = Mid$(Phrase$, AfterSpace%, 1)
      Select Case NxtChar$
        Case Chr$(32), "!", "?", ".", ";", ":", ","
          Answer% = AfterSpace%
        Case Else
          AfterSpace% = AfterSpace% + 1
      End Select
    Loop
    FindSeparator% = Answer%
End Function
```

This function starts by looking from one position farther along in the string than the position passed as a parameter. This takes into account any previous uses of the function.

The local variable Answer% plays a key role in what follows. As Visual Basic moves through the loop, this variable accumulates information either by staying equal to zero (in which case no separator was found) or becoming positive (the value is the location of the separator).

The Do loop has to stop if either the accumulator (the value of Answer%) signals the hunt was successful or there's no place else to look (the loop has finished searching all the characters in the string). Notice that instead of using a Do loop with two conditions (a *Eureka loop*, in the jargon), you could have used multiple Exit Loop commands.

**note:** *The function could have put all the tests on more than one line. However, by putting the tests on the same line we speed the program up. For example, if we used three lines, then the program would look a little cleaner, but if the separator were a comma, you would be asking Visual Basic to process three lines of code instead of one.*

Using a Select Case statement makes it easy to add another separator to this function; you need only add the appropriate case to the function. In any case, if the character wasn't a separator, you move on to the next character.

Finally, the value of the accumulator variable Answer% will be 0 if no separator was found; otherwise, it will be the position of the separator. (You could have also written this as a function of three variables, much like Instr itself is.)

## Parsing Text

Next, suppose you want to examine the contents of a text box and print out the words one by one in a second text box in response to each click on a command button. The screen might look like the one in Figure 8-2. You want each click to print the next word. Supposing the command button is called FindWords, here's how the whole program might go. (Notice that this uses the FindSeparator function from the last section.)

```
Sub FindWords_Click ()
  'This event program uses the function FindSeparator
  ' to parse a phrase by searching for the separators
  ' . , : ? ; ! and the space it finds all words
  'contained in the phrase

  ' local variables
  Static BeforeSpace%, AfterSpace%
  Dim Phrase$, LenPhrase%, SizeOfWord%

Phrase$ = Text1.Text
LenPhrase% = Len(Phrase$)
AfterSpace% = FindSeparator%(Phrase$, BeforeSpace%)
SizeOfWord% = AfterSpace% - BeforeSpace% - 1
Do Until (SizeOfWord% > 0) Or (AfterSpace% = 0)
   BeforeSpace% = AfterSpace%
```

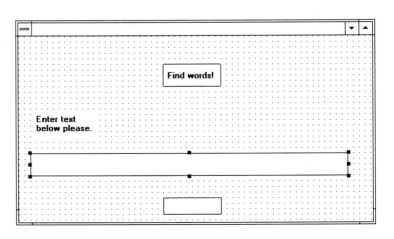

**Figure 8-2**

Form for MoreWords program

```
    AfterSpace% = FindSeparator%(Phrase$, BeforeSpace%)
    SizeOfWord% = AfterSpace% - BeforeSpace% - 1
  Loop
  If SizeOfWord% > 0 Then
    NextWord$ = Mid$(Phrase$, BeforeSpace% + 1, SizeOfWord%)
    BeforeSpace% = AfterSpace%
    Text2.Text = NextWord$
  Else
    Text2.Text = Mid$(Phrase$, BeforeSpace% + 1)
    MsgBox "No more words!"
    Text1.Text = ""
    BeforeSpace% = 0
  End If
End Sub
```

First, notice that the variables BeforeSpace% and AfterSpace% are static variables in order to preserve the information between clicks. If AfterSpace% = 0, then you've finished the text and won't enter the Do loop at all. If SizeOfWord% is also 0, then this small loop eliminates multiple spaces—another example of a Eureka loop.

The If clause changes the value of the static variables in preparation for the next function call and displays the word found in the second text box. The Else clause gives the last word and then a message box. Once the user clears the message box, the last line clears out the original text.

## An Example: A Pig Latin Generator

This section shows you how to write a "Pig Latin converter" that demonstrates many of the techniques you've learned so far. Pig Latin is a well-known variant on English that children often use: Ancay ouyay understandway isthay?

The rules are simple:

◆ All one-letter words stay the same.

◆ Words beginning with vowels get the suffix "way."

◆ Words beginning with a string of consonants have the consonants shifted to the end and the suffix "ay" added.

◆ Any q moved because of the preceding rule carries its u along with it.

◆ Y is a consonant.

◆ There are no more rules.

Here is an outline for a Pig Latin convertor in its simplest form:

While there are still words
        "Pig Latinize" the next word

To "Pig Latinize" a word, follow the rules just given. You will need two text boxes (Source and Translation) and a command button (with the control name Translate) to start the process:

```
' A pig latin generator
' This program translates a phrase into
' pig latin. It modifies the 'find word'
' program by adding a 'latinize' function
' Phrase$ is a form-level variable

Sub Translate_Click()

    Dim BeforeSpace As Integer, AfterSpace As Integer
    Dim SizeOfWord As Integer
    Dim NextWord$, PigWord$, FinalWord$, T$

    Phrase$ = Source.Text
    If Len(Phrase$) = 0 Then Exit Sub
    BeforeSpace = 0
    AfterSpace = FindSeparator (Phrase$, BeforeSpace)
    Do Until AfterSpace = 0
      SizeOfWord = AfterSpace - BeforeSpace - 1
      NextWord$ = Mid$(Phrase$, BeforeSpace + 1, SizeOfWord)
      If SizeOfWord > 0 Then
        PigWord$ = Latinfy$(NextWord$)
        T$ = T$ + PigWord$ + Space$(1)
      End If
      BeforeSpace = AfterSpace
      AfterSpace = FindSeparator(Phrase$, BeforeSpace)
    Loop
    FinalWord$ = Mid$(Phrase$, BeforeSpace + 1)
    PigWord$ = Latinfy(FinalWord$)
    Translation.Text = T$ + PigWord$ + Space$(1)
End   Sub

Function FindSeparator (Phrase$, Position% ) As Integer
    ' local variables are:
    Dim AfterSpace As Integer, Answer As Integer
```

```
    Dim LenString As Integer, NxtChar$

  AfterSpace  = Position  + 1
  Answer  = 0
  LenString  = Len(Phrase$)
  Do Until (Answer <> 0) Or (AfterSpace  > LenString)
    NxtChar$ = Mid$(Phrase$, AfterSpace, 1)
    Select Case NxtChar$
       Case Chr$(32), "!", "?", ".", ";", ":", ","
         Answer  = AfterSpace
       Case Else
         AfterSpace = AfterSpace  + 1
    End Select
  Loop
  FindSeparator  = Answer
End Function


Function Latinfy$ (A$)
  Dim FirstChar$
  If Len(A$) = 1 Then
    Latinfy$ = A$
  Else
    FirstChar$ = UCase$(Left$(A$, 1))
    Select Case FirstChar$
      Case "A", "E", "I", "O", "U"
        Latinfy$ = A$ + "way"
      Case Is < "A"
        Latinfy$ = A$
      Case Is > "Z"
        Latinfy$ = A$
      Case Else
        Latinfy$ = ShiftCons$(A$) + "ay"
    End Select
  End If
End Function


Function ShiftCons$ (A$)
  ' local variables
  Dim Count As Integer, Done As Integer
  Dim NextChar As String

  Count = 1
  Done = False
  Do
```

```
      NextChar = UCase$(Mid$(A$, Count, 1))
      Select Case NextChar
        Case "A", "E", "I", "O", "U"
          Done = True
        Case "Q"
          Count = Count + 2
        Case Else
          Count = Count + 1
      End Select
    Loop Until Done
    ShiftCons$ = Mid$(A$, Count) + Left$(A$, Count - 1)
End Function
```

As mentioned earlier, all you have to do is change the "find next word" program to one that, instead of printing the next word, prints the converted form. (Along the way, this function strips out all punctuation and spaces. It is left to you to change the program so that the converted phrase retains the original punctuation.)

The Latinfy function starts out by dealing with the special case of one-letter words and follows the first rule: it does nothing to them. The first case in the Select Case deals with vowels: words with a leading vowel add "way." The next case makes sure numbers and other special characters are not transformed. The Else case calls the most complicated function—the one that shifts consonants to the end.

The ShiftCons$ function works by using a flag to detect when, moving letter by letter, Visual Basic finally hits a vowel. By adding 2 to the count, you carry the *u* along with the *q* for this special case. The trick is that by starting with the count equal to 1 and incrementing the count every time a consonant shows up, Left$(A$, Count − 1) must, when the loop ends, contain the leading consonants.

This program is a good demonstration of how longer programs can be built from "building blocks." You'll see more about this later in the chapter under the section "Some General Words on Program Design."

# Sub Procedures

Function procedures can be made to do almost anything, provided that what you want to do is get an answer—a value—out of them. As mentioned before, although functions can change properties of a form or affect the value of form-level variables, it's not a good idea to do so unless the change is somehow related to what the function is designed to do. In any case, a function takes raw data, massages it, and then returns a single value. For example, although you can write a function that will work through a list and return the smallest or the largest value, it can't return both. A function can't directly return a sorted list. (You'll see many ways to sort lists in Chapters 9 and 16.) You tell Visual Basic you want to define a Sub procedure (some people call them *subprograms*) in much the same way you would with a Function procedure: use New Procedure on the View menu. Only this time, click the Sub option button.

Suppose, for example, you want to print a song, one with many verses but only a single chorus. The outline is clear:

```
While there are verses left
 − −     print verse
 − −     print chorus
Loop
```

Unless you wrote a truly bizarre function, you could not easily translate this outline into Visual Basic by using a function. You would need to include many statements of the form

```
X = Chorus ()
```

even though the Chorus function would not have any value to return. Unless you want to repeatedly type useless assignment statements or place the entire chorus in an event procedure, you'll need a new structure: the Sub procedure.

The structure of the simplest kind of Sub procedure—although one powerful enough to translate the outline—looks like this:

```
Sub Chorus( )
 − −     ' many print statements
End Sub
```

The first line has the keyword Sub followed by the procedure's name. A procedure name can be up to 40 characters. Next comes the parameter list, enclosed in parentheses, for the information the function will use. In this case, the Sub procedure uses no parameters. Even if your procedure uses no parameters, you must have the parentheses. After the parameter list come the statements that make up the procedure. Finally, there is the keyword End Sub, which, you've seen, ends all event procedures; it's used to indicate the end of general procedures as well. As with Function procedures, if you need to exit the Sub procedure prematurely, you can use the Exit Sub command in the body of the procedure as often as necessary.

If you imagine an event procedure as one of the main verses and the Sub and Function procedures as the choruses, then thinking of a program as a song with many choruses would be a good metaphor for designing any program, except that it misses one key point: each time you need the procedure, it's likely to be in a different situation. The procedure must change to meet new requirements. You need a way to transfer information between the main program and the procedure. You do this in much the same way as you did for functions: by using the parameter list. This parameter list is used to communicate between the main program and the procedure. When you call the procedure, you use the name of the subprocedure followed by the arguments (parameters), separated by commas if there is more than one:

NameOfProcedure argument1, argument2,...

You can also use the QuickBASIC version:

Call NameOfProcedure(Argument1, Argument2,...)

When you use the Call keyword, you must use parentheses around the argument list; when you omit the Call keyword, you must omit the parentheses. You can also call an event procedure directly in this way.

For example, suppose you want to print the old song "A Hundred Bottles of Beer on the Wall" on a blank form in response to a click. It begins this way:

100 bottles of beer on the wall,
100 bottles of beer,
If one of those bottles should happen to fall,
99 bottles of beer on the wall.

99 bottles of beer on the wall,
99 bottles of beer,
If one of those bottles should happen to fall,
98 bottles of beer on the wall.

98 bottles of beer on the wall,
98 bottles of beer,

If one of those bottles should happen to fall,
97 bottles of beer on the wall.

and so on.

Here's what you can write in the event procedure:

```
Sub Form_Click()
  Dim I As Integer

  For I = 100 To 1 Step -1
    Chorus I
  Next I
  Print "There are no more bottles of beer on the wall."
End Sub
```

The chorus Sub procedure looks like this:

```
Sub Chorus (X As Integer)
  Print X; " bottles of beer on the wall,"
  Print X; " bottles of beer,"
  Print "If one of those bottles should happen to fall,"
  Print (X - 1); " bottles of beer on the wall."
  Print
End Sub
```

On each pass through the loop, the current value of the variable I is sent to the procedure, where it replaces the formal parameter *X*. The I is also called the actual parameter, as was the case for functions. Also, just as with functions, the names you choose for your formal parameters are irrelevant; they just serve as placeholders. Finally, note that you do not use a type identifier for a Sub procedure. (Early versions of Visual Basic seem to have a problem with printing this many lines to a form; you might use a multiline text box instead.)

You may be thinking that this particular example seems a little forced; it's easy to rewrite the program using a For-Next loop. Of course this is true, but writing the program using a Sub procedure changes the emphasis a little; it's a lot closer to the outline. Now think about a more complicated program. Imagine a For-Next loop that surrounds 50 lines of code. In this situation, it's too easy to forget what the loop is doing. Most programmers prefer loops to be "digestible"—the whole loop ideally should not be more than a single screen of code.

Notice how in this program most of the nitty-gritty details have been pushed under the rug. This is quite common when you use procedures. Your event procedures will often have a fairly clean look, containing directions and repeated procedure and function calls. (In fact, some people would even put the directions into procedure calls and so make an event procedure into one long sequence of procedure and function calls. This too is a matter of taste.) In any case, it's unlikely that any event procedure will need to be very long.

In general, a Sub procedure (subprogram) is a part of a project that performs one or more related tasks, has its own name, is written as a separate part of the project, and is accessed by using its name followed by the correct number of parameters separated by commas.

A subprocedure must have the form

Sub *SubprocedureName(parameter1, parameter2, ...)*
  *statement(s)*
End Sub

When Visual Basic executes statements of the form

SubprocedureName argument1, argument2,...
Call *SubprocedureName (argument1, argument2, ...)*

the values (actually the memory locations) of the arguments are passed to the corresponding parameters and the statements inside the Sub procedure are executed. When the End Sub statement is reached, execution continues with the line following the call to the Sub procedure. As with Function procedures, you must use the same number of arguments as parameters and they must be of compatible types.

Using the Call keyword, the song program would look like this:

```
Sub Form_Click()
  Dim I As Integer

  For I = 100 To 1 Step -1
    Call Chorus(I)
  Next I
  Print "There are no more bottles of beer on the wall."
End Sub
```

QuickBASIC users should note that the DECLARE housekeeping statement is not normally used in Visual Basic and will usually not be accepted. The only time you need a version of the DECLARE statement is when you use Microsoft Windows' application programming interface functions (API) from within a Visual Basic program. (See "Accessing Windows Functions" later in this chapter and Appendixes A and E for more on these functions.)

**note:** *If you delete a control from a form, then any event procedures you may have written for that control become general Sub procedures for that form, using the same procedure names as before. For example, suppose you had a command button with a control name of Command1 and have written a Command1_Click procedure for it. Now you delete the command button from the form. The general procedure part of your form will now have a procedure called Command1_Click. This will also happen if you change the name of the control.*

**tip:** *To quickly work with any Sub or Function procedure attached to your form, pop up the View Procedures box by pressing F2 when you are in the code window. Figure 8-3 is an example of the View Procedures code window for the calculator sample application supplied with Visual Basic. To work with a specific procedure, move through this dialog box until the procedure you want to work with is highlighted and press ENTER. (You can also use the View menu or the CTRL+UP ARROW/DOWN ARROW shortcuts when you're in the code window to move through the procedures in your project.)*

## Some Simple But Useful Procedures

A sophisticated program may need to beep at the user to give feedback—more beeps may indicate more feedback. Having a general procedure called Many-Beeps in a program is quite common:

```
Sub ManyBeeps (X As Integer)
  Dim I As Integer

  For I = 1 To X
    Beep
  Next I
End Sub
```

Since I was dimensioned inside the procedure, it is a local variable. Now you can write

**Figure 8-3**

**View Procedures dialog box**

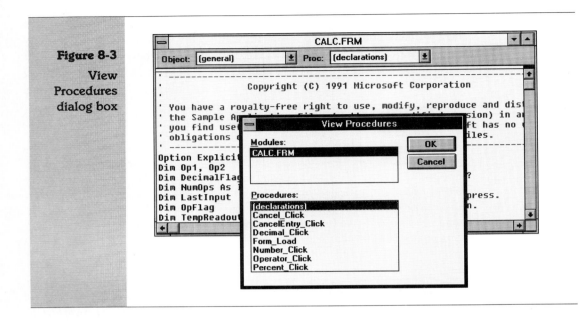

```
ManyBeeps 10
Call ManyBeeps(10)
```

for 10 beeps and

```
ManyBeeps 100
Call ManyBeeps(100)
```

for overkill.

Visual Basic lets you set up an event procedure that triggers itself after a set period of time has gone by (the Timer event is discussed in Chapter 10). Nonetheless, you may need to write a timer loop inside a procedure that stops processing for a fixed length of time. This is occasionally a useful debugging tool to use, rather than putting in a breakpoint (see Chapter 11) that stops the program in its tracks. To set up a timer loop to waste a fixed number of seconds in a Sub procedure, call the following:

```
Sub WasteTime(X As Single)
  Dim StartTime As Single
```

```
    StartTime = Timer
    Do Until (Timer - StartTime) > X
    Loop
End Sub
```

(Please see the section "The DoEvents Function" later in this chapter for more on this type of procedure.)

Since the Timer function returns only the number of seconds since midnight, this procedure would run into problems near midnight. One way around this is to use the DateValue function. Another way is to use the Mod function and the fact that there are 86400 seconds in a day. Just change the Do statement above to

```
Do Until (Timer - StartTime + 86400) Mod 86400 > X
```

To see that this works, assume that it is 2 seconds before midnight and that X is 3. StartTime will be 86398. Consider for now just the whole-number values that Timer will be taking on: 86399, 0(midnight), 1, 2, and so on. For these values, the expression involving Mod will be:

$$(86399 - 86398 + 86400) \text{ Mod } 86400 = 86401 \text{ Mod } 86400 = 1;$$

$$(\quad 0 - 86398 + 86400) \text{ Mod } 86400 = \quad 2 \text{ Mod } 86400 = 2;$$

$$(\quad 1 - 86398 + 86400) \text{ Mod } 86400 = \quad 3 \text{ Mod } 86400 = 3;$$

$$(\quad 2 - 86398 + 86400) \text{ Mod } 86400 = \quad 4 \text{ Mod } 86400 = 4;$$

from which it can be seen that the expression involving Mod will equal X (3) after 3 seconds and exceed X after 3 seconds, thus ending the loop.

**tip:**

*If you need to have a discernible time between beeps, place a short time interval between them with the Beep statement in the ManyBeeps procedure. You can do this by combining the ManyBeeps procedure with a call to the preceding WasteTime procedure.*

# Advanced Uses of Procedures and Functions: Passing by Reference/Passing by Value

There are two ways to pass a variable argument to a procedure: *passing by value* and *passing by reference*. When an argument variable is passed by reference, any changes to the corresponding parameter inside the procedure will change the value of the original argument when the procedure finishes. When passed by value, the argument variable retains its original value after the procedure terminates—regardless of what was done to the corresponding parameter inside the procedure. Argument variables are always passed by reference *unless* surrounded by an extra pair of parentheses.

For example, the statements

```
Display Variable1, (Variable2)
Call Display (Variable1, (Variable2))
```

for a Display Sub procedure pass Variable1 by reference and Variable2 by value. That is, the compiler creates a temporary copy of Variable2, passes that, and then abandons the copy after the routine finishes.

Consider the Sub procedure Triple, which triples the value of any argument passed to it:

```
Sub Triple (Num As Integer)
  Num = 3 * Num
  Print Num
End Sub
```

Notice the assignment to the parameter Num inside the procedure.

When the following lines of code are executed, the variable named Amt is passed by reference to the parameter Num.

```
Sub Form_Click ()
  'local variables:
  Dim Amt As Integer

  Amt = 2
  Print Amt
  Triple Amt
  Print Amt
End Sub
```

What you see is

2
6
6.

In this case, only one memory location is involved. Initially, the first line of code inside the Click procedure allocates a memory location to store the value of Amt. (See Figure 8-4(a).) When the Sub procedure is called, the parameter Num becomes the procedure's name for this memory location (Figure 8-4(b)). When the value of Num is tripled, the value in this memory location becomes 6 (Figure 8-4(c)). After the completion of the procedure, the parameter Num is forgotten. However, its value lives on in Amt (Figure 8-4(d)). (Note: Naming the parameter Amt produces the same result.)

Now consider the same Form Click procedure as above with the statement changed to Triple (Amt) so that the variable Amt is passed by value. The outcome of the revised code is shown here:

2
6
2.

This time two memory locations are involved. Initially, the first line of code allocates a memory location to store the value of Amt (Figure 8-5). When the Sub procedure is called, a temporary second memory location for the parameter Num is set aside for the procedure's use and the value of Amt is copied into this location (Figure 8-5(b)). When the value of Num is tripled, the value of Num becomes 6 (Figure 8-5(c)). After the completion of the procedure, Num's memory location disappears (Figure 8-5(d)). Since only the value in the procedure's memory location is tripled, the value of the variable Amt remains

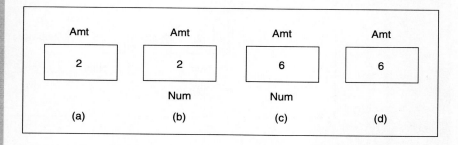

**Figure 8-4**

Passing a variable to a procedure by reference

the same. When the procedure is exited, the memory location for Num is released and the variable Num is forgotten. Note: The outcome of the program would be the same even if the parameter in the subprogram also was named Amt. There would still be two memory locations when the procedure was called—one for the argument Amt and the other for the parameter Amt.

Here's another example. The following Form_Click event procedure and its associated general procedure use passing by reference to validate what has been entered in an Inputbox. Here the value of the variable PhoneNum$ is changed.

```
Sub Form_Click ()
  'local variables:
  Dim PhoneNum$

  PhoneNum$ = InputBox$("Enter phone number (xxx-xxx-xxxx):")
  Validate PhoneNum$
  Print "Your phone number is "; PhoneNum$
End Sub

Sub Validate (Num$)
  Do While Len(Num$) <> 12
    Msgbox "Don't forget your area code."
    Num$ = InputBox$("Enter phone number (xxx-xxx-xxxx):")
  Loop
End Sub
```

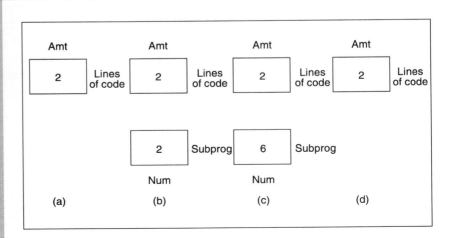

**Figure 8-5**

Passing a variable to a procedure by value

As another example, suppose you want to change a phrase by stripping out all the spaces inside a phrase—in other words, a more powerful version of the built-in function LTrim$. The outline is clear:

Find out where the spaces are and remove them.

You can use the Mid$ command to extract the nonspace character in the string. The code that strips out spaces is easy:

```
For Count = 1 To LenPhrase
  If Mid$(Phrase$, Count, 1) <> " " Then
    Temp$ = Temp$ + Mid$(Phrase$, Count, 1)
  End If
Next Count
```

When this loop ends, the value of Temp$ is the original phrase stripped of all its spaces. Now you have to decide whether you want to change the phrase or set up a new phrase. If you want the original phrase to change, incorporate the preceding fragment into a procedure:

```
Sub StripSpaces (X$)
  'local variables:
  Dim Count As Integer, LenPhrase As Integer, Temp$

  LenPhrase = Len(X$)
  For Count = 1 To LenPhrase
    If Mid$(X$, Count, 1) <> " " Then
      Temp$ = Temp$ + Mid$(X$, Count, 1)
    End If
  Next Count
  X$ = Temp$
End Sub
```

Now whenever you call the procedure via StripSpaces Phrase$, the original string Phrase$ changes. If you rewrote the preceding Sub procedure as a Function procedure, as in the following listing,

```
FunctionStripSpaces$ (X$)
  'local variables:
  Dim Count As Integer, LenPhrase As Integer, Temp$

  LenPhrase = Len(X$)
```

```
    For Count = 1 To LenPhrase
      If Mid$(X$, Count, 1) <>[{|"|}]" Then
        Temp$ = Temp$ + Mid$(X$, Count, 1)
      End If
    Next Count
    StripSpaces$ = Temp$
End Function
```

then the value of the function StripSpaces$(Phrase$) is the phrase stripped of all
its internal spaces, but the original Phrase$ is still intact. Of course, you can add
a line to the function to make it equivalent to the subprogram; all you need to
do is add the statement X$ = Temp$ at the end of the function.

In the following code fragment and function, the variable Bal is passed by
value to the function. The outcome is

8667.0178 is the future value of 1000

How would removing the parentheses surrounding Bal affect the outcome?

```
' Calculate future value after Yrs years with interest rate
' IntRate when Bal dollars is deposited and Dep dollars
' is added to the account at the end of each year
Din Bal As Currency
Bal = 1000
IntRate = .05
Dep = 100
Yrs = 26
Print NewBal((Bal), IntRate, Yrs, Dep);
Print "is the future value of"; Bal

Function NewBal (Bal, IntRate, Yrs, Dep)
  'local variables:
  Dim I As Integer

  For I = 1 To Yrs
    Bal = Bal + IntRate * Bal + Dep
  Next I
  NewBal = Bal
End Function
```

If you know that variables sent to a procedure should never be passed by
reference, you can specify that some or all of the parameters inside Function

and Sub procedures are to be passed *only* by value. For this, add the ByVal keyword before the parameter in the argument list. Here's an example of the syntax:

Function *Example* (*X* As Integer, ByVal *Y* As Single)

In this example, an integer variable passed to *X* may be passed by reference (the default) or by value (when enclosed in parentheses), but a single-precision variable passed to *Y* will always be passed by value, whether or not it is enclosed in parentheses.

Since procedures and functions can change the values of the variables used as actual parameters, any time you call a procedure attached to a form, you can think of yourself as temporarily making a new group of form-level variables. How do you decide whether to make a variable a form-level variable or send it as a parameter to a procedure? Most programmers follow the convention that form-level variables are for information that should be available to the whole form (like the value of π) and therefore you should rarely change the value of these variables inside a procedure. Procedures ideally should only change the values of the variables passed as parameters. The reason for this convention stems from the methods used to debug procedures. For more on this, see Chapter 11.

## An Example: Shuffling a Deck of Cards

Suppose you want to write a program to create and then shuffle a computer deck of cards. You can think of a deck of cards as being a string variable,

```
DeckOfCard$ = "2C3C4C5C6C7C8C9C0CJCQCKCAC2D..."
```

where a 0 is used for the 10—to keep all the cards the same length—and a *C* is used for clubs, a *D* for diamonds, and so on. (Windows doesn't support the low-order ASCII codes that give the clubs, hearts, diamonds, and spades symbols.) Obviously, since this string variable will have 104 characters, you'll want the computer to do some of the work. You'll see one slightly awkward method now and much better methods later, in Chapter 9.

In any case, since you want to change this variable when you shuffle the cards, you should write a Sub Shuffle(X$) Sub procedure, not a Function procedure. This procedure will be similar to the Jumble event procedure from Chapter 7. The only difference is that you have to move characters two at a time. (That's why a 0 was used for the 10.)

Here's the Jumble procedure rewritten as a procedure to do this:

```
Sub Shuffle (Phrase$)
  ' a Jumble program converted to a procedure
  ' jumbles by twos

' local variables are: LenPhrase,I
  Dim I As Integer, LenPhrase As Integer

  Randomize
  LenPhrase = Len(Phrase$) / 2
  For I = 1 To LenPhrase
    INum = Int((LenPhrase * Rnd) + 1)
    NewChar$ = Mid$(Phrase$, 2 * INum - 1, 2)
    OldChar$ = Mid$(Phrase$, 2 * I - 1, 2)
    Mid$(Phrase$, 2 * I - 1, 2) = NewChar$
    Mid$(Phrase$, 2 * INum - 1, 2) = OldChar$
  Next I
End Sub
```

In this case, the number of cards is half the length of the phrase, so you set the limits of the For-Next loop by taking half the length of the card string. Since the cards are located starting in the 1, 3, 5, 7... positions, you need to move two characters at a time inside the phrase in order to move to the next card. Otherwise, the Jumble procedure works exactly as before.

Now suppose you want to deal the cards in the course of writing a card program. Obviously, you should make the DeckOfCards$ variable a form-level variable:

```
Sub Deal
 'Form-level variable assumed to be DeckOfCards$
' local variable is Cards

  Dim Cards As Integer
  Call Shuffle(DeckOfCards$)
  For Cards = 1 To 52
    Print( Mid$(DeckOfCards$, 2*Cards - 1, 2) )
```

```
    Next Cards
End Sub
```

(Notice that we used the Call syntax in this example.) Again, the point of the 2 as the last parameter of the Mid$ function is that cards start in the first, third, and fifth positions, and so on.

# Passing Control and Form Information

You will often want to write a general procedure to manipulate properties of forms or controls or the forms and controls themselves. Properties of forms and controls can only be passed by value. For example, consider the following simple Sub procedure:

```
Sub ChangeText (ByVal X As String, Y As String)
    Y = X
End Sub
```

If you call it using

```
Call ChangeText(Form1.Caption, Y$)
```

then the current value of Y$ is the caption for Form1.

On the other hand, you will often want to affect the properties of a form or control by using a general procedure. For this, you have to declare the argument to be of the form or control data type.

The following code checks if a form is visible:

```
Sub BackAndForth (X As Form)

    If X.Visible Then
        X.Visible  = False
    Else
        X.Visible = True
    End If
End Sub
```

If it is, the procedure hides it; otherwise, it makes the form visible. Obviously, this kind of procedure must be in a module, since you will want to use it for many different forms.

Similarly, you can have a Sub or Function procedure that affects a property of a control. For example, a general procedure to change the caption on a control might look like this:

```
Sub ChangeCaption (X As Control, Y As String)
  X.Caption = Y
End Sub
```

However, suppose you tried to use this procedure in the form of

```
Call ChangeCaption(Text1, "New text")
```

where Text1 was the name of a text box. Then Visual Basic would give you a run-time error because text boxes do not have a Caption property.

The solution for this is to use a variant on the If-Then-Else loop in Visual Basic that allows you to determine what type of control is being manipulated. This takes the following form:

```
If TypeOf Control Is ControlType Then
  .
  .
  .
Else
  .
  .
  .
End If
```

(Use the online help to check the correct form of "ControlType.") For example:

```
Sub ChangeCaptionOrText (X As Control, Y As String)
  If TypeOf X Is TextBox Then
    X.Text = Y
   Else
    X.Caption = Y
   End If
End Sub
```

You cannot use the keyword Not in this type of control structure, so you will often find yourself using an empty If clause. A better way to write the ChangeCaption Sub procedure is

```
Sub ChangeCaption (X As Control, Y As String)
   If TypeOf X Is TextBox Then
     '  Do Nothing
   Else
     X.Caption = Y
   End If
End Sub
```

Another possibility is to use

```
If TypeOf X Is TextBox Then Exit Sub
```

Since there is also no version of the Select Case for controls, you may need the If–Then–ElseIf version of this control structure:

If TypeOf X Is...Then

.

.

ElseIf TypeOf X Is...Then

.

.

ElseIf TypeOf X Is...Then

.

.

Else

. .

.

End If

**tip:** *If you set the Tag property of the form or control to contain information otherwise not available at run time, you can use the techniques given in this section to process information that would otherwise not be available.*

## Object Variables

Object variables were new to Visual Basic 2.0 and give you even more flexibility in manipulating forms and controls than the techniques in the previous section did. For example, you can create a new copy of any form in your application that exists completely independent of the original. It can be manipulated or removed without affecting the original.

You declare an object variable with the same Dim or Static keyword you've already seen. (You can also have global object variables—see the section in this chapter on global variables.) Here's an example:

```
Dim FormVariable As Form1
Dim InfoBox As TextBox
Dim AButton As CommandButton
```

When you want to make an object variable refer to a specific object of that type in your project, use the Set keyword. For example, if your project has a form named Form1 and a command button named Command1, your code would look like this:

```
Set AForm = Form1
Set AButton = Command1
```

**note:** *When you are passing control and form information to a procedure, you are using an object variable implicitly.*

One reason object variables are important is that Visual Basic has two *collections* that give you information about all the forms in a project and all the controls on a specific form. The Count property of the Forms or Controls collection tells you how many forms you have or how many controls are on the form. You access individual forms or controls by saying, for example, Forms(0), Forms(1), and so on. Unfortunately, although the count starts at 0, Forms(0) is not necessarily the startup form. The order of the Forms( ) collection is unpredictable.

For example, the following code prints the captions of all the forms in your project:

```
Dim I As Integer
For I = 0 To Forms.Count - 1
  Print Forms(I).Caption
Next I
```

(Since the Count property starts at 0, we go to one less than Forms.Count − 1.)

## THE SET STATEMENT

The Set statement is useful when you need to refer to a form or control with specific properties. For example, suppose you need to know a non-enabled control on your form.

```
Dim AControl As Control, I As Integer
For I = 0 To Controls.Count -1
  If Not (Controls(I).Enabled) Then
     Set AControl = Controls(I)
     Exit For
  End If
Next I
```

This code moves through all the controls on a form until it finds one that is not enabled.

**tip:** *The Set command can also be used to simplify lengthy control references.*

Here's an example:

```
Set FooBar = HelpForm!HelpTextBox
```

Now you can write

```
FooBar.BackColor
```

instead of

```
HelpForm!HelpTextBox.BackColor
```

**note:** *The Set command does not make a copy of the object like a variable assignment would. Instead, the Set command points the object variable to the other object.*

This can occasionally lead to problems; if you change a property of an object variable that is Set to another object, the property of the original object changes as well (much like passing by reference in procedures does).

You can use the Is keyword to test if two object variables refer to (have been Set to) the same object. Suppose AControl and BControl are two object variables. A line of code like

If *AControl* Is *BControl* Then

lets you test whether they refer to the same object. (It is a wise precaution to find out if changing the properties of one variable will also change the properties of another!)

### THE NEW KEYWORD

You also can have object variables that refer to specific existing objects in your project. The syntax for this is a little different. Assume you have a form named Form1 in your project already. Then the statement

```
Dim AForm As New Form1
```

creates a new *instance* of Form1. This new instance has the same properties as the original Form1 at the time the code is executed. Use the New keyword only when you want Visual Basic to create a new instance of the original object when you use the object variable in code. For example,

```
Dim AForm As New Form1
Dim BForm As New Form1
AForm.Show
BForm.Show
AForm.Move Left - 199, Top + 100
BForm.Move Left - 399, Top + 200
```

shows two copies of the original Form1. The locations are determined by the value of the Left and Top properties of the original Form1. (We needed to change them to prevent them from stacking one on another because instances inherit all the properties of their parent.)

# Accessing Windows Functions

You have already seen that when you create a stand-alone Visual Basic program, you need to include the VBRUN300.DLL file (or a later version of this file)

with your program. A dynamic link library such as VBRUN300.DLL contains specialized functions that a Windows program can call on as needed. Microsoft Windows itself contains three dynamic link libraries that contain over 600 specialized functions. These are called Application Programming Interface (API) functions. Most of the time, Visual Basic is rich enough in functionality that you don't need to bother with API functions. But some tasks, like learning what chip (80286, 80386, or 80486) a computer is using or if a computer has a numeric coprocessor (80287, 80387, or 80486) must be done with an API function.

One problem to be aware of is that if you use API functions at all carelessly, your system will lock up and you will have to reboot.

Set the "Save before run" option when experimenting with API functions. An online version is supplied with Visual Basic Professional Edition (see Appendix A) and Microsoft at (206) 637-7099 may send it to you for a minimal cost if you call. It is also available for downloading from the MSBASIC forum on CompuServe. The printed version is in the *Microsoft Windows Programmers Reference* published by Microsoft Press. Another problem is that these functions are cumbersome to use and often require a fair amount of work before the information is usable to your Visual Basic program.

The DLL functions that you'll usually use are found in three dynamic link libraries: KERNEL.EXE, GDI.EXE, and USER.EXE. Before using a DLL function within a Visual Basic program, you must add a special declaration to the Declarations section of the form, module, or global module. For example, to find out what kind of chip is being used in the system, place the following statement in the Declarations section:

```
Declare Function GetWinFlags Lib "Kernel" () As Long
```

This tells Visual Basic that you will be using the Windows API function GetWinFlags, which is contained in the Kernel library ("Lib" stands for "library"). Since this is a function, you would expect it to return a value—in this case, a long integer because of the As Long clause. To use this function, you need to isolate individual bytes of the long integer by using masking techniques (see Chapter 7). For example, if the first byte of the value of this function is &H4 (decimal 4), then the chip used by the computer is an 80386. Here are the constants you need to fully analyze this value:

```
Const Is286 = &H2&
Const Is386 = &H4&
Const Is486 = &H8&
Const Has87 = &H400&
```

Now try the following Form_Click procedure after inserting the preceding Declare statement and defining the constants in the Declarations section of the form:

```
Sub Form_Click()
'this procedure analyzes the value of GetWinFlags
'in order to determine CPU type

  Dim CPUInfo As Long

  CPUInfo = GetWinFlags()
  If CPUInfo And Is286 Then
    Print "You're using a 286 chip."
  ElseIf CPUInfo And Is386 Then
    Print "You're using a 386."
  ElseIf CPUInfo And Is486 Then
    Print "You're using a 486."
  End If
  If CPUInfo And Has87 Then
    Print "You have a numeric co-processor."
  End If
End Sub
```

Another example of using a Windows API function is the GetSystemMetrics function contained in the "User" library. The Declare statement for this function looks like the following. (Like many API declarations, the Declare statement for GetSystemMetrics is too long to fit on one printed line. It must, however, be typed on one line in the code window. Some API declarations actually challenge the 255-character limit!)

```
Declare Function GetSystemMetrics Lib "User"
(ByVal WhatInfo%) As Integer
```

You send this function an integer value that tells the function what information you want reported back. This function gives you very detailed information about the system used by your application. For example, you can use this API function to find out if Windows is reporting that a mouse is in use. Here's a fragment that does this:

```
Const MousePresent = 19
If GetSystemMetrics(MousePresent) Then Print "Mouse is_
present"
```

Finally, most API functions expect the parameters used to be passed by value. As the preceding example indicates, you specify this in the Declare statement that specifies which API function you will be using.

It is extremely important that the Declare statement for an API function be *exactly* as Windows expects. Leaving off a ByVal keyword will almost certainly lock your system. One nice feature of Visual Basic Professional Edition is that it supplies a file with all the Declare statements for the Windows API functions. You can copy and paste this information inside your program freely. Obviously, for any serious use of API functions, having the necessary documentation (with the correct Declare statements!) is essential. Finally, if you want to go further with Windows API functions from within Visual Basic, I recommend Daniel Appleman's *Visual Basic Programmer's Guide to the Windows API* (Ziff Davis, 1993).

**note:** *See Appendix E for more uses of Windows API functions.*

# Code Modules: Global Procedures and Global Variables

The supplied (global) constant file CONSTANT.TXT discussed in Chapter 5 needed to be in a code module. (Remember that you add a code module by going to the File menu and choosing New Module—ALT+F+M.) The Code window for a code module is shown in Figure 8-6. This window looks much like the Code window attached to a form. Below the title bar, to the upper left of the Module window, is the Object list box. In Figure 8-6, the Object box tells you that you are working on general procedures for the module. To the right of the Object box is the Procedure list box, which gives a list of all the procedures for that module and the Declarations section. The display in Figure 8-6 also indicates that declarations are being worked on.

A code module can have declarations (such as DefType or Dim statements) that apply to all the procedures attached to that module. If you've written procedures attached to a code module, you can click the arrow in this box to see a list of them. Just as with the list box for event procedures attached to a form, you can then select a specific procedure to edit, press F2 to look at the Procedure list box, or choose the Next Procedure item from the Code menu to cycle through the procedures. (CTRL+DOWN ARROW is the shortcut.)

The Sub and Function procedures in code modules default so that they are available to the whole project. This is because where you place a procedure or

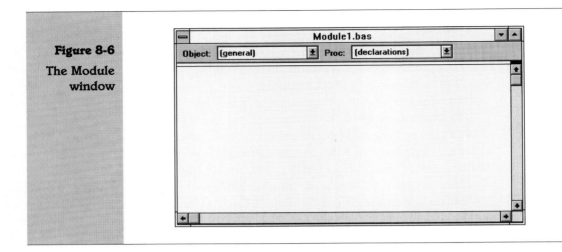

**Figure 8-6**

**The Module window**

declare a variable or constant determines which parts of the project can use it. If you attach a procedure to a form, the procedure will be usable only by procedures attached to the form. If you put the procedure in a module, the procedure will be available to the whole project. (Event procedures can be attached only to forms; Sub and Function procedures can be placed anywhere.)

Similarly, to make a variable into a global variable and so visible to every part of a project, place a statement of the form

Global *VariableName* As *VariableType*

in the Declarations section of any code module, as in this example:

```
Global Interest As Single
Global Years As Integer
```

The Global declaration can only be used in code modules; it may not be used in form modules.

Of course, just as form-level declarations can be superseded by declarations in procedures, global declarations will be superseded by declaring a form- or procedural-level variable.

Variables declared in a code module can be made to be local variables. To make a variable a global variable requires the Global keyword. If you use the ordinary Dim declaration syntax that you are familiar with in the Declarations section of a code module, then the variable is visible only to the procedures attached to that code module. Similarly, if you use the Dim statement inside a procedure attached to a code module, then that variable is local to the procedure. Figure 8-7 shows you the scope for variables within a Visual Basic project.

**tip:** *Although you may have many code modules and put global variables in each of them, it makes debugging easier if you keep all global variables in a single code module.*

You can also open up a code module window for any code module in the current project. To open an existing module, bring the Project window to the top of the screen and double-click on the name of the module.

Once you create a code module, saving it to disk is easy. When you are working with the module, open the File menu and choose Save File As (press CTRL+A or use ALT+F+A). You'll be presented with a dialog box. Enter the path name under which you want the module saved and press ENTER. Visual Basic will do the work. However, as in all the File menu operations, Visual Basic will save the code in a binary format not usually readable by other programs unless you check off the Save As Text option in the Save File As dialog box.

**Figure 8-7**

**Scope of variables**

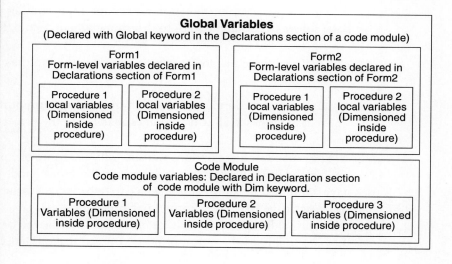

## Adding or Removing Code Modules

Just as you can add a form module to your project, you can add text or complete code modules that are stored on a disk. This lets you share code between projects (and often means you won't have to reinvent the wheel). On the other hand, code from one module may conflict with code from another module, especially if you are incorporating other people's code. (For example, names of procedures in modules must be unique, regardless of how many modules you have.)

To add an existing code module, open the File menu and choose the Add File option. A dialog box opens, asking for the name of the file. The convention is that code modules have a .BAS extension and form modules use .FRM. With work, you can reuse a great deal of QuickBASIC code by incorporating it into a code module (see Appendix A). To add code to a module choose Load Text and then the Merge option.

Occasionally, you will need to remove a code or form module from a project.

1. Open the Project window by clicking on any part that's visible or by choosing Project Window from the Window menu (ALT+W+P).

2. Select the code module or form module you want to remove.

3. From the File menu, choose Remove File (ALT+F+R).

## Fine Points About the Scope of Procedure

When you use a Sub or Function procedure inside another procedure, Visual Basic follows very simple steps to determine where to look for it:

1. Visual Basic first looks at procedures attached to the current form or module.

2. If the procedure is not found in the current form or module, Visual Basic looks at all code modules attached to the project.

The second of these options explains why the name of a procedure must be unique throughout all code modules. On the other hand, you certainly can have the same procedure name attached to two different forms; otherwise, forms could not have their own Form_Load procedures.

Finally, although the default for procedures attached to code modules is that they are visible to the entire project, you can make them visible only to the code module to which they are attached by using the keyword Private before the name of the procedure:

Private Sub *ProcedureName*
Private Function *FunctionName*

# The DoEvents Function

Usually you want Windows (and Visual Basic) to constantly monitor the environment for events to respond to. On the other hand, there can be a lot of idle time that you can use to do, for example, time-consuming numeric calculations or sorts. However, you don't want a Visual Basic application to stop responding to events completely. For example, this is something you may want to do when you write a procedure that wastes time, as you saw earlier in this chapter. Obviously, you need a way to tell Visual Basic to periodically respond to events in the environment and return to the calculation when nothing else needs to be done.

The function that does this is called DoEvents. Whenever Visual Basic processes a statement containing this function, it releases control to the Windows operating system to process all the events that have occurred. (Windows keeps track of events in an events queue and keypresses in the SendKeys queue.) Obviously, you should not use the DoEvents function inside an event procedure if it is possible to reenter the same event procedure again. For example, a Click event procedure may be called again by the user's clicking the mouse. If you forget about this possibility, your program may be caught in an infinite regression.

A loop that is processed only when no events are occurring is called an *idle loop*. Idle loops are written inside a special Sub procedure called Main that may be attached to any code module. You can have only one Sub Main procedure in any project. The format looks like this:

```
Sub Main ()
  Do While DoEvents()
    'Code you want to be processed during idle time
  Loop
End Sub
```

Next, you have to make the code module containing the Main procedure the startup module. To do this, go to the Options menu and choose Project

(ALT+O+P). In the dialog box that Visual Basic presents when you choose Start Up Form, choose Sub Main instead of a form. Once you've set a Sub Main as the startup object, Visual Basic does not load any forms automatically. You will have to write the code for this yourself using the Load and Show keywords.

Here's a simple example of an idle loop at work. Start a new project and add a code module. Next, add a global variable Count as a long integer by adding the statement

```
Global Counter As Long
```

to the code module. Next, add this code to the code module:

```
Sub Main ()
  Form1.Show
  Do While DoEvents()
    Counter = Counter + 1
  Loop
End Sub
```

Finally, make Sub Main the startup module and add a Form_Click procedure:

```
Sub Form_Click()
  Print Counter
End Sub
```

When you run this program, you'll notice that the number gets larger each time you click inside the form. The reason is that during the idle time (when you are not clicking), Visual Basic moves to the Main procedure and keeps adding 1 to the count. Since Count is a global variable, Visual Basic preserves the value for each call.

The DoEvents function actually gives you the number of forms loaded for the application. Idle loops stop when all forms are unloaded (or when Visual Basic processes an End statement).

Another common use of the DoEvents function is inside a Function procedure that is making a time-consuming numeric computation. Set up a timing loop or a counter so that Visual Basic periodically processes a DoEvents function to check what events may have taken place while it was calculating away. The little extra time that Visual Basic uses to manage the timing loop inside the function is well worth it.

# Error Trapping

Regardless of how carefully you debug your own program, it will often seem impossible to anticipate all the crazy things an inexperienced user may do. If you want your program to degrade gracefully and not just roll over, you'll want to prevent fatal errors. The command that activates (*enables*) error trapping within a given procedure is

```
On Error GoTo...
```

where the three dots stand for the label (line number) that defines the error trap. The labeled code must be in the current procedure. You cannot jump out of a procedure using an On Error GoTo command. On the other hand, the code for the error trap will often use other Sub or Function procedures.

A label is any identifier ending with a colon that satisfies the rules for variables. The label identifies the island of code starting on the next line, as shown here:

```
ErrorTrap:
  ' error code goes here
```

Since you do not want Visual Basic to inadvertently "fall" into the error-trapping code, it is quite common to have an Exit (Sub or Function) on the line immediately preceding the label for the error trap.

The On Error GoTo command can occur anywhere in an event, Sub, or Function procedure. Usually, the error-trapping code is inside that procedure. The only exception to this is when one procedure was called by another. In this case, Visual Basic will look to see if an error trap was enabled in the earlier procedure if one does not exist in the second procedure.

Once you start error trapping with the On Error GoTo command, a run-time error will no longer bomb the program. (Operating system errors cannot be helped, of course; Windows 3.1 will have fewer of them than Windows 3.0 had.) In any case, the On Error GoTo command should transfer control to a piece of code that identifies the problem and, if possible, fixes it.

If the error can be corrected, then the Resume statement takes you back to the statement that caused the error in the first place. However, you can't correct an error if you don't know why it happened. You identify the problem by means of the Err function. This gives you an integer that you can assign to a variable. For example, if you write

```
ErrorNumber = Err
```

the value of the variable ErrorNumber can help you pick up the type of error. Visual Basic can identify more than 80 run-time errors. The Trappable Errors item available from the Contents menu in the online help gives you the current list of errors, and you can even jump to short explanations of what might have caused any specific error. This table gives some examples:

| Error Code | Explanation |
| --- | --- |
| 57 | Device I/O error (for example, trying to print when the printer is off line) |
| 68 | Device unavailable (the device may not exist or is currently unavailable) |

The way you use this information is simple. Suppose an event procedure will be using the printer. Somewhere in the procedure, before the error can occur, place a statement such as this:

```
On Error GoTo PrinterCheck
```

Now, before the End Sub, add code that looks like this:

```
Exit Sub
PrinterCheck:
  ErrorNumber = Err
  Beep
  Select Case ErrorNumber
    Case  25
      MsgBox "Your printer may not be off-line."
    Case 27
      MsgBox "Is there a printer available?"
    Case Else
      M$ = "Please tell the operator (= program author?) that"
      M$ = M$ + Chr$(10) + Chr$(13)    'New Line
      M$ = M$ +"error number"+ Str$(ErrorNumber) +_" occurred."
      MsgBox M$
      End
  End Select

M$ = "If the error has been corrected click on OK."
M$ = M$ + Chr$(10) + Chr$(13)
M$ = M$ + "Otherwise click on Cancel."
Continue = MsgBox(M$, 1)
If Continue = 1 Then Resume Else End
```

The idea of this error trap is simple, and the Select Case statement is ideal. Each case tries to give some indication of where the problem is and, if possible, how to correct it. If you reach the Case Else, the error number has to be reported. In any case, the final block gives you the option of continuing or not by using a message box with two buttons. You might want to get into the habit of writing a general procedure that analyzes the error code. The error trap inside a procedure just sends control to the general procedure. If you do this, you can reuse the general procedure in many different projects.

Error trapping isn't a cure-all. Obviously, very little can be done about a hard disk crash or the user's running out of paper.

A variant on the Resume command lets you bypass the statement that may have caused the problem. If you use

```
Resume Next
```

Visual Basic begins processing at the statement following the one that caused the error. You can also resume execution at any line of code that has been previously identified with a label. For this, use

Resume *Label*

It is unusual to have labels in Visual Basic except in connection with error trapping. Nonetheless, for compatibility with older BASICs, Visual Basic does let you use the unconditional GoTo or GoSub to transfer to the line of code following the label, but there is almost never any reason to use an unconditional GoTo, and GoSubs are far less flexible than procedures.

Both the Resume and Resume Next commands behave differently if Visual Basic has to move backward to find the error trap in another procedure. Recall that this happens when one procedure is invoked by a previous procedure and the current procedure doesn't have an error trap. In both cases, the statement executed by Visual Basic will not be in the procedure where the error occurred. For the Resume command, Visual Basic will call the original procedure again. For the Resume Next command, Visual Basic will execute the statement after the call to the original procedure. You will never get back to the original procedure.

Suppose the chain of procedural calls goes back even further: Procedure1 calls Procedure2, which calls Function3. Now an error occurs in Function3, but the only error handler is in Procedure1. If there is a Resume command in the error handler in Procedure1, Visual Basic actually goes to the statement that called Procedure2.

Because this is unwieldy and so prone to problems, it is probably better to rely only on error handlers that occur in a specific procedure. If one procedure calls another, turn off the error handler in the calling routine.

Occasionally, when debugging a program, it's helpful to know what the error message for the last error was (for example, to place it in a message box). The command that does this is

```
ErrorMessage$ = Error$
```

You can also use

```
ErrorMessage$ = Error$(ErrorNumber)
```

to give the error message corresponding to a specific error number. Of course, Visual Basic gives the current error number as the value of the Err function.

There's one other error-handling function, Erl (Error Line). If you get really desperate and need to find the line that caused the error and Visual Basic isn't stopping the program at that line, you can do the following:

1. Add line numbers before every statement in the procedure.

2. Add a Debug.Print Erl statement inside the error trap.

When developing a program, you may want to test how your error handler works. Visual Basic includes the statement

```
Error(errorcode number)
```

which, when processed, makes Visual Basic behave as if the error described by the given error number had actually occurred. This makes it easier to develop the trap.

If you are confident that you will no longer need an error trap, you can disable error trapping with the statement

```
On Error GoTo 0
```

Similarly, you can change which error trap is in effect by using another On Error GoTo statement. Be sure to have an Exit command between the error traps. Visual Basic uses the last processed On Error GoTo statement to decide where to go.

# Some General Words on Program Design

The usual improved methods for writing programs—often called modular, top-down, structured program design—developed in the 1970s and 1980s from rules of thumb that programmers learned through experience in using conventional programming languages. An event-driven language like Visual Basic requires some obvious shifts. For one thing, there is no "top" of the program. Nonetheless, when you have something hard to do, you first divide it into several smaller jobs. Moreover, with most jobs, the *subtasks* (the smaller jobs) have a natural order in which they should be done. (You dig a hole for the foundation before you call the cement truck.) Write programs from the general to the particular. Stub out the code that you'll later implement more fully. After you design the interface for your Visual Basic project, start by looking at the big picture (what are the event procedures supposed to do?) and then, in stages, break that down. This lets you keep track of the forest even when there are lots of trees.

Your first outline lists the event procedures and the jobs they have to do. Keep on refining your outline by adding helper Sub and Function procedures for the jobs the event procedures are supposed to do until the pieces to be coded for all the procedures are well within your limits. Stop massaging the problem (breaking down the jobs) when you can shut your eyes and visualize the code for the procedure to accomplish the task you set out for it. Sometimes this "step-wise refinement" is described as "relentless massage." Since programmers often say "massage a problem" when they mean "chew it over and analyze it," the metaphor is striking—and useful.

Even if you can see how to program two completely separate jobs in one Sub or Function procedure, it's usually better not to do so. Sticking to one job per procedure makes it easier both to debug the procedure and to optimize the code in it.

Often, professional programmers are hired to modify programs written by other people. Imagine trying to modify a big program that wasn't written cleanly—if, for example, no distinction was made between local and global variables (all variables were global) and no attempt was made to write the program in digestible pieces with clear lines of communication between the pieces.

What happens? Because all variables are global, a little change you make in a small module could foul up the whole program. Because the pieces of the program aren't digestible and the way they communicate is unclear, you can't be sure how they relate. Anything you do, even to one line of code, may introduce side effects—possibly disastrous ones.

This kind of disaster was common until the late 1960s or early 1970s. Companies first spent millions of dollars having programs modified; then they spent more money trying to anticipate the potential side effects the changes they just paid for might cause. Finally, they hoped that more time (and more money) would fix the side effects. No matter where they stopped, they never could be certain that the programs were free of bugs. Top-down design, when combined with programming languages that allow local and global variables, can stop side effects completely; programs still have bugs, but these bugs don't cause epidemics. If you fix a small module in a giant, but well-designed program, then you know how the changes affect everything; it is clear how the parts of the program communicate with each other. Only global form-level variables and parameters need to be checked.

Ultimately, you will develop your own style for writing Visual Basic programs, and what works for one person may not work for another. Still, just as artists benefit from knowing what techniques have worked in the past, programmers can learn from what programmers have done before them.

The first rule is still "Think first—code later." You have some idea of what needs to be done and so you design the interface and start writing code. When your first attempt doesn't work, you keep on modifying your project until it does (or seems to) work. This is usually referred to (sometimes with pride, sometimes with disdain) as "hacking away at the keyboard."

Of course, almost everyone will occasionally write programs with little or no preparation (you may need a ten-line program to print out a label or something); that's one of the virtues of any BASIC, and Visual Basic is no exception. Where do you draw the line? How long must a program be before it can benefit from some paper and a pencil? The answer is to know your own limits. You may find it hard to write a program longer than one screen or with more than one event procedure without some sort of outline. If you try to do it without an outline, it might end up taking longer than if you had written an outline first.

Outlines don't have to be complicated. The complete outline for the Pig Latin program was as follows:

Two text boxes and a command button

text1 for text
text2 for translation

Command button starts process

While there are still words
  latinize the next word

To latinize a word
  one letter words stay the same
  beginning vowels -> add way
  beginning consonants (y, qu = conson) -> ROTATE and add ay
ROTATE
  find conson
  move it to end

This may be a little hard for others to use, but that's not the point of an outline. Your outlines are for you. In particular, outlines should help you fix the concepts that you'll use in the program. You may find it a good rule that when each line in your outline corresponds to ten or fewer lines of code, you've done enough outlining and should start writing. (Of course, only practice will let you see at a glance how long the coded version is likely to be.)

Some people like to expand their outlines to pseudocode. This is especially common if you are developing a program with or for someone else. *Pseudocode* is an ill-defined cross between a programming language and English. While everyone seems to have his or her own idea of what pseudocode should look like, most programmers do agree that a pseudocode description (unlike an outline) should be sufficiently clear and detailed that any competent programmer can translate it into a running program.

Here's a pseudocode version of part of the preceding outline:

```
Function(latinize NEXT WORD)
  IF Length(NEXT WORD) = 1 THEN do nothing
  IF FirstLetter(NEXT WORD) = a,i,e,o,u THEN
      latinize(NEXT WORD) = NEXT WORD + WAY
  ELSE
    Find(leading consonants of NEXT WORD)  ' (qu a consonant)
latinize(NEXT WORD) = NEXT WORD - leading consonants + ay
```

The point is that, although a phrase such as

latinize(NEXT WORD) = NEXT WORD – leading consonants + ay

doesn't seem on the surface to be very close to Visual Basic code, it is for an experienced programmer.

# Chapter 9

# Arrays, Grids, and Records

**W**HEN you use object variables (as shown in Chapter 8) to create a new control, you get an identical copy of the parent control. That means the event procedures for the new instance are *exactly* the same as those for the parent control. Suppose you need to create a new control with different event procedures attached to it. Visual Basic does this by grouping related controls in a structure called a *control array*. The controls in a control array share common properties but use a parameter to distinguish among them. This parameter identifies the specific control and gives you the flexibility you will need. You'll see how to handle control arrays in the first part of this chapter as well as more on the differences between them and object variables.

Next, you'll see variable arrays. You use a *variable array* (most people simply say an *array*) when you need to set aside space in the computer's memory that you can use in a systematic way while a program is running. You use these arrays to store lists and tables. Once you have a list, of course, you'll need to have fast and effective ways to search and sort the contents. This chapter covers some of the many methods known for searching and sorting. (Chapter 16 covers some more sophisticated methods.)

You'll also see how to use one of the three custom controls supplied with Visual Basic 3: the *grid* control. This control makes it easy to display tabular information. You can also use this control to write your own spreadsheet or display information from a database. Finally, you'll see how to create records. *Records* let you create variables that combine variables of many types into one.

## Control Arrays

You may have inadvertently given two controls of the same type the same control name or tried to copy a control using the Edit menu. If you did, then you saw a dialog box that looks like the one in Figure 9-1. Any time you use the same control name (the value of the Name property) more than once while designing a Visual Basic application, Visual Basic asks you whether you really want to create a control array. Click the Yes button (or press ENTER), and you now can add more controls of the same type while the application is running. Each new control in a control array is called an *element* of the control array. (To more easily follow this discussion, you might want to create two text boxes with the control name of Money and set up the same control array as in Figure 9-1.)

Since both controls now have the same name, Visual Basic needs a way to distinguish them. You do this with the Index property. When you ask Visual Basic to create a control array, Visual Basic gives the first control an Index property of zero and the second control an Index property of 1. Like any properties of Visual Basic objects, you can change them at design time using the properties box. In fact, if you assign any number to the Index property of a control at design time, Visual Basic automatically creates a control array. This lets you create a control array without having to use two controls at design time. In theory, you can have up to 255 elements in a control array (because you can have up to 255 controls on a form) but that would be very unusual—as it would waste too many of Windows' resources.

**note:**  *It's best to create the control array first before writing any event procedures for its first element.*

Suppose you want to work with the Change procedure for an element of the text box control array created as in Figure 9-1. When you move to the Code window by, say, double-clicking one of these text boxes from the control

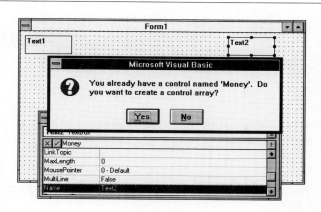

**Figure 9-1**

Message box to create a control array

array, you'll see something like the screen in Figure 9-2. Notice that the Change event procedure template looks a little different from anything you've seen before. Instead of having no parameters, as the Change procedure ordinarily does, this event procedure now uses a new parameter, *Index As Integer*.

This index parameter is the key to the smooth functioning of control arrays. If you want to use the Change procedure for any element of the control array, call it with the appropriate index parameter:

```
Money_Change(0)         'applies to the original text box
Money_Change(1)         'applies to the second text box
```

For example, add the following code to the event procedure template shown in Figure 9-2:

```
Sub Money_Change (Index As Integer)
   If Index = 0 Then
     Print "You typed in text box 0"
   Else
     Print "You typed in text box 1"
   End If
End Sub
```

Now, when you type in one of the text boxes, Visual Basic calls this event procedure *and* passes the index parameter to the procedure. In this way, the event procedure can use the index to determine what to do. When you type in the text box with the Index property of zero, Visual Basic activates the If clause inside this event procedure and so displays text telling you where you

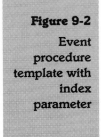

**Figure 9-2**

Event procedure template with index parameter

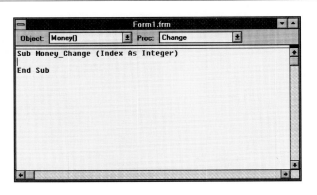

typed. Otherwise, Visual Basic processes the Else clause. The If-Then-Else combined with the index parameter lets the event procedure determine where you typed. (By the way, do you see why changing the Text1.Text property instead of using ordinary Print statements, as was done in the example, would not have worked?)

Any event procedure that would work for a single control can be used for a control array of that type while a program is running. Visual Basic adds an index parameter as the first parameter to the parameter list for the given event procedure. For example, the KeyPress event procedure for the control array of Money text boxes now starts out as

```
Sub Money_KeyPress(Index As Integer, KeyAscii As Integer)
```

instead of

```
Sub Money_KeyPress(KeyAscii As Integer)
```

as it would for an ordinary text box.

If you inadvertently added a control to a control array at design time, you can remove it by changing the control name or deleting the control. However, once Visual Basic creates a control array, you must change all the control names or delete all the controls that were in the array in order to eliminate the control array. At that point, you can reuse the name.

## Adding and Removing Controls in a Control Array

Once you've created a control array at design time, you can add controls while the application is running. To do this, you use a variation of the Load command that you already used to load a new form in an application with multiple forms. For example, suppose you want to add four new text boxes to the Money text box control array created in the previous section. To do this when the startup form loads, all you need to do is add the following code to the Form_Load event procedure for the startup form:

```
Sub Form_Load()
  Dim I As Integer

  For I = 2 To 5
    Load Money(I)
    Money(I).Text = "Text box #" + Str$(I)
```

```
    Next I
End Sub
```

Whenever Visual Basic loads a new element of a control array, the object is invisible—the visible property is set to False. All other properties (except the TAB Index and Control Array Index) are copied from the object that has the lowest index in the array. In particular, even if you modify the preceding Form_Load procedure to read

```
Sub Form_Load()
  Dim I As Integer
  For I = 2 To 5
    Load Money(I)
    Money(I).Text = "Text Box #" + Str$(I)
    Money(I).Visible = True
  Next I
End Sub
```

all you will see is the fifth text box. This is because the Left and Top properties start out the same for all the newly created controls. They are the same as Money(0).Left and Money(0).Top. This means that newly created controls in a control array default to being stacked one on top of the other. Because of this, you'll often find yourself applying the Move method to controls in a control array after you tell Visual Basic to load them. For example, suppose you want to place the newly loaded text boxes on the far left. Then, using the default size for the height of a text box, you might write

```
Sub Form_Load()
  Dim I As Integer

  For I = 2 To 5
    Load Money(I)
    Money(I).Text = "Text Box #" + Str$(I)
    Money(I).Move 0, 495*(I-2)
    Money(I).Visible = True
  Next I
End Sub
```

The key line

```
Money(I).Move 0, 495*(I-2)
```

starts at the top left when I = 2, because the command is then

```
Money(I).Move = 0, 0
```

On each pass through the loop, the location for the top of the box moves down by the default height of a text box (495 twips), as shown in Figure 9-3. You can use the UnLoad statement to remove any element of a control array that you added at run time. You cannot use the Unload statement to remove the original elements of the control array that you created at design time. For example, if you add the Click procedure

```
Sub Form_Click()
  Static I As Integer

  If I < 4 Then
    Unload Money(I+2)
    I = I + 1
  Else
    Exit Sub
  End If
End Sub
```

each click on an empty place in the form removes the next control in the control array, but this routine will not remove the initial element in the control array.

You must be careful, of course; you can only load or unload an element of a control array once. If you try to load or unload a control array element twice in succession, Visual Basic gives a run-time error you can trap (Err = 360).

**Figure 9-3**

Demonstration of loading labels in a control array

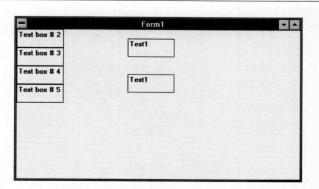

## An Example: A Square Control Array of Labels

The ability to position elements of a control array precisely is important. As an example, later in the chapter, in the section "An Example: Magic Squares," you'll see a program that creates magic squares. (A *magic square* is one in which the sum of all the rows, columns, and diagonals add up to the same number.) For this version, you'll need a control array of bordered labels named BoxLabel on a blank form with maximal size. You'll also need an odd number of rows and columns. Figure 9-4 shows an example of a magic square created by this program. Moreover, the labels should be square with a size in twips determined by a variable called LabelSize. (The section "The Grid Control" will show you a somewhat more efficient method of creating pigeonholes for displaying data.)

Here's the outline for the steps needed to put a square array of labels on a form for the magic square program:

1. Maximize the form and find its height and width using the Screen object.

2. Get the number *n* of labels and the size.

3. If either *n* * LabelSize > Screen.Height or *n* * LabelSize > Screen.Width, or if you would exceed the limits (255) on the number of controls on a form, the program displays a message box saying the label size is too big.

**Figure 9-4**

**7 × 7 magic square**

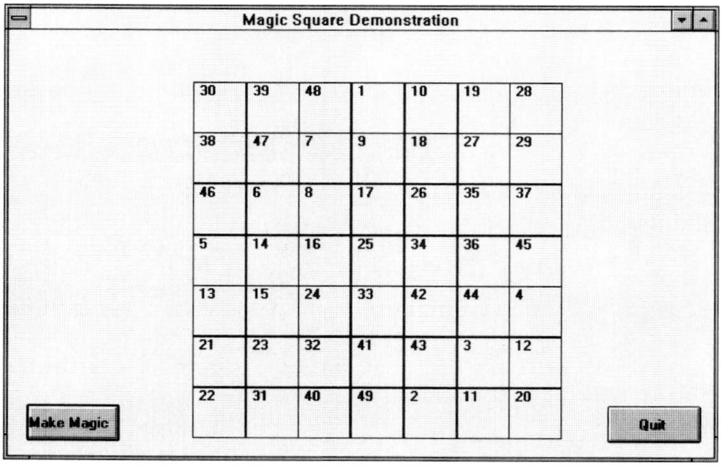

| Magic Square Demonstration | | | | | | |
|------|------|------|------|------|------|------|
| 30 | 39 | 48 | 1 | 10 | 19 | 28 |
| 38 | 47 | 7 | 9 | 18 | 27 | 29 |
| 46 | 6 | 8 | 17 | 26 | 35 | 37 |
| 5 | 14 | 16 | 25 | 34 | 36 | 45 |
| 13 | 15 | 24 | 33 | 42 | 44 | 4 |
| 21 | 23 | 32 | 41 | 43 | 3 | 12 |
| 22 | 31 | 40 | 49 | 2 | 11 | 20 |

Make Magic          Quit

4. Otherwise, load the labels.

5. Arrange the labels in a square on the form by moving them to the correct places.

Where should the labels be moved? Since Screen.Width/2 is the center of a horizontal line and Screen.Height/2 is the center of a vertical line, for the horizontal you start at

Screen.Width/2 − (*n*/2) * LabelSize

where *n* is the number of controls/rows, and use

Screen.Height/2 − (*n*/2) * LabelSize

for the vertical.

Here's the code. First, you'll need some form-level variables and constants. For these, enter

```
Dim NumberOfDim As Integer, Size As Integer
    Dim LabelSize As Integer
```

Next, the Form_Load procedure determines the number of rows and columns, as well as their size:

```
Sub Form_Load ()
  'Local variables
  Dim I As Integer
  Dim X As String, L As String

  WindowState = 2                            'maximal
  X = InputBox$("Number of dimensions?")
  NumberOfDim = Val(X)
  '   This loop makes sure you have an odd number
  '   And keeps you under the 255 controls/form Limit
  Do Until NumberOfDim Mod 2 = 1  And NumberOfDim < 16
     X = InputBox$("Number of dimensions must be odd and < 16!")
     NumberOfDim = Val(X)
  Loop
  L = InputBox$("Size of Labels?")
  LabelSize = Val(L)
  BoxSize = LabelSize * NumberOfDim
```

```
'  This loop makes sure things aren't too large
 Do Until BoxSize <= Screen.Height And BoxSize < Screen.Width
     L = InputBox$("Previous label size too big - label
size?")
     LabelSize = Val(L)
     BoxSize = LabelSize * NumberOfDim
 Loop
 Show
End Sub
```

Now you can set up the procedure to create the labels (which assumes you have already created the control array named BoxLabels):

```
Sub MakeBoxes(HowBig)
  Dim I as Integer

  Boxlabel(0).Visible = 0    'temp hide original label
  BoxLabel(0).Height = HowBig
  BoxLabel(0).Width = HowBig
  Size = NumberOfDim * NumberOfDim
  For I = 1 To Size - 1      'already have one label
                             'BoxLabel(0)
    Load BoxLabel(I)
    BoxLabel(I).Height = HowBig
    BoxLabel(I).Width = HowBig
  Next I
End Sub
```

Now you can call the MakeBoxes procedure to create and size the labels as needed:

```
Sub Form_Click()
  Static BoxesMade As Integer

  If Not (BoxesMade) Then
    MakeBoxes LabelSize
    BoxesMade =   True
  End If
  LocateBoxes LabelSize, NumberOfDim
End Sub
```

This doesn't put all the work in the Form_Click procedure. By not overloading a single procedure, you make the program more modular. This gives you added flexibility for reusing the code in a slightly different situation.

By setting up BoxesMade as a static variable, you can make sure the control array is loaded only once. This prevents the run-time error that would occur if you tried to load a control more than once. You also could have put this in the MakeBoxes procedure. Next, notice that the LocateBoxes procedure increases modularity. You can call the procedure by using the parameters set by the global variables LabelSize and NumberOfDim.

The LocateBoxes general procedure looks like this:

```
Sub LocateBoxes(HowBig as Integer, Number As Integer)

  Dim I As Integer, Row As Integer, Column As Integer

  StartHeight = Screen.Height/2 -((Number / 2) * HowBig)
  StartWidth = Screen.Width / 2 - ((Number / 2) * HowBig)
  For I = 0 To Size - 1
    Row = I \ Number
    Column = I Mod Number
    CurrentHeight = StartHeight + (Row * HowBig)
    CurrentWidth = StartWidth + (Column * HowBig)
    BoxLabel(I).Move CurrentWidth, CurrentHeight
    BoxLabel(I).Caption = Str$(I + 1)
    BoxLabel(I).Visible = True
  Next I
End Sub
```

Inside the procedure, the For-Next loop does all the work. By setting the starting width and height as indicated, you can use integer division to find the row. For example, when I is between 0 and NumberOfDim, then Row = 0; and when I is between NumberOfDim and one less than twice the number of dimensions, then Row = 1.

Columns are given by the remainder. The line BoxLabel(I).Caption=Str$(I+1) was put in to display the ordering of the boxes.

One nice point about this procedure is that you can easily adapt it to many situations. Minor changes allow you to use it whenever you'll need to load and position multiple controls on a form. For example, change the HowBig parameter to a control parameter and make the necessary changes in the code to reflect this.

## CONTROL ARRAYS VERSUS OBJECT VARIABLES

It's easy to get confused about the differences between these two concepts. At the lowest level the difference is that object variables are used to create new instances of a form. These are identical copies of the form with all the controls (including elements of a control array) placed on it at design time. Control arrays are used only with controls and allow you to create a new control at run time with its own event procedures. Even if you write a generic event procedure for handling a control in a certain way, such as

```
Sub WorkWithControl(Foo As Control, Bar As Control,...)
```

you still can only work with the controls created at design time—unless you add a control array at that time. Finally, object variables can be used in an array to create an array of controls, control arrays cannot.

# Lists: One-Dimensional Arrays

Suppose you need data for a 12-month period. You would like to say something like this:

```
For I = 1 to 12
  MonthI = Val(InputBox$(Data for MonthI))
Next I
```

If this kind of loop were possible, the information entered would still be available in the various MonthI variables. Unfortunately, this is not quite correct. In Visual Basic, MonthI is a perfectly good variable name—for a single variable. Visual Basic cannot separate the I from the Month. After you see a systematic way to name variables, it's easy to take care of this problem.

To Visual Basic, a *list* (often called a *one-dimensional array*) is just a collection of variables, each one of which is identified by two things:

◆ The name of the list

◆ The position of the item on the list

For example, you've already seen in Chapter 5 the Fonts list that Visual Basic uses to store font names. As another example, suppose you are writing a program that lets a user enter an "errand list" at the beginning of each day. You would probably choose to store the information on a list. The third errand might be stored as Errand$(3). The name of this list is Errand$. Notice the dollar sign ($) that indicates that the variables on this list will hold words (strings).

The number in the parentheses is usually called a *subscript, pointer,* or *index.* The term "subscript" comes from mathematics, where the item M(5) is more likely to be written $M_5$. The term "pointer" is used because the 5 "points" to the row holding the information. To Visual Basic, M5 is the name of a single variable, but M(5) is the name of the fifth element on a list called M. As you saw with the Fonts list, lists in Visual Basic default to having a zeroth entry.

## Fixed Versus Dynamic Lists

Lists can't be open-ended in Visual Basic. While the limits are quite large—Visual Basic 3 allows what programmers call *huge arrays* (see the online help)—you must tell Visual Basic how much memory to set aside for the list before you use it.

There are two kinds of lists in Visual Basic: *fixed lists,* where the memory allocation never changes, and *dynamic lists,* where you can change size on the fly. The advantage of a fixed list is that memory is set aside at the beginning of the program; you run a much smaller risk of running out of memory while the program is running. The advantage of dynamic lists is the flexibility they give. You can change the size in response to what the program has encountered.

**note:** *List boxes give you another way to store information (see Chapter 10). In many situations, using them can be the preferred way to store data.*

Both kinds of lists may be made visible to either the whole application, to a specific form or module, or only within an event procedure. To set up a fixed list in a form or module, place a statement like

```
Dim Errand(13) As String
```

in the Declarations section of the form or module. This sets up a 14-element list for strings visible to every procedure on that form or module. The items would be stored in Errand(0) through Errand(13).

To set up a dynamic list in a form or module, place a statement like

```
Dim Errand() As String
```

in the Declarations section of the form or module. You then use the ReDim statement inside a procedure to allocate the space:

```
Sub NameOfProcedure()
..Dim Number As Integer
  ReDim Errand(Number) As String
.

.
End Sub
```

Each time Visual Basic processes a ReDim statement, the information in the array is lost. The advantage, though, is clear: you can calculate how much space you need before issuing the ReDim command. In the preceding example, the value of the variable Number can change depending on the circumstances.

You can also use the ReDim statement in a procedure without needing a Dim statement in the declarations section of the form or module first. In this case, space is allocated for that list only while the procedure is active and disappears as soon as the procedure is exited.

A variation of the ReDim statement can be used to increase the size of a dynamic list while retaining any information already stored in the list. The statement

```
ReDim Preserve Errand(NewSize) As String
```

can be placed in a procedure to increase the number of entries in the array Errand( ) to NewSize + 1 without losing data already stored in the list.

To set up a fixed list that is global and therefore visible to the entire project, place a statement like

```
Global Errand(13) As String
```

in a module. This sets up a 14-element global list for strings. The items would be stored in Errand(0) through Errand(13).

To set up a dynamic list that is global, and therefore visible to the entire project, place a statement like

```
Global Errand() As String
```

in a module.

As before, Visual Basic actually reallocates the space each time it encounters a ReDim Errand(Number) statement inside a procedure.

Finally, you can set up a local fixed array inside a procedure by using the Static keyword:

```
Sub ProcedureName()

  Static Errand(13) As String
.
.
End Sub
```

As with static variables, the information you store in a list defined by static dimensioning remains intact. You cannot use a variable inside the parentheses when you do static dimensioning. Similarly, the information in a form or global list remains intact until you redimension it.

When you dynamically dimension a list or array, Visual Basic sets aside space at that time. If the program is very large, it's possible that you won't have enough room. If this happens, you'll get the dreaded "out of memory" error. Given Windows' memory-management skills, this is a much more rarely encountered error than you might think.

## Some Ways of Working with Lists

Values inside lists are most often assigned by using a For-Next loop or, since you often want to allow someone to stop before entering all the names, by using a Do loop, as in the following fragment:

```
Static Errand(30)  as String
Index = 0

Do
  M$ = "You've entered"+ Str$(Index)+ " entries so far."
  M$ = M$ + "Enter the next errand - ZZZ when done"
  NextErrand$ =InputBox$(M$)
  If NextErrand$ <> "ZZZ" Then
    Index = Index + 1
    Errand$(Index) = NextErrand$
  End If
Loop Until Index = 30 Or NextErrand$ = "ZZZ"

NumberOfItems = Index
```

Notice that a temporary variable, NextErrand$, was set up to hold the information before it is added to the list. This keeps the flag off the list. Once you know the entry is acceptable, you first move the pointer (add 1 to the index) and only then fill in the entry. Do you see why the order is important? Notice as well that this If–Then is completely skipped when "**ZZZ**" is entered. This also keeps the flag off the list. Enter "**ZZZ**", and you move immediately to the loop test and leave. The variable NumberOfItems keeps track of the number of items on the list. In a program that will manipulate this list in many ways, it's a good candidate for a global or form–level variable. (Of course, it is not really in keeping with the Visual Basic spirit to use so many input boxes. This is just a programming example to illustrate a concept. Most likely, in a situation like this, you'd use a command button and a text box.)

However, there are other ways to pass the information around than by using a global variable like NumberOfItems. For this, recall that in Visual Basic all lists default to having a zeroth entry. In the example, when you wrote

```
Static Errand(30) As String
```

Visual Basic actually set aside 31 slots, the extra one being Errand(0). This zeroth slot is useful for things like the number of significant items on the list. What you might want to do (rather than set up a new variable) is enter

```
Errand(0) = Str$(Index)
```

Now, to find the number of items (for example, to set up a For–Next loop), you can convert this entry back to a number by using the Val command.

Another, perhaps even more popular alternative is to keep a flag (like the "ZZZ") as the last item on a list. This lets you use an indeterminate loop to manipulate the list (test for the flag). To do this, modify the previous fragment as follows:

```
' A simple list demo revisited and revised

Static Errand(30) As String
Index = 0
Do
  M$ = "You've entered"+ Str$(Index)+ " entries so far."
  M$ = M$ + "Enter the next errand - ZZZ when done"
  NextErrand$ =InputBox$(M$)
  If NextErrand$ = "ZZZ" Then
    Errand$(Index) = "ZZZ"
```

```
   Else
     Errand$(Index) = Next Errand$
     Index = Index + 1
   End If
Loop Until Index = 30 Or Errand$(Index) = "ZZZ"
```

Notice that here, the If–Then–Else deals with the two possibilities—a real entry or the flag. Notice as well that the last entry could hold the flag. Of the two methods, the idea of keeping the number of items currently used in the zeroth entry (when possible) may be the most appealing, but this is clearly a matter of taste. You may find it comforting to always know how many entries are on a list. It makes debugging easier and, like most programmers, you may find For-Next loops easier to use than Do loops.

## An Example: Improving the Built-in Random Number Generator

The built-in random number generator (see Chapter 7) in Visual Basic doesn't give good results for some type of simulations and is not a particularly good method for developing encryption programs (see Chapter 14). If you find that the random number generator is a problem, there is a simple method of improving the random number generator by using a list. This gives you a way of generating numbers that seem even more random. (Technically, what the method does is eliminate sequential correlations.) All you need to do is the following:

1. Set up an array of random numbers.

2. Use the built-in random number generator to pick one element of the array.

3. Replace the element chosen with a new random number generated by the built-in random number generator.

If you use this method instead of the built-in random number generator, you should eliminate most of the problems of the built-in random number generator, with very few performance penalties. Essentially, what these steps do is shuffle the cards one more time. An array of about 100 works very well. (Actually, 101 works a bit better because 101 is a *prime number*—you can't factor 101 like you can 100 = 4 * 25.) To implement the method outlined previously, first set up a global array and fill it with 100 random numbers in an Initialize procedure:

```
Global RandomList(100)   'gives 101 entries

Sub Initialize()
  Dim I As Integer

  Randomize
  For I = 0 To 100
    RandomList(I) = Rnd
  Next I
End Sub
```

Now, whenever you need a random number, use the following function:

```
Function NewRandom()
  Dim Foo As Single, X As Integer
  Randomize
  Foo = Rnd
  X = Int(101*Foo)
  NewRandom=RandomList(X)
  RandomList(X) = Foo            'Replace used up entry
End Function
```

## Lists with Index Ranges

Some people never use the zeroth entry of a list; they just find it confusing. (And if you are not going to use it in a program, it certainly wastes space.) For this reason, Visual Basic (to keep compatibility with interpreted BASICs) has a command that eliminates the zeroth entry in all lists dimensioned in the module or form. It is the Option Base 1 statement. This statement is used in the Declarations section of a form or module and affects all lists in the module. All new lists dimensioned in that form or module now begin with item 1. After Option Base 1, Dim Errand$(30) sets aside 30 spots rather than 31. Of course, you can also use the statement Dim Zot(1 to 6) as Integer.

As usual, Visual Basic goes one step beyond interpreted BASICs. Suppose you want to write the input routine for a bar graph program for sales in the years 1980 through 1992. You could write something like

```
Static  SalesInYear(12) As Single
For I = 0 To 12
```

```
    Sales$=InputBox$("Enter the sales in year"+ Str$(1980 + I))
    SalesInYear(I) = Val(Sales$)
Next I
```

However, this program requires 13 additions (one for each pass through the loop) and is more complicated to boot. This situation is so common that QuickBASIC and Visual Basic enhance the language by allowing subscript ranges. Instead of writing

```
Dim SalesInYear(12)
```

you can now write

```
Dim SalesInYears(1980 To 1992)
```

The keyword To marks the range, smaller number first (from 1980 to 1992, in this case) for this extension of Dim, ReDim, and static dimensioning. Using this variant, you can rewrite the preceding fragment as

```
Static SalesInYear(1980 To 1992) As Single
Dim I As Integer

For I = 1980 To 1992
  Sales$=InputBox$("Enter the sales in year"+ Str$(I))
  SalesInYear(I) = Val(Sales$)
Next I
```

Besides being much cleaner, this new fragment runs more quickly. In a large program with lists containing thousands of entries, the savings can be substantial.

## The Erase Statement

As your programs grow longer, the possibility that you'll run out of space increases (although, given Visual Basic's rather large limits and Windows' memory management, it's never very likely). Visual Basic allows you to reclaim the space used by a dynamically dimensioned array. You do this with the Erase command. For example,

```
Erase Errands
```

would erase the Errands array and free up the space it occupied.

If an array was not dimensioned dynamically (that is, was not dimensioned using the ReDim statement inside a procedure), then the Erase command simply resets all the entries back to zero for numeric lists (and to the null string for string lists or to null for variants). Using the Erase command on a fixed (static) list gives a fast method to "zero out" the entries. (It sets them to the null string for string arrays.)

## Arrays with More Than One Dimension

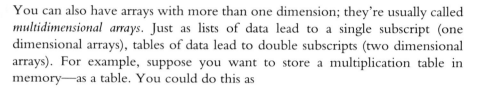

You can also have arrays with more than one dimension; they're usually called *multidimensional arrays*. Just as lists of data lead to a single subscript (one dimensional arrays), tables of data lead to double subscripts (two dimensional arrays). For example, suppose you want to store a multiplication table in memory—as a table. You could do this as

```
Static MultTable(12,12) As Integer
Dim I As Integer, J As Integer

For I = 1 To 12
 For J = 1 To 12
  MultTable(I, J) = I*J
 Next J
Next I
```

To compute the number of items in a multidimensional array, multiply the number of entries. The dimension statement here sets aside one of the following:

◆ 144 (12 * 12) entries if an Option Base 1 has been previously processed

◆ 169 (13 * 13) entries if an Option Base 1 has not been processed

So in this example, there are either 12 rows and 12 columns or 13 rows and 13 columns. In general, the number of entries in an array is either the product of the numbers or the product of one more than the individual numbers used in the dimension statement.

The convention is to refer to the first entry as giving the number of rows and the second the number of columns. Following this convention, you would describe this fragment as filling an entire row, column by column, before moving to the next row.

As you can see, in arrays, the extra space taken up by the zeroth row and zeroth column can dramatically increase the space requirements for your arrays. Also, the total number of entries cannot exceed the numbers given in the table presented earlier. For this reason, Visual Basic's Range feature is even more welcome. A statement like

```
Dim Salary(1 To 50, 1980 To 1992)
```

sets aside 50 rows, numbered 1 through 50, and 13 columns, "numbered" 1980 through 1992. Therefore, this Salary array has 650 entries.

Visual Basic allows you up to 60 dimensions with the Dim statement and 8 with the ReDim statement. A statement like

```
Dim LargeArray%(2,2,2,2,2,2,2,2)
```

would set aside either $2^8 = 256$ or $3^8 = 6561$ entries (depending on whether an Option Base 1 statement has been processed). But you almost never see more than 4 dimensions in a program, and even a 3-dimensional array is uncommon. Finally, note that you can use ReDim for multi-dimensional arrays in exactly the same way.

## An Example: Magic Squares

For a more serious example of a program using arrays, consider the following program, which constructs a magic square. A magic square is one in which all the rows, columns, and long diagonals add up to the same number. These squares were once thought to have magical properties. Many people have devised rules for constructing magic squares. The one used in this section is called Loubère's and works only for odd-order magic squares—those with an odd number of rows and columns. Here's the method:

1. Place a 1 in the center of the first row.

2. The numbers now go into the square in order by moving up on the diagonal to the right.

Of course, you're immediately met with the problem of where to put the 2. If you've placed a 1 in the top row, going up takes you off the square. The solution is:

3. If you go off the top, wrap around to the corresponding place in the bottom row.

On the other hand, going to the right eventually drops you off the side.

4. If you go off to the right end, wrap around to the left column.

5. Finally, if a square is already filled or the upper right-hand corner is reached, move down one row and continue applying these rules.

Here's a 5 × 5 magic square constructed with this rule.

| 17 | 24 | 1  | 8  | 15 |
|----|----|----|----|----|
| 23 | 5  | 7  | 14 | 16 |
| 4  | 6  | 13 | 20 | 22 |
| 10 | 12 | 19 | 21 | 3  |
| 11 | 18 | 25 | 2  | 9  |

This procedure assumes you've added a command button (MakeMagic) whose Click procedure will do all the work. It also assumes you've set up the control array for the labels using the code from the example program in the section "Control Arrays" at the beginning of this chapter. Set the boxes to be slightly smaller than the screen width and height. This lets you display up to 255 controls on a form.

Here are the form-level declarations for the magic square program:

```
' Magic squares by Loubere's rule
' Form-level declarations

Dim Magic() As Integer
Dim Size As Integer, NumberOfDim As Integer
Dim Limit As Integer, LabelSize As Integer
```

Here's the procedure that does all the work:

```
Sub MakeMagic_Click ()
   'local variables
   Dim I As Integer, Row As Integer, Col As Integer
   Dim NewRow As Integer, NewCol As Integer

   Limit = NumberOfDim - 1
   ReDim Magic(Limit, Limit)
   Row = 0
   Col = (NumberOfDim \ 2)
   Magic(Row, Col) = 1
```

```
      Boxlabel(Col + (NumberOfDim * Row)).Caption =_
Str$(Magic(Row,Col))

   For I = 2 To Size
     If Row = 0 And Col = Limit Then
       NewRow = 1
       NewCol = Col
     Else
       NewRow = Row - 1
       NewCol = Col + 1
       If NewRow < 0 Then NewRow = NewRow + NumberOfDim
       If NewCol > Limit Then Newcol = NewCol - NumberOfDim
     End If
   ' find empty slot
   Do Until Magic(Newrow, Newcol) = 0
       NewRow = Row + 1
       NewCol = Col
   Loop
   Row = NewRow
   Col = NewCol
     Magic(Row, Col) = I
     Boxlabel(Col + (NumberOfDim * Row)).Caption =_
Str$(Magic(Row,Col))                          'one line of text!
   Next I
End Sub
```

The If clause inside the For-Next loop corresponds to the special case of the upper right-hand corner. The two If statements inside the Else clause correspond to the first rule, "up and to the right." Of course, this row may be off the square, and the If-Thens take care of this.

The Do loop stops when you get to an unoccupied square. One of the nice properties of Loubère's method of constructing magic squares is that you know this will always work.

# Using Lists and Arrays with Procedures

Visual Basic has an extraordinary facility to use lists and arrays in procedures and functions. Unlike languages like Pascal, it's easy to send any size list or array to a procedure. One way to do this, of course, is to make the list or array a form or global variable, as you saw in the section "An Example: Improving the Built-in Random Number Generator" earlier in this chapter. However, using lists and arrays as parameters for procedures and functions is much more common.

The reasons for doing this are similar to why one usually prefers parameters to shared variables—they increase your flexibility. To send an array parameter to a procedure or function, put the name of the array followed by ( ) in the parameter list. For example, assume that List# is a one-dimensional array of double-precision variables. Array$ is a two-dimensional string array and BigArray% a three-dimensional array of integers. Then,

```
Sub Example(List#(), Array$(), BigArray%(), X%)
```

would allow this Example procedure to use (and change) a list of double-precision variables, an array of strings, a three-dimensional array of integers, and a final integer variable. Note that just as with variables, list and array parameters are placeholders; they have no independent existence. To call the procedure, you might have a fragment like this:

```
Dim PopChange#(50), CityState$(3,10), TotalPop%(2,2,2)
```

Now,

```
Example PopChange#(), CityState$(), TotalPop%(), X1#
```

would call this procedure by sending it the current location (passed by reference) of the three arrays and the integer variable. And just as before, since the compiler knows where the variable, list, or array is located, it can change the contents.

Suppose you want to write a function procedure that would take a list of numbers and return the maximum entry. Since you may want to do this for many different lists, you decide to write a procedure that follows this outline:

Function FindMaximum(List( ))
    Start at the top of the list
    If an entry is bigger than the current Max "swap it"
    Until you finish the list.
    Set the value of the function to the final "Max"

This kind of outline obviously calls for a For-Next loop. But the problem with translating this outline to a program is, how do you know where the list starts or ends? You could arrange for every list to have a flag at the end, but then you would have trouble combining this with Visual Basic's Range feature. Or you could use the trick of reserving one entry in the list for the number of items in the list.

Visual Basic makes this process easier with the commands LBound and UBound, which are not part of interpreted BASIC. LBound gives the lowest possible index and UBound the highest in a list. For example, you can easily translate the preceding outline to the following:

```
Function FindMax(A() As Single)
  ' local variables Start, Finish, I
  Dim Start As Integer, Finish As Integer, I As Integer

  Start = LBound(A)
  Finish = UBound(A)
  Max = A(Start)
  For I = Start  To Finish
    If A(I) > Max Then Max = A(I)
  Next I
  FindMax = Max
End Function
```

When this procedure is finished, the value of this function would be the largest entry on the list of single-precision variables.

In general, the command

LBound(*NameOfArray, I*)

gives the lower bound for the I'th dimension. (For a list (one-dimensional array), the I is optional, as in the preceding example.) Therefore,

```
Dim Test%(1 To 5,6 To 10,7 To 12)
Print LBound(Test%,2)
```

gives a 6 and

```
Print UBound(Test%,3)
```

gives a 12.

Here's another example. Suppose you want to write a general procedure to copy one two-dimensional string array to another. The LBound and UBound commands allow you to copy lists or arrays with different ranges, provided the total number of rows and columns is the same. (Subtract the LBound from the UBound for each dimension and see if they match.)

It's hard to stress enough the flexibility that Visual Basic's method for handling lists and arrays within procedures gives, especially when combined with the LBound and UBound commands. For example, you may have learned about matrices in math or engineering courses. It is close to impossible to write a general matrix package in standard Pascal, yet it's almost trivial in Visual Basic.

You should be aware that you cannot pass a control array by reference to a procedure; you can only pass by value a specific entry in the array. To do this, give the entry. For example,

```
Call Example(A(), BoxLabel(10))
```

would send a procedure a list named A and the value of the tenth entry in a control array named B. The actual procedure would look like this:

```
Sub Example(A(), X As Control)
.
.
.
End Sub
```

One last point: using LBound and UBound is not a cure-all. If part of the list or array hasn't yet been filled, they may not help. Therefore, although adding the number of items on a list as the zeroth item on the list was a more common programming trick for earlier BASICs (that didn't have UBound and LBound), it is still sometimes useful in Visual Basic.

**tip:** *You cannot use LBound and UBound with control arrays. Instead store this information in the Tag property of the original element of the control array.*

## Using Arrays of Object Variables

Object variables allow you to use an array of controls or forms in the same way that you use a variable array. For example, statements like

```
Dim FormsArray(10) As Form
Dim TextBoxArray(15) As Text
Dim ManyControls(20) As Control
```

allow you to work with arrays of 11 forms, 16 text boxes, and 21 (generic) controls. Just as with arrays of variables, you can use global, local, and static arrays of objects and use ReDim (or ReDim Preserve) to work with local arrays of objects or use index ranges or the Option Base Command.

To actually fill the array you use the Set keyword that you saw in Chapter 8 with existing objects (including new instances) of that type, such as

```
Set FormsArray(1) = Form1
Set FormsArray(2) = Form2
Set ManyControls(15) = Command1
```

and so on. The right hand side of the assignment using the Set keyword is the control (or form) name. You can fill up an array of forms in a similar way.

For arrays of forms you can also have Visual Basic automatically create instances of the form for each element of the array after it processes the appropriate ReDim statement. For this use the syntax:

```
Global Documents() As New Form1
Dim Documents() As New Form1
```

Once you've added an entry to an array of object variables you can use the Is command to check what type of object it is. For example, a statement like

```
If ManyControls(5) Is TextBox Then ...
```

checks if the sixth (fifth if Option Base 1 was processed) entry in the Many-Controls array was a Text box.

Finally if you are getting confused about the differences between arrays of control variables and control arrays, all you need to do is keep in mind that arrays of control variables are just a convenient method of grouping existing controls where as control arrays let you make new controls of the same type at run time.

# The Grid Control

The grid control lets you build spreadsheet-like features into your projects. As the screen in Figure 9-5 shows, this control displays a rectangular grid of rows and columns. Each grid member is usually called a *cell*. Cells can hold text, bitmaps, or icons or even mix text and graphics. You can specify the contents

**Figure 9-5**

**A sample grid control**

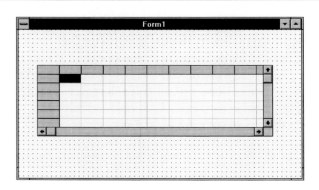

as well as the width and height of a row or column individually, and of course, you can use code to control each cell individually while your project is running. Users can move from cell to cell by using the arrow keys or the mouse; Visual Basic handles such movement automatically. The grid control even includes a built-in word-wrap feature so users can enter text more easily, but you must program in the ability for cells to actually accept text. In any case, a grid control, like a text box, can hold only text. Numbers must be translated back and forth using the Val and Str$ functions or the Variant data type.

Grids let you easily display the information stored in arrays neatly and efficiently. For example, you can use a grid control to display larger magic squares than the control array of labels allowed you to do earlier, with less use of Windows resources.

Users can work with contiguous groups of cells in the grid, usually called *regions,* by clicking a cell and dragging the mouse or by pressing SHIFT plus an arrow key to select the region. Once a region is selected, code can be used to analyze or change the contents.

The grid control is automatically added to your toolbox unless you modify the AUTOLOAD.MAK file that controls the initial startup features of Visual Basic 3.

**note:** *If you give someone an application that uses the grid control, you must install the GRID.VBX file in their \WINDOWS\SYSTEM directory or some other place that Windows knows about. See Appendix B on the SETUP wizard or Appendix A on the Professional Edition for how to do this.*

# General Properties of the Grid Control

Many of the properties of the grid control are the same as those for the controls that you're already familiar with such as, BackColor and ForeColor or the font properties. You can even use the picture property to place a bitmap or icon inside a specific cell. What this section will do is take you through the most important of the properties that are special to grids.

**Cols, Rows**  These properties determine the number of rows and columns in the grid. The default values for each of these properties is 2, but you can reset them in code or via the property box as needed. They obviously must be integers and the syntax is

    GridName.Cols = NumOfCols%
    GridName.Rows = NumOfRows%

You can also add an optional form name, as in this example:

```
DisplayForm.Cols = 10
```

**ColWidth, RowHeight**  These two properties specify the width of a specific column or height of a specific row. They can only be set via code. Both are measured in *twips*. The syntax is

    GridName.ColWidth*(ColNumber%)* = Width%
    GridName.RowHeight*(RowlNumber%)* = Height%

You can also add an optional form name.

**tip:**

*If text has been automatically word wrapped, then adjust the ColWidth or RowHeight to display it by checking the text's TextWidth and TextHeight properties.*

**Col, Row**  These properties (which shouldn't be confused with Cols and Rows!) set or return the current cell inside the grid. For this reason they are only available at run time. As the user moves around the grid, the values of these properties change. You then would use their values to determine where inside the grid the user was. By adjusting their values via code, you can specify the current cell directly. Since both Col and Row start out at zero, the top-left corner cell has Col index 0 and Row index 0.

*Text* This sets or returns the text inside the current cell (the one given by the values of the Col and Row properties). You can place up to 255 characters in an individual cell.

For example, if a grid (control name Grid1) has four rows and four columns, the following code fragment places text directly in the bottom-right corner and displays the contents of the top-left corner cell:

```
Grid1.Col = 3
Grid1.Row = 3
Grid1.Text = "This would go in the bottom-right corner"
Grid1.Col = 0
Grid1.Row = 0
Print Grid1.Text
```

(Note that because rows and columns in grids are numbered from 0, the bottom-right corner of a 4 × 4 grid has col (and row) index 3.)

*ColAlignment* There are three possible settings for data inside a column. You can left justify (value = 0), right justify (value = 1), or center the text (value = 2). The syntax is

GridName.ColAlignment(*Index%*) = *Setting%*

*FixedCols, FixedRows, FixedAlignment* Often when you are working with a grid you will want to use certain cells to display information at all times. For example, regardless of how the user scrolls through a spreadsheet, you may want to display the column headings. Fixed rows and columns are always displayed in gray and must be at the top and left sides of the grid. The FixedAlignment property works exactly as does the ColAlignment property, but applies only to fixed columns. The syntax for these three properties is

GridName.FixedCols = *NumberOfFixedCols%*
*GridName*.FixedRows = *NumberOfFixedRows%*
*GridName*.FixedAlignment = *SettingNumber%*

where, as before, the setting for the alignment property has the possible values 0, 1, and 2, and you can add an optional form name, of course.

**GridLines, ScrollBars** These two properties control whether grid lines (these make it easier to see cell boundaries) and scroll bars appear. The default is to show grid lines and to have both horizontal and vertical scroll bars.

**LeftCol, TopRow** These two properties control what is the leftmost column and highest row displayed from a grid. You use these properties when the entire grid is too large to fit on the form. These properties can only be set in code and the syntax for both of these properties is similar:

GridName.LeftCol = *LeftmostCol%*
*GridName*.TopRow = *HighestRow%*

### PROPERTIES OF SELECTED CELLS INSIDE GRIDS

Although grids are often used passively to display data (or pictures), it is even more common to make them responsive to the user. Users can select cells or regions and change their contents. This section takes you through the properties that let you work with regions selected by the user.

**CellSelected** This is a Boolean (True/False) property that tells you if the cell specified by the current value of the Row and Col properties is within the region selected by the user. You can use this property to check if the user has selected a region that includes the current cell.

**SelStartCol, SelEndCol, SelStartRow, SelEndRow** These properties are determined by the region currently selected. If all these values are the same, then a single cell was selected.

*Clip* This property is among the most important when dealing with selected regions. This sets or returns the contents of the selected region. The syntax is

GridName.Clip = *String$*

The string expression on the right-hand side contains the entire contents of the selected region. The contents of each cell on the same row are separated from the adjacent cell by the TAB character (ASCII 9), and each row is separated from the next by the carriage return character (ASCII 13). For example,

```
TabChar$ = Chr$(9)
CR$ = Chr$(13)
Grid1.SelStartCol = 0: Grid1.SelEndCol = 2
Grid1.SelStartRow = 0: Grid1.SelEndRow = 1
S$ = Str$(1) + TabChar$ + Str$(2) + TabChar$ + Str$(3)
S$ = S$ + CR$ + Str$(4) + TabChar$ + Str$(5) + TabChar$ + _
Str$(6)
Grid1.Clip = S$
```

fills up the first three columns and two rows with the string equivalents of the numbers 1 through 6.

*FillStyle* Sometimes you want what the user enters into one cell of the selected region to fill up the entire region. You can control this by changing the FillStyle property from its default value of 0 to the value 1. In addition, when FillStyle is 1, any image assigned to the Picture property automatically fills all cells whose CellSelected property is True.

*HighLight* This True/False property determines if the cells selected are highlighted. The default value (True) is that selected cells are highlighted.

## The Events and Methods for Grid Controls

Grids respond to many of the standard events; for example, you can use the Click event to determine whether the user has clicked inside the grid and the KeyPress event to send what a user is typing inside the grid directly to the currently selected cell. Using the KeyPress event to accumulate keystrokes with a static variable and then testing for the ENTER key is a common way to allow data direct entry into the grid. All you need to do after the ENTER key is pressed is assign the data accumulated by the static variable to the text property of the grid. However, since the code to activate a grid control must constantly monitor when the selected region changes, Visual Basic provides you with two events unique to grids that you might want to consider allowing along with (or instead of) the ENTER key. They are described below.

**RowColChange** This event is activated when the current cell changes—either because the user has moved around in the grid or you've used code to change one of the properties given in the previous section. If you make the variable used in the KeyPress event procedure a form level variable instead of a static variable you can use an assignment to the Text property of the grid in this event procedure to make the changes.

**SelChange** This event is activated when the selected region changes—either because the user has moved around in the grid or the code has directly changed one of the properties given in the previous section.

## METHODS FOR RESIZING A GRID

There are also two methods that are unique to grids. These let you insert or delete rows from a grid. The syntax to add a row is

GridName.AddItem *Item$* [*,Index%*]

The string given by Item$ is placed in the first column of the new row. The optional index parameter gives the position of the row that is added.

RemoveItem on the other hand removes a row from a grid. Its syntax is

GridName.RemoveItem *Index%*

For example, to remove the first row of a grid you might use

```
Grid1.RemoveItem 0
```

(because the first index starts out at zero).

# Sorting and Searching

Sorting and searching through lists of names is one of the most common tasks people use computers for. Let's start with the techniques needed for searching through a list.

## Searching

Suppose a long list of names is stored in the computer's memory. Now you want to find out whether a certain name is on the list. You can do this easily: Just write a program to compare the name you want with all the names on the list. Visual Basic generates code quickly, so this method is effective for short lists.

However, if the list has 5000 names, all in alphabetical order, this method would be a waste of time. If you are looking in a telephone book for a name beginning with "K," you don't start at page 1; you open the book roughly in the middle and proceed from there. When the information in the list you're searching is already ordered, you can speed things up by using an extension of this method: Each time, the program will look at a list that is only half the size of the previous list. This procedure speeds up a search almost beyond belief. Here's an outline for a program that searches through a list that is already in alphabetical order:

1. Divide the list in half.

2. Determine whether you have gone too far. (Is the entry at the halfway mark before or after the name you're looking for?)

3. If you have gone too far, look at the first half of the list; otherwise, look at the second half.

4. Go back to step 1 as long as there are names left to look at.

Suppose your list has 5000 names. After completing step 4, you will go back to step 1 with a list of 2500 names. Complete step 4 again and you will have only 1250 names, then only 625, and so on. By the twelfth time, you will have only two names to search. This type of search is called a *binary search*.

An extraordinary feature of the binary search is that it works almost as quickly for large lists as for small. For example, suppose you are searching through the New York City telephone directory, with roughly 10,000,000 entries, to find a name. Just by following this outline (and not doing any estimating of where the letters are), you would find the name, if it is in the directory, in no more than 25 applications of step 4.

The procedure is a bit tricky, so it's worth spending time on. What follows is a first attempt. (It has a subtle bug.)

```
Sub BinarySearch (X$(), Target$)
  ' LOCAL variables are Low, High, Middle
  ' A global integer variable called TargetPosition
  Dim Low As Integer, High As Integer, Middle As Integer
  TargetPosition = 0
  Low = LBound(X$)
  High = UBound(X$)

  Do
    Middle = (Low + High) \ 2
    Select Case X$(Middle)
      Case Is = Target$
        TargetPosition = Middle
      Case Is > Target$
        High = Middle - 1
      Case Is < Target$
        Low = Middle + 1
    End Select
  Loop Until TargetPosition <> 0
  Print TargetPosition
End Sub
```

Setting the variable TargetPosition to zero initializes the global variable at the beginning of the list. At the end of the procedure, this variable will contain the position of the target. (You also could set up another parameter for this information, and an even better idea would be to turn the whole procedure into a function whose value is the location of the target.)

Notice that this procedure uses the UBound/LBound method of finding the limits. The method described earlier for storing the number of entries in the list as the zeroth entry is not needed here because this procedure assumes that the entire list is ordered.

The Do loop does the work. First it finds the middle of the list by using the integer division operator. (List indexes are always integers.) There are three possibilities in the search, so it's a perfect candidate for the Select Case command. (You can also use If-Then-ElseIf, of course.) If the entry in the middle position is too large, you know that you should look at the first half of the list. Your target can't be the middle entry (you eliminated that in the first case), so you can move the "High" index down by one. (A similar situation holds in the next case.)

Now comes the problem in this preliminary version of a binary search routine: The loop stops only if TargetPosition has a nonzero value—in other words, if the function finds the target. But suppose the target isn't in the list? The loop never stops; the program is stuck in an infinite loop.

How can you fix this procedure so it stops when there are no more entries left to check? Consider the following example. Suppose you are down to a list that consists of two names, say in the forty-second and forty-third positions, and the forty-second entry is too small and the forty-third entry too large. What happens? The first time you're in this situation, the value of Middle is set to $(42+43)\backslash 2 = 42$. Since the value in the forty-second position is too small, the value of Low is set to one more than Middle—that is, to 43. The value of Low and High are now the same. What happens next? Both Low and High are the same, and the value of Middle is also the same. Now the entry in the Middle position is too large, so the value of High shrinks by one, to 42—less than the value of Low. This gives you one way to end the loop. Change it to read

```
Loop Until (TargetPosition <> 0) Or (High < Low)
```

There's another way to write this loop that some people find easier to understand. This method is based on the assumption that something special happens in small lists when the difference between the High and Low indices is 1. Arrange to leave the loop when the list has size 1 and add a few lines to take care of this special case:

```
If (High - Low) < = 1 Then
   If A$(High) = Target$ Then TargetPosition = High
Else
   If A$(Low) = Target$ Then TargetPosition = Low
End If
```

Notice that both these possibilities take care of the case when the list has only one entry, or even no entries. Remember: It's the boundary cases that often cause the most subtle bugs in a program.

On the subject of bugs, how do you write a test module for a binary search module in order to determine what was wrong with the preliminary program given earlier? Obviously, you need a long, ordered list. One way to test the program is to use a list that consists of all possible two-letter strings:

AA, AB, AC,...BA, BB,...ZZ

There are 26 * 26 = 676 two-letter combinations. (Using three-letter combinations allows a list of 26^3 = 17,576 entries.)

To create this list, you can use this fragment:

```
Dim A$(1 To 676)
Dim Index As Integer, I As Integer, J As Integer
Index = 1
For I = 65 To 90
  For J = 65 To 90
    A$(Index) = Chr$(I) + Chr$(J)
    Index = Index + 1
  Next J
Next I
```

Now you can test the binary search module by trying various possibilities, such as searching for a two-letter string that is on the list and another two-letter string that is not on the list or searching for the first entry and the last.

## Sorting

Programmers like ordered lists, just as people prefer alphabetized lists such as dictionaries and telephone books, because techniques such as binary searching work so quickly. Sorting data is one of the most common jobs a computer is asked to do. Unfortunately, sorting is also one of the most time-consuming tasks for a computer. Because of this, computer scientists have developed literally hundreds of different ways to sort lists, and it's impossible to say which is best in all possible circumstances. In this section we'll discuss four methods. The first two are useful for short lists. The third is often the method of choice, even for lists having thousands of entries. The last sort method is called the bubble sort and seems to be the sort most commonly given in elementary books. Unfortunately, it has few, if any, redeeming features, and you may find it better to not use it even if you are adapting code already written. It is usually better to switch to one of the other three sort procedures given here. Chapter 16 discusses three more sorting methods. Two of those three are usually better than even the fastest sort presented in this section, but unfortunately, they are much more difficult to program.

When you sit down to write a program, it's always a good idea to ask yourself if there's anything you do in real life that's analogous to what you want the computer to do. For sorting lists, what often comes to mind is ordering playing card hands. There seems to be two types of people: those who pick up all the cards at once and sort their hands by first finding the smallest card, then the next smallest, and so on; and those who pick up one card at a time, scan what they have already sorted, and then immediately place the new card in the correct place. (For what it's worth, computer scientists have proved that these two methods take roughly the same amount of time, with the second method usually being a tiny bit faster.) Each of the methods for ordering playing cards translates into a way to sort lists. We will take each up in turn.

### RIPPLE SORT

The sorting method analogous to the first way of sorting cards given above is usually called *ripple sort*. Here's an outline for it:

1. Start with the first entry.

2. Look at the remaining entries one by one. Whenever you find a smaller entry, swap it with the first.

3. Now shrink the list; start with the second entry and look at the remaining entries (3, 4, and so on).

4. Continue this until all items are worked through.

Notice that if, say, the list has 50 entries, you only have to do the fourth step of this outline 48 times. This is because by the time this procedure works its way to the last entry, enough switching has happened that it has to be the largest entry. Here's the procedure. (Like many of the sorts in this chapter, it assumes you've written a SWAP general procedure to interchange the values of two variables, filling in the gap left by the designers of Visual Basic.)

```
Sub RippleSort (A$())
  'Local variables NumOfEntries%, NumOfTimes%, I%, J%
  Dim NumOfEntries%, NumOfTImes%, I%, J%

  NumOfEntries% = UBound(A$)
  NumOfTimes% = NumOfEntries% - 1
  For I% = 1 To NumOfTimes%
    For J% = I% + 1 To NumOfEntries%
      If A$(J%) < A$(I%) Then SWAP A$(J%), A$(I%)
    Next J%
```

```
    Next I%
End Sub
```

This procedure assumes the list starts from one. An even more elegant idea is to make this procedure depend on two more parameters, say Low and High, and use these to establish the bounds on the loops.

## FIRST STEPS FOR TESTING SORTS

How do you write a module to test a sort? Well, you need a way of creating random lists of strings. Here's one way. Add the following lines to a Form_Click procedure:

```
Dim B$(100)
Dim I As Integer, RndInt1 As Integer, RndInt2 As Integer

Randomize
For I = 1 To 100
  RndInt1 = Int(26*RND(1)) + 1: RndInt2 = Int(26*Rnd(1)) + 1
  B$(I) = Chr$(RndInt1+ 65) + Chr$ (RndInt2 + 65)
Next I
```

At this point of course, you have only one sort to test, although this method can be used to test any sort. In any case, to test ripple sort use the following:

```
RippleSort B$()
```

Now print out the list to make sure it's been sorted:

```
I = 1 To 100
  Print B$(I);"    ";
Next I
```

## INSERTION SORT

The second method, usually called *insertion sort,* is no harder to program. In this sort, at every stage you'll have an already sorted, smaller list. Look through the list, from the first entry to what is currently the last, until you find something smaller than the new entry. Unfortunately, unlike the case of playing cards, you have to move all the entries down by one to make room for the new entry. This leads to a slight "tweak" (computer jargon meaning "a small change that improves performance"). The new version is even easier to program. Instead of moving forward from the start of the list, move backward from the end of the list. Now, each time the comparison fails, move the old entry down by one. If you do this, you'll be moving a "hole" along as you move through the list. When the comparison finally fails, you drop the new entry into the hole. Here's that procedure:

```
Sub InsertionSort (A$())
  'LOCAL Variables are NumOfEntries%, I%, J%, Temp$
  Dim NumOfEntries%, I%, J%, Temp$

  NumOfEntries% = UBound(A$)
  For I% = 2 To NumOfEntries%
   Temp$ = A$(I%)
   For J% = I% - 1 To 1 Step -1
     If Temp$ >= A$(J%) Then Exit For
     A$(J% + 1) = A$(J%)
   Next J%
   A$(J% + 1) = Temp$
  Next I%
End Sub
```

As with ripple sort, you might want to make this procedure depend on a Low and High parameter. Notice, however, that by starting the For-Next loop at 2 we take care of the special case of the list having one entry. The loop moves entries forward until conditions are ripe for the Exit For statement. This occurs when you have located the position of the hole—in preparation for the statement A$(J%+1) = Temp$, which fills the hole.

Since these methods follow the playing card analogy closely, they are not hard to program. Moreover, for small lists, they are reasonably fast. Sorting 100 strings by using the ripple sort takes about two-thirds of a second on a basic 33MHz 386. Unfortunately, sorting 200 entries takes about 2.75 seconds. Although the insertion sort is a little faster than the ripple sort (0.5 seconds for 100 items), both these types of sorts have the unfortunate property that doubling the list quadruples the time. Sorting a list of 13,000 names (by no means a very large list) would take about 3 hours, so you can see that these are not the methods to use for lists much longer than 200 or so entries. You need to turn to a faster method. (Now you can see why the binary search is so nice—doubling the list adds only one step.)

The next section shows you one of the very fastest all-purpose sorts.

## SHELL SORT

The faster sort discussed in this section, *Shell sort,* was discovered by Donald Shell around 30 years ago. (Three other fast sorts are discussed in Chapter 16.)

Shell sort is unusual because while the procedure is simple—and short—understanding what makes it work is not. This is partially because there is nothing that you do in real life that's analogous to Shell sort and partially because it's a really neat idea. Another problem is that even after you understand why it works, it's unclear why it's so much faster than the previous two methods.

To understand Shell sort, you should ask yourself what are the advantages and disadvantages of the two previous sorting methods. One obvious disadvantage of ripple sort is that most of the time, the comparisons in the various loops are wasted. The disadvantage of insertion sort is that most of the time it moves objects inefficiently. Even when the list is mostly sorted, you still have to move the entries one by one to make the hole. The big advantage of ripple sort is that it moves objects efficiently. Once the smallest object gets to the top, it stays there.

In a sense, then, insertion and ripple sorts are opposites. Donald Shell decided to improve insertion sort by moving the keys long distances, as is done in ripple sort. Consider the following list of numbers to sort:

57, 3, 12, 9, 1, 7, 8, 2, 5, 4, 97, 6

Suppose, instead of comparing the first entry to the second, you compare it with the seventh, and instead of comparing the second with the third, you compare it with the eighth. In short, you cut up the list into six different lists. Now do an insertion sort on these six small lists. After this, you have six lists, each of which is sorted, while the whole list is probably still not sorted. Merge the smaller lists and break up the result into three new lists (the first with the fourth, sixth, and so on, and the second with the fifth, eighth, and so on). Do an insertion sort on these three smaller lists and merge again. Now the resulting list is very close to being sorted. A final sort finishes the process. (Insertion sort is efficient when it doesn't have much work to do.)

If the numbers are already stored in a list, you never have to break up the list into smaller lists. Instead, you shift your point of view by concentrating on the different sublists. Also, because on the earlier passes the entries moved fairly long distances, when you're down to the final step not many more moves are needed. Here's a version of Shell sort:

```
Sub ShellSort (A$())
   'LOCAL variables are NumOfEntries%, Increm%, J%, Temp$
   Dim NumOfEntries%, Increm%, J%, Temp$
   NumOfEntries% = UBound(A$)
   Increm% = NumOfEntries% \ 2
   Do Until Increm% < 1
      For I% = Increm% + 1 To NumOfEntries%
         Temp$ = A$(I%)
         For J% = I% - Increm% To 1 Step -Increm%
            If Temp$ >= A$(J%) Then Exit For
            A$(J% + Increm%) = A$(J%)
         Next J%
         A$(J% + Increm%) = Temp$
      Next I%
      Increm% = Increm% \ 2
   Loop
End Sub
```

The Do loop gives you the way of dividing the lists into smaller lists. Inside the Do loop, the inner For-Next loop does an insertion sort on the smaller lists. Since each entry on the smaller list differs from the next by the number given in the variable Increm%, the Step command gives you a way of working with the smaller lists.

What's amazing about Shell sort is that it's so much faster than the ripple or insertion sort, although, surprisingly enough, nobody yet knows how much faster it will be in general. (A way to get a first-rate Ph.D. would be to fully analyze Shell sort.) In any case, sorting a list of 3600 names will take only about 10 seconds using Shell sort on a basic 33MHz 386.

The speed of Shell sort depends somewhat on the numbers you use to split the list into smaller ones. These are usually called the *increments* (the 6, 3, and 1 used in the preceding example), and they should be chosen with care. (Because the increments get smaller on each pass, Shell sort is sometimes known as a "diminishing increment" sort.) The numbers used in the example (half the current size of the list) are Shell's original choice. Today we know you can obtain slightly better results with other increments. One of the simpler choices that gives slightly better results is

...3280, 1093 364 121 40 13 4 1

where each number is arrived at by multiplying the preceding number by 3 and adding 1. (You start with the largest increment that's smaller than the size of your list, so a list with 5000 entries would start with an increment of 3280.) In any case, no one yet knows the best choice of increments. Try other sequences and see if you get better results.

How do you write a realistic test module for a fast sorting routine? Obviously, you want to create a long list of random strings. This is not very difficult to do, but it can sometimes take longer than the sort. For a list of random four-letter strings for Shell sort, use

```
Dim Test$(1 To 3600)
Dim I%, J%, CNumber
  For I% = 1 To 3600
    For J% = 1 To 4
      Cnumber = Int(26*RND(1))
      Test$(I%) = Test$(I%) + Chr$(CNumber + 65)
    Next J%
  Next I%
```

and call Shell sort. (We wouldn't recommend trying to sort a list of 3600 names with insertion or ripple sort.) Finally, add a routine to print out parts of the transformed list. If the results are ordered, then you can be satisfied. Once you are, then you might want to add a routine to time the various sorts. (If you devise your own sort or want to test these, you might want to also test the sorts on the two "boundary cases." For a sorting routine, this is usually thought of when the list is either already ordered or completely in reverse order.)

## A COMMON BUT BAD SORT: THE BUBBLE SORT

Finally, you should be aware of (or may already be using) a sort called *bubble sort*. It's very common in elementary programming books. The idea of bubble sort is the easiest of all: You constantly compare an entry with the one below it. This way, the smallest one "bubbles" to the top. The code for this is almost trivial:

```
For I = 2 To N
 For J = N To I Step -1
  If A$(J-1) > A$(J) Then
    ' need to SWAP A$(J-1), A$(J)
    Temp$ = A$(J-1)
    A$(J-1) = A$(J)
    A$(J) = Temp$
   End If
```

```
        Next J
   Next I
```

The problem is that bubble sort is almost always the slowest sort of all. Since it has few if any redeeming virtues, it should be replaced, at the very least, by an insertion or ripple sort (which are just as easy to program) for small lists and one of the faster sorts, such as Shell sort, for longer lists.

# Records

Suppose you want to have a three-dimensional array for 100 employees in a company. The first column is to be for names, the second for salaries, and the third for social security numbers. This common situation can't be programmed in a multidimensional array except using the variant data type. Some people would call using the variant data type in this situation a *kludge* (computer jargon for an awkward ad hoc method of solving a problem). The problem is that variants use more memory and are slower as well. For both speed and memory reasons, you might prefer to set up three parallel lists—one for the names, the second for salaries, and the third for social security numbers (they're strings to include the dashes), as shown here:

```
Dim Names$(100), Salary!(100), SocSec$(100)
```

Having done this, you now would use the same pointer (that is, the row number) to extract information from the three lists.

The way around this extra work is to use a new structure called a *record*. Records are not part of traditional BASICs, although they are common in programming languages such as C and Pascal. Essentially, a record is a type of "mixed" variable that you create as needed. It usually mixes different kinds of numbers and strings. Visual Basic makes it easy to avoid maintaining parallel structures or using arrays of variants.

Here's the first step: In the Declarations section of a code module, enter

```
Type  VitalInfo
     Name as String
     Salary as Long
     SocialSec as String
End Type
```

This defines the type. From this point on in the program, it's just as good a variable type for variables as single-precision, double-precision, or variants.

Now, to make (set up) a single variable of "type" VitalInfo, write

```
Dim YourName as VitalInfo
```

in the Declarations section of any form or module. You can also write

```
Static MyName As VitalInfo
```

inside a procedure. You can also set up global variables of this type using the Global statement.

Each of these statements sets up a single "mixed" variable. The jargon is to say, "YourName is a record variable of type VitalInfo."

Now you use a dot (period) to isolate the parts of this record:

```
YourName.Name = "Howard"
YourName.Salary = 100000
YourName.SocSecNumber = "036-78-9987"
```

You can also set up an array of these record variables:

```
Dim CompanyRecord(1 To 75) as VitalInfo
```

This sets up a list capable of holding 75 of these records.

Now imagine you wanted to design a form to allow inputting the data needed to fill the 75 records. Set up a form level array called CompanyRecord to hold the 75 records. Next, the form used for this input operation requires three labels to identify the text boxes, three text boxes (control names of Names, Salary, and SSNum), and a command button. If we give the command button the control name (value of Name property) AddButton and add to the Form the form name of DataForm, we can use the following code to add up to 75 records:

```
Sub AddEmpData_Click ()
  Static Count As Integer
  Count = Count + 1
  If Count > 75 Then
     MsgBox("Too Many records")
     Exit Sub
  End If
  DataForm.Caption = "Adding data for entry" + Str$(Count)
```

```
    CompanyRecord(Count).Name = Names.Text
    CompanyRecord(Count).Salary = Val(Salary.Text)
    CompanyRecord(Count).SocialSec = SSNum.Text
End Sub
```

Note that the caption on the form changes to reflect the number entered. By making Count a static variable and adding one before checking we make sure that at most 75 entries are allowed. Also note the periods for each component, or element, of the record.

You can even have a component of a record be a record itself. For example, you could make up a RecordOfSalary type to keep track of monthly earnings along with the previous year's salary:

```
Type RecordOfSalary
    SalInJan As Integer
    SalInFeb As Integer
    SalInMar As Integer
    SalInApr As Integer
    SalInMay As Integer
    SalInJun As Integer
    SalInJul As Integer
    SalInAug As Integer
    SalInSep As Integer
    SalInOct As Integer
    SalInNov As Integer
    SalInDec As Integer
    SalInPrevYear As Long
End Type
```

Now you can set up a record of records:

```
Type  ExpandedVitalInfo
    Name As String
    Salary As RecordOfSalary
    SocSecNumber As String * 11
End Type
```

Of course, filling out all the information needed for a single record is now that much harder. Filling in the record RecordOfSalary for a single employee requires at least 13 lines of code, so filling in a record of type ExpandedVitalInfo requires at least 15. It also gets a little messy to refer to the information in

ExpandedVitalInfo. You thread your way down by using more periods. After using

```
Dim GaryStats As ExpandedVitalInfo
```

to set up a variable of this new type, use a statement like

```
Print GaryStats.Salary.SalInPrevYr
```

to display the information on the previous year's salary. You can have records as one of the parameters in functions or subprograms. For example, you might write a general procedure to analyze salary data. The first line in the procedure would look like this:

```
Sub AnalyzeSalary (X As ExpandedVitalInfo)
```

This procedure allows (and in fact requires) that only variables of type ExpandedVitalInfo be passed to it. Now you can call it at any time by using a line of code like this:

```
AnalyzeSalary(BillStats)
```

This would analyze Bill's salary information. You also can pass individual components of a record whenever they match the type of the parameter.

Visual Basic inherited from the BASIC Professional Development System the ability to use arrays in user-defined records. You can set up an array inside the record:

```
Type RecordOfSalary
   Salaries(1 To 12) As Integers
   SalInPrevYear As Long
End Type
```

You can then use a loop plus one individual statement to fill a record rather than 13 using statements.

**tip:**

*By combining an array of records with the ReDim Preserve command, you can gain some of the features of pointers from Pascal or C.*

# Chapter 10

# Finishing the Interface

**n**OW that you have learned most of the programming techniques needed in Visual Basic it's time to turn to the user interface again. This chapter shows you how to use most of the remaining controls on the toolbox. These extra controls are what you need to perfect the user interface. For example, you'll see the techniques needed to add menus, toolbars, and status bars to your applications.

The controls covered in this chapter also let you add check boxes, option (radio) buttons, and various kinds of list and combo boxes to your Visual Basic projects. You'll also see another method besides double-clicking for quickly adding controls to a form at design time.

When you start adding many different controls to a form, the way they overlap becomes more important. So this chapter has a section on the order that Visual Basic uses to display interface elements. This section deals with what happens if you draw overlapping controls at design time or run time: which ones appear on top and how can this be changed. (It's called the ZOrder—and pronounced "zee order". The Z stands for the Z-axis, the conventional way to describe depth.)

Next, you'll see how to add standard Windows dialog boxes to your projects as well as a sophisticated method using MDI forms (*multiple document interface*) to add subsidiary (*child*) forms to a single parent form. In addition, you'll learn how to use timers to have parts of your program spring to life at specified time intervals and how to use picture boxes for displaying images.

Menus are covered next. Think of menu items as being specialized controls that you add to your forms. Menu items respond only to the click event, and unlike all the other controls in Visual Basic, menus are not added to forms by using the toolbox. Instead, you use the Menu Design window, which is available from the Window menu on the main menu bar. Visual Basic 3 also allows you to use pop-up menus and these are explained here as well.

The last section of the chapter is a (short) section on how the Windows interface for a program will usually look and feel to the user.

# The Toolbox Revisited

In Chapter 4 you saw the basic controls for a Visual Basic project: command buttons, line and shape controls, image controls, text boxes, and labels. Figure 10-1 shows you the controls covered in this chapter. Following is a brief description of each control. See the appropriate section of this chapter for more on the individual controls.

***Frames*** The icon for the frame control looks like a box with a bit of text (xyz) at the top. Frames give you a way to visually highlight and/or separate parts of a form by simply drawing a box around specific controls. You can also caption the frame if need be. (Chapter 12 gives you some more sophisticated methods of highlighting controls by drawing three-dimensional-looking frames around them.)

The frame control lets you group other Visual Basic controls visually but frames do much more than that. As you'll soon see, for design purposes, grouping controls inside a frame allows you to treat all the controls inside the frame as one unit. For example, they will move with the frame as you adjust its position.

***Picture Boxes*** The icon for picture boxes looks like a desert scene and reminds you that this control holds graphics images. Chapter 12 covers graphics in depth. Picture boxes gives you the simplest way of adding a toolbar or a status bar to

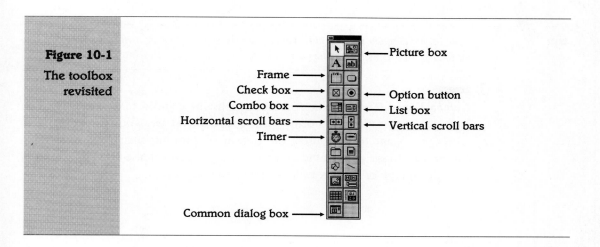

**Figure 10-1**

The toolbox revisited

Frame ⟶

Check box ⟶

Combo box ⟶

Horizontal scroll bars ⟶

Timer ⟶

Common dialog box ⟶

⟵ Picture box

⟵ Option button

⟵ List box

⟵ Vertical scroll bars

your applications. Picture boxes can also display icons, although image controls require fewer Windows resources and might be a better choice unless you also need to display text, add your own drawings to the control, or use an API function for special effects. Like frames, picture boxes can also act as containers for other controls.

■■■

***Check Boxes*** The icon for check boxes gives a good feel for what the control will look like on your form: a box with a cross. When your project is running, check boxes are toggled on and off via mouse clicks or the TAB+SPACEBAR combination. Check boxes are used when you want to allow users to select from various options but these options are not exclusive.

■■■

***Option (Radio) Buttons*** The icon for option buttons looks like an old-fashioned radio button—hence the other popular name for this control. Unlike check boxes, option buttons work in groups. When the user chooses one button in the group, all the others are turned off. This means option buttons are used for either/or situations. Option buttons are also toggled on and off via mouse clicks or the TAB+SPACEBAR combination.

■■■

***List Boxes*** Use list boxes when you want to give users a list of items from which they must make a choice. As the icon indicates, list boxes often come with scroll bars, which are automatically added if there are too many items to display for the current size of the list box.

**tip:**

*Since list boxes can be made to automatically sort themselves, they are useful for sorting small- to medium-sized lists without adding any code.*

■■■

***Combo Boxes*** Combo boxes combine a list box and a text box. The icon indicates this by showing a blank space above the list area. You use this control when you want to give users the option of entering their own choices in addition to those you provide on the list. This control also lets you display a specialized type of list box called a pull-down list box.

*Vertical and Horizontal Scroll Bars* The controls for vertical and horizontal scroll bars give you another way of getting user input. Another possibility is to use them to display how close you are to the beginning or end of a time-consuming process.

*Common Dialog Boxes* By now you've seen lots and lots of these usual Window dialog boxes. Whether opening or closing a file, choosing a font, printing a page, or changing the color of a Windows object, there are standard dialog boxes that users expect to see. This control lets you add them to your Visual Basic application.

*Timers* The icon for timers looks like an old-fashioned alarm clock. This reminds you that this control will wake up at specified time intervals. Unlike all other controls in the standard edition of Visual Basic, timers are always invisible to the user. You can see them only during the design phase of your project. You are restricted in the number of timers you can use both by Visual Basic and Windows itself. Do not go overboard on the timer control since it requires a large share of precious Windows resources.

## Frames

You rarely write event procedures for frames. In fact, frames only respond to mouse events. (See Chapter 13 for these events.) Instead, you usually use frames as passive containers to group images or controls. The screen in Figure 10-2 is an example of a form with multiple frames used to divide the form functionally.

There are 26 properties for frames, and all of them are similar to ones for the controls you are already familiar with. For example, the font properties control how the caption appears, MousePointer controls how the mouse pointer appears when it is inside the frame, and so on.

Finally, the important point to keep in mind when using a frame is that you must draw the frame first. Only after the frame is on the form should you place controls inside it. In this way, Visual Basic knows the controls are attached to the frame. (Otherwise, Visual Basic will not let the control respond to events that the frame can respond to and the controls will not move with the frame when you reposition it.) In particular, do *not* use the double-click method for creating a control when you want to attach a control to a frame. The double-click method places the control in the center of the screen, but even if

**Figure 10-2**

**Form with frames**

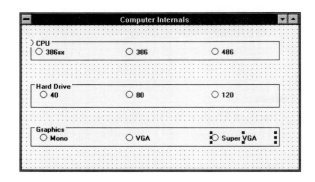

the frame is there, Visual Basic will not attach the control to the frame. Instead, use the method described in the next section or select the control from the toolbox and position the mouse pointer inside the frame before dragging and dropping the control. (See Chapter 4 for more details on this method for creating controls.)

**tip:**

*One of the least Windows-intensive ways to build a toolbar into an application is to use a frame with image controls inside it for the actions. Resize the frame to be the height of the image controls and the width of the form and use code to position it where you want. Finally, write the code for the toolbar operation in the Click event of the image control for the action.*

(See the section on picture boxes for the more usual ways to build toolbars.)

## The Sticky Click Method for Creating Controls

Visual Basic has one other way to create controls on a form. It is especially useful when working with frames. This method is a cross between the double-click and the drag-and-drop methods you've seen already. Using the *sticky click method,* you can create multiple copies of the same control but position and size them as you see fit. (Recall that the double-click method always gives you similarly sized controls, stacked one on another, in the center of the form.) To create controls using the sticky click method, follow these steps:

1. Move to the toolbox and press CTRL while clicking the left mouse button. The control in the toolbox is highlighted.

2. Move to the form or frame and click the left mouse button. The top-left corner of the new control is "stuck" at this location.

3. Hold the left mouse button down and drag until you are happy with the size of the control.

4. Release the mouse button and repeat steps 2 and 3 until you have finished placing all the controls of that type on the form or in the frame.

To change to another way of working with the toolbox, go back to the toolbox and click the pointer or any control other than the one you were working with, using the sticky click method.

## Picture Boxes

You can use picture boxes in many different contexts, not just as passive containers for graphics or icons. For example, because they respond to the Click and Double-click events, you can use them exactly as you would use a command button. (Although image controls would be a better choice if that is all you are doing with them.)

On the other hand, for display purposes at least, you can think of picture boxes as being "forms within forms." For example, you can print text directly to a picture box. Moreover, because picture boxes have the CurrentX and CurrentY properties as well as the same Scale properties as forms, you can accurately position the text inside them. (See Chapter 12 for more on the Scale properties.) Finally, just as with frames, picture boxes can have controls attached to them. To attach a control to a picture box use the same methods described above for attaching controls to a frame.

Picture boxes have over 50 properties and respond to 19 events, and you can use any one of 18 methods for them. (For the methods for picture boxes that are used for graphics—Circle, Line, and so on—see Chapter 12.) The picture box events that respond to mouse movements or clicks are covered in Chapter 13, and those for Link events are covered in Chapter 15. All the remaining events are those like Click, Double-click, or the Key events that you've already seen.

Many of the properties are already familiar to you: the font properties control how text appears, Visible and Enabled control whether the control is responsive or even visible, and so on. One property, AutoSize, which you've seen for labels, is even more important for picture boxes. This is because how much of the image your picture box will show depends on how large you designed (or programmed) it—unless you set the AutoSize property to True. If AutoSize is True, the picture box will automatically resize itself to fit the image. Of course, like text boxes, labels, and command buttons, you can also resize the picture box by manipulating the sizing handles when you've selected the control at design time or with code at run time.

**note:** *What AutoSize does is determined by the size of the image assigned to the Picture property of the picture box, not that of any controls that may be attached to the box.*

The Cls method works in much the same way for picture boxes as it does for forms with one extra point worth keeping in mind: Cls erases whatever image and text were placed on the picture box *while the program was running.* (You will see shortly how to clear graphics that were placed in a picture box or form at design time.)

The Move method lets you move the picture box around at run time. The TextHeight and TextWidth methods are used with the CurrentX and CurrentY properties to accurately position text inside a picture box. (The values associated to them depend on the current Scale.)

## Graphics and Picture Boxes

Picture boxes can also hold the three types of graphics that are common in Windows applications. Here are short descriptions of them.

**Bitmaps** Bitmaps are graphic images of the screen (or part of the screen). Each dot (or *pixel*) corresponds to 1 bit for black-and-white displays and many bits for color or gray-scale displays. Image controls are often used to display bitmaps. When bitmaps are stored in a file, the convention is to use a .BMP extension for the filename. The Windows Paintbrush program generates bitmaps, so this is a convenient source for them.

**Icons** You already saw icon files in Chapters 3 and 4. Besides the 400 or so icons supplied with Visual Basic, you can create custom icons with the IconWorks sample program supplied with Visual Basic. The convention is to use a .ICO extension for icons.

***Windows Metafiles*** Instead of a dot-by-dot description of the graphics image, think of Windows metafiles as containing descriptions of how and where to draw the object. Because they describe the picture in terms of circles, lines, and the like, they work much better than bitmaps that require you to shrink or enlarge a graphics image. Because of the calculations required to adjust their size, they are displayed slower than bitmaps. Many publishing programs (like Microsoft Publisher) come with libraries of Windows metafiles. No metafiles are supplied with Visual Basic, but over 80 are supplied with Visual Basic Professional Edition (see Appendix A for more information). The convention it to use a .WMF for metafiles.

**note:** *If you are using a Windows metafile as the value of the Picture property do not set the AutoSize property to be True. Visual Basic makes a very tiny picture box in this case.*

## ADDING IMAGES TO PICTURE BOXES AND FORMS

There are two ways to display an image inside a picture box (or form) at design time. The first is to load a picture by setting the Picture property via the Properties window just like you did for an image control. (You'll be presented with the same sort of dialog box when you click the ellipsis.)

Another possibility is to paste a picture directly into the picture box (or form). For example, you may be enamored of a picture you just drew using Microsoft Paintbrush and want to bring this image inside a Visual Basic project. You do this by using the Windows clipboard. For example, if the picture box is the active control, copy the picture from Windows Paintbrush to the clipboard. Then choose Paste from the Edit menu (ALT+E+P). Visual Basic then attaches the bitmap to the picture box or form. In particular, when you save the Visual Basic project, the image is saved at the same time. Pictures added at design time do not need to be supplied as individual files, as they would if you wanted to load the picture while the project was running.

Nonetheless, you will occasionally want to add (or allow the user to add) a picture while a Visual Basic project is running. There are also two ways to do this. The first requires you to have the picture already loaded in a form or a picture box on some form in the project. If this is true, you need only assign the Picture property of one object to the Picture property of the other. For example, suppose you have two picture boxes, Picture1 and Picture2. Picture1 has an image attached to it, and Picture2 does not. Then a line of code like

```
Picture2.Picture = Picture1.Picture
```

copies the image from the first picture box to the second.

More common, however, is to use the LoadPicture function to attach a file containing a graphics image to a picture box. The syntax for this function is

PictureBoxName.Picture = LoadPicture([*filename*])

or, for forms,

[*FormName.*]Picture = LoadPicture([*filename*])

The filename should include the full path name if the file isn't in the current directory. If you leave out the optional filename by writing

[*FormName.*]Picture = LoadPicture ( )

(the empty parentheses are necessary), then the current image is cleared from the form or picture box. Unlike the Cls method, which clears images and text placed only while the project is running, the LoadPicture statement without a filename will also clear a picture that was added at design time.

**note:** *Any pictures added to your project at design time become part of the project when made into an .EXE file. This means that the size of the file can grow very large, very quickly. A 256-color bitmap of the screen is around .5 megabytes, for example.*

## Adding Toolbars and Status Bars to Projects

Although you can use a frame to put a toolbar or a status bar on a form, most programmers prefer to use picture boxes. This is because placing a picture box on the bottom or top of a form is easy in Visual Basic 3 using the picture boxes' Align property.

The value of the Align property determines where the picture box appears. The Align property has three possible values and here is what they do.

| Align Property Value | Action |
| --- | --- |
| 0 | The default for ordinary forms. You can position the picture box anywhere you want |
| 1 | The value for a toolbar. The picture box will appear flush against the top and will automatically have the same width as the form (i.e. the value of the ScaleWidth property). This is the default for MDI forms (see the section in this chapter on them) |
| 2 | The value for a status bar. The picture box is flush with the bottom of the form and also automatically is the correct width |

**note:** *If you need to place a toolbar in another position (like the far left used in Windows Paintbrush) you have to use code to position the picture box. This is best done in the Paint event procedure of the Form.*

## BUILDING A TOOLBAR OR STATUS BAR

First, decide on the icons you want to use. Next, assign these icons to the Picture property of the image controls that will be on the toolbar.

**tip:** *Make the image controls you use in your Toolbar part of a control array. This makes the necessary code shorter.*

For example, suppose you wanted to prepare a form with a toolbar like the one shown in Figure 10–3.

Here's what you have to do:

1. Draw a large enough picture box to encompass the icons that are used on the toolbar.

2. Set the Align property of the picture box to 1.

3. Attach an image control to the picture box and make it part of a control array by adjusting the index property.

4. Add the image controls at design time or run time and adjust the Picture property of the image control to the correct icons.

**Figure 10-3**

**Form with toolbar**

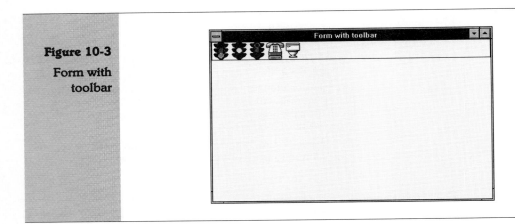

Now, to give the toolbar a professional look you should have the Form_Paint event adjust the size and position of the icons inside the Picture box with code that might look like this. (This code assumes that the image controls have already been loaded with equally sized pictures or icons and that they have AutoSize set to True. We also assume that you have five image controls in the control array named ToolImage and the picture box has a control name of ToolBar.):

```
Sub Form_Paint()
  Dim I As Integer, PositionIcon As Integer, ImageWidth As_
Integer
  ToolBar.Align = 1
  Toolbar.Height = ToolImage(0).Height
  ImageWidth = Image(0).Width
  For I = 0 To 4
    ToolImage(I).Move ImageWidth*I, 0
  Next I
  .
' other code for the Paint event
End Sub
```

What this code does is position the image controls sequentially with no space between them. We set the width before the loop to avoid having to check a property value within the loop. (This is a common way to speed up loops.) You could easily insert gaps between the icons by changing the values used in the Move method. Notice how the code also adjusts the size of the toolbar to be exactly as high as the image controls themselves.

Status bars tend to be text-oriented. Typically, the only graphics used are shaded lines to separate the text items to give a nicer look to the bar. These lines can be created using the Line control or the graphics methods from Chapter 12. Of course, you can write the code that sends the text to the status bar in whatever procedure necessitates your updating the status bar. However, the cleanest choice is always to call a general procedure that takes the text to be displayed and updates the status bar. (For example, this general procedure may need to parse the text so as to adjust where the separation lines are placed and, in any case, it is always best to have procedures concentrate on what they are supposed to be doing rather than having them update status bars as well!)

## Option (Radio) Buttons

Option buttons always work together. When the user chooses one button by clicking inside the button or caption area, all the other buttons in the group are turned off. For this reason, any application that uses more than one group of option buttons on a form *must* use a frame or picture box to separate the groups. (See the section "Frames" earlier in this chapter for how to do this.) Option buttons can be turned on whenever the focus is inside the button's area—this includes the caption of the button.

Add option (radio) buttons to a form when you want the user to choose from a finite list of possibilities. For example, the screen in Figure 10-4 shows how a form for a database might look.

The Value property of the option button tells you whether a button was selected by the user. If the Value property is True (−1), the user selected that button; otherwise, its Value property is False (0).

**Figure 10-4**

Form for possible database

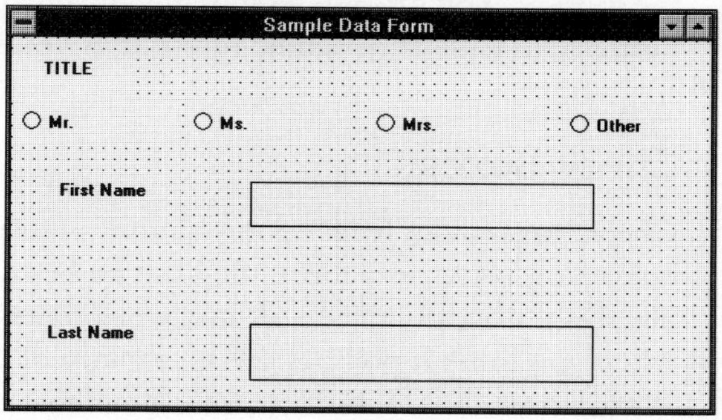

If you give control names to the option buttons in Figure 10-3 of "Mr.", "Ms.", "Mrs.", and "Other", you could use code like the following to pick up the information:

```
If Mr.Value Then
   Title$="Mr."
ElseIf Ms.Value Then
   Title$= "Ms."
ElseIf Mrs.Value Then
   Title$= "Mrs."
Else
   Title$=InputBox$("Please enter the title you want us to
use.")
End If
```

This code works because of the Boolean (True/False) nature of the Value property. For example, the clause "Ms.Value" will be True only when the user has chosen the Ms option button.

Option buttons respond to the Click and Double-click events as well as to the Key events and now can also repond to the mouse events. They can also detect if a button has received or lost the focus. Visual Basic generates the Click event when the user selects the button by clicking with the mouse or moving via the TAB key and pressing SPACEBAR. If you reset the Value property of the Option button to True (–1) inside code, then you also generate the Click event. This is occasionally useful for demonstration programs. You can also turn on one of the buttons at design time by setting its Value property to True via the Properties bar.

The properties of option buttons are a subset of those for command buttons. For example, you can set the Font properties to change how Visual Basic displays the caption. You can also temporarily disable the button by setting the Enabled property to False at design or run time as you see fit.

## Check Boxes

Check boxes differ from option buttons in that, regardless of how many check boxes you place on a form, they can all be turned on and off independently. For this reason, placing check boxes in a frame or picture box is necessary only when you think it polishes the appearance of your form.

However, like option buttons, whether a check box is on or off is also determined by its Value property. If the user has selected a check box, the Value property switches to True. It stays True until the user deselects that box. (This is unlike the situation with option buttons, where selecting one of the buttons flips the value of all the others to False.) If you want a check box to be on when the project starts up, either set the Value property of the box to True at design time or set it to True in the Form_Load procedure. Check boxes can be turned on whenever the focus is inside the check box—like option buttons this includes the caption area.

As an example of where you might want to use check boxes, consider the following form:

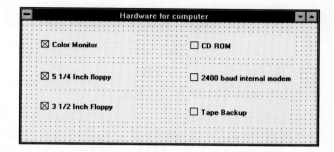

Notice that several of the check boxes are already defaulted to be on. (After all, most people want color monitors for their computers.) On the other hand, the user can still switch to a monochrome monitor by deselecting the check box.

You can combine check boxes and radio buttons. A good example of this is the Print dialog box on the File menu:

As with option buttons, check boxes will respond to the Click and Double-click events as well as to the Key events. They will also detect if a button has received or lost the focus. As with option buttons, Visual Basic generates the Click event when the user selects the button by clicking with the mouse or moving via the TAB key and pressing SPACEBAR. If you reset the Value property of the button to True inside code, you also generate the Click event.

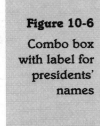

**Figure 10-5**

List box with presidents' names

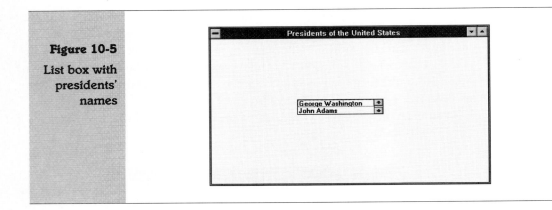

## List and Combo Boxes

Use list boxes when you have a fixed list of choices. For example, suppose you are designing an application to provide information about the United States presidents. The form might look like the one in Figure 10-5. Note that (as in this figure) Visual Basic automatically adds vertical scroll bars whenever the list box is too small for all the items it contains.

On the other hand, you might want this application to let the user select a president by number rather than by scrolling through the list. To allow users to input data as well as make choices from a list, use a combo box, as shown in Figure 10-6. Notice that this form has a label near the combo box to identify what the user should type into the input area of the combo box.

**Figure 10-6**

Combo box with label for presidents' names

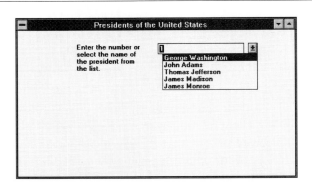

There are actually two types of combo boxes, and which one you get depends on the value of the Style property.

◆ If the value of the Style property is set to the default value of 0, you get a combo box with a detached arrow. If the user clicks the arrow, he or she will see the list of choices given in the box.

◆ If the value of the Style property of a combo box is 1, the user sees the combo box with the list already dropped down.

Here are examples of these two types of combo boxes:

Notice that in both these cases, the user still has a text area to enter information. On the other hand, the final possible choice for the Style property for combo boxes, a value of 2, gives you a pull-down list box, as in the following:

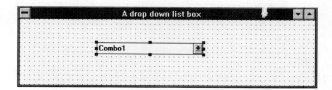

Thus, although you draw a pull-down list box by using the Combo Box icon, once you set the Style property to 2 (either via code or at design time), the text area disappears and what appears on the screen looks like a different version of a list box. On the other hand, the events that a pull-down list box will respond to are those of a combo box and not those of a list box.

Items in a list or combo box can be sorted in ASCII/ANSI order. This depends on the value of the Sorted property. If you set the Sorted property to True, Visual Basic will order the items in ASCII/ANSI order. Otherwise, the order of the items depends on the order in which you placed them in the list box. You can set the Sorted property to True at design or run time, as well as switch it back and forth via code as necessary.

## MANIPULATING THE ITEMS ON A LIST OR COMBO BOX

You can add or remove items from a list or combo box only while the project is running. Use the AddItem method to add an item to a list or combo box. The syntax for this method is

ListName.AddItem *Item$* [, *Index*]

ListName is the control name of the list or combo box, and *Item$* is a string or string expression. If the Sorted property is True for the list or combo box, then *Item$* goes where ASCII order places it. If the Sorted property is False, Visual Basic places *Item$* either at the position determined by the *Index* parameter or at the end of the list when you do not specify the index. The *Index* parameter must be an integer or integral expression. An *Index* value of 0 (not 1) means you are at the beginning of the list. The *Index* option has no effect on where the item is added to the list if the Sorted property of the list box is set to True.

The most common place to use the AddItem statement is in the Form_Load procedure. For example, if the list or combo box had the control name of Presidents, the code to build the list might start like this:

```
Sub Form_Load()
  Presidents.AddItem "George Washington"
  Presidents.AddItem "John Adams"
  Presidents.AddItem "Thomas Jefferson"
  Presidents.AddItem "James Madison"
  .
  .
  .
End Sub
```

**note:** *For GW-BASIC and QuickBASIC users: there is no direct analogue of the READ/DATA combination to build information into your program.*

Actually building the information into your program usually comes down to repeatedly typing in the necessary AddItem statements. One occasionally useful way around this chore is to store the information that will go in the box in a file (see Chapter 14).

You can also remove an item from a list while the program is running. The syntax for the RemoveItem method is

ListName.RemoveItem *Index*

where, as before, *ListName* is the control name for the list or combo box and *Index* is the position where the item was located.

In addition to removing individual items on a list, you can use the Clear method, which was new to Visual Basic 2.0, to remove all the entries. The syntax is

ListName.Clear

**tip:**

*Using Clear is much faster then removing all the items with a loop.*

## THE LIST AND COMBO BOX PROPERTIES

Many of the properties of list and combo boxes determine how the information should appear. These properties are the same as ones you've already seen. For example, the font properties control how the items appear in the list, and the BackColor and ForeColor properties control what colors are used for the background and foreground, respectively. Similarly, properties like Height, Left Top, and Width control the shape and location of the list or combo box. The properties special to list and combo boxes let you get at the information in the box or the item the user has moved to within the box. They also allow you to have multiple columns in a list box.

For example, when a user moves the focus to a list or combo box, he or she can select an item on the list or combo box by using the ordinary Windows conventions—the arrow keys, PGUP, PGDN, the END key, and so on. In fact, once the user moves the focus to the list or combo box, he or she can also use the Windows shortcut of pressing a letter key to move to the first item in the list box beginning with that letter. The item the user selects is always highlighted. (On the other hand, a combo box with the list pulled down also moves through the items but doesn't highlight the first match.) All these details are handled automatically by Visual Basic. The item selected by the user is the value of the Text property of the box.

Following are descriptions of the six list and combo box properties you'll need to work with these controls.

**ListIndex** The value of the ListIndex property gives the index number of the highlighted item, which is where the user has stopped in the list. If no item was selected, the value of this property is −1. For example, suppose you've stored information about the presidents in a string array named PresidentInfo$ and you need to get at the item in this array containing information about the president that the user has selected from the Presidents list box. A statement such as

```
If ListIndex = -1 Then
   MsgBox "No president selected!"
Else
   Info$ = PresidentInfo$(Presidents.ListIndex + 1)
End If
```

makes the value of the Info$ string variable the information you'll need. The code also assumes you've stored the information about George Washington in the first position in the PresidentInfo$ string array. If you've put the information about Washington in the zero slot, you don't need to add 1 to the value of President.ListIndex to get at this information.

**Text** The Text property gives the currently selected item stored as a string. (If you need the numeric equivalent, apply the Val function or do an implicit conversion via the Variant data type.)

**List** The List property is not a single value but actually is a string array that contains all the items on the list. The value of the *BoxName*.Text property for a list or combo box is the same as that of *BoxName*.List(*ListIndex*).

**ListCount** The ListCount property gives you the number of items on the list. Since the Index property starts at 0, to analyze the contents of the list using a For-Next loop, write the limits of the loop as

For I% = 0 To *BoxName*.ListCount−1

**Columns and MultiSelection** The Columns property controls the number of columns in a list box. If the value is 0 (the default), you get a normal single-column list box with vertical scrolling. If the value is 1, you get a single-column list box with horizontal scrolling. If the value is greater than 1, you allow (but do not require) multiple columns.

**tip:** *Multiple columns show up only when the items don't fit into the list box. To force multiple columns, reduce the height of the list box accordingly.*

The MultiSelect property controls whether the user can select more than one item from the list. (Of course, you may have to parse the resulting string assigned to the Text property to determine the individual items selected.) There are three possible values for this property:

| Type of Selection | Value | How It Works |
|---|---|---|
| No multiselection allowed | 0 | |
| Simple multiselection | 1 | Use ordinary Windows techniques and mouse dragging (SHIFT+arrow and so on) to select more items |
| Extended multiselection | 2 | SHIFT+mouse click extends the selection to include all list items between the current selection CTRL+click selects or deselects a single item |

## THE LIST BOX EVENTS

List boxes respond to 12 events. The KeyUp, KeyDown, and KeyPress events work exactly as before. The mouse events are covered in Chapter 13. List boxes can also tell you whether they've received or lost the focus.

However, the two most important events for list boxes are the Click and Double-click events. An important Windows convention is that clicking on an item selects the item but does not choose it. This is reserved for double-clicking on the item. In general, therefore, you do not write code for the Click event procedure for a list box but only for the Double-click event procedure.

Another reason not to write code for the Click event procedure is that each time the user moves through the list, Visual Basic generates the Click event. Landing on an item in a list box by using the keyboard is the functional equivalent of clicking on the item. (There is no keyboard equivalent for double-clicking, although you can write your own for a specific list box by using the Key events.)

## THE COMBO BOX EVENTS

Combo boxes respond to many of the same events as list boxes. You can analyze which keys were pressed or whether the box has received or lost the focus.

The first event that is different is the Change event. The Change event occurs only for pull-down combo boxes and simple combo boxes (Style = 0 or 1). Visual Basic does not generate this event if you are using a pull-down list box (Style = 2). Visual Basic generates this event whenever the user enters data in the text area of the combo box or you change the Text property of the combo box from code.

As an example of where you might use this, suppose you've set up the list of presidents using a simple combo box (Style = 0, control Name = Presidents). Again, let's assume the information you want to display about each president is stored in the string array: PresidentsInfo$. As the directions on the screen in Figure 10-6 indicate, you want to allow the user the possibility of entering the number of the president instead of scrolling through the list. Now, suppose someone typed a number in the text box. Then you might first try to use the following Change event procedure to give the user the information he or she might be looking for:

```
Sub Presidents_Change()
   PresidentNumber% = Val(Presidents.Text)
   If PresidentNumber% < 1 Or PresidentNumber% >42 Then
     MsgBox("Only 42 presidents with Clinton's election!")
   Else
     MsgBox(PresidentsInfo$(PresidentNumber%))
   End If
End Sub
```

The trouble with this is that the Change event procedure is *too* responsive for this particular task. Visual Basic calls this event procedure every time the user types a character in the text area of the combo box. This means that for all but the first nine presidents, the procedure is called twice. (For example, if the user entered **16**, he or she would see information about both Washington and Lincoln!) Also, if the user pulls down the list and clicks, text rather than a number fills the text box. A better way to analyze the information is to put this code inside the KeyPress event procedure but check that the user has pressed ENTER. You can do this with the following code:

```
Sub Presidents.KeyPress(KeyAscii As Integer)
  If KeyAscii = 13 Then                     'the Enter key
    PresidentNumber% = Val(Presidents.Text)
    Select Case PresidentNumber%
      Case 0
        MsgBox("Please enter a number or double-click on an
entry.")
      Case Is < 1
        MsgBox("No negative (numbered at least) presidents.")
      Case Is > 42
        MsgBox("Only 42 presidents so far.")
      Case Else
        MsgBox(PresidentsInfo$(PresidentNumber%))
    End Select
  End If
End Sub
```

You can easily modify this procedure to let the user select an item by scrolling through the list and pressing ENTER. (Change the Case 0 clause.)

Since simple combo boxes (Style = 1) recognize the Double-click event, another possibility is to code this in the Double-click event procedure. However, since there is no keyboard equivalent for double-clicking, you still might want to write a KeyPress event procedure to add keyboard equivalents for the user.

Visual Basic calls the DropDown event procedure right after the user clicks the detached arrow to pull the list box down or presses ALT+DOWN ARROW when the combo box has the focus—before the list drops down. For this reason, this event procedure is mostly used to update a combo box before the list appears. Since you can have a pull-down list only when the Style property is 0 or 2, this event is not invoked for simple combo boxes (Style = 1).

## ASSOCIATING NUMBERS TO ITEMS ON LIST OR COMBO BOXES

In the Checkbook Management Program (Chapter 18) we need to associate an account ID number to the account's name. Needing to associate integers to items in a list or combo is so common that a simple method of doing this was added to Visual Basic 2.0. Of course, you could create an array to store this information and keep track of this array yourself but you no longer need to do that—at least as long as all you need is a (long) integer associated to the item.

Whenever you create a list or combo box, Visual Basic automatically creates a long integer array called the ItemData array. This array is another property of the box like the List array that you saw previously. And, like any property of a Visual Basic control, you can examine it or modify it.

If you want to add the numeric data to an entry in this ItemData array, you need to know the array index of the item. This is taken care of by the NewIndex property of the box. This property gives you the index of the last item added to the box. (If the Sorted property is True this is particularly useful information.)

At this point you need to write the code to update the ItemData array. The code will always look something like this.

```
List1.AddItem ItemToBeAdded
List1.ItemData(List1.NewIndex) = LongIntegerData
```

(See Chapter 18 for how this might be used in a more realistic situation.)

## Scroll Bars

Scroll bars are used to get input or display output when you don't care about the exact value of an object but you do care whether the change is small or large. A good example of using scroll bars to accept input may be found in the Custom Color dialog box available from the color palette. As you saw in Chapter 3, this dialog box lets you adjust the amount of red, green, or blue for the custom color by moving the scroll bars. Although the common dialog box for colors is now built into Visual Basic (see the section on "Common Dialog Boxes" in this chapter), this box is often overwhelming to naive users. Therefore you will occasionally want to let users adjust the color of a form or picture box by using scroll bars alone. The next section shows you how to code this.

Vertical scroll bars and horizontal scroll bars work exactly the same way. Scroll bars span a range of values; the scroll box shows where the value is relative to the two extremes. Every scroll bar has a little box (called the *thumb* for some reason) inside of it. Users manipulate the bars either by clicking on the left or right pointing arrow or dragging the thumb.

Scroll bars work with 9 events and 22 properties. The events that are the key to using scroll bars are the Change event and the Scroll event. The Change event is activated whenever the user clicks on one of the arrows or drags the thumb and then releases the mouse button. The Scroll event is much more sensitive; it is called *continuously whenever the user manipulates the thumb.* The Scroll event is used to provide instantaneous feedback whereas the Change event is used more discretely.

**caution:** *Because the Scroll event is called essentially continuously as the user manipulates the bars, tighten up code inside of it as much as possible.*

So, use the Scroll event procedure very carefully. Use it only where you really need to give instantaneous feedback.

## SPECIAL PROPERTIES OF SCROLL BARS

Only 5 properties are special to scroll bars. What follows is a short description of those properties.

*Min*   The Min property is an integer that defines the smallest value for a scroll bar. For red, green, or blue color codes, which range from zero to 255, the Min property would be set to zero for a project that sets colors via scroll bars. Since Min takes integer values, the possible settings are from −32,768 to 32,767.

*Max*   The Max property is an integer that defines the largest value for a scroll bar. For the primary color codes, the Max property would be set to 255 for a project that sets the colors via a scroll bar. Since Max also takes integer values, the possible settings are also from −32,768 to 32,767. You can set the Max value to be less than the Min value. This causes the maximum value of the scroll bar to be reached at the left or top of the scroll bar, depending on whether it's a horizontal or vertical scroll bar. Both Max and Min are usually set at design time, but you can change them with code while a project is running.

*Value*   The Value property tells you where the scroll bar is. It is always an integer. The range is determined by the Min property and the Max property. The Value property can be as small as the Min value or as large as the Max value.

*SmallChange*   What you set the SmallChange property to determines how Visual Basic changes the Value property of the scroll bar in response to a user's clicking one of the scroll arrows or pressing UP ARROW or DOWN ARROW. If the user clicks the up scroll arrow, the Value property of the scroll bar increases by the amount of SmallChange until the Value property reaches the value of the Max property. If the user clicks the down scroll arrow, Visual Basic decreases the Value property similarly. The default value of SmallChange is 1, and it can be set to be any integer between 1 and 32,767. As with Min and Max, this property is usually set at design time but can be changed in code as well.

**LargeChange** What you set the LargeChange property to determines how Visual Basic changes the Value property of the scroll bar in response to a user's clicking between the thumb (scroll box) and the scroll arrow or pressing PGUP or PGDN. The default LargeChange value is also 1 but is usually set to be a multiple of the SmallChange value. It too is an integer between 1 and 32,767. As with Min, Max, and SmallChange, this property is usually set at design time but can also be changed at run time.

### AN EXAMPLE: ADJUSTING COLOR CODES VIA SCROLL BARS

Suppose you want to begin an application by letting the user adjust the background and foreground colors. The initial form might look like the one in Figure 10-7. Notice that this application has three vertical scroll bars, a picture box, and two radio buttons.

Here is a table describing the important properties of the controls that make up this application:

| Control Name | Property | Setting |
|---|---|---|
| RedBar | Min | 0 |
| | Max | 255 |
| | SmallChange | 5 |
| | LargeChange | 25 |
| GreenBar | Min | 0 |
| | Max | 255 |
| | SmallChange | 5 |
| | LargeChange | 25 |
| BlueBar | Min | 0 |
| | Max | 255 |
| | SmallChange | 5 |
| | LargeChange | 25 |
| BkColorButton | Caption | BackColor |
| FrColorButton | Caption | ForeColor |

Leave the picture box with the default name of Picture1. Here's an example of the code you'll need for this project:

**Figure 10-7**

**Form to adjust color using scroll bars**

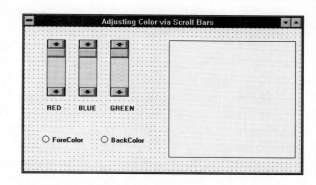

```
Sub RedBar_Change()
  If BkColorButton.Value Then
    Picture1.BackColor = RGB(RedBar.Value,GreenBar.Value,
BlueBar.Value)
  ElseIf FrColorButton.Value Then
    Picture1.ForeColor = RGB(RedBar.Value,GreenBar.Value,
BlueBar.Value)
    Picture1.Cls
    Picture1.Print "This is displayed in the current_
foreground
color."
  End If
End Sub
```

The other Change procedures work exactly the same way. Notice that to show the ForeColor change requires displaying some text inside the picture box. Finally, notice that in an actual application, you would probably add a command button called Finished, and have a click on that button hide this form, saving the BackColor and ForeColor information as the values of global variables to use for the other forms in your project. You might also combine all this code into a single general procedure that uses a color as the parameter. Notice that this would not be a good place to use the Scroll event. Color changes are too subtle to bother with instantaneous feedback.

## Timers

Use a timer control whenever you want something (or nothing; in other words, a pause) to happen periodically. You might want to have a program that wakes up periodically and checks stock prices. On a more prosaic level, if you want to display a "clock" on a form, you might want to update the clock's display every minute or even every second. Timers are not visible to the user; the icon appears only at design time. For this reason, where you place or how you size the timer control at design time is not important. Although timers are an important tool for Visual Basic programmers, they shouldn't be overused. In fact, Windows restricts all the applications (not just the Visual Basic applications) running at one time to 16 timers.

The screen in Figure 10-8 shows an example of a form at design time with a label and a timer control that you can use to develop a simple clock (see the next section).

Besides the control name of the timer (the defaults are Timer1, Timer2, and so on), there are two important properties of timer controls: Enabled and Interval.

### ENABLED

Enabled is a Boolean (True/False) property that determines if the timer should start ticking or not. If you set this to True (−1) at design time, the clock starts ticking when the form loads. "Ticking" is meant metaphorically; there's no noise unless you program one. Also, because timer controls are invisible to the user, he or she may well be unaware that a timer has been enabled. For this reason, you may want to notify the user that a timer is working by means of a message box, an image control, or a picture box with a clock icon inside of it.

**Figure 10-8**

**Form for a simple clock**

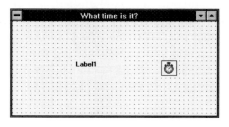

If you set the Enabled property to False at design time, the timer control starts working only when you switch this property to True in code. Similarly, you can disable a timer inside code by setting its Enabled property to False.

### INTERVAL

The Interval property determines how much time Visual Basic waits before calling the Timer event procedure (see the next section). The interval is measured in milliseconds, and the theoretical limits are between 1 millisecond and 65,535 milliseconds (a little more than one minute and five seconds). The reason these are only theoretical limits is that the underlying hardware reports the passage of only 18 clock ticks per second. Since this is a little less than 56 milliseconds per clock tick, you can't really use an Interval property any less than 56, and intervals that don't differ by at least this amount may give the same results. (Although you can use API functions for smaller event timings.)

The smaller you set the Interval property, the more CPU time is spent waking up the Timer event procedure. Set the Interval property too small and your system performance may slow to a crawl.

**note:**  *An Interval property of 0 disables the timer.*

Finally, since the CPU may be doing something else when the interval time elapses, you cannot be guaranteed that Visual Basic will call the Timer event procedure exactly when you want it. (Visual Basic will know when the interval has elapsed; it just may need to finish what it is doing before activating the Timer event.) If the interval has elapsed, Visual Basic will call the Timer event procedure as soon as it is free to do so. The next section explains how to deal with this problem.

### THE TIMER EVENT AND SOME SAMPLE USES

Suppose you want to develop a project with a clock that will update itself every second, following the form shown in Figure 10-8. To design the form, follow these steps:

1. Add a label and a timer to a blank form.

2. Set the AutoSize property of the label to be True and the FontSize to be 18. Set the Interval property of the timer control to be 1000 (1000 milliseconds = 1 second).

Now write the following code in the Timer event procedure for the Timer1 control:

```
Sub Timer1_Timer()
  Label1.Caption = "The time is " + Format$(Now,"hh:mm:ss:")
End Sub
```

Visual Basic will call this event procedure and update the clock's time roughly every second because the Interval property was 1000. (See Chapter 5 for how the Now function works with the Format$ function.) It would be easy enough to add an option button to let the user switch to an AM/PM display if he or she wanted.

Next, suppose you want to have a Timer event procedure do something even less frequently than the maximum setting for the Interval property—much more slowly than once a minute. The trick is to add a static variable to the Timer event procedure. For example, suppose you want to have a Timer event procedure wake up only once an hour. Set the Interval property to 60,000 (one minute):

```
Sub Timer1_Timer()
  Static TimerTimes As Integer
  TimerTimes = TimerTimes + 1
  If TimerTimes = 60 Then
    TimerTimes = 0             'reset counter
    'Here's where the once an hour code would go
  Else
    Exit Sub
  End If
End Sub
```

The If clause is activated only when the counter TimerTimes reaches 60. But this happens only when the Timer event procedure has been called 60 times, because TimerTimes is a static variable. Now, put whatever code you want inside the If clause. That code will be processed only once an hour (because you reset TimerTimes back to 0).

Finally, to take into account the possibility that Visual Basic was doing something else exactly when the timer elapsed, you can add code inside the

Timer event procedure to check the system clock if you feel this is necessary. (See Chapter 5 for the functions that check the clock.)

## AN EXAMPLE: SCREEN BLANKERS

Here is another example. One of the problems with computer screens is that they may be left on too long. This occasionally causes an image to be burned into the screen, its ghostly presence interfering with efficient use of the monitor forever after. Screen-blanking programs work by constantly drawing a different image in a different color. They were originally designed to prevent burn-in but now of course they are popular methods of expressing one's individuality. It is trivial to use a timer control to write a screen-blanking program. While commercial programs provide beautiful images, the following project gives you a randomly colored, randomly placed "Press any key to end" message.

For this, start up a new project and add a timer control to it. Next, make the BackColor property black. You can do this either by using the color palette or by directly setting the BackColor property color code to the color code for black (&H0&). Finally, since you want to have this screen take over the whole screen, set the Border property to None (0) and the WindowState property to Maximal (2).

Here's the code for the Timer1_Timer event procedure:

```
Sub Timer1_Timer()
  Cls
  CurrentX = Rnd*ScaleWidth
  CurrentY = Rnd*ScaleHeight
  ForeColor = QBColor(16*Rnd)
  Print "Press any key to end!"
End Sub
```

This program first clears the screen. Next, it calculates a random location on the screen and sets the ForeColor randomly using the QBColor function. (See Chapter 12 for more on this function.) Of course, since you are taking a percentage of the screen height and width, this may occasionally not give the program enough room to display the full message. If this bothers you, you can easily add code by using the TextHeight and TextWidth methods to make sure the text is always on the screen.

Now, having the program end when the user presses a key requires only a simple KeyDown event procedure:

```
Sub Form_KeyDown(KeyCode As Integer, Shift As Integer)
   End
End Sub
```

This procedure is invoked by Visual Basic whenever the user presses any key, thus ending the application.

To make this into a practical screen-blanking program, your first instinct might be to choose a large value for the Interval property like 1000 (one second) or even 2000 (two seconds) for the Interval property. This prevents the text from moving around like crazy. On the other hand, it would probably be better to use a small interval of, say, 100 for the Interval procedure and add a call to the DoEvents function inside of the Timer event (see Chapter 8). This would allow other processes to use the CPU. You could then keep track of the number of small intervals that passed with a Static variable, and move the text around (and reset the static variable) according to its value mod 10.

**note:** *Using the WinExec API function you can also call the built-in Windows screen savers from Visual Basic if need be.*

# Menus

Designing the right kind of menus will make your applications much more user-friendly. Visual Basic 3 lets you build up to six levels of menus and add pop-up menus as well. The screen in Figure 10-9 shows you a menu with four of the possible six levels. Menus that contain submenus are usually called *hierarchical menus*. Of course, using too many levels of menus can make the application confusing to the user. Four are almost certainly too many, and two or three levels are the most you will usually see. The user knows that a submenu lurks below a given menu item when he or she sees a ► following the menu item.

**tip:** *Instead of using lots of submenus, consider designing a custom dialog box for the options.*

Notice in the following illustration that each of the three items in the first level of menus in Figure 10-9 has the ► symbol and so conceals a submenu:

You can open a submenu by using the standard Windows conventions: press ENTER, click the item with the mouse, or press LEFT ARROW.

When designing a form, you add menus to the form using the Menu Design window available from the Window menu on the Visual Basic main menu bar. If you open the Window menu or press the ALT+W+M access key, you'll see a dialog box that looks like the one in Figure 10-10. What follows is a short description of each of the components of this dialog box.

**_Caption_** What you type in the Caption text box is what the user sees. The caption also shows up in the text area inside the dialog box. Unlike other Visual Basic controls, menu items do not have default captions. ALT+P is the access key for the Caption text box in the Menu Design window.

**tip:**

*If you set the Caption property for a non-main menu to a hyphen (-), a separator bar shows up. Separator bars have many uses; the simplest is to break long menus into groups. If you have more than five or six items on a menu, see if there is some way to use a separator bar to group them.*

**Figure 10-9**

**Hierarchical menus**

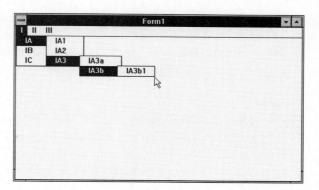

**Figure 10-10**

**Menu Design window**

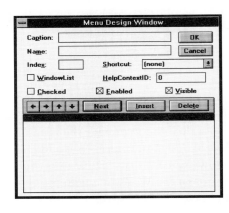

The Caption property is also where you add the three dots for the ellipses that the menu item may have in Windows programs. (Recall that ellipses in menu items indicates that clicking on the item will not do anything until the user makes more choices. Ellipses usually indicate that a dialog box will pop up when the user clicks on the item.)

**tip:**

*If the Caption property is blank, Visual Basic still reserves room for the menu item. This is one way to have the Help menu appear on the far right.*

**Name** Each menu item must have a control name. Unless the menu items are part of a control array (see Chapter 9), they must have different control names. What you enter in the Name text box becomes the control name that is used by Visual Basic for the Click event procedure for the menu item. Visual Basic will not let you leave the Menu Design window until you give each menu item a control name. The access key is ALT+M.

**The OK and Cancel Buttons** Click the OK button when you are finished designing the menu. Click the Cancel button if you decide not to build the menu at all. Even after you've finished designing a menu and clicked on the Done button, you can return to the Menu Design window and make changes.

**The Index Box** Use the Index box if you want to make a menu item part of a control array. As you saw in Chapter 9, control arrays let you add new instances of the control at run time. In the case of menu items, this would let you have the menu enlarge or shrink while the program was running. Once you've set a menu item to be part of a control array at run time, you add new menu items with the Load method you saw in Chapter 9. The new items are automatically on the same level as the initial element in the control array. For example, if the first item in the array was on the main menu bar, then all subsequent items must be as well. Similarly, you remove menu items from a control array by using the Unload method.

**The Shortcut Box** The shortcut box lets you add accelerator keys to your menu items. Recall that accelerator keys are either function keys or key combinations that activate a menu item without the user's needing to open the menu at all. If you click the down arrow to the right of the Shortcut box, a list box drops down with the choices for accelerator keys. You need only click the key you want.

tip:

*The ALT+F4 shortcut to close a window is not an allowable shortcut key. Response to this key combination is built into the form unless you remove the control box at design time. If you have a File menu and a control box on the form and want to show ALT+F4 as a shortcut for the Exit item, place this shortcut as part of the caption and use the QueryUnload event to call the Click procedure of the Exit item.*

**Window Lists** Window lists are used when you have MDI windows. (See the section "MDI Forms" in this chapter.)

**HelpContextId** This is used when you are working with the Help compiler— available in the Visual Basic Professional Edition.

**The Checked Check Box** The Checked check box determines whether a checkmark shows up in front of the menu item. As you'd expect, this box controls the setting of the Checked property of the menu item. The default is off. It is much more common to switch the Checked property to True when a user selects the item while the program is running than to set it at design time.

**The Enabled Check Box**    The Enabled check box determines the value of the Enabled property of the menu item. A menu item that is Enabled will respond to the Click event. An item that has been changed to False—either at design time by toggling the box off or at run time via code—shows up grayed.

**The Visible Check Box**    The Visible check box determines the value of the Visible property of the menu item. If a menu item is made invisible, all its submenus are also invisible and Visual Basic moves the menu items to fill in the gap.

**tip:**    *Setting the Visible property to False for the first item in a menu control array at design time lets you add items to the menu without any showing up at first. However, wait till you finish writing the code before doing so.*

**The Arrow Buttons**    The arrow buttons work with the current menu items. The menu item you're currently working with is highlighted in the large text window below the arrow buttons. Submenus are indicated by the indentation level in this text window, as you'll see in the next section. The left and right arrow buttons control the indentation level. Clicking on the left arrow button moves the highlighted item in one level; clicking on the right arrow button moves it one indentation level deeper. You cannot indent an item more than one level deeper than the item above it. If you try, Visual Basic will not let you leave the Menu Design window until you fix it.

Clicking on the up arrow button interchanges the highlighted menu item with the item above it; clicking on the down arrow button interchanges the highlighted item with the item below it. The up and down arrows do not change the indentation pattern of an item. See the section "A Sample Menu Design Window" for more on using the arrow buttons.

**The Next Button**    Clicking the Next button moves you to the next menu item or inserts a new item if you are at the end of the menu. The indentation of the new item is the same as the indentation of the previous item. ALT+N is the access key. You can also use the mouse to move among items.

**The Insert Button** Clicking the Insert button inserts a menu item above the currently highlighted menu item. ALT+I is the access key.

**The Delete Button** Clicking the Delete button removes the currently highlighted item. The access key is ALT+T. You cannot use the DEL key to remove menu items.

## A Sample Menu Design Window

The Menu Design window that led to the hierarchical menu in Figure 10-9 began like the screen in Figure 10-11. Notice that the menu item that is not indented appears on the main menu bar. Menu items that are indented once (preceded by four dots) appear as a menu item below the main menu bar. Items indented twice (8 dots) are submenus, items indented 12 dots are sub-submenus, and so on. You can always determine the main menu bar by looking for items that appear flush left in the text window in the Menu Design window.

**Figure 10-11**

Beginning of the Menu Design window for the menus in Figure 10-9

## Pop-Up Menus

Visual Basic 3 added the ability to pop up menus any place on the form. Using a specific pop-up menu when the user clicks the right mouse button in a specific place is becoming more and more common in Windows applications. (See Chapter 13 for how to determine where and if the right mouse button was pressed.)

**caution:** *When you display a pop-up menu Visual Basic stops executing code in the routine that pops up the menu until the user clicks on an item or cancels the pop-up by pressing* ESC.

Pop-up menus require some care at design time because you have to plan all the menus users will need first. The rule is you can pop up any menu that has at least one submenu *regardless of whether its Visible property is True or False.* The syntax is:

[*FormName*]PopUpMenu *MenuName* [*Flag* [, *X* [, *Y* ] ] ]

If you leave the optional *FormName* off, Visual Basic uses the current form. The flag's parameter determines where (in relation to the optional *X* and *Y* coordinates) the menu pops up. If Flag = 0, the left side of the menu is at the place on the form determined by the *X* parameter. If Flag = 4, the menu is centered at *X* and if *Flag* = 8, the right side of the menu is at *X*. The *X* and *Y* coordinates use the scale of the form. Ordinarily pop-up menus recognize only when the user clicks a menu with the left mouse button. By adding a 2 to the value of the *Flag* parameter you allow the right mouse button to activate the Click event as well.

**note:** *The CONSTANT.TXT file contains symbolic constants for the Flag parameter. These constants begin as POPUPMENU, for example, POPUPMENU_LEFTALIGN.*

## An Example of Working with Menus at Run Time

Suppose you want to write a program that would help people convert between various kinds of units—for example, between inches, centimeters, meters, and feet. A form for this application might look like the one in Figure 10-12. Notice

**Figure 10-12**

Form for conversion program

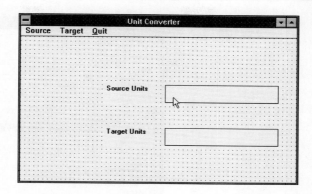

that this form has three items on the menu bar: Target, Source, and Quit. The Menu Design window for this form looks like the one in Figure 10-13.

The control names and captions for the menu items and controls are given in the following table:

| Control Name | Caption |
|---|---|
| Source | Source |
| Target | Target |
| FromInches | Inches |
| FromFeet | Feet |
| FromCentimeters | Centimeters |
| FromMeters | Meters |
| ToInches | Inches |
| ToFeet | Feet |
| ToCentimeters | Centimeters |
| ToMeters | Meters |
| Text1 | |
| Label1 | |
| Label2 | Source Units |
| Label3 | Target Units |

Notice that the Caption properties are the same for the items on the Target and Source menus; only the control names are different. The first label should have the BorderStyle property set to 1 so that it resembles a text box.

Whenever you write a conversion program, it's easiest to establish one unit as the basic unit and convert all the units using that as an intermediary. For this, set up the form–level variable

```
Dim BasicLength As Single
```

**Figure 10-13**

**Menu Design window for conversion program**

in the Declarations section of the form.

Now, suppose the user clicks the menu item marked Inches in the Source menu. The code should do the following:

◆ Put a checkmark next to the Inches item and remove checkmarks from all other items.

◆ Disable the Inches item in the Target menu and enable all the other items.

Here's the code for the Click procedure that implements this outline for one of the menu items. (The others work the same.)

```
Sub FromInches_Click()
   FromInches.Checked = True
   FromFeet.Checked = False
   FromCentimeters.Checked = False
   FromMeters.Checked = False
'change items on Target menu
   ToInches.Enabled = False
   ToFeet.Enabled = True
   ToCentimeters.Enabled = True
   ToMeters.Enabled = True
'set the caption for units
   Label2.Caption = "Inches"
End Sub
```

Now suppose the user clicks an item in the Target menu. You need to read the value from the text box, calculate the new value, and display the result in the first label. Suppose, for example, the user clicked the Meters item, indicating he or she wanted to convert from inches to meters. Here's the code that does this, using centimeters as the basic length:

```
Sub ToMeters_Click()
  Label3.Caption = "Meters"
  If FromInches.Checked Then
    BasicLength = Val(Text1.Text)*2.54'2.54 Centimeters/inch
  ElseIf FromFeet.Checked Then
    BasicLength = Val(Text1.Text)*2.54 *12
  ElseIf FromCentimeters.Checked Then
    BasicLength = Val(Text1.Text)
  End If
  Label1.Caption = Str$(BasicLength/100)
End Sub
```

This procedure uses the fact that clicking on an item in the Target menu changes the Checked property to False for all but the unit to be converted. If you add some directions to the Form_Load procedure, you can see the result shown in Figure 10-14.

**Figure 10-14**

Results of running the conversion program

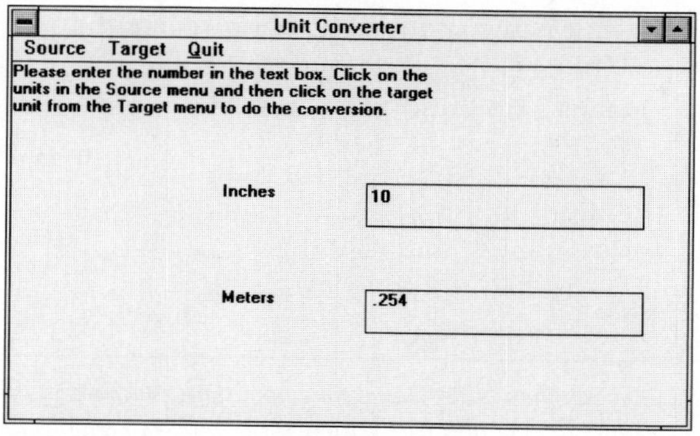

# Common Dialog Boxes

While working with Windows and Visual Basic you've become accustomed to seeing one of five standard dialog boxes for opening or saving a file, printing, choosing fonts, or setting colors. The ability to add these dialog boxes was always part of the high end of the Visual Basic line but in version 3, Microsoft decided (finally) to make it part of the standard edition. The file CMDIALOG.VBX contains the common dialog control and this file must be in your WINDOWS directory. (It is placed there during the installation process.)

Common dialog boxes are easy to use in principle but they are somewhat less easy to use in practice. This is because they require a fair amount of initializing to get them to look exactly the way you want. The online help is essential for working with common dialog boxes. This chapter can only give you a feeling for how to work with them.

The common dialog box control is automatically added to the toolbox unless you have changed your AUTOLOAD.MAK file to remove it. To use a common dialog box you need to place a common dialog control on the form. Here's a picture of this control:

This control is invisible to the user while the program is running. To actually pop up a specific common dialog box requires setting the Action property of the common dialog control while the program is running. For example, if you have an Open File item on the File menu and the associated Click procedure is in OpenFile_Click, the code to pop up a File Open dialog box using the default name of the control looks like this

```
OpenFile_Click ()
     .
     .
     CMDialog1.Action = 1
     .
```

**note:** *The common dialog boxes take no actions; they accept information only. You will always need to write the code that tells Visual Basic what to do with the information entered and then have this code processed when the user closes the common dialog box.*

## Working with Common Dialog Boxes

Before you pop up the box, you need to initialize the various properties that determine how the common dialog box looks. For example, you might want to make the default in the Print dialog box be that the Print Range is set to print only page 1 (see Figure 10-15). This is done by adjusting the value of the FromPage and ToPage properties of the common dialog control as shown in the following listing.

```
CMDialog1.FromPage = 1
CMDialog1.ToPage = 1
```

**tip:**

*Since common dialog boxes require a seemingly endless stream of specific integer values to get them to do anything, managing them can be very difficult without using symbolic constants. Incorporating the appropriate parts of the CONSTANT.TXT file into a .BAS module is practically essential.*

For example, here are the other possible values for the Action property along with the appropriate symbolic constant from CONSTANT.TXT:

| Action Value | Type Of Box | Symbolic Constant |
|---|---|---|
| 0 | Nothing shows | |
| 1 | File Open Box | DLG_FILE_OPEN |
| 2 | File Save Box | DLG_FILE_SAVE |
| 3 | Color Choice Box | DLG_COLOR |
| 4 | Choose Font Box | DLG_FONT |
| 5 | Printer Dialog Box | DLG_PRINT |

**Figure 10-15**

**Preset Print common dialog box**

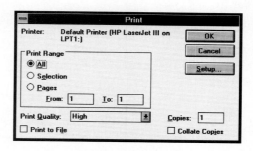

**note:** *Setting the Action property to 6 (DLG_HELP) calls the Windows Help engine. Because of this, you might want to add a common dialog box to any application that will use Windows Help (see Appendix A for more on the Windows Help engine).*

All the common dialog boxes allow you to generate an error if the user clicks the Cancel button. Setting up an error trap for this is necessary in most (if not all) cases. To do this, use the following code:

[*FormName*].*CMDialogName*.CancelError = True

The default is False and so no error is reported when the Cancel button is activated. Set it to True and an error with error number 32,755 is generated if the user clicks Cancel or presses ESC. (Again, since nobody would want to use this kind of number in their code—even if they could remember it—use the symbolic constant CDERR_CANCEL instead.)

Setting this property to be True and then trapping this error is important because whether the user clicks OK or Cancel, certain values may have changed. Since you only want to use the information when the OK button was clicked, you must have a way to know if the Cancel button was used to close the dialog box.

Here's a general framework for working with a common dialog box that uses an error trap to detect if the Cancel button was pressed.

```
CMDialog1.CancelError = True
On Error GoTo IsOK
  .
  .
  .

'Make sure the code after the IsOK label is always processed
IsOK:
  If Err = 0 Then  'no error so OK clicked
   'code to process data as needed
  ElseIf Err = CDERR_CANCEL
   'do nothing cancel invoked
  Else
   'wow you have a real error to handle
  End If
End Sub
```

## THE FILE OPEN AND FILE SAVE BOXES

Here is a table with descriptions of the most important properties used for these dialog boxes.

| Property | Use |
| --- | --- |
| DefaultExt | Sets the default extension for files shown in the box |
| DialogTitle | Sets the title bar. In particular you do not need to use Open and Save if you are using these boxes in other contexts |
| FileName | Gives the name and path of the file selected |
| FileTitle | Gives the name without the path |
| Filter | Effects the Type box. You can have multiple filters by separating them by a CHR$(124) (|). The format is the description string, the CHR$(124), the filter, another CHR$(124), and so on |
| FilterIndex | This is used when you set up many filters using the Filter property |
| Flags | This property is used to set various possible options on how the box will look. The values needed are stored in constants that begin with OFN_ in the CONSTANT.TXT file |
| InitDir | Specifies the initial directory |
| MaxFileSize | Sets the maximum size of the file name including all the path info |

The Flags property is very important in determining the final look and feel of the box. For example, a line of code like

```
CMDialog1.Flags = OFN_ALLOWMULTISELECT
```

allows the File name list box to use multiple selections. You can combine more than one flag with an OR and read back the values using bit-masking techniques with an AND.

Once the user clicks the OK button, you have to read back the information that was entered and take appropriate actions based on these values. For example, CMDialog1.FileName would contain the name of the file chosen.

## THE COLOR CHOICE BOX

Here is a table with descriptions of the important properties used for these dialog boxes.

| Property | Use |
| --- | --- |
| Color | Shows or gets the color |
| Flags | As with File Save/File Open specifies the form of the box |

The symbolic constants for this box begin with CC_. For example, CMDialog.Flags = CC_FULLOPEN would display the whole dialog box (including the one for defining custom colors). When the user clicks the OK button, the value of, for example, CMDialog1.Color is the long integer code for the color selected.

### THE FONT CHOICE BOX

Before we get to the table showing the remaining properties for this box, you'll need to know something about how the Flag property works here. Since you might want to have the font choice box reflect printer fonts only, screen fonts only, or both at once, Visual Basic requires you to set the Flag parameter correctly before it will display the Font box. The symbolic constants used are CF_PRINTERFONTS, CF_SCREENFONTS, or CF_BOTH. If you don't set the CMDialog.Flag property to one of these three values and still try to show the Font box (Action property = 4), the program generates an error and dies. There are 15 different Flag property values. As always, you combine them using the OR operator. You might want to look at the online help to see what the other flags do.

Here is a table with descriptions of the important remaining properties used for this dialog box.

| Property | Use |
| --- | --- |
| Color | Only used for color printers |
| FontBold, FontItalic, FontStrikeThru, FontUnderline | True/False properties. If the CC-EFFECTS flag is set you can allow the user to choose these properties |
| FontName | Sets or returns the font name |
| FontSize | Sets or returns the size of the font |
| Max, Min | These effect the point sizes shown in the size box. You need to have the CF_LIMITSIZE flag be set before you can use these properties |

You read back the value of the various font properties to see what the user wants. For example, the value of CMDialog1.FontName is the name of the font the user chose. Then have Visual Basic process the code to have the new value go into effect.

### THE PRINTER DIALOG BOX

As before, the Flags property controls how the box appears. For example, if the Flag parameter is PD_ALLPAGES then the All option button in the Print

Range frame is set. In particular this means you will need bit-masking techniques to check out what the user did with the box. Use code like this

```
If CMDialog1.Flags And PD_AllPages = PD_AllPages Then
  'all pages button checked
```

Check the online help for more details on the possible flags you can use.

Here is a table with descriptions of the remaining properties used for these dialog boxes.

| Property | Use |
|---|---|
| Copies | Sets or returns the number of copies the user wants |
| FromPage, ToPage | What pages are wanted |
| hDC | This is the device context number. It is used for API function calls |
| Max, Min | Specifies the maximum and minimum pages the user can put in the Print Range frame |
| PrinterDefault | Set this to True and the user can click the Setup button to change the WIN.INI file |

# MDI Forms

MDI stands for *multiple document interface,* which is Microsoft's term for a windowing environment like many word processors or spreadsheets where one window, usually called the MDI *container* or MDI *parent* form, contains many other windows, usually called *child* forms. For example, you can use an MDI container form to allow a user to work with two separate windows in the same application.

The MDI container form takes up the whole screen; the user can't resize the container form, although he or she can minimize the form to an icon. You can have only one MDI container form to a project and that form must, naturally enough, be the startup form.

To make an MDI container form, choose the New MDI Form option from the File menu. Next, create the additional forms (usually from the file menu as well). These will be the child forms to your newly created MDI form *after* you set the form's MDIChild property to True. (You can also turn an existing form into an MDI child form by adjusting this property.) At design time, child forms and the MDI parent form look similar—it's hard to tell the differences between them.

When you run the project, on the other hand, all the child forms must be explicitly shown (with the Show method) and are displayed within the MDI parent form's boundaries. Moreover, if the child form is minimized, its icon appears inside the MDI parent form, rather than in the Windows desktop. (If you maximize a child form, its caption replaces the caption of the parent form.) Finally, you can neither hide nor disable child forms without using Windows API. You can, of course, unload them.

**note:**    *Only in Windows 3.1 can you reset the values of the CommandBox, MinButton, and MaxButton properties for child forms.*

One of the nicest features of Visual Basic's MDI forms is that the menus of the container form change according to which child form has the focus. This lets you work with specific menus for each child form. What happens is that the menu for the child form that has the focus appears on the menu bar of the MDI container form—replacing whatever menu was previously there. In particular, the user only sees the menu for the child form when that child form has the focus.

### THE WINDOW MENU AND THE ARRANGE METHOD

Every MDI application should have a Window menu that allows the user to arrange or cascade the child windows—much like Windows itself does. The Window menu should also include a list of the MDI child windows. An example of such a menu is shown in Figure 10-16.

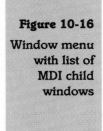

**Figure 10-16**

Window menu with list of MDI child windows

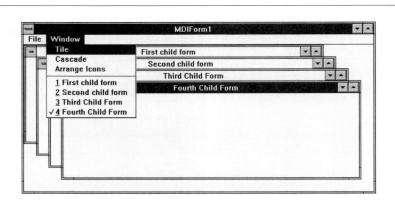

The list of MDI child windows is easy to put on the menu: set the WindowList check box on the menu design window to be on. Visual Basic will automatically display the list of the MDI child form captions—and even put a checkmark next to the one that most recently had the focus.

To activate the Tile, Cascade, and Arrange items on the Windows menu, first incorporate the CONSTANT.TXT file into your project and then write code like this:

```
Sub CascadeForms_Click()
  MDIParentForm.Arrange CASCADE
End Sub
```

This uses the CASCADE constant with the Arrange method. The other two constants are TILE_HORIZONTAL and ARRANGE_ICONS.

# More on How Visual Basic Displays Work: ZOrder

When Visual Basic paints the parts of your application it does so in three layers. The back (bottom) layer is where you draw information directly on the form using the graphical methods that you will see in Chapter 12. The middle layer contains the graphical controls (lines, shapes, picture boxes, and the image control). The top layer contains the non-graphical controls like command buttons, list boxes, and check and option buttons. Certain controls such as labels have a FontTransparent property that lets information from the layers below shine through.

Within each layer you can control the order in which controls appear. For example, if you use an MDI form, can you control which one is on top after you use the Arrange method? Or, if you overlap two command buttons, can you specify which one appears on top?

You can do this in two ways. At design time you can use the Bring To Front option and Send To Back option from the edit menu to effect the initial ordering of what's on top. To change it dynamically while the program is running you need the ZOrder method. Its syntax is:

[*object.*]ZOrder [*position*]

The position parameter can be 0 or 1. If it is 0 or omitted, the object named moves to the front. If it is 1, the object moves to the back. If you omit the object name the current form moves to the top.

# Some Words on Windows Design

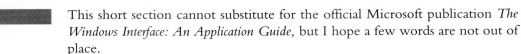

This short section cannot substitute for the official Microsoft publication *The Windows Interface: An Application Guide,* but I hope a few words are not out of place.

There's a temptation, especially for experienced DOS programmers, to force Visual Basic programs into a framework that is not Windows-oriented. The author himself has been guilty of this on more then one occasion when porting DOS programs to Windows. But this temptation should be resisted. For example, having a sequence of Input boxes to get data is very DOS—very linear—and not very Windows. Let the user stay in control; design input forms that the user can access from menus instead. Use DoEvents whenever your application is sitting around idle; don't hog resources. Just because Sub Main lets you write a standard old-fashioned linear program doesn't mean you should. Windows is to some degree multitasking but only if the applications cooperate in not hogging CPU resources.

Make sure you are giving enough feedback to the user. Change the MousePointer to an hourglass when the user is going to have to wait. Don't monkey with what users have grown to expect. Leave control boxes on forms and have ALT+F4 close the form (use the QueryUnload event for the needed clean-up code). Allow users to resize forms and move them around—unless there is some good reason not to do so. Scroll bars are helpful when the users are going to have to work through lots of information. Don't crowd your forms with too many buttons; use menus instead. On the other hand, don't make menus too deep. Use custom or common dialog boxes as appropriate.

Make the menus look like what users expect. Programs that handle files should have the standard order in the File menu, with the right captions and the right access keys (where appropriate). Users expect to see a file menu (with an ALT+F shortcut) that will have whatever subset of the following list is appropriate:

New
Open ...
Save
Save As ...
Print ...
Exit

Similarly, the Help menu (ALT+H access key) would usually have at least these three items:

Contents
Search ...
About

(See Appendix A for more on Help systems.)

The best advice is: when in doubt, look to Visual Basic itself for how to design your menus and forms!

Here's a short table on the actions users will expect:

| Action | Function |
|---|---|
| Click the left mouse button | Activates a control or selects an item from a list or combo box. In a Text box, moves the insertion point |
| Double-click left mouse button | Performs the action |
| Click right mouse button | Pops up context-sensitive menus |
| Drag with left button | Either encloses a specific area or moves an object |
| Press TAB key | Moves to the next control (watch your TAB order!) |

Of course, there are lots of keystroke combinations that should work as users expect. The nice thing about Visual Basic is that the objects usually default to have the expected response. For example, text boxes recognize the SHIFT+UP ARROW or DOWN ARROW keys to select text.

# Chapter 11

# Tools and Techniques for

# Testing and Debugging

411

ONCE a program becomes in any way complicated, no matter how carefully you outline your program or how carefully you plan it, it probably won't do what you expect—at first. This is one lesson programmers are forced to painfully relearn over and over again. It seems that no matter how robust you try to make a program, someone, somehow, will find a way to crash it. A realistic goal is not a perfect program, but one that is as bulletproof (or robust) as possible, that even while crashing, tries to save the user's work before fading away. So you might make it your goal to write programs that conform to a sign the author once saw. Slightly paraphrased, it read,

---

Our goal is a program
THAT SPUTTERS OUT AND DOESN'T BLOW UP!

---

The technical phrase for this is a program that *degrades gracefully*.

So after you write a program, you will need to test it for *bugs*. Once the testing process convinces you that there are bugs lurking, you need to find them and then eradicate them. Visual Basic has many tools to assist with this task, and this chapter will show you how to use them. Before trying to test and debug a program, you should first make a hard copy of the program source code. You might also want a copy of the specifications of the forms in ASCII format (see Chapter 4) so you can quickly check whether the initial properties of a form and its controls match what you expect.

Finally, this chapter gives you techniques for speeding up your programs that do the job but are unlikely to introduce new bugs (trying to over-optimize code is one of the most common sources of programming bugs) and some words on good programming style.

# The Debugging Tools and What They Do

You use the Debug menu to gain access to the tools needed for debugging, and most of the tools needed for testing and debugging can be found on the toolbar as well (see Figure 11-1). Usually, the debugging tools are used when the program is temporarily suspended (in *break mode*). The following table lists the debugging tools you can use.

| Tool | Keyboard Equivalent | Function |
|---|---|---|
| Run/Restart | ALT+R+S (F5/SHIFT+F5) | Starts the program anew |
| Break | CTRL+BREAK | Interrupts the program |
| End | | Ends the program |
| Breakpoint | ALT+D+T (F9) | Stops the program immediately before the line is executed |
| Instant Watch | ALT+D+I (SHIFT+F9) | Checks the value of the expression while the program is in break mode |
| Calls | ALT+D+C (CTRL+L ) | Shows how the procedure calls interrelate |
| Single Step | ALT+D+S (F8) | Moves through the program one statement at a time |
| Procedure Step | ALT+D+P (SHIFT+F8) | Performs like the single-step tool except procedure and function calls are treated as one step |

The first three tools provide the most common way of switching from project design, or design mode, to break mode—where you'll be doing most of your

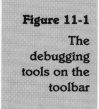

**Figure 11-1**

The debugging tools on the toolbar

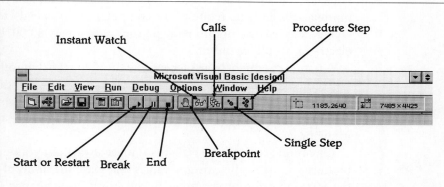

debugging. You can always tell what mode you're in by looking at the title bar. For example, when you stop a program by switching to break mode, the title bar switches to

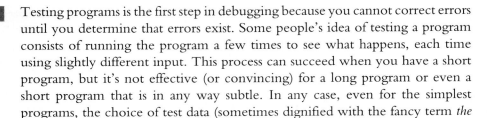

# Testing Programs

Testing programs is the first step in debugging because you cannot correct errors until you determine that errors exist. Some people's idea of testing a program consists of running the program a few times to see what happens, each time using slightly different input. This process can succeed when you have a short program, but it's not effective (or convincing) for a long program or even a short program that is in any way subtle. In any case, even for the simplest programs, the choice of test data (sometimes dignified with the fancy term *the testing suite*) is all–important.

Testing programs is an art, not a science. There's no procedure that always works. If your program is so long and complicated that you can't test all the possibilities, you have to be content with testing the reasonable ones.

The key to testing lies in the word *reasonable,* and the following story explains how subtle this concept can be. A utility company had a complicated but, they thought, carefully checked program to send out bills, follow up bills, and finally, automatically cut off service if no response to a bill was received. One day, the story goes, someone went on vacation and shut off the electricity. The computer sent out a bill for $0.00, which, understandably, wasn't paid. After the requisite number of follow–up requests, the computer finally issued a termination notice saying that if this unfortunate person didn't pay $0.00 by Thursday, his electricity would be cut off.

A frantic call might have succeeded in stopping the shut–off; the story doesn't say. If this story is true, the programmer forgot to test what the program would do if the bill was $0.00. To the programmer, this wasn't a "reasonable" possibility. (All the programmer had to do was change a >= to a > somewhere in the program.)

One moral of this story is that you must always test your programs using the boundary values—the extreme values that mark the limits of the problem, like the $0.00 that the programmer in the story forgot. For example, for sorting routines, a completely ordered or reverse-ordered list are good test cases. In programs that require input, the empty string (or 0) is always a good test case.

Since errors are often caused by bugs, error trapping can help you isolate what portion of a procedure caused the bug. For example, you can add line numbers to your program and then use the Erl statement to find out which half of the program caused the error. Continue this bisection process until you isolate the line that caused the bug. (Of course, Visual Basic ordinarily stops a program at the line that causes an error, but you will often need to insert line numbers to debug a program with an error trap.)

**tip:** *Having an active error trap (On Error Goto) can prevent your tests from doing their job. You often will need to temporarily disable any active error traps before starting the testing process. For more information on error traps, see Chapter 8.*

**note:** *Professionals might want to consider buying Microsoft's Test program. This comes with a language related to Visual Basic and lots of tools to make a professional testing procedure go smoother.*

# Designing Programs to Make Testing Easier

Long and complicated programs are never easy to test, but writing the programs in certain ways will make your job easier. (These methods also make programming in general easier.) By breaking the program into manageable pieces (giving the program *modularity,* in the jargon), each of which ideally does one task alone, you can make testing your programs much, much easier. After you finish each procedure or function, you can test it thoroughly to see whether it can handle all possible parameters that may be passed to it.

Next, combine all the procedures you've checked and test everything again. In some cases, a procedure or function may need results from a piece not yet written in order to run. In this case, the best technique, often called *stub programming,* substitutes constants, where necessary, for the results of as-yet-unwritten procedures or functions. Define the Sub procedure or Function procedure, but fill it with constants instead of having it do anything. The procedure calls will still work the same, but they receive only the constants from the stubs. You can then change the constants to vary the tests.

Now suppose you have eliminated the obvious syntax errors and can get the program to run—after a fashion. But testing the program has told you that it doesn't work as it's supposed to; it contains bugs that you need to isolate and eradicate. Don't be surprised or dismayed; bugs come with the territory. You have to find them and determine what kind they are.

There are essentially two kinds of bugs: grammatical and logical. An example of a grammatical error is a misspelled variable name, which leads to a default value that ruins the program. Surprisingly enough, they are often the most difficult kind of bug to detect. Probably the best way to avoid such bugs in Visual Basic is to prevent them in the first place by using the Option Explicit command (see Chapter 5), which forces you to declare all variables. Logical bugs are a vast family that encompasses all errors resulting from a misunderstanding of how a program works. This includes procedures that don't communicate properly and internal logic errors inside code.

Another useful tool for understanding how variables are used in your programs is a programmer's tool called a cross-reference (or XREF) program. This program works through the source code of a program and then lists the names of all variables and where they occur. A cross-referencing program is especially useful for detecting the common error of an incorrect variable in an assignment statement. Although using meaningful variable names can help to a certain extent, the mistake of using the variable ThisWeeksSales when you really meant the variable ThisMonthsSales is still easy to make. (The Option Explicit command doesn't help if the wrong variable was already dimensioned.) You'll learn about the tools needed to write an XREF program in Chapter 17. Commercial programs that do far more also are available. See Appendix D for more information on them.

## Logical Bugs

To get rid of subtle logical bugs, you have to isolate them—that is, find the part of the program that's causing the problem. If you've followed the modular approach, your task is a lot easier. The pieces are more manageable, so finding the bug means the haystack isn't *too* big.

If you've been testing the program as you develop it, then you should already know in what procedure or function the problem lies. Pinpointing the problematic procedure or function is usually easier if you developed the program, mostly because you start off with a good idea of the logic of the program. If the program is not yours or you've waited until the program is "finished," you can use the following techniques to check the pieces one at a time.

Assume that you've chosen a faulty procedure or function to test. There are only three possibilities:

♦ What's going in is wrong—what you've fed to the procedure or function is confusing it.

♦ What's going out is wrong—the procedure or function is sending incorrect information to other parts of the program (for example, it may be causing unplanned side effects).

♦ Something inside the procedure or function is wrong (for example, it's performing an operation too many times, or it's not clearing the screen at the right time).

In the first two cases, the fault can be traced to any or all of the following: the parameters you send to the procedure or function, what you've assigned to the parameters, or the form-level or global variables modified within the function or procedure.

How do you decide which situation you're dealing with? First, it's hard to imagine a correctly written short procedure or function that you can't analyze on a piece of paper to determine what should happen in most cases. Work through the procedure or function by hand, "playing computer" (this means don't make any assumptions other than what the computer would know at that point; don't assume variables have certain values unless you can convince yourself that they do). You now need to check that the functions and procedures are doing what they are supposed to.

# The Debug Window

Most versions of BASIC have a way to test program statements, procedures, and functions, and Visual Basic is no exception. Visual Basic uses the Debug window, shown in Figure 11-2.

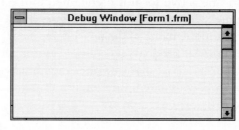

**Figure 11-2**

**The Debug window**

Debug Window [Form1.frm]

The main difference with non-Windows versions of BASIC is that you cannot use the Debug window to test programs when you are developing a program. The Debug window pops up only when you run a program and is available for testing when you press CTRL+BREAK (or choose the Break option from the Run menu or toolbar) to interrupt a program.

To bring the Debug window to the foreground, use the Window menu or click any part of the Debug window that is visible. The Debug window is moveable or resizeable by ordinary Windows technique. As in QuickBASIC, you can use the Debug window to test statements or to perform quick calculations when you are in break mode. If you type **Print 2 + 2** in the Debug window and press ENTER, Visual Basic quickly responds with a 4. You can use the ordinary Microsoft Window editing commands to modify the contents of a line in the Debug window. You can also cut and paste between lines. Keep in mind, though, that the moment you press ENTER, Visual Basic attempts to process the line.

Lines in the Debug window can use the colon separator and up to 255 characters. Because of these restrictions, you can write loops in the Debug window, although they'll look strange. For instance,

```
For I = 10 TO 1 STEP -1:Form1!Text1.Text = STR$(I)+CHR$(13)+_
CHR$(10): NEXT I
```

is a perfectly acceptable line of code for the Debug window. (Don't type the underscore that this book uses to indicate that the line runs beyond the width of the printed page. The line must fit on one line in the Debug window.)

Keep in mind that you can always reexecute any lines that currently appear in the Debug window by moving the cursor anywhere in the line and pressing ENTER. (Use the arrow keys or mouse to move around the Debug window.)

## More on Debugging in the Debug Window

When you stop a program the Debug window displays the title all the time. Also, the active form is highlighted in the Project list box, the title bar of the Debug window, as shown in Figure 11-3. It displays the name of the active form and the name of the procedure (if any) that Visual Basic was processing at the moment program execution was stopped—in this case, the Load procedure for Form1. It also shows the line about to be processed, in a box (which, incidentally, is drawn right on top of any embedded underscores, making them invisible).

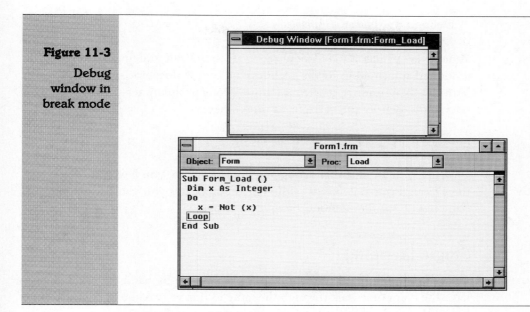

**Figure 11-3**

**Debug window in break mode**

The Debug window makes it easy to test an isolated procedure or function for its effects on certain values (for example, to see whether the results match with your hand calculations). You can test only procedures and functions that are attached to the form or module shown in the title bar of the Debug window.

Most debugging techniques use the Debug window to examine the current value of variables, but the only variables you can view from the Debug window are

◆ Variables local to the procedure listed in the title bar

◆ Form–level variables for the form listed in the title bar

◆ Global variables

To look at the value of a variable that fits one of these categories, use a simple Print statement inside the Debug window:

Print *NameOfVariable*

You can also add lines of code to your program that print values directly to the Debug window. For this, you use a predefined Visual Basic object called Debug:

Debug.Print *NameOfVariable*

Whenever Visual Basic encounters a Debug.Print statement, it sends the requested information to the Debug window. It does not stop the program. You can then examine it at your leisure. Many programmers like to have these statements identify the variable, as shown here:

```
Debug.Print "The value of X is";X
```

When you are through debugging your program, you'll want to remove all the Debug.Print statements, although theoretically you can leave them in a compiled .EXE file without the user noticing.

## Single Stepping

Often, when you have worked through a program by hand, you will want to have the computer walk through the same example, one line of code at a time. Visual Basic lets you execute one statement in your program at a time—single-stepping—by repeatedly pressing F8 or the single-step tool on the toolbar. (Of course, if Visual Basic is waiting for an event to happen, there won't be any statements to execute.)

When single-stepping is first used, the first executable statement of the program is boxed in the code window (see Figure 11-4). (Usually, the first statement will be in the Form_Load procedure, if there is one.) Each subsequent press of F8 or the single-step tool executes the boxed statement and boxes the next statement to be executed. As you can imagine, single-stepping through a program is ideal for tracing the logical flow of a program through decision structures and procedures.

Another possibility is to use the Debug window to check the values of constants, variables, or conditions by using Print statements. You also might want to consider having the Debug window and code window simultaneously on the screen. You can do this by resizing and relocating them as needed.

Whenever a procedure is called during single-stepping, the procedure code fills the code window. After its statements have been highlighted and executed (one at a time), the routine that called it reappears in the code window.

Besides the F8 key or single-step tool from the toolbar, you can also use SHIFT+F8 (or procedure-step tool) to single-step through a program. With this tool, each procedure is processed as if it were a single statement. In many cases, this is preferable to single-stepping through a complex function that you already know works.

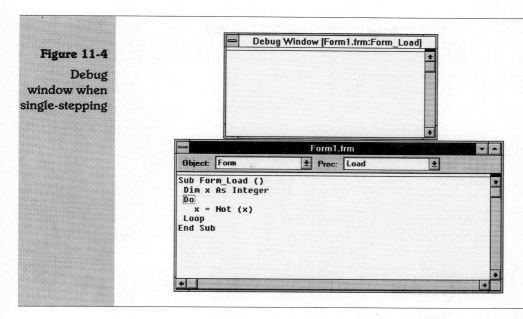

**Figure 11-4**

Debug window when single-stepping

Single-stepping through a program will probably take you to the place where you know a problem lurks. Now you want to place a break at that point before continuing the debugging process. This can be done with the Stop statement or, more commonly, by using a *breakpoint,* one of the tools available from the Debug menu or toolbar (see the next section).

# Stopping Programs Temporarily

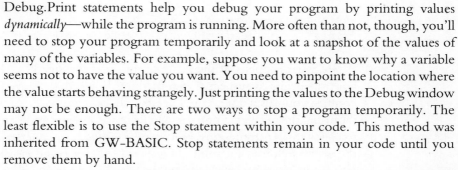

Debug.Print statements help you debug your program by printing values *dynamically*—while the program is running. More often than not, though, you'll need to stop your program temporarily and look at a snapshot of the values of many of the variables. For example, suppose you want to know why a variable seems not to have the value you want. You need to pinpoint the location where the value starts behaving strangely. Just printing the values to the Debug window may not be enough. There are two ways to stop a program temporarily. The least flexible is to use the Stop statement within your code. This method was inherited from GW-BASIC. Stop statements remain in your code until you remove them by hand.

Breakpoints, on the other hand, are toggled off or on by pressing F9 or using the hand-up tool from the toolbar. (You can also select Toggle Breakpoint from the Run menu by pressing ALT+R+D). Breakpoints are usually shown in red in your code. When you run the program and Visual Basic encounters a breakpoint, Visual Basic stops the code just before the statement with the breakpoint is executed and enters break mode.

You can set multiple breakpoints. To remove a breakpoint, position the cursor on the breakpoint and press ALT+D+B (or press F9). To clear all breakpoints from a program, press ALT+D+C (or choose the Clear All Breakpoints option on the Debug menu).

## Using Breakpoints to Test Programs

Now suppose you want to test a procedure. Put a breakpoint right before the call to the procedure or function you want to test. Once the program stops at the breakpoint, open up the Debug window, if necessary, and write a driver program. A *driver* is a program fragment that calls a function or procedure with specific values. For example, suppose you know that with the parameter

Variable1 = 10

and the parameter

Variable2 = 20

the result of a procedure of two parameters (a form-level variable named, say, FormLevel1) has the value 97. When you want to test how this procedure or function behaves at a particular place in a program, add the breakpoint at the appropriate point and use the Debug window to enter

```
WhateverYouAreTesting 10, 20
Print "The value of the variable FormLevel1 is: "; FormLevel1
```

See what happens. If the value of the variable FormLevel1 isn't right, then you can begin to suspect that something inside this procedure is wrong. To confirm your suspicions, you'll need to check that no other form-level variable is causing the problem. You can add Print statements inside the Debug window to check this. (Another possibility is to use Watch variables—see the section on these that follows.) Examine the values of the relevant variables, the variables whose values affect the value of the variable FormLevel1. This check may quickly tell you whether something is wrong inside the procedure or function. If the value of the variable FormLevel1 is correct, then determine, again by hand, what happens for some other values. Always remember to try the boundary values (the strange values, like the $0.00 that the programmer in the story forgot). If the values always match your expectations, there's probably nothing wrong with the procedure or function.

Of course, in practice, you have to make sure your driver fragment sends all the information needed by the procedure or function—and that's not likely to be only the values of two variables. Before calling the procedure, you can make all the necessary assignments in the Debug window while the program is stopped.

Assume that you've tested the procedure and know that the problem seems to be coming from outside it. Check each procedure that calls this procedure or function. Apply the same techniques to them: check what goes in and out of these procedures or functions.

**tip:**

*Use* SHIFT+F8 *or the procedure-step tool on the toolbar to treat a call to a Sub procedure or Function procedure as a single step. This way, you don't have to step through all the lines in all the functions and procedures in your program when you don't need to. Combine this with the Calls option on the Debug menu to see which procedure called the one you are in or to look at the entire chain of procedure calls if need be.*

### INSTANT WATCH

In every case, you eventually wind your way down to a procedure or function that just doesn't work. You now know that you have an error internal to a procedure or function. Although the Debug window can be used to examine the values of expressions while single-stepping through a program, using Visual Basic's *Instant Watch* provides a more efficient mechanism.

The Instant Watch item (SHIFT+F9) on the Debug menu lets you look at the value of any variable or expression. For example, you can look at the truth or falsity of an expression (see Figure 11-5). It complements Visual Basic's feature that lets you use the Debug window to look at the value of any variables inside a procedure when a program is stopped within the procedure.

To use Instant Watch,

1. Select the variable or expression you want to watch by moving the cursor to the item or highlighting the expression using SHIFT+arrow key combinations.

2. Choose Instant Watch from the Debug menu (ALT+D+I or SHIFT+F9).

**Figure 11-5**

**Instant Watch dialog box example**

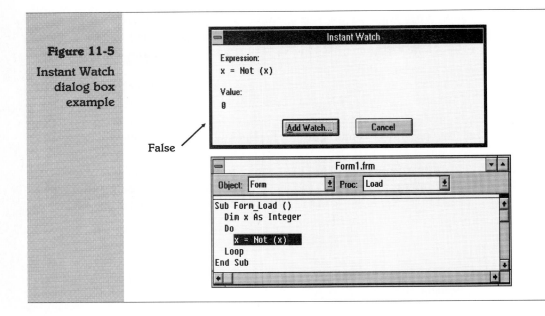

A dialog box like the one in Figure 11-5 appears.

If the value isn't currently available, Visual Basic will tell you. At this point, you can close the box with the ESC key or choose to add this variable as a Watch item.

### WATCH ITEMS

Watch items are variables, expressions, or conditions that are displayed in a special part of the Debug window (see Figure 11-6). Notice that the Debug window has split into two parts: the *Watch Pane* (where the watch items are shown) and the *Immediate Pane* (which you use for displaying information or checking code).

You can choose the watch items you want to examine either before you start the program or while the program is running and you have temporarily stopped it. Any variable, expression, or condition can be entered into the dialog box that pops up when you choose Add Watch from the Debug menu. However, you can watch only global variables or variables attached to the current form or module. When you press ENTER, the item will appear in the Watch Pane of the Debug window with a little pair of eyeglasses as the icon at the far left (see Figure 11-6). As Visual Basic executes the program, the values of the watch items will be updated in the Watch Pane of the Debug window.

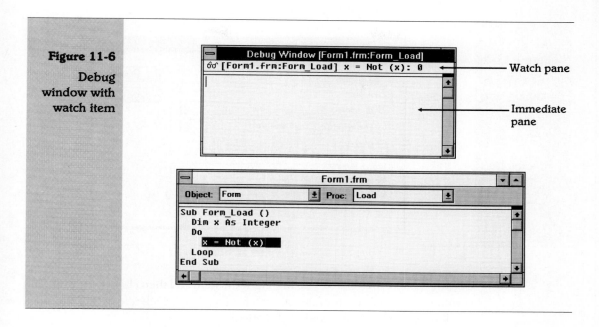

**Figure 11-6**

Debug window with watch item

To create a watch item, press ALT+D+A (the Add Watch option on the Debug menu). A dialog box will appear as shown in Figure 11-7. The expression box initially uses whatever expression you highlighted. The context option buttons are used to set the scope of the variables in the expression. You can restrict the scope to procedure-level, form-level, module, or global variables. The last option buttons offer two other ways of watching your program, covered in the next section.

To remove an item from the Debug window, press ALT+D+E (Edit Watch). This opens up a dialog box that looks like this:

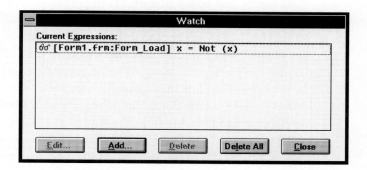

**Figure 11-7**

**Add Watch dialog box**

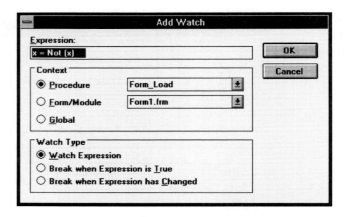

Use the DOWN ARROW key to highlight the item and then click the appropriate command button. To remove all watch items, click Delete All. To remove a specific item, highlight it and click Delete.

**tip:**

*If you have to watch a string variable, use an expression like*

*"{" + NameOfStringVariable + "}"*

*Then you can quickly detect whether the string is the empty string, because if it is, all you'll see in the Debug window is the brackets with nothing between them.*

## WATCHPOINTS

As mentioned above, sometimes the problem with a program appears to be tied to a variable or expression whose value falls outside some anticipated range, yet it is unclear in which line this occurs. In this case, setting a breakpoint at a specific line is not appropriate, and watching the variable and single-stepping may be too time-consuming. What is needed instead is the ability to suspend the program at the line that causes the variable or expression to reach or exceed some value. In Visual Basic, this debugging procedure is referred to as setting a watchpoint and is done from the Add Watch Item dialog box.

If you choose the Break When Expression Is True option button, Visual Basic stops the program as soon as the watched expression is True, and it highlights the line after the one that caused the expression to become True.

The other option button lets you stop execution when an expression has changed. The icons for these watch items in the Watch pane are a raised hand with an equal sign and a raised hand with a triangle.

### SETTING THE NEXT STATEMENT

Set Next Statement on the Debug menu lets you bypass part of a program while you are stepping through it. Sometimes (especially when using the stub programming technique described earlier) you'll want to start a program other than at the beginning of a procedure or function, or you may, while single-stepping, want to skip to another place in the program. To use this option, you need to be in a running program (usually one you are stepping through). To set this option, while in the code window, move the cursor to the line where you want to restart execution. Press ALT+D+S. When you tell Visual Basic to continue, Visual Basic starts executing at the line you just set. You can move both backwards and forwards within the procedure.

# Final Remarks on Debugging

Feeding a procedure or function specific numbers and using the debugging techniques described here are not cure–alls. No technique can help unless you have a good grip on what the procedure or function should do. If you are using an If–Then statement, are you testing for the right quantity? Should a >= be a >? Use watch items to check the value (True or False) of any Boolean relations that seem to be off (it is perfectly legal to enter X=19 as a watch value). Check any loops in the routine; loops are a common source of problems. Are counters initialized correctly (is there an off–by–one error)? Are you testing your indeterminate loops at the top when you should be testing them at the bottom?

### AN EXAMPLE: DEBUGGING A BUGGY LOOP

Recall in Chapter 6 we discussed a loop that looks like this:

```
Total = 0
PassNumber = 0
Do
  PassNumber = PassNumber + 1
  Total = Total + .1
Loop Until Total = 1
```

This loop would continue forever. Suppose you put a loop like this in a procedure, forgetting that you should never test single-precision numbers for equality. How can you use debugging techniques to find and then fix this bug?

Whenever you have a loop that is running amok, you'll need to either watch the loop variable, set up a watchpoint involving the loop variable, or both. In this case, you might first watch the value of Total. You would quickly discover that it is growing without bound. Knowing this, you need only set a watchpoint with the expression

PassNumber > 10

Once the program stops, you can examine the value of Total to discover that it isn't quite equal to 1—and that is the root of your problem.

**tip:** *When a Do loop seems to be running too long, add a temporary counter to the Do loop. Then use the counter in a watchpoint at some (fairly) large value. When the program stops, examine the state of the expression tested in the loop to help determine why your loops are running too long.*

## Event-Driven Bugs and Problems

When you debug an event-driven program, you have to be aware of certain problems that could never come up in older programming languages. "Event cascades" are perhaps the most common. These are bugs caused by an infinite sequence of one event procedure calling itself or another event procedure, with no way to break the chain. The most likely time such bugs are introduced is when you make a change in the Change event procedure for a control. The Change procedure is called again, which in turn is called again, and so on—theoretically forever, but in practice you'll get an "Out of Stack Space" error message.

Other special problems occur when you stop a program during a Mouse-Down or KeyDown event procedure. In both situations, during the debugging process you'll naturally release the mouse button or lift the key that invoked the event procedure. However, when Visual Basic resumes the program, it assumes the mouse button or the key is still down, and so the relevant MouseUp and KeyUp procedures will never be called. The usual solution is to call the MouseUp or KeyUp procedure from the Debug window as needed.

# Documentation and Program Style

Although you can remember the logic of a complicated program for a while, you can't remember it forever. Good documentation is the key that can open the lock. Some people include the pseudocode or outline for the program as multiple remark statements. Along with meaningful variable names, this is obviously the best form of documentation. Set up conventions for global, form, or local variables and stick to them. Try to avoid tricky code; if you need to do something extraordinarily clever, make sure it's extensively commented. (Most of the time, you'll find that the clever piece of code wasn't really needed.) Nothing is harder to change six months down the line than "cute" code. Cute code often comes from a misplaced attempt to get a program to run more quickly. While this is sometimes necessary, versions of Visual Basic after 1.0 are usually fast enough for most situations. The author once saw a sign that made this point clearly:

> **Rules for program optimization:**
>
> 1. Don't do it.
> 2. (For expert programmers only) DON'T DO IT!

The point is that when you start thinking of tricks to speed up your programs, you can too easily lose sight of the fundamental issue: making sure your programs run robustly in the first place. In fact, dramatic speedups usually come from shifts in the algorithms in the program, not from little "tweaks." Roughly speaking, an *algorithm* is the method you use to solve a problem. For example, in problems that involve sorting a list, the sort method you choose determines the speed of the sort. As you saw in Chapter 9, choosing the right sorting technique can speed up a program manyfold. This is more than any minor tweak can ever hope to accomplish. Discovering new (and, with luck, faster) algorithms is one of the main tasks of computer scientists and mathematicians.

This is not to say that *after* a program is running robustly, you might not want to consider ways of making it run faster. Making sure that variables are integers whenever possible is an obvious and not dangerous change. Don't use variant variables unless you need their special properties. Any statement using a variant that requires converting it to another type will run much slower. For-Next loops with counters that are variants instead of integers may run half as fast; using single-precision counters can slow a loop down 10-fold.

Try the following additional techniques to increase the speed of your program if necessary:

◆ Preload VBRUN300.DLL when the user starts Windows by putting a compiled Visual Basic program in the Windows Startup group. (This gives the appearance of speed but really doesn't speed up a program.)

◆ Use dynamic arrays whenever possible and free up the space if it is not needed.

◆ Unload forms when no longer needed.

◆ Delete code if it is no longer used in your project.

◆ Use local variables whenever possible.

◆ Use a Picture box for graphics rather than another form.

◆ Write a general purpose error handler and pass the error code to it instead of having complicated error handlers in every procedure.

Finally, for advanced users:

◆ Use Dynamic Link Library (DLL) routines in particular API calls when appropriate.

(Obviously it also helps to have as much RAM and as fast a hard disk space as possible.)

**caution:** *Some ways known to make Visual Basic programs run faster (such as using global variables instead of parameters) are usually more dangerous than the speed is worth.*

In any case, it's extremely difficult to modify or debug a program (even one that you, long ago, wrote yourself) that has few or no remark statements, little accompanying documentation, and uninformative variable names. A procedure called MakeMartini(Shaken,ButNot,Stirred) should be in a program about James Bond (and perhaps not even there), not in a program about trigonometric functions. In addition, since Visual Basic allows long variable names, don't make your programs a morass of variables named X, X13, X17, X39, and so on. If you strive for clarity in your programs rather than worry about efficiency at first, you'll be a lot better off.

Finally, if a procedure or function works well, remember to save it for reuse in other programs. Complicated programs will often have many procedures and functions. These procedures and functions may often have come up before in a slightly different context. This means that after you design the interface, sometimes all you have to do is modify and connect parts of a thoroughly debugged library of subprograms and functions to the event procedures for the interface. (This is one reason why commercial toolkits for Visual Basic are so useful. The time saved is worth the small cost.)

# Chapter 12

# An Introduction to Graphics

i
N Chapter 4 you saw how to use the graphical controls. This chapter discusses the graphical methods built into Visual Basic. Using the graphical methods can require writing a fair amount of code, but in return, these methods allow you to control every dot that appears on your screen or prints on your printer. Because Microsoft Windows is a graphically based environment, the graphics powers of Visual Basic can be astonishing. The screen in Figure 12-1 shows you what a short program from this chapter can do.

The graphics methods in Visual Basic allow you to control each dot (usually called a *pixel* or *picture element*) that appears on the screen. If you take a magnifying glass to a monitor, you can see that each character is made up of many of these pixels. In fact, certain combinations of software, hardware, and monitors can divide the screen into more than 1,000,000 dots and theoretically choose from a palette of more than 16,777,216 (256 × 256 × 256) colors for each pixel. And the same graphics statements that work for the screen apply to the Printer object. This lets you control every dot your printer can put out; on a laser printer, this is at least 300 dots per inch.

**Figure 12-1**
**Rotating squares**

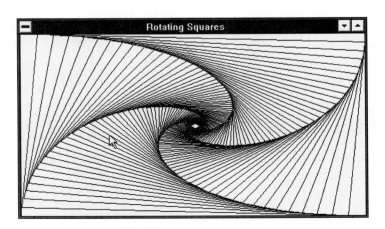

In addition to drawing pretty pictures, the graphical methods and controls also allow you to embellish your Visual Basic projects. As you'll see in this chapter, lines drawn around controls in special ways can dramatically change the look of your applications.

Computer graphics (especially three-dimensional drawings) is a subject in which mathematics must inevitably rear its head. However, this chapter uses nothing beyond a little trigonometry, and that only in the last few sections. Of course, you can just skip the math and use the programs; the results are pretty spectacular. Figure 12-2 shows an example of what you can do with polar coordinates.

Chapter 16 describes one other technique for creating graphics: using recursion to draw fractals. That chapter includes a short introduction to fractal graphics. Figure 12-3 is an example of what you can draw using those techniques.

You should be aware that in traditional programming languages, graphics are usually distinguished from text. This distinction is much less important with Windows and, therefore, with Visual Basic. With the exception of text boxes and labels, Visual Basic considers essentially everything placed on a form to be graphical. This is why forms can display text with such varied fonts and why you are able to use the CurrentX and CurrentY properties to position text accurately on the screen. Nonetheless, the graphics methods themselves work only on forms, picture boxes, and the printer. Since the ZOrder layer for controls (in particular picture boxes and text boxes) is above that of the form, you can often get dramatic special effects by combining the two.

**Figure 12-2**

Polar
coordinates
demonstration

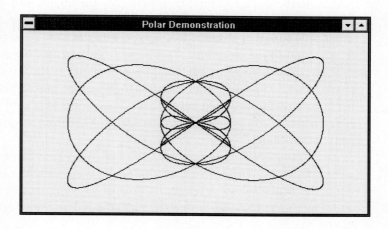

Polar Demonstration

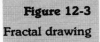

**Figure 12-3**
**Fractal drawing**

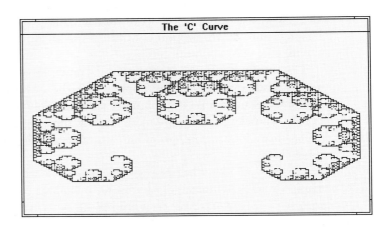

The 'C' Curve

Finally, although this chapter will show you the techniques needed to do presentation-style graphs and charts, the Visual Basic Professional Edition (see Appendix A) has these tools built in. If you need these facilities, you may want to upgrade to this rather than reprogram all the tools yourself.

## Fundamentals of Graphics

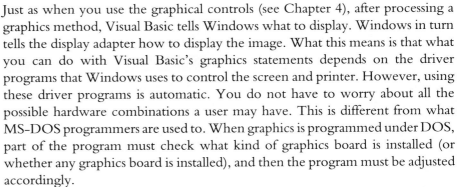

Just as when you use the graphical controls (see Chapter 4), after processing a graphics method, Visual Basic tells Windows what to display. Windows in turn tells the display adapter how to display the image. What this means is that what you can do with Visual Basic's graphics statements depends on the driver programs that Windows uses to control the screen and printer. However, using these driver programs is automatic. You do not have to worry about all the possible hardware combinations a user may have. This is different from what MS-DOS programmers are used to. When graphics is programmed under DOS, part of the program must check what kind of graphics board is installed (or whether any graphics board is installed), and then the program must be adjusted accordingly.

However, nothing comes for free. Windows has to do a lot to manage a graphics environment, and this forces trade-offs. For example, unless you set the AutoRedraw property to True so Visual Basic saves a copy of the object in memory, you will have to manage the redrawing of graphics yourself.

There are slight differences between how the AutoRedraw property being set to True works for forms and picture boxes:

◆ For a resizeable form, Visual Basic saves a copy of the entire screen. Thus, when you enlarge the form, no graphics information is lost. This option requires by far the most memory, but if your graphics do not currently fit on a form but will when the form is enlarged, choose this option.

◆ For a picture box, Visual Basic saves an image only as large as the current size of the box. Nothing new will appear even if the box is enlarged later.

Thus, drawing to picture boxes requires less memory than drawing to the form, even if the picture box fills up the form.

Visual Basic activates the Paint event each time a part of the form is newly exposed. If the ClipControls property is set to True and AutoRedraw is False, then Visual Basic repaints the entire object. If ClipControls is set to False, Visual Basic repaints only the newly exposed areas. You can write the necessary code in the Paint procedure whenever you want to redraw part of a form or picture box. Therefore, the least memory-intensive way to handle the problem of graphics disappearing because a user covered a form or picture box is to redraw the image in the form or picture box in the Paint event procedure. Again this solution involves a trade-off between memory-intensive and CPU-intensive programming activities. Setting AutoRedraw to True uses up memory (if you have it), potentially speeding up the program. Using the Paint event procedure (or the hard disk, if you don't have enough memory) uses up time. You have to choose what's best for the application. At the extremes, the choice is easy: If the amount of drawing to be done is minimal, using the Paint event procedure is better. In any case, Visual Basic calls the Paint procedure for the object only if the AutoRedraw property of the object is set to False.

**caution:** *Be very careful about including in the Paint event procedure any commands that move or resize the object. If you include such commands, Visual Basic will just call the Paint procedure again, and you'd be stuck in an infinite regress.*

Here is one other interesting feature of AutoRedraw: Suppose you change AutoRedraw to False while a program is running. Then you clear the object by using the Cls method. Whatever you drew before you changed the AutoRedraw property will remain, but everything that was drawn after the switch will disappear. This feature can be very useful. To see how it works, start a new project and try the following demonstration program (recall that text is treated as graphics output on a form). For the Form_Load procedure, write

```
Sub Form_Load ()
  AutoRedraw = True
  Print "Please click to see a demonstration of AutoRedraw."
  Print "These two lines will stay on the screen after you
  double click."
End Sub
```

Now, for the Click procedure, add

```
Sub Form_Click ()
  AutoRedraw = False              'keeps old stuff
  Cls
  Print: Print: Print      'third line
  Print "But this line will disappear after you double click."
End Sub
```

Finally, the Double_Click procedure is simply

```
Sub Form_DblClick ()
  Cls                            'Clears line from Click() procedure
End Sub
```

**tip:**    *If AutoRedraw is set to True, you can speed up your program by setting ClipControls to False.*

You will occasionally need to use the Refresh method when working with graphics. This method applies to both forms and controls. It forces an immediate refresh of the form or control and, as mentioned previously, will let you see an image develop even when AutoRedraw is True. If you use the Refresh method, Visual Basic will also call any Paint event procedure you have written for the object. This method is commonly used in the Form_ReSize procedure to redisplay any graphics that are calculated in the Paint event procedure. Also, while Visual Basic handles refreshing the screen during idle time, occasionally you will want to control this process yourself. Whenever Visual Basic processes an *Object*.Refresh statement, it will redraw the object immediately and generate the Paint event, if the object supports this feature.

Finally, Visual Basic makes it easy to save the pictures you've drawn to a form or picture box. The SavePicture statement uses the following syntax:

SavePicture *ObjectName.Image, Filename*

The operating system uses the Image property to identify the picture in the form or picture box. If you leave off *ObjectName*, then, as usual, Visual Basic uses the current form. The syntax for this version of the method is

SavePicture *Image, Filename*

If you originally loaded the picture from a file by assigning an image to the Picture property of the form or picture box (see Chapter 10), Visual Basic saves the picture in the same format as the original file. (For example, icon files stay icon files.) Otherwise, Visual Basic saves the picture as a bitmap (.BMP) file.

# Screen Scales

The default scale for forms and picture boxes uses twips. The default size for a form in ordinary VGA is 7485 twips long by 4425 twips wide. A twip is 1/1440 of an inch when printed, thus creating a form of roughly 5 inches by 3 inches. The following table gives you the coordinates in one column and the location of the point in the other for a form of the default size for a VGA monitor.

| Coordinates | Location |
| --- | --- |
| (0,0) | Top-left corner |
| (7485,0) | Top-right corner |
| (0,4425) | Bottom-left corner |
| (7485,4425) | Bottom-right corner |
| (3742,2212) | Roughly the center |

If two points have the same first coordinate, they're on the same vertical line; if they have the same second coordinate, they're on the same horizontal line.

There are six other possible scales besides the default scale, as well as a totally flexible user-defined scale that you'll see in the next section. These scales are set by changing the ScaleMode property at design or run time, as shown here:

| ScaleMode | Units |
| --- | --- |
| 1 | Twips (the default) |
| 2 | Points (72 per inch) |
| 3 | Pixels (the number of dots as reported by Windows) |
| 4 | Characters (units default as 12 points high and 20 points wide) |
| 5 | Inches |
| 6 | Millimeters |
| 7 | Centimeters |

Once you set the ScaleMode property, you can read off the size of the *drawing area,* which is the area inside the form or control or the printable area on the paper. This is reported in the current units when you use the ScaleHeight and ScaleWidth properties. Since both ScaleHeight and ScaleWidth report their results using the units selected by ScaleMode, they are very convenient for resetting form-level or global variables in a ReSize event procedure. On the other hand, the Height and Width properties of an object are less useful for graphics. This is because these properties give you the area of the object including the borders and title bar, if there are any. In graphics, you usually care more about the dimensions of the drawing area.

**tip:** *If you use global variables for the Height and Width properties of the Screen object and use percentages of these variables in your code, you'll find it easier to make the code independent of the particular monitor and card.*

## AN EXAMPLE: SIMPLE ANIMATION

Although Visual Basic has many powerful tools to perform animation (see the section, "Animation and DrawMode," later in this chapter), you now have the tools to simulate one kind: a so-called "drunkard's walk" (or, more technically, a random walk). All this means is that you imagine an object whose movements over time you can plot. If it seems to move randomly, you have a random walk. To simulate this, start with a form with a single command button, using the default settings. For this program, all you need to do is start a new project and double-click the command button. As you've seen, this puts the button at the default location in the middle of the screen.

The Click event procedure will have the code for moving the button around. However, instead of moving the button a fixed amount, this project will move up and down and left and right randomly 50 times. If you run the program, you'll see that the square will spend most of its time in a narrow range around the center. For this program, pixels (ScaleMode = 3) seems the appropriate choice:

```
Sub Command1_Click()
  ' moving squares to imitate a random walk
  Dim X As Single, Y As Single
  Dim I As Integer

  Randomize
  Form1.ScaleMode = 3                'pixel scale

  X = Form1.ScaleWidth/2             'start roughly in center
  Y = Form1.ScaleHeight/2

  For I = 0 To 50
    XMove = 3*Rnd
    YMove = 2*Rnd
    If Rnd < .5 Then
      X = X + XMove
    Else
      X = X - XMove
    End If
    If Rnd < .5 Then
      Y = Y + YMove
    Else Y = Y - YMove
    EndIf
    If X < 0 Or X > ScaleWidth Or Y < 0 Or Y > ScaleHeight Then
      ' DO NOTHING
    Else
      Command1.Move X, Y
    End If
  Next I
End Sub
```

The first two If-Then-Elses give the size of the random motion. The Else clause of the third If-Then-Else actually moves the command button up or down and left or right, depending on whether the random number generator delivers a number less than one-half or not. Later sections of this chapter show you how to add the code needed to give a trace of where the control has been. If you add the commands to change the background color of the command button (see the section "Colors" later in this chapter), the results are usually a quite attractive random pattern.

## Custom Scales

The screen is normally numbered with (0,0) as the top-left corner. This is obviously inconvenient for drawing tables, charts, graphs, and other mathematical objects. In most of these situations, you want the coordinates to decrease as you move from top to bottom and increase as you move from left to right. For example, mathematics usually uses an X-Y (Cartesian) system, with X measuring how much across you are from a central point (the origin) and Y measuring how much up or down from the center you are. For example, Figure 12-4 plots a few points on the X-Y plane.

The Scale method sets up new coordinates for forms and picture boxes that you can use in any of the graphics methods. For example,

```
Scale (-320,100) - (320,-100)
```

sets up a new coordinate system with the coordinates of the top-left corner being (−320,100) and the bottom-right corner being (320,−100). After this method, the four corners are described in a clockwise order, starting from the top left:

(−320,100)
(320,100)
(320,−100)
(−320,−100)

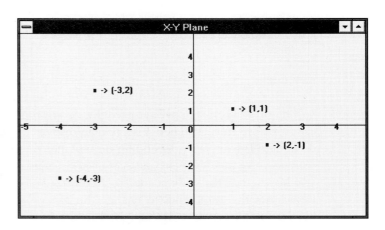

**Figure 12-4**

X-Y plane with points

Now 0,0 is roughly in the center of the screen. This placement occurs because whenever Visual Basic processes a Scale method that changes to a custom scale, Visual Basic automatically finds the pixel that corresponds to your coordinates (rounding if necessary).

On the other hand, a scale like

```
Scale (0,0) - (640,199)
```

would give you roughly the same detail as the previous scale, but (0,0) would be the coordinates of the top left-hand corner. (This scale would be useful in converting ordinary GW-BASIC or QuickBASIC SCREEN 2 graphics.)

In general, the Scale method looks like this:

Scale (*LeftX, TopY*) − (*RightX, BottomY*)

where *LeftX* is a single-precision real number that will represent the smallest X coordinate (leftmost), *TopY* is a single-precision number for the largest Y (top), *RightX* is the right corner, and *BottomY* the bottom edge. For example,

```
Scale (-1E38, 1E38) - (1E38,-1E38)
```

gives you the largest possible scale, which means the smallest amount of detail. Large X and Y changes are needed to light up adjacent pixels.

The line

```
Scale (-1,1) - (1,-1)
```

gives you a relatively small possible scale. Since a default-size form will be 268 by 491 pixels, you can get very fine detail. Only tiny X and Y changes are needed to light up adjacent pixels.

If you use the Scale method with no coordinates, Visual Basic will reset the coordinates back to the default scale of (0,0) for the top left-hand corner and the units being twips.

**note:**    *Some programmers prefer using a custom scale rather than percentages of the Screen.Height and Screen.Width objects in their code.*

## ANOTHER WAY TO SET UP CUSTOM SCALES

The Scale method is the simplest way to set up a custom scale. There is one other way that occasionally may be useful. You can specify the coordinates of the top left-hand corner and how Visual Basic should measure the vertical and horizontal scales. You do all this by using combinations of the ScaleLeft, ScaleTop, ScaleWidth, and ScaleHeight properties. For example, after Visual Basic processes

    Object.ScaleLeft = 1000
    *Object*.ScaleTop = 500

then the coordinates of the top left-hand corner of the object are (1000,500). After Visual Basic processes a statement like this one, all graphics methods for drawing within the object are calculated based on these new coordinates for the top left-hand corner. For example, if you made these changes to a form, then to place an object at the top left-hand corner now requires setting its Top property to 500 and its Left property to 1000.

Similarly, if you set the ScaleWidth to 320 and the ScaleHeight to 200, the horizontal units are 1/320 of the graphics area and the vertical units are 1/200 of the height of the graphics area.

Just as with the Scale method, you can use any single-precision number to reset these four properties. If you use a negative value for ScaleWidth or ScaleHeight, the orientation changes. If ScaleHeight is negative, the coordinates of the top of the object are higher values than those of the bottom. If ScaleWidth is negative, the coordinates of the left side of the object are higher values than those of the right side, as shown in Figure 12-5.

# Colors

The next step is to decide what colors you want. If you do not specify a color, Visual Basic uses the foreground color of the object for all the graphics methods. There are four ways to specify colors. The first way is directly from the hexadecimal coding (see Chapter 3).

The second way is to use the RGB function. The syntax for this function is

    RGB(*AmountOf Red, AmountOfGreen, AmountOf Blue*)

**Figure 12-5**

**ScaleHeight with negative value**

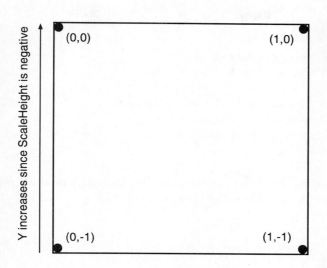

where the amount of color is an integer between zero (do not blend in that color) to 255 (maximal amount of that color blended in). Strangely enough, this is exactly the opposite order of that used in the &HBBGGRR coding. (This is unfortunate because what this function does is return a long integer corresponding to the codes chosen. Although you can still use this function in the Immediate window as another way to find the hex coding for a color.)

The third way is to include the CONSTANT.TXT file and use the color codes defined there.

If you are comfortable with QuickBASIC and want to use the color scheme from there, use the fourth way, the QBColor function. The syntax for this function is

QBColor(*ColorCode*)

where *ColorCode* is an integer between zero and 15. The colors this function gives are summarized in the following table:

| 0 | Black | 5 | Magenta | 10 | Light green |
|---|---|---|---|---|---|
| 1 | Blue | 6 | Brown | 11 | Light cyan |
| 2 | Green | 7 | White | 12 | Light red |
| 3 | Cyan | 8 | Gray | 13 | Light magenta |
| 4 | Red | 9 | Light blue | 14 | Yellow |
|   |       |   |            | 15 | High-intensity white |

For example, you can set up a blank form and try the following demonstration program:

```
Sub Form_Click()
    Static CNumber As Integer

    BackColor = QBColor(CNumber)
    CNumber = CNumber + 1
    CNumber = CNumber Mod 16     'recycle after 16 clicks
End Sub
```

Because CNumber is a static variable, each click on the form gives you the next color in the table as the background color.

# Pixel Control

Now you know how colors are assigned and can change the scale of your screen as you see fit. How do you turn a pixel on? The syntax for this method is

PSet(*Col, Row*) [, *ColorCode*]

Since the color code is optional (as indicated by the square brackets), all you need to do is replace the parameters with the values you want. The value of the first entry determines the column and the second determines the row. After Visual Basic processes this statement, the pixel defined by that point lights up. Obviously, where that point is depends on what scale you've chosen. For example, in the ordinary scale, using the default size for a form, the line

```
PSet(3722,2212)
```

would turn on the center pixel on a standard VGA screen, but after a ScaleMode=3 command, this would cause an overflow run-time error. It is possible to use PSet outside the current limits of the form, but if you exceed the limits on the size of the screen, you'll almost certainly get an overflow run-time error. When you use PSet to turn on a point that is outside the form, Visual Basic records this information but doesn't plot any points. This is where the AutoRedraw property's being set to True can help. Suppose you ask Visual Basic to plot a point that is too large to fit the current size of the form and

AutoRedraw is True for the form. Then the information isn't lost; set the WindowState property to 2 (maximized), and the point will show up.

For example, the following simple Form_Click procedure uses PSet to draw a straight line down the center of the screen and a line across the bottom of the screen. Notice that the vertical line goes a little bit beyond the default size of the form.

```
Sub Form_Click()
  ' line via PSet with a bit of 'clipping'
  Dim I As Integer
  AutoRedraw = True                        'slows things down a bit

  For I =0 To 5000
   PSet (3742,I)
  Next I
  For I =0 To 7485
    PSet (I, 3500)
  Next I
End Sub
```

The second For-Next loop gives you a horizontal line near the bottom of the screen. Figure 12-6 shows what you'll see. However, if you maximize the form, you can see that the graphics information wasn't lost, as shown in Figure 12-7.

Suppose you want to erase every other dot in this line. Although there are many ways to do this, at this point the simplest is to notice that redrawing a point in the background color obviously erases it. For example, you might add another loop that reads

```
For I =0 To 5000 Step 2
 PSet (3742,I), BackColor
Next I
```

You might suppose that this fragment would make Visual Basic erase every other point. However, because of how Visual Basic rounds off coordinates, this probably won't work on your monitor. In fact, adding this fragment to the previous program will probably accomplish nothing or too much. The coordinates of the points that are erased are so close to the ones that are turned on that either no changes show up or all the points are erased. This is because twips are a much finer scale than the actual screen resolution. For this reason, one possibility is to change the program to work in ScaleMode 3 (pixels) and modify

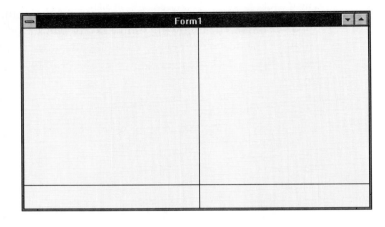

**Figure 12-6**

Line via PSet (parts are hidden)

the limits on the For–Next loop accordingly. Another possibility is to use a much larger Step. (Fifty seems to work well.)

**tip:**

*In a situation like this where you need to know how many twips correspond to a single pixel, turn to Visual Basic's built-in TwipsPerPixelX / TwipsPerPixelY functions.*

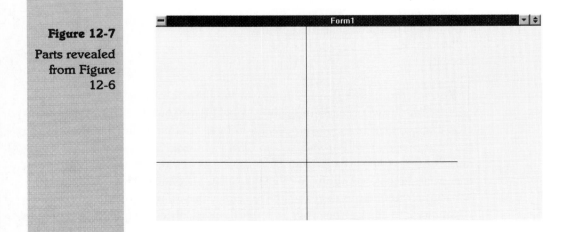

**Figure 12-7**

Parts revealed from Figure 12-6

## An Example Program: "Visual Basic A Sketch"

The following program shows how powerful even a seemingly trivial method like PSet can be when combined with Visual Basic's event-driven nature. Many people find this program appealing because of its similarity to a popular toy called "Etch-A-Sketch." This program imitates that toy. For those who aren't familiar with this toy, the idea is that you can control the growth of a line by twisting and turning two knobs that control the up/down and left/right directions. The trick (and what makes the game so appealing) is that the line has to be continuous; you can't break it up. Nonetheless, you can draw what appears to be circles and other complicated shapes by carefully combining twists of the up/down and left/right controls. It obviously isn't nearly as sophisticated as the Paint program supplied with Windows, but it is a lot of fun.

The following program imitates this game by using the KeyDown event procedure to detect the arrow keys. Each time you press UP ARROW, the pixel directly up from where you were turns on. Each time you press LEFT ARROW, the pixel directly to the left is turned on, and so on. If you hold an arrow key down, you can draw multiple pixels in the same direction.

The program needs two forms, one for directions (the startup form) and one for the drawing area, plus a code module for the CONSTANT.TXT file. The second form should have AutoRedraw set to True. The initial screen should look like the one in Figure 12-8. The two command buttons have control names: Directions and Start. The following table summarizes the properties of the command buttons set at design time:

| Control | Properties and Settings |
| --- | --- |
| First command button | Default: size, shape, color<br>ControlName = Directions<br>Caption = Directions<br>Location: left corner |
| Second command button | Default: size, shape, color<br>ControlName = Start<br>Caption = Start!<br>Location: right corner |

Here are the event procedures and what they do:

| Event Procedure | Task |
| --- | --- |
| Directions_Click | Prints directions on startup form |
| Start_Click | Loads the form for drawing |
| Key_Down | Interprets keystrokes, plots |

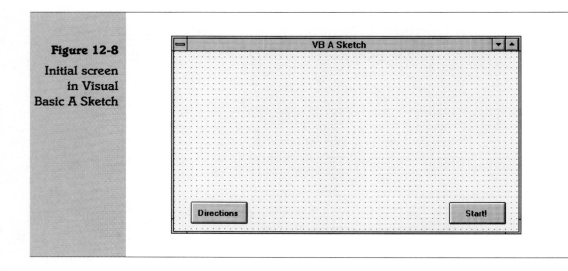

**Figure 12-8**

Initial screen
in Visual
Basic A Sketch

Here's the Directions_Click procedure:

```
Sub Directions_Click ()
  Print "This program imitates the Etch-A-Sketch (TM) game."
  Print "As you hold down an arrow key a line will grow in";
  Print " that direction starting"
  Print "from the center of the screen. Press the End key ";
  Print "to end while drawing.": Print
  Print "Click on the Start button to start."
End Sub
```

For the Start_Click procedure, you need to load the form that contains the drawing area and hide the directions:

```
Sub Start_Click ()
  Form2.Show
  Form1.Hide
End Sub
```

Now, the second form needs some form-level variables to contain information about how big the screen is.

```
Dim PixelHeight As Single, PixelWidth As Single
Dim WhereX As Single, WhereY As Single
```

The variables PixelHeight and PixelWidth hold the current size of the form. The program uses these variables to make sure the user doesn't go off the form. WhereX and WhereY give the current position on the screen.

The program sets all these variables as well as the ScaleMode in the Form_Load procedure for the form containing the drawing area.

```
Sub Form_Load ()
  AutoRedraw = True
  ScaleMode = 3                       'Pixels
  PixelHeight = ScaleHeight
  PixelWidth = ScaleWidth
  WhereX = PixelWidth / 2
  WhereY = PixelHeight / 2
End Sub
```

Next, to allow a user to resize the form, the program uses the ReSize event procedure. The ReSize event procedure is invoked by Visual Basic when the form is first displayed or if the user resizes it. This way you can change the allowable limits for drawing while the program is running.

```
Sub Form_ReSize()
  PixelHeight = ScaleHeight
  PixelWidth = ScaleWidth
End Sub
```

Note that these methods are needed in both the ReSize and Form_Load procedures in order to initialize the WhereX, WhereY variables in the Form_Load procedure. All the work is actually contained in the KeyDown event procedure attached to the second form. To make it easier to read the codes for the KeyDown procedure, this program assumes you've added the CONSTANT.TXT file to the .BAS module. Here's the KeyDown procedure:

```
Sub Form_KeyDown (KeyCode As Integer, Shift As Integer)
  Dim YesNo%
  Select Case KeyCode
    Case Key_Left                     'From CONSTANT.TXT
      If WhereX <= 0 Then             'don't go off drawing area
        WhereX = 0                      'but round down may occur
      Else
        WhereX = WhereX - 1           'move left 1
      End If
    Case Key_Right                    'From CONSTANT.TXT
```

```
        If WhereX >= PixelWidth Then
          WhereX = PixelWidth
        Else
          WhereX = WhereX + 1              ' right 1
        End If
      Case Key_Up                            'up 1
        If WhereY <= 0 Then
          WhereY = 0
        Else
          WhereY = WhereY - 1
        End If
      Case Key_Down
        If WhereY >= PixelHeight Then
          WhereY = PixelHeight
        Else
          WhereY = WhereY + 1
        End If
      Case Key_End
        YesNo% = MsgBox("Are you sure you want to end?", 4)
        If YesNo% = 6 Then End              '6 is Yes button click
      Case Else
        Beep
    End Select
     PSet (WhereX, WhereY)
End Sub
```

The message box uses Yes/No buttons and ends only if the user clicks the Yes button.

# Lines and Boxes

Obviously, if you had to draw everything by plotting individual points, graphics programming would be too time-consuming to be practical. In addition to line and shape controls, Visual Basic comes with a rich supply of graphics features, called *graphics primitives*, that allow you to plot such geometric figures as lines, boxes, circles, ellipses, and wedges with a single statement.

For example, the following fragment replaces the two For-Next loops in the PSet demonstration with the Line method:

```
Sub Form_Click()
  ' line via Line with a bit of 'clipping'
  AutoRedraw = True                        'slows things down a bit
  Line (3742,0) - (3742,5000)
  Line (0,3500) - (7485,3500)
End Sub
```

More generally, the statement

Line (*StartColumn, StartRow*) – (*EndCol, EndRow*), ColorCode

gives you a line connecting the two points with the given coordinates, using the color specified by ColorCode. For example, the following program gives you a starburst by drawing random lines in random colors from the center of the screen. This program uses a custom scale so that (0,0) is the center of the screen. Since the number of pixels in the default-size form is 491 across and 268 down, (−245,134) is the top right-hand corner and (245,−134) is the bottom right-hand corner:

```
Sub Form_Click()
  'random lines in random colors
  Dim I As Integer, CCode As Integer
  Dim Col As Single, Row As Single

  Randomize
  Cls
  Scale (-245, 134) - (245, -134)
  For I = 1 To 100
    Col = 245*Rnd
    If Rnd < .5 Then Col = -Col
    Row = 134*Rnd
    If Rnd < .5 Then Row = -Row
    CCode = 15*Rnd
    Line (0, 0) - (Col, Row), QBColor(CCode)
  Next I
End  Sub
```

The body of the For-Next loop calculates a random point and color code on each pass. Another use of Rnd determines whether the coordinates are positive or negative. Next, the Line method tells Visual Basic to draw a line from the center of the screen to that point. The screen in Figure 12-9 is an example of what you get.

**Figure 12-9**
**Starburst**

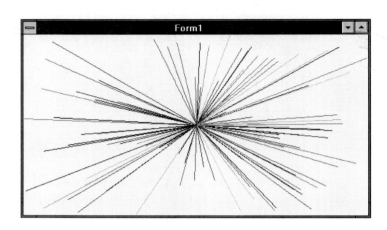

## LAST POINT REFERENCED

Visual Basic keeps track of where it stopped plotting. This location is usually called the *last point referenced (LPR)*, and the values of the CurrentX and CurrentY variables store this information. If you are continuing a line from the last point referenced, Visual Basic allows you to omit the LPR in the Line method.

For example,

```
Line - (160, 90)
```

draws a line from the last point referenced to the point with the coordinates (160,90). When you start any graphics mode with a ScaleMode method or a custom scale, the last point referenced has the coordinates (0,0) in that scale. For custom scales, this need not be the top left-hand corner. After a Line method, the last point referenced is the end point of the line (the second coordinate pair).

Up to now you've been using *absolute coordinates*. Each point is associated with a unique row and column. It's occasionally useful to use *relative coordinates*, where each point is defined by how far it is from the last point referenced. For example, if you write

```
PSet(12, 100)
```

which makes 12, 100 the last point referenced, then you can write

```
PSet Step(50, 10)
```

to turn on the point in column 62 (50 + 12) and row 110 (10 + 100). In general, when Visual Basic sees the statement

Step (X, Y)

in a graphics method, it uses the point whose coordinates are X units to the right or left and Y units up or down from the last point referenced (depending on whether X and Y are positive or negative).

## An Example: The X-Y Plane

Suppose you need to create an X-Y axis that allows numbers on the axes satisfying the following requirements:

–5<= X, Y <= 5

Here's a fragment that will do this:

```
Scale (-5,5) - (5,-5)
Line (-5,0) - (5,0)              'X Axis
Line (0,5) - (0,-5)             'Y Axis
' Now to label the axes add:
LetterHeight = TextHeight("X")   'How high is a letter
LetterWidth  = TextWidth("X")
CurrentX = -5 + LetterWidth
CurrentY =  2*LetterHeight
Print "X - Axis";
For I = 1 To 6
  CurrentX = LetterWidth
  CurrentY = (8-I)*LetterHeight
  Print Mid$("Y Axis", I ,1)
Next I
```

This fragment calculates how high a letter is, using the TextHeight function before resetting the CurrentX and CurrentY to allow a little space away from the axis. Since the CurrentX remains the same, all the letters are aligned, as shown in Figure 12-10. Finally, you might want to add numbers on the axes. You can do this by using the following fragment:

```
For I = -4 To 4
    CurrentX = I
    CurrentY = LetterHeight/2
    If I <> 0 Then Print I
Next I
For I = -4 To 4
    CurrentX = I
    CurrentY = LetterHeight/2
    CurrentY = I
    CurrentX = -LetterHeight/2
    Print I
Next I
```

The result looks like the screen in Figure 12-11.

## Grid Graphics

Suppose you want to draw a rocket ship, as shown in Figure 12-12. Since you can read off the coordinates from the diagram, it's easy (if a bit tedious) to write the following fragment.

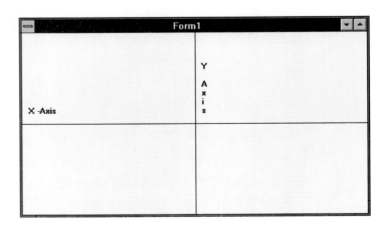

**Figure 12-10**

**X-Y plane**

**Figure 12-11**

Labeled X-Y plane

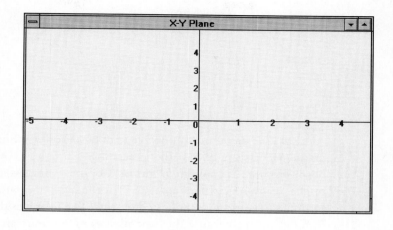

**Figure 12-12**

Rocket ship via grid graphics

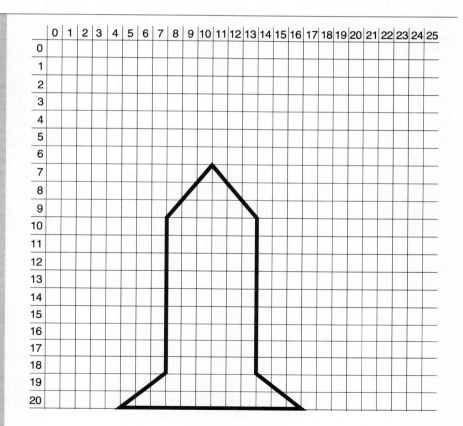

```
Scale (0,0) - (25,20)
Line  (6,20) - (14,20)
Line  - (12,18)
Line  - (12,9)
Line  - (10,6)
Line  - (8,9)
Line  - (8,18)
Line  - (6,20)
```

It's at least theoretically possible to draw almost anything by outlining it using graph paper; just mimic the preceding example. Obviously, as the object becomes more complicated, this method becomes less and less practical. One of the reasons that mathematics is needed for computer graphics is to give formulas for various complicated objects. The formulas then shorten the length of the program because they themselves incorporate an enormous amount of information. This makes it practical to write the program, whereas writing a few thousand PSet statements is obviously not.

## DrawWidth, DrawStyle

When you draw on the printer or the screen by using the PSet or Line method (and circles—see the section "Circles, Ellipses, and Pie Charts" later in this chapter), Visual Basic uses dots that are normally drawn one pixel wide. If you need to change the width of points or lines, use the DrawWidth property. The syntax for this method is

Object.DrawWidth = *Size%*

The theoretical maximum size for DrawWidth is 32,767.

For example, Figure 12-13 shows what you'll get if you run the following Click procedure on a blank form:

```
Sub Form_Click()
  ' Demonstrates DrawWidth
  WindowState = 2
  Dim I as Integer

  For I = 1 to 10
    DrawWidth = I    ' Form is default
    Line (0,I*ScaleHeight/12)-(ScaleWidth-15*TextWidth("D"), _
       I*ScaleHeight/12)
```

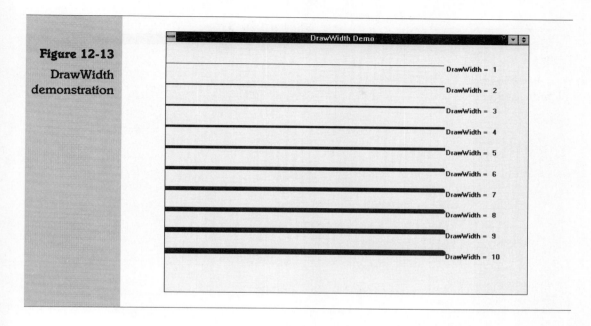

**Figure 12-13**

**DrawWidth**
**demonstration**

```
        Print " DrawWidth =";I
    Next I
End Sub
```

If you do not want a solid line, all you need to do is change the DrawStyle property. You can see the effect of DrawStyle only when the DrawWidth is 1. There are seven possible settings when DrawWidth is 1:

| Value of DrawStyle Property | Description |
| --- | --- |
| 0 (default) | Solid |
| 1 | Dashes |
| 2 | Dotted line |
| 3 | Dash-dot-dash-dot pattern |
| 4 | Dash-dot-dot pattern |
| 5 | Transparent—nothing shown |
| 6 | Inside solid (see the next section) |

Figure 12-14 shows what you get if you run the following demonstration program and then enlarge the screen.

**Figure 12-14**

**DrawStyle demonstration**

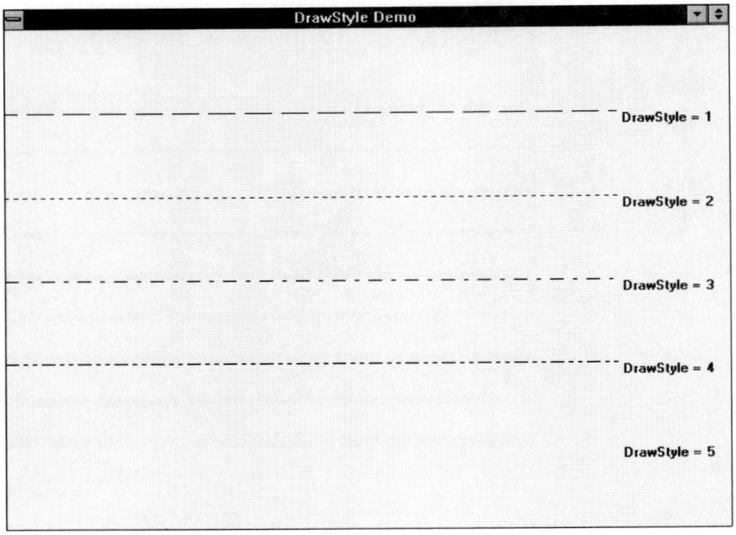

```
Sub Form_Click()
  ' Demonstrates DrawStyle
  AutoRedraw = True
  Dim I as Integer
  For I = 1 to 5
    DrawStyle = I
    Line (0,I*ScaleHeight/6) -(ScaleWidth, I*ScaleHeight/6)
    Print "DrawStyle =";I
  Next I
End Sub
```

## Boxes

A modification of the Line method lets you draw a rectangle. The statement

Line (*FirstCol, FirstRow*) − (*SecCol, SecRow*), *CCode,* B

draws a rectangle in the given color code (*CCode*) whose opposite corners are given by *FirstCol, FirstRow* and *SecCol, SecRow*. For example, the following fragment gives you nested boxes in a scale like QuickBASIC's SCREEN 2:

```
Sub Form_Click()
  Dim I As Integer
  Scale (0,0) - (639,199)

  For I = 1 To 65 Step 5
    Line (5*I,I) - (639 - 5*I,199-I), ,B
  Next I
End Sub
```

Notice that this program leaves off the color code but still keeps the comma to separate out the B. Without this comma, Visual Basic would think the B was the name of a variable rather than the Box command. Leave out the comma, and Visual Basic would think you're asking for a line connecting

$$(5*I, I)–(639-5*I, 199-I)$$

with color code the current value of B. (Since an uninitialized numeric variable 0 has value 0, you probably get a color code of 0.)

The width of the line defining the boundary of the box is determined by the current value of DrawWidth for the object on which you are drawing. When you have a fairly wide line for the boundary, you can see the effect of using the "inside solid" (DrawStyle = 6). As the following demonstration programs show, using the InsideSolid line makes for a boundary of the box that is half inside, half outside (see Figures 12-15 and 12-16).

Notice in Figure 12-15 the boundaries of the boxes merge whereas in Figure 12-16 they don't. This is because the inside solid style puts half the boundary of the box inside itself—so there's less of a common boundary. Here is a program that doesn't use InsideLine:

```
Sub Form_Click()
  ' Demonstrates Not Using InsideLine
  WindowState = 2
  DrawWidth = 10
  Line (100,100) - (ScaleWidth/2, ScaleHeight/2), , B
  Line(ScaleWidth/2, ScaleHeight/2) - (ScaleWidth-100,_
ScaleHeight-100), , B
End Sub
```

Now, to see InsideLine at work, run

```
Sub Form_Click()
  ' Demonstrates  Using InsideLine
```

**Figure 12-15**

Boxes with normal boundary

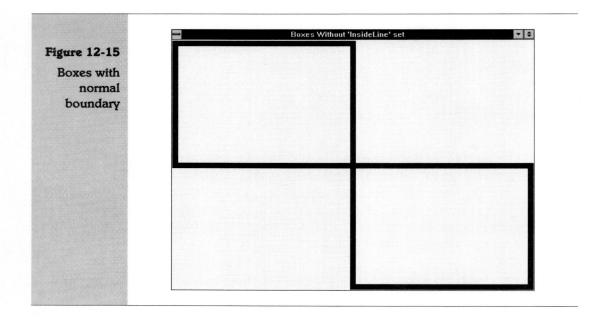

**Figure 12-16**

Boxes with inside/outside boundary

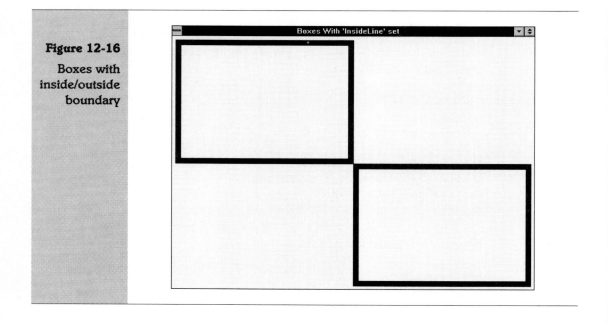

```
WindowState = 2
DrawStyle = 6
DrawWidth = 10
Line (100, 100) - (ScaleWidth/2, ScaleHeight/2),,B
 Line(ScaleWidth/2, ScaleHeight/2) - (ScaleWidth-100,_
ScaleHeight-100), , B
End Sub
```

## FILLED BOXES

You can arrange for the variant on the Line method that gives boxes to also fill the box. All you need to do is use BF rather than B, and you get a filled box. Therefore,

Line (*FirstCol, FirstRow*) − (*SecCol, SecRow*), *CCode*, BF

will yield a solid rectangle whose opposite corners are given by *FirstCol, FirstRow* and *SecCol, SecRow*. For example, change the nested box program so the code looks like this:

```
Dim I As Integer
Scale (0, 0) - (639, 199)
For I = 1 To 64 Step 5
 CCode = QBColor(I Mod 16)
 Line (5*I, I) - (639 - 5*I, 199-I), CCode, BF
Next I
```

You get a rather dramatic nesting of colored frames, as shown with shades in Figure 12-17. This happens for two reasons. The first is that the Mod function lets you cycle through the QuickBASIC color codes in order, and the second is that when Visual Basic draws each smaller rectangle, it overdraws part of the previous one using the new color.

## FILLSTYLE, FILLCOLOR

Boxes (and circles—see the next section) are usually empty or solid, but Visual Basic allows you seven different patterns to fill boxes. To do this, you need to change the FillStyle property of the form or picture box:

**Figure 12-17**

Demonstration
of colored
boxes

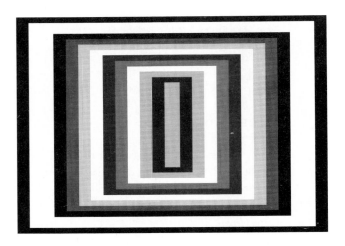

| Value of FillStyle Property | Description |
| --- | --- |
| 0 | Solid |
| 1 (default) | Empty |
| 2 | Horizontal line |
| 3 | Vertical line |
| 4 | Upward diagonal |
| 5 | Downward diagonal |
| 6 | Cross |
| 7 | Diagonal cross |

The screen in Figure 12-18 shows you the results of the following demonstration program:

```
Sub Form_Click()
  ' demonstrates FillStyle
  Dim I%
  Scale (0, 0) - (25, 25)
  For I% = 0 To 7
    FillStyle = I%
    Line (0, 3*I%) - (4, 3*(I%+.8)), , B
    CurrentX = 4.1: CurrentY = 3*I% + .5
    Print "This is FillStyle #";I%
  Next I%
End Sub
```

**Figure 12-18**

**Fill patterns**

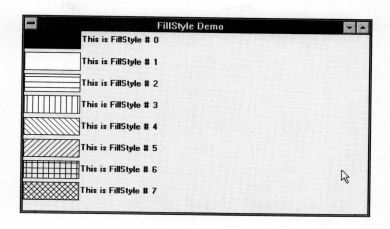

Once you have changed the FillStyle property from its transparent default (FillStyle = 1), you can use the FillColor property to set the color used for FillStyle. This property has the syntax

Object.FillColor = ColorCode

where, as usual, you can set the color code in any of the four ways mentioned previously.

## An Example: Embellishing a Control

Windows 3.1 was much more visually appealing than Windows 3.0 for many reasons, but some of the little things turned out to matter the most. One was the way controls looked. For example, command buttons gave the impression of being pressed when clicked. You can also make your application much more appealing by framing controls in various ways other than simply using the frame control or changing the BorderStyle property of the control. For example, you can make controls (and hence images) appear to be recessed or raised—give them a three-dimensional look that users find appealing.

To do this you need to draw different-colored lines of various thicknesses around the control. If the colors you choose contrast with the background color of the form, you can get dramatic effects. Here's a routine that puts a frame around a single control:

```
Sub FrameControl (X As Control, CTop%, CRight%, CBot%, _
CLeft%, WidthOfFrame As Single)

  Dim LeftBoundary As Single
  Dim TopOfControl As Single
  Dim HeightOFControl As Single

  DrawWidth = 1
  FillStyle = 1
  ScaleMode = 1

  LeftBoundary = X.Left
  TopOfControl = X.Top
  HeightOfControl = X.Height
  WidthOfControl = X.Width

  Line (LeftBoundary, TopOfControl -_
WidthOfFrame)-(LeftBoundary_
+ WidthOfControl + WidthOfFrame, TopOfControl),_
QBColor(CTop%), BF
  Line -(LeftBoundary + WidthOfControl, TopOfControl + _
HeightOfControl + WidthOfFrame), QBColor(CRight%), BF
  Line -(LeftBoundary - WidthOfFrame, TopOfControl + _
HeightOfControl), QBColor(CBot%), BF
  Line -(LeftBoundary, TopOfControl - WidthOfFrame), _
QBColor(CLeft%), BF
End Sub
```

The idea of this routine is simple. We draw four narrow filled boxes around the four sides of the controls. This version of the routine accepts a control, four color codes for the sides, and a width.

If you call this routine three times, first with a thicker width and one set of color codes and then with successively narrower widths and different sets of color codes, the effects become even more dramatic. For example, if the BackColor of the form is light gray, try this routine with a black boundary around the box (QBColor(0)), a thick light gray box, and then thin white lines across the top and left (QBColor(15)) and dark gray across the bottom and right (QBColor(8)). Figure 12-19 was created using the following additional lines of code to surround a metafile that came with the Professional Edition.

```
Call FrameControl(Picture1, 0, 0, 0, 0, 100)
Call FrameControl(Picture1, 7, 7, 7, 7, 75)
Call FrameControl(Picture1, 15, 8, 8, 15, 25)
```

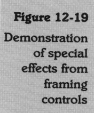

**Figure 12-19**

Demonstration of special effects from framing controls

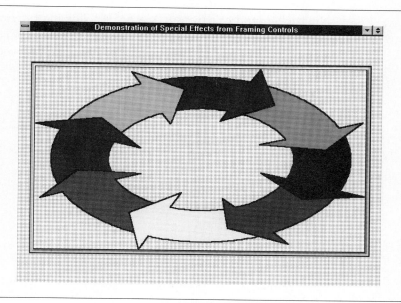

There are many other possibilities. Try reversing the white and gray lines; try leaving out the outer black lines. Experiment!

**tip:**

*For a routine that can frame many controls at once, replace the Control parameter in the above routine by four additional parameters that come from the leftmost control, the top control, the bottom control, and the rightmost control. Use these in place of the information provided by the control in the routine above. One way to obtain these parameters is to set up an array of the controls you want to frame. Next, write a routine to find out this information by passing the array to the routine and analyzing the position properties of the controls in the array.*

## ANIMATION AND DRAWMODE

The main problem with animation in Visual Basic is in redrawing what was there before the moving object obscured it. Redrawing the whole screen would take too long. Drawing the line in the background color wouldn't work because this would erase what was there before.

The key to successful animation is to use the analogue for drawing of the Xor operator that you saw in Chapter 7. Recall that when you use this logical operator twice, it brings you back to where you started. When you set the DrawMode property to 7 for a form or picture box, then drawing a line restores the background exactly as it was before. The most dramatic way to see this is to run the following demonstration program, which combines the starburst demonstration given earlier with a box that moves randomly each time you click the form:

```
Sub StarBurst()
  'random lines in random colors
  Dim I As Integer, CCode As Integer
  Dim Col As Single, Row As Single
  WindowState = 2
  Randomize

  Scale (-245,134) - (245,-134)
  For I = 1 To 100
    Col = 245*Rnd
    If Rnd < .5 Then Col = -Col
    Row = 134*Rnd
    If Rnd < .5 Then Row = -Row
    CCode = 15*Rnd
    Line (0,0) - (Col, Row) , QBColor(CCode)
  Next I
End  Sub
```

A Form_ReSize procedure can simply call the StartBurst routine. Now, for the Form_Click procedure, try the following with the DrawMode line commented out and then with the line being executable:

```
Sub Form_Click()
  Static Col, Row As Single
  Static CCode As Integer
  DrawMode = 7

  'This line erases the box and restores the background
  Line (0, 0) - (Col, Row), QBColor(CCode), BF
  'These lines move the box randomly
  Col = 100*Rnd
  If Rnd < .5 Then Col = -Col
  Row = 50*Rnd
  If Rnd < .5 Then Row = -Row
  CCode = 15*Rnd
  Line (0, 0) - (Col, Row), QBColor(CCode), BF
End Sub
```

(Use the Run menu or the CTRL+BREAK combination to stop the demonstration.)

There are 15 other possible settings for DrawMode. In all cases, Visual Basic compares the color code for each pixel in the object that it is in the process of drawing with the color code of the pixel that was already there. This is done at the bit level by converting the color code to a bit pattern. For example, the DrawMode value of 7 that you've just seen applies the Xor operator to the color codes. A DrawMode property of 6 draws the new object by applying the Not operator to the color code of the original object. With a DrawMode of 4, Visual Basic applies the Not operator to the color code of the foreground and uses that code for drawing. You can find a complete list of the 16 possible settings for DrawMode in the online help, but 4, 6, and 7 are the most common values.

To see this at work, use the starburst fragment in the Form_Paint procedure and add the following Form_Click procedure:

```
Sub Form_Click()
  DrawWidth = 10
  DrawMode = 4
  Line (-245, 134) - (245, -134)
  DrawMode = 6
  Line (245, 134) - (-245, -134)
End Sub
```

# Circles, Ellipses, and Pie Charts

Normally, to describe a circle in Visual Basic, you give its center and radius. The following fragment draws a circle of radius .5 units starting at the center of the screen:

```
Scale (-1,1) - (1,-1)
Circle (0,0), .5
```

The last point referenced (*CurrentX, CurrentY*) after a Circle method is always the center of the circle. You can also add a color code to the Circle method. For example,

```
Circle (0,0), .5 , CCode
```

would draw a circle of radius .5 in the color code indicated here by the variable CCode. The following demonstration program shows off the Circle method, which produces the nested circles shown in Figure 12-20:

```
Sub Form_Click()
  Dim I As Single, CCode As Single
  WindowState = 2

  ' nested circles
  Scale (-1,1) - (1,-1)
  For I = .1 To .7 Step .05
    CCode = 16*Rnd
    Circle (0,0), I, CCode
  Next I
End  Sub
```

You may be wondering what exactly the radius is. Is it measured in column units or row units, or is the measure the same in both the horizontal and vertical directions, as a mathematical radius would be? It turns out that the Circle method usually counts pixels by columns (horizontal units) to determine the radius. If you use the same horizontal units as vertical units, then the only problems will come from the aspect ratio of the screen (the aspect ratio is the

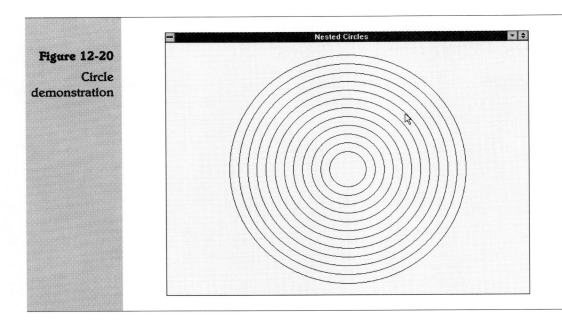

**Figure 12-20**

**Circle demonstration**

ratio between the height and width of your screen). Usually Windows takes care of any aspect ratio problems automatically. In fact, the major screen resolutions (640 * 480, 800 * 600, 1024 * 768) all have the same ratio. It's in the EGA area that you might have problems. You can take care of any aspect ratio problems with a variant on the Circle method that we'll discuss shortly.

You may have seen pie charts used to display data. Visual Basic sets up a pie chart with a modification of the Circle method. First, some terminology: a *sector* is a pie-shaped region of a circle, and an *arc* is the outer boundary of a sector, as shown in Figure 12-21.

To draw a sector or an arc, you have to tell Visual Basic which angle to start at and which angle to finish at. You do this using radian measure, which you may have seen in school. (It is also used in the trigonometric functions in Visual Basic.) Radian measure isn't very difficult. It measures angles by what percentage of the circumference of a circle of radius 1 that the radian measure would give. For example, all the way around a circle of radius 1 is $2\pi$ units. It is also 360 degrees, so 360 degrees is equal to $2\pi$ radians. One-half of a circle of radius 1 is 180 degrees and is p units. Therefore, 180 degrees is $\pi$ radians. Similarly, one-quarter of a circle (90 degrees) is $2/\pi$ radians, and so on. To go from degrees to radians, multiply by $180/\pi$; to go back, multiply by $180/\pi$. (Since $\pi$ is roughly 3.14159, 360 degrees is roughly 6.28 radians.) In any case, the statement that follows

Circle (*XRad, YRad), Radius, CCode, StartAngle, EndAngle*

**Figure 12-21**

**Arc versus sector**

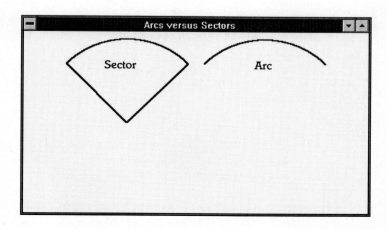

draws an arc of the circle starting at the angle given in radians by StartAngle and ending with EndAngle. To get a sector, use negative signs. Therefore, assuming you've set up Scale as $(-1, 1) - (1, -1)$ and have set up a global variable called Pie = 3.14159 (or better yet, set Pie = 4*Atn(1) as a global variable), then the screen in Figure 12-20 may be obtained from the following code:

```
Scale (-1, 1) - (1, -1)
Circle (-.4, 0), .5, , -Pie/4, -3*Pie/4
' above line gives you the sector in Figure 12-20. And:
Circle (.4, 0), .5, , Pie/4, 3*Pie/4
' gives you the arc.
```

There are a few peculiarities of these methods that you should be aware of. The first is that although mathematics allows negative angles, Visual Basic does not. The negative sign only serves to indicate, "Draw a sector rather than an arc." The second is that if you want your arc to start with a vertical line pointed due east (that is, 0 degrees = 0 radians), you shouldn't use $-0$ for the StartAngle or EndAngle. Instead, use $-2 *\pi (= -6.28 \dots)$. The final peculiarity is that angles in the Circle method can only have values between $-2\pi (-6.28 \dots)$ and $2\pi (6.28 \dots)$. (In the current version of Visual Basic, using 8*Atn (1) rather than 6.28 for $2*\pi$ seems to result in an error message.)

## An Example: Pie Charts

Suppose you want to write a general pie chart program. This program takes a bunch of numbers (stored in an array) and sets up a pie chart using the numbers. Essentially, what you need to do is determine what percentage of the total each positive number is and set up an arc using that percentage. This should be a general procedure that is sent an array as a parameter:

```
Sub MakePie( A() As Single )
   ' This procedure takes an array of positive entries and
   ' creates a pie chart using proportions determined by the
   ' array.

   ' LOCAL variables: I,First,Last,Total,StartAngle,EndAngle
   ' Global variable is assumed to be TwoPie
   ' TwoPie should be 6.28 and not 8*Atn(1)

   Dim I As Integer, First As Integer, Last As Integer
   Dim Total As Single, StartAngle As Single
```

```
    Dim EndAngle As Single, LastAngle As Single

    First = LBound(A,1)
    Last = UBound(A,1)
    Total = 0
    For I = First To Last
      Total = Total + A(I)
    Next I
    Scale (-1,1) - (1,-1)
    StartAngle = -TwoPie
    For I = First To Last
      EndAngle = ((A(I)/Total)*TwoPie) + StartAngle
      Circle (0,0),.5, , StartAngle,EndAngle
      StartAngle = EndAngle
    Next I
End Sub
```

The key to this program is the statement determining the EndAngle. This statement determines what fraction of the total a particular entry is. Multiplying by TwoPie (roughly 2 * 3.14159) gives you the radian equivalent. Since the StartAngle is $-2*\pi$, adding this angle gives you the necessary negative number for the size of the sector starting due east and going counterclockwise.

You can add other parameters to control the size of the circle used and the scale used. You could also change the procedure to pass an array of strings that you could use to label the sectors.

How can you test this procedure? Simply create some random arrays of random sizes with random positive entries and call the procedure.

This is only a sample of the kind of business-related graphics you can produce with Visual Basic. It would be very easy to modify this program to produce bar charts if that was what you needed. However, if you are constantly using presentation-style graphs, you should consider getting the Visual Basic Professional Edition (see Appendix A). This product has almost all the graphing capabilities you'd ever want available to you via a custom control (including three-dimensional bar and pie charts).

## Ellipses and the Aspect Ratio

You convert the Circle drawing method to an Ellipse drawing command by adding one more option. This also lets you override Visual Basic's default settings if you need to adjust the aspect ratio for your monitor. The syntax for this method is

Circle [*Step*] (*XCenter, YCenter*), *radius, , , , aspect*

The four commas must be there even if you are not using the color code and angle options that you saw earlier. (Step is optional, of course.) This version of the Circle method lets you change the default ratio of columns to rows. (It's really an Ellipse command.)

If the aspect parameter is less than 1, the radius is taken in the column direction and the ellipse is stretched in the horizontal direction. If the aspect parameter is greater than 1, the radius is taken in the row direction and the ellipse is stretched in the vertical. The following program demonstrates this:

```
Sub Form_Click()
   Scale (-2,2) -(2,-2)
   Static I As Single

   Cls
   Circle (0, 0), .5, , , , I+ .1
   CurrentX = -2: CurrentY = 2
   Print "This is aspect ratio";Format$(I+.1,"#.#");
   Print ". Click to see the next size ellipse"
   I = I + .1
End Sub
```

As the aspect ratio gets larger, the ellipse gets closer and closer to a vertical line.

# Curves

This is where the math starts. The first of the following sections uses the X–Y plane (Cartesian plane) and therefore a tiny bit of analytic geometry. The next section uses polar coordinates, and the last section uses some trigonometry.

The Scale method makes graphing any mathematical function trivial. The only problems come in deciding the maximum and minimum values to use for the Scale statement, which often takes calculus. However, as before, Visual Basic will clip any figure that is off the axis, so no problems result from setting the wrong scale, unless you are way out of line. In this case, you'll have to trap the overflow error that may result. You could have the error trap call a ReSize procedure that would rescale the drawing area to allow the new information to be used. This might require recalculating all the points already drawn, however.

For example, here's a fragment that draws a cosine graph, as shown in Figure 12-22:

```
Dim I As Single, TwoPie As Single
TwoPie = 8*Atn(1)
Scale (-TwoPie, 1) - (TwoPie, -1)

For I = -TwoPie To TwoPie Step .01
  PSet (I, Cos(I))
Next I
```

You saw earlier in this chapter how to put in the axes and mark them. If you want to experiment with other functions, you'll need to change the scale accordingly.

## Pictures Without Too Many Formulas

Now that you know about the Scale method, you can get to some serious picture drawing. The first method you'll see depends on the following simple idea. Imagine two points in the plane (say, with a tortoise at one and a hare at the other) chasing each other. As the second point (the hare) moves, draw the line connecting the first point's (the tortoise's) old position to the new position of the second point. Now move the tortoise down this line a little bit (say, ten

**Figure 12-22**

**A cosine graph**

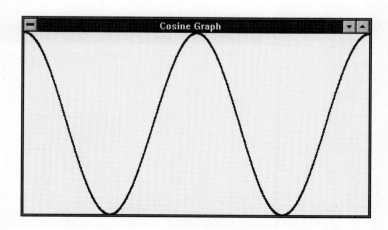

Cosine Graph

percent of the way). Continue the process. The screen shown in Figure 12-23 is what you get after a few stages if the second point (the hare) moves directly down five units and the first always moves ten percent of the way.

To implement this idea, you need a formula that calculates the new coordinate. Suppose first that you want the point halfway down on the line connecting, say, 50,100 to 100,200. It's pretty obvious that it has to be 75,150. Suppose, though, you wanted a point that was only ten percent of the way along this line. This turns out to be 55,110 (since, in a sense, you have 50 X units to move and 100 Y units to move). In general, the formula to move T% of the way on a line connecting *X1, Y1* to *X2, Y2* is

$$(1-T) * X1 + T * X2$$

for the new X coordinate and

$$(1-T) * Y1 + T * Y2$$

for the new Y coordinate. Here, *T* is the percentage moved, expressed as a decimal. (Some people like to think of this as a weighing formula.) Here is the listing that implements this method, and the result is shown in Figure 12-24:

```
Sub Form_Click()
  ' parabolic arch by tortoise and hare
  Dim PerCent As Single, X1 As Single, X2 As Single
```

**Figure 12-23**

First steps in tortoises and hares

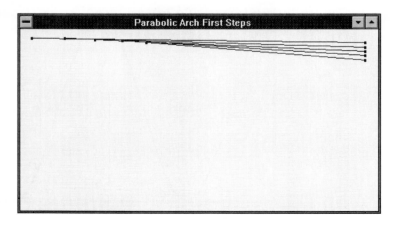

**Figure 12-24**

**Parabolic arch**

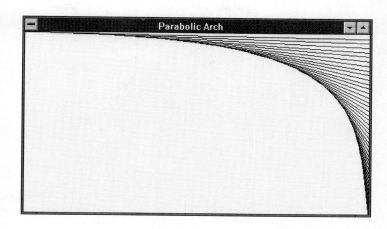

```
Dim Y1 As Single, Y2 As Single

Scale (-300, 100)-(300, -100)
PerCent = .1
X1 = -300: X2 = 300
Y1 = 100: Y2 = 100
Do Until Y2 < -100
   Y2 = Y2 - 5                              'down five units
   Line (X1, Y1)-(X2, Y2)                   'connect the points
   X1 = (1 - PerCent) * X1 + (PerCent * X2)    'move down line
   Y1 = (1 - PerCent) * Y1 + (PerCent * Y2)
Loop
End Sub
```

Although this is not a bad start, you don't really begin getting results until you add more animals (points). Imagine that four animals start at the corners of a square. The first animal chases the second, the second chases the third, the third the fourth, and the fourth chases the first. The screen in Figure 12-25 shows you what you get after only four moves. Obviously, what is happening is that each square is both rotating and shrinking. If you continue this process, then you get what was shown in Figure 12-1. Before you can work through the program, though, you'll need one more formula: the *distance formula* for points in the plane. This says that the distance between two points, *X1, Y1* and *X2, Y2*, in the plane is

**Figure 12-25**

First steps in rotating squares

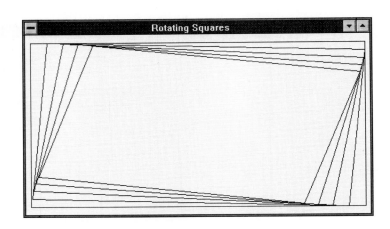

$$\text{Sqr}((X2 - X1)\char`\^2 + (Y2 - Y1)\char`\^2)$$

where Sqr is the square root function. In Visual Basic, you'll want to make a function out of it:

```
Function Dist(X1, Y1, X2, Y2) As Single
   Dim A As Single, B As Single

   A = (X2 - X1)*(X2 - X1)
   B = (Y2 - Y1)*(Y2 - Y1)
   Dist = Sqr(A + B)
End Function
```

The purpose of the distance function is to tell the program when to stop, to know when the animals are "close enough." Next, you need a MoveIt procedure for the chase:

```
Sub MoveIt (A, B, T)
  A = (1 - T) * A + T * B
End Sub
```

Here's the Form_Click( ) procedure that does all the work:

```
Sub Form_Click()
   Dim T As Single, X1 As Single, Y1 As Single
   Dim X2 As Single, Y2 As Single, X3 As Single
```

```
Dim Y3 As Single, X4 As Single, Y4 As Single

Scale (-320, 200)-(320, -200)
T = .05                          'Percentage moved if 5%
X1 = -320: Y1 = 200
X2 = 320: Y2 = 200
X3 = 320: Y3 = -200
X4 = -320: Y4 = -200
Do Until Dist(X1, Y1, X2, Y2) < 10
  Line (X1, Y1)-(X2, Y2)
  Line -(X3, Y3)
  Line -(X4, Y4)
  Line -(X1, Y1)
  MoveIt X1, X2, T
  MoveIt Y1, Y2, T
  MoveIt X2, X3, T
  MoveIt Y2, Y3, T
  MoveIt X3, X4, T
  MoveIt Y3, Y4, T
  MoveIt X4, X1, T
  MoveIt Y4, Y1, T
Loop
End Sub
```

The Do loop ends when the points get close enough—less than ten units from each other. Notice that you can't use the Box command because the square is rotated.

The block of repeated calls to the MoveIt function finds the new coordinates for each of the four points. By adding more parameters, you could have made the MoveIt subprogram make the changes one point at a time instead of one coordinate at a time.

If you imagine the animals are moving independently along curves, then the kind of pictures produced can be even more dramatic. The screen in Figure 12-26 shows one of the simplest ones. In this picture, you should imagine that one point is constantly moving around a circle around the origin while the other point chases it by moving along the line of sight. To write a program to do this or to construct one whose results are even more dramatic (chases along more complicated curves), you'll need formulas for the curves. That's the subject of the next section. That section shows you how to write the program that will draw what you see in Figure 12-26.

**Figure 12-26**

Circle chase

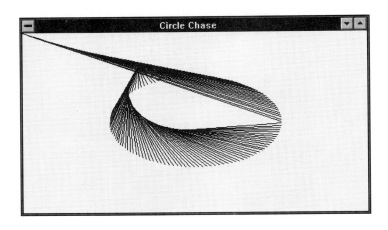

## Polar Coordinates

Most complicated mathematical curves are more easily described by using polar coordinates. With polar coordinates, you describe the position of a point by saying how far it is from the origin and what angle a line connecting the origin to it makes with the positive X axis. Figure 12-27 shows this.

**Figure 12-27**

Polar coordinates

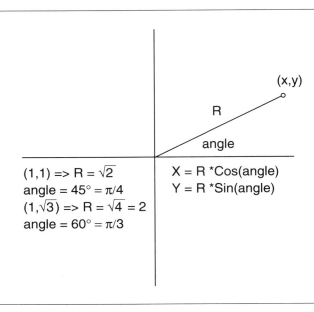

$$(1,1) => R = \sqrt{2}$$
$$\text{angle} = 45° = \pi/4$$
$$(1,\sqrt{3}) => R = \sqrt{4} = 2$$
$$\text{angle} = 60° = \pi/3$$

$$X = R * \text{Cos(angle)}$$
$$Y = R * \text{Sin(angle)}$$

To go from polar coordinates to X–Y coordinates, use the formulas

X=R * Cos(Angle)

and

Y=R * Sin(Angle)

where *Angle* is the angle indicated in Figure 12-26. (These formulas come from dropping a perpendicular to the X axis and making a right triangle.)

To go from X–Y coordinates to polar coordinates, use

$R = \sqrt{X^2 + Y^2}$ (in Visual Basic, Sqr($X*X + Y*Y$))

and the angle is Atn(Y/X) (unless X is zero).

The point of polar coordinates for computer graphics is that the equation of a curve may have a much simpler formula than in rectangular (X–Y) coordinates. For example, the equation of a circle of radius .5 around the origin is simply $R = .5$ (instead of $X^2 + Y^2 = .25$). This means

R * Cos(Theta)

R * Sin(Theta)

where the angle *Theta* runs from zero to $2\pi$ radians are the X and Y coordinates of a circle in polar coordinates.

Here's the program that runs a chase around a circle, as was shown in Figure 12-25:

```
Sub Form_Click ()
   Dim X1 As Single, Y1 As Single, X2 As Single
   Dim Y2 As Single, TwoPie As Single, I As Single

   Scale (-1, 1) - (1, -1)
   X1 = -1
   Y1 = 1
   TwoPie = 8 * Atn(1)
   For I = 0 To TwoPie Step .05
      X2 = .5 * Cos(I)
      Y2 = .5 * Sin(I)
      Line (X1, Y1)-(X2, Y2)
```

```
    X1 = (.95 * X1) + (.05 * X2)
    Y1 = (.95 * Y1) + (.05 * Y2)
  Next I
End Sub
```

Polar coordinates let you draw much more complicated figures. For example, you can easily draw objects like a four-leaf clover, as shown in Figure 12-28. The formula for the four-leaf clover curve is

$$Cos(2*Angle)$$

as the angle runs from zero to $2\pi$ (0° to 360°). (The rectangular X–Y version is very messy.) Combine this formula with the conversion formulas for X and Y given previously, and you have the following simple fragment that draws a four-leaf clover:

```
Sub Form_Click ()
  Dim X As Single, Y As Single
  Dim TwoPie As Single, I As Single, R As Single

  TwoPie = 8 * Atn(1)
  Scale (-2, 2) - (2, -2)
  For I = 0 To TwoPie Step .01
    R = Cos(2 * I)
    X = R * Cos(I)
```

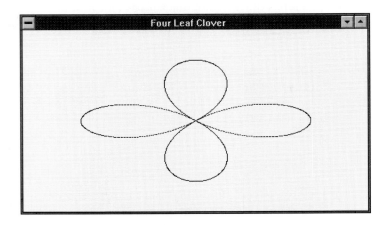

**Figure 12-28**

Four-leaf
clover

```
      Y = R * Sin(I)
      PSet (X, Y)
    Next I
End Sub
```

Don't be surprised if this takes a bit of time. After all, it requires a few thousand sine and cosine computations.

Combine this with a chase and you get something like what is shown in Figure 12-29. (You can easily modify the "Circle Chase" program given previously to draw this.)

Of course, you have to know the formula for whatever object you're trying to draw. Over the years, people have collected this information, and you can find books with massive lists of figures and their polar equations. Here's a short list of some of the more common ones:

| Polar Equation | Figure |
|---|---|
| R = PositiveNumber | Circle of that radius |
| R = 1 + Sin(2*z) | Infinity symbol on angle |
| R = 1 + Cos(z) | A cardioid (heart-shaped) |
| R = 1 + 2*Cos(z) | A limacon (Write a program to find out what this is!) |
| R = Sin(n*z) | A petaled rose—number of leaves depends on n>2 |
| R = z/c | A spiral |
| R =1 + 2*Cos(2*z) | A loop-the-loop |
| R = Sec(z) + Tan(z) | A strophoid (z <> 0,90,180...) |
| R = Sec(z) + 1 | A conchoid |
| R^2 = Cos(2*z) | A lemniscate |
| x = Cos(z)^3 | An astroid |
| y = Sin(t)^3 | |
| x = 3*Cos(z)–Cos(3*z) | A nephroid |
| y = 3*Sin(z)–Sin(3*z) | |

It's easy to modify the four-leaf clover program to draw any one of these objects—or see the program in the following section.

## A POLAR DEMONSTRATION PROGRAM

The following demonstration program collects a large number of examples from the list given in the previous section through the use of the random number generator. It also uses the following observation: if you slightly twist the conversion formulas from, for example,

**Figure 12-29**

**Four-leaf clover chase**

R * Cos(Angle)

to

R * Cos(RandomInteger * Angle)

then the pictures are even more dramatic.

The following program is long, but nothing in it is very difficult. The program uses two forms: one for the demonstration and one for the directions. It also needs a .BAS module for general code. For this program, you should set the form Name for the form containing the graph to PolarDemo. You might also want to set the AutoRedraw property of this form to True. The trouble with this is that Visual Basic will then wait for idle time to refresh the screen, and you would not be able to see the object being drawn. (Using the Refresh method constantly slows things down so much that you might want to add a counter to call the Refresh method periodically.)

The form Name for the form holding the directions will be simply Directions. The two forms look like the screen in Figure 12-30. As you can see, the top form contains two option (radio) buttons that let the user choose whether to use ordinary or twisted polar coordinates and a menu. The menu allows the

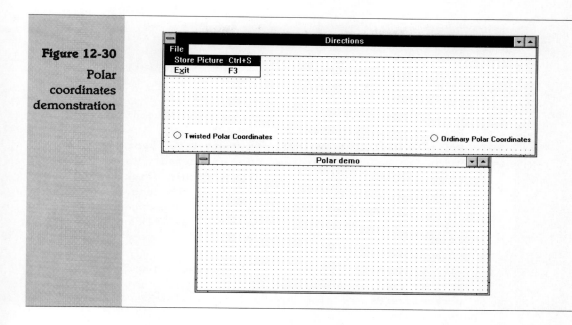

**Figure 12-30**

Polar
coordinates
demonstration

user to exit or toggle to save the picture. The code for the click procedure on
the StorePicture menu item is

```
Sub StorePicture_Click ()
  PolarDemo.AutoRedraw = Not (PolarDemo.AutoRedraw)
  StorePictureFlag = Not (StorePictureFlag)
  StorePicture.Checked = Not (StorePicture.Checked)
End Sub
```

Besides toggling the AutoRedraw property to true, this module toggles the
check marks and also toggles a global flag variable "StorePictureFlag".

Here are the global constants and variables that need to be in the code
module:

```
Global FFactr() As Integer    'will store 8 random integers
Global TwoPie As Single
Global CurveNumber As Integer
Global Limit As Integer
Global Complicated As Integer
Global StorePictureFlag As Integer
```

The Sub procedure for giving the directions is

```
Sub GiveDirections ()
  PolarDemo.Hide
  Directions.Show
  Directions.AutoRedraw = True   'Want the directions to _
persist
  Cls
  Print "This shows off the power of polar coordinates. You ";
  Print "can use ordinary or twisted"
  Print "coordinates depending on whether you want the graph ";
  Print "to be complicated or not. The default is to use"
  Print "twisted coordinates. Please double click on any ";
  Print "blank area in this form to see the demo. The mouse"
  Print "pointer will resume its normal shape when the curve";
  Print "is finished. You may then double click on any part"
  Print "to see another graph."
  Directions.Print
  Directions.Print "To save the picture use the file menu.
Note this will "
  Directions.Print "slow down the display of the picture -_
have patience!"
End Sub
```

The procedure that performs the initialization at the beginning of the program is in the code module, and each time the user wants to reuse the program, the program calls this procedure. It looks like this:

```
Sub Initialize ()
  'Assign to global variables Complicated, CurveNumber
  'Limit and FFactr
  Dim I As Integer

  Randomize
  ReDim FFactr(1 To 7)
  For I = 1 To 7
    FFactr(I) = Int(8 * Rnd) + 1
  Next I
  Limit = MaxSize%(CurveNumber)
  PolarDemo.Scale (-Limit, Limit)-(Limit, -Limit)
  CurveNumber = FFactr(7)
  If Directions.Twisted.Value Then
    Complicated = True
  Else
    Complicated = False
```

```
    End If
End Sub
```

The Form_Load procedure for the startup (Directions form) is

```
Sub Form_Load()
  TwoPie = 8*Atn(1)
  GiveDirections
End Sub
```

Next, you need to change the normal polar graphing module to allow twisted coordinates, as described earlier. This procedure should be placed in the .BAS module and takes two parameters: The first is for the curve, and the second acts as a switch to determine whether or not to twist the coordinates.

```
Sub PolarPlot (Curve%, Tf%)
Dim I As Single, X As Single, Y  As Single
  Dim FileName As String
  PolarDemo.Cls
  PolarDemo.Show
  Directions.MousePointer = 11
  PolarDemo.MousePointer = 11    ' Hourglass
  ' Global variables Pie, Limit, FFactr()
  ' This procedure plots the graph using either normal or
  'twisted polar coordinates
  For I = 0 To TwoPie Step .001
    If Tf% Then                        'Fudge it
      X = RofTheta(I, Curve%) * Cos(FFactr(5) * I)
      Y = RofTheta(I, Curve%) * Sin(FFactr(6) * I)
    Else                               'reg polar cord
      X = RofTheta(I, Curve%) * Cos(I)
      Y = RofTheta(I, Curve%) * Sin(I)
    End If
    PolarDemo.PSet (X, Y)
  Next I
  PolarDemo.MousePointer = 0
  Directions.MousePointer = 0 'Back to normal
  If StorePictureFlag Then
    FileName = InputBox$("Name of file to save picture as?")
    SavePicture PolarDemo.Image, FileName
  End If
  Directions.SetFocus
End Sub
```

Notice that if StorePictureFlag is set, this module pops up an input box that asks the name of the file for saving the bitmap.

Next comes the .BAS procedure that sets up the function RofTheta used in the preceding procedure. This procedure uses the array of fudge factors previously set up as the global variable FFactr. This array lets you make the curves even more complicated when desired.

```
Function RofTheta (Theta As Single, Curv%) As Single
  ' Global variables array FFactr() As Integer
  Dim A As Single, B As Single
  Select Case Curv%
   Case 1
     RofTheta = 1 + (2 * Cos(2 * Theta))
   Case 2
     RofTheta = 3 * Cos(4 * Theta)
   Case 3
     RofTheta = Theta
   Case 4
     RofTheta = (2 * Sin(FFactr(3) * Theta)) - 2 *
Cos(FFactr(4) * Theta)
   Case 5
     RofTheta = 3 * Cos(FFactr(1) * Theta)
   Case 6
     RofTheta = FFactr(2) + (FFactr(1) * Cos(FFactr(3) *
FFactr(4) * Theta))
   Case 7
     RofTheta = FFactr(2) + (FFactr(1) * Cos(FFactr(2) * Theta))
   Case 8
     RofTheta = ((FFactr(1) + FFactr(2)) * Sin(Theta)) / (2 +
Cos(Theta))
   Case Else
     A = (FFactr(1) * Cos(FFactr(3) * Theta))
     B = (FFactr(2) * Sin(FFactr(4) * Theta))
     RofTheta = A + B
  End Select
End Function
```

Now the direction form Form_DblClick procedure has only to call the plotting routine, passing the information regarding the curve number and whether or not twisted coordinates are used:

```
Sub Form_DblClick ()
  Initialize
```

```
    PolarPlot CurveNumber, Complicated
End Sub
```

Finally, you need a MaxSize function in the .BAS module to compute the limits:

```
Function MaxSize%(X As Integer)
  If X < 6 Then
    MaxSize% = 4
  Else
    MaxSize% = FFactr(1) + FFactr(2)
  End If
End Sub
```

If you choose the complicated option, the figures this demonstration program creates can be quite spectacular. Figures 12-2 and 12-31 show examples.

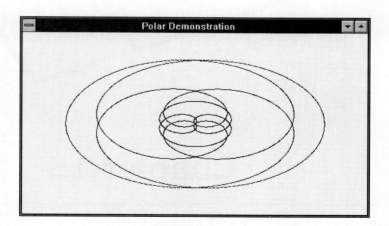

**Figure 12-31**

Curve from twisted polar demonstration

# Chapter 13

# Monitoring Mouse Activity

W I N D O W S , and therefore Visual Basic, constantly monitors what the user is doing with the mouse. Up to this point, all you have used are the Click and Double Click events. These detect whether the user clicked the mouse once or twice in a form or control. This chapter shows you how to obtain and use more subtle information. Was a mouse button pressed? Which button was it? Is the mouse pointer over a control? Did the user release a button, and if so, which one? Did the user move the mouse out of one form and into another? Exactly where inside the form is the mouse? Visual Basic can detect all these events. Of course, as with all Visual Basic operations, you must write the event procedures that determine how Visual Basic will respond to the event. For example, if you want to pop up a menu after a right mouse click, you'll need to write the necessary lines of code.

**note:** *To allow the possibility of context-sensitive pop-up menus, all controls in Visual Basic 3 are now mouse-sensitive.*

Finally, just as designing a Visual Basic application involves dragging controls around a blank form, Visual Basic lets you write applications that let the user move controls around by dragging and dropping. The last section of this chapter shows you how.

## The Mouse Event Procedures

There are three fundamental mouse event procedures:

| Name | Event That Caused It |
|------|----------------------|
| MouseDown | User clicks one of the mouse buttons |

| Name | Event That Caused It |
|------|----------------------|
| MouseUp | User releases a mouse button |
| MouseMove | User moves the mouse pointer |

In many ways, these procedures are analogous to the KeyUp, KeyDown event procedures that you saw in Chapter 7. For example, as with those event procedures, Visual Basic lets you use bit masking to determine if the user was holding down the SHIFT, ALT, or CTRL key at the same time he or she pressed or released a mouse button.

Only forms and picture boxes return where the mouse pointer is in terms of their internal scales. For the other controls, it's necessary to calculate this information by using the scale of the surrounding container—a method that may or may not be practical.

Controls recognize a mouse event only when the mouse pointer is inside the control; the underlying form recognizes the mouse event in all other cases. However, if a mouse button is pressed *and held* while the mouse pointer is inside a control or form, that object *captures the mouse*. This means that no other Visual Basic object can react to mouse events until the user releases the mouse button, regardless of where the user moves the mouse.

All mouse event procedures take the same form and use the same parameters:

*Object_MouseEvent*(*Button* As Integer, *Shift* As Integer, *X* As Single, *Y* As Single)

If the object was part of a control array, then, as usual, there is an optional first *Index* parameter:

*ObjectIn*ControlArray_*MouseEvent*(*Index* As Integer, *Button* As Integer, *Shift* As Integer, *X* As Single, *Y* As Single)

As the next sections show, bit masking lets you use the *Button* argument to determine which mouse button was pressed. Similarly, you can find out if the user was holding down any combination with the SHIFT, CTRL, or ALT key by bit masking, using the *Shift* parameter. Finally, *X* and *Y* give you the information you need to determine the position of the mouse pointer, using the internal coordinates of the object if they exist (forms and picture boxes).

## The MouseUp/MouseDown Events

To see the event procedure given in this section at work, start up a new project. Double-click to open the Code window and move to the MouseDown event procedure. Now enter the following:

```
Sub Form_MouseDown(Button As Integer, Shift As Integer, X As
Single, Y As Single)
   Circle (X,Y), 75
End Sub
```

This simple event procedure uses the positioning information passed by *X* and *Y*. Each time you click a mouse button, a small circle is centered exactly where you clicked—namely, at CurrentX = X and CurrentY = Y, of size 75 twips. If you add a MouseUp event procedure that looks like

```
Sub Form_MouseUp(Button As Integer, Shift As Integer, X As
Single, Y As Single)
   Dim CCode As Integer
   Randomize
   CCode = Int(15*Rnd)
   FillStyle = 0
   FillColor = QBColor(CCode)
   Circle (X,Y), 75
End Sub
```

then each time you release the same button, Visual Basic fills the circle with a random color. On the other hand, even though you may have two or even three mouse buttons, Visual Basic will not generate another MouseDown event until you release the original mouse button. This prevents you from making some circles filled and others empty when using these two procedures.

Suppose, however, you wanted to make some circles filled and some empty. One way to do this is to use the added information given by the *Button* argument. For example, suppose the user has a two-button mouse. You can easily write code so that if the user presses the right mouse button, he or she gets a filled circle, and otherwise all he or she gets is a colored circular outline. The *Button* argument uses the lowest three bits of the value of the integer, as shown here:

| Button | Value of Button Argument |
| --- | --- |
| Left | 1 |
| Right | 2 |
| Middle | 4 |

Visual Basic will tell you about only one button for the MouseUp/Mouse-Down combination. You cannot detect if both the left and right buttons are down simultaneously, for example. Thus you can rewrite the MouseUp event procedure to allow both filled and empty circles using the left/right buttons:

```
Sub Form_MouseUp(Button As Integer, Shift As Integer, X As
Single, Y As Single)
  Dim CCode As Integer
  Randomize
  CCode = Int(15*Rnd)
  Select Case Button
    Case 1, 4
      Circle (X,Y), 75, QBColor(CCode)
      FillColor = &HFFFFFF&
    Case 2
      FillStyle = 0
      FillColor = QBColor(CCode)
      Circle (X,Y), 75
   End Select
End Sub
```

If you want a pop-up menu in response to a right mouse click, use a line of code like this:

If Button = 2 Then PopUpMenu *MenuName*

(See Chapter 10 for more on pop-up menus.)

You can also let the user combine the keyboard with a mouse. For example, you can have the SHIFT+right mouse button combination drop down a special menu. This uses the *Shift* argument in the MouseUp or MouseDown event procedure. Here's a table of the possible values for the lower three bits of the *Shift* parameter:

| Action | Bit Set and Value |
| --- | --- |
| SHIFT key down | Bit 0: Value = 1 |
| CTRL key down | Bit 1: Value = 2 |
| ALT key down | Bit 2: Value = 4 |

| Action | Bit Set and Value |
|---|---|
| SHIFT+CTRL keys down | Bit 0 and 1: Value = 3 |
| SHIFT+ALT keys down | Bit 0 and 2: Value = 5 |
| CTRL+ALT keys down | Bit 1 and 2: Value = 6 |
| SHIFT+CTRL+ALT keys down | Bits 0, 1, and 2: Value = 7 |

At the present time, most people seem to be writing code for the SHIFT key by using a Select Case statement, as follows,

```
Select Case Shift
  Case 1
   Print "You pressed the Shift key."
  Case 2
   Print "You pressed the Ctrl key."
  Case 3
   Print "You pressed the Shift + Ctrl keys."
  Case 4
   Print "You pressed the Alt key."
```

and so on.

Microsoft discourages this practice because they reserve the possibility of using the higher order bits for something else. It's preferable then to use the And operator to isolate the first three bits before proceeding. As you saw with the KeyUp event procedure in Chapter 7, you can do this as follows:

```
Bits = Shift And 7
Select Case Bits
  Case 1
    Print "You pressed the Shift key."
  Case 2
    Print "You pressed the Ctrl key."
  Case 3
    Print "You pressed the Shift + Ctrl keys."
  Case 4
    Print "You pressed the Alt key."
```

By Anding with 7 (binary pattern = 111), you eliminate any information that may eventually be contained in the higher order bits, letting the program concentrate on the information contained in the lowest three bits. You might also want to apply the same preventative against future problems for the *Button* argument.

The CONSTANT.TXT file assigns the values you'll need for the mouse events to the following global constants:

| Name of Constant | Value |
| --- | --- |
| LEFT_BUTTON | 1 |
| RIGHT_BUTTON | 2 |
| MIDDLE_BUTTON | 4 |
| SHIFT_MASK | 1 |
| CTRL_MASK | 2 |
| ALT_MASK | 4 |

You may find it easier to incorporate the approprate part of the CON-STANT.TXT file into a code module and use these symbolic constants.

The MouseUp/MouseDown event procedures work similarly for picture boxes, the only difference being that, as you've seen, you must use the control name of the picture box (and the index if the picture box is part of a control array), as shown here:

Sub *CntrlName*_MouseDown(*Button* As Integer, *Shift* As Integer,
*X* As Single, *Y* As Single)

Microsoft Windows has begun to adopt the convention that the right mouse button pops up a context-sensitive menu. This was first used (by Microsoft, at least) in Excel 4.0. Another possibility is to have this button give context-sensitive help.

## THE MOUSEMOVE EVENT

Visual Basic calls the MouseMove event procedure whenever the user moves the mouse. This is the most powerful of the mouse event procedures because, unlike the MouseUp/MouseDown event pair, you can use it to analyze completely the state of the mouse buttons. For this event procedure, the *Button* argument tells you whether some, all, or none of the mouse buttons are down.

You should not get into the habit of thinking that the MouseMove event is generated continuously as the mouse pointer moves across objects. In fact, a combination of the user's software and hardware determines how often the MouseMove event is generated. To see the MouseMove event at work, start a new project and enter the following MouseMove event procedure:

```
Sub Form_MouseMove(Button As Integer, Shift As Integer, X As
Single, Y As Single)
  DrawWidth = 3
  PSet (X,Y)
End Sub
```

Now run the project and move your mouse around the form at different speeds. Figure 13-1 shows an example of what is obtained as you decrease your speed, moving from left to right in a vaguely rectangular motion. As you can see, the dots are more tightly packed when you move the mouse slowly than when you move it rapidly. This happens because Visual Basic relies on the underlying operating system to report mouse events, and such events are generated frequently but not continuously. Because the MouseMove event procedure is *not* called continuously, the dots are relatively sparse when the mouse is moved rapidly.

Nonetheless, since the MouseMove event procedure will be called relatively frequently, any code inside this event procedure will be executed often. For this reason, you will want to tighten the code inside the MouseMove event procedure as much as possible or provide a flag to prevent repetitive processing. For example, use integer variables for counters and do not recompute the value of variables inside this procedure unless the new value depends on the parameters for the event. Always remember that accessing object properties is *much* slower than using a variable.

As mentioned in the introduction to this section, the MouseMove event uses the three lower bits of the value of the *Button* parameter to tell you the complete state of the mouse buttons, as shown here:

**Figure 13-1**

Demonstration
of
MouseMove
response time

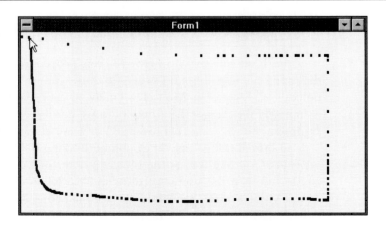

| Button | Value |
|---|---|
| Left button | 1 |
| Right button | 2 |
| Middle button | 4 |
| Left + right | 3 |
| Left + middle | 5 |
| Right + middle | 6 |
| All three | 7 |

Of course, if you don't have a three-button mouse, the third bit will always be zero. As with the *Shift* parameter in the MouseUp/MouseDown event procedures, you are safest masking out all but the lowest three bits before using this information:

```
Bits = Shift And 7
Select Case Bits
  Case 1
    Print "The left mouse button is down."
  Case 2
    Print "The right mouse button is down."
  Case 3
   Print "The left and right mouse buttons are down."
  Case 4
   Print "The middle mouse button is down."
   .
   .
```

# Dragging and Dropping Operations

To move a control as you are designing the interface in your Visual Basic project, you hold down a mouse button (the left one) and then move the mouse pointer to where you want the control to end up. A gray outline of the control moves with the mouse pointer. When you are happy with the location, you release the mouse button. The Microsoft Windows documentation calls moving an object with the mouse button depressed *dragging* and calls the release of the mouse button *dropping*. Visual Basic makes it easy to program this potential into your projects. You can even drag and drop from one form to another if your project uses multiple forms.

Controls permit two types of dragging. These correspond to two different values of the DragMode property. The default is to not allow you to drag controls around except under special circumstances. (As always, you'll need to write the code for these special circumstances; see the next section.) This is called *manual dragging,* and the DragMode property will have the value zero. Changing the value of this property to 1, *automatic,* means that the user may drag the control around the project. Regardless of the setting for the DragMode property, the control will actually move only if you write the code using the Move method to reposition it, as shown in the next example.

For this example, start up a new project and add a single command button to it. Set the DragMode property of that command button to 1 (automatic). The event that recognizes dragging and dropping operations is called the DragDrop event, and it is associated with the control or form where the "drop" occurs. Thus, if you want to drag a control to a new location on a form, you write code for the form's DragDrop event procedure. For example, to allow dragging and dropping to move the single command button around the form in this example, use the following:

```
Sub Form_DragDrop(Source As Control, X As Single, Y As Single)
   Source.Move X, Y
End Sub
```

Since the type of the *Source* parameter is a control, you can refer to its properties and methods by using the dot notation, as in the preceding example. If you need to know more information about what type of control is being dragged before applying a method or setting a property, use the If TypeOf Control Is... statement you saw in Chapter 8.

If you run this example, you will notice that the object remains visible in its original location while the gray outline moves. You cannot use the DragDrop event to make a control invisible while the dragging/dropping operation takes place. This is because this event procedure is called only after the user drops the object. In fact, the DragDrop event need not move the control at all. You often use this event to allow the user just to initiate some action. This is especially common when dragging from one form to another. The reason is that the only way a similar control can appear on a new form in Visual Basic is if you created it on another to place an invisible control of the same type on the new form at design time, to make the control part of a control array, or to use object variables.

If you get tired of the gray outline that Visual Basic uses during a drag operation, you can change it. The easiest way to do this is to set the DragIcon property of the control at design time. To do this, select the DragIcon property from the Properties box. Now click the three dots to the left of the Settings box, as shown here:

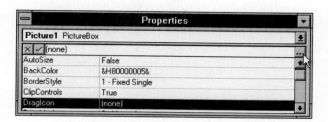

This opens up the Load Icon dialog box for choosing icons. You can also assign the drag icon of one object to another:

   *FirstControl*.DragIcon = *SecondControl*.DragIcon

The final possibility is to use the LoadPicture function. For example:

   *Control*.DragIcon=LoadPicture("C\VB\ICONS\MISC\CLOCK01.ICO")

If you design a custom icon, a common practice is to reverse the colors for the drag icon. The IconWorks program supplied with Visual Basic makes this easy to do.

The following table summarizes the events, methods, and properties used for dragging and dropping:

| Item | Description |
|---|---|
| DragMode property | Allows automatic dragging (value = 1) or manual dragging (value = 0) |
| DragIcon property | Set this to change from the gray rectangle to a custom icon when dragging |
| DragDrop event | Associated with the target of the operation; generated when the source is dropped on the target control |
| DragOver event | Associated with any control the source control passes over during dragging |
| Drag Method | Starts or stops dragging when DragMode is set to manual |

## MANUAL DRAGGING

If you have left the value of the DragMode property at its default value of zero, then you must use the Drag method to allow dragging of the control. The syntax for this method is

*Control*.Drag *TypeOfAction*

The *TypeOfAction* is an integer value from zero to 2, as shown here:

| | |
|---|---|
| Control.Drag 0 | Cancel dragging |
| Control.Drag 1 | Begin dragging |
| Control.Drag 2 | Drop the control |

If you omit the *TypeOfAction* argument, the method has the same effect as the statement Control.Drag 1. That is, Visual Basic initiates the dragging operation for the control.

One way to use the flexibility this method gives you is to allow expert users to drag and drop controls but make the default that users cannot do this. For example, use the CTRL+MouseDown combination to allow dragging to take place. You can do this by beginning the MouseDown event procedure with the following:

```
Sub CntrlName_MouseDown(Button As Integer, Shift As Integer,
X As Single, Y As Single)
   If (Shift And 7) = 2 Then   'or CTRL_MASK
     CntrlName.DragMode = 1
 .
 .
 .
End Sub
```

Another example of where you might want to use this method is in self-running demonstration programs. You can use a value of 1 to start the dragging operation and a value of 2 to drop the control. This lets you show off dragging and dropping operations.

## THE DRAGOVER EVENT

All Visual Basic objects except menus and timers will detect if a control is passing over them. You can use the DragOver event to allow even greater flexibility for your projects. This event lets you monitor the path a control takes while being dragged. You might consider changing the background color of the control being passed over. The event procedure template for forms is

```
Sub Form_DragOver(Source As Control, X As Single, Y As
Single, State As Integer)
.
.
.
End Sub
```

For controls, this event procedure template takes the form

```
Sub CtrlName_DragOver([Index As Integer,]Source As Control,
X As Single, Y As Single, State As Integer)
.
.
.
End Sub
```

As usual, the optional *Index* parameter is used if the control is part of a control array. The *Source* is the control being dragged, but the event procedure is associated with the control being passed over. The *X* and *Y* parameters give you the CurrentX and CurrentY values in terms of the scale of the object being passed over for forms and picture boxes and the underlying form for all other controls. The *State* parameter has three possible values:

| Value of State Parameter | Description |
| --- | --- |
| 0 | Source is now inside target |
| 1 | Source is just left of target |
| 2 | Source moved inside target |

### AN EXAMPLE: DELETING FILES VIA DRAG/DROP

The idea of letting the user drag an icon of a file to another icon representing a disposal unit has been around as long as graphical user interfaces. Apple's Macintosh uses a simple trash can; the Next computer uses a black hole. Since Apple has caused problems for those who use a simple trash can for this type of application, this example presents a slightly different form. The Trash03 icon supplied with Visual Basic seems to work well.

Figure 13-2 shows an example of what the screen might look like. As you can see, the files are represented by labeled icons. The project in this section allows the user to drag one of the icons representing a file into the disposal unit, at which point (after a warning, of course) the file is deleted from the disk. Since

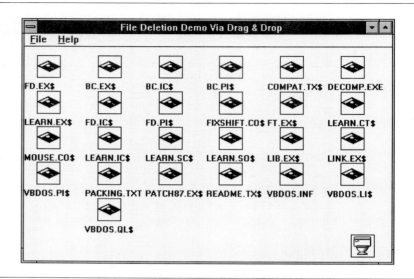

**Figure 13-2**

Form for drag and drop demo

you haven't yet seen the file-handling controls from the toolbox (Chapter 14), this project is a little less user friendly than it could be. Nonetheless, it demonstrates the techniques needed for handling dragging and dropping in one of its most common contexts.

To follow this discussion, start up a new project with two forms. Add a picture box (or image control) in the lower-right corner of the startup form. Set the picture property of this control to the icon found in the TRASH03.ICO file. This file may be found in the Computer subdirectory of the Icon library. Set the AutoSize property to True if you use a picture box (or set the Stretch property to False if you choose an image control).

Next, set up two control arrays: an array of labels with the control name of FileName and an array of image controls named Files. Set the DragMode property of the image control to 1 (Automatic). Make both the label and the image control invisible at run time by setting the Visible property to False. As usual, all subsequent elements in these control arrays will inherit these properties.

Most of the work in this project is in the following simple DragDrop event procedure:

```
Sub Garbage_DragDrop (Source As Control, X As Single, Y As
Single)
   'local variables
```

```
    Dim Msg As String
    Dim ControlIndex As Integer, YesNo As Integer
    ControlIndex = Source.Index
    Form1.FileName(ControlIndex).Visible = False
    Form1.Files(ControlIndex).Visible = False
    Msg = "Do you really want to delete " +
Form1.FileName(ControlIndex).Caption
    YesNo = MsgBox(Msg, 4, "Confirmation Box")
    If YesNo = 6 Then
      Kill (Form1.FileName(ControlIndex).Caption)
      Unload Form1.Files(ControlIndex)
      Unload Form1.FileName(ControlIndex)
    Else
      Form1.FileName(ControlIndex).Visible = True
      Form1.Files(ControlIndex).Visible = True
    End If
End Sub
```

The ControlIndex line in this event procedure finds out the index array of the control being dragged. The next two lines make the picture box and label temporarily invisible after the drop operation. The ControlIndex variable lets Visual Basic extract the caption (which will be the name of the file) from the label. The message box has type = 4 so it's a Yes/No message box. The title is Confirmation Box. The Kill command deletes a file from a disk. (You'll learn more about this command in Chapter 14.) Once the program deletes the file, the program unloads the label and picture box from the control array. If the user has made a mistake, this code makes the original picture box and label visible again.

Next, you need a general procedure called Directions that will give the user the information needed for this application:

```
Sub Directions ()
  Form1.Hide
  Form2.Show
  Form2.Cls
  Form2.Print "This program illustrates dragging and dropping
mouse operations."
  Form2.Print "The user gives a file spec inside the message
box and a form"
  Form2.Print "appears with icons labelled by all the files
with that file specification."
  Form2.Print "The user can drag the icon to be 'flushed' away
i.e. deleted."
```

```
      Form2.Print
      Form2.Print "Click on any part of this form to continue."
   End Sub
```

The program displays this information on the second form in this project. It gives you a screen like the one shown in Figure 13-3.

The Form_Load procedure for the initial form needs to load the directions form and call the general procedure that gives the directions. It looks like this:

```
Sub Form_Load ()
   Load Form2
   Directions
End Sub
```

The File menu on the startup form has two items:

New File Spec
Exit

Clicking the New File Spec menu item will let the user examine a new directory or drive. Clicking this menu item will call a general procedure called GetFile that reads the names of the files from the disk.

Now the question is how to deal with a new file specification. The first time the user uses this application, Visual Basic loads a certain number of elements

**Figure 13-3**

Information screen for drag and drop demo

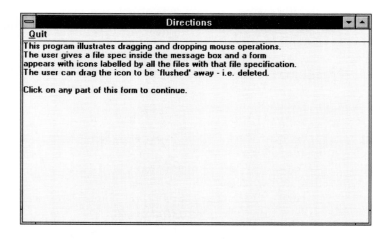

```
┌─────────────────────────────────────────────────────────┐
│═                        Directions                    ▼ ▲ │
│ Quit                                                       │
├───────────────────────────────────────────────────────────┤
│This program illustrates dragging and dropping mouse operations.│
│The user gives a file spec inside the message box and a form│
│appears with icons labelled by all the files with that file specification.│
│The user can drag the icon to be `flushed' away - i.e. deleted.│
│                                                           │
│Click on any part of this form to continue.                │
│                                                           │
│                                                           │
│                                                           │
└───────────────────────────────────────────────────────────┘
```

in the two control arrays. The program needs to change the information contained in the captions. These captions contain the names of the files to delete. There are various ways of changing the information. The easiest is to unload the form and then reload it. This automatically clears out the old information contained in the control array. It also avoids any error messages that might result from loading the same element of a control array twice. Then the procedure can reload new members of the control arrays that represent the files.

One other way you might consider is a bit more complicated to code. However, it will often be somewhat faster when the program runs. To use this method, load the two control arrays only once. Then set up a string array that reads the file information from the disk using the Dir$ command. Finally, assign the entries in this array to the Caption property of the labels. The code for this is more complicated as you must read the disk information twice to redimension the arrays appropriately.

Regarding the menu item, since the "N" is underlined, the user can press N as a shortcut to activate this item. Once the menu is open, the control name for this menu item is set to be NewFileSpec. The Click event procedure for this control is

```
Sub NewFileSpec_Click ()
   Unload Form1
   Load Form1
   GetFile
End Sub
```

The Unload Form1 line clears out the old elements of the control array. The GetFile general procedure looks like this:

```
Sub GetFile ()
   'local variables
   Dim FileSpec As String

   Form2.Hide
   FileSpec = InputBox$("File specification?")
   If FileSpec = "" Then
     Directions
   Else
     Form1.Show
     DisplayFiles (FileSpec)
   End If
End Sub
```

As you can see, the details of displaying the files on the startup form are contained in a general procedure with one string parameter called *DisplayFiles*. This procedure allows up to 30 files. It looks like this:

```
Sub DisplayFiles (FileSpec As String)
  'local variables
  Dim NameOfFile As String
  Dim ControlIndex As Integer

  Form1.Show
  Form1.Width = 8000              'slightly larger for 30 files
  Form1.Height = 5500
  Form1.Garbage.Move 7000, 4200  'move the garbage can icon
  NameOfFile = Dir$(FileSpec)
  If NameOfFile = "" Then
    MsgBox "No Files found with that file specification!"
  End If
  ControlIndex = ControlIndex + 1      'start with index = 1
  Do While NameOfFile <> ""
    Load Form1.Files(ControlIndex)
    Load Form1.FileName(ControlIndex)
    Column = (ControlIndex Mod 6)
    Row = (ControlIndex - 1) \6
    Form1.Files(ControlIndex).Move (1300 * Column) + 275, 800
* Row + 200                           'to allow for menu
    Form1.FileName(ControlIndex).Move 1300 * Column, 800 *
(Row + 1)
    Form1.Files(ControlIndex).Visible = True
    Form1.FileName(ControlIndex).Visible = True
    Form1.FileName(ControlIndex).Caption = NameOfFile
    ControlIndex = ControlIndex + 1
    If ControlIndex > 30 Then
      MsgBox ("Too many files!")
      Exit Do
    End If
    NameOfFile = Dir$
  Loop
End Sub
```

The Do loop does the work of spacing the picture boxes and labels. The spacing was determined by experimenting with different values. As with all new elements in a control array, they remain invisible until you set the Visible property to True.

Clicking the menu item marked Help calls the Directions general procedure:

```
Sub Help_Click ()
  Directions
End Sub
```

You'll need a Click procedure on the second form to bring back the startup form:

```
Sub Form_Click ()     'Bring back startup form
  Form2.Hide
  Form1.Show
End Sub
```

To finish the program, you need only associate the simplest of event procedures with each of the two Quit menu items on the different forms:

```
Sub Quit2_Click ()
  End
End Sub
```

```
Sub Quit_Click ()
  End
End Sub
```

# Chapter 14

# Working with Files

511

T H I S chapter shows you how to handle disks and disk files within Visual Basic. You'll also see how to work with the executable version of a Visual Basic project. In particular, you'll see two techniques for adding licensing screens to your completed applications. (Much like Microsoft itself does—you see to whom the copy is licensed whenever Visual Basic starts up.)

The first section explains the commands in Visual Basic that interact with DOS. For example, you can tell DOS to rename files, change the logged drive, or switch directories. Then you'll see the commands introduced in Visual Basic 2.0 that make handling disk files easier. For example, now you can copy files from within a Visual Basic program with a single command. Next you'll see how to use the file system controls on the toolbox. Finally, there's an extensive introduction to file handling in Visual Basic, including a discussion on how to keep file information confidential by encrypting the information in the files.

Although Visual Basic 3 now contains many features for handling databases (see Chapter 17), the ability to set up and work with files directly remains very important. Random Access files are still useful for setting up certain kinds of databases and binary file techniques are needed to work with files stored in non-ASCII format and to add licensing screens. In addition these techniques are important when you need to write your own file conversion routines.

Finally, use the common dialog boxes that you saw in Chapter 10 when manipulating files for other users. Windows users expect to see these boxes when working with the files!

## DOS-Related File Commands

Visual Basic has six commands that interact directly with DOS and mimic the usual operating system commands. You already saw one of the commands in Chapter 13: the Kill command, which lets you delete a file. The following table summarizes these commands.

| Command | Function |
| --- | --- |
| ChDrive | Changes the logged drive for DOS |
| ChDir | Changes the default directory |
| MkDir | Makes a new directory |
| RmDir | Removes a directory |
| Name | Changes the name of a file or moves a file from one directory to another |
| Kill | Deletes a file from a disk |

You use these commands by following them with a string or string variable. For example,

```
MkDir "TESTDIR"
```

would add a subdirectory called TESTDIR to the current directory. The line

```
MkDir "C:\TESTDIR"
```

would add the subdirectory to the root directory of the C drive.

The commands that handle files also accept the normal DOS wildcards. For example,

```
Kill "*.*"
```

deletes all the files in the current directory (not to be done casually!). As the preceding table indicates, the Name command can actually do a bit more than the DOS REN command; with DOS 3.3 or later it can copy files from one directory in the current drive to another. To do this, give the full path name. For example,

```
Name "C:\VB\TEST.BAS" As "C:\EXAMPLES\TEST.BAS"
```

moves the TEST.BAS file from the VB directory to one named EXAMPLES.

In addition, the CurDir$ function returns a string that gives the path for the current drive. You can also specify a drive:

CurDir$ (*Drive*)

The first character of *Drive* determines the drive. When used in this form, the function now gives the path for the specified drive. (You can also use CurDir, which returns something of the variant type rather than a string.)

As with any function that uses disk drives, you can generate a run-time error if DOS cannot perform the function asked. See the section "Making a File Program Robust: Error Handling" later in this chapter for more on dealing with these types of errors.

### AN EXAMPLE: HOW TO RESET THE LOGGED DRIVE

Programs for other users that change the logged drive or path will often need to reset the drive back to where it was when the program started. (It's the neighborly thing to do.) The original logged drive and path information is often stored in global variables in the Form_Load procedure of the startup form. If there is a chance that the Form_Load will be called more than once, you'll need to modify the obvious code. Here's an example of the modifications needed.

```
Sub Form_Load ()
  'Global variables OldDrive$ and OldPath$
  Static AlreadyLoadedOnce As Integer
  If Not (AlreadyLoadedOnce) Then
    OldDrive$ = Left(CurDir$, 2) 'get current drive
    OldPath$ = CurDir$    'and path so can reset at end
    AlreadyLoadedOnce = True
    'other code you want to use once goes here
    'Examples are copyright notices and such
  End If
End Sub
```

## The Shell Function

Although a few of DOS's utility programs are built into Visual Basic commands—usually with slightly different names, such as Kill for Del—most are not. Experienced users can move to the Program Manager or File Manager within Microsoft Windows to format disks or copy multiple files. On the other hand, inexperienced users might not be comfortable doing this. You can always use the Shell function to run any .COM, .EXE, or .BAT file from within a Visual Basic program. For example, if you want to allow a user to format a disk, add a line like this:

```
X% = Shell "FORMAT A:"
```

For this to work, of course, DOS must know where the FORMAT.COM file is located. It can know this if FORMAT.COM (or a FORMAT.BAT file that points to it) is located in a directory in the DOS path, in the WINDOWS directory, in the WINDOWS\SYSTEM directory, or in the current directory. If you give the full path name of the application, then you can use files not in these directories.

When Visual Basic shells to a program, it generates a new iconized window and gives it the focus. You can change this behavior with the general form of the Shell function, as follows:

$X\% = $ Shell(*string,* WindowStyle)

where *string* contains the full path name of the stand-alone program (or batch file) that you want to execute along with any information needed by the program, and WindowStyle sets the type of window the program runs in. The possible values for WindowStyle are as follows:

| Value | Type of Window |
| --- | --- |
| 1, 5, 9 | Normal with the focus |
| 2 | Minimized with the focus |
| 3 | Maximized with the focus |
| 4, 8 | Normal without the focus |
| 6, 7 | Minimized without the focus |

Use the Shell function with care, especially while you're developing the program from within Visual Basic. Ideally, you should have enough memory to keep Windows, Visual Basic, all programs currently running, a new copy of DOS, and the program to which you are "shelling" all simultaneously in memory. Otherwise, you have to rely on Windows to manage the memory for you by swapping to disk.

The integer returned by the Shell function identifies the task identification number of the program. This information is not needed in Visual Basic programs (but is used in API calls).

**note:** *You can use the Shell function only with programs that have an .EXE, .COM, .BAT, or .PIF extension.*

## Command-line Information

Most professional programs allow (or require) the user to type in additional information when he or she invokes the program. This extra information is usually called *command-line information*. For example, when you write

COPY A:*.* B:

the command-line information is the string "A:*.* B:". The utility program COPY uses this information to know what to do. Unlike interpreted BASICs, Visual Basic makes it easy to read this information. When you run any program from the File Manager and use the form

*FileExeName info1 info2 info3...*

then the value of the reserved string variable Command$ (or Command if you want a variant) is the string whose value is "*info1 info2...*". Since you have already seen in Chapter 7 how to write a program that parses a string, you now know how to analyze the command-line information by breaking the string Command$ into its component parts.

Obviously, you need a way to create sample pieces of command-line information while developing the program; otherwise, you wouldn't have any test data with which to debug the program. You do this with the Project option on the Options menu. This opens the dialog box shown here:

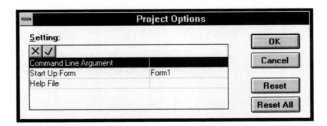

In the setting box, choose Command Line Argument and the string that would be used in the Command$ command within the program.

You can also pass command-line information to Visual Basic itself when Visual Basic starts up. For this, start Visual Basic from the File Manager and use the form

VB /CMD *CommandLineInfo*

Now, anything after the /CMD switch is sent to Visual Basic as command-line information.

## The File Handling Functions

Certain tasks are so common that the designers of Visual Basic 2.0 decided to add them to the language itself rather than make you use Windows API calls or shell to DOS. There are four of these functions.

**The FileCopy Function** The FileCopy function copies a file from the source path to another path. It does not use SHELL to activate the DOS copy routine or call the File Manager. The syntax is

   FileCopy *SourcePath$, DestPath$*

The FileCopy function does not allow wildcards. (Use SHELL "COPY..." if you need wildcards.)

**The FileDateTime Function** The FileDateTime function returns the date and time a file was created or last modified. The syntax is

   FileDateTime (*FileName$*)

**The GetAttr Function** The GetAttr function returns an integer. Using masking techniques to get at the individual bits, you can determine how the various attributes are set. The syntax for this function is

   GetAttr (*FileName$*) As Integer

Constants for the various attributes are stored in CONSTANT.TXT. The following table summarizes these values.

| Attribute | Constant | Value |
| --- | --- | --- |
| Normal | ATTR_NORMAL | 0 |
| Read Only | ATTR_READONLY | 1 |
| Hidden | ATTR_HIDDEN | 2 |

| Attribute | Constant | Value |
|-----------|----------|-------|
| System | ATTR_SYSTEM | 4 |
| Volume | ATTR_VOLUME | 8 |
| Directory | ATTR_DIRECTORY | 16 |
| Archive | ATTR_ARCHIVE | 32 |

For example, if

GetAttrib(*FileName*) = 3

then the file is hidden and read-only.

**tip:** *You can use this masking technique with the Dir$ (or Dir) function to find files that match both a file specification and a file attribute. The syntax is*

Dir$*(FileSpec, AttributeMask)*

*where you add together the various values to specify the types of files to be looked for.*

**The SetAttr Function** The SetAttr function sets attribute information for files. Using the same bit values given in the preceding table, you can change the various attributes. The syntax for this function is

SetAttr *FileName$, AttributeValue*

For example, because 1 is the ReadOnly attribute and 2 is the Hidden attribute mask,

SetAttr *FileName$, 3*

would hide the file and set it as read-only (because 3 = 2 + 1).

**tip:** *Use the SetAttr function to hide files that you don't want users to know about.*

For example, putting an encrypted password in a hidden file and then examining that file is a common (and reasonably secure) method of making sure that a program is being used by the right person. (See the section "Adding Licensing Screens" later in this chapter.)

# The File System Controls

The file system controls in Visual Basic allow users to select a new drive, see the hierarchical directory structure of a disk, or see the names of the files in a given directory. As with all Visual Basic controls, you need to write code to take full advantage of the power of the file system controls. In addition, if you want to tell DOS to change drives or directories as the result of a mouse click by a user, you need to write code using the commands listed in the first section in this chapter. The file system controls complement the common dialog boxes you saw in Chapter 10.

Figure 14-1 shows the toolbox with the file system controls marked. The file system controls are designed to work together. Your code checks what the user has done to the drive list box and passes this information on to the directory list box. The changes in the directory list box are passed on to the file list box. (See the section "Tying All the File Controls Together" a little later in this chapter.)

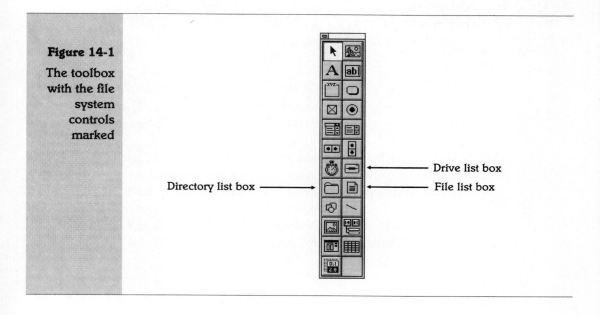

**Figure 14-1**

The toolbox with the file system controls marked

Directory list box ⟶

Drive list box ⟵

File list box ⟵

## File List Boxes

A file list box defaults to displaying the files in the current directory. As with any list box, you can control the position, size, color, and font characteristic at design time or via code.

```
ch5_7.frm
ch5_7.mak
constant.txt
decomp.dll
form2.frm
packing.lst
readme.txt
```

Most of the properties o a file list box are identical to those of ordinary list boxes. For example, as with all list boxes, when the number of items can't fit the current size of the control, Visual Basic automatically adds vertical scroll bars. This lets the user move through the list of files using the scroll bars. You can set the size, position, or font properties of file list boxes via the Properties box or via code as needed. Similarly, file list boxes can respond to all the events that list boxes can detect. In addition, you can write event procedures for a keypress or a mouse movement. One point is worth remembering, though: the Windows convention is that double-clicking a file, not single-clicking, chooses the file. This is especially important when using a file list box because using an arrow key to move through a file list box would call any Click procedure that you have written. (Recall that arrow movements are functionally equivalent to a single mouse click for a list box.)

It is quite common to use the List, ListCount, and ListIndex properties to analyze the information contained in a file list box rather than use the Dir$ command. For example, suppose the file list box has the default name of File1 and you have already set up a string array for the information contained in the box. Then a fragment like

```
For I% = 0 To File1.ListCount -1
  FileNames$(I%) = File1.List(I%)
Next I%
```

fills a string array with the information contained in the file list box named File1. If you need to find out the name of the file that a user selects, you can use File1.List(ListIndex) or the FileName property which, when read, has the same function.

You can have a file list box display only files that are read-only (good for novice users) or those that have the Archive bit turned on or off (that is, to indicate whether or not the files have been backed up since the last change). There are five Boolean properties (True, False) that control what type of files are shown in a file list box: Archive, Hidden, Normal, ReadOnly, and System. The default setting is True for Archive, Normal, and ReadOnly and False for Hidden and System.

As an example of this, consider the code to activate the form shown in Figure 14-2, which has a single file list box and five check boxes to specify the type of files the file list box shows. For example, if the file list box is named File1 and one of the check boxes is named ShowHidden, a line of code like

```
File1.Hidden = ShowHidden.Value
```

would tell the file list box to display (or not display) hidden files depending on whether or not the box was checked.

## PATTERN AND PATH

The most important properties for file list boxes are Pattern and Path. The Pattern property determines which files are displayed in the file list box. The Pattern property accepts the ordinary DOS wildcards—the * (match any) and the ? (match a single character). The default pattern is set to *.* to display all files. (Of course, the Pattern property works with the attribute properties discussed earlier before Visual Basic displays the files.) When you change the Pattern property, Visual Basic looks to see if you have written a PatternChange event procedure for the file list box and, if so, activates it.

The Path property sets or returns the current path for the file list box, but not for DOS. To tell DOS to change the current path from within Visual Basic, you need the ChDir command. On the other hand, you may just need to

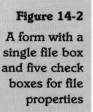

**Figure 14-2**

A form with a single file box and five check boxes for file properties

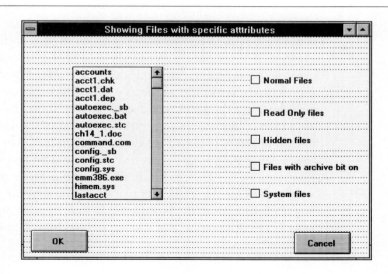

accumulate this information for use by your program without disturbing the default path. When you change the Path property, Visual Basic looks to see if you have written a PathChange event procedure for the file list box and, if so, activates it.

Changing the FileName property activates the PathChange event or the PatternChange event (or both), depending on how you change the FileName property. For example, suppose you are in the C:\ root directory. Setting

```
File1.Filename ="C:\DOS\*.COM"
```

activates both the PathChange and PatternChange events.

## Directory List Boxes

A directory list box displays the directory structure of the current drive. The current directory shows up as an open file folder. Subdirectories of the current directory are shown as closed folders, and directories above the current directory are shown as nonshaded open folders.

**note:** *When the user clicks on an item or moves through the list that item is highlighted. When he or she double-clicks, Visual Basic automatically updates the directory list box.*

The List property for a directory list box works a little differently than it does for file list boxes. While subdirectories of the current directory are numbered from zero to ListCount–1, Visual Basic uses negative indexes for the current directory and its parent and grandparent directories. For example, –1 is the index for the current directory, –2 for its parent directory, and so on. Unfortunately, you cannot use the LBound function to determine the number of directories above a given directory; you must either count the number of backslashes in the Path property or move backward through the items in the Dir1 list box.

As an example of how powerful the file system controls can be when they begin to work together, put a directory list box and a file list box together on a new project, as shown in Figure 14-3. Now suppose you want a change by the user in the Dir1 list box to tell Visual Basic to update the file list box immediately. All you have to do is enter one line of code in the Dir1_Change event procedure:

**Figure 14-3**

A project with
a directory list
box and a file
list box

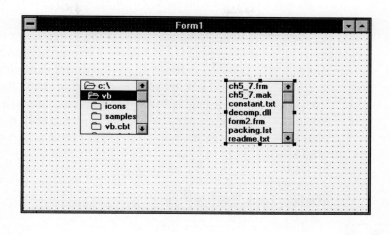

```
Sub Dir1_Change()
   File1.Path = Dir1.Path
End Sub
```

This is all it takes to update the file list box whenever a user changes the
current directory. To activate this event procedure, the user must double-click
a new directory in the Dir1 list box.

**note:** *Directory list boxes do not recognize the DoubleClick event; instead they call the Change procedure
in response to a double-click and reassign the Path property.*

Again, Visual Basic cannot use a single click to activate the Change event
because then users could not use the arrow keys to move through the list box.
If you want to have pressing ENTER update the file list box as well, use the
Dir1_KeyPress event procedure as follows:

```
Sub Dir1_KeyPress(KeyAscii As Integer)
   If KeyAscii = 13 Then      'Or Key_Return from CONSTANT.TXT
     Dir1.Path = Dir1.List(Dir1.ListIndex)
   End If
End Sub
```

You can also write a procedure that calls the previous event procedure when the user presses ENTER.

Again, this procedure didn't change the Path property directly because doing so is superfluous. Visual Basic calls the Change event procedure for a directory list box whenever you change the value of the Path property.

Finally, it's important to keep in mind that while the meaning of the Path property for file list boxes and directory lists boxes is similar, they are not identical. For directory list boxes, the Path property specifies which directory was selected; for file list boxes, the Path property specifies where to look for files to display.

## Drive List Boxes

Unlike file and directory list boxes, drive list boxes are pull-down boxes. Drive list boxes begin by displaying the current drive, and then when the user clicks on the arrow, Visual Basic pulls down a list of all valid drives.

The key property for a drive list box is the Drive property, which can be used to return or reset the current drive. For example, to synchronize a drive list box with a directory list box, all you need is code that looks like this:

```
Sub Drive1_Change()
   Dir1.Path = Drive1.Drive
End Sub
```

On the other hand, if you also want to change the logged drive that DOS is using, write

```
Sub Drive1_Change()
   Dir1.Path = Drive1.Drive
   ChDrive Drive1.Drive
End Sub
```

## Tying All the File Controls Together

When you have all three file system controls on a form, you have to communicate the changes among the controls in order to have Visual Basic show what the user wants to see. For example, if the user selects a new drive, the Drive1_Change event procedure is activated. Then the following occurs:

1. The Drive1_Change event procedure assigns the Drive1_Drive property to the Dir1.Path property.

2. This changes the display in the directory list box by activating the Dir1_Change event procedure.

3. Inside the Drive1_Change event procedure, you assign the Dir1.Path property to the File1.Path property. This updates the File1 list box.

It is easy to add a text box for a file pattern (assign the box to the File1.Pattern property) and check boxes to allow the user to choose what type of files to view in the file list box, as shown in Figure 14-4. Including all this information gives you something that looks like the usual Microsoft Windows file control box that you saw in Chapter 10. Occasionally you will need the extra flexibility that using file controls provides.

**caution:** *Often you will combine the path name obtained from the Path property with the file name taken from the FileName property to get the full path name of a file. Unfortunately, if you are in the root directory there is a "\" at the end of the path name property that would lead to two backslashes in a row if you naively combined the two properties. Instead, use code such as the following:*

**Figure 14-4**

**A form with a text box and check boxes**

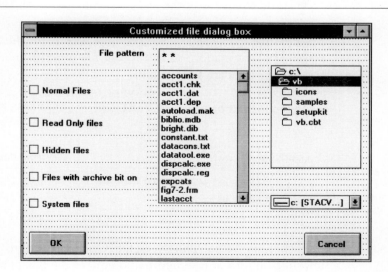

```
If Right(File1.Path, 1) <> "\" Then
   NameOfFile = File1.Path + "\" + File1.FileName
Else
   NameOfFile = File1.Path + File1.FileName
End If
```

# Sequential Files

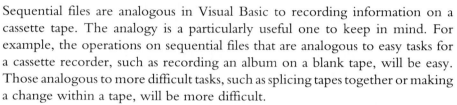 Sequential files are analogous in Visual Basic to recording information on a cassette tape. The analogy is a particularly useful one to keep in mind. For example, the operations on sequential files that are analogous to easy tasks for a cassette recorder, such as recording an album on a blank tape, will be easy. Those analogous to more difficult tasks, such as splicing tapes together or making a change within a tape, will be more difficult.

To avoid unnecessary work, use a sequential file only when you know that you will

◆ Rarely make changes within the file

◆ Massage (process) the information the file contains from start to finish, without needing to constantly jump around

◆ Add to the file at the end of the file

It's not that you can't make changes within the file, jump around when processing information, or add to the file other than at the end; it's just that these procedures are a bit painful.

Here's a table of some common operations on a cassette tape and the analogous operations on a sequential text file called TEST in the currently active directory:

| Operation | Visual Basic Equivalent |
| --- | --- |
| Put the machine in playback mode and pause | Open "TEST" for input as #1 |
| Put the machine in record mode and pause | Open "TEST" for output as #1 |
| Push Stop | Close #1 |

Each time Visual Basic sees the Open command, it gets ready to send information into or take information out of the file. (The jargon is that it "sets up a channel" to communicate with the file.) What follows the Open command is the name of the file you are working with. The filename must be a string variable or enclosed in quotation marks, and unless it is in the current directory, you need to provide enough information to identify its path. (The value of a string variable must be a legal filename.) The rules for filenames are the rules that DOS imposes:

◆ The filename can be at most eight characters with an optional three-character extension following the period.

◆ The characters you can use are

```
A - Z 0 - 9 ( ) { } @ # $ % & ! - _ ' / ~
```

◆ Lowercase letters are automatically converted to uppercase.

◆ You need a file identifier. This is a number between 1 and 255 preceded by the # sign that you will use to identify the file. Although you can't change this number until you close the file, the next time you need the file you can open it with a different ID number. The number of possible files you can have open at once is limited by DOS to eight unless you raise the limit in your CONFIG.SYS file.

When Visual Basic processes an Open command, it also reserves a file buffer in the computer's memory. Without a buffer, each piece of information sent to (or from) the disk would be recorded (or played back) separately. Since mechanical operations like writing to a disk are much slower than writing to RAM, this would waste a lot of time. Instead, when a file buffer fills up, Visual Basic tells DOS to activate the appropriate drive, and a whole packet of information is sent in a continuous stream to the disk. The number of buffers can also be changed from your CONFIG.SYS file.

The Close command usually empties the buffer and tells DOS to update the FAT (file allocation table). But because of Windows' own buffering techniques this may not happen precisely when Visual Basic processes the Close command. For this reason, a sudden power outage when you have a file open almost inevitably leads to lost information and occasionally even to a corrupted disk. (The CHKDSK/f command is often necessary when this happens.)

**tip:** *The Reset command, unlike the Close command, seems to force DOS to flush the buffers. Use this command in critical situations to make it more likely that the DOS file buffer is flushed.*

The Print command sends information to a form. A slight modification, Print #, provides one way to send information to a file. Here is an example of a fragment that sends one piece of information to a file named TEST:

```
' Writing to a file
Open "TEST" For Output As #1
Print #1, "TESTING, 1 2 3"
Close #1
```

After the usual remark statement, the first executable statement tells Visual Basic that you are going to set up a file named TEST having file identifier #1.

**caution:** *If a file in the current directory already exists with the name TEST, it is erased by this statement. Opening a file for output starts a new file; the contents of a previous file with the same name are lost.*

Next comes the statement that actually sends the information to the file. The comma is necessary, but what follows the comma can be anything that might occur in an ordinary Print statement. And what appears in the file is the exact image of what would have occurred on the screen. For example, the file does not contain quotation marks. More precisely, the file will contain the word "TESTING", followed by a comma, followed by a space, followed by the numeral 1, followed by another space, followed by the numeral 2, followed by a space, followed by the numeral 3, and then, although you may not have thought of it, the characters that define a carriage return/line feed combination—a CHR$(13) (carriage return) and a CHR$(10) (line feed).

It is extremely important that you keep in mind that the Print # command works exactly like the Print command. By now you know of the automatic carriage return/line feed combination that follows an ordinary Print statement. More precisely, if the line read

```
Print #1, "TESTING, 1 2 3";
```

then the file would contain two fewer characters. The CHR$(13) and CHR$(10) would no longer be there because the semicolon (just as for an ordinary Print statement) suppresses the carriage return/line feed combination. This is important because the cardinal rule of file handling is that you must know the exact structure of a file if you want to be able to efficiently reuse the information it contains.

As a third example, suppose you change the line to read

```
Print #1, "TESTING",1,2,3
```

Now the file contains many spaces (occurrences of CHR\$(32)) that were not there before. To see why this must be true, just recall that a comma in a Print statement moves the cursor to the next print zone by inserting spaces. Use a comma in a Print # statement, and the same spaces are placed in your file.

Finally, the Close command (followed by a file identifier) *flushes,* or moves, whatever is in the appropriate file buffer to the disk. The Close command without a file ID flushes all open buffers—that is, it closes all open files.

Instead of using FileLen, once a file is open you can use the Visual Basic command LOF( ) (Length Of File) to learn how large the file is. To use this command, place the appropriate file identifier number within the parentheses. To see this command at work (and to confirm what was said earlier about the sizes of the various versions of the TEST file), try the following Click procedure in a new project:

```
Sub Form_Click()
' a file tester
' demonstrates the 'exact' image property of Print #
  Open "Test1" For Output As #1
  Open "Test2" For Output As #2
  Open "Test3" For Output As #3
  Print #1,"TESTING, 1,2,3"
  Print #2,"TESTING, 1,2,3";
  Print #3,"TESTING",1,2,3
  Print LOF(1)
  Print LOF(2)
  Print LOF(3)
  Close
End Sub
```

If you run this program, you'll see

```
16
14
47
```

As you can see, the first file does contain 2 more characters (bytes) than the second (to account for the carriage return/line feed combination). And the third contains far more than the 14 characters (bytes) in the phrase "TESTING, 1 2 3". The extra characters, as you'll soon see, are indeed spaces (CHR$(32)).

## Reading Back Information from a File

To read information back from a file, you must open the file for input using its name (again, the full path name if it's not in the currently active directory) and give it a file identifier that is not currently being used within the program. (It doesn't have to be the same identifier that it was set up with originally.) The easiest way to find an unused file identifier is with the command FreeFile. The value of FreeFile is always the next unused file ID number. Therefore, you merely have to have a statement like

```
FileNumber% = FreeFile
```

at the appropriate point in your program followed by

Open *FileName* For Input As #FileNumber%.

**caution:**

*Never use Open File Name For Input as #FreeFile.*

Next, you choose a variant on the PC-BASIC Input command to retrieve the information. For example, suppose you want to read back the file TEST1. This contains the word "TESTING", followed by a comma, followed by the numbers. It ends with the carriage return/line feed combination. For those who know some form of PC-BASIC, to choose how to read this information back from this file, pretend for a second that you were going to enter this information into the computer via the keyboard in the older version of BASIC. You could not say INPUT A$ because that would pick up only the word "TESTING". (The INPUT command would read information only up to the first comma.) So you would likely use LINE INPUT A$ because the LINE INPUT command from ordinary BASIC disregards any spaces or commas that may have been typed; it accepts all the information typed until ENTER is pressed. (The carriage return/line feed combination corresponds to the ENTER key.) In general, you use the Line Input # statement to read information in a sequential file one line at a time. Here is a fragment that reads back and displays the contents of the file named TEST1:

```
' Reading back a file
Open "TEST1" For Input As #1
Line Input #1, A$
Print A$
Close #1
```

As an alternative you could have used

```
Open "TEST1" For Input As #1
Input #1, A$, B$, C$, D$
Print A$; " "; B$; " "; C$; " "; D$
Close #1
```

or

```
Open "TEST1" For Input As #1
Input #1, A$, B, C, D
Print A$; B; C; D
Close #1
```

both of which seem clumsier and yield slightly different results. For example, the last program has recovered the numbers as numbers (values of numeric variables) rather than as strings of numerals (part of a larger string). If you have stored numbers in a file, this is often the method to choose to retrieve them.

If you know how many entries there are in a file, a For-Next loop is often the easiest way to read the information back. For example, suppose you're a teacher with a class of 25 students. You know the currently active disk contains a file called CLASS that stores the information about the class in the following form:

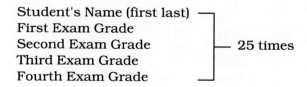

Student's Name (first last)
First Exam Grade
Second Exam Grade — 25 times
Third Exam Grade
Fourth Exam Grade

Two useful terms that recur often in file handling are "fields" and "records." (Field is now a keyword in Visual Basic 3 and used for the new data access features of Visual Basic 3. It is an object type that's part of a recordset—see Chapter 17.) Think of this file as being made up of 25 records and each record as consisting of five fields. Usually, a program that manipulates this file will read back the information by records—that is, five fields at a time. And each field can be picked up by a single Input # rather than needing the Line Input command. The similarity with user-defined records (see Chapter 9) is not a coincidence. You'll often find yourself filling in the components of a record from a file.

Knowing the exact format of this file means you can easily write a procedure that will retrieve this information. First set up a record type:

```
Type StudentRecord
   Name As String
   FirstExam As Integer
   SecondExam As Integer
   ThirdExam As Integer
   FourthExam As Integer
End Type
```

Now make up an array of StudentRecords as a global variable:

```
Global StudentGrades() As StudentRecord
```

and then use the following general procedure:

```
Sub RetrieveGrade()
  Dim FileNum As Integer, I As Integer
  ReDim StudentGrades(1 To 25)
  FileNum = FreeFile
  Open "GRADES" For Input As #FileNum
  For I = 1 To 25
   Input #FileNum, StudentGrades(I).Name
   Input #FileNum, StudentGrades(I).FirstExam
   Input #FileNum, StudentGrades(I).SecondExam
   Input #FileNum, StudentGrades(I).ThirdExam
   Input #FileNum, StudentGrades(I).FourthExam
  Next I
  Close FileNum
End Sub
```

Now each row of the array StudentGrades contains a record with the name and grades of a student. You could easily incorporate this type of general Sub procedure into a program that analyzes the grades or places the information on a grid.

This file has a simple structure because the cardinal rule remains: You can't do anything with a file until you bring into memory the information you need from it.

The more complicated the structure of the file, the harder it is to work with. If you can keep the structure of your files simple, then filling up an array is often the method of choice. The reason is that once the information contained in the file is stored, massaging it is easy, usually requiring only a few For–Next loops to run through the array.

For example, suppose you want to write a procedure that can return the average and number absent on each exam. As always when dealing with an array of records, you could choose to store this information in two parallel arrays or in one string array. In this case, if you chose to store this information in an array of strings rather than in the array of records given earlier, you could write a Sub that would take a parameter for the exam number, as in the following listing:

```
Sub AnalysisOfExams(ExamNumber As Integer)
  Dim NumAbsent As Integer, Total As Integer, I As Integer
  ' StudentGrades() is a global string array
  NumAbsent = 0
  Total = 0
  For I = 1 To 25
    If StudentGrades(I, ExamNumber) = "absent" Then
    NumAbsent = NumAbsent + 1
    Else
    Total = Total + Val(StudentGrades(I, ExamNumber))
    End If
  Next I
  Print "The number absent was"; NumAbsent
  Print "The class average was"; Total/(25 - NumAbsent)
End Sub
```

This procedure is straightforward. The parameter tells the procedure what exam number (column of the array) to look at, and the For–Next loop runs through each row. (The Val command is needed because the exam grades are stored in a string array.)

## Adding to an Existing File

The GRADE file contains each student's name followed by a list of his or her grades. This is a bit unnatural. A different, more natural kind of file structure would occur if the teacher entered everything in steps: first the student's name and then, after a while, the results of the first exam, and so on. To write a program to do this, you need a command that lets you add information to the end of an already existing file. The statement Open *FileName* For Append As *File#* causes three things to occur at once:

◆ Visual Basic opens the file (if the file doesn't exist, it creates it) and sets up the appropriate buffer.

◆ Visual Basic locates the end of the file on the disk.

◆ Visual Basic prepares to output to the file at its end.

Recall that if you open an existing file for output, you erase it. Only by using the Append command can you add to an existing file.

If you are writing this type of program for yourself, for a single class's records, you might want to update this file, using a short fragment that reads the students' names and stores them in an array before the appending:

```
Dim I As Integer
ReDim StudentNames$(25)
Open "StudentGrades" For Input As # 1
For I = 1 To 25
  Input #1, StudentNames$(I)
Next I
Close #1
Open "StudentGrades" For Append As #1
For I = 1 To 25
  M$ = "The grade for " + StudentNames$(I) + " is ?"
  StudentGrade$ = InputBox$(M$)
  Print #1, StudentGrade$
Next I
Close
```

This fragment assumes the file was already created and contains the names of the students. The point of the Close command is that to change a sequential file's status from reading to writing, it must first be closed. Once the file is closed, the Append command lets you add to it.

You will probably find yourself writing lots of these "quick and dirty" programs as you become more familiar with file-handling techniques. Although they're never very robust, they do get the job done. (You need special techniques to make file-handling programs robust; see the next section of this chapter.)

**tip:**

*For quick and dirty file-handling jobs, consider using the Data Manager that comes with Visual Basic 3 (see Chapter 17).*

Suppose, however, you were teaching five classes, each with a different number of students. Then the "quick and dirty" approach is not worthwhile. It's possible to get the classes mixed up, leading to an error message or even to losing a student's grades. To prevent this kind of mishap, write a header to all your files. Use this header to put standard information about the file at the beginning of the file. You can then use this information to build a grid to allow data entry.

To write a usable grade book program, you can use the first few entries in the file for the name of the class, the semester, the number of exams, and the number of students. This kind of information isn't likely to change. (If you want to change it, see the section "Binary Files" later in this chapter.) Also, it has the added advantage that you can use it to set up the bounds on the loops that will read and process the information contained in the file. The following table shows you the form that lets the user fill in this header information inside various text boxes:

| Type of Object | Control (Form) Name | Caption (Text) |
| --- | --- | --- |
| Form | HeaderForm | General Information |
| Label | Label1 | File Name |
| Label | Label2 | Class Name |
| Text box | NameOfFile | |
| Text box | NameOfClass | |
| Text box | NumberOfExams | |
| Text box | NumberOfStudents | |
| Command button | SetUp | Set Up File |

Now you could have the following general procedure that sets up a grade book on a disk in the currently active directory. (This procedure assumes you've checked that the filename is acceptable already and it does not contain the error trap that is needed for any serious file-handling program.)

```
Sub SetUp_Click()
' local variables
Dim ExamNum As Integer, StuNum As Integer, FileNum As Integer

FileNum = FreeFile
Open NameOfFile.Text For Output As #FileNum
 Print #FileNum,NameOfClass.Text
 Print #FileNum, Val(NumberOfExams.Text)
 Print #FileNum, Val(NumberOfStudents.Text)
Close #FileNum
End Sub
```

## General Sequential Files

Although For-Next loops are a convenient way to read back information contained in a file, obviously there are times when they are not practical. There may be too much information in the file, or you don't know what limits to use. You need a way to implement the following outline:

> While there's information left in the file
>   Get next piece of INFO
>   Process it
> Loop

To do this, you need a way to test when you're at the end of a file. The statement in Visual Basic that lets you do this is mnemonic: it's called EOF( ) (End Of File), where the parentheses hold the file ID number. A quite general program to read back the information contained in a file set up with Print # statements looks like this:

```
FileNum = FreeFile
Open FileName$ For Input As #FileNum
Do Until EOF(FileNum)
   Line Input #FileNum, A$
   ' process line - this would probably be a procedure call or
   ' function call
Loop
Close #FileNum
```

You use a loop at the top to take into account the unlikely possibility that the file exists but doesn't contain any information—that is, it was opened for output but nothing was actually sent to the file. This fragment is a more or less direct translation of the outline. It picks up a line of data (that is, all the data up to a carriage return/line feed pair), and it continues doing this until it gets to the end of the file.

Use this kind of fragment to write a simple print formatter for text files. All you need to know is that you can enter each line (that is, that the lines are not too long or too short); then add the lines to the current value of a string variable. When you're done, make the lines the Text property of a multiline text box with vertical scroll bars.

**tip:**

*It's much faster in Visual Basic to create the string first and then assign the Text property when you're finished retrieving the information than to repeatedly change the Text property itself.*

By the way, a lot of people use the Do While form of these loops. They prefer

```
Do While Not EOF(1)/Loop
```

or

```
While Not EOF(1)/WEnd
```

Since all three forms are equivalent, which you choose is a matter of taste.

One common use of the EOF statement is to read back the information contained in a file character by character. The analogy to keep in mind if you know PC–BASIC is that you read a file as if it were the keyboard. The command that picks individual characters from the keyboard is Input$. In Visual Basic, you pick up individual characters from a file with the statement

A$ = Input$(*NumberOfChars, File Id*)

where the first entry holds the number of characters and the second holds the file ID. Therefore,

```
SixChar$ = Input$(6,#2)
```

picks up six characters from a file opened for input with file ID #2 and assigns it to a string variable named SixChar$.

Here is a fragment that reads the contents of a file named FileName$ character by character and prints both the ASCII code and the character on the same line:

```
' A 'semi' master file reader
FileNum = FreeFile
Open FileName$ For Input As #FileNum
Do Until EOF(FileNum)
 A$ = Input$(1,#FileNum)
 Print  A$, ASC(A$)
Loop
Close FileNum
```

If you use this program on the files TEST1, TEST2, and TEST3 created earlier, you can easily check that the spaces and carriage return/line feed combinations the Print # sends to a file (as stated earlier) are, in fact, there.

Although the Input$(,) statement lets you examine the structure of many files character by character, it shouldn't be overused. For example, it's usually much slower than using the Line Input # or even the Input # function. (If you read many characters at once Input$ speeds up considerably.) Moreover, it's possible for files created by word processors or programs not to be readable by this method. This is because Visual Basic stops reading the file when it encounters a CTRL+Z combination (CHR$(26)), the traditional end–of–file character. (Some files created by programs use CHR$(26)'s internally for purposes other than to indicate the end of the file.) You can see this by trying to use the previous program to read back the file created with the following fragment:

```
'demonstrates Ctrl+Z (=^Z=CHR$(26)) as EOF
Dim FileNum As Integer, I As Integer
FileNum = FreeFile
Open "TEST" For Output As #FileNum
Print #FileNum, CHR$(26)
For I = 1 To 10
Print #FileNum, "The previous program can't ever read this"
Next I
Close #FileNum
```

**tip:**  *Placing a CHR$(26) at the beginning of your file is a simple yet effective way to keep casual snoopers out of your files.*

Since it can be very important to massage non–ASCII files (like spreadsheet files), Visual Basic has another method of reading back files that, among its other powers, gets around this CTRL+Z problem. (See the section "Binary Files" later in this chapter.)

In any case, even if a file can be read with the Input$ function, it's usually better to think of a file as being made up of fields, possibly grouped into records. Each field is separated from the next by a delimiter—that is, a comma or carriage return/line feed combination. The delimiter is what lets you use a single Input # to pick up the field. This is much faster than doing it character by character.

## Sending Special Characters to a File

Since you send information to a file as if it were the screen, you again have to solve the following problems:

◆ How do you send special characters (like quotation marks) to the screen?

◆ How do you nicely format a file?

Visual Basic uses the Write # statement to send items to a file separated by commas and with quotes around strings. For example,

```
Write #3, "Testing 1,2,3"
```

sends everything (including the quotes and the commas) to the output (or append) file with ID #3. This is exactly the same as (and of course less cumbersome than) writing

```
Print #3, Chr$(34);
Print #3, "Testing";
Print #3, Chr$(34)
Print #3, "1, 2, 3";
```

(Note the three semicolons to prevent inadvertent carriage return/line feed combinations.)

As long as you send individual pieces of information to a file, the Print # and Write # commands can be used interchangeably. For example,

```
Print #FileNum, "Hello"
```

and

```
Write #FileNum, "Hello"
```

both put a single piece of information into a file. In either case, you can read back the information by using the Input # command. (Although the files won't be the same size, the Write command adds two quotation marks (Chr$(34)) to the file.) It's only when you send more than one piece of information at a time that the differences really emerge. For example, to send three numbers to a file using

```
Print #FileNum, 1, 2, 3
```

sends a rather large number of superfluous spaces. The command

```
Write #FileNum, 1,2,3
```

sends the appropriate commas to the file, saving space and making it easier to read back the information. It's equivalent to the cumbersome

```
Print #FileNum, 1; ","; 2; ","; 3
```

Simply put, use Write # together with Input # and use Print # with Line Input #.

## Making Changes Inside a Sequential File

The information inside a sequential file is packed tight and is hard to change, but that doesn't mean you can't do it. If the changes you're making don't alter the size of the file, then the methods described in the "Binary Files" section of this chapter are your best bet. This section explains some other ways that do not use these techniques.

The Open FileName For Append As #FileNum command lets you add information to the end of a sequential file. Suppose you now want to add information to the beginning of a file. Proceed as follows:

1. Open a temporary file for output.

2. Use Print # or Write # to place the new information in the temporary file.

3. Close the temporary file.

4. Append the information from the original file onto the end of the temporary file. Two techniques are available to perform this task:

The first technique involves reopening the temporary file For Append. The original file is then opened for input, and information is read from the original file and appended to the temporary file. Finally, the temporary file is closed again.

The second technique is much faster when the original file is large. Visual Basic's Shell command is used to execute DOS's COPY command. The DOS command

COPY *file1*+*file2*

appends the file named *file2* onto the file named *file1*. Thus, the Shell command would take the form

Shell "COPY *TempFileName*+*OriginalFileName*"

or alternatively

Shell "COPY" + *TempFileName$* +"+" + *OriginalFileName$*

5. Delete the original file using the Kill command.

6. Rename the temporary file to the original file's name by using the Name command.

Suppose the information does not go right at the beginning of the file, or you want to remove or replace information already in the file. To do this, imagine what you might do if you were to make these modifications on a cassette tape. First, you'd record the words to be added on a separate tape with a little bit of leader, which means you'd leave some blank tape so you can cut and paste. Then you'd find where on the tape the new information is to go and splice (or cut) the tapes.

For example, suppose you want to change all occurrences of the word "QuickBASIC" in a file to "Visual Basic" (or, more generally, to write your own search and replace function). Follow these steps:

1. Read the information in the file into a temporary file, stopping whenever you get to the string "QuickBASIC".

2. Write "Visual Basic" into the temporary file.

3. Move past the occurrence of the word "QuickBASIC" and continue repeating steps 1 and 2 until you reach the end of the file.

4. Now kill the original file and rename the temporary file with the original file's name.

Because you have to read the information back character by character, a program that implements this outline can run for a long time if done in this naive manner. Binary techniques can work much faster. See the section on "Binary Files" for more on this.

On the other hand, the program will run more quickly (and is also simpler to program) if you know that each occurrence of the string you're searching for is in a separate field. If this is true, you can use a loop that in pseudocode is

```
OPEN Original File
OPEN Temp File
INPUT Field from Original File
DO UNTIL EOF(Original File)
    If field <>"QuickBASIC" THEN
     WRITE It To Temp File
    ELSE
     WRITE "Visual Basic" to Temp File
    END IF
    INPUT nextfield
LOOP
KILL Original File
ReNAME Temp File as Original File
```

# Making a File Program Robust: Error Trapping

Usually, when you're testing a program, you don't care if you get a run-time error and your program crashes. However, when an open file is around, then after a crash, strange things may get written into your files or information you need may never get there. Even if you've thoroughly debugged the program, someone may try to send information to a full disk or try to access a file that doesn't exist. To solve these problems, you must stop the program when, for example, it faces a full disk. The command that activates error trapping, as you saw in Chapter 8, is

```
On Error GoTo ...
```

where the three dots are for the label (line number) that defines the error trap. (Recall that labels must be unique across a module or form.)

Now you need to transfer control to a part of the procedure that identifies the problem and, if possible, fixes it. If the error can be corrected, you can use the Resume statement to pick up where you left off. However, you can't correct an error if you don't know why it happened. Table 14-1 gives the error codes most common to file-handling programs and their likely causes. You would use this information just as was outlined in Chapter 8. For example, place the following statement somewhere in the program before the error can occur:

```
On Error GoTo DiskCheck0
```

Now add code to your event procedure like the fragment given here:

| Error Code | Explanation |
|---|---|
| 53 | File not found (probably a typo) |
| 55 | File already opened (You obviously can't open a file that is already opened unless you use a different identification number.) |
| 57 | Device I/O error (Big problems! Your hardware is acting up. I/O stands for Input/Output, but check the disk drive anyway.) |
| 61 | Disk full (not enough room to do what you want) |
| 62 | Input past end (You put the test for EOF in the wrong place.) |
| 64 | Bad file name (You didn't follow the DOS naming conventions for a file name.) |
| 67 | Too many files open (number determined by CONFIG.SYS) |
| 70 | Permission denied (The disk you're writing to has the write-protect notch covered.) |
| 71 | Drive not ready (The door is open, or where's the floppy?) |
| 72 | Disk media error (Time to throw out the floppy or start thinking about the state of your hard disk.) |
| 76 | Path not found (Probably a typo—you asked to open a file on a nonexistent path.) |

**Table 14-1**
**Common Error Codes for File Handling**

```
Diskcheck0:
  Dim ErrorNumber As Integer
  ErrorNumber = ERR
    Beep

  Select Case ErrorNumber

    Case 53
      Print "Your file was not found. Please check on the "
      Print "spelling or call your operator for assistance."
    Case 61
      Print "The disk is full. Please replace with a slightly"
      Print "less used model"  'could Shell to FORMAT.COM here
    Case 71
      Print "I think the drive door is open - please check"
    Case 72
      Print "Possibly big problems on your hard disk. You"
      Print "definitely should call for help."
      Print "definitely time to call your operator for_
assistance"
    Case 57
      Print "Possibly big problems on your hardware. You"
      Print "definitely should call your operator for_
assistance"
    Case Else
      Print "Please tell the operator (= program author?) that"
      Print " error number ";ErrorNumber; " occurred."
  End Select
  M$ = "If the error has been corrected click on retry"
  M$ = M$ + "Otherwise click on cancel."
  YN% = MsgBox(M$, 5)      'retry/cancel message box
  If YN% = 4 Then Resume Else End
```

The idea of this error trap is simple—the Select Case statement is ideal for handling the many possibilities. Each Case tries to give some indication of where the problem is and, if possible, how to correct it. If you reach the Case Else, the error number has to be reported. In any case, the final block gives you the option of continuing or not, using a Retry/Cancel message box (Type = 5). (Depending on the situation, you may prefer to replace the Print statements with message boxes.)

Error trapping isn't a cure-all. Obviously, very little can be done about a hard disk crash. On the other hand, if you can "shell" to the FORMAT command, then not having a formatted (empty) floppy around is not a crisis for the novice user. (Experienced Windows users can always use the File Manager to format a disk, of course.)

Adding a complete DiskCheck fragment to your file-handling programs is the only way to make them robust. You can merge the same module containing this kind of error trap into all your serious file-handling programs, using the Load Text option in the file menu or the clipboard.

As mentioned in Chapter 8, probably the simplest and cleanest way to put error trapping in your program is to write a function in a code module that analyzes the error code and gives the user the necessary feedback. A global function can do the work once the program passes the error code to it as a parameter. In any case, writing a serious file-handling program without an error trap is an awful idea.

# Random-Access Files

Suppose you are tired of having to search through entire cassettes for certain songs. To avoid this, you decide to put songs that you want instant access to on individual cassettes. The advantages of doing this are obvious, but there are disadvantages as well. First, to gain more or less instant access to an individual song, you're going to waste a considerable amount of blank tape on each cassette. If, to prevent this, you decide to create a standard size tape—one that holds, say, four minutes—you're sure to have at least a couple of songs that run more than four minutes. It's clear that no matter what you do, you'll either waste space or have a few songs that won't fit. Also, if you single out too many songs for separate tapes, you increase the number of cassettes you have to store. If you have hundreds of tapes, each containing an individual song, then you're almost back where you started. It can't possibly be easy to find an individual song if you have to search through a hundred tapes. At this point you would probably choose to alphabetize the tapes by some key feature (such as singer or title), set up an index, or both.

Random-access files are stored on a disk in such a way that they have much the same advantages and disadvantages as the song collector's tapes. You gain instant access to individual pieces of information, but only at some cost. You must standardize the packets of information involved, which means that some things may not fit or that space is not efficiently used, and if the file grows too big—with too many pieces of information—you'll have to set up another file to index the first.

**note:** *The data-handling features of Visual Basic 3 make random-access files somewhat less important. But the amount of overhead involved with using data access sometimes makes setting up your own random-access files the right choice. This is especially true for small files.*

When setting up a sequential file, it's occasionally useful to think of a group of fields as forming a single record. For example, grouping the fields by fives gave a logical and convenient way to read back the information contained in the grade book program. It's worth stressing that this particular grouping was not intrinsic to the file—it's only the way the program looks at the file. The only intrinsic divisions within a sequential file are those created by the delimiters (commas or carriage return/line feed combinations). When you read back information, you read it field by field, with the delimiters acting as barriers.

In a random-access file, however, the notion of a record is built in. A *random-access file* is a special disk file arranged by records. This lets you immediately move to the 15th record without having to pass through the 14th before it, which saves a considerable amount of time.

When you first set up a random-access file, you specify the maximum length for each record. When you enter data for an individual record, you can, of course, put in less information than this preset limit, but you can never put in more. So just like the song collector, you might need to prepare for the worst possible situation.

The command that sets up a random-access file is analogous to the one for opening a sequential file. For example,

```
Open "SAMPLE.RND" As #5 Len = 100
```

opens a random-access file called SAMPLE.RND on the current directory with a file ID of 5, and each record can hold 100 bytes (characters). Note that, unlike the situation for sequential files, you don't have to specify whether you're opening the file for input, output, or appending. As you'll soon see, this distinction is taken care of in the commands that manipulate a random-access file; an open random-access file can be read from and written to essentially simultaneously. You can have any mixture of random-access and sequential files open at the same time. The only restrictions are set by DOS (the FILES command in your CONFIG.SYS file). To prevent confusion between file types, many programmers use an extension like .RND for all random-access files, as in the preceding example.

Similarly, you close a file opened for random access by using the Close command followed by the file ID number. As before, the Close command alone closes all open files, regardless of whether they were opened for sequential or random access. This is especially useful because a sophisticated program for random files often has many files open simultaneously—both sequential and random.

Suppose you want to write a random-access file that would keep track of someone's library. You start by designing the form. You decide on five categories—AUTHOR, TITLE, SUBJECT, PUBLISHER, and MISCELLANEOUS, and after looking over your library, you decide on the following limits for the categories:

| Category | Size |
| --- | --- |
| AUTHOR | 20 |
| TITLE | 30 |
| SUBJECT | 15 |
| PUBLISHER | 20 |
| MISCELLANEOUS | 13 |

Therefore, the total for each record is 98. A random-access file to fit this form is set up (via FileNum = FreeFile, as always):

```
Open "MYLIB.RND" As FileNum Len = 98
```

Just as each file has an ID number, each record within a random-access file has a record number. A single random-access file can hold from 1 to 16,777,216 records. Moreover, you don't have to fill the records in order. As you'll see, you can place information in the 15th record without ever having touched the first 14. The disadvantage of doing this, however, is that Visual Basic would automatically set aside enough space for the first 14 records on the disk, even if nothing was in them.

The word "record" has been used frequently in this chapter. This is no coincidence. One of the main reasons QuickBASIC and then Visual Basic implemented record types was to simplify working with random-access files. First, set up a type:

```
Type Bookinfo
   Author As String*20
   Title As String*30
   Subject As String*15
   Publisher As String*20
   Miscellaneous As String*13
End Type
```

You must use fixed-length strings in order to work within the limitations of a random-access file because of the record length.

Next, suppose ExampleOfBook had been previously dimensioned as being of type Bookinfo. Then the command

```
Get FileNum, 10, ExampleOfBook
```

would transfer the contents of the 10th record from the random-access file into the record variable ExampleOfBook, automatically filling in the correct components of ExampleOfBook.

The command

```
Put FileNum, 37, ExampleOfBook
```

would send the components of ExampleofBook to the 37th record of file #FileNum.

This method of sending information to a random-access file is unique to QuickBASIC and Visual Basic, and it's a very valuable improvement over older PC-BASIC. Visual Basic does not allow you to use the older (and much clumsier) method, which requires what are called field variables.

The record types you create determine the size of the random-access file. Since records can hold numbers as well as text, it's a bit messy to compute the length of a record variable of a given record type. (You have to remember that an integer takes 2 bytes, a long integer 4, and so on.) Visual Basic makes it simple, however, because the Len command not only gives the length of a string, it gives you the length of a record as well. Take any variable of the given type—for example,

```
Dim ExampleOfRecord As ThisType
LenOfRecord = Len(ExampleOfRecord)
```

and use this to set the length for the Open command used to create the random-access file.

## Headers and Indexes for Random-Access Files

If you have the information you want to transfer to a newly created random-access file stored in an array of records, you can use a loop to send the information there. The loop counter determines where to put the record. Usually, however, you set up a variable whose value is the number of the next record you want to read from or write to.

Similarly, you can read back all the information in a random-access file by using the EOF flag after making the dimensions of the array records sufficiently large:

```
Do Until EOF(FileNum)
 I = I + 1
 Get FileNum, I, Records(I)
Loop
```

There are many problems with doing this. For one, you're unlikely to want all the information contained in the file at once, and it may not fit, anyway—suppose you have 1,000,000 records. Also, go back to square one: how do you even know what length to use to open the random-access file? While there are many ways to determine this, a common practice is to set up another file that contains this (and other) vital information about the random-access file. At the very least, this sequential file will contain information about the sizes and types of the fields, possibly names for the fields, and the number of records stored to date. In fact, it may even contain an index of certain keys and the numbers of the records that contain those keys.

Indexes are vital to a random-access file. Many database managers are nothing more than elaborate programs to manage random-access files. Their speed depends on how the program finds the record containing keyed information. This can only be done effectively through indexes. (The alternative is to examine the relevant component of each record one by one.)

An index can be as simple as a sequential file containing a list of keys followed by a record number, or it can be a more elaborately ordered one.

**note:** *Given the database-handling features of Visual Basic 3 you are unlikely to want to go to the trouble of creating a random-access file if it needs an elaborate index. If you do need an index for a random-access file, then a good choice for the index are binary trees (Chapter 16). Other possibilities are to Quicksort (Chapter 16) or Shell sort (Chapter 9) the keys once you've read this information into memory. In all cases, however, you're likely to read the index into an array or arrays.*

# Binary Files

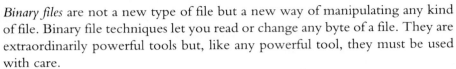

*Binary files* are not a new type of file but a new way of manipulating any kind of file. Binary file techniques let you read or change any byte of a file. They are extraordinarily powerful tools but, like any powerful tool, they must be used with care.

Among other features, binary file techniques do not care about any embedded EOFs (CTRL+Z = Chr$(26)) that the file may have. (Recall that it was impossible to read back the file created earlier in the chapter using sequential file techniques because of the CTRL+Z sequences in the file.)

The command

Open *FileName* For Binary As # *FileNum*

sets up a file to be read with these new techniques.

Just as with random-access files, you can now both read and write to the file. For example, one way to pick up the information from a file open in binary file mode is with the Input$( , ) function you saw earlier. This function works the same way for binary file techniques. The first slot still holds the number of characters and the second the file ID number. For example, the following listing gives a module that prints the contents of any file, regardless of any embedded control characters:

```
Sub PrintAFile(A$)
' example of binary input
Dim I As Integer, FileNum As Integer, Char$
FileNum = FreeFile                ' get free file i.d.
Open A$ For Binary As #FileNum

For I = 1 To LOF(FileNum)
 Char$ = Input$(1,#FileNum)
 Print Char$;
Next I
Close #FileNum
End Sub
```

More often than not, however, you'll want to modify this module by adding some filtering lines—for example, to make it strip out the control characters or those with ASCII codes greater than 127. Once you strip such a file, it can be displayed with the DOS TYPE command or more easily sent by a modem.

For example, the WordStar word processing program normally stores a file in such a way that if you use the DOS TYPE command, you will have trouble reading the file. Stated simply, here's what WordStar does:

◆ It uses certain control codes inside the file (such as CTRL+B for bold).

◆ Each word-wrapped line ends with CHR$(141)+CHR$(10). Note that 141 = 13 + 128. Thus, 141 corresponds to a carriage return with the high-order bit set. Also, the first letter of each word in a word-wrapped line may have its high-order bit set.

◆ WordStar uses the carriage return/line feed combination (CHR$(13)+CHR$(10)) for hard returns. This means that someone has pressed ENTER rather than that the program performed word wrapping.

It's easy to modify the procedure given earlier to strip out all formatting (control) codes and then convert characters with their high-order bits set. (For those who do use WordStar, the procedure will not strip out dot commands; the changes needed for that are left to you.) Here's how to modify the procedure:

```
Sub StripAFile (A$)
  Dim FileNum As Integer, I As Integer
  Dim Char$

' Example Of Binary Input
  FileNum = Freefile                       ' get free file i.d.
  Open A$ For Binary As #FileNum
  For I = 1 To LOF(FileNum)
    Char$ = Input$(1, #FileNum)
    ' strip high-order bit, if any
    If Asc(Char$) > 127 Then
      CharCode = Asc(Char$)
      Char$ = Chr$(CharCode - 128)
    End If
    ' Ignore All Control Codes Except Line Feed
    If Char$ >= Chr$(32) Then
      Print Char$
    Elseif Char$ = Chr$(10) Then
      'Issue A Chr$(13) And A Chr$(10)
      Print
    End If
```

```
        Next I
      End Sub
```

Of course, in a more general program, you'd probably want to do something more than print the character.

**note:** *This program reads the information one byte at a time. This is often inefficient. Consider reading in the information in larger chunks as described in the following tip.*

**tip:** *The optimum setting seems to be 4096 character chunks. Read in chunks this size and then analyze the characters in the string after they've picked up the information contained in the file.*

Visual Basic maintains a file pointer within a file opened for binary access. Each time you use Input$, the file pointer moves one position farther within the file. The Seek command is a fast forward command and a rewind command combined into one. More precisely,

Seek *filenum, position number*

moves the file pointer for the file with *filenum* directly to the byte in that position. Any Input$ would start picking up characters from this location.

Seek has another use. Seek(*filenum*) tells you the position number for the last byte read for either a binary or sequential file. You can also use the Seek function with random-access files. Now it will return the record number of the next record.

To place information within a file opened for binary access, use a modification of the Put command. For example,

```
Put #1, 100, A$
```

would place the contents of the string value directly into the file with file ID #1 starting at the 100th byte. The number of characters sent to this file is, of course, given by Len(A$). The Put command overwrites whatever was there. If you leave a space for the byte position but don't specify it in the Put command, like this:

```
Put #1, , A$
```

then the information is placed wherever the file pointer is currently located.

The Get command also works with a binary file. Here, though, you are best off dimensioning the variable as a fixed-length string. This is because the command

Get *file#, position,* A$

picks up only as many characters as are currently stored in A$. For example, if A$ = "Many", then the statement above would pick up four characters. (This means you can use normal string variables if you are careful to initialize them to have the correct length.)

Now that you know the commands for working on the byte level for a file, you're in a position to write any file utility you like. You also now can use the information contained in a book like *File Formats for Popular PC Software,* second edition, by Jeff Walden (New York: John Wiley & Sons, 1991). The manual to your favorite program probably contains this information as well. Now you can massage the output of any application program.

For example, the features of the Seek command make it easy to write a function to search through a file for a string and even replace it as well (see the next section). To find a string read the file back in chunks. Use the Instr function to search for the string inside the chunk. If the string is found, exit the function and report success. If the string was not found in a specific chunk, reset the Seek pointer back by one less than the length of the string searched for and repeat until the file is processed. (You have to reset the file pointer back to allow for the string being only partially digested by the Input$ command.)

If you want to allow for replacement, combine the above technique with a temporary file as you saw in the section "Making Changes Inside a Sequential File." If the replacement string is exactly the same size, you can use the Put command instead of a temporary file.

## Whose Program Is It?: The App Object

If you are going to distribute your program, you'll probably want to add a startup licensing screen. This section describes two techniques for doing this. One involves making a change to the .EXE file itself and seems to be the most popular. The author actually prefers a second method: storing an encrypted hidden file in the same directory as the application.

**caution:** *It is possible that the method shown here for changing the .EXE file will not work in future versions of Visual Basic.*

Both these techniques ultimately depend on using binary file techniques to carefully examine and make some subtle changes in a file. The routine in the next section is a quite general purpose procedure for doing that. After explaining this routine, you'll see how to apply it to add a licensing screen to your program in the two ways mentioned above.

First, though, you'll need to learn about the App object. This is a very useful Visual Basic object because it can tell you the full path name of the Application (App.Path) or the root name of the .EXE file (App.EXEName) as well as the Help file associated with the application, the Title, or whether another copy of it is running at the present time.

### A GENERAL FILE MODIFIER

The following procedure takes any file and replaces all occurrences of one string inside of it by another. It adjusts the size of the replacement string by padding or truncating to match the original string.

Here's the procedure:

```
Const ChunkSize = 4096

Sub ChangeFile(FName$, IdString$, NString$)
   Dim PosString As Integer, WhereString As Integer
   Dim FileNumber As Integer, A$, NewString$
   Dim AString As String*ChunkSize

   FileNumber = FreeFile
   PosString = 1
   WhereString = 0
   AString = Space$(ChunkSize)

   'Make sure strings have same size
   If Len(IdString$) > Len(NString$) Then
     NewString$ = NString$ + Space$(Len(IdString$) -_
Len(NString$))
   Else
     NewString$ = Left$(NString$, Len(IdString$))
   End If
```

```
Open FName$ For Binary As FileNumber
If LOF(File Number) < ChunkSize Then
   A$ = Space$(LOF(File Number))
   Get #File Number, 1, A$
   WhereString = InStr(1, A$, IdString$)
Else
  Get #File Number, 1, AString
  WhereString = InStr(1, AString, IdString$)
End If


If WhereString <> 0 Then
  Put #File Number, WhereString, NewString$
End If
PosString = ChunkSize + PosString - Len(IdString$)


Do Until EOF(File Number) Or PosString > LOF(File Number)
   If PosString + ChunkSize > LOF(File Number) Then
      A$ = Space$(LOF(File Number) - PosString)
      Get #File Number, PosString, A$
      WhereString = InStr(1, A$, IdString$)
   Else
      Get #File Number, PosString, AString
      WhereString = InStr(1, AString, IdString$)
   End If
   If WhereString <> 0 Then
     Put #File Number, PosString + WhereString - 1,
NewString$
   End If
    PosString = ChunkSize + PosString - Len(IdString$)
  Loop
  Close
End Sub

Problems:
  ' error trap goes here
End Sub
```

This procedure is fairly subtle so let's go over it carefully. First, it sets up a constant for the size of each chunk. As mentioned earlier, 4096 seems to give the best performance on the author's machines but your experience may vary.

Next come the declarations for the various counters used in this program. In particular, there is a fixed-length string equal in size to the chunk size. Since binary file techniques require that the strings replaced be exactly the same size, the first If–Then–Else takes care of this by setting up a correctly sized local variable NewString$ to hold the replacement string.

The procedure then starts picking up pieces of the file. Because we are reading the file in chunks we have to be careful not to go past the boundaries of the file. We use a temporary value A$ in case the file is smaller than the size of the chunks. Because Get only reads as many characters as are currently stored in the file, we need to initialize A$ properly.

Next, we use the Instr command to search for the IdString$. If we find it, we put the NewString in its place. Next comes the Loop that looks through the rest of the file. This allows us to do multiple replacements. At each step we have to slightly adjust the pointer back because of the possibility that we picked up part of the target string in a chunk. Notice as well that the chunk size again requires us to monitor the remaining characters in the file inside the loop. Finally, this procedure indicates where the error trap would go, although to save space we haven't included one.

**note:** *You can easily modify this procedure to change it into a function that returns True or False depending on whether the string is found or not.*

### ADDING LICENSING SCREENS

Now that you have the procedure to make changes inside any file and the needed properties of the APP object, you can move on to the techniques for adding licensing screens. By far the easiest (and the author's preference) is to have the Form_Load (or Sub_Main) look for a hidden file in the same directory as the application. Install this hidden file at the same time as the program. During the installation procedure open this hidden file and modify a string so as to give the licensee's name. (If you want to also encrypt this information inside the file, see the end of the chapter.) You can use the Path property of the App object to determine the directory to examine. If you can't find the required information inside the hidden file, or can't find the hidden file, do not permit the program to proceed.

To modify the hidden file, you can use a Form_Load procedure in the installation program that looks something like this.

```
Form_Load ()
On Error GoTo Problems
   Dim InstallTries As Integer, Install$, Person$
```

```
Person$ = ""
Do Until Person$ <> "" Or InstallTries > 2
  Person$ = InputBox$("Please enter your name.")
  InstallTries = InstallTries + 1
Loop
If InstallTries > 3 Then
  MsgBox "Installation Failure - no name supplied "
  End
End If
User$ = "Program licensed by " + Person$
IdString$ = "This program has not been licensed to anybody. "
Call ChangeFile(HiddenFileName$, IdString$, Person$)
```

This program assumes you would supply the hidden file name as the value of the HiddenFileName$ variable and that the IdString$ to search for (and change) is, "This program has not been licensed to anybody."

Once you modify the hidden file, the Form_Load of the .EXE file can use the function variation on the ChangeFile mentioned in the previous section to insure that the string "This program has not been licensed to anybody." no longer occurs.

## MODIFYING AN .EXE FILE DIRECTLY

This method of determining to whom the program is licensed is popular but the author really doesn't like it. It depends on a feature of Visual Basic that may eventually disappear. But if you like the idea of actually encoding the user information in the .EXE file, here it is.

The method works because in the current version of Visual Basic assignments to Global variables remain intact in the .EXE file. For example, if you have a Sub_Main startup module with the following code:

```
Global ProgramId$

Sub Main ()
ProgramId$ = "This program has not been licensed to anybody. "
 Load StartForm
End Sub
```

and create an .EXE file then the string "This program has not been licensed to anybody." will actually occur unchanged in the .EXE file. (You can use

DEBUG.COM or a program editor to check.) If you now make sure that the program contains no other assignments of variables to this string, then in the *current version* of Visual Basic, the .EXE file will contain a unique copy of this string and *it will be the value of the global variable ProgramId$.*

Now, if you modify the .EXE file by changing this string using the techniques you have seen previously, you will change the value of the global variable ProgramId$. So, if your Form_Load program of the StartForm has code that looks like this:

```
Sub Form_Load ()
If ProgramId$ Like "*licensed to anybody*" Then
   M$ = ProgramId$ + " Please install program correctly. _
Terminating NOW!"
   MsgBox M$
   End
End If
 MsgBox "Program licensed to " + ProgramId$
End Sub
```

your program will actually display the licensee.

This trick works because by working directly on the byte level with the .EXE file we have changed the value of the global variable ProgramId$ directly!

**caution:** *Again, keep in mind that this technique depends on there being a unique version of the string in your program and the technology currently used in Visual Basic 3. The author makes no guarantees that this will work in your version or in future versions.*

(On the other hand, it's amazing that you can currently modify an .EXE file in this way!)

## Keeping File Information Secret

Since a simple utility program using binary file techniques can read back the information contained in any file, the data contained in your files is readily available to anyone with a compatible computer, a little programming skill, and a copy of your disk. In the next few sections you'll see how to encode a file so that only people having the right key can easily read your file. These methods work very well with the hidden file technique described above for handling licensing screens. Of course, the methods here aren't perfect, but considering how easy they are to implement, they are surprisingly secure.

First, a little history. All the earliest ciphers that we know about use simple substitutions. For example, Julius Caesar kept his messages secret by taking each letter in the message and replacing it with the one three letters further on; the letter "A" would be replaced by "D," "B" by "E," and so on, until you got to the letters after "X." Since "X" is the 24th letter of the alphabet, you have to wrap around to the beginning of the alphabet, and "X" becomes "A," "Y" becomes "B," and "Z" becomes "C." Here is a normal alphabet and below it a complete Caesar alphabet:

ABCDEFGHIJKLMNOPQRSTUVWXYZ
DEFGHIJKLMNOPQRSTUVWXYZABC

(Actually, in Caesar's time, the alphabet had fewer letters—23 instead of 26. For example, "U" and "V" developed out of "V" around a thousand years ago, and "J" came around 500 years after that.) For example, the sentence, "Can you read this" becomes

FDQ BRX UHDG WKLV

Shift ciphers go back further than Caesar; one occurs in the Bible. In Jeremiah 25-26, the prophet conceals his prophecy by changing the name of Babylon using a cipher that splits the Hebrew alphabet in half and replaces the first letter with the middle letter, the second by the middle + 1, and so on.

Here is a general procedure that shifts any character by any number of characters, wrapping around if necessary.

```
Sub CaesarShift(A$, Shift%)
  Dim CharNum As Integer
  CharNum = (Asc(A$) + Shift%) Mod(256)
  A$ = Chr$(CharNum)
End Sub
```

It wouldn't be hard to incorporate this procedure into a file encrypter; just pass the procedure the contents of the file character by character. The trouble is that a shift cipher is easy to break; you can even do it by hand. Look at the coded message and run back down the alphabet by steps, shifting the letters back step by step. After, at most, 25 steps, you're done. Here's what you get at each step in the example:

| | | | |
|---|---|---|---|
| FDQ | BRX | UHDG | WKLV |
| ECP | AQW | TGCF | VJKU |
| DBO | ZPV | SFBE | UIJT |
| CAN | YOU | READ | THIS |

Note that it's better to work with the whole message than with individual words because occasionally English words (*clear text*) show up by mistake. For example, the word "HTQI" backs up to the word "FROG" on the second try and to the word "COLD" on the fifth.

Decoding a Caesar cipher, simple as it is, stresses the usefulness of the computer and its limitations. It can do the drudgery, but you have to recognize when to stop. For the more complicated ciphers described in what follows, this division of labor is essential.

## More Complicated Ciphers

Since a shift cipher provides virtually no security, the next step is to change the letters in a more random manner. Write down the alphabet and below it write all the letters in some arbitrary order:

ABCDEFGHIJKLMNOPQRSTUVWXYZ
QAZXSWEDCVFRBGTYHNUJMIKOPL

Now, every time you see an "A" in your original message, replace it with a "Q," replace each "B" with an "A," each "C" with a "Z," and so on. This cipher can't be broken by the techniques used for shift ciphers, but it's extremely hard to remember the random alphabet used for the code. Around 1600, in an attempt to combine the virtues of this method with the ease of shift codes, people began to use a keyword cipher. The idea is to replace the letters of the alphabet with the letters in the key phrase, using the order in which they occur there. For example, suppose the key is THE RAY GUN ZAPPED ME QUICKLY. Now look at the following:

ABCDEFGHIJKLMNOPQRSTUVWXYZ
THERAYGUNZPDMQICKLBFJOSVWX

What this does is take the individual letters from the key phrase, avoiding duplicates as needed, and place them below the normal alphabet. Since the phrase contains only 18 different letters, the unused letters went at the end. To encipher a message using this code, replace the letters in the original message with the ones directly below them—"A" with "T," "B" with "H," and so on.

Here's one possible outline for a procedure that takes a key phrase and creates the code:

```
Get keyphrase
  Run through each letter in key phrase
  Check if already used
    if not used:
    store in next place in 'cipher' list
    mark that letter as used
  Until no more letters are in the keyphrase
Now store unused letters from normal alphabet into key
```

However, this outline turns out to be not quite the best way of proceeding. For example, suppose you want to decipher a message enciphered this way. Say you see an "A" in the coded message; then, because an "A" is below an "E" in the alphabets just given, the original letter must have been an "E."

To set up the two lists to be used for encoding and decoding, start with two ordinary alphabets. Now, since "T" replaces "A," you swap the "A" in the first alphabet with the "T" in the second. Next, you swap the "B" and the "H." How can you tell if a letter is already used? Just look at that letter's position in the second alphabet. If the letter is still in its original position, that letter has not been used. When you are done with the letters in the key phrase, any remaining letters should be swapped out of the first alphabet into the second one.

To actually write this program, set up two lists. To make life easier, use two global arrays of integers dimensioned to run from 65 to 90 (the ASCII codes for A to Z):

```
Global Dim EncodeAlph() As Integer, DecodeAlph() As Integer
```

Now call an initialize procedure from the Form_Load procedure:

```
Sub Initialize( )
  Dim I As Integer
  Redim EncodeAlph(65 To 90) As Integer
  Redim DecodeAlph(65 To 90) As Integer
```

```
   For I = 65 To 90
     EncodeAlph(I) = I
     DecodeAlph(I) = I
   Next I
End Sub
```

Now you can write the Sub that creates both lists by translating the preceding outline. To do this, you need to keep track of where you are in the original alphabet because that determines where the letter will go. Suppose you call this variable PosOfLet. Each time you use a letter from the key, swap the letter determined by this position number with its counterpart in the other alphabet, determined from the key, and increase PosOfLet by one. The tricky part comes when you've used up all the letters in the key. Then you have to decide where to put the letters remaining from the first alphabet. The problem occurs because there is no convenient pointer to the unused letters in the second alphabet. To take care of this, set the letters you use to the negative of their ASCII values. For example, if "X," "Y," and "Z" were the only letters not used in the key, then they would be the only ones that were still positive in the Decode alphabet.

```
Sub Makelists (Key$)
   'Uses Global Variables EncodeAlph(), DecodeAlph()
   'Local Variables
   Dim LenKey As Integer, PosOfLetUsed As Integer
   Dim I As Integer, A As Integer
   Dim A1$

   LenKey = Len(Key$)
   PosOfLetUsed = 65                        'start with Asc("A")

   For I = 1 To LenKey
     A1$ = Mid$(Key$, I, 1): A$ = UCase$(A1$)
     Select Case A$
      Case "A" To "Z"
        A = Asc(A$)
        If DecodeAlph(A) = A Then          'Character Not Yet_
Used
          EncodeAlph(PosOfLetUsed) = A
          DecodeAlph(A) = -PosOfLetUsed    'Swap The_
Encode/Decode
                                           'And Flag A Used Char
          PosOfLetUsed = PosOfLetUsed + 1
        End If
      Case Else
```

```
      ' Not A Letter - Of Course You Can
      ' Do Something With These Too
    End Select
  Next I
  ' Now Throw In Unused Letters
  ' This Loop Should End If You've Used Up All 26 Letters Or
  ' You Can't Find Any New Letters To Swap
  For I = 65 To 90                 ' Start Looking In Second Alph
                                   ' Here.
    If DecodeAlph(I) = I Then
        EncodeAlph(PosOfLetUsed) = I
        DecodeAlph(I) = -PosOfLetUsed    'Swap The Encode /_
Decode
        PosOfLetUsed = PosOfLetUsed + 1
    End If
  Next I
End Sub
```

Now encoding or decoding a letter is almost a trivial task. Suppose you want to encode a "C" (ASCII code 67). You just look at the value of Encode(67) to find the ASCII value for the coded version. Similarly (and this is the nice part), to decode a "C," you just have to look at the absolute value of the entry in Decode(67). Thus, you can pass the appropriate array as a parameter and use the following listing:

```
Sub EncodeDecode(A(),X$)
  Dim X1 As Integer
  X1 = Asc (UCase$(X$))
  X$ = Chr$(Abs(A(X1)))
End Sub
```

## A More Secure Cipher

Having spent all of the previous section on a fairly subtle program to create a keyword cipher, you might expect it to be secure—or at least difficult to break. (It does work quickly, though.) Unfortunately, any substitution cipher can be broken, given enough text. In fact, assuming the encoded text was originally written in standard, everyday English, it's pretty easy to find the encoding algorithm if you have, say, a thousand words of encoded text. The key to breaking a substitution code is that letters do not exist in isolation. "E" is almost certainly the most common letter, "T" is likely to be the next most common, and "A" is likely to be third highest. Over the years, cryptographers have examined thousands of pages of texts to determine the frequency of letters in standard English. The problem with a simple substitution cipher is that if you always replace a letter with the same symbol, someone can break it by using frequency analysis.

One way to avoid this method of breaking a code is to change the substitution. Instead of always replacing, say, an "E" with the letter "T," use a "T" the first time and a "Z" the next. This way, each time an "E" occurs, it is replaced with another letter. This method is called a *multi-alphabet substitution cipher*. It's much more difficult to break this cipher, but it's also much more difficult to set up. After all, you have to devise a way of getting these multiple alphabets.

However, you can use the built-in random number generator in Visual Basic to generate the alphabets. Recall that the command

```
X = Rnd        'or X = Rnd(1)
```

gives you a different random number between zero and 1. However—and this is the key to breaking the cipher—given enough data, a professional cryptographer (or a good amateur) can find out the next number in the sequence. Cryptographers would say the random number generator in Visual Basic isn't "cryptographically secure." Finding (and then proving that you have) a cryptographically secure random number generator is probably the most important problem in cryptography.

The idea for the cipher that follows is that you scale this number and use it to determine the "Caesar shift." Now, instead of using the same shift for the next letter, use the random number generator to get a different shift for each letter. Each time you encode a letter, it's transformed differently.

Unfortunately, this method won't quite work. Since the patterns don't obviously repeat (that's what is meant by random), there isn't any reasonable method of decoding the message. You would never know what to shift back by. You have to modify this approach slightly. The first idea that might come to mind is that the Rnd function, when given a negative number as an argument, is supposed to give a repeatable sequence. Thus, if you precede all other uses of Rnd with a statement of the form

Randomize *Seed*

where *Seed* is a negative number, then Visual Basic is always supposed to give you the same sequence of random numbers. Each seed is *supposed* to yield a different, repeatable sequence of random numbers. *Unfortunately, because of a bug in the current version of Visual Basic, this feature won't work as it is supposed to.* You need to modify the procedure slightly. To get a repeatable sequence of random numbers, you must have Visual Basic process the following statement before generating the next random number in the sequence:

X = Rnd(*the negative number*)

To use random Caesar shifts, you need only ask the user for a key—say, a four-digit positive number. Use this to reseed the random number generator:

```
X = Rnd(-Key)
```

Now you can generate a list of shifts, one for each character in the file:

```
NextShift = Int(256 * Rnd)
```

Use these shifts just as in a Caesar cipher—call this shift generator for each letter in the message.

Now the question is how to decode. The whole point of repeatability is that if you process the command

```
X = Rnd(-Key)
```

again, then when you generate Caesar shifts, you get the same series of numbers as you did before. As before, if you know what the original shift was, you can reverse it just as easily.

However, rather than using this procedure as presented, you can use a more elegant and faster approach. Recall from the bit twiddling section of Chapter 7 that the Xor operator has a convenient property: If

```
B = A Xor Shift
```

and you enter

```
C = B Xor Shift
```

again, then the value of C is the same as the original value of A. Thus, by Xoring twice, you get back to where you started. Thus, you can use the same procedure to both encode and decode. Here's the procedure to do that:

```
Sub EncodeDecode (FileName$, KeyValue)
  ' local variables:
  Dim FileNum As Integer, X As Single, I As Integer
  Dim CharNum As Integer, RandomInteger As Integer

  Dim SingleChar As String * 1          'for use in GET and PUT

  X = Rnd(-KeyValue)
  FileNum = FreeFile
  Open FileName$ For Binary As #FileNum
    For I = 1 To LOF(FileNum)
    Get #FileNum, I, SingleChar
    CharNum = Asc(SingleChar)
    RandomInteger = Int(256 * Rnd)
    CharNum = CharNum Xor RandomInteger 'this is it
    SingleChar = Chr$(CharNum)
    Put #FileNum, I, SingleChar
  Next I
  Close FileNum
End Sub
```

As mentioned before, you will find that the program works faster if you read the information from the file in larger (4096–character) chunks. You can also choose the improved version of the random number generator presented in Chapter 9 to make this approach even more secure. Finally, you should be aware that a quick but insecure way to encrypt a file is to Xor the contents of the file with a single password.

# Chapter 15

# Communicating with Other

## Windows Applications

ICROSOFT Windows can *multitask,* or run several applications at once. (Although applications must cooperate by releasing the CPU for this to be really effective.) As you'll soon see, Visual Basic lets you take advantage of this with ways of writing code that activate any Windows application or that send commands directly to the active application from within a Visual Basic project.

Multitasking is even more powerful if the various applications can work with each other. Suppose you could write a Visual Basic program that monitors what a spreadsheet like Excel or Lotus 1-2-3 for Windows is doing. This would make it possible to use Visual Basic to add a feature that isn't built into the spreadsheet. For example, you might want to notify the user if a crucial quantity has changed or reached a target. Perhaps you want to write a program that analyzes a document being written in a Windows word processor like Word for Windows in real time, notifying the user when he or she has written a certain number of words. All this and more are possible through *dynamic data exchange* (DDE for short) and *object linking and embedding* (OLE for short).

DDE seems mysterious at first, but if you think of it as automated use of the Windows clipboard, the mystery should disappear. The first section of this chapter covers the clipboard. If you haven't spent much time using the clipboard, you'll see that it is much more than a passive place to store objects for cutting and pasting. Essentially, what your Visual Basic program does in DDE is tell the other application what to put into or take out of the clipboard.

**note:** *Although you must use a registered clipboard format, DDE doesn't use the clipboard the way an ordinary cut and paste operation does. Any data already there doesn't get overwritten, and you can have multiple simultaneous DDE conversations.*

OLE in the second version that Visual Basic 3 supports is potentially an even more powerful way to have Windows applications communicate through Visual Basic. OLE lets you build your own integrated Windows applications as a Visual Basic project. Unfortunately, while OLE 2.0 support may one day be very common in Windows applications, right now very few applications support it. For this reason the section on OLE 2 in this chapter is more a survey of what you will be able to do with it someday rather than what you can do with it now. In particular, we do not cover what Microsoft calls OLE automation, which is the theoretical ability of one application to actually program another application.

# The Clipboard

The Windows clipboard lets you exchange both graphics and text between Windows applications and is often used for cut-and-paste operations inside a specific Windows application. In particular, Visual Basic uses the clipboard for its cut-and-paste editing feature, and you can use the clipboard together with the properties given in the section "Selecting Text in Visual Basic" to implement similar features into your projects.

However, users of Microsoft Windows rarely think of the clipboard at all, and if they do they usually think of it as a passive feature of Windows. This is not true; the clipboard viewer is an independent program, usually available in the Windows Main program group. The screen in Figure 15-1 is what you'll see if you run the clipboard viewer program on its own.

**Figure 15-1**

**The clipboard**

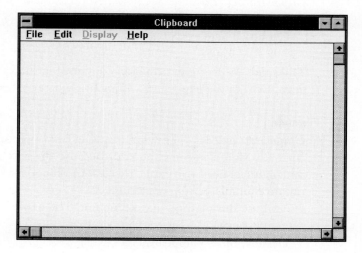

You can use the File menu on the clipboard viewer to view graphics files or to save the contents of the clipboard as an independent file. Moreover, the clipboard viewer program is often smart enough to convert images from one format to another. This is why you can use the clipboard to transfer text to Visual Basic from a non–ASCII word processor like Word for Windows. (As you saw in Chapter 14, writing conversion programs from scratch requires binary file techniques.)

Since most of this chapter is about automating clipboard operations, you may want to have the clipboard viewer up and running while working through it. That way you can look at the contents of the clipboard to check that what you think you've put there (automatically) really is there.

The clipboard can hold only one piece of the same kind of data at a time. If you send new information of the same format to the clipboard, you wipe out what was there before. Sometimes, however, you will want to make sure that the clipboard is completely free before working with it. To do this, add a line of code inside your project that looks like this:

```
Clipboard.Clear
```

As you might expect, this applies the Clear method to the predefined Clipboard object.

If you need to send text to and from the clipboard, use the two additional methods described next.

**Clipboard.SetText**  The SetText method is usually used in the following form:

```
Clipboard.SetText StringData
```

This sends the string information contained in the variable or string expression StringData to the clipboard, wiping out whatever text was there.

**Clipboard.GetText**  The Clipboard.GetText method takes a copy of the text currently stored in the clipboard. Because the text contents of the clipboard remain intact until you explicitly clear the clipboard or send new text to it, you can do multiple pasting operations.

You use this method like a function. The general form is

```
Destination = Clipboard.GetText( )
```

# Selecting Text in Visual Basic

When you use a text box or a combo box on a Visual Basic form, users can select text following the usual Windows convention: press SHIFT and use an arrow key, PGUP, or PGDN. Sending selected text to other Windows applications is quite common. Moreover, especially for multiline text boxes, you will often want to add to your project cut-and-paste editing functions that work with selected text. To do this within Visual Basic, you refer to selected text by three properties, two of which have long integer values and the third of which is a string.

**SelStart** The SelStart long integer gives you the place where the selected text starts. If the value is 0, the user has started selecting text from the beginning of the text or combo box. If the value is equal to the length of the text string—Len(Text1.Text), for example—the user wants the code to start working after all the text that's currently in the box. You can specify where selected text starts (for example, in a demonstration program) by setting the value of this property from code. For example, for a text box named Text1, a line of code like

```
Text1.SelStart = Len(Text1.Text)/2
```

starts the selected text in midstream.

**SelLength** SelLength gives you the number of characters the user has selected. If SelLength equals 0, no text was selected. If SelLength is equal to the length of the text string, all the characters in the control were selected. To highlight the first half of the contents of a text box, you would use code like this:

```
Text1.SelStart = 0
Text1.SelLength = Len(Text1.Text)/2
```

**SelText** SelText is the actual string the user has selected. If the user hasn't selected any text, this is the empty (null) string. If you add the following line of code to the fragment just given:

```
FirstHalfOfText$ = Text1.SelText
```

then the value of the string variable FirstHalfOfText$ is the selected string.

If you assign a new string value to the SelText property, Visual Basic replaces the selected string with the new value. To allow users to copy selected text, combine these properties with the SetText method. For a menu item named Copy and a text box named Text1, all you need to do is use

```
Sub Copy_Click()
  Clipboard.SetText Text1.SelText
End Sub
```

To change this to a procedure that cuts out the selected text, use the following code:

```
Sub Cut_Click()
  Clipboard.SetText Text1.SelText
  Text1.SelText = ""
End Sub
```

By adding the line that resets the value of SelText to the empty string, you have cut the selected text out of the text box.

For example, to implement a Paste_Click procedure at the place where the user has set the insertion point inside a text box named Text1, use the following code:

```
Sub Paste_Click()
  Text1.Text = Clipboard.GetText()
End Sub
```

Notice that if the user hasn't selected any text, this acts as an insertion method. Otherwise, it replaces the selected text.

## Clipboard Formats and Graphics Transfers

To retrieve graphics images from the clipboard, Visual Basic must know what type of image is stored there. Similarly, to transfer images to the clipboard, the program must tell the clipboard what type of graphics it is sending. (See Chapters 10 and 12 for more on these formats.) The following table summarizes this information. The last column of the table gives the name of the constant that the CONSTANT.TXT file uses for the format. (As usual, if you want to use these constants instead of the values, incorporate the relevant part of the CONSTANT.TXT file into a code module.)

| Value | Format | Symbolic Constant |
|-------|--------|-------------------|
| 1 | Text (.TXT ) | CF_TEXT |
| 2 | Ordinary bitmap (.BMP) | CF_BITMAP |
| 3 | Windows metafile (.WMF) | CF_METAFILE |
| 8 | Device-independent bitmap (.DIB) | CF_DIB |

You ask the clipboard what type of image it is currently storing by using the GetFormat method. The syntax for this method is

Clipboard.GetFormat(*Format%*)

where *Format%* is one of the values given in the previous table. This method returns True if the image in the clipboard has the right format, for example:

```
If Clipboard.GetFormat(2) Then MsgBox "Clipboard has a bitmap"
```

To retrieve an image from the clipboard, you use the GetData method. The syntax for this method looks like this:

Clipboard.GetData(*Format%*)

where *Format%* has the value 2, 3, or 8, as in the preceding table. (Remember, you use the GetText method to retrieve text data from the clipboard.)

## A Clipboard Example Program

As an example of how to use the clipboard methods, start up a new project and add a picture box and a multilevel text box with vertical scroll bars and four command buttons. The screen in Figure 15-2 shows you what the form might look like. Suppose you give the command buttons the following control names: TextCopy, TextGet, PictureCopy, and PictureGet. Then the code that activates the Click procedures for these four buttons looks like this:

```
Sub TextCopy_Click ()
  If Text1.Text = "" Then
    MsgBox ("No text to copy.")
  Else
    Clipboard.Clear
    Clipboard.SetText Text1.Text
  End If
End Sub
```

**Figure 15-2**

Form for clipboard example

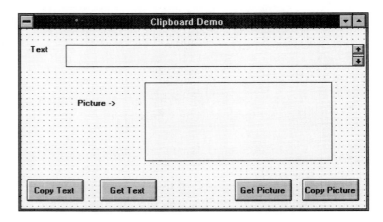

This code checks the contents of the Text1 text box. If there is nothing there, it tells Visual Basic to inform the user. Otherwise, it clears the clipboard and sends the text contained in the box to the clipboard. (Strictly speaking, the Clear method isn't needed except in unusual circumstances; sending new text to the clipboard wipes out whatever text was there.)

To retrieve text from the clipboard, you first have to make sure the clipboard contains text. The If clause in the following procedure does this, using the GetFormat statement:

```
Sub TextGet_Click ()
  If Clipboard.GetFormat(1) Then  'CF_TEXT
    Text1.Text = Clipboard.GetText()
  Else
    MsgBox ("No text in Clipboard")
  End If
End Sub
```

Retrieving a graphics image requires checking the format by using GetFormat and then modifying the parameter for the GetData method accordingly. Here's the procedure:

```
Sub PictureGet_Click ()
  If Clipboard.GetFormat(1) Then  'CF_TEXT
    MsgBox ("Only text in Clipboard")
```

```
    ElseIf Clipboard.GetFormat(2) Then   'CF_BITMAP
      Picture1.Picture = Clipboard.GetData(2)
    ElseIf Clipboard.GetFormat(3) Then   'CF_METAFILE
      Picture1.Picture = Clipboard.GetData(3)
    ElseIf Clipboard.GetFormat(8) Then   'CF_DIB
      Picture1.Picture = Clipboard.GetData(8)
    Else
      MsgBox "No recognizable picture in Clipboard"
    End If
End Sub
```

To copy images from the picture box to the clipboard as a bitmap, use

```
Sub PictureCopy_Click ()
  ' As BITMAP
  Clipboard.Clear
  Clipboard.SetData Picture1.Picture, 2
End Sub
```

Finally, you might want to consider using menus rather than command buttons. The control names can remain the same. The Menu Design window would look like the screen shown in Figure 15-3.

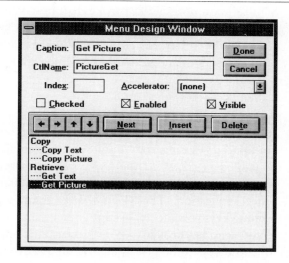

**Figure 15-3**

Menu Design window for clipboard example

# Activating Windows Applications

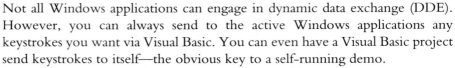

Not all Windows applications can engage in dynamic data exchange (DDE). However, you can always send to the active Windows applications any keystrokes you want via Visual Basic. You can even have a Visual Basic project send keystrokes to itself—the obvious key to a self-running demo.

The AppActivate statement moves the focus to another project currently running on the Windows desktop; it does not start a program. (Use the Shell command you saw in Chapter 14 for that.) The syntax for this statement is

AppActivate *TitleBar$*

The string expression for *TitleBar$* must match the name that appears in the title bar of the application when its window isn't minimized. The comparison isn't case-sensitive. For example, both of the following lines of code activate the Windows File Manager:

```
AppActivate "File Manager"
AppActivate "file manager"
```

## Sending Keystrokes to an Application

Once you've activated another Windows application by using AppActivate, you use the SendKeys statement to send keystrokes to the active window. SendKeys cannot send keystrokes to a non-Windows application that happens to be running under Windows in a virtual DOS window. If no other window is active, the keystrokes go to the Visual Basic project itself. (This is useful in testing programs and self-running demos.) The syntax for this statement is

SendKeys *Text$* [,*WaitOrNot%*]

If the *WaitOrNot%* integral expression is True (nonzero), Visual Basic will not continue processing code until the other application processes the keystrokes contained in *Text$*. If the expression is False (0, the default), Visual Basic continues with the procedure immediately after it sends the keystrokes to the other application. The *WaitOrNot%* argument matters only when you are sending keystrokes to applications other than your Visual Basic application itself. If you send keystrokes to your Visual Basic application and you need to wait for those keys to be processed, use the DoEvents function (see Chapter 8).

The value of the *Text$* string is the keystrokes you want to send. For keyboard characters, use the characters. For example,

```
SendKeys "Foo is not Bar", 0
```

sends the keystrokes "F", "o", "o", and so on, to the active application, exactly as if the user had typed them on the screen. Since the *WaitOrNot%* parameter is False, Visual Basic does not wait for these keystrokes to be processed by the active application. The only exceptions to this are the plus sign (+), caret (^), percent sign (%), brackets ([ ]), tilde (~), parentheses (( )), and braces ({ }). As you'll soon see, these have special uses in the SendKeys statement. If you need to send these keys, enclose them in braces. For example, to send "2+2" to the active application, use this:

```
SendKeys "23+32"
```

You'll often need to send control key combinations, function keys, and so on, in addition to the ordinary alphanumeric keys (A to Z, 0 to 9). To send a function key, use {F1} for the first function key, {F2} for the second, and so on. For other keys, such as BACKSPACE, use the following codes:

| Key | Code | Key | Code |
| --- | --- | --- | --- |
| BACKSPACE | {BACKSPACE} or {BS} or {BKSP} | HOME<br>INS | {HOME}<br>{INSERT} |
| BREAK | {BREAK} | LEFT ARROW | {LEFT} |
| CAPS LOCK | {CAPSLOCK} | NUM LOCK | {NUMLOCK} |
| CLEAR | {CLEAR} | PGDN | {PGDN} |
| DEL | {DELETE} or {DEL} | PGUP | {PGUP} |
| DOWN ARROW | {DOWN} | PRTSCRN | {PRTSC} |
| END | {END} | RIGHT ARROW | {RIGHT} |
| ENTER | {ENTER} or ~ | SCROLL LOCK | {SCROLLOCK} |
| ESC | {ESCAPE} or {ESC} | TAB | {TAB} |
| HELP | {HELP} | UP ARROW | {UP} |

For combinations of the SHIFT, CTRL, and ALT keys, use the codes just given, but place one or more of these codes first:

| Key | Code |
|-----|------|
| SHIFT | + |
| CTRL | ^ |
| ALT | % |

To indicate that one (or all) of the SHIFT, CTRL, and ALT keys should be used with a key combination, enclose the keys in parentheses. For example, to hold down CTRL while pressing A and then B (that is, what this book would symbolize as CTRL+A+B), use "^(AB)". The string "^AB" would give you the three keystrokes individually.

You can also send repeated keys more easily by using the string in the form *Keystrokes$ Number%*. There must be a space between the keystrokes and the number. For example, SendKeys "UP 10" sends ten presses of the UP ARROW to the active application.

As an example of putting all this together, the following fragment activates the File Manager and maximizes the window in which it is running by sending the keystrokes needed to open the control box and then choosing the Maximize item on its control box menu:

```
AppActivate "File Manager"
SendKeys "% {Down 4}{Enter}", -1
```

The SendKeys statement sends the ALT key followed by a press of the SPACEBAR (because the quotes enclose a space). These keystrokes open the control menu. The next strokes move you to the Maximize menu item and choose that item.

**note:**   *This technique (using cursor keys instead of the accelerator letters) also works in the international version of Visual Basic where the words may not be the same.*

# Dynamic Data Exchange (DDE)

The way DDE works is that one Windows application (called the client) tells another Windows application (called the server) that it wants information. (Technically, a DDE conversation is between two *windows*, and from the point of view of Microsoft Windows it turns out that most controls are windows as, of course, are forms themselves.)

This is called setting up a DDE conversation or DDE link. For Visual Basic, only forms can be DDE servers, but text boxes, picture boxes, or labels can be DDE clients. Although technically only forms can be servers, the controls on the form will probably be providing the information via their properties, so this isn't usually much of a problem. Information generally flows from the server to the client, although the client can, if necessary, send information back to the server.

Windows allows an application to engage in many DDE conversations at the same time. An application can even play the role of server and client simultaneously. For example, your Visual Basic project can send information to Word for Windows while receiving it from Excel. However, only one piece of information may be sent at any one time.

You must know the name of the application you want to talk to. If an application supports DDE, the DDE name will be given in the documentation. For example, as far as DDE is concerned, the name for Word for Windows is "WinWord." The DDE name for Excel is still "Excel." The DDE name for any Visual Basic form acting as a DDE server is the name you chose when you made it into an executable file. If you are running the project within the Visual Basic development environment, the DDE name is the name of the project without any extension.

Next, you need to know the *topic* of the DDE conversation. Usually this is a specific filename. For example, Excel recognizes a full file name (a path name) ending in .XLS or .XLC as a suitable topic. Finally, you need to know what you are currently talking about. This is called the *item* of the DDE conversation. For example, if Excel is the DDE server, the item for a DDE conversation could be a cell or range of cells. If Visual Basic is the DDE server, the control name of a picture box, text box, or label can be the item for a DDE conversation.

**note:** *The one exception to this rule is the System topic. This allows a program to find out information about the application as a whole (for instance, what data formats it supports, what the other valid topics are, and so on). The System topic also allows you access to DDEExecute commands, which typically run macros (or, in the case of Visual Basic, become parameters to subroutines).*

You can have three kinds of DDE conversations (links). A *hot link* means that the server sends the data contained in the item specified for the DDE conversation whenever it changes in the server application. Hot links occur in real time. A *cold link* means that the client must explicitly request updates. A *notification link* is one where the server tells the client that data has changed, but the destination is only changed after a LinkRequest method is processed (see below for this event).

## Creating DDE Links at Design Time

This section uses Microsoft Excel for the examples. If you do not have Excel, you should still be able to follow the discussion. All you need to know is that spreadsheets like Excel are organized into rows and columns and that Excel, like Visual Basic itself, has a Copy menu on its main menu bar with similar items.

For the following discussion, start up a new project and add a text box and label to it. Next, start up Excel (or imagine that you are starting it). You might want to resize the windows and change the Caption property for the label to look something like the screen in Figure 15-4.

To set up a client link with Excel as the DDE server and the contents of the first row and column as the item for this DDE conversation, do the following:

1. Move to the Excel window and highlight (select) the contents of the cell in the first row and first column.

2. From the Edit menu in Excel, choose the Copy command.

3. Move to the Visual Basic window and select the text box by moving the mouse and clicking.

4. From the Edit menu in Visual Basic, choose Paste Link. (If you followed steps 1 through 3, this should be enabled.)

**Figure 15-4**

Excel and Visual Basic windows for DDE example

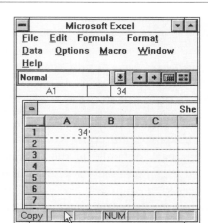
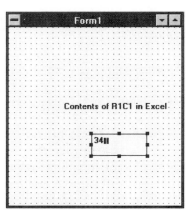

Now you can test whether the link was successfully made. For this, move back to the Excel window and type something in the cell in the first row and first column. Whatever you type should instantaneously appear in the text box in the Visual Basic window, because links made at design time are hot links. In addition, every time the DDE server updates the information for a Visual Basic control acting as the DDE client, Visual Basic generates the Change event. This lets you act on the information in real time as well.

Note that when you switch from designing a Visual Basic project to running it within the development environment, Visual Basic must break the DDE link. Many applications will automatically attempt to reestablish the DDE link, but you may find that server links, especially, need to be established by code. (See the section "Links via Code" later in this chapter.)

This link is permanent. If you save the project, Visual Basic preserves the information about the link as the value of certain properties. You'll see these properties in the next section. In particular, try the following for the DDE link set up previously:

1. Close Excel and save the Visual Basic project.

2. Start up a new project temporarily.

3. Open the Visual Basic project with the DDE link.

You may see the message box given here if Visual Basic can not start up Excel:

As the message box indicates, Visual Basic will always attempt to start up the application that was the server for a DDE conversation set up at design time.

You can also make a Visual Basic form the server at design time (although ultimately the contents of a control provide the data) by essentially interchanging the roles of Visual Basic and Excel in the previous outline. For example, to have the contents of a text box sent automatically to the cell in the first row and first column of an Excel spreadsheet, follow these steps:

1. In the Visual Basic project, select the text box.

2. From the Edit menu in Visual Basic, choose the Copy command.

3. Move to the Excel window and select the cell in the first column and first row.

4. From the Edit menu in Excel, choose Paste Link.

As before, this link is permanent, but this time Excel will tell Windows to try to start up the Visual Basic project when you load this spreadsheet into Excel.

## DDE Properties

As you might expect, DDE conversations—at least as far as Visual Basic is concerned—are determined by the value of certain properties. Manipulating the values of these properties via code will make your DDE conversations far more flexible than DDE links made at design time can ever be.

*LinkTopic*   The value of the LinkTopic property always takes the form

> ServerName | *Topic*

The name of the application is separated from the topic by the pipe symbol ( | , found above the backslash on most keyboards, or ASCII code 124). For example, for the default Excel worksheet SHEET1.XLS found in the \EXCEL directory, this property takes the form

> Excel | C:\EXCEL\SHEET1.XLS

You can set the value of this property for any text box, picture box, or label.

If a Visual Basic form is acting as the server, the LinkTopic property for the form determines which DDE requests the form will respond to. For example, suppose the name of the Visual Basic project is IaServer and you set the LinkTopic property of a form in that project to AskForInfo. Then any DDE client application that asks for a conversation named

> IaServer | AskForInfo

will link up with the project named IaServer. Moreover, if this project were made into an .EXE file that Windows had access to, then Windows would try to start it up. Any controls on the form whose link property was AskForInfo could be items for this DDE link.

If you change the LinkTopic property at design time or run time, all conversations on that topic are ended. This lets client applications switch topics.

**LinkItem** The LinkItem property identifies what data is actually going to be passed from server to client. For example, if Excel was the server, the item can be R1C1—the contents of the cell in the first row and first column. The syntax for this property is

   [*FormName.*] *ControlName.LinkItem* = *Item$*

You only set the LinkItem for the client control, so ControlName in the previous syntax statement must identify a text box, picture box, or label. *Item$* is the string expression that identifies the item the server should send, such as R1C1.

If the DDE server determines what kind of item to send, the value of the LinkItem property is set to the string "DDE_LINK" for the first link, "DDE_LINK2" for the second, and so on. These generic LinkItems are used if the application doesn't have a way to name items systematically, as Excel does by rows and columns. Visual Basic uses the control name of the control for the DDE item.

**LinkMode** Setting the LinkTopic and LinkItem properties is not enough to activate a DDE link; you must also change the LinkMode property to Hot (a value of 1) or Cold (a value of 2). The default value of this property is None (0). Once you change the LinkMode property to a nonzero value, Visual Basic tries to establish the link using whatever topic you specified as the value of the LinkTopic property.

Any time you change the value of LinkMode, Visual Basic ends the link. The standard programming practice is to set LinkMode to 0 (None) before you fiddle with the LinkTopic or LinkItem properties.

**LinkTimeOut** The LinkTimeOut property specifies how long Visual Basic will try to establish the link. The default value is five seconds. However, the

LinkTimeOut property uses tenths of seconds, so to double the time to ten seconds, for example, change the value of this property to 100 (instead of the default value of 50). (Some applications are slower to respond than others.)

## The DDE Events

There are four link events. Like any Visual Basic events, you can write code to respond to these events as you see fit. The four events are described here.

**LinkOpen** Visual Basic generates the LinkOpen event when a DDE link succeeds. One common use of this event procedure is to generate a message telling the user that the link is open, for example:

```
Sub Picture1_LinkOpen(Cancel As Integer)
  M$ = "DDE link made with" + Picture1.LinkTopic
  M$ = M$ + " concerning "+ Picture1.LinkItem
  MsgBox M$
End Sub
```

If you change the value of the Cancel parameter to a nonzero value (True) in the course of a LinkOpen event procedure, Visual Basic will not immediately cancel the link.

**LinkClose** The template for the LinkClose event procedure starts out like

Sub *FormName*_LinkClose( )

for forms or

Sub *ControlName*_LinkClose([*Index As Integer*])

for controls. As always, the optional index parameter identifies an element of a control array. Visual Basic calls this event procedure when the DDE link ends.

**LinkExecute** The LinkExecute event procedure is used only when the DDE client wants the DDE server to do something. This event is generated when the DDE client sends a command to the server (see the upcoming section "The DDE Methods"). The template for this event procedure starts out like this:

Sub Form_LinkExecute(*CommandString As String, Cancel As Integer*)

The syntax for the command string depends completely on the application you are talking to. You must consult the documentation provided with that application to see what to say.

▬▬▬▬

*LinkError* Visual Basic calls the LinkError event procedure whenever something goes wrong in a DDE conversation. The syntax for this event procedure template starts out like this for forms:

Sub Form_LinkError(LinkErr As Integer)

and like this for controls:

Sub *ControlName*_LinkError(LinkErr As Integer)

There are 12 possible error codes. Visual Basic will supply these as the value of the LinkErr parameter. The following table gives these codes:

| LinkErr Value | Reason |
|---|---|
| 1 | The other application requested data in the wrong format |
| 2 | The other application tried to get data before a link was established |
| 3 | The other application tried to send data before a link was established |
| 4 | The other application tried to change an item before establishing a link |
| 5 | The other application tried to poke data (see the LinkPoke method in the next section) before a link was established |
| 6 | After you cut links by changing LinkMode to 0 (None), the other application tried to continue the conversation |
| 7 | Too many DDE links for Windows to handle |
| 8 | Text too long to send via DDE |
| 9 | Client specified wrong control array index |
| 10 | Unexpected DDE message |
| 11 | Too little memory for DDE |
| 12 | The server tried to switch roles and become the client |

The LinkError event is not generated for ordinary run-time errors, such as your project accepting a value of 0 from a server and then trying to divide by 0. You handle these errors by using an ordinary error trap (see Chapter 8). Roughly speaking, Visual Basic generates the LinkError event only when no code is running—for example, when a client tries unsuccessfully to send data automatically because of a previously established hot link.

*LinkNotify*  This event occurs only when the LinkMode property is set to 3 (Notify). This is used when the server has changed the source and needs to tell the client that. Use the LinkRequest method to actually get the new data.

## The DDE Methods

There are four DDE methods you can use with Visual Basic controls that are acting as clients for a DDE link.

*LinkExecute*  Use the LinkExecute method to send a command to the DDE server. The syntax for this method is

    ControlName.LinkExecute *CommandString$*

where, as with the LinkExecute event procedure, the form of the command string depends on what the server application will accept.

*LinkPoke*  The LinkPoke method is the only way for a DDE client to send data to the server. You can use this method to transfer the contents of any DDE client control on your Visual Basic project to the server. The syntax for this method takes the form

    ControlName.LinkPoke

If the client control is a text box, Visual Basic sends the string that is the value of the Text property. For a label, it's the value of the Caption property. For a picture box, it's the value of the Picture property.

■

***LinkRequest***  You use the LinkRequest method to request the DDE server to send information to the control. This method is needed only if you've set the value of LinkMode to 2 (Cold). (Recall that for hot links, the server sends updates automatically.) The syntax for this method takes the form

    ControlName.LinkRequest

■

***LinkSend***  The LinkSend method is used when you have a form acting as a DDE server and want to send the contents of a picture box. Although hot links normally work automatically, the designers of Visual Basic felt that resending the contents of a picture box every time even one pixel is changed would cut down performance too much. For this reason, you must use the LinkSend method to tell the DDE client that the contents of a picture box have changed. (For example, you could use this method after you make a significant change to the image stored in a picture box.) The syntax for this method takes the form

    PictureBoxControlName.LinkSend

The picture box must be a control on the form that is the DDE server.

## Links via Code

As an example of putting all the link properties and methods together, suppose you want to have a Visual Basic project set up a hot DDE link with an Excel spreadsheet. The user should be allowed to supply the full pathname for the spreadsheet as well as the row and column he or she wants to keep tabs on. The form might look like the one in Figure 15-5. Notice that in this figure there are four labels, four text boxes, and a command button to start the link as well as one to end the program. Suppose you set the control names for the text boxes to be NameOfFile, RowNumber, ColumnNumber, and CellData. The command buttons might have control names of MakeLink and Quit.

Here's the MakeLink_Click event procedure that does all the work:

```
Sub MakeLink_Click()
  Const HOT = 1, NONE = 0
```

**Figure 15-5**

Form for example setting DDE links via code

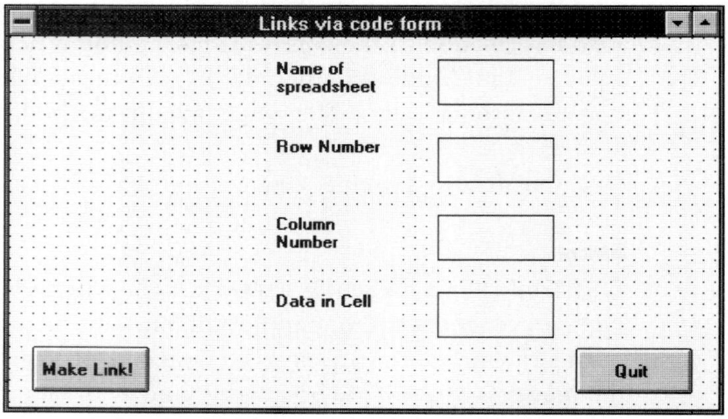

```
On Error GoTo ErrorHandler
StartExcel$ = "C:\EXCEL\EXCEL" + NameOfFile.Text
X% = Shell(StartExcel$)
CellData.LinkMode = NONE
Topic$ = "Excel|" + NameOfFile.Text
CellData.LinkTopic = Topic$

Item$ = "R" + LTrim$(RTrim$(RowNumber.Text))
Item$ = Item$ + "C" + LTrim$(RTrim$(ColumnNumber.Text))
CellData.LinkItem = Item$
CellData.LinkMode = HOT
Exit Sub

Errorhandler:
  M$ = Error$(Err)
  MsgBox(M$)
End Sub
```

The idea behind this event procedure is simple. You assume the text box named NameOfFile has the full pathname of the Excel file you want to communicate with. You then use the Shell command to start up Excel for that file. Next, you switch LinkMode to None to cut any links for the text box that will hold the Excel information. The LinkTopic property is set to the correct form using the pipe symbol (|), and then all spaces are stripped from the contents of the two text boxes that hold the row and column information. Finally, you set LinkItem to the right value and make the link hot.

The error handler in the preceding procedure just describes the error to the user; it doesn't allow the user to correct it. (You saw in Chapter 8 how to use the Resume statement to allow this.) Finally, notice that the previous code does not take into account the fact that an instance of Excel may already be running. You can easily add the code to take care of this situation.

## ADDING HOT LINK OPTIONS TO A VISUAL BASIC PROJECT

Although using PasteLink and Copy to start DDE hot links is inflexible, there are still times when you want to add this capability to your Visual Basic projects. Suppose you add a menu subitem with a control name of PasteLink to your project. There are four steps you must follow in writing the code to activate a PasteLink menu item. Usually you'll add them to the Click event procedure:

1. Find out from the clipboard what type of information is stored there. You do this with the statement

   Item$ = Clipboard.GetText(&HBF00)

   (You can also use the constant CF_LINK if you add the CONSTANT.TXT file to your project.) The data is always in the form

   ApplicationName | Topic!Item

2. Parse the string data obtained in step 1 into the name of the application, the topic, and the item.

3. Use the results from step 2 to set the LinkTopic and LinkItem properties for the active control (the one you're pasting into).

The following listing implements this outline and adds the feature of telling the user if he or she can't make the link. First, you need these constants:

```
Const CF_LINK = &HBF00, CF_DIB = 8, CF_BITMAP = 2
Const CF_TEXT = 1, NONE = 0
Const HOT = 1
```

Next, you need the function that tells the user if he or she can use PasteLink. (If this is impossible, you can disable the PasteLink item from the menu.)

```
Function CanIPaste() As Integer
  CanIPaste = False
  If Not(Clipboard.GetFormat(CF_LINK)) Then
    MsgBox("Nothing to link to!")
    Exit Function
  End If
  If TypeOf Screen.ActiveControl Is PictureBox Then
    If Clipboard.GetFormat(CF_TEXT) Then
      MsgBox "Only text in clipboard!"
      Exit Function
    ElseIf Clipboard.GetFormat(CF_BITMAP) Then
      CanIPaste = True
    End If
  End If
  If TypeOf Screen.ActiveControl Is TextBox Then
    If Clipboard.GetFormat(CF_TEXT) Then
      CanIPaste = True
    Else
      MsgBox("Only images in Clipboard!")
      Exit Function
    End If
  End If
End Sub
```

Now the PasteLink_Click event procedure can use the results of the CanIPaste function:

```
Sub PasteLink_Click()
  If Not CanIPaste Then Exit Sub
  LinkInfo$ = Clipboard.GetText(CF_Link)
  LocOfBang = Instr(LinkInfo$,"!")
  If LocOfBang <> 0 Then
    Screen.ActiveControl.LinkMode = NONE
    Screen.ActiveControl.LinkTopic =_
Left$(LinkInfo$,LocOfBang-1)
    Screen.ActiveControl.LinkItem =_
Mid$(LinkInfo$,LocOfBang+1)
    Screen.ActiveControl.LinkMode = HOT
  ElseIf Instr(LinkInfo$,"|") Then
    Screen.ActiveControl.LinkMode = NONE
    Screen.ActiveControl.LinkTopic = LinkInfo$
    Screen.ActiveControl.LinkItem$ =""
    Screen.ActiveControl.LinkMode = HOT
```

```
      End If
End Sub
```

What this procedure does is find the location of the ! separator and use that to isolate LinkTopic and LinkItem. Then it switches LinkMode to hot. If it can't find the ! separator, it looks for the | separator.

You can create a server link similarly via a copy command. This time, what you do is place the information needed, using the same format as before:

ApplicationName | *Topic!Item*

One problem is that *Item* must be the control name for the control supplying the information. Unfortunately, Visual Basic has no way to give the control name of a control while a project is running. The usual way around this is, at design time, to set the value of the Tag property of the control to the control name. (In general, setting the Tag property of a control at design time lets you get at information that is not available at run time.)

It's a good idea to send the contents of the control that will supply the information at the same time you send the link information. You can send more than one piece of data to the clipboard, provided that the formats are different for each piece. The code attached to a Copy_Click event procedure might look like this:

```
Sub Copy_Click()
  If Not(ControlOK) Then
    MsgBox("This procedure only works for picture boxes and _
text boxes!")  'this and preceding are one line
    Exit Sub
  End If
  Clipboard.Clear
  Name$ = AppName + "|" + LinkTopic
  Name$ = Name$ = "!" +Screen.ActiveControl.Tag
  If TypeOfScreen.ActiveControl Is TextBox Then
    Clipboard.SetText Name$, CF_LINK
    Clipboard.SetText Screen.ActiveControl.Text
  ElseIf TypeOfScreen.ActiveControl Is PictureBox Then
    Clipboard.SetText Name$, CF_LINK
    Clipboard.SetText Screen.ActiveControl.Picture
  End If
End Sub
```

This code assumes that the name of the application is given by the value of the global string variable called AppName and that the Tag property of the control contains the control name. It also assumes that you have already written a function called ControlOk that has the value True if the active control is a picture box or text box; otherwise, the value of this function should be False.

# OLE 2

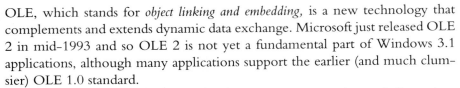

OLE, which stands for *object linking and embedding,* is a new technology that complements and extends dynamic data exchange. Microsoft just released OLE 2 in mid-1993 and so OLE 2 is not yet a fundamental part of Windows 3.1 applications, although many applications support the earlier (and much clumsier) OLE 1.0 standard.

OLE goes beyond DDE in that, instead of merely transferring information, information passed with OLE is presented in the same way it would appear in the originating application. Spreadsheets appear as spreadsheets, word-processed documents as they would in the word processor, and so on. When you add an OLE 2 client control to your Visual Basic project, you give the user a bridge to another Windows application.

There are three parts to OLE. The *objects* are the data supplied by the Windows applications that support OLE—for example, an Excel worksheet (or, more likely, part of an Excel worksheet).

To understand *linking,* imagine that you are part of the group working on this book. Besides the author, there are a technical editor, a copyeditor, a proofreader, and others involved. The most efficient method for your group to work would be to maintain a single copy of the document and have each person involved be able to link to it and make changes. *There should still be only one copy of the document* (on a central server) *involved*; that way your group doesn't have to worry about important changes being missed. (In the jargon, it allows work in a parallel rather than a serial way.) With a linked object, the data stays in the application that created it. Think of linking as attaching a chain to preexisting data—like any chained objects, you can effect changes by jerking on the chain. Technically what linking does is insert a placeholder into the Visual Basic application and an image of the data is stored in the OLE 2 control.

The idea of the *embedding* part of OLE is that you create documents that integrate various Windows applications under one roof. Embedding in OLE 2 allows the custom control to maintain the data in the object inside itself. When Visual Basic activates the OLE 2 control, control switches back to the application that created the data and you can use that application's power to modify the data in place.

One of the main ideas behind the introduction of OLE was that Microsoft wanted to get users away from thinking of applications as being paramount. Instead you think of the document itself as central. For example, suppose you are preparing a complicated report that uses spreadsheet data and a graphics package. You want parts of the document to be under the control of the word processor and parts to be under the control of the spreadsheet. In OLE 2, the other application temporarily takes over to work with the data embedded in the control. When you embed an object in an OLE client control, then no other application can access the data (as opposed to linking it where they can). Moreover, the application that created the embedded data is automatically started up whenever the user works with the embedded data.

## Using OLE

When you add an OLE 2 client control to your Visual Basic projects, you create what Microsoft calls an *OLE compound document*. (In fact, the moment you add a client control, Visual Basic pops up a dialog box asking you for the name of the application it should hook into. See the next section for more on this dialog box.) The OLE client control is one of the three custom tools supplied with the standard edition of Visual Basic; the icon is at the bottom of the toolbox with a grid and an "OLE 2" in a box.

As with DDE, your Visual Basic project can be the *client* (or *container*) application that receives the information or the *server* (*source*) application that sends it out. In most cases with OLE, your Visual Basic project receives the information and serves as the client. In any case, the OLE control supplied with Visual Basic is an OLE client control and does not allow a Visual Basic application to become an OLE server. This would have to be done by writing code or using a custom control.

Some important terminology for dealing with OLE is explained in the following sections.

**OLE Objects** This is any data the OLE control can work with. It can be a single graph, a range of cells in a spreadsheet, a whole spreadsheet, or part or all of a word–processed document.

**OLE Class** This is the application that produces the OLE object. Any application that supports OLE has a unique OLE class name. For example, "Word-Document" or "ExcelWorksheet." (Class names can be case-sensitive.) You can get a list of the class names available by clicking on the ellipses for the Class property in the Property window.

## Using OLE 2 at Design Time

Compared to OLE 1.0, creating links or embeddings at design time is easy. Essentially, you need only work with the dialog boxes that will be described in this section.

If you have added an OLE 2 client control to a form, you immediately got a dialog box like Figure 15-6. (The more applications you have, the more items will appear.) This gives you the names of all the Windows applications you can hook into. As Figure 15-6 indicates, you can have the object show up as an icon or with the data visible in the OLE 2 control. The two radio buttons on the far left determine whether you will work with an existing file created by the application (a linked object) or want the other application to create one anew (an embedded object). If you choose to link the control by choosing the Create from File option, the dialog box changes to Figure 15-7. You can click on the Browse button to open a dialog box that lets you pick the file. When you have done that check the Link box in Figure 15-7.

**note:** *You can click on cancel if you want to set the OLE properties via code. You do not need to use this dialog box in order to work with OLE. In fact, if you create an executable file with an OLE connection made at design time, the file will be much larger than if you create the connection at run time with code.*

**Figure 15-6**

Insert Object dialog box for OLE control

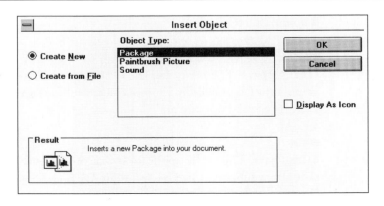

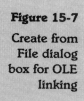

**Figure 15-7**

Create from File dialog box for OLE linking

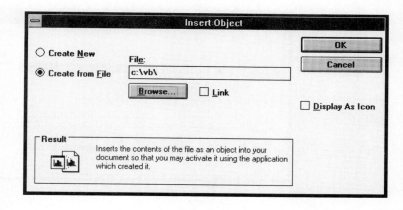

## Paste Special

Sometimes you want to create linked or embedded objects by using information stored in the Windows clipboard to determine the SourceDoc and SourceItem properties. To do this you first need to copy the data from the application to the clipboard by using the copy command in the application. You then need to use the Paste Special dialog box which is available at design time by clicking the right mouse button when the focus is in the OLE control and choosing Paste Special from the pop-up menu that results. This dialog box automatically examines the contents of the clipboard to determine the needed OLE properties. Figure 15-8 shows this dialog box. If you want to create an embedded object, click the Paste option button; for a linked object choose Paste Link and then click OK.

## The OLE Properties

As you might expect, the dialog box only makes it simpler to set the properties of the OLE control. You can always change them via the Property window or code (and of course you will have to do this to enable OLE at run time).

For example, the Icon/Display Data choice in Figure 15-6 actually sets the DisplayType property. The SizeMode property allows you to change how the control looks at run time. If the value is 0 then the control clips the data displayed at run time. If you want to stretch the image to fit the current size of the OLE control, set the value of this property to be 1. Finally, you can have the control automatically resize the control (value = 2).

**Figure 15-8**

**Paste Special dialog box**

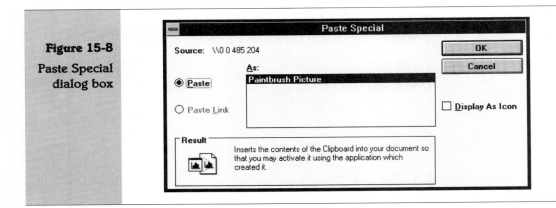

The dialog box that pops up is also setting the crucial *Class* property which specifies the application containing the data. The *OLETypeAction* property determines what type of object you have created. Is it linked, embedded, or either? The *SourceDoc* property gives the name of the linked object or the file to be used as a template for an embedded object. The *SourceItem* property is used for linked objects to specify what portion of the linked document the Visual Basic application can work with. (For example a spreadsheet range might be indicated by setting this property to "R1C1:R1C10.")

### THE ACTION PROPERTY

Finally, there is the very important *Action* property which specifies just exactly what should be done to the OLE object. Do you want to update the object, create the object, delete the object, save the information in the object to a file, retrieve it from a file, and so on? The syntax is always

OLEControlName.Action = *Value*

What follows is a short discussion of what settings of this property do. (The symbolic constant stored in CONSTANT.TXT is also given.)

■■■■

*0 (Constant is OLE_CREATE_EMBED)* This creates an embedded OLE object. To do this, you must first set (via the OLE dialog box or code) both the Class and OleTypeAllowed properties. Recall that the OleTypeAllowed property is 1 for Embedded or 2 for either and the Class property determines the type of OLE object. (Class names are available from the OLE dialog box or the

Property window.) When you create a new embedded OLE object, the application must either be active (use AppActivate) or in the system's path.

**1 (OLE_CREATE_LINK)** This creates a linked OLE object from an existing file. To do this first set the OleTypeAllowed and SourceDoc properties. In this case the OleTypeAllowed is 0 (Linked) or 2 (Either).

The SourceDoc property gives the name of the file for the linked object. If you want to restrict yourself to working with a portion of the linked object, set the SourceItem property as well.

Just as with embedding a document, the application must either be active or in the path.

**4 (OLE_COPY)** This sends all the data and linking properties of the object to the Windows clipboard. Both embedded and linked information can be copied to the clipboard.

**5 (OLE_PASTE)** This copies data from the clipboard to an OLE control. You'll need to check the PasteOK property of the control.

**6 (OLE_UPDATE)** This is a very important action because it pulls the current data from the application and gives you a view of it in the OLE control.

**7 (OLE_ACTIVATE)** This activates an OLE object. To use this action, you will need to set the Verb property of the control which specifies what operation you want performed.

**note:** *If you set the AutoActivate property of the control to double-click (value = 2), the OLE control will automatically activate the current object when the user double-clicks in the control. If the application supports "In Place Activation" then you can arrange it so that the application is activated whenever the OLE control gets the focus (set AutoActivate to 1).*

**9 (OLE_CLOSE)** This is used only for embedded objects since it closes the OLE object and cancels the connection with the application that controlled the object.

**10  (OLE_DELETE)**  Use this if you want to delete the object. OLE Objects are automatically deleted when a form is closed.

**11  (OLE_SAVE_TO_FILE)**  If the OLE object is embedded, then this action is vital because the OLE control data is maintained by the OLE control and will be lost unless you save it by tying together the necessary code with setting the Action property to this value (see below).

If the OLE object is linked, then only the link information and an image of the data is saved to the specified file. This is because the actual object's data is stored in the file that was created and maintained by the other application.

The code to save the information will always look something like this:

```
Sub SaveOLE_Click
  Dim FileNum As Integer

  FileNum = FreeFile
  Open Objectname$ For Binary As #FileNum
  OLECLIent1.FileNumber = FileNum
  OLEClient1.Action = 11    'Action = 11 is SaveToFile
  Close #FileNum
End Sub
```

This program opens the file using the value of the form-level variable Object-Name$ in binary mode. (Files for handling OLE data must be opened in binary mode.) We then use the correct value of the Action property to tell Visual Basic to save the data.

**12  (READ_FROM_FILE)**  If you used the SaveToFile action discussed previously, this Action value reloads an OLE object from the data file created using the SaveToFile action. The code needed for this action is similar to that for saving data, except, of course, this time you'll be reading the data back.

**14  (INSERT_OBJ_DLG)**  This pops up the same Insert Object dialog box that Visual Basic uses when you put an OLE control on a form. At run time, use this action to allow the user a friendly way to create a linked or embedded object.

*15 (OLE_PASTE_SPECIAL_DLG)* This displays the Paste Special dialog box. At run time, you display this dialog to allow the user to paste an object from the clipboard.

*17 (OLE_FETCH_VERBS)* Gets the list of verbs supported by the application.

*18 (OLE_SAVE_TO_OLE1FILE)* Use this if you need backward compatibility with the earlier version of OLE.

## MORE ON CREATING OLE CONNECTIONS AT RUN TIME

To create a linked object at run time

1. Set the SourceDoc property to the name of the file.

2. Set the Action property to OLE_CREATE_LINK.

   (If the AutoActivate property is set to 2, then these steps are not needed.)

To create an embedded object at run time

1. Set the Class property to determine the object used.

2. Set the SourceDoc property to the name of the template to use.

3. Set the Action property to OLE_CREATE_EMBED.

Finally, in the future, applications may allow you to perform many actions on OLE data. The list of these will be stored in the Verbs collection. At present, most applications only support Edit and Play. (If you set AutoVerb to True for the OLE control then after clicking the right mouse button, instead of a pop-up menu, the user will see a list of the verb actions he or she can ask the server application to perform on the data.)

# Chapter 16

# Recursion

**r**E C U R S I O N is a general method of solving problems by reducing them to simpler problems of a similar type. For the experienced programmer, thinking recursively presents a unique perspective on certain problems, often leading to particularly elegant solutions and, therefore, equally elegant programs. In Visual Basic, you usually use recursion in general procedures to make event procedures or the whole project run more smoothly or quickly. For example, this chapter shows you how to use recursion to build three very fast sorting routines. Among them is what most programmers regard as the best general-purpose sort—it's called, naturally enough, Quicksort.

This chapter also shows you how recursion makes it easy to construct efficient indexes and so build a cross-reference program to make your programming jobs easier. This chapter also has a section that introduces you to recursive graphics, called *fractals*. The screen in Figure 16-1 shows an example of the Koch Snowflake. This is just one of the figures that can be drawn using the programs in this section.

**Figure 16-1**

**A fractal drawing**

Like many powerful tools, recursion can be overused. At the end of this chapter, you will find a short section on when not to use recursion.

If you are an experienced GW-BASIC programmer, you may be wondering why you haven't used recursion before. In fact, recursion is not supported in GW-BASIC, and in spite of its power, recursion is too often slighted in books on languages like QuickBASIC and Visual Basic that do support it. This is sometimes because recursion is thought of as too sophisticated for BASIC, but modern BASICs (like Visual Basic) are essentially as powerful as languages like Pascal and C, where recursion is commonly used. Another reason is that recursion is sometimes thought of as a mysterious, even mystical, process, but this reputation is undeserved. See, for example, the Pulitzer prize-winning book, *Gödel, Escher, Bach,* by Douglas Hofstadter (New York: Basic Books, 1979). It's a book some people swear by and others swear at.

## Getting Started with Recursion

Before this chapter shows you how to program recursive procedures and functions, let's look at some typical examples of recursive problem solving. Discovering a recursive solution to at least one problem seems innate—at least with children. Have you ever met a three-year-old who didn't intuitively know how to solve the following problem with the solution given here:

PROBLEM:        How do I deal with my parents?
SOLUTION:       Deal with father first, then deal with mother (or vice versa).

This method of solving a problem is, naturally enough, called *divide and conquer,* and it clearly has a long history.

For a more serious example of divide and conquer, consider the following old problem: You have 7 balls and a balance scale. One ball is heavier than the other 6. Find the heaviest ball in just two weighings. To solve this, first try a simpler case—3 balls. Notice that if you try to balance 2 balls, there are only two possibilities:

◆ They balance (in which case the remaining ball is the heaviest).

◆ They don't balance (in which case the heaviest one is obvious).

Now, to do the 7-ball problem, divide the balls into two groups of 3 with 1 left over. If they balance, then, as before, the heaviest one is the one left over. If they don't balance, then whichever side is heavier is also obvious. This reduces the problem to the previous case. (Similarly, you can do 15 balls in three weighings, 31 in four, and so forth.)

As a final example of divide and conquer, here's an outline of a recursive method for sorting (called merge sort) that you'll see soon. Merge sort follows this outline:

    To SORT a LIST
      If a list has one entry stop
    Otherwise:
      SORT(the first half)
      SORT(the second half)
      Combine (merge) the two halves

As long as the operation of combining the two takes substantially less time than the sorting process, you have a viable method of sorting. As you'll soon see, it does take less time.

Finally, any operation on a directory that is supposed to work similarly on subdirectories will need recursion when the operation is programmed. For example, when you use

    XCOPY *.* *NewPath* /S

to copy files in all subdirectories to a new place, you are using recursion. The XCOPY routine constantly calls itself on lower and lower subdirectories until it finishes.

A recursive solution to a problem will always follow this outline:

    Solve recursively (problem)
        If the problem is trivial, do the obvious
        Simplify the problem
      Solve recursively (simpler problem)
        (Possibly) combine the solution to the simpler problem(s)
        into a solution of the original problem

A recursive procedure constantly calls itself, each time in a simpler situation, until it gets to the trivial case, at which point it stops. (There's also indirect recursion, where a function or procedure calls itself via an intermediary. For example, function A calls function B, which in turn calls function C, which calls function A, and so on.)

## Recursive Functions

You know a function can call another function. (These are called nested function calls.) Recursion occurs when a function eventually calls itself. Before looking at an example of a recursive program in Visual Basic, stop and think for a second what Visual Basic must do when one function calls another. Obviously, Visual Basic has to communicate the current value or location of all the parameter variables to the new function. To do this, Visual Basic places the locations of the variables (or the location of a copy of the values, if you are passing by value) to a reserved area in its memory called the *stack*. Now suppose this second function needs the results from a third function. This requires yet another storing of the locations of variables, and so on. However, this process can take place regardless of the nature of the other functions. It is this that makes recursion possible.

Here's an example. The factorial of a positive integer is the product of the numbers from 1 up to the integer and the custom is to use the ! to symbolize it. For example:

| | |
|---|---|
| $2! = 2*1$ | $(=2)$ |
| $3! = 3*2*1$ | $(=6)$ |
| $4! = 4*3*2*1$ | $(=4*3! = 24)$ |
| $5! = 5*4!$ | |

As you can see, the factorial of an integer can be written using the factorial of the previous integer and a multiplication. Using this idea, here's a recursive definition of the factorial:

```
Function Factorial (N As Integer) As Long
  If N <= 1 Then
    Factorial = 1                        'factorial not usually
  Else                                   'defined for N<0
    Factorial = N * Factorial(N - 1)     'note the call to
  End If                                 'itself in a simpler
End Function                             'situation
```

Suppose you now write Print Factorial(4). Then Visual Basic does the following:

1. It calls the function with N = 4. The first statement processed is the If-Then test. Since the If clause is false, it processes the Else clause.

2. This says compute 4*Factorial(3).

3. It tries to compute Factorial(3). And so it now has to start building up its stack. The stack will hold partial results—those obtained to date. Think of what gets pushed onto the stack as a little card containing the status, location, and values of all the variables as well as what is still left "up in the air." In this case, the card would say

    3. Need to compute 4 * (an as yet unknown number = Factorial(3))

4. Now Visual Basic repeats the process, calling the factorial function with a variable now having the value 3. And so another card gets pushed onto the stack:

    2. Need to compute 3  * (an as yet unknown number = Factorial(2))

5. Repeat the process again so the stack contains three cards:

    1. Need to compute 2 *  (an as yet unknown number = Factorial(1))

Now Visual Basic does one final call, with the variable N having the value 1, and sets up a fourth card. But at this point the process can stop—the top card no longer contains an unknown quantity. By the first clause, Factorial(1) is 1, so Visual Basic can start "popping the stack." The results of the top card (the number 1) feed into the second card. Now Visual Basic can figure out what the second card stands for (the number 2), and so Visual Basic can pop the stack one more time and feed the information accumulated to the third card (the number 6). Finally, Visual Basic feeds the results to the bottom card and comes out with 24 = 4!. Since the stack is empty, this is the answer. Figure 16-2 shows you one way of imagining the stack.

The explanation of the process, of course, takes much longer than the actual solution via Visual Basic. Visual Basic keeps track of the partial results of any recursive operation via its stack. You don't need to be aware of the stack—most of the time. The only time you do worry about the stack is when it "overflows" and your program crashes or behaves erratically. The disastrous error message you'll see is number 28, "Out of stack space." Unfortunately, unlike in QuickBASIC or Visual Basic for DOS, where you can enlarge the stack, you have to rely on Windows to handle the stack; there is no way to enlarge the stack from within a Visual Basic program. This is not usually a problem, however, as the stack has more than enough for normal needs. (The number of recursive calls you can make varies with how much information the stack needs to keep track of. With minimal use of the stack in each call you can get around 450 recursive calls. Heavy use of the stack, where many variables are being passed, could cut this down by a factor of 2.)

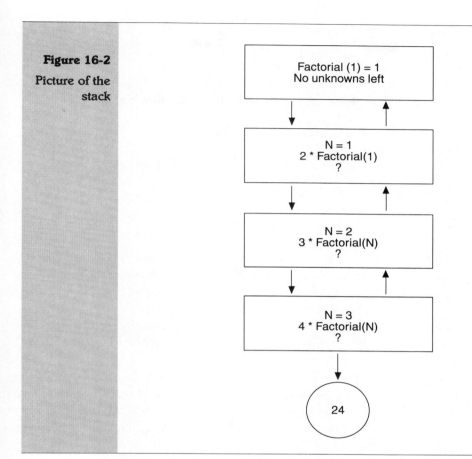

**Figure 16-2**

Picture of the stack

There are many other examples of recursive functions. For example, the Fibonacci numbers are defined as follows:

◆ The first Fibonacci number is 1 (in symbols, Fib(1) = 1).

◆ The second Fibonacci number is also 1 (in symbols, Fib(2) = 1).

◆ From that point on, the next Fibonacci number is the sum of the two preceding ones (in symbols, Fib($n$) = Fib($n$–1) + Fib($n$–2)).

For example:

$$Fib(3) = Fib(2) + Fib(1) \quad (= 1 + 1 = 2)$$
$$Fib(4) = Fib(3) + Fib(2) \quad (= 2 + 1 = 3)$$
$$Fib(5) = Fib(4) + Fib(3) \quad (= 3 + 2 = 5)$$

and so on. The recursive definition of the Fibonacci numbers is almost simple:

```
Function Fib (N As Integer) As Integer
  If N <= 2 Then
    Fib = 1                    'Making negative Fibonacci numbers = 1
  Else
    Fib = Fib(N - 1) + Fib(N - 2)
  End If
End Function
```

Note the pattern. The simple case is taken care of first. This is followed by reducing the calculation to a simpler case. Finally, the results of the simpler case or cases are combined to finish the definition. (Also, the Fibonacci numbers were arbitrarily defined at negative N to be 1.)

However elegant this may seem, it turns out to be an incredibly inefficient way to calculate these numbers. See the section "When Not to Use Recursion" later in this chapter for more on this.

As a final example of a recursive function, consider the calculation of the greatest common divisor (GCD) of two numbers. (For those who have forgotten their high school mathematics, this is defined as the largest number that divides both of them. It's used when you need to add fractions.) Therefore,

◆ GCD(4,6) = 2 (because 2 is the largest number that divides both 4 and 6)

◆ GCD(12,7) = 1 (because no integer greater than 1 divides them both; 1 is the largest "common divisor")

Around 2,000 years ago, Euclid gave the following method of computing the GCD of two integers, *a* and *b*:

If *b* divides *a*, then the GCD is *b*. Otherwise,
  GCD(*a*,*b*) = GCD(*b*, a Mod *b*)

**note:** *This is usually called the Euclidean algorithm. Algorithms are what programming is ultimately about. More precisely, an algorithm is a method of solving a problem that is both precise (no* *ambiguity allowed) and finite (the method must not go on forever). In the case of the Euclidean algorithm, since the Mod operation shrinks the integer each time, the process must stop.*

Recall that the Mod function gives the remainder you get by dividing $b$ into $a$; it's obviously less than $b$. If a Mod $b$ is zero, then $b$ divides $a$. Here is this recursive outline translated into a Visual Basic function:

```
Function GCD (P As Long, Q As Long) As Long
   If Q Mod P = 0 Then
      GCD = P
   Else
      GCD = GCD(Q, P Mod Q)
   End If
End Function
```

Here, the pattern is a trivial case followed by a reduction to a simpler case, with no need to combine results. (Since the Mod function is not restricted to long integers, it's easy enough to change the function to work with short integers as well. The advantage of this is that you can use the preceding code for both kinds of integers by converting the integer to a long integer before calling the function.)

## Simple Recursive Procedures

Just as you can have recursive functions, you can have, through the magic of the stack, recursive procedures. A good example of this is a rewritten version of the binary search method for looking through an ordered list:

If list has length one
   then check directly (the simple case)
Else
   look at the middle of the list
If middle entry is too big then
   search the first half
Else
   search the second half

Note that this outline for a recursive solution is quite close to one's intuitive notion of how to search an ordered list. Here is this outline translated to a procedure:

```
Sub RecursiveBinSearch (X$, A$(), Low as Integer, High as _
Integer)
'LOCAL variable is: Middle
 Dim Middle As Integer
    If Low >= High Then      'If list is empty or has 1 item
      If A$(Low) = X$ Then
        MsgBox ("Target found at entry" + Str$(Low))
      Else MsgBox ("Target not found!")
      End If
      Exit Sub
    End If

 Middle = (Low + High) \ 2
 If A$(Middle) = X$ Then
     MsgBox ("Target found at entry" + Str$(Middle))
     Exit Sub
  Else If A$(Middle) > X$ Then
     RecursiveBinSearch X$, A$(), Low, Middle - 1
  Else
     RecursiveBinSearch X$, A$(), Middle, High
 End If
End Sub
```

To test this you can use the same techniques as for testing the nonrecursive binary search mentioned in Chapter 9.

Whenever you're trying to understand a recursive program, it's a good idea to think about what is on the stack and what happens when the stack is finally popped. In this case, each "card" on the stack contains

◆ The address of the array

◆ The current values (actually the addresses) of the variables Low and High and the location of a new copy of the local variable Middle

Knowing what is on the stack is also essential when you are debugging a recursive procedure. After all, watching the variables on the stack is useless if you don't know what values they're supposed to have.

## An Example—The Tower of Hanoi

By now you may be thinking that recursion is just a fancy way of avoiding loops. There's some truth to this (see the last section of this chapter), but there are many problems for which it would be hard to find the loop equivalent. Perhaps the most famous example of this is the "Tower of Hanoi" problem. (As the quote that follows indicates, it was originally called the "Tower of Brahma.") Here's the problem, extracted from *Mathematical Recreations and Essays* by W. W. Rouse Ball and H. S. M. Coxeter (New York: Dover, 1987):

> In the great temple at Benares, says he, beneath the dome which marks the center of the world, rests a brass plate in which are fixed three diamond needles, each a cubit high and as thick as the body of a bee. On one of these needles, at the creation, God placed sixty-four discs of pure gold, the largest disc resting on the brass plate, and the others getting smaller and smaller up to the top one. This is the Tower of Brahma. Day and night unceasingly the priests transfer the discs from one diamond needle to another according to the fixed and immutable laws of Brahma, which require that the priest on duty must not move more than one disc at a time and that he must place this disc on a needle so that there is no smaller disc below it. When the sixty-four discs shall have been thus transferred from the needle on which at the creation God placed them to one of the other needles, tower, temple and Brahmins alike will crumble into dust, and with a thunderclap the world will vanish.

(There's also a famous Arthur C. Clarke story on a similar theme.)

The idea, then, is to transfer the disks one at a time, taking care to never put a larger disk on a smaller one. The explanation that follows continues to use 64 disks, but solving this problem with this many disks would take the priests (or a super computer, for that matter) more time than scientists say the universe has been around or is likely to be around. For $n$ disks, the solution takes $2^n - 1$ steps; for 64 disks, this has 19 digits (approximately 1.844674E+19, according to Visual Basic). The graphically based solution found in the next section limits you to 15 disks, and that many disks take about 15 minutes to solve the problem on a 386.

To solve this problem recursively, you need to decide on the "trivial" case—the one that the recursion stops on. Obviously, when the tower is down to 1 disk (height 1), you can just move that disk. Next, you have to find a way to simplify the problem while retaining the same form (and making sure that this process does eventually lead to the trivial case). The key is to note that the bottom disk is irrelevant when you move the first 63 disks from the first tower to any other tower. Since it's larger than any disk, you can just as well regard a peg with it alone as being empty when it comes to moving disks around. Next, note that you can change the destination temporarily if this helps to simplify the problem. Given all this, here's an outline of a solution to the Tower of Hanoi:

Move the top 63 disks to tower 3 using tower 2 (a simpler case)
Move the bottom disk to its destination (tower 2)
Move the top 62 disks to tower 1 using tower 2
(Of course, to move 62 disks is a problem of smaller size. And just as before, the bottom disk will be irrelevant.)

Here is procedure code that implements this outline. This procedure only gives directions for a solution:

```
Sub SolveTowerOfHanoi (Height As Integer, FromTower As
Integer, ToTower As Integer, UsingTower As Integer)

  If Height = 1 Then
    Print "Move a disk from tower #"; FromTower; "to tower#";
ToTower
  Else
    SolveTowerOfHanoi Height - 1, FromTower, UsingTower,ToTower
    Print "Move a disk from tower #"; FromTower; "to tower
#";ToTower
    SolveTowerOfHanoi Height - 1, UsingTower, ToTower,FromTower
  End If
End Sub
```

If you've set up a global variable called NumberOfDisks, then to actually see the directions for solving the problem, all you have to do is write

```
SolveTowerOfHanoi NumberOfDisks, 1, 2, 3
```

As mentioned in the outline, the key to this solution is the switch in the destinations between the two procedure calls:

```
SolveTowerOfHanoi Height-1,FromTower,UsingTower,ToTower
```

and

```
SolveTowerOfHanoi Height-1,UsingTower,ToTower,FromTower
```

If this is confusing, try analyzing the stack for the simple case of three disks by "playing computer." Work through this case using the outline and the procedure. Next, get a printout of the steps by changing the Print statements to Printer.Print statements. Finally, compare your hand solution to the solution that Visual Basic will print out using the preceding program.

## A VISUAL VERSION OF THE TOWERS

While the preceding section gives the directions for solving the problem, it would be much more interesting to have Visual Basic move disks around. The initial screen might look like the one in Figure 16-3.

If you use two forms, you can use the second form for directions and the first for the solution. To follow this discussion, you need to start up a new project and add another form. The second form will need to have the Caption property set to Directions but otherwise needs no special treatment. The directions form would just tell the user about the problem and ask him or her to click a command button to start the project. To get to the screen in Figure 16-3, the first form should have the following properties:

| Property | Setting |
| --- | --- |
| Caption | Tower of Hanoi/Brahma |
| BorderStyle | Fixed single (=1) |
| ControlBox | False |
| MaxButton | False |

**Figure 16-3**

**Initial screen for Tower of Hanoi/Brahma**

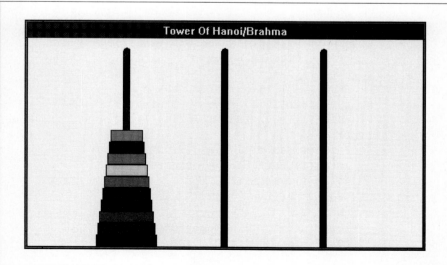

Tower Of Hanoi/Brahma

| Property | Setting |
|----------|---------|
| MinButton | False |
| Auto Redraw | True |

Next, add a text box called Disk and set the Index property to zero for this control, thus setting up a control array. Change the Height property to 285 to make the text boxes flatter and make the Text property the empty string. Now, the code to initialize the first form in order to get the screen in Figure 16-3 uses the following:

```
Sub Initialize ()
 Dim I As Integer

 HowWide = Form1.ScaleWidth        'global variable
 HowHigh = Form1.ScaleHeight       'ditto
    Form1.Show
    Form1.Cls
    DrawWidth = 9
    For I = 1 To 3
      Line ((I / 4) * HowWide, HowHigh)-((I / 4) *
HowWide,ScaleTop - 250)       'on one line
    Next I
    M$ = InputBox$("Number of disks - 15 or less?")
    NumberOfDisks = Val(M$)
    Do Until NumberOfDisks > 0 And NumberOfDisks < 16
      M$ = InputBox$("Number of disks - 15 or less?")
      NumberOfDisks = Val(M$)
    Loop

 ReDim DiskInfo(NumberOfDisks, 3)
 ' Put Picture boxes

 For I = 1 To NumberOfDisks
 DiskInfo(I, 1) = NumberOfDisks + 1 - I
 Disk(I).Move (HowWide / 4) - 600 + 30 * I, HowHigh - (285 *_
I),
 1200 - (65 * I), 285
 Disk(I).BackColor = QBColor(I)
 Disk(I).Visible = -1                'TRUE
 Form1.Refresh
 Next I
 DiskInfo(0, 1) = NumberOfDisks
 DiskInfo(0, 2) = 0
```

```
DiskInfo(0, 3) = 0
End Sub
```

The DiskInfo global array will hold the information as to which disks are on which towers. The zeroth position holds the number of disks. Because of the previous For-Next loop, DiskInfo(1,1) holds the number of the bottom disk, DiskInfo(2,1) the number of the second disk, and so on. The Move method is used to stack the disks in the right place.

As the initialization routine showed, you'll need the following global variables:

```
Global DiskInfo() As Integer
Global HowWide, HowHigh As Single
Global NumberOfDisks As Integer
```

The Form_Load procedure hides the original text box (disk), sets the AutoRedraw property to True, and loads 15 new disks (text boxes) but keeps them invisible. When Visual Basic finishes loading the text boxes (disks), you call a procedure to display the second form with directions:

```
Sub Form_Load ()
  Disk(0).Visible = 0 : AutoRedraw = True
  For I% = 1 To 15
    Load Disk(I%)
  Next I%
  GiveDirections        'should give the directions
End Sub
```

The Directions form tells the user to click the first form to start the process.

The procedure to actually solve the puzzle replaces the Print statements by a call to a procedure that will move the disks around using the information contained in the DiskInfo( ) array:

```
Sub SolveTowerOfHanoi (Disks As Integer, FromTower As Integer,
ToTower As Integer, UsingTower As Integer)

If Disks = 1 Then
   MoveADisk FromTower, ToTower
Else
   SolveTowerOfHanoi (Disks - 1), FromTower, UsingTower, _
ToTower
   MoveADisk FromTower, ToTower
```

```
      SolveTowerOfHanoi (Disks - 1), UsingTower, ToTower, _
FromTower
   End If
End Sub
```

Now the key MoveADisk procedure replaces the simple Print statement in the solution from the previous section:

```
Sub MoveADisk (FromTower As Integer, ToTower As Integer)
  DiskNumber = DiskInfo(0, FromTower)
  DiskIndex = DiskInfo(DiskNumber, FromTower)
  DiskInfo(DiskNumber, FromTower) = 0
  DiskInfo(0, FromTower) = DiskInfo(0, FromTower) -1
  DiskInfo(0, ToTower) = DiskInfo(0, ToTower) +1
  DiskNumber = DiskInfo(0, ToTower)
  If DiskNumber > NumberOfDisks Then
     Exit Sub
  Else
     DiskInfo(DiskNumber, ToTower) = DiskIndex
  End If

  NewLeft = (HowWide * ToTower / 4) - Disk(NumberOfDisks + 1 -
  DiskIndex).Width / 2
  NewTop = HowHigh - (DiskNumber * 285)
  Disk(NumberOfDisks + 1 - DiskIndex).Move NewLeft, NewTop
  Form1.Refresh
End Sub
```

The click procedure that starts the process is now pretty simple:

```
Sub Form_Click ()
  Initialize
  Form1.Enabled = 0   'no user input needed
  SolveTowerOfHanoi NumberOfDisks, 1, 2, 3
End Sub
```

# Recursive Sorts

In Chapter 9, you saw three useful methods for sorting: insertion, ripple, and Shell sorts. Insertion and ripple sorts are good for short lists, and Shell sort is good for moderately sized lists. The sorts you'll see in this section are among the fastest known; they are often the sorts of choice for very large lists.

## Merge Sort

The first sort, called merge sort, has the easiest outline. You saw it in the first section of this chapter:

> To SORT a LIST
>   If a list has one entry stop
> Otherwise:
>   SORT(the first half)
>   SORT(the second half)
>   Combine (merge) the two

Once you write the merge procedure, the procedure to sort a list is easy. Here's the sort procedure:

```
Sub MergeSort (A$(), Start As Integer, Finish As Integer)

  'LOCAL  Variable is Middle
  Dim Middle As Integer

  If Start < Finish Then
    Middle = (Start + Finish) 2
    MergeSort A$(), Start, Middle
    MergeSort A$(), Middle + 1, Finish
    Merge A$(), Start, Middle, Finish
  End If
End Sub
```

This procedure keeps on splitting the list. When it gets to $n$ lists of size one, the merge procedure combines them into $n/2$ ordered lists of size two, $n/4$ ordered lists of size four, $n/8$ ordered lists of size eight, and so on. (At this point, the details have been swept under the rug by moving them to the as-yet-unwritten merge procedure.)

Merging two ordered files (or ordered parts of the same file) is intuitively obvious but a bit tricky to program. What you have to do is set up a temporary array and work your way slowly through the lists, filling up the temporary array with the appropriate entry from one of the two lists. When you're done, you have to write the temporary array back to the original array.

Here's the Merge procedure:

```
Sub Merge (A$(), Start As Integer, Middle As Integer, Finish
As Integer)
  'local variables are:
  'Temp$(),Begin1,End1,Begin2,End2,TempLocation,I

  ReDim Temp$(Start To Finish)
  Dim  Begin1 As Integer,End1 As Integer,Begin2 As Integer
  Dim  End2 As Integer,TempLocation As Integer,I As Integer
  Begin1 = Start
  End1 = Middle
  Begin2 = End1 + 1
  End2 = Finish
  TempLocation = Start
  Do While Begin1 <= End1 And Begin2 <= End2
    If A$(Begin1) <= A$(Begin2) Then
      Temp$(TempLocation) = A$(Begin1)
      TempLocation = TempLocation + 1
      Begin1 = Begin1 + 1
    Else
      Temp$(TempLocation) = A$(Begin2)
      TempLocation = TempLocation + 1
      Begin2 = Begin2 + 1
    End If
  Loop
  If Begin1 <= End1 Then
    For I = Begin1 To End1
      Temp$(TempLocation) = A$(I)
      TempLocation = TempLocation + 1
    Next I
  ElseIf Begin2 <= End2 Then
    For I = Begin2 To End2
      Temp$(TempLocation) = A$(I)
      TempLocation = TempLocation + 1
    Next I
  End If

  For I = Start To Finish
   A$(I) = Temp$(I)
  Next I
End Sub
```

The Do loop runs through the list that is passed to the procedure. It systematically compares entries in the two parts of the list and moves the smaller one to the temporary list. After every move, it shifts a pointer (TempLocation) that moves one step forward within the temporary list. Similarly, it moves a pointer within a given sublist (either Begin1 or Begin2) whenever it does a swap. The loop constantly checks the status of these pointers to avoid going past the boundaries of the individual sublists.

You get to the If statement following the Do loop when one of the sublists is "used up." This block copies the remainder of the other list to the temporary array.

The final For-Next loop copies the temporary array back to the original array. Without this, the recursion would fail.

Although merge sort is theoretically one of the fastest sorts, in practice the simple formulation just given is not very fast for small or moderate-sized lists. A list of 300 random four-letter strings takes about the same amount of time for insertion sort and merge sort (approximately three-fourths of a second), and both are far slower than Shell sort, which takes only about one second for this problem on a 33MHz 386. However, unlike insertion sort, doubling the size of the list no longer quadruples the time; it slightly more than doubles it. Therefore, even this simple formulation of merge sort will be much faster than insertion sort for a list of 600 items. (The rounded time for insertion sort is 2.5 seconds and for merge sort is 1.75 seconds. Shell sort still remains much faster; it takes about 0.5 seconds.)

One problem is that copying the temporary array back to the original list takes too much time. Unfortunately, there's little you can do about this without writing a low-level-language program. (Wouldn't it be nice to have a built-in Swap for lists as well as variables in the next version of Visual Basic?)

**tip:** *These functions are available in the add-on libraries from Crescent and MicroHelp—see Appendix D.*

The procedure also spends too much time (and stack space) on the trivial cases of lists of size one and two. You can dramatically speed up merge sort (and save a lot of stack space) by modifying what the procedure regards as the "trivial case." For example, suppose you directly sort all lists of length one or two by swapping entries as needed. Change the original procedure to read like the following:

```
Sub MergeSort(A$(),Start As Integer,Finish As Integer)
  'local variables
  Dim Middle As Integer

  If  Finish - Start <= 1 Then
   If A$(Finish) < A$(Start) Then
    'SWAP A$(Finish),A$(Start)
    Temp$ = A$(Finish)
    A$(Finish) = A$(Start)
    A$(Start) = Temp$
   End If
  Else
   Middle = (Start + Finish) \ 2
     MergeSort A$(),Start,Middle
     MergeSort A$(),Middle+1,Finish
     Merge A$(),Start,Middle,Finish
  End If
End Sub
```

Now you are directly swapping the entries when the lists are tiny. The savings are dramatic. For 1,000 random four-letter combinations, which take 8 seconds for insertion sort and approximately 2.9 seconds for the original version of merge sort, this tweaked version of merge sort takes approximately 2.25 seconds— around a 20 percent improvement. (Shell sort is still the fastest; it takes approximately 0.6 second.)

Slightly more savings result from modifying the "trivial case" even further. Recall that insertion (or ripple) sort is very fast for small lists (say, lists of size 64 or less). Modify insertion sort's procedure to allow a start and a finish location within the array. Then modify the procedure for the merge sort by rewriting the fundamental procedure, as in the following:

```
Sub MergeSort (A$(), Start As Integer, Finish As Integer)
  If Finish - Start <= 7 Then
    InsertionSort A$(),Start,Finish
  Else
    Middle = (Start + Finish)
    MergeSort A$(),Start,Middle
    MergeSort A$(),Middle+1,Finish
    Merge A$(),Start,Middle,Finish
  End If
End Sub
```

In any case, all these tweaks preserve the essential advantage of the original merge sort—doubling the list still only slightly more than doubles the time needed. Unfortunately, all the versions of merge sort do have one big disadvantage, and ironically this disadvantage shows up only for the very large lists on which merge sort should shine: you need twice as much space as is needed for Shell sort because of the temporary array used in the merge procedure. This means that you're likely to run out of space for very large lists. It turns out that merge sort is of more theoretical than practical interest in most situations, but see the section "Making Sorts Stable" for these exceptional situations.

## Quicksort

As many people have remarked, finding a better general-purpose sort is the "better mousetrap" of computer science. Unfortunately, the best general-purpose sort currently known, usually called Quicksort, unlike the various modifications of merge sort, is not guaranteed to work quickly. In very unlikely situations, it can be the slowest sort of all.

If the merge sort is a "divide-and-conquer" recursion, then Quicksort can be thought of as a "conquer-by-dividing" recursion. To understand this, consider this list of numbers:

5,12,4,9,17,21,19,41,39

The number 17 is in an enviable place: all the numbers to the left of it are smaller than it and all the numbers to the right of it are greater than it. This means that 17 is in the correct position for when this list is sorted. It *partitions* the list and will not have to be moved by any sort. The idea of Quicksort is to create these "splitters" artificially, on smaller and smaller lists. Here's the basic outline:

1. Take the middle entry of a list.

2. By swapping elements within the list, make this element into a splitter. (Note that this element may need to move, and this is obviously the most difficult part to program.)

3. Divide the list into two at the splitter and repeat steps 1 and 2.

4. Continue until both the lists created by making a splitter have a size of at most one.

The following code translates this outline into a procedure. (All numeric variables are assumed to be integers unless otherwise specified, say by a DEFINT A–Z statement in the Declarations section of the form or module.)

```
Sub QuickSort (A$(), Start As Integer, Finish As Integer)
  'Local variable PosOfSplitter
  Dim PosOfSplitter As Integer

  If finish > Start Then
     Partition A$(), Start, Finish, PosOfSplitter
     QuickSort A$(), Start, PosOfSplitter - 1
     QuickSort A$(), PosOfSplitter + 1, Finish
  End If
End Sub
```

Now you need to write the procedure that forces the splitter. This procedure is subtle and makes Quicksort harder to program than merge sort. Luckily, there are many ways to do this. The one shown here is inspired by insertion sort. You move the splitter "out of the way" first. Next, you start from the left end of the list and look for any entries that are smaller than the splitter. Whenever you find one, you move it, keeping track of how many elements you've moved. When you get to the end of the list, this marker will tell you where to put back the splitter. Here is that procedure. (It assumes you've written a Swap procedure to interchange two elements in the array, fixing the gap in Visual Basic.)

```
Sub Partition (A$(), Start As Integer, Finish As Integer,
 LocOfSplitter As Integer)
' LOCAL variables are: SplitPos,NewStart,I,Splitter$
Dim SplitPos As Integer, NewStart As Integer
Dim I As Integer, Splitter$

  SplitPos = (start + finish) \ 2
  Splitter$ = A$(SplitPos)
  SWAP A$(SplitPos), A$(start)              'get it out of the way
  LeftPos = start                          'needs to be written!
     For I = start + 1 To finish
       If A$(i) < Splitter$ Then
          LeftPos = LeftPos + 1
          SWAP A$(LeftPos), A$(i)
       End If
     Next i
  SWAP A$(start), A$(LeftPos)        ' LeftPos marks the hole
```

```
    LocOfSplitter = LeftPos        ' This gets passed
    End Sub                        'to the original procedure
```

Quicksort is usually quite fast. (It will actually be a bit faster to write the Swap routine inside the module instead of using another procedure.) For example, sorting a list of 2,000 random four-letter strings takes approximately 4.25 seconds on a 33MHz 386—roughly on a par with Shell sort. Quicksort is usually faster than Shell sort for larger lists.

However, how fast Quicksort works depends completely on how much the splitter splits; the ideal is when it splits the list in two. If each time you sort the smaller list, the element you are trying to make into a splitter is the smallest (or largest) in the list, then in one of the recursive calls, too little work is done, and in the other, too much is done. This makes Quicksort slow down; for all practical purposes, it becomes a complicated version of insertion sort. If this unfortunate situation should come to pass, you may end up waiting a long time to sort a list of 2,000 entries. Luckily, this worst case is quite unlikely, but it can happen.

To prevent this situation, computer scientists offer some suggestions. The first is that you use an insertion or ripple sort for small lists, much like the tweaked version of the merge sort. (This appears to work best when you use insertion sort or ripple sort on lists of size eight or smaller.) Using an insertion or ripple sort for small lists speeds up the program by around 10 percent. It also saves stack space.

Second, and most important, to eliminate the chance of the worst case happening, don't use the middle element as the potential splitter. One idea is to use the random number generator to find a "random" element on the list. Change the lines

```
SplitPos = (Start + Finish) \ 2
Splitter$ = A$(SplitPos)
```

to

```
SplitPos = Start + Int((Finish -Start+1)*Rnd)
```

Doing this makes it almost inconceivable that you'll end up with the worst case. The problem is that using the random number generator takes time. While it makes the worst case almost inconceivable, it does appear to slow down the average case around 25 percent. On the other hand, if you use this idea in the tweaked version described earlier, the deterioration is much less. This combination seems to cause only a 10 percent reduction, and it's still faster than the original version of Quicksort. Far fewer calls to the random number generator are necessary because Visual Basic is not dealing recursively with small lists. (This is the author's favorite version of Quicksort.)

Another possibility that many people prefer is to keep on using insertion or ripple sort for small lists but, instead of calling the random number generator to find a candidate for the splitter, use the median of the start of the list, the middle term, and the end of the list. The code for finding the median of three items is simple (and doesn't take very much time).

## Making Sorts Stable

Finally, why so many sorts? One reason for presenting them is that they illustrate programming techniques so well, but there's a more serious reason. Although Quicksort and Shell sort are fast, they do have one disadvantage that insertion, ripple, and merge sorts do not have. They are not *stable*. To understand what stability means, suppose you have a list of names and addresses that is already ordered alphabetically by name. Suppose now that you want to re-sort the list by city and state. Obviously, you want the list to be ordered alphabetically by name within each state. Unfortunately, if you use Quicksort or Shell sort, the alphabetical order of the names will disappear. With merge sort, you can preserve the old order within the new.

There is one other way to deal with the problem of making your sorts stable. You can set up an integer array and fill the entries with consecutive integers. These entries serve as pointers to the items in the list you want to re-sort. Next, sort the pointer array using the entries in the original list, but leave the original list intact. This solution requires a lot more programming to print the list in the new order because you have to check both lists at the end. In addition, this solution adds to the space requirement since you need to maintain two arrays instead of one, but it can be faster if you need to move many large entries in an array around.

## Binary Trees

In many cases, you don't really need to sort a list; rather, you sort the list so you can easily search through the list later (using a binary search). Or suppose you have a person entering random names and you want to be able to prevent duplicates. If the list were ordered, this would be easy, but a new entry requires re-sorting the list. (If you choose this option, use insertion sort; it's obviously the best way to insert a new item.) Finally, you may know that at some point in the future you'll frequently need to search through the list, possibly ordering the list as well. Stopping and re-sorting the list each time the user enters a new name is obviously not the method of choice if the final ordering happens in the far future.

It should come as no surprise that programmers have long searched for methods of accepting information for a list so you can still search through the list as quickly as through an ordered list (that is, as fast as a binary search) and, at some future time, sort it quickly as well. And all this should take place without having to stop and constantly re-sort.

Of course, you can't expect to get something for nothing. The methods that programmers invented require more sophisticated programs and use a lot more space. Moreover, unless you use very sophisticated methods (which are not described here), the method given here works only if the names are entered in a "random" order. If someone applies these methods when entering an ordered list, the results will be disastrously slow.

To understand this method, called binary trees, first suppose you have a list of names:

**Mary, Susan, Gary, Karen, Ted, Saul, David, Fran, Harry, Hal**

Start by putting the first name at the center of the top of a piece of paper:

**Mary**

Since the name Susan comes in the alphabet after Mary, draw an arrow pointing to the right. (It's sometimes called an "after" or "right" arrow.):

Gary comes before Mary, so draw a left arrow (a "before" arrow):

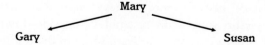

Karen comes before Mary but after Gary, so the picture looks like this:

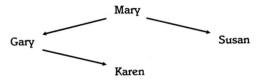

Ted comes after Mary and after Susan, so the picture now looks like this:

The idea is that when you insert a new name, follow the "branches" in the right order. Saul comes after Mary and before Susan. At the next step, the picture looks like this:

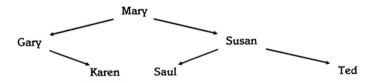

Finally, the picture looks like this:

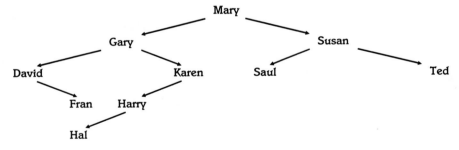

Naturally enough, programmers call the resulting diagram a *binary tree*—"binary" because there are never more than two branches, and "tree" because the picture supposedly resembles an upside-down tree.

It's a good idea to learn some of the terminology computer scientists use to describe binary trees. For example, they say that each of the names forms (or sits in) a *node* on the binary tree. The top node is called the *root* of the tree. The node directly above (that points to) a node is called the *parent* of that node. For example, Karen is the parent node for Harry, and Gary is the parent node for David and Karen. Every parent in a tree can have either no children, a younger (left) child, an older (right) child, or both. A node that has no children is said to be a *leaf*.

When you enter names and form a binary tree by following the procedure just given, you are said to have *loaded* the tree. Adding a new name to a loaded tree is fairly quick, almost as fast as just sticking the name at the end of an ordinary list. Although now, instead of merely sticking it at the end, you follow the correct branch of the tree until you can go no farther. At that point, stick the new name where the hole is. Note that searching a tree and loading a tree are basically the same operation.

Note as well that a binary tree is inherently a recursive object. After all, start from any node at all; then all the nodes that are attached to it form a binary tree as well, with the first node as the new root (usually called a *subtree*). The left child of a parent gives you the left subtree, and the right child of a parent gives you the right subtree. It is this recursive property that makes most of the operations on a binary tree simple.

A recursive version of loading a tree will be a procedure that depends on the contents of the current position in the tree as well as the subtree. An outline in something close to pseudocode might look like this:

```
Procedure LoadATree(Tree,NodeInTree,ThingToAdd)
  If the current node is empty, add the word there
  Else
    If the word precedes the contents of the node
    LoadATree(Left Tree, LeftChild, ThingToAdd)
    Else
    LoadATree(Right Tree, RightChild, ThingToAdd)
```

To write a program that implements this, you have to decide how you're going to represent the arrows and the holes. This is usually called the *data structure*. The ideal situation would be to use a three-column array. Each row on the array would use the first column for the contents of the node, the second column for the row the left child is on, and the third column for the row the right child is pointing to.

The trouble with this is that if you use a string array, you can't use numbers for the entries in the second and third columns (the rows of the children). If you use an array of variants you will build in a fair amount of additional overhead.

Instead, you might turn to a list of records as follows:

```
Type ContentsOfTree
  NodeContents As String
```

```
    RowOfLftChil As Integer
    RowOfRtChild As Integer
End Type
```

In the example, the 10×3 array would look like this (using −1 if there's nothing to point to):

| Row Number<br>(= node number) | Contents of Node | Row "Before"<br>Arrow Points To | Row "After"<br>Arrow Points To |
|---|---|---|---|
| 1 | Mary | 3 | 2 |
| 2 | Susan | 6 | 5 |
| 3 | Gary | 7 | 4 |
| 4 | Karen | 9 | −1 |
| 5 | Ted | −1 | −1 |
| 6 | Saul | −1 | −1 |
| 7 | David | −1 | 8 |
| 8 | Fran | −1 | −1 |
| 9 | Harry | 10 | −1 |
| 10 | Hal | −1 | −1 |

For example, the third row of the array of records that will represent the tree would contain three entries—one in each column:

```
"Gary"   7   4
```

Note that the first column has the entries in the order in which they were entered. It's the other two columns that give you the extra information needed to quickly search through the tree.

The method used here employs the idea of parallel lists (discussed in Chapter 9), which save space. Ultimately, which method you use is a matter of taste.

The first list will hold the contents of the nodes. It will be a string array, with a two-column integer array for the pointers to the left and right children.

Here is the procedure to load a tree:

```
Sub LoadATree (Nodes$(), Arrows%(), Item$, CurrentPos%)
  ' LOCAL variables are: Items%,WhereToGo%,Direction$
  Dim Items%, WhereToGo As Integer, Direction$
  Items% = Val(nodes$(0))
  If Items% = 0 Then
    Nodes$(0) = "1"
    Nodes$(1) = Item$
    Arrows%(1, 0) = -1
    Arrows%(1, 1) = -1
    Exit Sub
```

```
      End If
      If Item$ < Nodes$(CurrentPos%) Then
        WhereToGo% = Arrows%(CurrentPos%, 0)
        Direction$ = "left"
      Else
        WhereToGo% = Arrows%(CurrentPos%, 1)
        Direction$ = "right"
      End If
      If WhereToGo% = -1 Then
        Items% = Items% + 1
        Nodes$(Items%) = Item$
        Arrows%(Items%, 0) = -1
        Arrows%(Items%, 1) = -1
        Nodes$(0) = Str$(Items%)
    ' Now change pointers on parent node
        Select Case Direction$
          Case "left"
            Arrows%(CurrentPos%, 0) = Items%
          Case "right"
            Arrows%(CurrentPos%, 1) = Items%
        End Select
      Else
          LoadATree Nodes$(), Arrows%(), Item$, WhereToGo%
      End If
End Sub
```

As mentioned earlier, the contents of the nodes are stored in a string array indicated by the parameter array Nodes$, with Nodes$(0) being the string equivalent of the number of items. The arrows are stored in an array Arrows% ( , ). The parameter Item$ is for the item to be loaded, and the parameter CurrentPos% is used to indicate where you are in the tree. (To load the tree, call this procedure with CurrentPos% = 1.)

You need a special case when you're setting up the tree. Note that the zeroth position of the nodes is used to keep track of the number of items in the first If statement. This is necessary for two reasons. The first is that you have to know in which row of the array you'll add the next entry. The second is that when using this procedure, you have to have previously dimensioned the arrays. A robust program would constantly monitor this number.

The final If gives you a way out of the recursion. When the arrow is pointing to a hole, it's time to place the entry. The Else starts the recursion.

Of course, in a more serious example you would have to use a ReDim Preserve command to add more room as needed. In any case, to print out the table in the current form for debugging purposes, you can use something like this:

```
Sub PrintaTree (Nodes$(), arrows%())
  ' LOCAL variable is NumberOfItems
  Cls
  Print "Row           Contents     Row 'before'     Row _
'after'"
  Print "Number     of Node     arrow points     arrow _
points"
  Print "(= node                  to               to"
  Print "number)"
  Print : Print
  NumberOfItems = Val(Nodes$(0))
  For I = 1 To NumberOfItems
    Print I, Nodes$(I), arrows%(I, 0), arrows%(I, 1)
  Next I
End Sub
```

Another possibility for debugging is to replace the Print statement with Printer.Print statements. Modifying the LoadATree to SearchATree is simple and is left to you. In any case, you should be aware that the efficiency of SearchATree depends on the shape of the tree.

The best situation (usually called a complete or balanced tree) is when the tree is as "bushy" as possible:

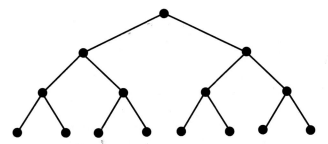

In this case, it works as fast as an ordinary binary search. The worst case is when someone gives you an ordered list, in which case the tree is unbalanced and is as narrow as possible:

With an unbalanced tree, if you use SearchATree, you'll end up searching the list one item at a time.

When users enter data randomly, then most of the time they'll be very close to the balanced tree and very far from an unbalanced tree. This is why one technique for rebalancing a tree consists merely in pulling out entries from the array that defines the tree at random and rebuilding the tree randomly. This requires adjusting all the pointers again as you rebuild the tree.

## Tree Sort

One of the nicest features of trees is that you can sort the items in the tree quite quickly—about as quickly as for the Quicksort. To do this, you have to traverse (move through) nodes cleverly. (It's usually called *inorder traversal*). Here is an outline of how this is done:

1. Go left as far as you can. Print the node.

2. Print the parent of the node from step 1.

3. From the parent, if you can, go right and repeat step 1. If you can't go right, move up to the grandparent from step 1 and repeat step 3.

This outline obviously describes a recursive procedure. The following listing shows you one version:

```
Sub TreeSort (Nodes$(), Arrows%(), CurrentPos%)
  'LOCAL variable is: WhereToGo%
  Dim WhereToGo%
  If Arrows%(CurrentPos%, 0) <> -1 Then
    WhereToGo% = Arrows%(CurrentPos%, 0)
      TreeSort Nodes$(), Arrows%(), WhereToGo%
  End If
  Print Nodes$(CurrentPos%)
  If Arrows%(CurrentPos%, 1) <> -1 Then
```

```
        WhereToGo% = Arrows%(CurrentPos%, 1)
          TreeSort Nodes$(), Arrows%(), WhereToGo%
      End If
    End Sub
```

To use this in the preceding example, call

```
TreeSort Nodes$(), Arrows%(), 1
```

The only problem with using this method to sort a list is that, just as when you use SearchATree, its efficiency completely depends on the shape of the tree. The closer the tree is to being balanced (maximum bushiness), the more quickly this works. On the other hand, if the tree degenerates because the names entered were already ordered, then TreeSort does as well. Consult an advanced book like R. Sedgwick's *Algorithms* (Reading, MA: Addison–Wesley, 1990) to learn how to make sure your trees stay balanced. Doing so requires careful monitoring of the shape of the tree and making some rather complicated switches, and you may prefer to use the random method mentioned in the previous section.

Trees do have one other problem, especially when you're using arrays to represent the contents of the nodes and the pointers: it's quite painful to delete a node. (In fact, it's almost never worth the trouble to try to reclaim the space.) Probably the best method to delete a node is to follow the outline given here. (The details are left to you.)

1. If the node has no children, simply delete it by zeroing out the contents.

2. If the node has one child, attach the parent of the node to be deleted to the lone child by changing the pointers.

3. If the node to be deleted has two children, go to its left child and then as far right as possible. This is the entry that alphabetically comes right in front of the entry being deleted. Swap it with the entry to be deleted.

In spite of the occasional problems they cause, binary trees are an extremely useful technique. Most of the time they are the best way to build an index. As you saw in Chapter 14, an efficient index program is the key to writing an XREF program to cross reference your programs (which, if you stop to think about it, is exactly the same problem as writing any other kind of index).

# Fractals

This section depends on an understanding of recursion and trigonometry. Benoit Mandelbrot of IBM, who coined the term "fractal" and is doing much to show how useful the idea is, begins his book *The Fractal Geometry of Nature* (San Francisco, CA: W. H. Freeman, 1982) with the following:

> Why is geometry often described as "cold" and "dry"? One reason lies in its inability to describe the shape of a cloud, a mountain, a coastline, or a tree. Clouds are not spheres, mountains are not cones, coastlines are not circles, and bark is not smooth, nor does lightning travel in a straight line.

A little bit later he goes on to say that these objects are most often "identical at all scales." This is the simplest way to understand fractals; they are objects that, no matter how powerful the magnifying glass, remain essentially the same. The large-scale structure is repeated ad infinitum in the small structure. One of Mandelbrot's standard examples is a coastline: from an airplane, from afoot, or using a magnifying glass, you get the same pattern on an ever-smaller scale. A pseudocode description of a general fractal is

Draw the object in the large
Replace pieces of the large object with smaller versions of itself

This is obviously a description of a recursive process. Before you get to any of the classic fractals, look at Figure 16-4. As you can see, this figure consists of squares, the corners of which are replaced by still smaller squares. The pseudocode for this program might be something like:

Sub Draw A Square
  At each corner of the square
  Draw a square of smaller size,
    Draw a square unless the squares are already too small
End Sub

Here's a Form_Click procedure that implements this outline:

```
Sub Form_Click()
  ' recursive squares
  Scale (-2000, 2000)-(2000, -2000)
```

**Figure 16-4**

Beginning of
recursive
squares

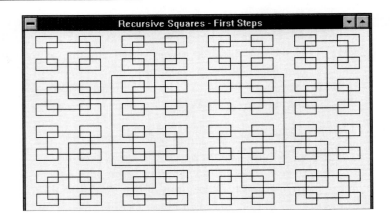

```
      Square -1000, 1000, 2000
End Sub

Sub Square (x, y, Size)
   'To end recursion
   If Size < 50 Then Exit Sub
   Line (x, y)-(x + Size, y - Size), , B    'Draws the large
                                            'square

   Square x - Size / 4, y + Size / 4, Size / 2    'Recursive
                                                  'call
   Square x + Size - Size / 4, y + Size / 4, Size / 2
   Square x - Size / 4, y - Size + Size / 4, Size / 2
   Square x + Size - Size / 4, y - Size + Size / 4, Size / 2
End Sub
```

On each recursion, there are four new corners. Each one is moved one-quarter of the size of the previous one in or out from the previous one and is half as big.

Figure 16-5 is a screen dump of the start of one of the first fractals to be discovered. It's the beginning of a fractal called the Koch Snowflake that you saw in Figure 16-1. As you can see, this consists of a star repeated on an ever-smaller scale. The key to programming this is to notice that if you start from the center of the star of, say, size eight, then each vertex has a one-, two-, or four-unit shift in the X or Y level.

**Figure 16-5**

**Start of the Koch Snowflake**

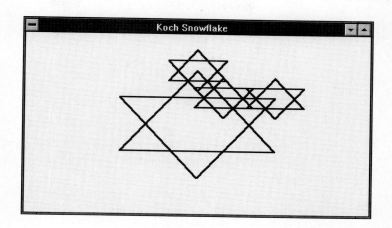

Once you understand this, then writing the program only requires setting up an array that, on each call, holds the current values for the 12 vertexes. Here's a fragment that does this:

```
Sub Koch (Xpos, Ypos, size)
' The Koch Snowflake
 'local variables are X(),Y(),shift,i,colnum
 ReDim x(12), y(12)
 Dim shift As Single, I As Integer
  If size < 4 Then Exit Sub
  shift = size / 8
  x(1) = Xpos: y(1) = Ypos + 4 * shift
  x(2) = Xpos + shift: y(2) = Ypos + 2 * shift
  x(3) = Xpos + 3 * shift: y(3) = y(2)
  x(4) = Xpos + 2 * shift: y(4) = Ypos
  x(5) = x(3): y(5) = Ypos - 2 * shift
  x(6) = x(2): y(6) = y(5)
  x(7) = Xpos: y(7) = Ypos - 4 * shift
  x(8) = Xpos - shift: y(8) = y(5)
  x(9) = Xpos - 3 * shift: y(9) = y(5)
  x(10) = Xpos - 2 * shift: y(10) = Ypos
  x(11) = x(9): y(11) = y(2)
  x(12) = x(8): y(12) = y(2)
  Line (x(1), y(1))-(x(5), y(5))
  Line -(x(9), y(9))
  Line -(x(1), y(1))
```

```
   Line (x(3), y(3))-(x(7), y(7))
   Line -(x(11), y(11))
   Line -(x(3), y(3))
      Koch Xpos, Ypos, 2 * shift
      For I = 1 To 12
          Koch x(i), y(i), 3 * shift
      Next I
End Sub
```

If you have a color monitor, you might want to experiment by adding color to the routine by changing the ForeColor property. The results can be fascinating.

To actually use this procedure, you need to put this fragment in the event procedure that will start the process:

```
Scale (-100,100) -(100,-100)
Koch 0, 0, 120
```

## Other Fractal Curves

To better understand the fractal curves described in this section, observe that there's another way to think of the Koch Snowflake. What you're doing is replacing each straight line segment with a line segment that looks like this:

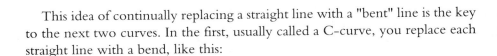

This idea of continually replacing a straight line with a "bent" line is the key to the next two curves. In the first, usually called a C-curve, you replace each straight line with a bend, like this:

This eventually gives you a figure that looks like the one in Figure 16-6. You can modify the C-curve for the next fractal, called the Dragon curve, by putting the bends on opposite sides. The replacement parts alternately go out and in. The screen in Figure 16-7 shows a picture of what you get. The pseudocode for both these programs is the same:

```
Sub DrawAFractal with MakeABend
  If the line isn't too small
  Replace the line with the bent one.
```

**Figure 16-6**

**The C-curve**

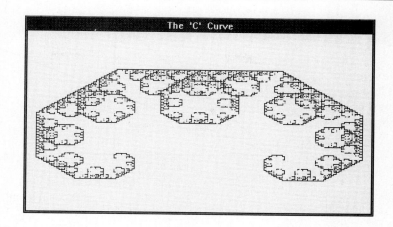

```
Sub for the smaller line
End Sub
```

The only point remaining is to describe, mathematically, "making a bend." This is where trigonometry comes in. What you need is a formula that, given a line connecting any two points and angle, finds the coordinates of the new point that gives the bent line. Look at Figure 16-8. Notice that if the angle is 45 degrees, as it is in the C- and Dragon curves, then the size of the spike is

**Figure 16-7**

**The Dragon curve**

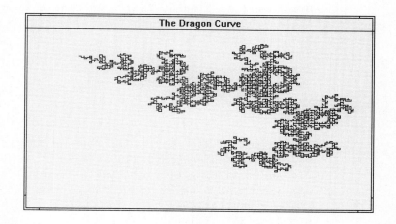

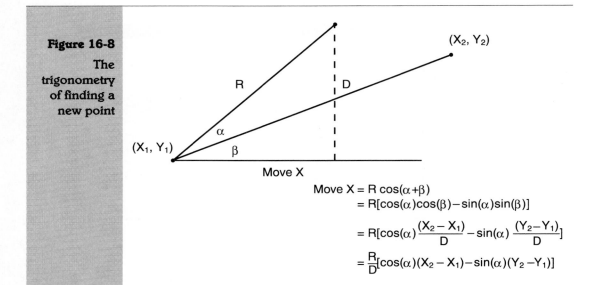

**Figure 16-8**

**The trigonometry of finding a new point**

$$\text{Move X} = R\cos(\alpha+\beta)$$
$$= R[\cos(\alpha)\cos(\beta)-\sin(\alpha)\sin(\beta)]$$
$$= R[\cos(\alpha)\frac{(X_2-X_1)}{D}-\sin(\alpha)\frac{(Y_2-Y_1)}{D}]$$
$$= \frac{R}{D}[\cos(\alpha)(X_2-X_1)-\sin(\alpha)(Y_2-Y_1)]$$

$$\text{COS}(45°)*D = (\text{SQR}(2)/2)*D$$

because the triangle is a 45°-45°-90° right triangle. Using this, the keys to a program for the C-curve are the following MoveX and MoveY functions:

```
Function MoveX (X1!, Y1!, X2!, Y2!) As Single
  ' local variables: Angle(in radians),D,XShift,YShift
  Dim Angle As Single, D As Single
  Dim XShift As Single, YShift As Single
  Angle = Radians(45)
  D = Dist(X1!, Y1!, X2!, Y2!)
  R = (SQR(2) / 2) * D
  XShift = Cos(Angle) * (X2! - X1!)
  YShift = Sin(Angle) * (Y2! - Y1!)
MoveX = R / D * (XShift - YShift)
End Function

Function MoveY (X1!, Y1!, X2!, Y2!) As Single
  ' local variables: Angle(in radians),D,XShift,YShift
  Dim Angle As Single, D As Single
  Dim XShift As Single, YShift As Single
  Angle = Radians(45)
  D = Dist(X1!, Y1!, X2!, Y2!)
```

```
   R = (SQR(2) / 2) * D
   XShift = Sin(Angle) * (X2! - X1!)
   YShift = Cos(Angle) * (Y2! - Y1!)

   MoveY = (R / D) * (XShift + YShift)
End Function
```

Before you can get to the main recursive procedure, you need the distance function and a function to convert to radian measure:

```
Function Dist (X1!, Y1!, X2!, Y2!) As Single
   ' finds the distance between points
   ' local variables are: x,y
   Dim X As Single, Y As Single
   X = (X2! - X1!) * (X2! - X1!)
   Y = (Y2! - Y1!) * (Y2! - Y1!)
   Dist = SQR(X + Y)
End Function
```

```
Function Radians! (X!)
   ' converts degrees to radians
   ' Needs global variable PI = 4*Atn(1)
   Radians! = X! * PI / 180
End Function
```

Next, you have the main (recursive) Sub:

```
Sub Curve (X1!, Y1!, X2!, Y2!)
   Dim DistPt As Single, NX1 As Single, NY1 As Single
   DistPt = Dist(X1!, Y1!, X2!, Y2!)
   If DistPt < 10 Then
     Exit Sub
   End If
   NX1 = X1 + MoveX(X1!, Y1!, X2!, Y2!)        'find the coord _
for
   NY1 = Y1 + MoveY(X1!, Y1!, X2!, Y2!)        'the spike
   ' If these are in a module replace Line with FormName.Line
     Line (X1!, Y1!)-(X2!, Y2!), BackColor     'erase previous _
line
     Line (X1!, Y1!)-(NX1, NY1)                'make the spike
     Line -(X2!, Y2!)
   Curve X1!, Y1!, NX1, NY1                    'now recurse on _
the
```

```
        Curve NX1, NY1, X2!, Y2!                    'spikes
    End Sub
```

Here's the rest of the program for the C-curve. First, as commented in the Radians function, you need a form-level variable, Pi, for the value of $\pi$. Then all you have to do is set Pi = 4*Atn(1) in the Form_Load procedure and do the following:

```
Sub Form_Click()
    Dim X1!, X2!, Y1!, Y2!
    Scale (-500, 500)-(500, -500)
    X1! = -250: Y1! = -200
    X2! = 250: Y2! = -200
    Curve X1!, Y1!, X2!, Y2!
End Sub
```

The nice thing about these kinds of fractals is that all you ever have to do is change the MoveX and MoveY functions. For the Dragon curve, you need to modify them so they alternate sides each time—a perfect situation for static variables. For example, here's what you need to do to modify the MoveX function—the MoveY function is similar and left to you.

```
Function MoveX (X1!, Y1!, X2!, Y2!) As Single
    ' modified mover for Dragon curve
    ' local variables: Angle(in radians),D,XShift,YShift
    Dim D As Single, XShift As Single, YShift As Single
    Static J As Integer
    J = J + 1
    Angle = Radians!(45)
    If J Mod 2 = 0 Then Angle = -Angle:J=0  'alternate on each
                                            'call!
    D = Dist(X1!, Y1!, X2!, Y2!)
    R = (SQR(2) / 2) * D
    XShift = Cos(Angle) * (X2! - X1!)
    YShift = Sin(Angle) * (Y2! - Y1!)
    MoveX = R / D * (XShift - YShift)
End Function
```

The screen in Figure 16-9 shows the result of a program to draw a model of a landscape. Modification of this program can give extremely realistic three-dimensional pictures. Even clicking twice gives a more three-dimensional effect, as you can also see in Figure 16-9. (For example, fractal techniques were used

**Figure 16-9**

**A fractal landscape**

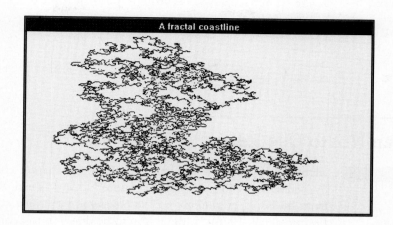

A fractal coastline

to create the Genesis sequence in the Star Trek movie *The Wrath of Khan*.) The only difference between this and the two preceding curves is that this time the angle is to be random, as is the size of each "spike." To do this, you have to change the Move functions by incorporating a random factor for the angle (instead of 45 degrees) and for the size of the spike (instead of Cos(45°*D). For example, the following listing does this for MoveX.

```
Function MoveX (X1!, Y1!, X2!, Y2!) As Single
   ' local variables: Angle(in radians),D,XShift,YShift
   Dim Angle As Single, D As Single, R As Single
   Dim XShift As Single, YShift As Single
   Angle = Radians!(15 + 60 * Rnd)
   If Rnd(1) > .5 Then Angle = -Angle
   D = Dist(X1!, Y1!, X2!, Y2!)
   R = (.15 + (.6 * RND(1))) * D
   XShift = Cos(Angle) * (X2! - X1!)
   YShift = Sin(Angle) * (Y2! - Y1!)
   MoveX = (R / D) * (XShift - YShift)
End Function
```

Finally, instead of one call that acts recursively on a single line, this time you'll build the shoreline out of three recursive calls to three lines that form a triangle. The following fragment will do this:

```
Scale (-500!, 500!)-(500!, -500!)
X1! = -250: Y1! = 200
X2! = 250: Y2! = 200
Curve X1!, Y1!, X2!, Y2!
Curve X2!, Y2!, 0, -Y2!
Curve 0, -Y2!, X1!, Y1!
```

# When Not to Use Recursion

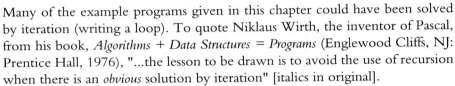

Many of the example programs given in this chapter could have been solved by iteration (writing a loop). To quote Niklaus Wirth, the inventor of Pascal, from his book, *Algorithms + Data Structures = Programs* (Englewood Cliffs, NJ: Prentice Hall, 1976), "...the lesson to be drawn is to avoid the use of recursion when there is an *obvious* solution by iteration" [italics in original].

The reason is that although a recursive procedure is often shorter to write, it almost inevitably takes longer and uses much more memory to run. (You may counter that memory is cheap, but no matter what you do in Visual Basic, the stack is limited to what Visual Basic provides.)

In fact, as Wirth and others have pointed out, what should be the standard examples of when not to use recursion are also the examples most commonly given of recursion: the factorial and the Fibonacci numbers. (They're used as they were in this chapter because they illustrate the techniques well.)

Both the factorial and Fibonacci numbers can be computed more easily and quickly (and using much less memory) by using loops. The factorial is obvious, the Fibonacci numbers only slightly less so. You need to keep track of the previous two Fibonacci numbers, as in the following listing:

```
Function Fib% (n as Integer)
' LOCAL variables are: I,First,Sec,CurrentFib
Dim First As Integer, Sec As Integer
Dim I As Integer, CurrentFib As Integer
  If N <= 1 Then
    Fib% = N
    Exit Function
  Else
    First = 0
    Sec = 1
    For I = 2 To N
      CurrentFib = First + Sec
      First = Sec
```

```
        Sec = CurrentFib
      Next I
    Fib% = CurrentFib
  End If
End Function
```

Although you can use the Timer command to demonstrate the difference between the two versions, a more graphic demonstration is obtained by drawing a diagram of how much wasted effort there is in the recursive version of Fibonacci, as shown in Figure 16-10.

Note that to compute Fib(5) recursively, a program has to compute Fib(3) twice, Fib(2) three times, and get to the trivial case eight times. It never saves the information it so laboriously computes—it just recomputes it constantly.

Another example of where you can replace recursion is in the LoadATree and SearchATree procedures. Since the recursive call happens only at the end (when a hole has not yet been detected), you can rewrite that part of the procedure in, for example, LoadATree, as follows:

```
Do Until WhereToGo% = -1
  If Item$ < Nodes$(CurrentPos%) Then
    WhereToGo% = Arrows%(CurrentPos%,0)
    Direction$ = "left"
  Else
```

**Figure 16-10**

Calls needed for recursive Fib

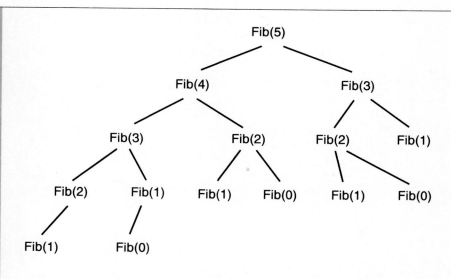

```
      WhereToGo% = Arrows%(CurrentPos%,1)
      Direction$ = "right"
    End If
Loop
```

The reason it's easy to change the original version to a nonrecursive, iterative version is that LoadATree is a *tail recursive program*. This means that when you make the recursive call, nothing is left to be done on the stack; it doesn't need to remember anything. Any tail recursive program can be changed to a loop controlled by the trivial case, exactly as was done earlier. On the other hand, TreeSort is not tail recursive because the stack contains many requests to "Print a node."

One other point that may be of interest to you is that you can theoretically translate any recursive procedure, tail recursive or not, into an iterative version. The trouble is that you do it by setting up a stack and keeping track of everything—work that is best done by the compiler.

# Chapter 17

# Data Access

**t**HIS chapter introduces you to the faculties added to the standard edition of Visual Basic 3 for working with databases. You'll first see a little bit of what modern *relational* databases are all about. These concepts will be illustrated with the sample database supplied with Visual Basic and the help of the Data Manager application that is also supplied with Visual Basic. After this introduction, you'll see how to use the Data Manager to build your own simple databases.

Next, you'll see how Visual Basic can work with an existing database through the data control. Finally, you'll see how to use Visual Basic code to move beyond the simplest database manipulations built into the data control.

This chapter can only be an introduction because you will quickly discover that if you want to do any serious work with databases using Visual Basic, you will both need and want the extra functionality provided by the Professional Edition (see Appendix A). And, once you have upgraded, you will discover just as quickly that you need to consult more specialized books. Database programming, whether done from Visual Basic Professional or from a full-fledged database manager like Microsoft Access, is not trivial. (It is worth noting that Microsoft Access includes much of the power of Visual Basic, and Visual Basic Professional includes much of the power of Microsoft Access but they work best together.) It would take a book at least as large as this one to explain any substantial part of the database programming power available to you with the Professional Edition of Visual Basic. (See Appendix E for more advanced information which Microsoft has provided.)

**note:** *If you are not running Windows For Workgroups, you must have SHARE.EXE running to use the data access features of Visual Basic. The minimum settings in your CONFIG.SYS file are:*

*SHARE /L:500 /F:5100*

*(SHARE.EXE can also be run from the DOS prompt before you start Windows.)*

# Some General Words on Modern Databases

Before you start working with data access it is a good idea to get a feel for what modern databases are all about. This section tries, without getting too technical, to explain what is usually called "the relational model" for a database. This is the model used by Visual Basic, Microsoft Access, and many other programmable PC databases such as FoxPro.

Before we get into the more sophisticated relational model of a database, let's return to the simpler databases. A rolodex is a good example to keep in mind of this kind of simpler database, called a *flat file* database. This kind of database is merely an indexed set of "cards," and can easily be created using the techniques you saw in Chapter 14. To build these kinds of databases, random-access files are ideal because they are easy to set up and manipulate and don't require massive resources. Notice that in these kinds of databases the data exists in a set form. Indices are added as a way of quickly getting to specific records but are not essential—especially for small sets of data.

The trouble with using only (indexed) random-access files for all database applications is that they are too limited. Suppose, for example, you were running a business. This business maintained a list of customers in one indexed system and a list of bills in another. Someone's address changes; ideally you would want the address to change in both places automatically. This is impossible without a lot of work as long as data for each situation is kept in separate databases.

More sophisticated databases, like the ones you can begin to build with the Data Manager (and build completely with Microsoft Access or the data access power of Visual Basic Professional), don't fit the indexed card model. This makes it easy to avoid the update problem mentioned in the previous paragraph. They have many other advantages as well, although the extra power comes at a cost. The extra cost usually will be the need for more powerful computers and more code.

There really is no convenient way to describe the underlying structure of the databases that you can build using the Access engine supplied with Visual Basic; that is what actually lies on the user's hard disk. In fact, for now, think of a database as a large amount of data that exists in no fixed form; it is merely "out there" in some sort of nebulous glob. However, the data is controlled by an oracle with great powers. These powers let the oracle bring order out of chaos.

For example, suppose the database was all computer books published (or even all books published!). You want to ask this oracle a specific question about computer books. There are a lot of computer books out there, often many on the same subject with the same title (as authors well know). There are also a lot of authors out there (as publishers well know). So there is a lot of information out there. The oracle being very powerful, with lots of storage space, has all possible information about computer books stored away in some form or other and, moreover, knows everything that's out there. So the oracle knows the authors, the titles, the page counts, the publishers, and lots more. The information kept by the oracle could be used in lots of ways. You might need all books by a specific author, all books with a specific string in the title, all books by a specific publisher, or all books that satisfy the three conditions.

Now, imagine that you ask the oracle a question like, "Present me with all books published by Osborne/McGraw-Hill in 1992. Show me the title, the author, and the page count." The oracle works through all its data and then presents you with a gridlike arrangement of the books satisfying the question you just asked. Notice that you neither know nor care how the oracle does this. You also neither know nor care how the information is actually stored and processed by the oracle. You end up with a grid and you can manipulate it easily.

Next, notice that a random-access file really can't handle this type of situation. If you had a single record associated to each author, you would simply have no way of knowing how many fields to add to allow for all an author's books. He or she may continue to write and write and write. Of course, you could have a separate record for each book but this forces a lot of duplication—the vital statistics of the author would need to be repeated each time, for example.

But, if the data is simply out there in some vague formless mass, the oracle can use lots of internal bookkeeping tricks to avoid redundancies, to compact the data, to search through the data, and so on.

**note:**

*In modern database terminology, the questions you ask are called queries and the grid you are presented with is either a table or a view.*

The difference between a table and a view is that a table is built into the database structures and a view is a way of looking at information that might span many tables. The oracle (in Visual Basic it's the Microsoft Access engine) will respond to different queries with different tables (views), although there is still only one (potentially huge) database out there.

The usual language for asking queries of relational database is called SQL (which stands for *structured query language* and is usually pronounced like "seekel" or "sequel"). Essentially this language is built into Visual Basic Professional and a subset is built into the standard edition.

Now, in real life oracles don't exist and data can't be nebulous. So, as you'll see in the next section, data is essentially stored in overlapping tables (grids) that are joined together as needed by the database engine. The columns of these tables (grids) are called fields and the rows are called records.

When you make a query, the Access engine either sends you a subset of one of the tables that already exists or temporarily creates a new grid (view) in memory by combining data from all the tables it has already stored. Since the grid is made up of a set of records extracted from the database, the object on Visual Basic is called, naturally enough, a RecordSet.

**note:** *Microsoft does not follow standard relational database terminology completely. Instead of the term "view" they use the term "dynaset" if the grid is updatable and "snapshot" if it is not. This book uses the term view if we are not specifying whether the table is updatable, and we use Microsoft's terms if we are distinguishing between the table being updatable or not.*

# The Data Manager

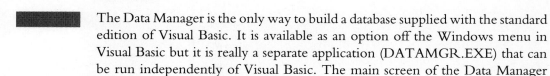

The Data Manager is the only way to build a database supplied with the standard edition of Visual Basic. It is available as an option off the Windows menu in Visual Basic but it is really a separate application (DATAMGR.EXE) that can be run independently of Visual Basic. The main screen of the Data Manager looks like Figure 17-1.

The Data Manager lets you look at the structure of an existing database in many formats, such as dBASE or Paradox. It also can build a new database in Microsoft Access format. (This is usually called MDB format and the convention is to use an .MDB extension for the file name.)

The Data Manager can also add information to databases in other formats such as existing Paradox, dBASE, or FoxPro databases. It can also delete information. Translation from one format to Microsoft Access format is handled essentially automatically. What the Data Manager can't do is create a database from scratch in these other formats.

## Using the Data Manager to Examine Existing Databases

As a way to get more comfortable with data access, let's use the Data Manager to examine the BIBLIO.MDB database that is supplied with Visual Basic. Open

**Figure 17-1**

Main screen of
Data Manager

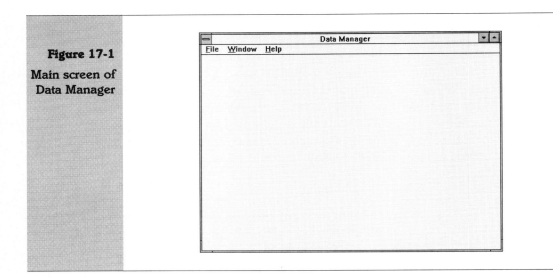

the File menu in the Data Manager and choose Open. This brings up a submenu
that looks like this:

Since the sample database is in Access format, click that as well. This pops
up the usual common dialog box for opening a file. The BIBLIO.MDB database
is usually stored in the same directory as Visual Basic. Your screen looks like this:

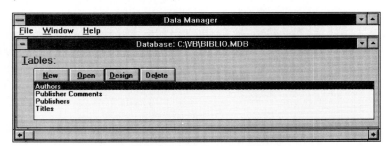

Notice that there are four tables in this database: one for the Authors, one for
Publisher Comments, one for Publishers, and one for Titles. Notice as well that
these names do not fit normal DOS file name conventions. (Since the Access
engine stores all the information in the database file, the parts of the database

do not need to follow ordinary DOS naming conventions. This is different from many earlier database managers such as dBASE III.)

Highlight the Authors table, click Design (or just double-click the name), and then expand the window to full size. This takes you to Figure 17-2. Notice that the Authors table has only two fields in it. The first field seems strange: it is a long integer called Au_ID, which stands for Author ID. This field exists because of the requirement that every table have at least one field (or combination of fields) that is unique. In this case the author's name alone would not satisfy this requirement. Next, notice that the Author field is a text field and can hold up to 255 characters.

Let's turn our attention to the second part of Figure 17-2, the boxes marked Indexes. Notice that +Au_ID is listed as a "unique, primary index." The + means that we want things ordered in an increasing fashion. The words "unique primary index" mean that the Au_ID number is unique and that the Access engine should use this field to determine if someone is trying to enter duplicate data. Therefore, the engine will allow you to enter the same author twice but will demand a different author ID number each time. (It turns out that in this database, author IDs are merely arbitrary integers that correspond to the order in which the title was entered.)

Notice that this particular table is *not* indexed on the authors' names at present. Setting up another index is worthwhile if you will need to search through the data using criteria derived from that index. For example, adding Authors as an index would certainly be worth considering in a more realistic

**Figure 17-2**

Screen for designing a database

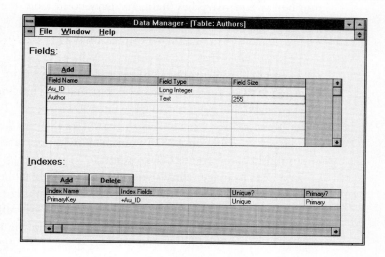

database about books. You almost certainly would like to look for specific authors. This kind of index is allowable because index entries with the Access engine need not be unique. That way you can index on the Author field even though one author may have written many books. Obviously, multiple indexes speed-search through the data. The cost is more overhead, just as it is with random-access files. (See the next section for how to add new indexes.)

A special type of primary index is derived from what is called a primary key. Primary keys are special fields whose contents must be unique for that table. Primary keys are necessary when you want to connect (join) the information in two tables together. (That is why they must be unique—how else could the Access engine know that it is not making a mistake in tying the information together?) Roughly speaking, what you do is tie the tables together by a common primary key and then have the common fields talk to each other. You need to have a primary key in a field only when you want to join that table in the database together with another table.

**note:** *Other tables in the database need not have a primary key set up for that field to allow them to be joined with the first table.*

An example of this is when a table of customer records has a unique customer ID as the primary key, but another table in the same database for orders by customers has the customer ID as a field. Obviously, since a customer may order more than once, the second table could not possibly have the customer ID number as a primary key field. In the second table the customer ID number would be an ordinary (but possibly index) field. This is called a *many to one relationship* and is the hallmark of relational databases.

To see a table that has a primary key in it, close the Author table by using CTRL+F4 or the control box in its window and open up the Titles table. When enlarged to full screen this takes you to something like Figure 17-3. Notice here that you have five fields in this table, one of which, Au_ID, is also in the Authors table. Next, notice the indexes shown. The ISBN is listed as the primary key (which is reasonable since ISBN numbers are unique and are used by bookstores and publishers to process book orders.)

The Data Manager allows you to keep multiple tables open at once. Having multiple tables available is convenient when thinking about how fields relate. To have more than one table available at once, open up another table without closing the previous ones. The Window menu in the Data Manager makes it

---

**Figure 17-3**

Titles table in
BIBLIO.MDB

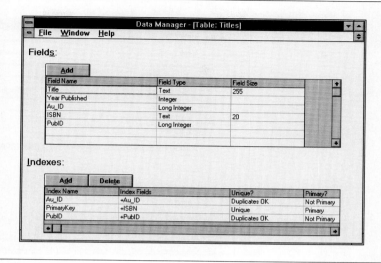

easy to manipulate multiple windows. Figure 17-4 shows all the tables and the main screen of the BIBLIO.MDB database cascaded.

**tip:**

*Since the Data Manager is an MDI application (written in Visual Basic Professional!), you can use* CTRL+F6 *or* CTRL+TAB *to move through the panes and* CTRL+F4 *to close a pane.*

Finally, whenever two tables share a common field, one could easily program them to be joined (using the Professional Edition or Microsoft Access). After they are joined, a change in one would affect the other (and usually vice-versa).

### ADDING INFORMATION TO THE DATABASE

Let's suppose you want to add the book *Windows 3.1 Made Easy* by Tom Sheldon, published by Osborne/McGraw-Hill, to this database. The ISBN number for this book is 0-07-881725-0. Information in a relational database is not added globally but must be added to specific tables.

To add data to a table, you have to open the table. If any of the tables are still open in design mode, close them. Return to the main screen of the BIBLIO.MDB, select Authors, and click Open. You are taken to a screen that looks something like Figure 17-5. Click at the button with the ► | symbol.

**Figure 17-4**

The parts of
BIBLIO.MDB
cascaded

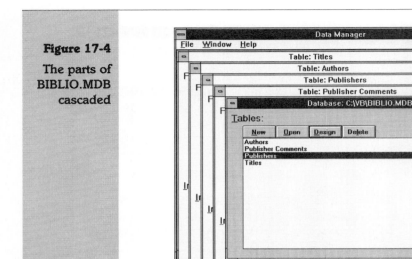

This takes you to the last record. From that you can determine the next unused author ID.

Click on the Add button and enter the data required. When you are satisfied click the Update button or move to another record by clicking any one of the arrow keys. Click on the Refresh button to cancel the entry and close this screen (CTRL+F4) when you are satisfied.

The Data Manager is not programmed to make it easy to use data entered in one table again in another table. This could be added as a feature via code in data applications you write with Visual Basic. (You would need to save the information for reuse as it is entered.) In our case, if you wanted to enter this book into the only other table that would be appropriate, the Titles table, you would need to reenter whatever data is duplicated between the tables. You would also need to look up the publisher ID for McGraw-Hill which you could get by using the arrow keys at the bottom of the add/record screen to move through the list of records. (As indicated in Figure 17-5, the forward-pointing arrow moves forward one record at a time, the backward-pointing arrow moves back. The arrows with bars next to them move to the beginning or end of the table, respectively.)

The Find button in the Data Manager has a great deal of power to search for records in an open table. You can use pattern matching to look for records with specific fields, for example. However, this requires entering an expression using

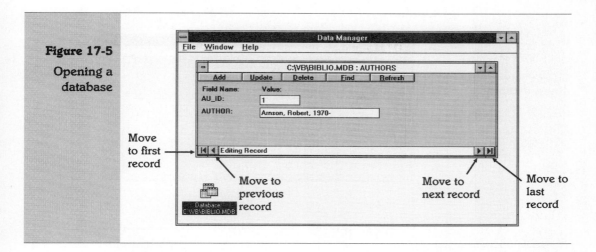

**Figure 17-5**

Opening a database

Move to first record

Move to previous record

Move to next record

Move to last record

SQL syntax in the message box that pops up when you click Find. Please see the section on SQL in this chapter for how to write these expressions.

## Using the Data Manager to Create New Databases

Let's suppose that you want to build a new database from scratch. Open the File menu in the Data Manager and click New. Your screen looks like this:

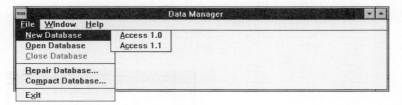

Notice that the Data Manager allows you to create databases in either Microsoft Access 1.0 or 1.1 format. Regardless of which one you choose, you are presented with a common dialog box for the name of the database. Let's suppose we want to create a database for information about cities in the United States. So, set the file name to CITY.MDB and press ENTER. Your screen looks like Figure 17-6.

As it turns out the oracle may be all powerful but in reality you will have to build the framework for all the tables used by your database unless you get the Professional Edition of Visual Basic. With the Professional Edition you can define the structure of tables via code. This is often much easier. (On the other

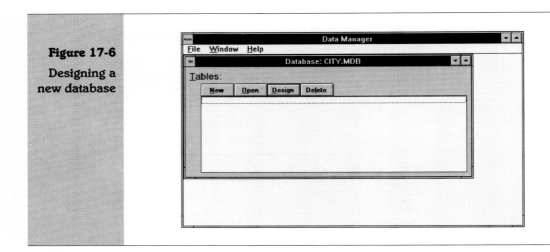

**Figure 17-6**

Designing a
new database

hand, even in the standard edition with a little bit of code you can arrange it so
that you don't have to reenter duplicate data.)

The screen looks much like it did for working with the BIBLIO.MDB
database. When you click New, a message box pops up asking for the name of
the table. The name need only follow the ordinary Visual Basic conventions
for object names. (Of course, if you intend to use the database with another
type of database manager, you would have to conform to both sets of requirements: Visual Basic's and the other data manager's.) Once you enter an
acceptable table name you are taken to the Table defining screen. Suppose you
use CityInfo as the table name. Your screen will look something like Figure
17-7. Click on the Add button and a message box that looks like this pops up:

Set the field name to be City Name and then move to the text box for field
type. If you click the down arrow, you see a list of the possible types for fields.
In this case we want to choose text. Similarly, set up another text field named
State and a long integer field called Population. When you are done, your screen
will look like Figure 17-8.

**Figure 17-7**

Table
definition
screen

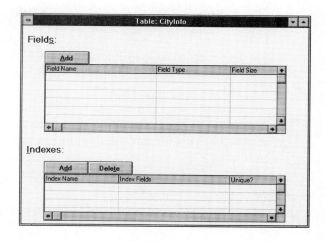

**note:** *Besides text and numbers, fields can accept binary input (for pictures, these are called BLOBS which stands for binary large objects), Boolean (for True/False), and what are called Memo fields for large amounts of text that will be stored as comments.*

**Figure 17-8**

Completed
table
definition
screen

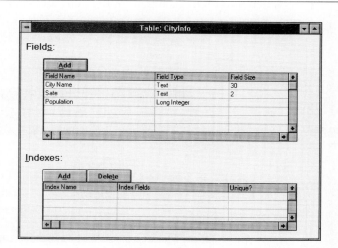

Now you need to allow at least one index for this table. (Each table in the database can have one or more indexes and you can index any text or numeric field.) For this, click the Add button. A dialog box like the one shown in Figure 17-9 will appear. Make the index name BYCity, Select City Name, and then click the Add (Asc) button. (The Asc stands for ascending order—in our case from A–Z.)

We are now done with designing this particular table. You can either close this box (ALT+F4, for example) or leave it on the screen. In any case, you now want to work with the table definition box again. In a similar way, construct another table called City History with two fields, one called City Name, and the other one (an integer value) called Date Founded. Index this table on Date Founded in ascending order also.

Now you have to fill each table with data. You'll soon see how to do this programmatically but for now click the Add button and use the information in the following table to fill in the two tables.

| City Name | State | Population | Year Founded |
|-----------|-------|------------|--------------|
| Detroit | MI | 1027974 | 1701 |
| Atlanta | GA | 394017 | 1837 |
| Boston | MA | 574283 | 1630 |

**note:** *Because we are using the Data Manager to fill in the information, we cannot use any shortcuts that arise because the two tables share a common field. Only code will let you do this.*

When you fill in each field of the table and click the Update button (or the right-pointing arrow), you are said to have *added a record to the table.* When you

**Figure 17-9**

Screen for adding index

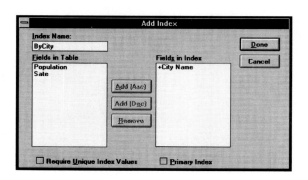

have finished entering all the data you want, click the Close database command from the file menu after closing all subsidiary windows. Click on the refresh button if you make a mistake entering the data.

## Other Operations You Can Do with the Data Manager

Besides adding records to tables, you can also delete them. Move to the record you want using the arrow buttons and click the Delete button.

The Data Manager also lets you add new fields to an existing table in the database. Open the existing database and then click the design button. Now the Add button allows you to update the table. Unfortunately, the Data Manager doesn't let you delete fields, rename them, or modify any of their properties. You would need to delete the whole table and start again. (With the Professional Edition you can do this with only a few lines of code.)

Finally, as you delete records and add records, your databases will seem to grow very quickly. For this reason you may want to periodically use the Compact Database option on the File Menu. You can only compact databases in Microsoft Access format.

**caution:**

*Although you can use the same name for both the original database and its compacted version, you are better off using a new name and, after the compaction is over, deleting the original and renaming the compacted version. This is because if you use the same name you run the risk of losing both versions if anything goes wrong.*

**tip:**

*The Repair DataBase option on the File menu of the Data Manager can sometimes repair databases that are corrupted because of buffer problems (such as a power failure). There are no guarantees, however.*

# Using the Data Control

Roughly speaking, here's how the data control works:

◆ By setting properties of the data control, you hook the data control to a specific database and a table in it. (Code lets you query the database in order to create a dynaset or a snapshot.)

◆ You then add controls to a form that will display the data.

The data control itself displays no data. Think of the data control as only conducting the flow of information back and forth between your project and the database. You use ordinary Visual Basic controls to display the data.

Controls that can work with the data control to access data are said to be *data-aware,* and the process of tying a data-aware control to a data control is called *binding* the data-aware control. In the standard edition of Visual Basic, text boxes, labels, check boxes, image controls, and picture boxes are the only data-aware controls. Data aware controls must be on the same form as the data control, but they need not be visible in order to pick up the information. Once these controls pick up the information sent to them by the data control, the information will be stored as values of properties of the controls.

**note:** *Neither the grid control nor list and combo boxes are data-aware. This is unfortunate and professionals might consider adding a custom control with the same functionality that is data-aware. See Appendix D for more information.*

## Seeing The Data Control at Work

If you look at the toolbox, the data control looks a little bit like a VCR control panel.

When you work with a data control on a form, you need to stretch it out in order to see the caption and the buttons for moving through the database table. If you stretch out the data control, it looks like this:

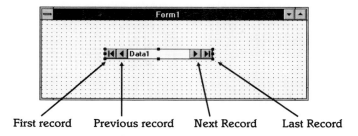

As noted in the illustration, the arrows that look like VCR buttons move to the beginning of the table, back one record, forward one record, and to the end of the table. Each time you press one of these arrow keys the bound controls are automatically updated. You do not have to write any code for this to take place.

You can have many data controls in a single project, each of which can be connected to a different database, or a different table in the same database (or with code to a query about a database and so to a dynaset or snapshot). The properties that control this are easiest to set at design time but can be set (or reset) at run time as well.

The DataBaseName property of the data control determines which database the data control will (try) to connect to. If you go to the properties window and click the ellipses for the DataBaseName property of the data control, you are presented with a common dialog box, as shown here:

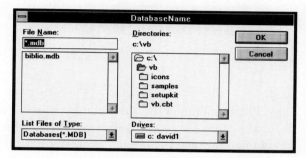

Notice that you can use the Type list box on the left to change what kind of extensions are shown. The default is to show only .MDB extensions.

Next you need to set the RecordSource property to the specific table in the database. If Visual Basic can find the database determined by the DataBaseName property, it will list the tables in the database when you click the ellipsis for the RecordSource property.

**note:** *With code you can set the RecordSource property to an SQL query and so get a view from your database. Please see the section on SQL for how to do this.*

Now you need to add the data-aware controls to the form and bind them to the data control. Pick the kind of control that best suits the information to be picked up. Use a Picture or Image control if it is a graphic image or a check box if it is a Boolean. You might want to use a label if you don't want someone to be able to update it or a text box if you do.

The DataSource property must be set to the name of the data control for each data-aware control. Only after you adjust the DataSource property to the name of the data control can the data-aware control display data from the database.

Next, you have to tell the newly data-aware control what field of the table to take the information to. This is done by setting the DataField property of the data-aware control to the field. If Visual Basic can access the database at design time, then clicking on the ellipsis for the DataField property will give you a list of the fields in the table that are connected by the DataSource property.

For example, the following table summarizes the properties you would need to set up controls to accept all the data available in the Authors table in the BIBLIO.MDB database.

| Control | Needed Properties | Settings |
|---------|-------------------|----------|
| Data1 | DataBaseName | C:\VB\BIBLIO.MDB |
|  | RecordSource | Authors |
| Text1 | DataSource | Data1 |
|  | DataField | Author |
| Text2 | DataSource | Data1 |
|  | DataField | Au_ID |

The nice thing is that once you have set this up, the user can now do simple lookups merely by clicking the arrow keys on the data control. The data control automatically gets the needed information from the database and passes it on to the bound controls.

**note:**   *Each click of one of the buttons changes the current record. (Think of the current record as being the row that Visual Basic is currently looking at.)*

**caution:**   *If data is changed in a bound control and you click an arrow key in the data control to move to a new record, Visual Basic will update the database with this new information. (See the section on "Monitoring Changes to the Database" for more on how to work with this.)*

## OTHER PROPERTIES COMMONLY SET AT DESIGN TIME

There are three other properties of the data control that are commonly set at design time (although they are equally often reset as needed at run time). Here are short descriptions of them.

**Connect**   This property specifies the type of database. You do not need to set this property if you are working with a database in Microsoft Access format. The connect string is usually the name of the program: for example, FoxPro2.5.

Different parameters in the connect string (like the password) are separated by semicolons and the entire connect string must end with a semicolon.

**Exclusive** Set this True/False property to True and no one else will be able to gain access to the database until you relinquish it by closing the database. The default is False.

**note:** *It is possible to change this property at run time but you will have to close and reopen the database in order for it to take effect.*

**ReadOnly** This True/False property is set to True when you want to be able to look at the database, but don't want to affect it in any way. One common way to use this property is to set it at design time to True and change it to False only in response to a password at run time. (See the Refresh method in the section on Data Control methods for more on this property.)

# Programming with the Data Control

Although you can do many things with the data control without code, only code lets you take full advantage of its powers. However, for the data control in particular, there is no need to go overboard on setting properties at run time. This is because although the data control properties *can* be set at run time, it is easiest to set properties like RecordSource, DataSource, and DataField at design time when dialog boxes will pop up with the needed information.

To give you an idea of what code for working with the data control will look like, suppose you want to check whether you can update the RecordSet. This is done with code that looks like this:

```
If Data1.RecordSet.Updatable Then
   'RecordSet will be updatable by the user
Else
   'RecordSet is viewable only
End If
```

As you can see, code for working with a data control looks only slightly different from code for working with any Visual Basic object. The difference is that we are actually using a property of the RecordSet object associated to the data control rather than a property of the data control.

Similarly, to determine if you are at the first or last record, you need to use the BOF (beginning of file) and EOF (end of file) properties of the RecordSet. The code might look like this:

```
If Data1.Recordset.BOF
If Data1.Recordset.EOF
```

**note:** *In almost all cases you will be working with properties of the RecordSet object associated to the data control rather than properties of the data control itself.*

This is because the standard edition of Visual Basic does not allow you to create the necessary database objects independently of the data control. The Professional Edition of Visual Basic does allow database objects to have independent existence. Think of the RecordSet object as pointing to the underlying table, dynaset, or snapshot that is created by the data control.

Every press on a button of the data control at run time has a corresponding method. The following table summarizes this correspondence for a data control named DATA1 using the current recordset.

| Control Action | Data1.Method |
| --- | --- |
| Click the \| ◄ | Data1.RecordSet.MoveFirst |
| Click the ◄ | Data1.RecordSet.MovePrevious |
| Click the ► \| | Data1.RecordSet.MoveLast |
| Click the ► | Data1.RecordSet.MoveNext |

All these methods change the current record.

### THE FIELD OBJECT

The most important object associated to the RecordSet object is the Field object. Think of this as giving you the name and properties of a single column in the grid. By reading or resetting the value of this object you can analyze or update information in the current record of the database. For example, the following line of code might be used to print the name of the author in the current record.

```
Print Data1.RecordSet.Fields("Author")
```

**tip:** *The default property of the RecordSet object is the Field property. This means you could also use the following line of code.*

```
Print Data1.RecordSet("Author")
```

The following table summarizes the most common properties of the important Field object. (Check the online help for more information.) To understand this table you might want to imagine you are at a specific row (the current record) in the database. Also, keep in mind that the Field object refers to a specific column.

| Property | What It Tells You |
|----------|-------------------|
| Attributes | What characteristics the field has. For example, is it updatable? |
| Size | How large the field can be. |
| Type | What type of data is contained in the field. |
| Value | What is actually in the row and column. |

You can analyze other properties of the data control, recordset, or Field object to analyze the database's structural properties. This lets you find out lots of information about the database or recordset. Please see the section entitled "Database Objects" in this chapter for more information.

## Other Useful Methods and Events for the Data Control

This section discusses most other methods that are needed to go beyond what the data control can do on its own.

**Refresh**  The Refresh method, when applied to a data control, opens a database. If you have changed either the DataBaseName, ReadOnly, Exclusive, or Connect properties, you must have Visual Basic process a line of code containing this method. The syntax looks like this:

*DataControlName*.Refresh

The Refresh method also resets the current record back to the first record (row) in the table or view.

**AddNew**  The Access engine maintains a buffer (called the *copy buffer*) where it keeps pending data that it will be writing to the database. The AddNew method clears the copy buffer and moves the current record to the end. (Think of this as potentially adding a new row to the grid.)

Since the copy buffer is empty you will be able to send new information to the table (and so to the database). The syntax is

*DataControlName*.RecordSet.Addnew

The AddNew method doesn't actually add the information to the database. This is the function of the Update method discussed next.

**tip:** *Always make the default that users must confirm that they want the data added (you can let them change this default, of course). Since the AddNew method lets you clear out the information in the copy buffer without actually copying it, use this method if the user doesn't confirm the update operation.*

**Update**  This method actually sends the contents of the copy buffer to the Table or dynaset. (You cannot use Update on a snapshot, of course.) The syntax is

*DataControlName*.RecordSet.Update

Suppose you have a table attached to the Data1 control and want to add a record. You have an Author and a Title field only in this table. The code to add this record might look like this:

```
Data1.RecordSet.AddNew
Data1.RecordSet.Fields("Author") = "Homer"
Data1.RecordSet.Fields("Title") = "Iliad"
Data1.RecordSet.Update
```

If the Update was not successful, Visual Basic generates a trappable error.

**note:**  *Any method that moves the current record will cause an automatic update. If the data control is available, then pressing any of the arrow buttons will do this.*

**UpdateControls**  Suppose the current record sent data to the bound control and someone changed this data. Since the current record is still current there ought to be a quick way to have Visual Basic, for instance, refresh the data without needing to actually move forward and backward. This is exactly what this method does.

*Use this method to reset the contents of bound controls to their original values when the user clicks on a cancel button. (Always provide some method of cancelling a database transaction.)*

**Edit** Visual Basic is always maintaining a pointer into the current table or dynaset. This method copies the current record into the copy buffer for editing. (Just moving to the record doesn't do this.) If the database or recordset is read–only or the current record is not updatable, then trying to use this method gives a trappable error.

Suppose you have a table attached to the Data1 control and want to edit the Author field in the current record. Suppose the procedure to allow changes to a specific field (via a custom dialog box, say) is called ChangeField. Then code to use this method might look like this:

```
Data1.RecordSet.Edit
AuthorName = Data1.RecordSet.Fields("Author")
Call ChangeField(AuthorName)
Data1.RecordSet.Fields("Author") = AuthorName
Data1.RecordSet.Update
```

(This code assumes the procedure displays the old name and then, since we are passing by reference (see Chapter 8), we can use the same variable to pass on the new information).

**UpdateRecord** If you want to quickly save the contents of the bound controls to the current record, use this method. It is exactly the same as using the Edit method, moving to a different record and clearing the copy buffer with the Update method, except that this is a little more dangerous because UpdateRecord does not activate the Validate event (see the section of this chapter "Monitoring Changes to the Database").

**Delete** This method deletes the current record in the RecordSet. If the RecordSet is read-only, then Visual Basic returns a trappable error. This method deletes one record at a time. The syntax is

> *DataControlName*.RecordSet.Delete

After you delete a record, you must move the record pointer away from the deleted record by a Move method (MoveNext, MoveFirst, and so on). For example, the following code will delete all the records in a table.

```
Data1.RecordSet.MoveFirst
Do While Not Data1.RecordSet.EOF
  Data1.RecordSet.Delete
  Data1.RecordSet.MoveNext
Loop
```

**note:** *This is probably overkill. You can use SQL statements to delete all records that satisfy specific criteria.*

**Close** This method closes the database attached to a control or the specific recordset currently attached to the control. The syntax is either

> *DataControlName*.Close

or

> *DataControlName*.RecordSet.Close

When you close a database or RecordSet, Visual Basic automatically processes the Update method to take care of any pending operations.

**note:** *A database or recordset must be open to use the Close method and is closed whenever the form containing the data control is unloaded or the program ends.*

## AN EXAMPLE: CYCLING THROUGH A TABLE

We now have enough of the methods and properties to write many useful routines. A good example of tying all the methods and properties that you have seen together is a slideshow routine. By that we mean a program that on its own cycles through all the records in a table without user intervention. The Timer control makes it very easy to do this—just set the Interval property to the space between slides that you desire. Every time the Timer wakes up we move to the next record. The data control automatically updates the information to bound control.

Suppose we bind a data control to three labels (we don't want the user updating things in a slide show). The form might look like Figure 17-10.

Let's suppose you have bound the labels to the data control and the data control to the right database. A click of the command button refreshes the database and then activates the Timer control. Here's the code for this:

```
Sub StartShow_Click ()
   Datal.Recordset.Refresh
   Timer1.Enabled
End Sub
```

The code inside the Timer event is

```
Sub Timer1.Timer ()
   If Not Datal.RecordSet.EOF Then Datal.RecordSet.MoveNext
End Sub
```

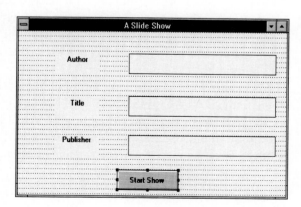

**Figure 17-10**

Form for slide show

**tip:** *If you use a database that contains graphics images, adding a bound picture box to a form and using the above code gives you an easy and efficient method of creating true automatic slide-show demonstrations.*

## Setting Properties via Code

Setting the various startup properties of the data control is easier at design time but this is not always possible. You may not know the name of the database, for example.

Here is an example of the code needed to connect to a FoxPro database at run time.

```
Data1.DataBase = "C:\FOXPRO\DATA\Business"
Data1.Exclusive = True
Data1.ReadOnly = False
Data1.Connect = "FoxPro;"
```

(Notice the needed semicolon at the end of the connect string.)

One property you haven't seen yet that you will often need to set is the Options property. This is discussed next.

### OPTIONS

This property is often set in the Form_Load and reset whenever you access a new table. Here is a short description of this important property.

Options is an integer parameter that controls what the user can do with the database. For example, you can deny other users the ability to write or read from the tables that are the sources of the data contained in the table you created. The reason for this parameter is that you must have the ability to control what is happening to the source of your information if, for example, you are going to change it. (Imagine the problems if everyone is changing the same data at the same time!)

The values for this parameter (as for all the data–access global constants) are stored in the DATACONS.TXT file. There are seven possible options but only six are relevant to the standard edition of Visual Basic. You can combine the options by adding the relevant constants together. The following table summarizes what will happen if you set a specific option.

| DATACONS.TXT Value | Effect |
|---|---|
| DB_DENYWRITE | Users cannot write to the source tables. |
| DB_DENYREAD | Users cannot read from the source tables. |
| DB_READONLY | Determines whether users can write to the dynaset created (and so to the tables in the database) |
| DB_APPENDONLY | Only allows additions to the recordset. |
| DB_INCONSISTENT | A change in one field can affect many rows. |
| DB_CONSISTENT | (Default) A change in one field can affect only one row. |

## PUTTING BOOKMARKS IN A TABLE

Generally one should not think of a table as being made up of records in a fixed order, because the order can change depending on what index you are using. Nonetheless, there are times when you will want to tag a specific record for quick access at a later time. This is done using the Bookmark property of the RecordSet. The idea is when you are at the record you want to tag, have Visual Basic process code that looks like this:

```
Dim ABookMark As String   'or As Variant
ABookMark = Data1.RecordSet.BookMark
```

Now, if you need to get to that record quickly, have Visual Basic process a line of code that looks like this:

```
Data1.Recordset.BookMark = ABookmark
```

Once the above line of code is processed, the record specified by the bookmark immediately becomes the current record.

**tip:** *One common use for a bookmark is to monitor the record that was last modified. You can do this with a line of code that looks like this:*

```
Data1.RecordSet.BookMark = Data1.RecordSet.LastModified
```

# Monitoring Changes to the Database

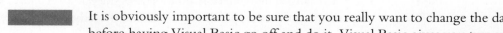

It is obviously important to be sure that you really want to change the database before having Visual Basic go off and do it. Visual Basic gives you two ways of changing your mind. The first is the Validate event which Visual Basic generates whenever the current record is going to change, for example, by a MoveFirst method or before it processes the Update, Delete, or Close methods. The syntax for this event procedure is as follows:

Sub *DataControlName*_Validate ([ Index As Integer,] Action As Integer, *Save* As Integer)

**caution:** *Do not put any method in this event that changes the current record. The result would be an infinite event cascade.*

The only data–access methods you can put into this event are UpdateRecord and UpdateControls, because neither one generates the Validate event. This gives you a way of updating the database or bound controls in this event procedure.

As always, the optional Index parameter is used if the data control is part of a control array. The Action parameter is sent by Visual Basic to the event procedure and tells what actually caused the Validate event to be generated. Here is a list of the possible values using the symbolic constants contained in the CONSTANT.TXT file.

| Constant | What Caused the Validate Event |
| --- | --- |
| DATA_ACTIONMOVEFIRST | The MoveFirst method |
| DATA_ACTIONMOVEPREVIOUS | The MovePrevious method |
| DATA_ACTIONMOVENEXT | The MoveNext method |
| DATA_ACTIONMOVELAST | The MoveLast method |
| DATA_ACTIONADDNEW | The AddNew method |
| DATA_ACTIONUPDATE | The Update method |
| DATA_ACTIONDELETE | The Delete method |
| DATA_ACTIONFIND | The Find method |
| DATA_ACTIONBOOKMARK | The Bookmark property was set |
| DATA_ACTIONCLOSE | The Close method |
| DATA_ACTIONUNLOAD | The form is about to be unloaded |

If you change the Action parameter to

DATA_ACTIONCANCEL

then Visual Basic will cancel the operation after it leaves the Sub procedure. In addition, if you change the Action parameter to one of the other values, then

Visual Basic will actually perform that operation instead of the original operation when the procedure is over. For example, if the Validate event procedure was caused by a MoveFirstMethod and in the course of the Sub Procedure you have a line like

```
Action = DATA_ACTIONMOVELAST
```

then Visual Basic will actually move the current record to the end of the table. You can only use this possibility if the actions are compatible. For example, you cannot change a MoveFirst action parameter to a DATA_ACTIONUNLOAD parameter without an error.

The Save parameter is either True or False. If any information in the bound data-aware controls have been changed, this parameter is True. This gives you a way of analyzing the information contained in the bound control before updating the database. To determine which data-aware controls were changed, use the DataChanged property of the control. This will be True if the contents of the control were changed and False otherwise.

tip:

*To make it easier to use this feature, set up an array for the data-aware controls on the form in the Form_Load event. That way you can use a loop to run through all the data-aware controls, checking the DataChanged property of each.*

## Transaction Control

Even if you allow a change to be made to a database, the changes made by Visual Basic need not be irrevocable. You have the ability to keep track of any changes you have made and cancel them if need be, provided, of course, that the database is sophisticated enough to handle this—Microsoft Access databases certainly can. Consult the documentation of your database to see if it supports *transaction processing,* as this capability is usually called.

Technically, a transaction in database terminology is a sequence of alterations made to a table in the database. What you need to do is tell Visual Basic to store all the transactions it is making so that it can undo them. This is done using the BeginTrans statement discussed next.

**━━━**

***BeginTrans*** This statement tells Visual Basic to start logging the changes for possible cancellation later on. Once Visual Basic processes this statement, it must process one of the two following statements in order to continue working with the database.

*It is possible to nest transactions. This gives you the ability to undo only small portions of the changes without needing to undo them all. You can have up to five transactions logs going at the same time. This is called nesting transactions.*

**CommitTrans** This statement tells Visual Basic to go ahead and make the changes. If you are nesting transactions, then this closes the innermost transaction log. However, no changes would be made to the actual database until Visual Basic closes all transaction logs.

**RollBack** This is the statement you need to undo all the changes made once transaction logging (by processing a BeginTrans statement) has started. If you are nesting transactions, this statement closes the innermost log.

# Structured Query Language (SQL) Basics

There are many whole books on using SQL; this section can only give you a feel for it. The idea of SQL, though, is very simple. The language consists of statements in what appears to be very close to English designed to select out records from tables according to criteria that you give. As you'll soon see, SQL query statements can be used at run time to set the RecordSource property of a data control. This lets you create dynasets and snapshots associated with a data control programmatically, using only the standard edition of Visual Basic. (A snapshot would be created if the ReadOnly property was also set to True.)

Most commonly, SQL criteria use the SQL keyword SELECT followed by one of these keywords: WHERE, SELECT, FROM, HAVING, GROUP BY, or ORDER BY. (By convention, SQL statements are written in all caps, although this is not necessary.) For example, suppose we wanted to work with a Table named Publishers in a database named BOWKER.MDB. This table has four fields: "Name", "Address", "State", and "Phone Number".

If a data control (named Data1, say) had its DataBase property set to BOWKER.MDB, then you could use the following statement (called an *SQL query*) to create a dynaset that consists only of the Names contained in the Publishers table.

```
Data1.RecordSource = "SELECT [Name] FROM Publishers"
```

The FROM statement is required in every SQL select statement. The FROM clause tells Visual Basic which table(s) or query(s) to examine to find the data.

**caution:** *After any query you must use the Refresh method to actually get the records you want from the database.*

## More on SELECT Statements

The SELECT statement usually occurs first in an SQL statement. It is almost inevitably followed by the field names. You can have multiple field names by using a comma between them:

```
Data1.RecordSource = "SELECT [Name], [State] FROM Publishers
```

(Strictly speaking, the brackets around field names are only necessary if the field names have spaces in them. Most people use them all the time because it makes it easier to read the SQL statement.)

When you use a FROM clause to select data from more than one table or query simultaneously, you run the risk of having the same field name occur in two different places. In this case you use a variant on the dot notation that you've already seen for Visual Basic properties to specify which field. For example, if you had a database containing customer IDs (field name CuID) in both the Address table and the Orders table and wanted to extract this information from the Address table only, use

```
Dat1.RecordSource = "SELECT [Addresses.CuID] FROM ...
```

Finally, you can use an asterisk (*) to say you want all fields from the table.

```
Data1.RecordSource = "SELECT * FROM Publishers"
```

Now suppose you wanted to create a dynaset with even more restrictions: for example, the list of publishers located in New York. This can be done by adding a Where clause to the previous SQL query. It would look like this:

```
Data1.RecordSource = "SELECT [Name] FROM Publishers Where _
State = 'NY'"
```

Notice the single quotes inside the SQL statement. This is how you identify a string inside an SQL statement (which is itself a string).

**note:**

---

*SQL statements must occur on a single line or be a single string.*

---

The Where clause can use pattern matching using the Like operator.

```
Data1.RecordSource = "SELECT [Name] FROM Publishers Where _
State Like 'New*'"
```

This statement builds a grid consisting of all publishers' names from states beginning with the word "New" (New Hampshire, New Jersey, New Mexico, and New York).

**Finding Records Using SQL** You can use the four Find methods combined with an SQL statement to examine the contents of a current recordset attached to a data control. These functions are FindFirst to find the first record, FindLast to find the last record, FindNext to find the next record, and FindPrevious to find the previous record. Here's an example of what this syntax looks like:

*DataControlName*.RecordSet.FindFirst *SQL criterion*

**note:**

---

*The standard edition requires you to use this syntax. Only the Professional Edition allows you dimension objects as recordsets that exist independently of the data control.*

---

The SQL criteria for the Find method is what would follow the Where clause in an SQL SELECT statement. For example,

*Data1*.RecordSet.FindFirst *"State = 'CA'"*

(Use the NoMatch property of the recordset object to determine if a match was found.)

To use the Find button in the Data Manager, enter the SQL query in the message box that pops up. An example of this is shown in Figure 17-11.

## Modifying a Table's Structure Through SQL

To this point you have only seen SQL statements that look through the tables in a database and extract information from them. It is also possible to write *action queries* that actually change data that match the conditions given in an SQL statement. For example, suppose you have a store with a table named Items and fields named Current Price and Placed On Shelf. You want to reduce the current price of all items that have not sold since Jan 1 1993 by 10%. This is the kind of situation for which action queries are ideal. Using an action query is much faster than examining each record to see if it matches the necessary condition. The SQL keywords you need to perform an action query like this are UPDATE and SET combined with the Execute method of the DataBase object. UPDATE tells the Access engine that changes should be made and the SET keyword tells it how (and which field) should be changed. The Execute property actually carries out the change (although you could be running transaction control to buffer this change for possible cancellation, of course.)

Here's what the action query for this situation might look like:

```
ActionQuery$ = "UPDATE [Items] "
ActionQuery$ = ActionQuery$ + "SET [Current Price] = _
```

**Figure 17-11**

SQL query for Find in Data Manager

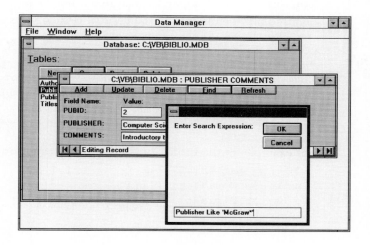

```
[Current Price]*.9
ActionQuery$ = ActionQuery$ + " WHERE [Placed On Shelf] <_
1993"
Data1.Database.Execute ActionQuery$
```

Similarly you can use change several fields at the same time by separating them by commas. There are many other SQL keywords you can use in an action query. Probably the most important besides UPDATE is DELETE, which allows the query to delete those records that satisfy certain criteria.

**tip:** *SQL comes with built-in functions for taking averages, finding maximums and minimums in a field, and a whole lot more. Consult the online help or a book on SQL for more about what you can do with action queries.*

## Database Objects

When Visual Basic works with a database it does so through the creation of special Visual Basic objects and collections associated with the database. You have already seen the RecordSet object. Analyzing properties of these objects and collections can give you much finer information about the database you are working with. For example, every Visual Basic collection has the Count property associated with it. You can use the Count property to find out how many tables there are in the database or how many fields there are in a table. You can then write a loop to analyze this information. What follows is a short discussion of the other important Visual Basic objects and collections.

**note:** *Visual Basic Professional Edition lets you create your own objects for working with databases. You are no longer restricted to using only the ones that Visual Basic supplies. In particular, data access need no longer be tied to the data control.*

For example, in the Professional Edition you can use a statement like

```
Dim Foo As Database
Dim Bar As Dynaset
```

and then use the Set operator to tie these object variables to a database or SQL query.

```
Set Foo = OpenDatabase("C:\VB3\BIBLIO.MDB")
```

***The DataBase Object*** You can analyze properties of this object to find out what you can do with the object. For example, to store the name of the database, you can use

```
NameDBase$ = Data1.Database.Name
```

Similarly, to find out if the database supports transaction control, you can use:

```
TransacFlag% = Data1.Database.Transactions
```

Or to find out if the database is updatable (before trying to update a record), you can use:

```
UpdateFlag% = Data1.DataBase.Updatable
```

There are a couple of other properties, such as CollatingOrder, which are less important—please consult the online help for information on them.

***The TableDef Object and TableDefs Collection*** Think of a TableDef object as giving the framework of the grid that stores the table. You can use the DateCreated property of a Table object to find out when it was created and the LastUpdated property to find out when it was last changed.

The TableDefs collection, on the other hand, is a property of the Database object and collects all the TableDef objects in the database into a single group.

For example, to print the name of all the tables in the database and when they were last updated, use

```
For I = 1 To Data1.Database.TableDefs.Count - 1
  Print Data1.Database.TableDefs(I).Name
  Print Data1.Database.TableDefs(I).LastUpdated
Next I
```

*The Field Object and the Fields Collection* You have already seen the Field object associated to a RecordSet. Field objects are also associated to each TablefDef object. (In practice there really isn't that much difference if all you are doing is checking the names of the fields. The main difference is that the Value property of a Field object is only available when a Table is bound to a data control, thus creating a RecordSet.)

The Fields collection is the set of all Fields associated to a given TableDef. For example, you can nest the previous loop together with another loop to analyze the fields belonging to all the TableDefs in the database.

```
For I = 1 To Data1.Database.TableDefs.Count - 1
  Print Data1.Database.TableDefs(I).Name
  For J = 1 To Data1.Database.TableDefs(I).Fields.Count - 1
    Print Data1.Database.TableDefs(I).Fields(J).Name
    Print Data1.Database.TableDefs(I).Fields(J).Type
    Print Data1.Database.TableDefs(I).Fields(J).Size
    Print Data1.Database.TableDefs(I).Fields(J).Attributes
  Next J
Next I
```

*The Index Object and the Indexes Collection* A table may have many indexes or it may not be indexed at all. The Name property of the Index object tells you the name used by the database for this object. The Indexes collection is all the indexes for a specific table. Using loops similar to ones you have seen in the previous section, you can map out the Index collection as well.

# Chapter 18

# A Checkbook

# Management Program

**t** H E purpose of this chapter is to take you through the design and implementation of a professional quality checkbook management program. The program is supposed to be user-friendly. Therefore it showcases many of the techniques and tools available in Visual Basic.

The length of the program notwithstanding, there are few, if any, techniques in this program that you've not yet seen. And so, although this program will be far longer than any other program in this book, none of the pieces that make it up will be surprising or difficult. However, many people do find the jump from small, one-objective programs, to more sophisticated programs with multiple objectives, daunting. This chapter should make the transition easier.

In the author's opinion, nothing in this book better demonstrates the power of Visual Basic than this chapter. That a user-friendly checkbook program can be written by designing eight forms and using only 1000 or so lines of code clearly shows the power of Visual Basic to improve the productivity of programmers. It is easy to imagine an entire finance program, along the lines of ones that have generated literally tens of millions of dollars of sales, being written in only a few weeks using Visual Basic! Of course, if you don't want to enter all the code by hand, the optional companion disk includes it. (See the end of the introduction to this book for the order form.)

Finally, this chapter is organized somewhat differently from the other chapters. We explain the design of the forms and some of the code early on. Then we place the entire code for each form together with a table for the controls on the form at the end of the chapter.

**note:** *To save space the code in this chapter has most of the error-trapping code removed. You can easily put the error-trapping code back in—it's the same as the one that is attached to the startup (Finance) form (see the listing in the section called "The Finance Form" later in this chapter).*

# Designing the Program

Although there are many commercial home finance programs available, they have added so many bells and whistles that the original purpose of keeping track of your checks and reporting amounts spent by various categories has become obscured. The program in this chapter is designed to be a user-friendly checkbook program. It will keep track of deposits and expenditures and is able to report totals by categories. It would be easy enough to add a reconciliation feature to the program (the grid control is ideal for this). We have not included one because this would have roughly doubled the length of the program.

Imagine for a moment that your boss came in and said: "I want you to write me a friendly checkbook management program." Like many bosses, he or she has some vague idea for this in mind but this is a far cry from having enough information for a programmer to proceed (although programmers often regard "ability to read boss's mind" as an unstated job requirement). You start questioning him or her: "Do you want to handle multiple accounts?," "What kind of information should the program keep track of?," and so on.

After some give-and-take, you find out that the general design goals are that the program should have the following features:

◆ Ability to handle multiple accounts, with the account names the same as the ones used by the bank.

◆ Ability to categorize each check as well as specify tax-deductible status.

◆ Ability to categorize the source of each deposit.

◆ The account's statistics should be available to the user at all times when working with an account.

The report facility should be able to:

◆ Report on either checks or deposits.

◆ Specify the dates to be included.

◆ Include, exclude, or ignore tax status.

◆ Pick one specific category or all categories for totals.

◆ Send reports to the screen, printer—or both.

Now, as a programmer, you realize that some of these goals will be easier to achieve than others. (And quite often what your boss thinks of as hard may turn out to be easy and, unfortunately, vice-versa.) For example, getting reports done is a standard programming task. The information will be stored in files and read back and processed as need be.

On the other hand, some of these requirements may require some thought and therefore be harder to achieve than your boss thought. For example, the first requirement means that account names should not be restricted to the ordinary DOS file conventions of eight characters plus a three-character extension. This in turn means that the programmer has to figure out some way to keep track of the account name other than the obvious step of making it the name of a file.

Since this decision will affect the whole program, you think about it first. After some thought, you decide to use a common programming trick to set up the accounts. Internally, the accounts are numbered ACCT1, ACCT2, and so on. You'll maintain a separately sequential file in the current directory (called, say, ACCOUNTS) that allows the program to translate these internal file names (gotten from the ID number strings "1", "2", and so on) to what the user sees. Associated to each account are three files, one for the account statistics, one for the checks, and one for the deposits. Internally, as far as the program is concerned, they are called ACCT1.DAT, ACCT1.CHK, and ACCT1.DEP. The value of the global variable AccountId$ is the digit string that identifies the account. For "ACCT1.DAT" this would be a "1". Finally, we assume the boss means that the categories should be available to all accounts in the current directory and we will store this information in files called INCATS for deposits and EXPCATS for checks.

**tip:**    *Files like these that contain information useful only to a program are best left with the read-only attribute set when the program ends. Another possibility is to hide the files when the program ends.*

# The User Interface

At this point, the design process moves on to the user interface. All the programmer was told was, "Make it friendly." After some thought we decide we need:

♦ A main menu-driven form.

♦ A form to change the directory. (A common dialog box doesn't quite fit.)

♦ A form for choosing from existing accounts or creating a new account.

♦ A form for working with new or existing accounts that lets you modify (or set up) account data.

♦ A form to record checks (make this look like a check).

♦ A form to record deposits (make this look like a deposit form).

♦ A form to specify the kinds of reports.

♦ A form to display the reports.

Then comes the question of how to give the user the information about the current state of the account. After many iterations, it seemed that what best fit the Windows look and feel was to attach a status bar to the main form, the deposit form, and the check writing form. This status bar would be the same in all cases. As with any status bar, the easiest choice is to use a picture box with the Align property equal to 1. Labels attached to the picture box can display the needed information.

# The Startup Form and the Set Directory Form

The startup form is the form that the user sees when he or she starts the program. We decided to set the Name and caption properties for this form to be Finance and have it fill up roughly 80% of the screen at the start. It should be menu-driven and follow the Windows convention of having a File menu with an Exit option plus menus for the other operations. For simplicity we decided to design the form in the location we wanted it to appear, although the user can move it. We also decided not to allow the user to maximize this form.

To insure that the account statistics will always fit on the form, we do not allow the user to shrink the form smaller than the minimum size needed to display the picture box used for this information. Figure 18-1 shows you the initial screen and Figure 18-2 shows you the menu design window for this form.

The Form_Load procedure, as is very common, calls a procedure to position the form nicely. This general procedure that centers any form is sent the Me object variable, so the Center procedure knows which form to work on. Next

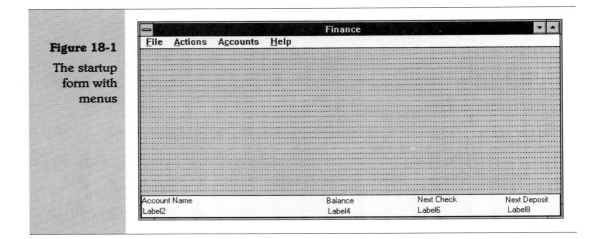

**Figure 18-1**

The startup form with menus

comes the call to the procedure that initializes everything. Finally come the calls to the procedures that update the status bars (picture boxes) on the three forms where they appear.

The Initialize procedure is actually located in the GENERAL.BAS module and what it does is use a static integer variable (AlreadyLoadedOnce) to determine if it has been called once already. The Initialize procedure first clears out the list and combo boxes for both expenses and income categories before

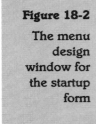

**Figure 18-2**

The menu design window for the startup form

reloading. The filenames for these categories are hard-wired by name into the program and so are not associated to the individual accounts but rather to individual directories. However, you can easily make the changes needed to attach categories to specific accounts rather than to all accounts stored in the directory if you choose to do so. If no account exists, a new one is created with the default name of Account 1, with ID string "1". If accounts exist, then the account name and other information needed is loaded into the combo box displayed on the EStats ("**E**dit **Stat**istic**s**") form. Finally, notice that this procedure (like any procedure handling files or other devices) has an error trap. The error trap sends the error number to a (global) function for processing.

Here is the code for the Form_Load, the Center procedure, and the Initialize procedure.

```
Sub Form_Load ()
    Center Me
    Initialize
    Call UpdateStats(Me)
    Call UpdateStats(Checks)
    Call UpdateStats(Deposits)
    SetFocus
End Sub

Sub Initialize ()
'from GENERAL.BAS
    Dim ErrorNumber As Integer
    On Error GoTo Problems0
    Static AlreadyLoadedOnce As Integer
    If Not (AlreadyLoadedOnce) Then
        gOldDrive$ = Left(CurDir$, 2) 'get current drive
        gOldPath$ = CurDir$              'and path so can reset at end
        AlreadyLoadedOnce = True
        M$ = "This program is copyright 1993 by Gary Cornell."
        MsgBox M$
    End If

    Call OpenAccount
    Call LoadCatLists
    Finance.Show
    Exit Sub
Problems0:
    ErrorNumber = Err
    If ProcessErrorOK(ErrorNumber) Then Resume
End Sub
```

```
Sub Center (frm As Form)
'from GENERAL.BAS
  frm.Move (Screen.Width - frm.Width) / 2, (Screen.Height - _
frm.Height) / 2
End Sub
```

Notice that the global variables in the general procedures begin with a lowercase "g." This is a quite common programming practice and makes it easier to identify these important (but nonetheless potentially bug-breeding) objects.

The code for all the Click procedures attached to each of the menu items is pretty straightforward. The Set Directory Click procedure shows the form to choose the directory. Notice in Figure 18-3 that we have placed three labels, a drive, a directory list box, and two command buttons on this form. This form will usually be invisible but if the user decides to switch to another directory from the file menu—see Figures 18-1 and 18-2—we will make it appear again.

The Exit procedure ends the program after writing the data to the appropriate file. This is done using the value of the global variable gAccountId$ that internally tracks the account and attaches the ".DAT" suffix and "ACCT" prefix to give the filename. We also save the last account accessed so that will be the default account next time in a (tiny) sequential file called "LASTACCT". The directory will then change back to what it was before the program started. (This is a good programming practice—and in any case, it's not neighborly to leave the logged drive changed.)

**Figure 18-3**

The form for resetting a directory

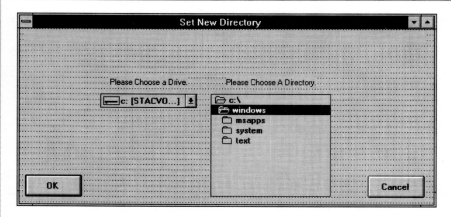

Each of the other menu items when clicked shows the appropriate form and initializes the various objects on the form. Here, for example, is the Check_Click procedure that a user activates if he or she wants to write a check.

```
Sub Check_Click ()
  Checks.Number.Text = Format$(gNextChk, "0")
  Checks.CrtDate.Text = ""
  Checks.PayTo.Text = ""
  Checks.Amount.Text = ""
  Checks.Memo.Text = ""
  Checks.Category.Text = ""
  Checks.Tax.Value = False
  Finance.Hide
  Call UpdateStats(Checks)
  Checks.Show 1
  Finance.Show
End Sub
```

This resets the values of all the text boxes to be blank except that it adds the current check number (using the value of the global variable gNextChk) to the Number text box and uses a general procedure to update the picture box on the Checks form with the current account statistics.

## The Picture Box Used for Account Statistics Forms

We use what is essentially the same picture box on every form where it needs to show up. Using exactly the same names for all the labels makes it easy to update the picture box by passing the name of the form to a general procedure. There are eight labels in this picture box. Four are used for identification and the other four will be used to show the data.

| Account Name | Balance | Next Check | Next Deposit |
|---|---|---|---|
| Label2 | **Label4** | Label6 | Label8 |

Here's the general code that updates this picture box on every form.

```
Sub UpdateStats (X As Form)
  X!AcctName.Caption = gAccountName$
  X!AcctBalance.Caption = Format$(gBalance, "0,0.00")
  X!AcctNextChk.Caption = Format$(gNextChk, "0")
```

```
X!AcctNextDep.Caption = Format$(gNextDep, "0")
End Sub
```

Again, notice how simple this procedure can be because we used the same control names on each picture box.

## Remaining Code for Finance Form

As with all forms in this project, the complete code attached to the form is given at the end of the chapter without a break save for a table that gives the controls. When you do examine the code notice the error-trapping routine in each procedure that works with files. (We need a different label in each routine because labels must be unique across a module.)

The two most interesting procedures left in this form are the QueryUnload procedure and the Form_Resize procedure. The QueryUnload procedure is very important to give the finance form the proper Windows behavior of shutting down in response to the ALT+F4 combination. We need to unload all the remaining forms in order to end the program properly. The Form_Resize procedure is there to insure that the user cannot make the form too small to display the account statistics. The user can minimize the form but, as long as it is not iconized, the form must (by the design goals) be large enough to display the account information.

## The Accounts Form

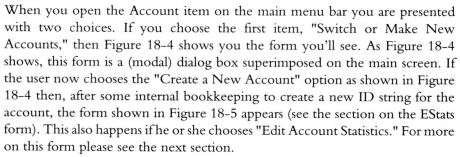

When you open the Account item on the main menu bar you are presented with two choices. If you choose the first item, "Switch or Make New Accounts," then Figure 18-4 shows you the form you'll see. As Figure 18-4 shows, this form is a (modal) dialog box superimposed on the main screen. If the user now chooses the "Create a New Account" option as shown in Figure 18-4 then, after some internal bookkeeping to create a new ID string for the account, the form shown in Figure 18-5 appears (see the section on the EStats form). This also happens if he or she chooses "Edit Account Statistics." For more on this form please see the next section.

The list box shows all the currently assigned account names, with the first item used to create a new account. All user account names are trimmed if necessary to have length 30 (the value of the global constant gMaxAcctName-

**Figure 18-4**

The form for working with an account

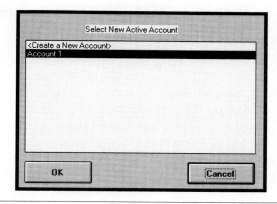

Len—this can easily be changed). The ID string is kept as the value of the ItemData property for the particular entry in the list box.

When the user clicks the OK button (or double-clicks an item), we call the Click procedure. This procedure first saves the current account information and closes the file that handles that account. The procedure then checks the name via a call to the ChangeName procedure. This assigns the account name to its internal account ID string and finally updates the sequential file that contains the user's version of the account name as well.

**note:** *This program does not hide these files or change the read attribute. It is best to add any code that modifies file attributes after most of the testing and development of your project is finished.*

Since the Form_Load procedure for the startup (Finance) form clears the old information in the list box and then loads the account information stored in the current directory into the list box on this form, the whole procedure is completely transparent to the user. This Form_Load procedure also loads the data for the account that was last used. Or, if this is the first time the user has used the program in the current directory, it sets up an account with the default name of Account 1 and pops the user in the EditStats form (see the next section). The user can, of course, click the Accounts main menu item and choose the Switch or Make New Accounts item to choose another account or add a new account.

There are two interesting procedures attached to this form. The GetNextId procedure is simple: it looks at the master account file ("ACCOUNTS") and finds out how many accounts exist in order to create the next ID number string.

When the user clicks the OK button, then the OK_Click procedure is activated. This procedure records the current account statistics using the internal ID string given by the variable AccountId$. Then it checks whether the user clicked on the New Account menu item. He or she is then asked to confirm the choice. If confirmed, then this procedure generates a new ID string using the CreateAccountId Sub procedure. Otherwise, the program finds the account ID by looking at the value of the ItemData property of the current entry in the list box.

```
Sub AccountNames_DblClick ()
  Call OK_Click
End Sub

Sub GetNextId (Id$)
  'This routine opens the list of accounts to find out the
  ' next valid id number - valid accounts are numbered
  ' consecutively

  'local variables
  Dim NextId As Integer, N$

  NextId = 1
  Open "ACCOUNTS" For Input As #1
  Do While Not EOF(1)
    Input #1, N$, Id$
    If Val(Id$) >= NextId Then NextId = Val(Id$) + 1
  Loop
  Close #1
  Id$ = Format$(NextId, "#")
End Sub

Sub OK_Click ()
  'This routine opens up a file with the account info
  ' the file ideas are of the form ACCT1.DAT ACCT2.DAT etc
  'the global variable gAccountId$ provides the "1" "2" etc

  'local variables:
  Dim Id$, Index As Integer

  'record stats on current account
```

```
Open "ACCT" + gAccountId$ + ".DAT" For Output As 1
Write #1, gBalance, gNextChk, gNextDep
Close #1

'These lines of code check for the < that is the
'first few characters on the Create New Account item in
'the list box. This shows the user wants to
'define a new account. Of course, if someone enters
' an account name with these leading characters the program
'bombs you can easily add the code to check for this

Index = AccountNames.ListIndex
If Left$(AccountNames.List(Index), 7) = "Create" Then
    'user has asked to create a new account
    If MsgBox("Please confirm: Create a New Account", 4) <> 6_
Then Exit Sub
    Accounts.Hide
    Call GetNextId(Id$)
    Call CreateAccount(Id$)
Else
    'switch to new account
    Accounts.Hide
    gAccountName$ = Trim$(Left$(AccountNames.List(Index), _
MaxAcctNameLen))
    gAccountId$ = Trim$(Str$(AccountNames.ItemData(Index)))
    Open "ACCT" + gAccountId$ + ".DAT" For Input As #1
    Input #1, gBalance, gNextChk, gNextDep
    Close #1
End If
Call UpdateStats(Finance)
Call UpdateStats(Checks)
Call UpdateStats(Deposits)
End Sub
```

# The EStats (Edit Statistics) Form

This form (shown in Figure 18-5) is accessed from the Accounts item on the main menu bar by choosing the "Edit Account Statistics" item. Also, if the user starts the program before any accounts exist or wants to create a new account, he or she will be sent to this form with a default name of Account 1 showing in the first text box. Whether working with a new or existing account this form lets them enter a new balance, the next check number, or the next deposit number in the appropriate text boxes.

Once the user enters a name, changes the account statistics, and clicks the OK button, the OK_Click procedure checks if the name is already in use. If it is, it pops you back in the form after a message box pops up telling you to choose a new name. On the other hand, if the name entered in the first text box hasn't changed or if it has but the user hasn't tried to create a new account by choosing that option from the appropriate menu, then the program allows this by rewriting the ACCOUNTS file with the new information. Otherwise, the program uses the ID string created in the Accounts form and adds that account name and ID string to the list box and the Accounts file.

## The Forms for Entering Checks and Deposits

Figures 18-6 and 18-7 show the forms for these two tasks. As you can see in these figures, we use a frame to visually set off the deposit and check from the combo box listing categories or the command buttons that actually activate the event procedures. Both of these forms have a default cancel button—so the user can press ESC to go back to the main screen (the Finance form).

As an example of user friendliness that is easy to add using Visual Basic, we decided to have the current date show up if the user moved the focus away

**Figure 18-5**

**The EditStats form**

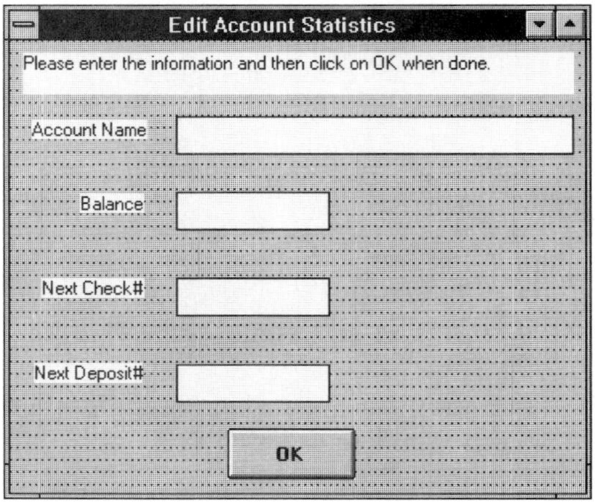

```
┌─────────────────────────────────────────────────┐
│ ─        Edit Account Statistics         ▼ ▲     │
├─────────────────────────────────────────────────┤
│ Please enter the information and then click on OK when done. │
│                                                  │
│  Account Name   ┌──────────────────────────────┐ │
│                 └──────────────────────────────┘ │
│                                                  │
│       Balance   ┌──────────────┐                 │
│                 └──────────────┘                 │
│                                                  │
│   Next Check#   ┌──────────────┐                 │
│                 └──────────────┘                 │
│                                                  │
│  Next Deposit#  ┌──────────────┐                 │
│                 └──────────────┘                 │
│                       ┌──────────┐               │
│                       │    OK    │               │
│                       └──────────┘               │
└─────────────────────────────────────────────────┘
```

**Figure 18-6**

Form for entering checks

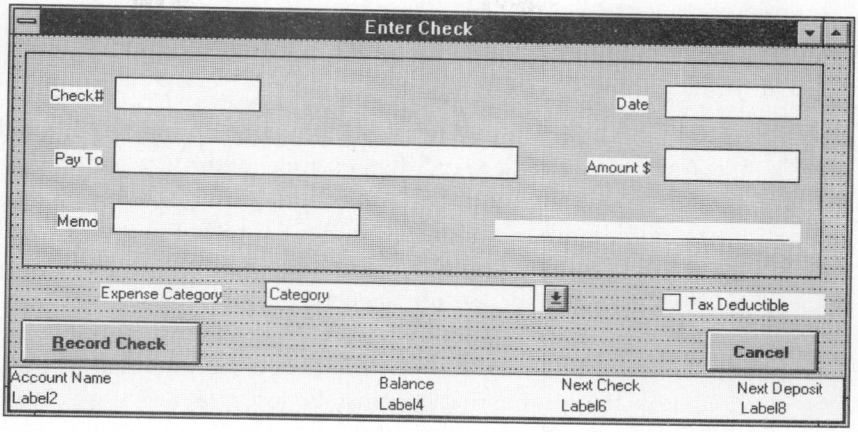

from the date box without entering a date. This requires only two lines of code in the LostFocus event procedure:

```
Sub CrtDate_LostFocus ()
  CrtDate.Text = Trim$(CrtDate.Text)
  If Len(CrtDate.Text) = 0 Then CrtDate.Text = Date$
End Sub
```

**Figure 18-7**

Form for entering deposits

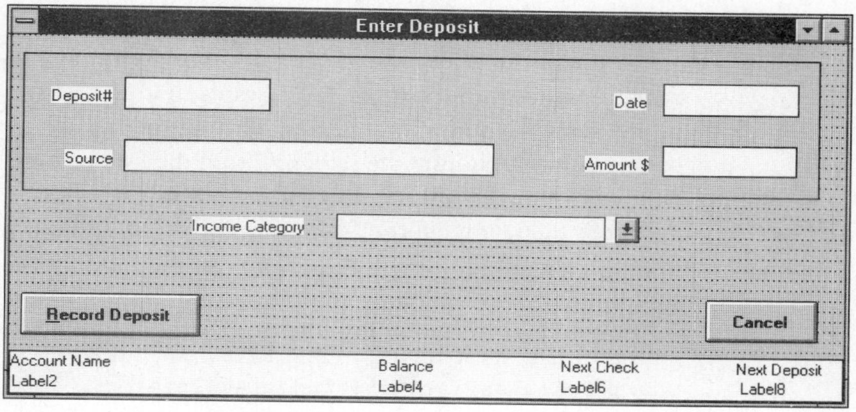

**note:** *We're assuming that if nothing but blanks were entered, then the user wants the current date.*

Both these forms use a similar Function procedure to validate the data entered before writing it to disk. For example, if the user hasn't entered a numeric string for the value, we notify him or her. We do not restrict the string to only digits and commas—although you saw the techniques for this additional method of bulletproofing a program in Chapter 7. Just as we use a general function to validate the date, we use a general function to validate values. Whenever a check is written or a deposit is made, the sequential file (identified by the Account-Name$ ID string) is immediately updated—but because of Windows buffering it is still possible that data may be lost if there is a system crash.

**tip:** *Remember the Reset command to flush file buffers in critical situations.*

# The Reports Form

Most of the hard work in this program is contained in the procedures and functions attached to the form that gives reports. The form (shown in Figure 18-8) is quite complicated. It has six framed areas. As you can see in Figure 18-8, some of these are for visual effects but three are absolutely necessary because they contain independent groups of option buttons. For example, the frame on the top-left corner asks the user whether he or she wants a report on checks or deposits. The one in the bottom-right corner asks whether the report is to go to the screen, the printer, or both.

To understand how the procedures work, let's suppose the user specifies dates, picks a specific category, and wants to know what checks were written in that category during those dates. The user makes the appropriate choices of option buttons, chooses the category from the list box, and clicks the Generate Report command button.

Here's the GenReport_Click procedure

```
Sub GenReport_Click ()
  'local variables:
  Dim Total As Currency, SubTotal As Currency
  Dim DoAll As Integer, Index As Integer
```

```
    Dim StartDate As String, StopDate As String
    Dim TaxVal As Integer, SearchCat As String

    Reports.RepTotal.Visible = False
    If ReportOptionsOk(DoAll, Index, StartDate, StopDate,_
TaxVal) Then
       Call TitleReport(StartDate, StopDate)
       Total = 0
       Do
          SearchCat = Trim$(Reports.Category.List(Index))
          SubTotal = 0
          Call ReportOnOneCategory(SearchCat, SubTotal,_
StartDate, StopDate, TaxVal)
          Call ReportSubTotal(SearchCat, SubTotal)
          Index = Index + 1
          Total = Total + SubTotal
       Loop Until (Not DoAll) Or (Index >_
Reports.Category.ListCount - 1)
       Reports.CheckReport.SetFocus
       Call ReportTotal(Total)
    End If
End Sub
```

This procedure first calls the ReportsOptionsOK function to check if what the user is asking for is acceptable. Because this function passes the key variable

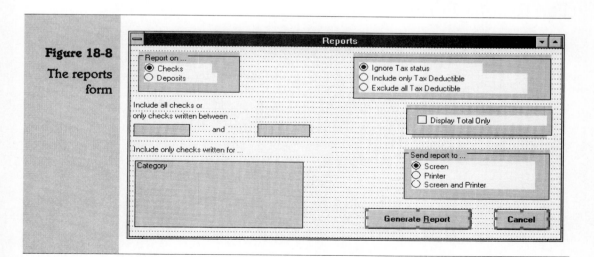

**Figure 18-8**

The reports form

DoAll by reference, it can modify this to be True or False depending on whether the first (all categories) or a specific category (any of the others given in the list box) was selected. The function also checks the start date and stop dates to see if they are valid. If no date is selected, the values are set to "0000000000" and "999999999" respectively. Since these values are used as serial numbers by the Ymd function, this effectively gives all checks (well, actually those written after 1900).

So, suppose the user chooses a single category and specific dates. The key DoAll variable is set to False in the ReportsOptionsOK function. Next, notice the Do Loop inside the Click procedure is tested at the bottom. This insures that we always pass through it at least once. However, if the key DoAll variable is False, then we pass though it *only* once. Otherwise, the Do Loop continues until we run out of categories.

What happens inside this loop? We display the title of the report by calling a procedure for it. Next, we identify the category to be analyzed by the line:

```
SearchCat = Trim$(Reports.Category.List(Index))
```

This procedure than calls a ReportOnOneCategory Sub procedure that analyzes the data contained in the sequential file for either the checks or deposits in the account using this category to identify the acceptable data.

## The Results Form

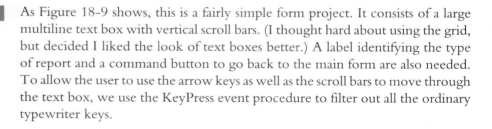

As Figure 18-9 shows, this is a fairly simple form project. It consists of a large multiline text box with vertical scroll bars. (I thought hard about using the grid, but decided I liked the look of text boxes better.) A label identifying the type of report and a command button to go back to the main form are also needed. To allow the user to use the arrow keys as well as the scroll bars to move through the text box, we use the KeyPress event procedure to filter out all the ordinary typewriter keys.

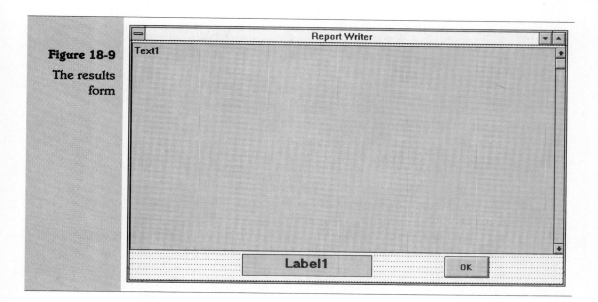

**Figure 18-9**
The results
form

# The General Code for the Program

First off, here's the part of the .MAK file that lists the forms and modules with the names we chose:

```
FINANCE.FRM
CHECKS.FRM
REPORTS.FRM
DEPOSITS.FRM
ESTATS.FRM
SETDIR.FRM
RESULTS.FRM
ACCOUNTS.FRM
GENPROCS.BAS
CONSTANT.BAS
```

The CONSTANT.BAS file contains the global variables and constants. Here it is:

```
'global variables and constants
Global gAccountName$, gAccountId$
Global gCurrentDrive$, gCurrentPath$
Global gOldDrive$, gOldPath$
Global gBalance As Currency
Global gNextChk As Integer, gNextDep As Integer
Global Const MaxAcctNameLen = 30
```

As you can see this sets up nine global variables, each with the "g" prefix identifier. These are used to identify the original path and drive, the current path and drive, the account name, an ID number (actually a string of digits) used by the program to identify the account being worked with, the current balance, the number of the next check, and the number of the next deposit. Since this sort of information really needs to be available to the whole program, making them global variables in a code module is the obvious way to proceed.

## The General Procedures Module

You've already seen the general procedures used to initialize the program, update the stats picture box, and center a form. We needed a few other Sub procedures and Function procedures that were accessible to the entire program. As is common with big programs, one of the Function procedures was used for analyzing errors.

Since adding a category to the various combo and list boxes is such a common operation, we made a general Sub procedure out of this. By making all the combo boxes have the same control name (Category) we can simplify the code a little bit. We don't need to pass the name of the combo box—passing the form name is enough.

In the AddCat procedure given below, the loop runs through the items in the combo box on the form being worked with and checks whether the category is included (by using the UCase$ function, case is ignored). If the category doesn't exist, the user is given the option of adding the category by means of a message box. The program then appends the category to the sequential file named by the CatFile$ string variable and the item is added to the combo box as well. The code to load the list of categories uses the Clear method first to reset the box before actually loading the information.

The CreateAccount procedure that creates an account sets up a sequential file called "ACCOUNTS" in the current directory. (The user can change the current directory from the file menu on the startup form.) This file contains the user's name for the account (his or her name, the business name, and so on) and the ID number string that is passed to this procedure. This procedure also creates the basic data file, list of checks, and list of deposits (".DAT", ".CHK", ".DEP"). This way the code that opens an account by reading in the needed information looks for the file named "ACCOUNTS" in the current directory in order to read back this information. The EditStats procedure resets the display in the Edit Statistics (EStat) form.

The functions that checks whether a date or number is valid uses the IsDate and IsNumeric functions which work with variants. These functions pass either True or False back to the calling procedure.

Finally, there's the error handler. This function would analyze the error number sent to it and give the user some feedback. This is a pretty bare bones version and you could easily make it much more elaborate. (I would probably not change file attributes in an error handler. If the program ends abnormally, the designer should see the state it is in. One exception sometimes worth making is using the Reset command to flush buffers.)

## THE COMPLETE GENPROC.BAS CODE

```
Sub AddCat (NewItem$, Op As Form, CatFile$)
    'local variables:
    Dim I As Integer

    'check to see if category is already listed
    For I = 0 To Op.Category.ListCount
        If Trim$(UCase$(Op.Category.List(I))) =_
Trim$(UCase$(NewItem$)) Then
            Exit For
        End If
    Next I
    'if category not listed, confirm and add to list and file
    If I = Op.Category.ListCount + 1 Then
        I = MsgBox("Add new category " + NewItem$ + " to list?",_
1)
        If I = 1 Then
            Op.Category.AddItem NewItem$
            Open CatFile$ For Append As 1
            Write #1, NewItem$
            Close 1
```

```
      Else
        NewItem$ = ""
        Op.Category.Text = ""
      End If
    End If
End Sub

Sub Center (frm As Form)
  frm.Move (Screen.Width - frm.Width) / 2, (Screen.Height - _
frm.Height) / 2
  'Finance.Move (Screen.Width - Finance.Width) / 2,_
Screen.Height - _
Stats.Height - Finance.Height
End Sub

Sub CreateAccount (Id$)
  'add account name and id to ACCOUNTS file
  Open "ACCOUNTS" For Append As #1
  gAccountName$ = "Account " + Id$
  gAccountId$ = Id$
  Write #1, gAccountName$, gAccountId$
  Close #1
  'create ACCT#.DAT, ACCT#.CHK, and ACCT#.DEP
  Open "ACCT" + gAccountId$ + ".DAT" For Output As #1
  gBalance = 0
  gNextChk = 1
  gNextDep = 1
  Write #1, gBalance, gNextChk, gNextDep
  Close #1
  Open "ACCT" + gAccountId$ + ".CHK" For Output As #1
  Close #1
  Open "ACCT" + gAccountId$ + ".DEP" For Output As #1
  Close #1
  'mark new account as the last account accessed
  Open "LASTACCT" For Output As 1
  Write #1, gAccountName$, gAccountId$
  Close #1
  'add account name (and id) to AccountNames list
  Accounts!AccountNames.AddItem gAccountName$ + Space$_
(MaxAcctNameLen - Len(gAccountName$))
Accounts!AccountNames.ItemData(Accounts!AccountNames.NewIndex)_
= Val(gAccountId$)
  Call EditStats
End Sub
```

```
Sub EditStats ()
  Estats!AcctName.Text = gAccountName$
  Estats!AcctBalance.Text = Format$(gBalance, "00.00")
  Estats!AcctNextChk.Text = Format$(gNextChk, "0")
  Estats!AcctNextDep.Text = Format$(gNextDep, "0")
  Estats.Show 1
End Sub


Sub Initialize ()
  Dim ErrorNumber As Integer
  On Error GoTo Problems0
  Static AlreadyLoadedOnce As Integer
  If Not (AlreadyLoadedOnce) Then
    gOldDrive$ = Left(CurDir$, 2) 'get current drive
    gOldPath$ = CurDir$            'and path so can reset at end
    AlreadyLoadedOnce = True
    M$ = "This program is copyright 1993 by Gary Cornell."
    MsgBox M$
  End If

    Call OpenAccount
    Call LoadCatLists
    Finance.Show
    UpDateStats Finance
    UpDateStats Checks
    UpDateStats Deposits

    Exit Sub
Problems0:
  ErrorNumber = Err
  If ProcessErrorOK(ErrorNumber) Then Resume
End Sub


Sub LoadCatLists ()
  'load list of expense categories
  'by looking for a file in the current directory
  'set from the initial form
  Dim ErrorNumber As Integer
  Checks.Category.Clear
  Deposits.Category.Clear
  On Error GoTo Problems1
  If Dir$("EXPCATS") = "EXPCATS" Then
    Open "EXPCATS" For Input As #1
```

```
      Do While Not EOF(1)
         Input #1, catname$
         Checks.Category.AddItem catname$
      Loop
      Close #1
   End If
   'load list of income categories
   If Dir$("INCCATS") = "INCCATS" Then
      Open "INCCATS" For Input As 1
      Do While Not EOF(1)
         Input #1, catname$
         Deposits.Category.AddItem catname$
      Loop
      Close 1
   End If

Exit Sub
Problems1:
 ErrorNumber = Err
 If ProcessErrorOK(ErrorNumber) Then Resume
End Sub

Sub OpenAccount ()
   Dim ErrorNumber As Integer
   On Error GoTo Problems3
   If Not (Dir$("ACCOUNTS") = "ACCOUNTS") Then
      'setup initial account files the first time program is run
      Call CreateAccount("1")
   Else
      Accounts!AccountNames.Clear
      'load list of account names into Accounts combo box
      Open "ACCOUNTS" For Input As #1
      Do While Not EOF(1)
         Input #1, gAccountName$, gAccountId$

         Accounts!AccountNames.AddItem gAccountName$ + _
Space$(MaxAcctNameLen - Len(gAccountName$))
Accounts!AccountNames.ItemData(Accounts!AccountNames.NewIndex)_
= Val(gAccountId$)
      Loop
      Close #1
      'open last account accessed as the default account
      Open "LASTACCT" For Input As #1
      Input #1, gAccountName$, gAccountId$
```

```
     Close #1
     Open "ACCT" + gAccountId$ + ".DAT" For Input As #1
     Input #1, gBalance, gNextChk, gNextDep
     Close #1
   End If
   'add an entry for the user to select when a new account is
'to be created
   Accounts.AccountNames.AddItem "Create a New Account"
   'make the first account created the default when switching _
'accounts the first time
   Accounts.AccountNames.ListIndex = 1
Exit Sub
Problems3:
 ErrorNumber = Err
 If ProcessErrorOK(Err) Then Resume
End Sub

Sub UpDateStats (X As Form)
  X.AcctName.Caption = gAccountName$
  X.AcctBalance.Caption = Format$(gBalance, "0,0.00")
  X.AcctNextChk.Caption = Format$(gNextChk, "0")
  X.AcctNextDep.Caption = Format$(gNextDep, "0")
End Sub

Function ValidDate (D$) As Integer
   'local variables:
   Dim Hold As Variant
   Hold = D$
   ValidDate = IsDate(Hold)
End Function

Function ValidNumber (D$) As Integer
   'local variables:
   Dim Hold As Variant
   Hold = D$
   ValidNumber = IsNumeric(Hold)
End Function

Function ProcessErrorOK (A As Integer) As Integer
 Dim Msg$, MsgType As Integer, ErrorResponse As Integer
 Select Case A
  Case 57
   Msg$ = "I/O error."
   MsgType = 5
```

```
   Case 61
     Msg$ = "Disk full"
     MsgType = 5
   Case 68    'Device unavailable
    Msg$ = "Can't use that device now - check drive."
    MsgType = 5
   Case 71
    Msg$ = "Disk Not ready."
    MsgType = 5
   Case 482
    Msg$ = "Printer error."
    MsgType = 5

 End Select

 ErrorResponse = MsgBox(Msg$, MsgType, "Errors!")

 Select Case ErrorResponse
   Case 1, 4
     ProcessErrorOK = True
   Case Else
     Msg$ = "Please report error number" + Str$(A) + " to your _
operator"
     Msg$ = Msg$ + Chr$(13) + Chr$(10) + "am shutting down now."
     Close
     MsgBox Msg$
     End
   End Select
End Function
```

# The Finance Form

We begin with a table that gives the controls followed by their name, followed by the caption or text property if appropriate. Controls inside frames follow the frame in this table, making it easier to match the controls up with Figure 18-1.

| Control Type | Name | Caption (or Text) Property Value |
|---|---|---|
| Form | Finance | Finance |
| PictureBox | Picture1 | |
| Label | AcctNextDep | Label8 |
| Label | Label1 | Next Deposit |

| Control Type | Name | Caption (or Text) Property Value |
|---|---|---|
| Label | AcctNextChk | Label6 |
| Label | Label3 | Next Check |
| Label | AcctBalance | Label4 |
| Label | Label5 | Balance |
| Label | AcctName | Label2 |
| Label | Label7 | Account Name |
| Menu | FileMenu | &File |
| Menu | SetDir | &Set Directory ... |
| Menu | Exit | E&xit |
| Menu | Actions | &Actions |
| Menu | Deposit | Enter &Deposit |
| Menu | Check | Enter &Check |
| Menu | Report | Create &Report ... |
| Menu | Accts | A&ccounts |
| Menu | Switch | &Switch or Make New Account ... |
| Menu | EditStats | &Edit Account Statistics ... |
| Menu | Help | &Help |

Here's the complete code attached to this form

```
Sub Check_Click ()
  Checks.Number.Text = Format$(gNextChk, "0")
  Checks.CrtDate.Text = ""
  Checks.PayTo.Text = ""
  Checks.Amount.Text = ""
  Checks.Memo.Text = ""
  Checks.Category.Text = ""
  Checks.Tax.Value = False
  Finance.Hide
  Call UpDateStats(Checks)
  Checks.Show 1
  Finance.Show
End Sub

Sub Deposit_Click ()
  Deposits.Number.Text = Format$(gNextDep, "0")
  Deposits.CrtDate.Text = ""
  Deposits.Source.Text = ""
  Deposits.Amount.Text = ""
```

```
      Deposits.Category.Text = ""
      Finance.Hide
      Call UpDateStats(Deposits)
      Deposits.Show 1
      Finance.Show
End Sub

Sub EditStats_Click ()
   Finance.Hide
   Call EditStats
   Finance.Show
End Sub

Sub Exit_Click ()
   Dim ErrorNumber As Integer
   On Error GoTo Problems5
   'record final stats on account
   Open "ACCT" + gAccountId$ + ".DAT" For Output As 1
   Write #1, gBalance, gNextChk, gNextDep
   Close #1
   'record last account accessed so it can be the default
'account next time
   Open "LASTACCT" For Output As 1
   Write #1, gAccountName$, gAccountId$
   Close #1
   'clear screen and exit

   Finance.Hide
   Cls
   ChDrive gOldDrive$
   ChDir gOldPath$
   'here's a good place to change the attributes or hide the
'files
   End

Problems5:
   ErrorNumber = Err
  If ProcessErrorOK(ErrorNumber) Then Resume

End Sub

Sub Form_Load ()
   Center Me
   Initialize
```

```
      Call UpDateStats(Me)
      Call UpDateStats(Checks)
      Call UpDateStats(Deposits)
      SetFocus
End Sub


Sub Form_QueryUnload (Cancel As Integer, UnloadMode As_
Integer)
      Unload Accounts
      Unload Checks
      Unload Deposits
      Unload Estats
      Unload Reports
      Unload Results
      Unload SetDirForm
      Unload Me
      ChDrive gOldDrive$
      ChDir OldPath
End
End Sub


Sub Form_Resize ()
      If WindowState <> 1 And Width < 9000 Then
        Width = 9000   'large enough for stats to show
        Center Me
      End If
End Sub


Sub Help_Click ()
  MsgBox ("Help feature not implemented yet.")
End Sub


Sub Report_Click ()
      Reports.Date1.Text = ""
      Reports.Date2.Text = ""
      Reports.Category.ListIndex = -1
      Finance.Hide
      Reports.Show 1
      Finance.Show
End Sub


Sub SetDir_Click ()
      gCurrentDrive$ = Left(CurDir$, 1)
      gCurrentPath$ = CurDir$
```

```
    Finance.Hide
    SetDirForm.Show
End Sub

Sub Switch_Click ()
    'of course where you position and size things is up to you
    Finance.Hide
    Accounts.Show 1
    Finance.Show
End Sub
```

## The SetDir Form

As before, we begin with the table that gives the controls, followed by their name, followed by the caption or text property if appropriate. This makes it easier to match up with Figure 18–3.

| Control Type | Name | Caption (or Text) Property Value |
| --- | --- | --- |
| Form | SetDirForm | Set New Directory |
| CommandButton | Ok | OK |
| CommandButton | Cancel | Cancel |
| DirListBox | Dir1 | |
| DriveListBox | Drive1 | |
| Label | Direction | |
| Label | Label2 | Please Choose A Directory |
| Label | Label1 | Please Choose a Drive |

Here's the complete code attached to this form

```
Sub Cancel_Click ()
    SetDirForm.Hide
    Finance.Show
    Drive1.Drive = gCurrentDrive$
    Dir1.Path = CurrentPath$
End Sub
```

```
Sub Drive1_Change ()
  Dim ErrorNumber As Integer
  On Error GoTo Problems4
  Dir1.Path = Drive1.Drive
  Exit Sub

Problems4:
  ErrorNumber = Err
  If ProcessErrorOK(ErrorNumber) Then Resume
End Sub

Sub Form_Load ()
  Center Me
  C$ = "To change where the program looks for files, change "
  C$ = C$ + "the drive if necessary and then highlight the "
  C$ = C$ + "directory. (Double click on a directory to move "
  C$ = C$ + "to its subdirectories.) When you have "
  C$ = C$ + "highlighted the correct (sub)directory, "
  C$ = C$ + "click on OK for the changes to go into effect. "
  C$ = C$ + "You can always click on Cancel  (or press Esc) "
  C$ = C$ + "to  use the current path with no changes."
  DirectionLabel.Caption = C$
End Sub

Sub OK_Click ()
  'This changes the logged drive and directory
  'and hides all the controls used to work with directories
'and drives
  Dim ErrorNumber As Integer
  On Error GoTo Problems2
  ChDrive Drive1.Drive
  ChDir Dir1.Path
  SetDirForm.Hide
  Finance.Show
  Call Initialize
  Exit Sub

Problems2:
  ErrorNumber = Err
  If ProcessErrorOK(ErrorNumber) Then Resume
End Sub
```

## The Accounts Form

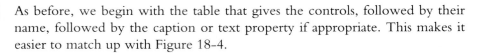

As before, we begin with the table that gives the controls, followed by their name, followed by the caption or text property if appropriate. This makes it easier to match up with Figure 18-4.

| Control Type | Name | Caption (or Text) Property Value |
| --- | --- | --- |
| Form | Accounts | |
| ListBox | AccountNames | |
| CommandButton | Ok | OK |
| CommandButton | Cancel | Cancel |
| Label | Label1 | Select New Active Account |

Here's the complete code attached to this form

```
Sub AccountNames_DblClick ()
  Call OK_Click
End Sub

Sub Cancel_Click ()
  Accounts.Hide
End Sub

Sub Form_Load ()
  Center Me
End Sub

Sub GetNextId (Id$)
  'This routine opens the list of accounts to find out the
  ' next valid id number - valid accounts are numbered
  ' consecutively

  'local variables
  Dim NextId As Integer, N$

  NextId = 1
  Open "ACCOUNTS" For Input As #1
  Do While Not EOF(1)
    Input #1, N$, Id$
    If Val(Id$) >= NextId Then NextId = Val(Id$) + 1
  Loop
```

```
   Close #1
   Id$ = Format$(NextId, "#")
End Sub

Sub OK_Click ()
   'This routine opens up a file with the account info
   ' the file ideas are of the form ACCT1.DAT ACCT2.DAT etc
   'the global variable gAccountId$ provides the "1" "2" etc

   'local variables:
   Dim Id$, Index As Integer

   'record stats on current account
   Open "ACCT" + gAccountId$ + ".DAT" For Output As 1
   Write #1, gBalance, gNextChk, gNextDep
   Close #1

   'These lines of code check for the < that is the
   'first few characters on the Create New Account item in
   'the list box. This shows the user wants to
   'define a new account. Of course, if someone enters
   ' an account name with these leading characters the program
'bombs you can easily add the code to check for this

   Index = AccountNames.ListIndex
   If Left$(AccountNames.List(Index), 7) = "Create" The
      'user has asked to create a new account
      If MsgBox("Please confirm: Create a New Account", 4) <> 6
Then Exit Sub
      Accounts.Hide
      Call GetNextId(Id$)
      Call CreateAccount(Id$)
   Else
      'switch to new account
      Accounts.Hide
      gAccountName$ = Trim$(Left$(AccountNames.List(Index), _
MaxAcctNameLen))
      gAccountId$ = Trim$(Str$(AccountNames.ItemData(Index)))
      Open "ACCT" + gAccountId$ + ".DAT" For Input As #1
      Input #1, gBalance, gNextChk, gNextDep
      Close #1
   End If
   Call UpDateStats(Finance)
   Call UpDateStats(Checks)
```

```
      Call UpDateStats(Deposits)
End Sub
```

## The EStats Form

Here's the table that gives the controls, followed by their name, followed by the caption or text property if appropriate. This makes it easier to match up with Figure 18-5.

| Control Type | Name | Caption (or Text) Property Value |
|---|---|---|
| Form | Estats | Edit Account Statistics |
| TextBox | AcctName | |
| TextBox | AcctBalance | |
| TextBox | AcctNextChk | |
| CommandButton | OK | |
| TextBox | AcctNextDep | |
| Label | Label5 | Please enter the information and then click on OK when done |
| Label | Label2 | Balance |
| Label | Label3 | Next Check# |
| Label | Label4 | Next Deposit# |
| Label | Label1 | Account Name |

Here's the complete code attached to this form

```
Sub Cancel_Click ()
  AcctName.SetFocus
  EStats.Hide
End Sub

Sub ChangeName (NewName$)
  'local variables:
  Dim N$, Id$, I As Integer

  Open "ACCOUNTS" For Input As #1
  Open "_t_e_m_p" For Output As #2
  Do While Not EOF(1)
    Input #1, N$, Id$
    If Id$ = gAccountId$ Then N$ = NewName$
```

```
      Write #2, N$, Id$
   Loop
   Close #1, #2
   Kill "ACCOUNTS"
   Name "_t_e_m_p" As "ACCOUNTS"
   For I = 0 To Accounts.AccountNames.ListCount - 1
      If Accounts.AccountNames.ItemData(I) = Val(gAccountId$)_
Then
      Accounts.AccountNames.List(I) = NewName$ + _
Space$(MaxAcctNameLen - Len(NewName$))
      Accounts.AccountNames.ItemData(I) = Val(gAccountId$)
      Exit For
      End If
   Next I
End Sub


Sub Form_Load ()
   Cls
   Print "please"
   Center Me
End Sub


Function NotGoodName (A$) As Integer
   Dim I As Integer
     For I = 0 To Accounts.AccountNames.ListCount - 1
       If Trim$(Accounts.AccountNames.List(I)) = A$ Then
         MsgBox ("Name already in use!. Choose another name.")
         NotGoodName = True
         Exit Function
       End If
     Next I
   NotGoodName = False
End Function


Sub OK_Click ()
   'local variables:
   Dim NewName$, D$
   NewName$ = Trim$(Left$(AcctName.Text, MaxAcctNameLen))
   If NewName$ <> gAccountName$ Then
     'adjust the account name in the ACCOUNTS file &_
AccountNames list
     If NotGoodName(NewName$) Then Exit Sub
     Call ChangeName(NewName$)
     gAccountName$ = NewName$
```

```
      End If
      D$ = AcctBalance.Text
      If Not ValidNumber(D$) Then
        MsgBox ("Please enter a valid balance")
        AcctBalance.Text = ""
        AcctBalance.SetFocus
        Exit Sub
      Else
        gBalance = Val(AcctBalance.Text)
      End If
      gNextChk = Val(AcctNextChk.Text)
      gNextDep = Val(AcctNextDep.Text)
      Call UpDateStats(Finance)
      Call UpDateStats(Deposits)
      Call UpDateStats(Checks)
      EStats.Hide
    End Sub
```

## The Checks Form

Here's the table that gives the controls, followed by their name, followed by the caption or text property if appropriate. (Notice that the picture box containing the account statistics is identical for the one on the Finance form.) The Checks form is shown in Figure 18-6.

| Control Type | Name | Caption (or Text) Property Value |
| --- | --- | --- |
| Form | Checks | Enter Check |
| PictureBox | Picture1 | |
| Label | AcctNextDep | Label8 |
| Label | Title4 | Next Deposit |
| Label | AcctNextChk | Label6 |
| Label | Title3 | Next Check |
| Label | AcctBalance | Label4 |
| Label | Title2 | Balance |
| Label | AcctName | Label2 |
| Label | Title1 | Account Name |
| CheckBox | Tax | Tax Deductible |
| ComboBox | Category | Category |
| Frame | Frame1 | |

| Control Type | Name | Caption (or Text) Property Value |
|---|---|---|
| TextBox | Number | |
| TextBox | CrtDate | |
| TextBox | PayTo | |
| TextBox | Amount | |
| TextBox | Memo | |
| Label | Label1 | Check# |
| Label | Label2 | Date |
| Label | Label3 | Pay To |
| Label | Label4 | Amount $ |
| Label | Label5 | Memo _____ |
| CommandButton | Record | Record Check |
| CommandButton | Cancel | Cancel |
| Label | Label7 | Expense Category |

Here's the complete code attached to this form

```
Sub Cancel_Click ()
  Number.SetFocus
  Checks.Hide
End Sub


Function CheckDataOk (ExpCat$) As Integer
  'local variables:
  Dim D$


  'verify that all needed check information has been given
  'some people would prefer not to use the Exit function in_
this code
  'you can do that by carrying the flag through
  CheckDataOk = False
  If Val(Number.Text) = 0 Then
    MsgBox "Check Number must be indicated"
    Number.SetFocus
    Number.Text = ""
    Exit Function
  End If
  D$ = CrtDate.Text
  'ValidDate is a function that uses IsDate to check
  If Not ValidDate(D$) Then
    MsgBox "A valid date must be given"
```

```
        CrtDate.SetFocus
        CrtDate.Text = ""
        Exit Function
      End If
      If Len(Payto.Text) = 0 Then
        MsgBox "A Payee must be indicated"
        Payto.SetFocus
        Exit Function
      End If
      D$ = Amount.Text
      If Val(D$) = 0 Or Not ValidNumber(D$) Then
        MsgBox "An amount must be indicated"
        Amount.Text = ""
        Amount.SetFocus
        Exit Function
      End If
      If Len(ExpCat$) = 0 Then
        MsgBox "An expense category must be chosen"
        Category.SetFocus
        Exit Function
      End If
      CheckDataOk = True
    End Function

    Sub CrtDate_LostFocus ()
      'this shows how easy it is to add a user friendly feature_
    in VB
      'if the user tabs away from the date box we place the_
    current
      'date there

      D$ = Trim$(CrtDate.Text)
      If Len(D$) = 0 Then
        CrtDate.Text = Format$(Date$, "MM-DD-YY")
      End If
    End Sub

    Sub Form_Load ()
      Center Me
      Call UpDateStats(Me)
    End Sub
```

```
Sub Record_Click ()
   'This routine records the info in a file
   'because of bufferring the program should be
   'ended from the file menu and not by ctrl+break - else the_
data
   'may not be writtten
   'local variables:
   Dim ExpCat$, CNumber As Integer, CAmount As Currency

   'if a new expense category is given, add it to the list
   ExpCat$ = Trim$(Category.Text)
   If Len(ExpCat$) <> 0 Then
      Call AddCat(ExpCat$, Checks, "EXPCATS")  'routine to_
check for
                                           'new category
   Else
      ExpCat$ = Category.List(Category.ListIndex)
   End If
   If CheckDataOk(ExpCat$) Then
      'record new check and update account statistics
      Open "ACCT" + gAccountId$ + ".CHK" For Append As 1
      CNumber = Val(Number.Text)
      CAmount = Val(Amount.Text)
      Write #1, CNumber, CrtDate.Text, Payto.Text, CAmount, _
Memo.Text, ExpCat$, Tax.Value
      Close 1
      gBalance = gBalance - CAmount
      gNextChk = gNextChk + 1
      Call UpDateStats(Me)
      Call UpDateStats(Finance)
      Call UpDateStats(Checks)
      Checks.Number.SetFocus
      Checks.Hide
   End If
End Sub
```

# The Deposits Form

Here's the table; use it to make it easier to match up with Figure 18-7.

| Control Type | Name | Caption (or Text) Property Value |
|---|---|---|
| Form | Deposits | Enter Deposit |
| PictureBox | Picture1 | |
| Label | AcctNextDep | Label8 |
| Label | Title4 | Next Deposit |
| Label | AcctNextChk | Label6 |
| Label | Title3 | Next Check |
| Label | AcctBalance | Label4 |
| Label | Title2 | Balance |
| Label | AcctName | Label2 |
| Label | Title1 | Account Name |
| ComboBox | Category | |
| Frame | Frame1 | |
| TextBox | Number | |
| TextBox | CrtDate | |
| TextBox | Source | |
| TextBox | Amount | |
| Label | Label1 | Deposit# |
| Label | Label2 | Date |
| Label | Label3 | Source |
| Label | Label4 | Amount $ |
| CommandButton | Record | &Record Deposit |
| CommandButton | Cancel | Cancel |
| Label | Label7 | Income Category |

Here's the complete code attached to this form

```
Sub Cancel_Click ()
  Number.SetFocus
  Deposits.Hide
End Sub

Sub CrtDate_LostFocus ()
  Dim D$
  D$ = Trim$(CrtDate.Text)
  If Len(D$) = 0 Then
    CrtDate.Text = Format$(Date$, "MM-DD-YY")
  End If
End Sub
```

```
Function DepositDataOk (IncCat$) As Integer
  'local variables:
  Dim D$

  'verify that all needed information has been given
  DepositDataOk = False
  D$ = Number.Text
  If Val(D$) = 0 Or Not ValidNumber(D$) Then
    MsgBox "Deposit Number must be indicated"
    Number.SetFocus
    Number.Text = ""
    Exit Function
  End If
  If Len(Source.Text) = 0 Then
    MsgBox "A Source must be indicated"
    Source.SetFocus
    Exit Function
  End If
  If Len(IncCat$) = 0 Then
    MsgBox "An income category must be chosen"
    Category.SetFocus
    Exit Function
  End If
  D$ = Amount.Text
  If Val(D$) = 0 Or Not ValidNumber(D$) Then
    MsgBox "An amount must be indicated"
    Amount.Text = ""
    Amount.SetFocus
    Exit Function
  End If
  D$ = CrtDate.Text
  If Not ValidDate(D$) Then
    MsgBox "A valid date must be given"
    CrtDate.SetFocus
    CrtDate.Text = ""
    Exit Function
  Else
    CrtDate.Text = Format$(D$, "MM-DD-YY")
  End If

  DepositDataOk = True
End Function
```

```
Sub Form_Load ()
  Center Me
  Call UpDateStats(Me)
End Sub

Sub Record_Click ()
  'local variables:
  Dim IncCat$, DNumber As Integer, DAmount As Currency

  'if a new income category is given, add it to the list
  IncCat$ = Trim$(Category.Text)
  If Len(IncCat$) <> 0 Then
    Call AddCat(IncCat$, Deposits, "INCCATS")
  Else
    IncCat$ = Category.List(Category.ListIndex)
  End If
  If DepositDataOk(IncCat$) Then
    'record new deposit and update account statistics
    Open "ACCT" + gAccountId$ + ".DEP" For Append As 1
    DNumber = Val(Number.Text)
    DAmount = Val(Amount.Text)
    Write #1, DNumber, CrtDate.Text, Source.Text, DAmount,_
IncCat$
    Close 1
    gBalance = gBalance + DAmount
    gNextDep = gNextDep + 1
    Call UpDateStats(Me)
    Call UpDateStats(Finance)
    Call UpDateStats(Checks)
    Deposits.Number.SetFocus
    Deposits.Hide
  End If
End Sub
```

## The Reports Form

 In this table controls attached to frames follow the frame. This makes it easier to match up with Figure 18-8.

| Control Type | Name | Caption (or Text) Property Value |
| --- | --- | --- |
| Form | Reports | Reports |

| Control Type | Name | Caption (or Text) Property Value |
|---|---|---|
| ListBox | Category | |
| Frame | Frame3 | Send report to ... |
| OptionButton | OnScreen | Screen |
| OptionButton | OnPrinter | Printer |
| OptionButton | OnBoth | Screen and Printer |
| TextBox | Date1 | |
| TextBox | Date2 | |
| Frame | Frame1 | Report on ... |
| OptionButton | CheckReport | Checks |
| OptionButton | DepositReport | Deposits |
| CommandButton | GenReport | Generate &Report |
| Frame | Frame2 | |
| CheckBox | TotalOnly | Display Total Only |
| CommandButton | Cancel | Cancel |
| Frame | Frame4 | |
| OptionButton | IgnoreTax | Ignore Tax status |
| OptionButton | TaxOnly | Include only Tax Deductible |
| OptionButton | NonTaxOnly | Exclude all Tax Deductible |
| Label | CatLabel | Include only checks written for ... |
| Label | DateLabel | only checks written between ... |
| Label | Label6 | and |
| Label | RepTotal | |
| Label | Label7 | Include all checks or |

Here's the complete code attached to this form.

```
Sub Cancel_Click ()
  Reports.CheckReport.SetFocus
  Reports.Hide
End Sub

Sub CheckReport_Click ()
  'local variables:
  Dim I As Integer
  Reports.Category.Clear
  Reports.Category.AddItem " <Include All Categories>"
  For I = 0 To Checks!Category.ListCount - 1
    Reports.Category.AddItem Checks!Category.List(I)
```

```
        Next I
        AllLabel.Caption = "Include all checks or"
        CatLabel.Caption = "Include only checks written for ..."
        DateLabel.Caption = "Include only checks written between"
        IgnoreTax.Enabled = True
        TaxOnly.Enabled = True
        NonTaxOnly.Enabled = True
End Sub

Sub DepositReport_Click ()
    'local variables:
    Dim I As Integer

    Reports.Category.Clear
    Reports.Category.AddItem " <Include All Categories>"
    For I = 0 To Deposits!Category.ListCount - 1
        Reports.Category.AddItem Deposits!Category.List(I)
    Next I
    AllLabel.Caption = "Include all deposits or"
    CatLabel.Caption = "Include only deposits written for ..."
    DateLabel.Caption = "Include only deposits written between"
    IgnoreTax.Enabled = False
    TaxOnly.Enabled = False
    NonTaxOnly.Enabled = False
End Sub

Sub Form_Load ()
    Center Me
    Call CheckReport_Click
End Sub

Sub GenReport_Click ()
    'local variables:
    Dim Total As Currency, SubTotal As Currency
    Dim DoAll As Integer, Index As Integer
    Dim StartDate As String, StopDate As String
    Dim TaxVal As Integer, SearchCat As String

    Reports.RepTotal.Visible = False
    If ReportOptionsOk(DoAll, Index, StartDate, StopDate,_
TaxVal) Then
        Call TitleReport(StartDate, StopDate)
        Total = 0
        Do
```

```
      SearchCat = Trim$(Reports.Category.List(Index))
      SubTotal = 0
      Call ReportOnOneCategory(SearchCat, SubTotal,
StartDate, StopDate, TaxVal)
      Call ReportSubTotal(SearchCat, SubTotal)
      Index = Index + 1
      Total = Total + SubTotal
    Loop Until (Not DoAll) Or (Index >
Reports.Category.ListCount - 1)
    Reports.CheckReport.SetFocus
    Call ReportTotal(Total)
  End If
End Sub


Sub ReportOnOneCategory (SearchCat As String, SubTotal As
Currency, StartDate As String, StopDate As String, TaxVal As Integer)
  'local variables:
  Dim N$, D$, W$, A$, Number As Integer, ItemDate$
  Dim Amount As Currency, Memo$, ItemCat$, Tax As Integer
  Dim UCat$
  'allocate space for items appearing in each line of report
  N$ = Space$(10)
  D$ = Space$(15)
  W$ = Space$(25)
  A$ = Space$(15)
  UCat$ = UCase$(Trim$(SearchCat)) 'make upper case and trim
  'open appropriate database
  If CheckReport.Value Then
    Open "ACCT" + gAccountId$ + ".CHK" For Input As 1
  Else
    Open "ACCT" + gAccountId$ + ".DEP" For Input As 1
  End If
  Do While Not EOF(1)
    If CheckReport.Value Then
      Input #1, Number, ItemDate$, Who$, Amount, Memo$,_
ItemCat$, Tax
    Else
      Input #1, Number, ItemDate$, Who$, Amount, ItemCat$
    End If
    'only process items which meet search criteria
    If (UCase$(Trim$(ItemCat$)) = UCat$) And (YMD(ItemDate$)_
>= StartDate) And (YMD(ItemDate$) <= StopDate) And (TaxVal = 99_
Or TaxVal = Tax) Then
      SubTotal = SubTotal + Amount
```

```
      If TotalOnly.Value = False Then
        RSet N$ = Str$(Number)
        RSet D$ = ItemDate$
        RSet W$ = Who$
        RSet A$ = Format$(Amount, "0,0.00")
        If OnScreen.Value Or OnBoth.Value Then
          Results.Info.Text = Results.Info.Text + Chr$(13) + _
Chr$(10) + N$ + Space$(3) + D$ + Space$(3) + A$ + Space$(3) + W$
        End If
        If OnPrinter.Value Or OnBoth.Value Then
          Printer.Print N$ + "   " + D$ + "   " + A$ + "   " + W$
        End If
      End If
    End If
  Loop
  Close 1
End Sub

Function ReportOptionsOk (DoAll As Integer, Index As Integer,
StartDate As String, StopDate As String, TaxVal As Integer)
As Integer
  'local variables:
  Dim D$

  ReportOptionsOk = False
  If Reports.Category.ListIndex = 0 Then
    DoAll = True
    Index = 1
  ElseIf Reports.Category.ListIndex > 0 Then
    DoAll = False
    Index = Reports.Category.ListIndex
  Else
    MsgBox "Category must be selected"
    Exit Function
  End If
  D$ = Reports.Date1.Text
  If Len(Trim$(D$)) = 0 Then
    StartDate = "00000000"
  ElseIf ValidDate(D$) Then
    StartDate = YMD(D$)
  Else
    MsgBox "Starting date is not a valid date"
    Exit Function
  End If
```

```
    D$ = Reports.Date2.Text
    If Len(Trim$(D$)) = 0 Then
      StopDate = "99999999"
    ElseIf ValidDate(D$) Then
      StopDate = YMD(D$)
    Else
      MsgBox "Ending date is not a valid date"
      Exit Function
    End If
    If CheckReport.Value Then
      If IgnoreTax.Value Then
        TaxVal = 99
      ElseIf TaxOnly.Value Then
        TaxVal = 1
      ElseIf NonTaxOnly.Value Then
        TaxVal = 0
      End If
    Else
      TaxVal = 99
    End If
    ReportOptionsOk = True
End Function


Sub ReportSubTotal (SearchCat As String, SubTotal As Currency)
    If OnPrinter.Value Or OnBoth.Value Then
      Printer.Print
      Printer.Print "Subtotal for " + SearchCat + ": " + _
Format$(SubTotal, "$0,0.00")
      Printer.Print
      Printer.Print
    End If
    If OnScreen.Value Or OnBoth.Value Then
      Results.Info.Text = Results.Info.Text + Chr$(13) +_
Chr$(10)
      Results.Info.Text = Results.Info.Text + Chr$(13) +_
Chr$(10) + _
"Subtotal for " + SearchCat + ": " + Format$(SubTotal,_
"$0,0.00")
      Results.Info.Text = Results.Info.Text + Chr$(13) +_
Chr$(10)
      Results.Info.Text = Results.Info.Text + Chr$(13) +_
Chr$(10)
    End If
End Sub
```

```
Sub ReportTotal (Total As Currency)
  If OnPrinter.Value Or OnBoth.Value Then
    Printer.Print
    Printer.Print "Total: " + Format$(Total, "$0,0.00")
    Printer.NewPage    'form feed
  End If
  If OnScreen.Value Or OnBoth.Value Then
    Results.RepTotal.Caption = "Total: " + Format$(Total,_
"$0,0.00")
  End If
  Finance.Hide
  Reports.Hide
  Results.Show 1
End Sub

Sub TitleReport (StartDate As String, StopDate As String)
  Dim ReportTitle As String, Header1 As String, Header2 As_
String
  Dim SDate$, EDate$

  SDate$ = Format$(StartDate, "MM-DD-YY")
  EDate$ = Format$(StopDate, "MM-DD-YY")
  If CheckReport.Value Then
    ReportTitle = "Report on checks "
    Header1 = "   Number           Date           Amount    _
Paid to"
  Else
    ReportTitle = "Report on deposits "
    Header1 = "   Number           Date           Amount    _
Received from"
  End If
    Header2 ="============================================_
="
  If StartDate <> "00000000" And StopDate = "99999999" Then
    ReportTitle = ReportTitle + "written on or after " +_
SDate$
  ElseIf StartDate = "00000000" And StopDate <> "99999999"_
Then
    ReportTitle = ReportTitle + "written on or before " +_
EDate$
  ElseIf StartDate <> "00000000" And StopDate <> "99999999"_
Then
    ReportTitle = ReportTitle + "written between " +_
```

```
       StartDate + _
" and " + StopDate
   End If
   If OnPrinter.Value Or OnBoth.Value Then
     Printer.Print ReportTitle
     Printer.Print
     Printer.Print Header1
     Printer.Print Header2
   End If
   If OnScreen.Value Or OnBoth.Value Then
     Results.Caption = ReportTitle
     Results.Info.Text = Header1 + Chr$(13) + Chr$(10) +_
Header2 + _
Chr$(13) + Chr$(10)
   End If
End Sub


Function YMD (D$) As String
   YMD = Str$(DateValue(D$))
End Function
```

# The Results Form

Finally, here's the table followed by the code for the final form (Figure 18-9).

| Control Type | Name | Caption (or Text) Property Value |
| --- | --- | --- |
| Form | Results | Report Writer |
| CommandButton | OK | OK |
| TextBox | Info | Text1 |
| Label | RepTotal | Label1 |

```
Sub Form_Resize ()
 Center Me
 If Height < 4 * Ok.Height Then Height = 4 * Ok.Height
 If Width < 3 * RepTotal.Width Then Width = 3 * RepTotal.Width
 Info.Width = ScaleWidth
 Info.Height = ScaleHeight - (1.5 * Ok.Height)
 Ok.Move 2 * ScaleWidth / 3, Info.Height + .25 * Ok.Height
 RepTotal.Move ScaleWidth / 4, Info.Height + .25 * Ok.Height
End Sub
```

```
Sub Info_KeyPress (KeyAscii As Integer)
  KeyAscii = 0
End Sub

Sub OK_Click ()
  Results.Hide
End Sub
```

# Appendix A

# Visual Basic

---

## Professional Edition

---

VISUAL Basic Professional Edition comes either as an add-on for Visual Basic or as a stand-alone product. It is designed for both professional and serious amateur Visual Basic programmers. Visual Basic Professional Edition adds capabilities to Visual Basic that will make your programming jobs easier, your projects look more impressive, or both.

This appendix explains what Visual Basic Professional Edition can do for you by briefly describing the features of the custom controls. The purpose of this appendix is to give you enough information to make an informed decision about whether to upgrade. In particular, since there are 23 custom controls and full programmatic access to databases, covering all their features would require another book. Of course, using a custom control is no different than using one of the built-in controls or the three custom controls supplied with Visual Basic: in both cases, set properties via code or the Properties window to get them to behave as you want. The properties supported by the custom controls are described in the more than 500 pages of documentation and extensive online help supplied with Visual Basic Professional Edition. If you need the facilities supported by even one of the custom controls, buying Visual Basic Professional Edition will quickly pay for itself with the time it saves you. Programming databases is a specialized subject and to really do it effectively you need to own a database manager, preferably Microsoft's own "Access," in addition to the Professional Edition.

What this appendix does cover in some depth are the basics of using the Windows 3.1 Help compiler—the documentation for all its features is more than 100 pages, so we can't cover it in depth. It also covers a bit about the Setup kit. The Setup kit is the companion to the Setup Wizard (see Appendix B). If the Wizard can do the job, don't bother with the Setup kit. (But the Setup Kit does come with a large number of useful file-handling functions as well; you will often find yourself using these functions in other contexts.) Both the Help compiler and the Setup kit are absolutely essential to anyone who wants to distribute applications built with Visual Basic. You need Visual Basic Professional Edition in order to get them, although the Windows Help compiler does come with Microsoft C, and the standard edition does include the Setup Wizard for basic tasks.

**note:** *This appendix does not go into writing a custom control or using the database features supplied with Visual Basic Professional Edition.*

Visual Basic Professional Edition is shipped two ways. The first includes Visual Basic, and the other contains only the extra features of the Professional Edition version. If you are intrigued by what this appendix tells you about Visual Basic Professional Edition and want to add it to your Visual Basic system, contact Microsoft. The company may be running one of its periodic specials to upgrade to the Professional Edition (another reason you should send in your registration card).

**caution:** *Be sure to remove earlier versions of custom controls if any still exist after installing Visual Basic Professional Edition.*

# An Overview of Visual Basic Professional Edition

Visual Basic Professional Edition extends Visual Basic; it doesn't replace it. You'll get the following benefits from Visual Basic Professional Edition:

◆ You can add a help system to your projects that uses the ordinary built-in Windows help system.

◆ You can write automated setup programs that go beyond what you can do with the Setup Wizard. Moreover, you can use the functions supplied with this feature to make many routine file tasks, like compressing files, fast and easy.

◆ You can gain programmatic access to large databases including the ability to do sophisticated reporting based on Crystal Reports' acclaimed "Report Writer." This program is called "Crystal Reports for Visual Basic."

◆ If you know C and the Windows Software Development Kit well, you can add custom controls to Visual Basic.

◆    You receive an online "Visual Design Guide" that gives you hints on Windows user interfaces.

Also, Visual Basic Professional Edition gives you online access to the Windows 3.1 API reference files (see the section on them later in this chapter).

There are also 23 custom controls that either add new functionality to Visual Basic, make programming tasks easier, or both. For example, Visual Basic Professional Edition adds a powerful graphing facility to Visual Basic that makes it easy to produce presentation-quality graphs.

Finally, Visual Basic Professional Edition comes with over 80 Windows metafiles and more than 100 bitmaps useful for business art. There is a lot of sample code to study and emulate, both in the examples supplied and in the Visual Basic Online Knowledge Base. Finally, there are over 500 pages of printed documentation, and most of the information written there is also available online.

# The Help Compiler

A professional Windows project needs a help system that does what Windows users expect. If your online help doesn't have the look and feel of a Windows help system, users will have to learn too much (and you'll probably be working too hard to teach them).

Visual Basic Professional Edition comes with the Windows Help compiler and the printed and online documentation you need to work with it. Roughly speaking, the way you use the Help compiler is simple: you write a text file containing certain formatting codes that the Help compiler translates into jumps, definitions, and so on. The text file must be written with a word processor that supports what Microsoft calls RTF (rich text format). Many full-featured word processors support this format. Obviously, you're best off using a Windows word processor when preparing the text files to feed to the Help compiler. This way you can work with the Help compiler in one window and the word processor in the other.

**tip:**    *There are also several third party tools (Doc-To-Help from WexTech amd RoboHelp from Blue Sky being the most popular) as well as a couple of tools (WHAT—the "Windows Help Authoring Templates" and WHPE—the "Windows Help Project Editor") on the Microsoft Software Developers CD-ROM that can make writing help files easier. (Check out the WinHelp Lib of the WINSDK forum on CompuServe for additional tools.)*

A Help system should also feature the customary menu that users are accustomed to from Windows. The Help menu should have Contents, Search, and About items. The Search item should lead to the list of keywords the user can search through. These keywords will connect to the topics that you write. Various parts of your application (like Visual Basic itself) should have context-sensitive help. This way all users know that if they press F1 they can get help about a specific item on a form.

## Writing Help Topics

At the core of your online help system are the Help topics you write. Ideally, these are short (one or two screen lengths is ideal), self-contained expositions of a single idea. Topics are usually arranged hierarchically. This way users can navigate from general to specific topics when needed. However, within each topic the user should find enough jumps to make navigation possible without having to move through a (possibly) laborious hierarchy.

While topics should ideally be self-contained, complete self-containment is rarely possible. You may need to add pop-up or secondary windows, described in the following sections.

*Pop-Up Windows* These are windows that pop up and give definitions of terms. They are occasionally used for lists of information. Places where the user can pop up a window are indicated by having the text appear with a dotted underline in the window. (Such places are called *jumps* or *hotspots*.) Figure A-1 shows a typical pop-up definition window.

*Secondary Windows* Secondary windows also are used when you need to display information without leaving the current topic. Unlike pop-up windows, secondary windows have their own title bars (and scroll bars, if needed). Figure A-2 shows a typical secondary window.

### THE NITTY-GRITTY OF A HELP TOPIC

As mentioned earlier, you'll need to have a word processor that supports Microsoft's RTF (rich text format) in order to write the files that will be compiled by the Windows Help compiler. Each topic must be separated from the next by a hard page break. (A *hard page break* is one that you insert manually rather than one calculated by the word processor. This is accomplished by

**Figure A-1**

**A pop-up window**

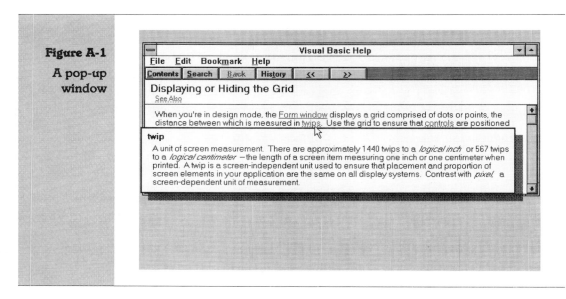

pressing CTRL+ENTER on Microsoft's family of word processors.) Each topic should have a *context string identifier*, a title, and a list of keywords attached to it. The context string is used for jumps, so context strings have to be unique. The keywords are used for the search feature built into the Windows Help engine, so many topics can share keywords.

**Figure A-2**

**A secondary window**

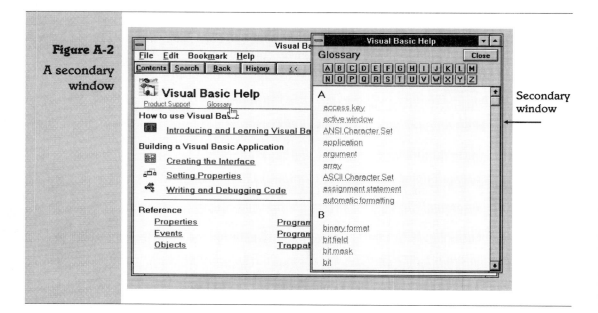

Secondary window

Footnotes using specific identifiers are the key to unleashing the Help engine's power. For example, context strings are indicated by placing a footnote with the # footnote identifier. Context strings can use A through Z, numerals, a period, and an underscore. They must be less than 255 characters.

The title of the topic is indicated by a footnote using a dollar sign ($). Titles can be up to 128 characters long and can use any of the Windows characters. Finally, keywords are indicated by the use of a capital "K" as the footnote identifier. (Keywords are optional, but you can place more than one keyword for a specific topic by separating the keywords by semicolons. Keywords can use any characters in the Windows character set (including spaces) and have a maximum length of 255 characters.)

Look at Figure A-3. Notice the footnotes, which use the three identifiers mentioned above. This means that the topic shown in Figure A-3 corresponds to the context string "EDITOR_FILE_MENU". The topic page has the title "File Menu." The keywords for this page are "File Menu," "New," "Open," "Save," "Save As," "Exit," "Viewer," and "Menu." Finally, the "+" footnote indicates a *browse sequence*. Next notice the .bmp references surrounded by braces. These indicate that a bitmap will appear in the corresponding help screen (see Figure A-4).

Browse sequences are optional; you've seen them while using Visual Basic's Help system. They let you specify the order in which users can browse through topics (if you build a Browse button into your Help system). Next, notice in

**Figure A-3**

**Help file in a word processor**

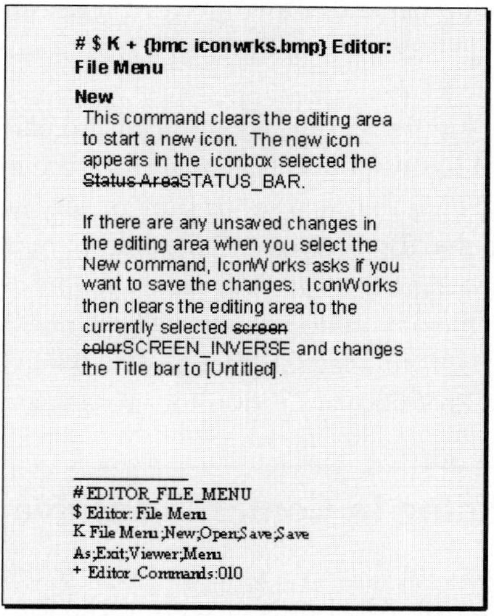

# $ K + {bmc iconwrks.bmp} Editor: File Menu

**New**
This command clears the editing area to start a new icon. The new icon appears in the iconbox selected the Status AreaSTATUS_BAR.

If there are any unsaved changes in the editing area when you select the New command, IconWorks asks if you want to save the changes. IconWorks then clears the editing area to the currently selected screen colorSCREEN_INVERSE and changes the Title bar to [Untitled].

# EDITOR_FILE_MENU
$ Editor: File Menu
K File Menu ;New;Open;Save ;Save As;Exit;Viewer;Menu
+ Editor_Commands:010

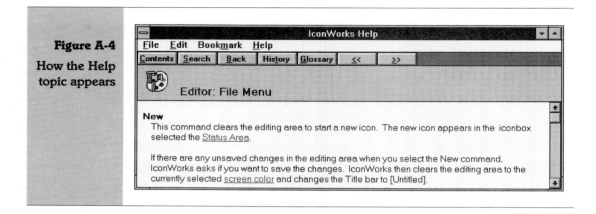

**Figure A-4**

**How the Help topic appears**

Figure A-3 that certain text, like the term "Status Area," is stricken through (it could also be double-underlined). Stricken (or double-underlined) text indicates a jump. Hidden text placed right after the jump indicates where the jump should go. The syntax is

JumpString *STRING*

where the context string must be formatted in your word processor as hidden text. Similarly, you place a hidden context string that follows the single-underlined text to indicate where the definition can be found. How hidden strings show up depends on your word processor. In Figure A-3, they show up in all capital letters, for example, as STATUS_BAR. Figure A-4 is the corresponding help screen.

As Figure A-4 shows, you can also place bitmaps in a topic page. If you have Word for Windows, you can place the bitmap directly in the file by using the Insert Picture function. (If they're very large, you should include your bitmaps using the "By Reference" method.) Graphics themselves can act as hotspots for jumps. (As Figure A-3 also shows, you can place references to bitmaps in your topic files if you do not have Word for Windows. This has both advantages and disadvantages. See Chapter 5 of the Help compiler manual supplied with Visual Basic Professional Edition for more information on this.)

## Building In Context-Sensitive Help

You create context-sensitive help by setting the HelpContextID of the form or control. All controls except those for the line, shape, image, and label have this property. You can use the common dialog control to access the Windows Help engine.

**tip:**  *If you want to assign context-sensitive help to an image control that doesn't have a HelpContextID property, replace it by a picture box that does.*

Once you assign the value of the HelpContextID property, you have to tell the Help compiler how to *map* the HelpContextID property to specific topics (see the next section).

On the other hand, the HelpFile property is a global property of the Application object. You need to set this property to the name of the Help file for the application. To do this:

1. Choose Project from the Options menu.

2. Choose HelpFile from the list of project options.

3. Set the value of this property to the name of the help file.

If you need to use the general Windows Help engine (for example, to have a "Help On Help" option), call the WinHelp API function. (See the API online help for more on this function.) If you use WinHelp, you will have to call WinHelp again to close down the extra Help files that Windows opens.

# Building and Compiling the Help Files

The Help project file contains the information needed for the Help compiler to do its job. The Help project file must be an ordinary ASCII file. The custom is to use .HPJ as the extension on all Help project files. The Help compiler changes this to .HLP for the compiled version. The Help project file lists all the topic files and can optionally add bitmaps or a map between context strings and context numbers. You can also assign two context strings to the same topic by modifying the project file.

To map Help context numbers to specific topics for context-sensitive help, place the topic after the keyword [MAP], followed by white space (press the SPACEBAR or TAB), followed by the Help context numbers. Here's a sample of what you might have in the [MAP] section of the Help project file.

```
[MAP]
first_context_string          5        ;5 is context number
                                       ;Comments follow semicolons
second_context_string        10        ;5 is context number
third_context_string         15        ;15 is context number
```

The context number is passed by the Visual Basic program as the value of the HelpContextID property.

After you build the Help project file, you need only call the Help compiler. (The Help compiler must be in a directory known to the PATH command, or else you need to specify the full path name when calling it.) The syntax is

C:\VB\HC\HC31 *NameOfHelpProjectFile*

if you left the Help compiler in the default directory for Visual Basic Professional Edition, or

HC31 *NameOfHelpProjectFile*

if the directory containing the Help compiler is in your path.

**tip:** *Although the Help compiler is a DOS application, you may find it preferable to run it under Windows 3.1 in order to benefit from Windows' memory-management techniques.*

(The Help compiler is a *big* program and uses a lot of memory.)

There is a lot more to the Help compiler: You can compile only certain parts of your file at one time, or control the size and shape of the windows in it. You can use a rich supply of macros that Microsoft wrote to extend the power of the Help compiler. The documentation is quite detailed, and if you closely study the ICONWRKS.RTF file and refer to the documentation as needed, you should have all the information you need.

## The Setup Kit

If you want to write a professional-looking installation program for your Visual Basic projects and the Setup Wizard doesn't do it for you, turn to the "Setup

Kit" supplied with Visual Basic Professional Edition. The Setup Kit makes it easy to produce a customized setup program with the look and feel of the one supplied with any Microsoft Windows product—for example, the SETUP program for Visual Basic itself. The Setup Kit lets you write a customized setup program that copies VBRUN300.DLL and any other needed files to the appropriate Windows subdirectories without worrying about where they are or what the user has called them. You can even provide a level of security for yourself by using the Windows-version stamping facility to decide if you need (or want) to copy a specific file to the user's machine. Moreover, the Setup Kit comes with programs to automatically compress and decompress the files in your application to save floppies. The main tool that the Setup Kit uses is a subset of Microsoft Test, which uses a Visual Basic-like scripting language.

## How to Use the Setup Kit

The Setup Kit comes with an executable Windows program called SETUP.EXE. This program looks for a special ASCII file called SETUP.LST that contains the names of the files SETUP should install. SETUP.LST is an ordinary text file, and the first line of this file must be the name of the customized SETUP program that you wrote in Visual Basic and compiled to an .EXE file. For example, suppose you wanted to install a program called TEST.EXE that used the GRID and OLE client controls. Here is an example of what the SETUP.LST file might look like:

```
INS_TEST.EXE
SETUPKIT.DLL
VER.DLL
VBRUN300.DLL
GRID.VBX
MSOLE2.VBX
```

The first line indicates that the customized SETUP program is called INS_TEST. This executable file is created by making changes in the SETUP1.MAK project supplied with the Setup Kit and then compiling the result to an .EXE file. SETUPKIT.DLL is used by the SETUP program.

The VER.DLL dynamic link library contains functions to work with the user's \WINDOWS directory and its subdirectories. VBRUN300.DLL is the dynamic link library needed for Visual Basic itself. The next two files are needed for the GRID and OLE client controls. The files listed in SETUP.LST are those that need to be installed before your application. This is why you do not put your application (TEST.EXE, in our example) in the SETUP.LST file. The SETUP.EXE program installs the files listed in SETUP.LST after the INS_TEST.EXE file. Then it calls the INS_TEST program, which will copy the TEST.EXE program and any other files needed.

**note:** *While you can have more than one disk in an automated SETUP program, files cannot be split between disks. They could be split ahead of time, and concatenated together during the installation process, however.*

(You can use the COMPRESS programs supplied with the Setup Kit to minimize the amount of floppy disk space you use. See the section on Compress/Decompress later in this chapter.)

## Modifying SETUP1.FRM

To actually change the SETUP1.MAK file supplied with the Setup Kit into your own customized setup routine, you only have to modify the Form_Load procedure of the SETUP1.FRM module. Suppose you want to install a program that fits on a single disk. All you need to do is the following:

1. Change certain SETUP1.FRM constants.

2. Use the PromptForNextDisk function to check if the disk the user inserts has a specific file that identifies the distribution disks.

3. Call the CopyFile function for each of the files on the distribution disks.

The PromptForNextDisk function tells the user via a message box to enter another disk. The syntax is

Function PromptForNextDisk (*DiskNum%, FileToLookFor$*) As Integer

This function returns True (−1) if a disk containing the file was inserted and False (0) otherwise.

**tip:** *As with many of the functions supplied with the Setup Kit, this function is useful in many other contexts.*

You can use the PromptForNextDisk function to check if a specific file exists on a newly inserted disk. The syntax used inside the Form_Load procedure is

If Not PromptForNextDisk (*DiskNum%, FileToLookFor$*) Then GoTo ErrorSetup

(ErrorSetup is the general error-handling routine supplied in SETUP1.FRM.)

Next, the CopyFile function copies a file from a source path to another path. It does not use SHELL to activate the DOS copy routine or call the File Manager. The syntax is

Function CopyFile (ByVal *SourcePath$*, ByVal *DestPath$*, ByVal *SourceFileName$*, ByVal *DestFileName$*) As Integer

This function uses the VerInstallFile API function. Since it uses this API function (which calls the expand DLL, LZEXPAND.DLL) this function both copies and expands the files if necessary. The CopyFile function does not allow wildcards. (Use SHELL "COPY..." if you need wildcards, and then call the EXPAND program directly on them.) You need to repeat a call to CopyFunction for each file to be copied. The syntax inside the Form_Load procedure is similar to the use of PromptForNextDisk:

If Not CopyFile (*SourcePath$, DestPath$, FileName$*) *Then GoTo ErrorSetup*

All files to be copied must be indicated in successive lines of the above type.

## THE CONSTANTS USED IN THE SETUP ROUTINE

The constants you need to change are described in the following sections.

**APPNAME**    APPNAME is the name of your application. This is not the compressed .EXE name, but the name you want displayed during the installation procedure.

**APPDIR**   APPDIR is the default directory where you want the application installed. (You can allow or forbid the user to change this, as you see fit.)

**WINSYSNEEDED**   This is how much space your file will take up in the \WINDOWS and \WINDOWS\SYSTEM directories. As you would expect, the setup program checks whether there is enough space in the drive holding these directories to install the files you want to place. For example, if the files needed in these directories totaled 200,000 bytes, you would change the Const declaration for SETUP1.FRM to read

```
Const WINSYSNEEDED = 200000
```

**OTHERNEEDED**   This is the total size of all the files that will be installed in the directory chosen by the user (or preset by you).

### APPLICATIONS NEEDING MULTIPLE DISKS

The automated program easily handles applications needing multiple disks. (Although if you use the supplied compression programs, the source files would have to be fairly large to need more than one disk. Image files compress best, .EXE files less well. The overall compression achieved is often 2 to 1 or better.)

To install an application that requires multiple disks, you need to know which files can be found on which disks. Then add another call to the PromptForNextDisk function after you finish copying all the files on the first disk, using a file on the second disk as the FileToLookFor$ parameter.

Next, the program must again use the CopyFile function as often as needed to copy all files on the second disk. If there is a third disk, place another call to the PromptForNextDisk function after the program copies all the files on the second distribution disk. Continue by copying its files and repeating the process.

### OTHER FUNCTIONS SUPPLIED WITH THE SETUP1 PROJECT

The SETUP1 project contains a module of powerful Visual Basic functions (in SETUP1.BAS). You've already seen the PromptForNextDisk and CopyFile functions, but all these functions give good examples of combining Windows API calls with Visual Basic functions to accomplish common tasks. The source code is supplied, of course, so you can pick up many useful programming tricks from studying these functions. Moreover, you are not confined to using these functions for setup programs alone. You can use these functions in any of your Visual Basic projects where these common tasks show up.

**■■■**

***Center a Form*** The CenterForm subprogram moves the specified form to slightly above the screen's center. You can use this subprogram to display dialog boxes centered on the screen. The syntax is

Sub CenterForm (X As Form)

**■■■**

***Create a Path*** The CreatePath function creates the specified path on the user's disk. This function is more useful than MKDIR because it can create paths more than one level deep. The syntax is

Function CreatePath (ByVal *DestPath$*) As Integer

**■■■**

***Create a Windows Program Manager Group*** The subprogram CreateProgManGroup sets up a DDE link with the Program Manager and creates a new Microsoft Windows Program Manager group. The syntax is

Sub CreateProgManGroup (X As Form, *ProgGroupName$*, *ProgGroupPath$*)

**■■■**

***Create a Windows Program Manager Item*** The CreateProgManItem subprogram sets up a DDE link with the Program Manager and creates a new Microsoft Windows Program Manager item. The syntax is

Sub CreateProgManItem (X As Form, CommandLineInfo$, IconTitle$)

**■■■**

***Find Out If a Specific File Exists*** The FileExists function tells you if a specified file already exists. The syntax is

Function FileExists (*FilePathName$*) As Integer

As you might expect, this function returns True (–1) if the file specified by FileName$ exists; otherwise it returns False (0). The *Filename$* parameter must contain the full path name of the file you want to check.

▬▬▬

**Find Out the Free Disk Space** The GetDiskSpaceFree function uses a Windows API call to find out the amount of free disk space on a drive. The syntax is

Function GetDiskSpaceFree (*Drive$*) As Long

This function uses the DiskSpaceFree function supplied in SETUP.DLL.

▬▬▬

**How Large Are the Allocation Units (Clusters) on a Drive?** The function Get DrivesAllocUnit returns the size of the disk allocation unit for a drive. (An *allocation unit* is the minimum number of bytes DOS uses for a file, regardless of how small it is.) The syntax is

Function GetDriveAllocUnit (*Drive$*) As Long

This function uses the AllocUnit function supplied in SETUP.DLL.

▬▬▬

**How Large Is a File?** The GetFileSize function uses binary file techniques to determine the size, in bytes, of a specified file. The syntax is

Function GetFileSize (*FileName$*) As Long

and the *FileName$* parameter must contain a full path name. The source code for this function is a nice application of binary file techniques (all it does is open the file for Binary input and call the LOF function).

▬▬▬

**Find Out Where Windows Is Located** The GetWindowsDir function tells you where the current Microsoft Windows directory is. This function returns the path for the current Windows directory. The syntax is

Function GetWindowsDir ( ) As String

***Find Out Where the WINDOWS\SYSTEM Subdirectory Is Located*** The GetWindowsSysDir function tells you where the current Microsoft Windows directory is. This function returns the path for the current directory. The syntax is

Function GetWindowsSysDir ( ) As String

***Check Whether Path Name Is Valid*** The IsValidPath function tells you if a specified path is valid. The syntax is

Function IsValidPath (*Path$*, ByVal *DefaultDrive$*) As Integer

This function returns True (−1) if the path specified by *Path$* is acceptable and False (0) otherwise. This function actually reconstructs Path$ so it is in the correct format: Drive:. If Path$ doesn't contain a drive letter, DefaultDrive$ is added before the string given in Path$. The default drive specification must be in the format "Drive:".

***Change a File's Date and Time Stamp*** The SetFileDateTime function sets the destination file's date and time to the source file's date and time. The syntax is

Function SetFileDateTime (*SourceFile$*, *DestinationFile$*) As Integer

This function uses the SetTime function supplied with SETUPKIT.DLL.

***Update How the Installation Procedure Is Progressing*** The subprogram Update Status updates the progress of a status bar found in the form named STATUS.FRM (supplied with the SETUP1 project). This function gives the user a measure of the progress made while the program is copying files or performing some other lengthy process. The code for this subprogram is a good example of using a gauge to provide feedback to a user.

## COMPRESSING AND DECOMPRESSING FILES

Most files contain a fair amount of redundancy. This is the key to file-compression programs. For example, "the" is by far the most common word in

English. Thus, if a file written in English replaced the word "the" with a single character, it would likely save a fair amount of space—even taking into account the extra overhead to manage the translation back and forth. Since compressed files automatically decompress back to their original forms when you use the Setup Kit, you should compress files if you do not have the room to fit all the files needed on a single disk. COMPRESS.EXE is an ordinary MS-DOS program, not a Windows program. The usual syntax for COMPRESS.EXE is

COMPRESS -R *filename*

The –R flag automatically replaces the last character of the compressed file with an underscore. For example,

```
COMPRESS - R TEST.EXE
```

gives you a file named TEST.EX_.

The Setup Kit also comes with an EXPAND.EXE stand-alone DOS program that you can use to independently expand compressed files (although the functions in the SETUP program do this automatically).

**note:** *If you compress a file, use the compressed file name in the SETUP.LST file.*

## Surveying the Custom Controls

There are 23 custom controls included in Visual Basic Professional Edition. As with the Grid control, the OLE client control, and the common dialog box control, custom control files always have a .VBX extension and consist of a specialized dynamic link library containing the information needed to define the control's properties, events, and methods. As with any custom control, if you need the capabilities of that control for your project, you must add the control to Visual Basic at design time. To do this, follow these steps:

1. Open the File menu and choose Add File.

2. Specify the .VBX file in the dialog box.

**tip:**

*Adjust the AUTOLOAD.MAK file to reflect exactly those custom controls you always want loaded.*

(The AUTOLOAD.MAK file already automatically loads the common dialog, GRID, and OLE client custom controls supplied with Visual Basic's standard version.)

The icon for the custom control will appear in the toolbox. When you add a custom control to Visual Basic, it becomes as easily accessible via the toolbox and properties bar as any of Visual Basic's built-in controls. Figure A-5 shows what your toolbox might look like if you loaded most of the custom controls supplied with Visual Basic Professional Edition at once.

Note that each time you start up a new Visual Basic project, you must load the custom controls you'll need. Once you save a project, though, the custom controls are saved with the project.

If you use a custom control to develop a Visual Basic project, you need to supply the specific .VBX file (really a specialized dynamic link library file) to the user. The SETUP program supplied with Visual Basic Professional Edition (or the Setup Wizard supplied with both the standard and professional editions) makes this easy, and you may freely distribute the needed files (supplied with Visual Basic Professional Edition) when you create an .EXE file using a custom control. (Users who don't have Visual Basic Professional Edition gain access

**Figure A-5**

The toolbox and Project window with all the custom controls

only to the functionality of the custom control; they can't use it to design their own applications.)

The custom controls with Visual Basic Professional Edition were developed by both Microsoft and outside vendors. Figure A-6 (from the Demonstration program supplied with Visual Basic Professional Edition) gives you information on these vendors, which all sell very interesting products that go way beyond the ones they supplied for Visual Basic Professional Edition. You might want to contact them and see if they have a product that can make your programming life easier. (See Appendix D for more information.)

## Animated Buttons

You can use animated buttons anywhere you would use a command button (or where you are using a picture box or image control as a command button substitute). They also let you store many bitmaps in one control. This gives you quick access to many bitmap images without tying up scarce Windows resources.

Animated buttons work much the way animation does in the movies. You load multiple images in the button and display them sequentially in a way that gives the appearance of animation. Although you can't see how the animation is done in the demonstration captured in Figure A-7, you'd certainly find it amusing. For example, each click on the open book in the top-left corner turns

**Figure A-6**

**The vendors for the custom controls**

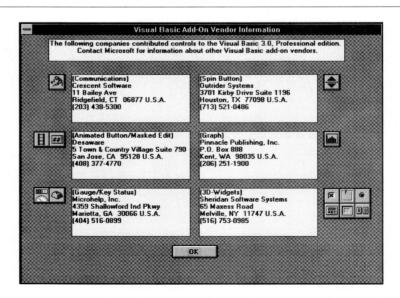

**Figure A-7**

*Animated buttons at work*

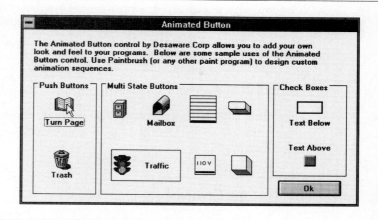

a page, and each click on the trash can in the bottom-left corner alternately opens and closes the top of the trash can.

In practice, this control can be hard to use if you really want to do animation. You must construct the needed images for the animation in some fashion. (There are commercial products that let you do this.)

On the other hand, animated buttons are perfect for replacing an image control you are using as a command button. This is especially true when you want to have multiple images displayed. Animated buttons will work more quickly and use fewer Windows resources than will updating the image multiple times. Use an animated button and you no longer need to confine yourself to having only a caption, as on ordinary command buttons.

**note:**

*The 3D group buttons support pictures too, and are a lot easier to program. They are also faster when actually used. Repainting the AniButton can be slow.*

## Communications

One of the gaps between the first version of Visual Basic and its elderly cousin QuickBASIC 4.5 or its new cousin Visual Basic for DOS was the lack of an easy way to talk to the communication port. The communications control, a subset of Crescent Software's Comm control (see Appendix D), makes it easy for you to design a communications package customized for your needs. The various properties of this control let you set the communications port and the settings needed, such as baud rate, number of data bits, or parity.

As you would expect, an event-driven language is ideal for dealing with communications. You can program the communications custom control so that it wakes up only when the hardware detects activity at the comm port.

## The Crystal Report Control

This control gives you an easy way to generate reports from data stored in a database. It includes much of the functionality of Crystal's own award-winning "Report Writer."

## The Gauge Control

The gauge control lets you add either linear-style gauges or circular (needle) gauges. You can add a custom bitmap or use one of the five bitmaps supplied with Visual Basic Professional Edition for this control. Gauges are a dramatic way to replace scroll bars whenever you want to display what percentage of a job is finished. Figure A-8 shows examples of the four types of gauges supplied.

## Graphs

The graph control adds a professional-quality graphing facility to Visual Basic. If you use a lot of graphs and don't want to spend the many hours required to write the Visual Basic programs needed for doing them, this control alone is worth the cost of Visual Basic Professional Edition.

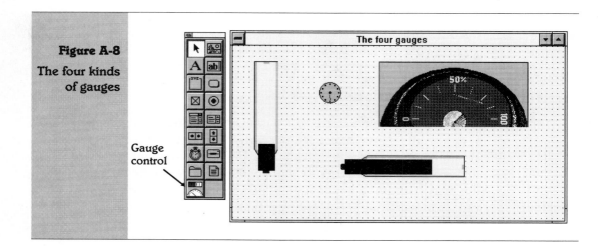

**Figure A-8**

**The four kinds of gauges**

Gauge control

The graph control lets you construct 11 types of graphs:

◆ Two- and three-dimensional pie charts (either exploded or not):

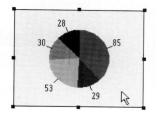 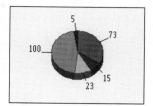

◆ Two- and three-dimensional bar charts:

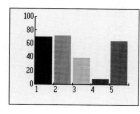 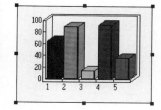

◆ Line charts:

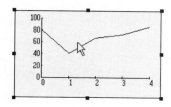

◆ Log/line charts:

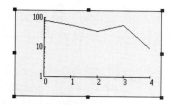

◆ Area charts:

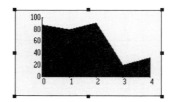

◆ Scatter charts:

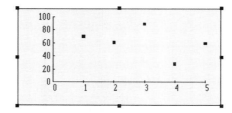

◆ High-low close charts, Gantt charts, and polar charts (for more special-ized uses, such as stock market plotting)

Although you design the graphs when you're building your project, you're not restricted to that. In fact, the graphing facility that the graph control adds to Visual Basic is so useful because you can easily write code that allows the user to do the following while the project is running:

◆ Change or add to the data used for the graph. Given new data, the graph control will redraw the graph automatically.

◆ Rescale the graph, change labels, or switch to a new kind of graph that displays the data from a different point of view.

◆ Send either a bitmap or Windows metafile version of the graph to the printer.

◆ Use the clipboard (or DDE) to incorporate graphs into other Windows applications, such as word processors and desktop publishers.

You release all of these features by changing the values of the 36 new properties associated with the graph control. The code needed for doing this is no different than the code needed to change any other Visual Basic property.

For example, suppose you started with a two-dimensional bar chart at design time. Now you want to switch to a three-dimensional bar chart while the program is running. All you need to do is have Visual Basic process the following line of code:

```
Graph1.GraphStyle=G_BAR3D
```

This uses a symbolic constant supplied in a file with Visual Basic Professional Edition.

## Key Status

The key status control has two purposes:

◆ To show the user (or to let him or her modify) the state of the CAPS LOCK, NUM LOCK, INS, and SCROLL LOCK keys

◆ To avoid your having to use an API function call to check or modify the state of these keys

Using this control is simple. All you need to do is manipulate or read off the setting of the Value property associated with the key. Here's a typical way that the key status control would appear on your form:

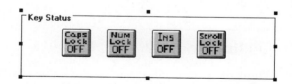

## MAPI Controls

MAPI (which stands for *messaging application program interface*) allows you to work certain electronic mail packages (E-mail, in the jargon) such as Version 3.0 of Microsoft Mail for Windows (or later versions of it). There are two MAPI controls; the first establishes the MAPI session and the second is used to gain access to special features of the E-mail program. MAPI controls are invisible to the user, so you would need to have a command button or image control to establish the MAPI session.

## Masked Edit

This control saves you a lot of code work needed to control the input to text boxes. For most purposes, it seems like an ordinary text box. The difference is that you can restrict the characters entered without having to write code in the Key events (see Chapters 6 and 7 for discussions of these events). Similarly, you can show certain characters in the control—to give people a visual cue that they should be entering a social security number, for example. This control is data-aware (see Chapter 17 for information on using data-aware controls).

## Multimedia MCI Device Control

Multimedia devices such as CD-ROM players will become more and more important to computer users. The idea of combining text, images, and sound on a computer is clearly the wave of the future. The multimedia device control lets users initiate what are called media control interface (MCI) commands. MCI commands are designed to be device-independent and control audio-visual peripherals. You use the multimedia device control to tell the multimedia device to start up, move forward, move back, pause, and so on.

Using this control requires Windows 3.1 or the Multimedia extension to Windows 3.0.

## Outline Control

Think of this control as a specialized list box that displays the text in a hierarchical manner (for example the way the drive list box works). Moreover, you can collapse or expand the levels at will.

## Pen Edit Controls

Although computers that use handwriting (pens) for input are still uncommon, Microsoft has already designed a version of Windows for this. It's called Microsoft Windows for Pen Computing. If you have this extension of Windows, you can use the pen edit controls to allow pen input.

## Picture Clip Control

The picture clip control gives you another way to store multiple icons or bitmaps in one control. Just as with animated buttons, this conserves Windows resources and speeds up access to the image. The obvious place to use this control is if you are adding a toolbox of controls to a Visual Basic project for the user to manipulate. Instead of loading each tool as a separate bitmap, you could use a picture clip to build them in all at once. Here is a typical example of a picture clip:

## Spin Buttons

Spin buttons give you yet another way to have users change a counter if you are tired of scroll bars. Spin buttons are especially useful if you want to give users feedback when they are adding to or subtracting from a counter. Here's an illustration of a typical spin button:

Once the user moves to one of the arrows indicated above and clicks, Visual Basic activates one of the two events for this control: SpinUp or SpinDown. The nice feature is that Visual Basic keeps on generating these events until the user releases the mouse button.

## The 3-D Controls

There are six 3-D controls based on Sheridan's 3D Widgets supplied with Visual Basic Professional Edition. These controls give another way besides framing the control (see Chapter 12) to give a three-dimensional look to your forms. Even text on these controls can appear three-dimensional.

***3-D Check Boxes*** The 3-D check boxes can replace the standard Visual Basic check boxes if you like the look they give. This control is data-aware.

***3-D Command Buttons*** The 3-D command buttons can replace the standard Visual Basic command buttons.

***3-D Frames*** The 3-D frames can replace the standard Visual Basic frames.

***3-D Option Buttons*** The 3-D option buttons can replace the standard Visual Basic option (radio) buttons. You use them in groups just like you would ordinary option buttons.

***3-D Group Push Buttons*** The 3-D group push buttons are also designed to replace radio (option) buttons. Within each group of buttons (use a 3-D frame for more than one group), clicking one button makes it appear pushed in. This also releases the previously pressed button.

***3-D Panel*** The 3-D panel tool combines the properties of a frame with a text box—all in three dimensions, of course. This control is data aware. Here's an example of a 3-D panel:

# The API Tools

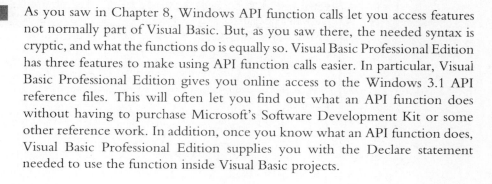

As you saw in Chapter 8, Windows API function calls let you access features not normally part of Visual Basic. But, as you saw there, the needed syntax is cryptic, and what the functions do is equally so. Visual Basic Professional Edition has three features to make using API function calls easier. In particular, Visual Basic Professional Edition gives you online access to the Windows 3.1 API reference files. This will often let you find out what an API function does without having to purchase Microsoft's Software Development Kit or some other reference work. In addition, once you know what an API function does, Visual Basic Professional Edition supplies you with the Declare statement needed to use the function inside Visual Basic projects.

**tip:**

*Copy the API declarations directly from the API help file. (As you've seen, API function declarations are quite messy. This tip can save you a lot of grief.)*

Moreover, there are lots of samples of using API calls inside a Visual Basic project. (See Chapter 8 for more information on how to use API function calls.)

*API Help* A Windows help file named WINSDK.HLP contains complete information for the Microsoft Windows API. You can use this to look up online any of the functions, data structures, or error messages you need to work with the Windows API. Figure A-9 shows a typical example of a help screen for an API function. It explains in more detail the GetWinFlags API function you saw in Chapter 8. As this figure indicates, with API help you have complete online access to what this function can do. (This is essentially the same as the help system supplied with the Microsoft Windows Software Development Kit.)

*The Windows API Declarations and Constant File* The Windows API declarations and constant file is a very large ASCII file containing all the constants and Declare statements you need to use Windows API functions from Visual Basic. As mentioned in Chapter 8, it is extremely important that the Declare statements be perfect before you use an API function. For this reason, the best way to use this file is to load it into Windows Write. (It's too large to fit into Visual Basic or even in the Windows Notebook.) Then cut and paste the

**Figure A-9**

Help screen for an API function

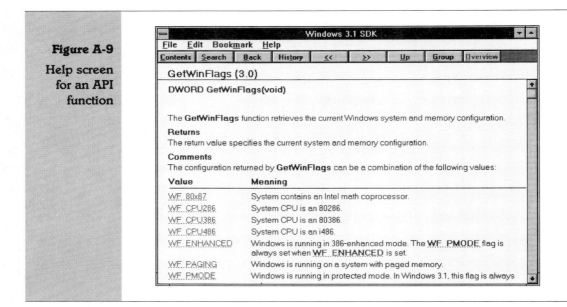

declarations you want into your Visual Basic project. (Be sure that when you do copy them into your Visual Basic project, they remain single lines.)

# The Visual Basic Online Knowledge Base

The Visual Basic Online Knowledge Base is a Windows help system with lots of ideas, example code, and tips about the Visual Basic Windows programming environment. The full Visual Basic knowledge base wouldn't fit on a floppy; it is included in the developer CD-ROM (see Appendix D).

# Appendix B

# The Setup Wizard

HE Setup Wizard makes it easy to distribute most Visual Basic applications. (In special situations you'll need to go in and work with the setup kit directly; see Appendix A.)

The Setup Wizard is a stand–alone Windows application written in Visual Basic itself. Don't run it while Visual Basic is running. The Visual Basic installation process adds this application as a program item in the Visual Basic program group. If you double-click on the icon, you are taken to the initial setup screen which looks likes Figure B-1.

Let's go over the items in the main screen. First, there is a Help button which takes you to the (short) on-line help file and an Exit button to close the Wizard. Here are descriptions of the other items.

**Figure B-1**

**Initial Wizard setup screen**

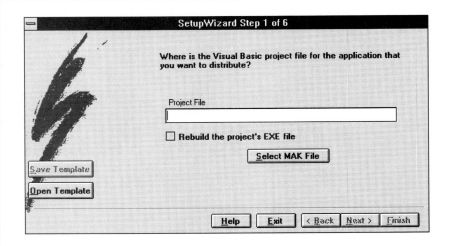

**Project File, Select MAK file**  The project file is the name of the make (.MAK) file. You can click on Select MAK File to open up a dialog box that lets you search for the MAK file.

**Rebuild EXE file**  Files you distribute are stand–alone executable. If you need to recreate a stand-alone product, set this check box to be on. The Wizard will automatically build the EXE file if it doesn't find one.

**Open Template**  This is used to create a template for future uses of the Wizard. If you habitually use certain files in your applications you can include them by clicking on this button and working with the dialog box that appears. This button is available at all times so you can add frequently-used options at any time.

## Using the Wizard

Let's suppose you want to distribute the Checkbook management program from Chapter 18. The MAK file is called FINANCE.MAK. Once you enter the name of the MAK file, the main screen of the Wizard would look something like Figure B-2.

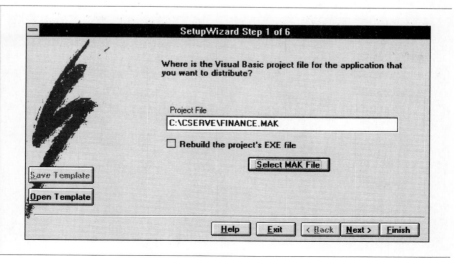

**Figure B-2**

Initial Wizard screen after choosing MAK file

**Figure B-3**

Extra features
that need to
be included

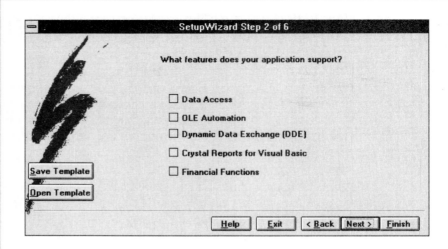

Notice that the Next button in Figure B-2 is now enabled. Click on it and after a short delay, while the Wizard processes the files and Visual Basic itself is invoked, you are taken to Figure B-3. (That's providing Visual Basic isn't running; if it is, you'll be told to first close Visual Basic so the Wizard can take control of Visual Basic itself.)

The checkbook program doesn't use any of the features listed. (If you used any of these features, clicking on the check box would tell the Wizard to include the necessary files for that feature in your distribution disks.) So we click on Next, which takes us to Figure B-4.

**Figure B-4**

Disk
controlling
screen

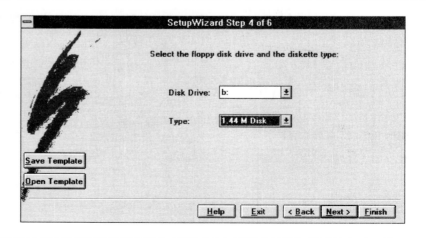

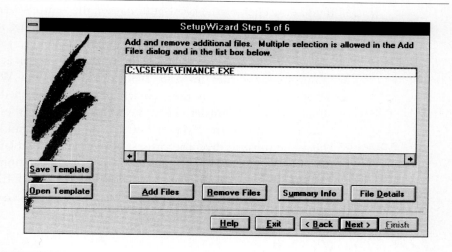

**Figure B-5**

Screen for adding and removing files

This screen is where you tell the Wizard where you want the files stored and on what type of disk. In Figure B-4, I am storing the files in the B: drive on a 1.4MB floppy. Click on the Next button and you are taken to Figure B-5. This screen allows you to add or remove files.

By clicking on the Summary Info button you are taken to a message box that looks like Figure B-6. This screen gives you important information on what the distribution disk will look like.

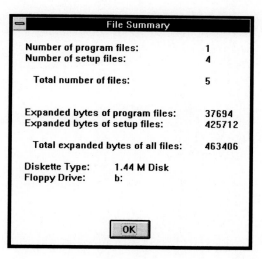

**Figure B-6**

File Summary screen

If you now click on the Next button, then the Setup Wizard first checks that there is enough space on your hard disk for the processing it will need to do. After the Setup Wizard shells to DOS in order to compress the needed files, it re-invokes Visual Basic to create the SETUP.EXE file that actually installs (and decompresses) the files in your application. After the Wizard creates the SETUP.EXE program, it then copies all the files needed to the disk you previously specified. Finally, when the Setup Wizard finishes copying the files, you are notified that the "Master distribution disks are finished" (and warned to check the finished disks for viruses). Users can now install your application simply by placing the distribution disk into a drive and running from Windows the SETUP.EXE program that is contained on the first distribution disk.

# Appendix C

# From QuickBASIC to

## Visual Basic

779

ALTHOUGH QuickBASIC and Visual Basic code are similar, their styles of programming are sufficiently different that you may want to rethink the code anyway. The user interface is fundamental in Visual Basic and pretty much ignored in QuickBASIC. On the other hand, general procedures that are used by other parts of the program to sort, parse data, and so on, can be reused with only minor changes.

This appendix briefly describes the differences between QuickBASIC and Visual Basic and presents the commands and statements in QuickBASIC that are not supported by or work differently in Visual Basic. Where possible, you'll see which features in Visual Basic give the same functionality.

**note:** *Microsoft also sells Visual Basic for DOS. Going from Visual Basic for DOS to Visual Basic for Windows is not usually too difficult. (You'll need to save your projects in text format for best results.) Consult the documentation that came with either product for help on converting from one platform to another.*

## Some General Information

The Load Text command on the File menu lets you bring QuickBASIC code into your Visual Basic project. You can also cut and paste from another Windows application. Visual Basic has no line-continuation character, so you'll have to go in by hand and combine lines that used one. When you import a QuickBASIC program, Visual Basic keeps Sub and Function procedures intact but puts any obvious declarations in the Declarations section of the current form or module.

If your QuickBASIC program used the older DEF FN form of function definition, rewrite it as a Function procedure. Unlike QuickBASIC, GoSubs and GoTos must stay inside a single procedure or function. (It's hard to imagine why you would need many—or even any—GoTos, though.) Similarly, error traps must remain inside the same Sub or Function procedure. Obviously, any event-trapping code in QuickBASIC can be easily adapted to Visual Basic; after all, event trapping is the essence of a Visual Basic program.

Since QuickBASIC doesn't require all executable code to be inside a module, you may need to move any executable statements from the main body of your QuickBASIC program to the Form_Load or Sub Main procedure. Declarations and definers can stay in the Declarations section of the form or module, where Visual Basic will put them when you import the file. An exception is the Type declaration, which must be in a code module. The DECLARE housekeeping statements that QuickBASIC uses are acceptable in Visual Basic only for function procedures that use no arguments and calls to DLLs; it's best to remove them. On the other hand, you must use parentheses when you call a function procedure in Visual Basic unless you have left the DECLARE statement for it intact.

Global variables in QuickBASIC (that is, COMMON SHARED variables) can be recast as form or global variables as needed. Conversely, you cannot use the SHARED keyword to make a Visual Basic variable visible to some procedures but not to others.

Since the period has a special meaning in Visual Basic, you must remove any periods from QuickBASIC variable names. Also, Visual Basic does not allow you to use two variables with the same name but different type identifiers visible in the same procedure. Having the variables A% and A$ will lead to an error message.

# The Keyword Changes

Many QuickBASIC commands either are not supported in Visual Basic or work differently. Sometimes you can make a simple replacement that gives a similar effect—an InputBox$ for an Input command, for example. Often, however, a change this simplistic runs contrary to the spirit of Visual Basic. For example, text boxes are the usual way to get information into a Visual Basic program, and transferring a Print command from a QuickBASIC program would, at best, send information to the current form, where it is likely to be obscured. This is why you're best off rethinking the user interface first.

Here are the QuickBASIC commands that work differently or are not supported in Visual Basic. If there is a reasonable way to work around the gap, you'll see that as well. In certain cases, you can use Windows API functions or commercial products to fill the gap. For example, Crescent Software (QuickPak Professional for Windows) and MicroHelp (VB Tools and Muscle) are comprehensive packages that, in addition to providing custom controls and many useful routines for general programming tasks, also provide replacements for many of these omitted functions. Both these tools are worth the serious Visual Basic programmer's attention. (Appendix D provides telephone numbers for the two companies that manufacture these products.) If you want to use Windows API functions, you should probably get the Visual Basic Professional Edition (see Appendix A). The documentation and examples supplied with that product will often help you replace a specific QuickBASIC function with an API call.

**BLOAD, BSAVE** If you are using BLOAD or BSAVE to load or save screen images, you might be able to substitute the LoadPicture/SavePicture functions. To do this, you'll need a way of recasting the image as a bitmap. There are commercial programs for this, or you can write your own (a rather laborious undertaking). One possibility that may work is to use the Windows clipboard to transfer the image to Windows Paintbrush, where you can then store it as a bitmap. If you need to save a memory image, Crescent Software's package can help you do this with its replacements for BLOAD and BSAVE.

**CALL ABSOLUTE, CALLS** You would not normally call from Visual Basic a machine-language program that is not part of a DLL. If the operation makes sense for Windows, you can theoretically convert the machine-language program into a DLL and then call it from Visual Basic. Usually, though, you would be better off writing it in C.

**CHAIN** If you want to run another program in the Windows environment, use Shell or AppActivate, as appropriate.

**CLEAR** There is no way to resize the stack inside Visual Basic, so this use of the CLEAR statement is impossible. If you need to close open files, the Close statement does that. The ReDim command lets you clear an array, and you'll need to reinitialize variables one by one unless you save all the values with ReDim Preserve.

**COLOR** Visual Basic's facilities with color (see Chapter 12) make it easy to convert the COLOR command. For example, the ForeColor and BackColor properties can be set independently for most Visual Basic objects.

**COM, WAIT** Unfortunately, Visual Basic does not yet have equivalents for the COM and WAIT commands. It is possible (but quite cumbersome) to write the equivalents by using API calls (see Chapter 8 and Appendix A), but when you buy the Visual Basic Professional Edition, you get a communication custom control as part of the package.

**CSRLIN** The CurrentY command gives you much more precise information. Divide CurrentY by FontHeight and subtract 1, and you know what line of the form you're on.

**CVD, CVDMBF, CVI, CVS, CVSMF, FIELD, MKD$, MKI$, MKL$, MKS$, MKSMBF$** Since you have user-defined records available to read information back from a random access file, the CVD, CVDMBF, CVI, CVS, CVSMF, FIELD, MKD$, MKI$, MKL$, MKS$, and MKSMBF$ statements are no longer needed. If you need to read a random-access file written with these older formats, the Crescent package supplies Visual Basic replacements. You can also use binary file techniques, though this is quite labor-intensive.

**DATA, RESTORE** The best you can do is build the information into a Form_Load procedure or a general procedure, item by item.

**DEF FN** Replace DEF FN with a function procedure.

**DEF SEG, PEEK, POKE, SADD, SETMEM** Windows handles memory management. The last thing you want to do is interfere with individual memory locations.

*DRAW* Unfortunately, DRAW is not supported. You can use the various graphics primitives built into Visual Basic to draw objects. This will sometimes be a little more time-consuming.

*ERDEV, ERDEV$* Sometimes the Error$ statement can give you equivalent information.

*FILES* Use the Dir$ command or a file or directory list box.

*FRE* You can use Windows API calls to find out the amount of free memory, but otherwise you are out of luck. (Crescent Software's package does supply a replacement for FRE.) You cannot increase the stack, for example, no matter what you do.

*INKEY$* The Key events (KeyUp/KeyDown and KeyPress) are far more flexible.

*INP* Visual Basic currently has no way to read specific information from a port. There are commercial products like the ones from Crescent and MicroHelp that restore this capability. You can also use Windows API functions.

*INPUT* Use a text box or the InputBox$ function. To replace statements like INPUT A, B, C$, you will need to parse the text to get at more than one piece of information.

*IOCTL, IOCTL$* You must rely on Windows to supply the device drivers. API function calls can often provide this functionality.

*KEY* The Key events in Visual Basic are far more flexible.

**LOCATE** CurrentX and CurrentY combined with TextHeight and TextWidth give you far more flexibility. You cannot change the cursor shape, but you can change the mouse pointer.

**LPOS, LPRINT** The Printer object in Visual Basic lets you completely control the printer. Its methods give you far more flexibility.

**ON COM, ON PLAY, ON STRIG** Light pens and joysticks are not currently supported by Visual Basic. Windows API functions or a commercial package can replace these commands, if need be.

**ON KEY, ON TIMER** Use the Key events for ON KEY; use a timer control for ON TIMER.

**OUT** API functions can communicate with specific ports, as can certain commercial Visual Basic products like the ones from MicroHelp and Crescent.

**PAINT** If the graphics primitives built into Visual Basic aren't sufficient, you can use Windows API functions to replace the PAINT command.

**PEEK, POKE** Don't even think about interfering with Windows' ever-so-delicate Memory Manager.

**PEN, ON PEN, STICK, STRIG** Light pens, joysticks, and game controllers aren't supported by Visual Basic. Since they all use specific ports, given the documentation and the *Windows API Reference Guide* (available online in the Visual Basic Professional Edition), you can probably contrive something.

**PLAY** API functions let you recover the PLAY capability. In fact, this is one of the examples that the Visual Basic Professional Edition uses to illustrate API calls.

---

***PMAP, VIEW, WINDOW*** The Scale method gives you far more power and flexibility. In addition, you don't ever have to worry about doing the conversions between different scales yourself. Let Visual Basic handle it.

---

***PRESET*** Use PSet in the background color to erase.

---

***PRINT USING$*** The Format$ command is even more flexible.

---

***RUN*** You wouldn't want to run a program from inside itself, anyway. If what you are doing is a self-running demo, you can change the appropriate properties in code and use the SendKey statement (refer to Chapter 15).

---

***SCREEN*** Since Windows handles the graphics, Visual Basic graphics commands do the best they can. In particular, you don't have to worry about what screen modes a person's hardware supports.

---

***SHARED*** The scope of variables in Visual Basic is actually easier to follow than in QuickBASIC. Using SHARED to make a variable visible to a specific procedure is not possible without a kludge. (Make it a global variable, but use the Dim statement to make it local in the procedures you want to hide the variable from.)

---

***SLEEP*** Use a timer loop inside a procedure or a timer control, as needed.

---

***SOUND*** Windows API calls can handle this (see the PLAY example in the Visual Basic Professional Edition for specifics).

---

***SWAP*** It's not clear why Visual Basic left out SWAP, but it's easy enough to write as a general procedure for each variable type. Crescent Software has a replacement for it.

**SYSTEM** Use the End command.

**TRON, TROFF** Single-stepping, watch variables, and using Debug.Print are far more flexible.

**UEVENT** Visual Basic should be responsive enough to events for most users. It is quite likely that Visual Basic responds to the event or something close enough to that event already.

**VARPTR, VARPTR$, VARSEG** Visual Basic does not provide this facility. If you need it, it is part of Crescent's package.

**VIEW, VIEW PRINT** Use a picture box or text box, as appropriate.

**WIDTH** A text box with scroll bars is far more flexible.

**WINDOW** Use the Scale command (see Chapter 12).

# Appendix D

# Third-Party Tools and

## Other Resources

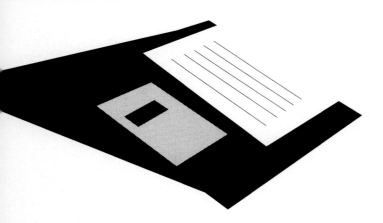

HIRD-PARTY tools can make Visual Basic programs easier, faster, more powerful—or all three. This appendix tries to give you a quick overview of some of what is available. The number of third-party tools is growing rapidly; this section can only give you a start. (Of course, probably first on your list should be the upgrade to the Professional Edition.)

## Tools

Tools can be divided into groups roughly as follows.

1. Those that make the nitty-gritty of design and debugging easier. Included in this are tools to make writing help files easier.

2. Tools that, for speed or convenience, add low-level routines or make it easier to use the ones supplied with Windows.

3. Custom controls.

### Design and Debugging Tools

The first tool that the author uses to make design and debugging easier is MicroHelp's cross-reference program "VBXRef" (1-800-922-3383). Cross-reference programs are extremely helpful when doing serious programming (and alas, the concomitant debugging) and MicroHelp's version is first rate. Both MicroHelp's "Muscle" and Crescent Software's "QuickPak" (1-800-35BASIC) provide routines for sending debugging information to a secondary (monochrome) monitor. Sheridan Software's "VBAssist" (1-516-753-0985) enhances the ordinary Visual Basic environment in too many ways to list all of them here. Features include tools to make aligning controls on a form, adding graphics, and accessing data easier. Another feature called the "Code Assistant" makes combining different code fragments trivial as well as helping you with Windows API calls. Finally, VideoSoft's "VB/Manager" (1-510-547-7295) is also a useful add-on for managing Visual Basic projects (and includes two custom controls, as well).

## Tools for Speed and Convenience

The tools that the author uses all the time for speedy low-level routines (including adding capabilities like sound that were mysteriously left out of Visual Basic) are: Crescent Software's "QuickPak Professional" and MicroHelp's "Muscle." Both these products are essential when porting QuickBasic, the Basic PDS, or even Visual Basic for DOS programs to Visual Basic for Windows. But, in addition, they have literally hundreds of useful, *fast* routines for everything from matrix handling to swapping variables and arrays.

Desaware's "SpyWorks-VB" (1-408-377-4770) is for people who have mastered standard Windows API calls and want to move to full control of Windows at the very lowest levels. For those people, this tool is essential and highly recommended.

Scientists can benefit from two toolkits with scientific routines: Crescent Software's "QuickPak Scientific" and TerraTech's (1-800-447-9120 x1036) "ProMath VB."

People working in finance can also look at TerraTech's "Financial Library VB" if the Crescent QuickPak doesn't have the appropriate function and it is not built into Visual Basic 3.

## Custom Controls

Custom controls probably could use a book of their own. Which control you want to look at depends completely on what you want to do. Doing it yourself is often akin to reinventing the wheel and is an overstated virtue in programming—especially in the '90s. If you need to write an interface to a mainframe, a report generator, or a graphics manipulator, you would be a lot better off looking for a custom control than trying to do it yourself.

Chances are someone has developed a tool to make your job easier, your application slicker, or both. Vendors sometimes (as in Crescent Software's "Quick-Pak Professional") include both custom controls and low-level routines in their packages so that you are getting either one or the other essentially for free.

Visual Basic Programmer's Journal (see the next section) is a very good source for learning what custom controls are being developed and what are already out there. Another place to turn to is the vendors who contributed the custom controls in Visual Basic Professional (see Appendix A). If you need to go beyond what those controls can do, chances are the original vendor has a fancier version available. For example, Crescent Software's "PDQComm" offers much more than the controls they supplied for VB Professional. Desaware's (1-408-377-4770) "Custom Control Factory" (it should be called the "Custom Button Factory") also goes far beyond the animated buttons included in the Professional Edition. (Desaware also has a nifty tool for adding custom cursors/mouse pointers called "CCF-Cursors.") Similarly, Sheridan Software's Widgets package far exceeds the 3D controls they supplied to Microsoft in the Professional Edition and Pinnacle Publishing's (1-206-251-1900) "Chart Builder" goes far beyond the graph control they supplied for Visual Basic Professional.

One of the great failings of Visual Basic 3 is the lack of a data-aware grid control or list and combo boxes. For the data-aware grid, contact FarPoint Technologies (1-800-645-5913) for their "Visual Architect," which includes a dynamite spreadsheet control that should be data-aware by the time you read this. (This control has virtually all the functionality of a commercial spreadsheet.)

**note:** *Crescent, MicroHelp, and Sheridan all have data-aware controls that are worth checking out.*

Just as FarPoint has essentially a complete spreadsheet as a custom control, MicroHelp's "HighEdit" (1-800-922-3383) is basically a complete word processor in a control. MicroHelp also sells "VBTools" with around 30 custom controls for common tasks.

Database add-ons used to be the biggest add-on area for earlier versions of Visual Basic. With the data access features added to Visual Basic 3 this area is in flux. There are still tools out there that are vital in special situations. For example, "VB/ISAM MX" from Software Source (1-510-632-7854) is a wonderful product for small, fast, flat database jobs where you don't want the overhead (not to mention the disk space) of the relational database Access engine. Similarly, Pioneer's "Q+E DataLink/VB" (1-800-876-3101) supports a much larger number of database formats than does Microsoft's Access engine. MicroHelp's "Report Generator" is very useful if you need bar codes on mailing labels.

**note:** *Some people feel that third-party custom controls should not be used because they may not work as planned in new versions of Visual Basic. The author feels that this is an overstated worry, and* *custom control vendors are likely to be very quick about upgrading to new versions. On the other hand, it may not be worth using a custom control if all you are getting out of it is a minor improvement—which might very well be obtainable by a clever use of Windows API calls.*

# Resources

The best resource the author knows for Visual Basic is the MSBASIC forum on Compuserve. Many knowledgeable people frequent this forum and Microsoft technical support is omnipresent there as well. Between the two, almost any question will find an answer. If you don't have a Compuserve account, Microsoft provides a coupon for a free month in the Visual Basic package. You can also call Compuserve directly to get an account (1-800-848-8990).

**caution:** *Compuserve can quickly become very expensive when you spend too much time exploring the forums.*

A bulletin board worth checking out is VB Online (1-216-861-0467). The board itself (1-216-694-5734) requires setting your terminal program to 2400-9600 baud with parameters 8/1/N. Browsing is free but downloading privileges are $39.50/year.

Among periodical resources that the author knows about, first, it is hard for me to imagine a serious Visual Basic programmer who won't like (and get a lot out of) Visual Basic Programmer's Journal (formerly BASICPro Magazine) (1-800-848-5523, around $28/year for 6 issues). Next, and somewhat more expensive, is "Inside Visual Basic" (1-800-223-8720, $59/year for twelve 16-page issues). Next, and in many ways the most interesting for developers, is Microsoft's Developer CD Program available by subscription for $200/year for four CDs (1-800-759-5474, Dept OABB3). The developer CD is not addressed specifically to Visual Basic programmers—it's for Windows developers generally. Nonetheless there are tens of megabytes of information that a VB programmer will find useful, including the current complete version of the Visual Basic Knowledge Base.

Not focusing completely on Visual Basic but having a useful article or two each month are "Windows Tech Journal" (1-800-234-0386) and "Windows/DOS Developer's Journal" (1-913-841-1631). In addition, Jonathan Zuck has an electronic newsletter called "VBZ" that I recommend. (Contact him via CSERVE at 76702, 1605 or at 1-202-785-3607 for details.)

# Appendix E

# Microsoft's Top Twenty

## Visual Basic

## Technical Support Questions

**note:** *We asked Microsoft for permission to include their answers to the most frequently asked questions about Visual Basic. They most graciously agreed to provide this information. We decided to include this information because, although technical support from Microsoft is free, it is often time consuming to get through and may turn out to be not free after all (half-hour toll calls during business hours can add up). We are providing this information essentially unchanged except for formatting and minor editorial changes.)*

The following frequently asked questions apply to Microsoft Visual Basic for Windows, version 3. They are not listed in order of importance, because the information was collected from several Microsoft sources.

1. I am having problems connecting to my database using open data base connectivity (ODBC) and Microsoft Visual Basic for Windows. What am I doing wrong?

2. How do I establish a network dynamic date exchange (DDE) link using Microsoft Visual Basic under Microsoft Windows for Workgroups?

3. What are the steps necessary to initiate DDE between a Microsoft Visual Basic destination application and a Visual Basic source application?

4. What are the steps necessary to initiate DDE between a Microsoft Visual Basic destination application and a Microsoft Excel source application?

5. What are the steps necessary to initiate DDE between a Microsoft Visual Basic destination application and a Microsoft Word for Windows (WINWORD.EXE) source document?

6. How do I send DDE interface commands to the Microsoft Windows Program Manager from within Microsoft Visual Basic for Windows?

7. How can I copy the entire screen into a picture box in Visual Basic for Windows?

8. How can I print a bitmap contained in a picture box control to the printer using Microsoft Visual Basic for Windows?

9. How can I print a control or a form in Microsoft Visual Basic for Windows?

10. How can I set the orientation of the printer to either landscape or portrait from within a Visual Basic application?

11. How can I access the information in the Windows initialization files from within a Visual Basic application?

12. How can I create a bitmap with a transparent background in Visual Basic for Windows?

13. How can I create a *floating window*—a window that always stays on top of every other window on the desktop?

14. Under Microsoft Visual Basic for Windows, how can I determine when a shelled process has terminated?

15. How can I use the LPSTR returned from an API function call to get the string data it points to?

16. How can I create a scrollable viewport using Microsoft Visual Basic for Windows?

17. How can I determine if a specific application is running under Windows?

18. How can I use the data control in Microsoft Visual Basic for Windows to scroll up and down in a recordset?

19. I have VC++ and VBWIN Pro. Do I still need the Visual Control Pack?

20. I have multiple .DLL and .VBX files. Which ones should I use?

# Q: I am having problems connecting to my database using ODBC and Microsoft Visual Basic for Windows. What am I doing wrong?

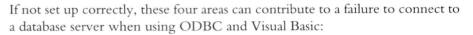

If not set up correctly, these four areas can contribute to a failure to connect to a database server when using ODBC and Visual Basic:

◆ .INI file settings must be correct.

◆ Correct dynamic link libraries (DLLs) must be in the right place.

◆ Server information needed to connect to a server correctly must be available.

◆ Information must also meet the needs of Microsoft and Sybase SQL servers.

The following sections describe these four areas, giving possible errors and problems that can arise.

## .INI File Settings

There are two .INI files (ODBCINST.INI and ODBC.INI) that must reside in the Windows directory and must contain correct information about the installed ODBC drivers and servers.

ODBCINST.INI contains the ODBC driver information needed to register new servers using the RegisterDataBase( ) statement in Visual Basic. Here is an example of an .INI file for the SQL Server driver that ships with Visual Basic:

```
[ODBC Drivers]
SQL Server=Installed

[SQL Server]
Driver=C:\WINDOWS\SYSTEM\sqlsrvr.dll
Setup=C:\WINDOWS\SYSTEM\sqlsetup.dll
```

The [ODBC Drivers] section tells the driver manager the names of the installed drivers. The [SQL Server] section tells the ODBC driver manager the names of the DLLs to use to access data from a server set up as a SQL Server. The order of the two sections and their entries is arbitrary.

ODBC.INI contains the data for each installed driver. The driver manager uses this information to determine which DLL to use to access data from a particular database backend. Here is an example of a file containing three data sources all using the SQL Server driver:

```
[ODBC Data Sources]
MySQL=SQL Server
CorpSQL=SQL Server

[MySQL]
Driver=C:\WINDOWS\SYSTEM\sqlsrvr.dll
Description=SQL Server on server MySQL
OemToAnsi=No
Network=dbnmp3
Address=\\mysql\pipe\sql\query

[CorpSQL]
Driver=C:\WINDOWS\SYSTEM\sqlsrvr.dll
Description=SQL Server on server CorpSQL
OemToAnsi=No
Network=dbnmp3
Address=\\corpsql\pipe\sql\query
```

The first section tells the driver manager which sections appearing below it define the data source. As you can see, each entry has a value (in this case, SQL Server) that matches a value from the ODBCINST.INI file.

If the information on a data source is incorrect or missing, you may get the following error:

ODBC – SQLConnect failure 'IM002[Microsoft][ODBC DLL] Data source not found and no default driver specified'

If the DLL listed on the Driver=... line cannot be found or is corrupt, the following error may occur:

ODBC – SQLConnect failure 'IM003[Microsoft][ODBC DLL] Driver specified by data source could not be loaded'

## ODBC and Driver DLLs

The following DLLs must be on the path or in the Windows system directory in order for ODBC to be accessible from Visual Basic:

ODBC.DLL – driver manager
ODBCINST.DLL – driver setup manager
VBDB300.DLL – Visual Basic programming layer

If VBDB300.DLL is missing or corrupt, you see the following error in Visual Basic when you try to run the application:

ODBC Objects require VBDB300.DLL

If either the ODBC.DLL or ODBCINST.DLL file is missing or corrupt, you see the following error in Visual Basic when you try to run the application:

Cannot Find ODBC.DLL, File not Found

The SQL Server driver requires the following files:

SQLSRVR.DLL – actual driver
SQLSETUP.DLL – driver setup routines
DBNMP3.DLL– named pipe routines needed by SQL server

If the SQLSRVR.DLL is missing or corrupt, you see the following error when calling the OpenDataBase( ) function with a SQL Server data source:

ODBC – SQLConnect failure 'IM003[Microsoft][ODBC DLL] Driver specified by data source could not be loaded'

If the SQLSETUP.DLL is missing or corrupt, you see the following error when calling the RegisterDataBase statement with SQL Server as the driver name:

The configuration DLL (C:\WINDOWS\SYSTEM\SQLSETUP.DLL) for the ODBC SQL server driver could not be loaded.

## Server Information Needed to Connect to a Data Source

Certain information is needed to connect to a data source using the OpenData-Base() function. This information is obtainable from the server administrator in the case of SQL Server. The following is an example of a call to the OpenDataBase() function to connect to a SQL Server called CorpSQL as a user named Guest with password set to taco:

```
Dim db As DataBase
Set db = OpenDataBase( "corpsql", False, False, "UID=guest;PWD=taco")
```

If any of this information is missing, an ODBC dialog box appears to give a user a chance to supply the needed data. If the information is incorrect, the following error occurs:

ODBC - SQLConnect failure '28000
[Microsoft] [ODBC SQL Server Driver]
[SQL Server]  Login failed'

## Information Specific to Microsoft and Sybase SQL Servers

For Microsoft and Sybase SQL Servers, you need to add stored procedures to the server itself by running a batch file of SQL statements to make a Microsoft or Sybase SQL Server ODBC-aware. In other words, before you can run a Visual Basic ODBC application using the SQL Server driver, you must first update the ODBC catalog of stored procedures. These procedures are provided in the INSTCAT.SQL file. The system administrator for the SQL Server should install the procedures by using the SQL Server Interactive SQL (ISQL) utility.

If the INSTCAT.SQL file is not processed on the server, the following error occurs:

ODBC - SQL Connect Failure
"08001" [Microsoft ODBC SQL Server Driver]
'unable to connect to data source 'number: 606'

To install the catalog stored procedures by using the INSTCAT.SQL file, run INSTCAT.SQL from the command line using ISQL. Do not use the SAF utility provided with SQL Server. Microsoft SAF for MS-DOS and OS/2 is limited to 511 lines of code in a SQL script, and INSTCAT.SQL contains more than 511 lines of code.

Run ISQL from the OS/2 command line using the following syntax. Enter the two lines as one, single line, and do not include the angle braces (<>).

ISQL /U <sa login name > /n /P <password> /S <F128QL server name /i <drive: \path\INSTCAT.SQL > /o <drive:\path\output file name>

The parameters in the preceding command line are as follows:

/U      The login name for the system administrator.

/n      Eliminates line numbering and prompting for user input.

/P      Password used for the system administrator. This switch is case sensitive.

/S      The name of the server to set up.

/i      Provides the drive and fully qualified path for the location of INSTCAT.SQL.

/o      Provides ISQL with an output file destination for results including error listings.

Here's an example (shown here on two lines but actually entered on one):

```
ISQL /U sa /n /P squeeze /S BLUEDWARF /i C: \SQL\INSTCAT.SQL /o
C: \SQL OUTPUT.TXT
```

# Q: How do I establish a network DDE link using Microsoft Visual Basic under Microsoft Windows for Workgroups?

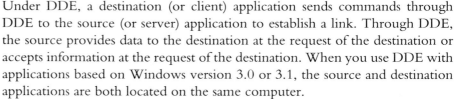

Under DDE, a destination (or client) application sends commands through DDE to the source (or server) application to establish a link. Through DDE, the source provides data to the destination at the request of the destination or accepts information at the request of the destination. When you use DDE with applications based on Windows version 3.0 or 3.1, the source and destination applications are both located on the same computer.

When you use network DDE with Windows for Workgroups based applications, DDE functions exactly the same way as standard DDE, except that the source and destination applications are located on different computers. There are three steps involved in establishing a network DDE link.

## Step One: Add DDE Share by Calling the NDdeShareAdd() Function

To establish a network DDE link, you must first establish a network DDE share for the conversation by calling the API NDdeShareAdd( ) function located in the NDDEAPI.DLL file. Here is the Visual Basic declaration:

```
Declare Function NDdeShareAdd Lib "NDDEAPI.DLL" (Server As Any, _
ByVal LevelAs Integer, ShareInfo As NDDESHAREINFO, ByVal _
nSize As Long) As Integer
```

Enter the entire statement as a single line. The first parameter is always a zero and is passed with ByVal 0& from Visual Basic. The second parameter is always 2. The next parameter is a filled ShareInfo structure (given in the following example).

The last parameter is the size of the ShareInfo structure.

Here is the structure of the NDDESHAREINFO structure:

```
Type NDDESHAREINFO
szShareName As String * MAX_NDDESHARENAME_PLUSONE
lpszTargetApp As Long      'LPSTR lpszTargetApp
lpszTargetTopic As Long    'LPSTR lpszTargetTopic
lpbPassword1 As Long       'LPBYTE lpbPassword1
cbPassword1 As Long        'DWORD  cbPassword1:
dwPermissions1 As Long     'DWORD  dwPermissions1;
lpbPassword2 As Long       'LPBYTE lpbPassword2;
cbPassword2 As Long        'DWORD  cbPassword2:
dwPermissions2 As Long     'DWORD  dwPermissions2;
lpszItem As Long           'LPSTR  lpszItem;
cAddItems As Long          'LONGcAddItems;
lpNDdeShareItemInfo As Long
End Type
```

The following table describes each field of the NDDESHAREINFO type:

| Field Name | Purpose |
| --- | --- |
| szShareName | Name of the share to add. |
| lpszTargetApp | Pointer to null-terminated string containing the service or application name. |
| lpszTargetTopic | Pointer to null-terminated string holding the topic name. |

| Field Name | Purpose |
|---|---|
| lpbPassword1 | Pointer to the read-only password—uppercase, null-terminated string. If null, pass null string, not zero. |
| cbPassword1 | Length of read-only password. |
| dwPermissions1 | Full-access password. |
| cbPassword2 | Length of the full-access password. |
| dwPermissions2 | Permissions allowed by the full-access password. |

Here are the permissions allowed for dwPermissions:

| Name | Value | Function |
|---|---|---|
| NDDEACCESS_REQUEST | &H1 | Allows LinkRequest |
| NDDEACCESS_ADVISE | &H2 | Allows LinkAdvise |
| NDDEACCESS_POKE | &H4 | Allows LinkPoke |
| NDDEACCESS_EXECUTE | &H8 | Allows LinkExecute |
| NDDEACCESS_START_APP | &H10 | Starts source application on connect |

Here are the possible return values from NDdeShareAdd( ):

| Name | Value | Meaning |
|---|---|---|
| NDDE_NO_ERROR | 0 | No error. |
| NDDE_BUF_TOO_SMALL | 2 | Buffer is too small to hold information. |
| NDDE_INVALID_APPNAME | 13 | Application name is not valid. |
| NDDE_INVALID_ITEMNAME | 9 | Item name is not valid. |
| NDDE_INVALID_LEVEL | 7 | Invalid level; nLevel parameter must be 2. |
| NDDE_INVALID_PASSWORD | 8 | Password is not valid. |
| NDDE_INVALID_SERVER | 4 | Computer name is not valid; lpszServer parameter must be NULL. |
| NDDE_INVALID_SHARE | 5 | Share name is not valid. |
| NDDE_INVALID_TOPIC | 10 | Topic name is not valid. |
| NDDE_OUT_OF_MEMORY | 12 | Not enough memory to complete request. |
| NDDE_SHARE_ALREADY_EXISTS | 15 | Existing shares cannot be replaced. |

## Step Two: Create DDE Source Application

The following steps show you how to create a Visual Basic DDE source and destination application that communicates through a network DDE link.

1. From the DDE source computer, start Visual Basic. If Visual Basic is already running, from the File menu, choose New Project (ALT, F, N).

   Form1 is created by default.

2. Change the LinkTopic property of Form1 to VBTopic.

3. If you are running Visual Basic version 2.0 or 3.0 for Windows, change the LinkMode property of Form1 to 1 – Source. In Visual Basic version 1.0, this property is already set to 1 – Server; don't change it.

4. Add a text box (Text1) to Form1.

5. Change the Name property (CTlName in version 1.0) of Text1 to VBItem.

6. Add a timer (Timer1) to Form1.

7. From the File menu, choose New Module (ALT, F, M). Module1 is created.

8. Add the following code to the General Declarations section of Module1, and enter all lines as a single line even though they may be shown on multiple lines for readability:

```
' DDE access options
Global Const NDDEACCESS_REQUEST = &H1
Global Const NDDEACCESS_ADVISE = &H2
Global Const NDDEACCESS_POKE = &H4
Global Const NDDEACCESS_EXECUTE = &H8
Global Const NDDEACCESS_START_APP = &H10
Global Const MAX_NDDESHARENAME_PLUSONE = 65

Type NDDESHAREINFO
szShareName As String * MAX_NDDESHARENAME_PLUSONE
lpszTargetApp As Long      'LPSTR lpszTargetApp
```

```
lpszTargetTopic As Long    'LPSTR lpszTargetTopic
lpbPassword1 As Long       'LPBYTE lpbPassword1
cbPassword1 As Long        'DWORD  cbPassword1;
dwPermissions1 As Long     'DWORD  dwPermissions1;
lpbPassword2 As Long       'LPBYTE lpbPassword2;
cbPassword2 As Long        'DWORD cbPassword2;
dwPermissions2  As Long    'DWORD  dwPermissions2;
lpszItem As Long           'LPSTR  lpszItem;
cAddItems As Long          'LONGcAddItems;
lpNDdeShareItemInfo As Long
End Type

Declare Function NDdeShareAdd Lib "NDDEAPI.DLL" (Server As Any,_
ByVal Level As Integer, ShareInfo As NDDESHAREINFO,_
ByVal Size As Long)
Declare Function lstrcpy Lib "KERNEL" (szDest As Any, szSource As_
Any)
'If using Visual Basic version 1.0,
'add the following constant declarations
'Global Const False = 0
'Global Const True = Not False
```

  9. Add the following code to the Form_Load event of Form1:

```
Sub Form_Load ()
Dim r As Integer
Dim szShareName As String ' Net DDE share name
Dim szTargetName As String' Net DDE target name
Dim szTopicName As String ' Net DDE source topic name
Dim szItemName As String
Dim szReadOnlyPassword As String ' Read-only password Net DDE share
Dim szFullAccessPassword As String ' Full access password
Dim ShareInfo As NDDESHAREINFO
Dim ShareInfoSize As Long
Dim Result As Integer
szShareName = "VBDDESource$" + Chr$(0)
szTargetName = "VBTARGET" + Chr$(0)
szTopicName = "VBTopic" + Chr$(0)
szItemName = Chr$(0)   'All items are allowed
szReadOnlyPassword = Chr$(0)'No password
szFullAccessPassword = Chr$(0)s
```

```
'Provide the share, target, topic and item names along with passwords
'that identify the network DDE share
ShareInfo.szShareName = szShareName
ShareInfo.lpszTargetApp = lstrcpy(ByVal szTargetName,
ByVal szTargetName)
ShareInfo.lpszTargetTopic = lstrcpy(ByVal szTopicName,
ByVal szTopicName)
ShareInfo.lpszItem = lstrcpy(ByVal szItemName, ByVal szItemName)
ShareInfo.cbPassword1 = 0
ShareInfo.lpbPassword1 = lstrcpy(ByVal szReadOnlyPassword,
ByVal szReadOnlyPassword)
ShareInfo.dwPermissions1 = NDDEACCESS_REQUEST Or NDDEACCESS_ADVISE Or
NDDEACCESS_POKE Or NDDEACCESS_EXECUTE Or NDDEACCESS_START_APP
ShareInfo.cbPassword2 = 0
ShareInfo.lpbPassword2 = lstrcpy(ByVal szFullAccessPassword,
ByVal szFullAccessPassword)
ShareInfo.dwPermissions2 = NDDEACCESS_REQUEST Or NDDEACCESS_ADVISE Or
NDDEACCESS_POKE Or NDDEACCESS_EXECUTE Or NDDEACCESS_START_APP
ShareInfo.lpNDdeShareItemInfo = 15
Result = NDdeShareAdd(ByVal 0&, 2, ShareInfo, Len(ShareInfo))
' Start the timer that will continually update the text box and
' the DDE link item with random data.
timer1.Interval = 1000
timer1.Enabled = True
End Sub
```

10. Add the following code to the Timer1_Timer event procedure:

```
Sub Timer1_Timer ()
 ' Display random value 0 - 99 in the text box (DDE source data).
 Randomize Timer
 VBItem.Text = Format$(Rnd * 100, "0")
 End Sub
```

11. From the File menu, choose Make EXE File.

12. Name the file VBTARGET.EXE and choose OK to create the .EXE file.

13. From the File Manager or Program Manager, run VBTARGET.EXE to display a random value in the text box every second.

---

# Step Three: Create the DDE Destination Application

14. From the DDE destination computer, start Visual Basic. If Visual Basic is already running, from the File menu, choose New Project (ALT, F, N). Form1 is created by default.

15. Add a text box (Text1) to Form1.

16. Add the following code to the Form_Load event of Form1:

```
Sub Form_Load ()
Dim r As Long
Dim szComputer As String   ' Network server name.
Dim szTopic As String
' Identify the network server where the DDE source application
' is running. The following statement assumes the source computer
' name is COMPUTER1. Change it to your source computer name.
szComputer = "\\COMPUTER1"
' Identify the DDE share established by the source application
szTopic = "VBDDESource$"
Text1.LinkMode = 0
' The link topic identifies the computer name and link topic
' as established by the DDE source application
Text1.LinkTopic = szComputer + "\" + "NDDE$" + "|" + szTopic
Text1.LinkItem = "VBItem" ' Name of text box in DDE source app
Text1.LinkMode = 1   ' Automatic link.
End Sub
'For this program to work, set the szComputer variable (above)
'to the computer name that holds the DDE source application.
'Find the computer name in the Network section of Windows
'for Workgroups Control Panel.
```

17. From the Run menu, choose Start to run the program.

You should see the same random values generated on the source computer displayed in the text box of the destination computer. If you receive the error message "DDE method invoked with no channel open" on the Text1.Link-Mode = 1 statement in step 16, make sure the szComputer variable is set correctly.

# Q: What are the steps necessary to initiate DDE between a Microsoft Visual Basic destination application and a Visual Basic source application?

 The following examples will demonstrate how to:

◆ Create a Visual Basic application to function as a DDE source.

◆ Create a Visual Basic application to function as a DDE destination.

◆ Initiate a manual DDE link (information updated upon request from the destination) between the destination application and the source application.

◆ Use LinkRequest to update information in the destination application from information in the source application.

◆ Initiate a automatic DDE link (information updated automatically from source to destination) between the destination application and the source application.

◆ Use LinkPoke to send information from the destination application to the source application.

◆ Change the LinkMode property between automatic and manual.

A destination application sends commands through DDE to the source application to establish a link. Through DDE, the source provides data to the destination at the request of the destination or accepts information at the request of the destination.

The following steps give an example of how to establish a DDE conversation between two Visual Basic applications.

## Step One: Create the Source Application in Visual Basic

1. Start Visual Basic, and Form1 will be created by default.

2. Change the Caption property of Form1 to Source.

3. Put a Text Box (Text1) on Form1.

4. Save the form and project with the name SOURCE.

5. From the File menu, choose Make EXE File. In the Make EXE File dialog box, choose OK to accept SOURCE.EXE as the name of the .EXE file.

## Step Two: Create the Destination Application in Visual Basic

1. From the File menu, choose New Project. Form1 will be created by default.

2. Change the Caption property of Form1 to Destination.

3. Create the following controls with the following properties on Form1:

| Default Name | Caption | Name |
|---|---|---|
| Text1 | (Not applicable) | Text1 |
| Option1 | Manual Link | ManualLink |
| Option2 | Automatic Link | AutomaticLink |
| Command1 | Poke | Poke |
| Command2 | Request | Request |

4. Add the following code to the General Declarations section of Form1:

```
Const AUTOMATIC= 1
Const MANUAL = 2
Const NONE = 0
```

5. Add the following code to the Load event procedure of Form1:

```
Sub Form_Load ()
'This procedure will start the VB source application that was
'created earlier
z% = Shell("SOURCE", 1)
z% = DoEvents()  'Causes Windows to finish
                 'processing the Shell command.
Text1.LinkMode = NONE          'Clears DDE link if it already
                    'exists.
```

```
  Text1.LinkTopic = "Source|Form1"    'Sets up link with VB source.
  Text1.LinkItem = "Text1"            'Set link to text box on source.
  Text1.LinkMode = MANUAL             'Establish a manual DDE link.
  ManualLink.Value = TRUE             'Sets appropriate option button.
End Sub
```

6. Add the following code to the Click event procedure of ManualLink:

```
Sub ManualLink_Click ()
  Request.Visible = TRUE    'Make request button valid.
  Text1.LinkMode = NONE     'Clear DDE Link.
  Text1.LinkMode = MANUAL   'Reestablish new LinkMode.
End Sub
```

7. Add the following code to the Clink event procedure of
   AutomaticLink:

```
Sub AutomaticLink_Click ()
  Request.Visible = FALSE       'No need for button with automatic link.
  Text1.LinkMode = NONE     'Clear DDE Link.
  Text1.LinkMode = AUTOMATIC   'Reestablish new LinkMode.
End Sub
```

8. Add the following code to the Click event procedure of Request:

```
Sub Request_Click ()
 'With a manual DDE link, this button will be visible, and when
 'selected it will request an update of information from the source
 'application to the destination application.
  Text1.LinkRequest
End Sub
```

9. Add the following code to the Click event procedure of Poke:

```
Sub Poke_Click ()
 'With any DDE link, this button will be visible, and when it's
 'selected, will poke information from the destination application
 'into the source application.
  Text1.LinkPoke
End Sub
```

## Step Three: Try It Out

You can now run the Visual Basic destination application from the VB.EXE environment (skip to step 4 here) or you can save the application and create an .EXE file and run that from Windows by beginning with step 1 here.

1. From the File menu, choose Save and save the form and project with the name DEST.

2. From the File menu, choose Make EXE File with the name DEST.EXE.

3. Exit the Visual Basic environment (VB.EXE).

4. Run the application (from Windows if an .EXE file, or from the Run menu if from the VB.EXE environment).

5. Form1 of the destination application will load and the source application will automatically start.

## Step Four: Experiment

You can now experiment with DDE between Visual Basic applications:

1. Try typing some text into the source's text box and then click the Request button. The text appears in the destination's text box.

2. Click the Automatic Link button and then type some more text into the source's text box. The text is automatically updated in the destination's text box.

3. Type some text into the destination's text box and click the Poke button. The text is sent to the source's text box.

## Q: What are the steps necessary to initiate DDE between a Microsoft Visual Basic destination application and a Microsoft Excel source application?

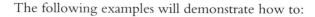

The following examples will demonstrate how to:

◆ Prepare a Microsoft Excel for Windows document for active DDE.

◆ Initiate a manual DDE link (information updated upon request from the destination) between Visual Basic (the destination) and Excel (the source).

◆ Use the LinkRequest method to update information in Visual Basic (the destination) based on information contained in Excel (the source).

◆ Initiate an automatic DDE link (information updated automatically from source to destination) between Visual Basic (the destination) and Excel (the source).

◆ Use the LinkPoke method to send information from Visual Basic (the destination) to Excel (the source).

◆ Change the LinkMode property between automatic and manual.

A destination application sends commands through DDE to the source application to establish a link. Through DDE, the source provides data to the destination at the request of the destination or accepts information at the request of the destination.

The following procedure is an example of how to establish a DDE conversation between Visual Basic and Excel for Windows.

First, create the source spreadsheet in Excel:

1. Start Excel. A document titled "SHEET1" will be created by default.

2. From the File menu, choose Save As, and save the document with the name SOURCE.XLS.

3. Exit Excel. For this example to function properly, Excel must not be loaded and running.

Next, create the destination application in Visual Basic. The destination is the application that performs the link operations. It prompts the source to send information or informs the source that information is being sent.

1. Start Visual Basic (VB.EXE). Form1 will be created by default.

2. Create the following controls with the following properties on Form1:

| Default Name | Caption | Name |
|---|---|---|
| Text1 | (not applicable) | Text1 |
| Option1 | Manual Link | ManualLink |
| Option2 | Automatic Link | AutomaticLink |
| Command1 | Poke | Poke |
| Command2 | Request | Request |

3. Add the following code to the General Declarations section of Form1:

```
Const AUTOMATIC = 1
Const MANUAL = 2
Const NONE = 0
```

4. Add the following code to the Load event procedure of Form1:

```
Sub Form_Load ()
 'This procedure will start Excel and load SOURCE.XLS, the
 'spreadsheet that was created earlier.

 z% = Shell("EXCEL SOURCE.XLS", 1)
 z% = DoEvents()    'Process Windows events. This insures
        'that Excel will be executed before
        'any attempt is made to perform DDE.
 Text1.LinkMode = NONE           'Clears DDE link if it already exists.
 Text1.LinkTopic = "Excel|source.xls"        'Sets up link with Excel.
 Text1.LinkItem = "R1C1"         'Set link to first cell on spreadsheet.
 Text1.LinkMode = MANUAL         'Establish a manual DDE link.
 ManualLink.Value = TRUE
End Sub
```

5. Add the following code to the Click event procedure of the Manual Link button:

```
Sub ManualLink_Click ()
  Request.Visible = TRUE         'Make request button valid.
  Text1.LinkMode = NONE          'Clear DDE Link.
  Text1.LinkMode = MANUAL        'Reestablish new LinkMode.
End Sub
```

6. Add the following code to the Click event procedure of the
Automatic Link button:

```
Sub AutomaticLink_Click ()
   Request.Visible = FALSE          'No need for button with automatic
   Text1.LinkMode = NONE            'Clear DDE Link.
   Text1.LinkMode = AUTOMATIC       'Reestablish new LinkMode.
End Sub
```

7. Add the following code to the Click event procedure of the Request
button:

```
Sub Request_Click ()
'With a manual DDE link this button will be visible and when
'selected it will request an update of information from the source
'application to the destination application.
  Text1.LinkRequest
End Sub
```

8. Add the following code to the Click event procedure of the Poke
button:

```
Sub Poke_Click ()
 'With any DDE link this button will be visible and when selected
 'it will poke information from the destination application to the
 'source application.
  Text1.LinkPoke
End Sub
```

You can now run the Visual Basic destination application from the Visual
Basic environment (skip to step 4 here) or you can save the application and
create an .EXE file and run that from Windows (start from step 1 here):

1. From the Visual Basic File menu, choose Save, and save the Form
   and Project with the name DEST.

2. From the File menu, choose Make EXE File, and name it
   DEST.EXE.

3. Exit Visual Basic.

4. Run the application (from Windows if an .EXE file or from the Run menu if from the Visual Basic environment).

5. Form1 of the destination application will be loaded and Excel will automatically be started with the document SOURCE.XLS loaded.

6. Make sure the main title bar in Excel reads "Microsoft Excel," NOT "Microsoft Excel – SOURCE.XLS." If the title bar is incorrect, then from the Window menu choose Arrange All.

You can now experiment with DDE between Visual Basic and Excel:

1. Try typing some text in R1C1 in the spreadsheet, and then select the Request button. The text appears in the text box.

Be sure to press ENTER after entering text into an Excel cell before clicking the Request button in the Visual Basic program, or else a "Timeout while waiting for DDE response" error message will be displayed from the TEXT1.LINKREQUEST statement.

This occurs because, while entering text into a cell, Excel is in a polling loop for data entry, and no real data is transferred to the cell until you press ENTER. Therefore, Visual Basic keeps attempting to request the data from the cell, but Excel does not pay attention to the request until it exits the polling loop, which results in the DDE time-out message.

2. Choose the Automatic Link button and then type some more text in R1C1 of the spreadsheet. The text is automatically updated in the Visual Basic text box.

3. Type some text in the text box in the Visual Basic application and choose the Poke button. The text is sent to R1C1 in the Excel spreadsheet.

**note:** *If you have the Ignore Remote Requests option selected in the Excel Workspace dialog box, you will not be able to establish DDE from Visual Basic. Make sure the Ignore Remote Requests option is NOT selected.*

# Q: What are the steps necessary to initiate DDE between a Microsoft Visual Basic destination application and a Microsoft Word for Windows (WINWORD.EXE) source document?

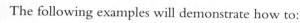 The following examples will demonstrate how to:

◆ Prepare a Word for Windows document for active DDE.

◆ Initiate a manual DDE link (information updated upon request from the destination) between the Visual Basic application (the destination) and the document loaded into Word for Windows (the source).

◆ Use LinkRequest to update information in the Visual Basic destination based on information contained in the Word for Windows source.

◆ Initiate an automatic DDE link (information updated automatically from source to destination) between the Visual Basic destination and the Word for Windows source.

◆ Use LinkPoke to send information from the Visual Basic destination to the Word for Windows source.

◆ Change the LinkMode property between automatic and manual.

A destination application sends commands through DDE to the source application to establish a link. Through DDE, the source provides data to the destination at the request of the destination or accepts information at the request of the destination.

The following steps give an example of how to establish a DDE conversation between a Visual Basic application and a document loaded into Word for Windows (WINWORD.EXE).

## Step One: Create the Source Document in Word for Windows

1. Start Word for Windows. Document1 is created by default.

2. From the Window menu, choose Arrange All. This removes maximization if the document was maximized. Note that the title at the top of the WINWORD.EXE main title bar is now:

Microsoft Word

instead of:

Microsoft Word – Document1

3. Press CTRL+SHIFT+END to select to the end of the document.

4. From the Insert menu, choose Bookmark. Under Bookmark Name, type:

```
DDE_Link
```

Press ENTER. This sets a bookmark for the entire document. This bookmark functions as the LinkItem in the DDE conversation.

5. From the File menu, choose Save As, and save the document with the name SOURCE.DOC.

6. Exit Word for Windows. For this particular example to function correctly, WINWORD.EXE must not be loaded and running.

## Step Two: Create the Destination Application in Visual Basic

1. Start Visual Basic. Form1 is created by default.

2. Create the following controls on Form1, giving the controls the properties shown in the table:

| Default Name | Caption | Name |
| --- | --- | --- |
| Text1 | (Not applicable) | Text1 |
| Option1 | Manual Link | ManualLink |
| Option2 | Automatic Link | AutomaticLink |
| Command1 | Poke | Poke |
| Command2 | Request | Request |

3. Add the following code to the General Declarations section of Form1:

```
Const AUTOMATIC = 1
Const MANUAL = 2
Const NONE = 0
```

4. Add the following code to the Load event procedure of Form1:

```
Sub Form_Load ()
'This procedure starts WINWORD.EXE, loads the document that was
'created earlier, and prepares for DDE by creating a bookmark to
'the whole document. This bookmark is necessary because it
'functions as the LinkItem for the source in the DDE conversation.
z% = Shell("WinWord Source.Doc",1)
z% = DoEvents ()  'Process Windows events to ensure that
'WINWORD.EXE is executed before any attempt is
'made to perform DDE with it.
Text1.LinkMode = NONE  'Clears DDE link if it exists.
Text1.LinkTopic = "WinWord|Source" 'Sets up link with WINWORD.EXE.
Text1.LinkItem = "DDE_Link"  'Set link to bookmark on document.
Text1.LinkMode = MANUAL'Establish a manual DDE link.
ManualLink.Value = TRUE
End Sub
```

5. Add the following code to the Click event procedure of the Manual Link button:

```
Sub ManualLink_Click ()
Request.Visible = TRUE  'Make request button valid.
Text1.LinkMode = NONE'Clear DDE Link.
Text1.LinkMode = MANUAL 'Reestablish new LinkMode.
End Sub
```

6. Add the following code to the Click event procedure of the Automatic Link button:

```
Sub AutomaticLink_Click ()
Request.Visible = FALSE  'No need for button with automatic link.
Text1.LinkMode = NONE 'Clear DDE Link.
Text1.LinkMode = AUTOMATIC  'Reestablish new LinkMode.
End Sub
```

7. Add the following code to the Click event procedure of the Request button:

```
Sub Request_Click ()
'With a manual DDE link this button is visible. Clicking this button
'requests an update of information from the source application to the
'destination application.
Text1.LinkRequest
End Sub
```

8. Add the following code to the Click event procedure of the Poke button:

```
Sub Poke_Click ()
'With any DDE link, this button is visible. Clicking this button
'pokes information from the destination application into the source
'application.
Text1.LinkPoke
End Sub
```

## Step Three: Try It Out

Now, you have two choices. You can run the Visual Basic destination application from the Visual Basic VB.EXE environment by skipping to step 4 here, or you can save the application, create an .EXE file, and run that from Windows by beginning with step 1 here.

1. From the File menu, choose Save, and save the form and project with the name DEST.

2. From the File menu, choose Make EXE File with the name DEST.EXE.

3. Exit the Visual Basic environment (VB.EXE).

4. Run the application. Run an .EXE file from Windows, or if you're in the Visual Basic environment, from the Run menu, choose Start.

Form1 of the Visual Basic destination application will be loaded, and Word for Windows will automatically start and load SOURCE.DOC.

5. Make sure that the main title bar in WINWORD.EXE reads "Microsoft Word," not "Microsoft Word – SOURCE.DOC." If the title bar is incorrect, choose Arrange All from the Window menu.

## Step Four: Experiment

Experiment with DDE between Visual Basic and Word for Windows:

1. Try typing some text into the document in Word for Windows. Then click the Request button. The text appears in the text box.

2. Click the Automatic Link button. Then type some more text into the document in Word for Windows. The text is automatically updated in the Visual Basic text box.

3. Type some text in the text box in the Visual Basic application. Then click the Poke button. The text goes to the Word for Windows document.

Note that if in the WINWORD.EXE document you delete the total contents of the bookmark, the bookmark is also deleted. Any attempt to perform DDE with this WINWORD.EXE session after deleting the bookmark causes this error:

Foreign applications won't perform DDE method or operation.

If this happens, you must re-create the bookmark in the document in Word for Windows before performing any further DDE operations.

# Q: How do I send DDE interface commands to the Microsoft Windows Program Manager from within Microsoft Visual Basic for Windows?

 The following examples will demonstrate how to use selected interface commands available through DDE with the Windows Program Manager:

```
CreateGroup(GroupName,GroupPath)
ShowGroup(GroupName,ShowCommand)
```

```
AddItem(CommandLine,Name,IconPath,IconIndex,XPos,YPos)
DeleteGroup(GroupName)
ExitProgman(bSaveState)
```

A full explanation of these commands can be found in Chapter 22, pages 19-22, of the *Microsoft Windows Software Development Kit Guide to Programming* version 3.0 manual.

An application can also obtain a list of Windows groups from the Windows Program Manager by issuing a LinkRequest to the "PROGMAN" item.

The following program demonstrates how to use four of the five Windows Program Manager DDE interface commands and the one DDE request:

1. Run Visual Basic for Windows, or from the File menu, choose New Project (press ALT, F, N) if Visual Basic for Windows is already running. Form1 is created by default.

2. Create the following controls with the given properties on Form1:

| Object | Name | Caption |
|--------|------|---------|
| TextBox | Text1 | |
| Button | Command1 | Make |
| Button | Command2 | Delete |
| Button | Command3 | Request |

(In Visual Basic version 1.0 for Windows set the CtlName Property for these objects instead of the Name property.)

3. Add the following code to the Command1_Click event:

```
Sub Command1_Click ()
  Text1.LinkTopic = "ProgMan|Progman"
  Text1.LinkMode = 2' Establish manual link.
  Text1.LinkExecute "[CreateGroup(Test Group)]"
' Make a group in Windows Program Manager.
  Text1.LinkExecute "[AddItem(c:\vb\vb.exe, Visual Basic)]"
' Add an item to that group.
  Text1.LinkExecute "[ShowGroup(Test Group, 7)]"
' Iconize the group and focus to VB application.
  On Error Resume Next  ' Disconnecting link with Windows Program
  Text1.LinkMode = 0 ' Manager causes an error in Windows 3.0.
```

```
 ' This is a known problem with Windows Program Manager.
End Sub
```

4. Add the following code to the Command2_Click event:

```
Sub Command2_Click ()
  Text1.LinkTopic = "ProgMan|Progman"
  Text1.LinkMode = 2 ' Establish manual link.
  Text1.LinkExecute "[DeleteGroup(Test Group)]"
 ' Delete the group and all items within it.
 On Error Resume Next  ' Disconnecting link with Windows Program
  Text1.LinkMode = 0 ' Manager causes an error in Windows 3.0.
  ' This is a known problem with Windows Program Manager.
End Sub
```

5. Add the following code to the Command3_Click event:

```
Sub Command3_Click ()
  Text1.LinkTopic = "ProgMan|Progman"
  Text1.LinkItem = "PROGMAN"
  Text1.LinkMode = 2' Establish manual link.
  Text1.LinkRequest ' Get a list of the groups.
 On Error Resume Next  ' Disconnecting link with Windows Program
  Text1.LinkMode = 0 ' Manager causes an error in Windows 3.0.
  ' This is a known problem with Windows Program Manager.
End Sub
```

6. Press F5 to run the program.

7. Choose the Make button, then choose the Delete button. Note the result.

8. Choose the Request button. This will put a list of the groups in the Windows Program Manager to be placed in the text box. The individual items are delimited by a carriage return plus linefeed.

As noted in the Windows Software Development Kit (SDK) manual mentioned above, the ExitProgman( ) command will only work if Windows Program Manager is NOT the shell (the startup program when you start Windows).

# Q: How can I copy the entire screen into a picture box in Visual Basic for Windows?

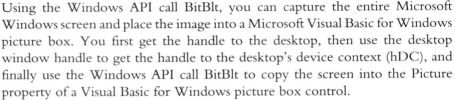Using the Windows API call BitBlt, you can capture the entire Microsoft Windows screen and place the image into a Microsoft Visual Basic for Windows picture box. You first get the handle to the desktop, then use the desktop window handle to get the handle to the desktop's device context (hDC), and finally use the Windows API call BitBlt to copy the screen into the Picture property of a Visual Basic for Windows picture box control.

Here is an example:

1. Start Visual Basic for Windows (VB.EXE). Form1 is created by default.

2. Create a picture box (Picture1) on Form1.

3. Set the following properties:

| Control | Property | Value |
|---------|----------|-------|
| Picture1 | AutoRedraw | True |
| Picture1 | Visible | False |

4. Add the following code:

```
Global.Bas
Type lrect
 left As Integer
 top As Integer
 right As Integer
 bottom As Integer
End Type
Declare Function GetDesktopWindow Lib "user" () As Integer
Declare Function GetDC Lib "user" (ByVal hWnd%) As Integer
' Note: The following Declare should be on one line:
Declare Function BitBlt Lib "GDI" (ByVal hDestDC%,
   ByVal X%, ByVal Y%, ByVal nWidth%, ByVal nHeight%,
   ByVal hSrcDC%, ByVal XSrc%, ByVal YSrc%, ByVal dwRop&
   ) As Integer
' Note: The following Declare should be on one line:
Declare Function ReleaseDC Lib "User"(ByVal hWnd As Integer,
  ByVal hDC As Integer) As Integer
```

```
Declare Sub GetWindowRect Lib "User" (ByVal hWnd%, lpRect As lrect)
'Global Const True = -1
'Global Const False = 0
Global TwipsPerPixel As Single
Sub Form_Click ()
  Call GrabScreen
End Sub


Sub GrabScreen ()

 Dim winSize As lrect
 ' Assign information of the source bitmap.
 ' Note that BitBlt requires coordinates in pixels.
 hwndSrc% = GetDesktopWindow()
 hSrcDC% = GetDC(hwndSrc%)
 XSrc% = 0: YSrc% = 0
 Call GetWindowRect(hwndSrc%, winSize)
 nWidth% = winSize.right ' Units in pixels.
 nHeight% = winSize.bottom  ' Units in pixels.
 ' Assign informate of the destination bitmap.
 hDestDC% = Form1.Picture1.hDC
 x% = 0: Y% = 0
 ' Set global variable TwipsPerPixel and use to set
 ' picture box to same size as screen being grabbed.
 ' If picture box not the same size as picture being
 ' BitBlt'ed to it, it will chop off all that does not
 ' fit in the picture box.
 GetTwipsPerPixel
 Form1.Picture1.Top = 0
 Form1.Picture1.Left = 0
 Form1.Picture1.Width = (nWidth% + 1) * TwipsPerPixel
 Form1.Picture1.Height = (nHeight% + 1) * TwipsPerPixel
 ' Assign the value of the constant SRCOPYY to the Raster operation.
 dwRop& = &HCC0020
 ' Note function call must be on one line:
 Suc% = BitBlt(hDestDC%, x%, Y%, nWidth%, nHeight%,
hSrcDC%, XSrc%, YSrc%, dwRop&)
 ' Release the DeskTopWindow's hDC to Windows.
 ' Windows may hang if this is not done.
 Dmy% = ReleaseDC(hwndSrc%, hSrcDC%)
 'Make the picture box visible.
 Form1.Picture1.Visible = True
End Sub
```

```
Sub GetTwipsPerPixel ()
 ' Set a global variable with the Twips to Pixel ratio.
 Form1.ScaleMode = 3
 NumPix = Form1.ScaleHeight
 Form1.ScaleMode = 1
 TwipsPerPixel = Form1.ScaleHeight / NumPix
End Sub
```

5. Run the program and click on the form.

6. With the mouse, change the size of the form to see more of the picture box. With a little work, you can use this as a screen saver program.

## Q: How can I print a bitmap contained in a picture box control to the printer using Microsoft Visual Basic for Windows?

The following example will explain how to print a Visual Basic picture control to a printer using several Windows 3.x API function calls.

**note:**    *This example will not work correctly on PostScript printers.*

Instead of the picture control printing, two blank sheets are ejected from the printer when using a printer configured to use the PostScript printer driver. For the example to work correctly, the printer must use a standard non-PostScript laser printer configuration (such as PCL/HP).

To print a picture control from Visual Basic, you must use the PrintForm method. Although this can be very useful, there is no straightforward method of printing just a picture control without the use of API function calls. Printing a picture control to the printer is useful when you want to control the location or size of the printed image. Calling API functions to print a picture control is also useful if you want to include other images or text along with the picture image on a single sheet of paper.

To print a bitmap, you need to do the following:

1. Create a memory device context that is compatible with the bitmap (CreateCompatibleDC). A memory device context is a block of memory that represents a display surface. It is used to prepare images before copying them to the actual device surface of the compatible device.

2. Save the present object (SelectObject), and select the picture control using the handle from the memory device context.

3. Use the BitBlt or StretchBlt function to copy the bitmap from the memory device context to the printer.

4. Remove the bitmap from the memory device context (SelectObject), and delete the device context (DeleteDC).

The following steps demonstrate this process:

1. Run Visual Basic, or from the File menu, choose New Project (ALT, F, N) if Visual Basic is already running. Form1 is created by default.

2. Add a picture (Picture1) control to Form1 and set the AutoRedraw property to True from the Properties bar.

3. Add a command (Command1) button.

4. Display some graphics in Picture1 by loading from a picture file or pasting from the clipboard at design time. You can load a picture from a file as follows:

   a. Select the Picture property from the Properties window.

   b. Click the arrow at the right of the Settings box, then select the desired picture file (such as a .BMP or .ICO file supplied with Microsoft Windows) from the dialog box.

5. Add the following declarations to the global Declarations section of the Code window. Note that each Declare statement must be on one line:

```
Declare Function CreateCompatibleDC% Lib "GDI" (ByVal hDC%)
Declare Function SelectObject% Lib "GDI" (ByVal hDC%, ByVal hObject%)
Declare Function StretchBlt% Lib "GDI" (ByVal hDC%, ByVal X%,
ByVal Y%, ByVal nWidth%, ByVal nHght%, ByVal hSrcDC%,
ByVal XSrc%, ByVal YSrc%, ByVal nSrcWidth%, ByVal nSrcHeight%,
ByVal dwRop&)
```

```
Declare Function DeleteDC% Lib "GDI" (ByVal hDC%)
Declare Function Escape% Lib "GDI" (ByVal hDC As Integer,
ByVal nEscape As Integer, ByVal nCount As Integer,
LpInData As Any, LpOutData As Any)
```

6. Add the following code to the Command_Click event:

```
Sub Command1_Click ()
' Const NULL = 0&
Const SRCCOPY = &HCC0020
Const NEWFRAME = 1
Const PIXEL = 3

'* display hour glass
MousePointer = 11
Picture1.Picture = Picture1.Image

'* StretchBlt requires pixel coordinates.
Picture1.ScaleMode = PIXEL
Printer.ScaleMode = PIXEL
Printer.Print " "
hMemoryDC% = CreateCompatibleDC(Picture1.hDC)
hOldBitMap% = SelectObject(hMemoryDC%, Picture1.Picture)
ApiError% = StretchBlt(Printer.hDC, 0, 0,
    Printer.ScaleWidth, Printer.ScaleHeight,
    hMemoryDC%, 0, 0, Picture1.ScaleWidth,
    Picture1.ScaleHeight, SRCCOPY)
hOldBitMap% = SelectObject(hMemoryDC%, hOldBitMap%)
ApiError% = DeleteDC(hMemoryDC%)
Print Escape(Printer.hDC, NEWFRAME, 0, NULL, NULL)
Printer.EndDoc
MousePointer = 1
End Sub
```

7. Run the program to copy the bitmap to the printer. If you have selected a low resolution from the Print Manager, printing the bitmap will proceed quickly (the lower the resolution, the faster the print time). While designing your software, you may want to keep this at the lowest possible resolution. The print resolution can be changed from the Windows Control Panel.

For more information, consult the following references:

Programming Windows: The Microsoft Guide to Writing Applications for Windows 3, Charles Petzold, Microsoft Press, 1990

Microsoft Windows Software Development Kit: Reference Volume 1, version 3.0

Microsoft Windows Software Development Kit: Guide to Programming, version 3.0.

WINSDK.HLP file shipped with Microsoft Windows 3.0 Software Development Kit.

# Q: How can I print a control or a form in Microsoft Visual Basic for Windows?

The following example will demonstrate two Visual Basic procedures: Print-Window and PrintClient. Both procedures allow you to print a control or form at a specified location and size on a printed page or to another form or picture control. The PrintWindow procedure allows you to print the entire control including border, caption, and menus. The PrintClient procedure prints everything contained within the form or control excluding the border, caption, and menus. When passed a form, the PrintClient procedure works just like Visual Basic's PrintForm method. Both procedures will print all child controls contained on the form or control.

The PrintWindow and PrintClient procedures use the StretchDIBits Windows API function as well as other Windows API functions to print a form or control. These functions will print to both PostScript and PCL (printer control language) or HP-type LaserJet printers.

Perform the following steps to create a sample program that demonstrates how to print a form to the printer:

1. Run Visual Basic, or from the File menu select New Project (ALT, F, N) if Visual Basic is already running. Form1 will be created by default.

2. Add two command buttons (Command1 and Command2) to Form1.

3. Load the WINLOGO.BMP file (or some other large bitmap) into the Picture property of Form1. WINLOGO.BMP should be located in your Windows directory.

4. From the File menu, select New Module (ALT, F, M). Module1 will be created.

5. Add the following code to the General Declarations section of Module1:

```
DefInt A-Z
Type BITMAPINFOHEADER_Type
 biSize As Long
 biWidth As Long
 biHeight As Long
 biPlanes As Integer
 biBitCount As Integer
 biCompression As Long
 biSizeImage As Long
 biXPelsPerMeter As Long
 biYPelsPerMeter As Long
 biClrUsed As Long
 biClrImportant As Long
End Type

Type BITMAPINFO_Type
 BitmapInfoHeader As BITMAPINFOHEADER_Type
 bmiColors As String * 1024
End Type

Type RectType
 Left As Integer
 Top As Integer
 Right As Integer
 Bottom As Integer
End Type

Type PointType
 x As Integer
 y As Integer
End Type

' DC related API
Declare Function CreateCompatibleDC Lib "gdi" (ByVal hDC)
Declare Function GetWindowDC Lib "user" (ByVal hWnd)
Declare Function GetDC Lib "user" (ByVal hWnd)
Declare Function ReleaseDC Lib "user" (ByVal hWnd, ByVal hDC)
Declare Function DeleteDC Lib "gdi" (ByVal hDC)
```

```
' Graphics related API
Declare Function BitBlt Lib "gdi" (ByVal hDC, ByVal x, ByVal y,
ByVal w, ByVal h, ByVal hDC, ByVal x, ByVal y, ByVal o As Long)
Declare Function GetDIBits Lib "gdi" (ByVal hDC, ByVal hBitmap,
ByVal nStartScan, ByVal nNumScans, ByVal lpBits As Long,
BitmapInfo As BITMAPINFO_Type, ByVal wUsage)
Declare Function StretchDIBits Lib "gdi" (ByVal hDC, ByVal DestX,
ByVal DestY, ByVal wDestWidth, ByVal wDestHeight, ByVal SrcX,
ByVal SrcY, ByVal wSrcWidth, ByVal wSrcHeight, ByVal lpBits&,
BitsInfo As BITMAPINFO_Type, ByVal wUsage, ByVal dwRop&)

' General attribute related API
Declare Function GetDeviceCaps Lib "gdi" (ByVal hDC, ByVal nIndex)
Declare Function GetWindowRect Lib "user" (ByVal hWnd, lpRect As
RectType)
Declare Function GetClientRect Lib "user" (ByVal hWnd, lpRect As
RectType)

' Memory allocation related API
Declare Function GlobalAlloc Lib "kernel" (ByVal wFlags, ByVal lMem&)
Declare Function GlobalLock Lib "kernel" (ByVal hMem) As Long
Declare Function GlobalUnlock Lib "kernel" (ByVal hMem)
Declare Function GlobalFree Lib "kernel" (ByVal hMem)

' Graphics object related API
Declare Function CreateCompatibleBitmap Lib "gdi" (ByVal hDC,
ByVal nWidth, ByVal nHeight)
Declare Function DeleteObject Lib "gdi" (ByVal hObject)
Declare Function SelectObject Lib "gdi" (ByVal hDC, ByVal hObject)
Declare Function ClientToScreen Lib "user" (ByVal hWnd,
As PointType)
Declare Function LPToDP Lib "gdi" (ByVal hDC, p As PointType,
ByVal nCount)
Const HORZRES = 8
Const VERTRES = 10
Const SRCCOPY = &HCC0020
Const NEWFRAME = 1
Const BITSPIXEL = 12
Const PLANES = 14
Const BI_RGB = 0
Const BI_RLE8 = 1
Const BI_RLE4 = 2
Const DIB_PAL_COLORS = 1
```

```
Const DIB_RGB_COLORS = 0
Const GMEM_MOVEABLE = 2
```

6. Add the following function, PrintWindow, to Module1:

```
Function PrintWindow (ByVal hDC_Dest, ByVal DestX, ByVal DestY,
ByVal DestDevWidth, ByVal DestDevHeight, ByVal hWnd_SrcWindow)
 Dim Rect As RectType
 Dim BitmapInfo As BITMAPINFO_Type
 cr$ = Chr$(13)
 ' Get the DC for the entire window including the non-client area.
 hDC_Window = GetWindowDC(hWnd_SrcWindow)
 hDC_Mem = CreateCompatibleDC(hDC_Window)
 ' Get the pixel dimensions of the screen. This is necessary so
 ' that we can determine the relative size of the window compared to
 ' the screen
 ScreenWidth = GetDeviceCaps(hDC_Window, HORZRES)
 ScreenHeight = GetDeviceCaps(hDC_Window, VERTRES)
 ' Get the pixel dimensions of the window to be printed.
 r = GetWindowRect(hWnd_SrcWindow, Rect)
 Window_Width = Abs(Rect.Right - Rect.Left)
 Window_Height = Abs(Rect.Bottom - Rect.Top)
 ' Create a bitmap compatible with the window DC.
 hBmp_Window = CreateCompatibleBitmap(hDC_Window, Window_Width,
Window_Height)
 ' Select the bitmap to hold the window image into the memory DC.
 hPrevBmp = SelectObject(hDC_Mem, hBmp_Window)
 ' Copy the image of the window to the memory DC.
 r1 = BitBlt(hDC_Mem, 0, 0, Window_Width, Window_Height,
  hDC_Window, 0, 0, SRCCOPY)
 BitsPerPixel = GetDeviceCaps(hDC_Mem, BITSPIXEL)
 ColorPlanes = GetDeviceCaps(hDC_Mem, PLANES)
 BitmapInfo.BitmapInfoHeader.biSize = 40
 BitmapInfo.BitmapInfoHeader.biWidth = Window_Width
 BitmapInfo.BitmapInfoHeader.biHeight = Window_Height
 BitmapInfo.BitmapInfoHeader.biPlanes = 1
 BitmapInfo.BitmapInfoHeader.biBitCount = BitsPerPixel * ColorPlanes
 BitmapInfo.BitmapInfoHeader.biCompression = BI_RGB
 BitmapInfo.BitmapInfoHeader.biSizeImage = 0
 BitmapInfo.BitmapInfoHeader.biXPelsPerMeter = 0
 BitmapInfo.BitmapInfoHeader.biYPelsPerMeter = 0
 BitmapInfo.BitmapInfoHeader.biClrUsed = 0
 BitmapInfo.BitmapInfoHeader.biClrImportant = 0
 ' Calculate the ratios based on the source and destination
```

```
' devices. This will help to cause the size of the window image
' to be approximately the same proportion on another device
' such as a printer.
WidthRatio! = Window_Width / ScreenWidth
HeightAspectRatio! = Window_Height / Window_Width
PrintWidth = WidthRatio! * DestDevWidth
PrintHeight = HeightAspectRatio! * PrintWidth
' Calculate the number of bytes needed to store the image assuming
' 8 bits/pixel.
BytesNeeded& = CLng(Window_Width + 1) * (Window_Height + 1)
' Allocate a buffer to hold the bitmap bits.
hMem = GlobalAlloc(GMEM_MOVEABLE, BytesNeeded&)
If hDC_Window <> 0 And hBmp_Window <> 0 And hDC_Dest <> 0 And
hMem <> 0 Then
  lpBits& = GlobalLock(hMem)
  ' Get the bits that make up the image and copy them to the
  ' destination device.
  r2 = GetDIBits(hDC_Mem, hBmp_Window, 0, Window_Height, lpBits&,
BitmapInfo, DIB_RGB_COLORS)
  r3 = StretchDIBits(hDC_Dest, DestX, DestY, PrintWidth,
PrintHeight, 0, 0, Window_Width,
Window_Height, lpBits&, BitmapInfo,
DIB_RGB_COLORS, SRCCOPY)
End If
' Reselect in the previous bitmap and select out the source
' image bitmap.
r = SelectObject(hDC_Mem, hPrevBmp)
' Release or delete DC's, memory and objects.
r = GlobalUnlock(hMem)
r = GlobalFree(hMem)
r = DeleteDC(hDC_Window)
r = DeleteObject(hBmp_Window)
r = ReleaseDC(hWnd_SrcWindow, hDC_Form)
' Return true if the window was successfully printed.
If r2 <> 0 And r3 <> 0 Then
  PrintWindow = True
Else
  PrintWindow = False
End If
End Function
```

7. Add the following function, PrintClient, to Module1:

```
Function PrintClient (ByVal hDC_Dest, ByVal DestX, ByVal DestY,
ByVal DestDevWidth, ByVal DestDevHeight, ByVal hWnd_SrcWindow)
 Dim Rect As RectType, RectClient As RectType
 Dim BitmapInfo As BITMAPINFO_Type
 Dim pWindow As PointType, pClient As PointType, pDiff As PointType
 cr$ = Chr$(13)
 ' Get the DC for the entire window including the non-client area.
 hDC_Window = GetWindowDC(hWnd_SrcWindow)
 hDC_Mem = CreateCompatibleDC(hDC_Window)
 ' Get the pixel dimensions of the screen.
 ScreenWidth = GetDeviceCaps(hDC_Window, HORZRES)
 ScreenHeight = GetDeviceCaps(hDC_Window, VERTRES)
 ' Get the pixel dimensions of the window to be printed.
 r = GetWindowRect(hWnd_SrcWindow, Rect)
 Window_Width = Abs(Rect.Right - Rect.Left)
 Window_Height = Abs(Rect.Bottom - Rect.Top)
 ' Create a bitmap compatible with the window DC.
 hBmp_Window = CreateCompatibleBitmap(hDC_Window, Window_Width,
 Window_Height)
 ' Select the bitmap to hold the window image into the memory DC.
 hPrevBmp = SelectObject(hDC_Mem, hBmp_Window)
 ' Copy the image of the window to the memory DC.
 r1 = BitBlt(hDC_Mem, 0, 0, Window_Width, Window_Height,
 hDC_Window, 0, 0, SRCCOPY)
 ' Get the dimensions of the client area.
 r = GetClientRect(hWnd_SrcWindow, RectClient)
 Client_Width = Abs(RectClient.Right - RectClient.Left)
 Client_Height = Abs(RectClient.Bottom - RectClient.Top)
 ' Calculate the pixel difference (x and y) between the upper-left
 ' corner of the non-client area and the upper-left corner of the
 ' client area.
 pClient.x = RectClient.Left
 pClient.y = RectClient.Top
 r = ClientToScreen(hWnd_SrcWindow, pClient)
 xDiff = Abs(pClient.x - Rect.Left)
 yDiff = Abs(pClient.y - Rect.Top)
 ' Create a DC and bitmap to represent the client area of the
 ' window.
 hDC_MemClient = CreateCompatibleDC(hDC_Window)
 hBmp_Client = CreateCompatibleBitmap(hDC_Window, Client_Width,
 Client_Height)
 hBmpClientPrev = SelectObject(hDC_MemClient, hBmp_Client)
```

```
' Bitblt client area of window to memory bitmap representing the
' client area.
r = BitBlt(hDC_MemClient, 0, 0, Client_Width, Client_Height,
hDC_Mem, xDiff, yDiff, SRCCOPY)
' Reselect in the previous bitmap and select out the source
' image bitmap.
r = SelectObject(hDC_Mem, hPrevBmp)
' Delete the DC a and bitmap associated with the window.
r = DeleteDC(hDC_Window)
r = DeleteObject(hBmp_Window)
BitsPerPixel = GetDeviceCaps(hDC_MemClient, BITSPIXEL)
ColorPlanes = GetDeviceCaps(hDC_MemClient, PLANES)
BitmapInfo.BitmapInfoHeader.biSize = 40
BitmapInfo.BitmapInfoHeader.biWidth = Client_Width
BitmapInfo.BitmapInfoHeader.biHeight = Client_Height
BitmapInfo.BitmapInfoHeader.biPlanes = 1
BitmapInfo.BitmapInfoHeader.biBitCount = BitsPerPixel * ColorPlanes
BitmapInfo.BitmapInfoHeader.biCompression = BI_RGB
BitmapInfo.BitmapInfoHeader.biSizeImage = 0
BitmapInfo.BitmapInfoHeader.biXPelsPerMeter = 0
BitmapInfo.BitmapInfoHeader.biYPelsPerMeter = 0
BitmapInfo.BitmapInfoHeader.biClrUsed = 0
BitmapInfo.BitmapInfoHeader.biClrImportant = 0
' Calculate the ratios based on the source and destination
' devices. This will help to cause the size of the window image to
' be approximately the same proportion on another device such as
' a printer.
WidthRatio! = Client_Width / ScreenWidth
HeightAspectRatio! = Client_Height / Client_Width
PrintWidth = WidthRatio! * DestDevWidth
PrintHeight = HeightAspectRatio! * PrintWidth
' Calculate the number of bytes needed to store the image assuming
' 8 bits/pixel.
BytesNeeded& = CLng(Window_Width + 1) * (Window_Height + 1)
' Allocate a buffer to hold the bitmap bits.
hMem = GlobalAlloc(GMEM_MOVEABLE, BytesNeeded&)
If hDC_Window <> 0 And hBmp_Window <> 0 And hDC_Dest <> 0 And
 hMem <> 0 Then
 lpBits& = GlobalLock(hMem)
 ' Get the bits that make up the image and copy them to the
 ' destination device.
 r2 = GetDIBits(hDC_MemClient, hBmp_Client, 0, Client_Height,
```

```
lpBits&, BitmapInfo, DIB_RGB_COLORS)
  r3 = StretchDIBits(hDC_Dest, DestX, DestY, PrintWidth,
PrintHeight, 0, 0, Client_Width,
Client_Height, lpBits&, BitmapInfo,
DIB_RGB_COLORS, SRCCOPY)
End If
' Select in the previous bitmap.
r = SelectObject(hDC_MemClient, hBmpClientPrev)
' Release or delete DC's, memory and objects.
r = GlobalUnlock(hMem)
r = GlobalFree(hMem)
r = DeleteDC(hDC_MemClient)
r = DeleteObject(hBmp_Client)
r = ReleaseDC(hWnd_SrcWindow, hDC_Form)
' Return true if the window was successfully printed.
If r2 <> 0 And r3 <> 0 Then
  PrintClient = True
Else
  PrintClient = False
End If
End Function
```

8. Add DefInt A–Z to the General Declarations section of Form1.

9. Add the following code to the Command1_Click event:

```
Sub Command1_Click ()
  ' The ScaleMode must be set to pixels for the PrintWindow
  ' routine to print correctly.
  Printer.ScaleMode = 3
  ' Change MousePointer to an hourglass.
  Screen.MousePointer = 11
  ' Initialize the printer.
  Printer.Print ""
  ' Copy the image of the form to the printer.
  ' To print Command1 instead, you can substitute Command1.hWnd for
Form1.hWnd
  ' as the last argument.
  r = PrintClient(Printer.hDC, 100, 100,
Printer.ScaleWidth, Printer.ScaleHeight,
Form1.hWnd)
```

```
' Display an error if the return value from PrintWindow is zero.
If Not r Then
 MsgBox "Unable to print the form"
Else
 Printer.EndDoc
End If
 Screen.MousePointer = 0
End Sub
```

10. Add the following code to the Command2_Click event:

```
Sub Command2_Click ()
 ' The ScaleMode must be set to pixels for the PrintWindow
 ' routine to print correctly.
 Printer.ScaleMode = 3
 ' Change MousePointer to an hourglass.
 Screen.MousePointer = 11
 ' Initialize the printer.
 Printer.Print ""
 ' Copy the image of the form to the printer.
 ' To print Command1 instead, you can substitute Command1.hWnd for
Form1.hWnd
 ' as the last argument.
 r = PrintWindow(Printer.hDC, 100, 100,
Printer.ScaleWidth, Printer.ScaleHeight,
Form1.hWnd)
 ' Display an error if the return value from PrintWindow is zero.
 If Not r Then
  MsgBox "Unable to print the form"
 Else
  Printer.EndDoc
 End If
 Screen.MousePointer = 0
End Sub
```

Run the program. Choosing Command1 prints just the client area of Form1. Choosing Command2 prints the entire area of the form. Note that you can print any of the forms or controls in a project using this method and control the size and placement of the forms by changing the second, third, fourth, and fifth parameters of the call to StretchDIBits. In the preceding example, the form or control is sized in proportion to the size of the screen.

# Q: How can I set the orientation of the printer to either landscape or portrait mode from within a Visual Basic application?

Some printers support changing the orientation of the paper output to landscape. With the Windows 3.0 API Escape function, you can change the settings of the printer to either landscape or portrait.

The following is an example of invoking the Windows 3.0 API Escape function from Microsoft Visual Basic programming system version 1.0 for Windows.

**note:**

*The Windows API Escape function used below is provided in Windows 3.0 only for backward compatibility with earlier Microsoft Windows releases. New applications should use the GDI DeviceCapabilities and ExtDeviceMode functions instead of the Escape function shown below.*

Normally, output for the printer is in portrait mode, where output is printed horizontally across the narrower dimension of the paper. In landscape mode, the output is printed horizontally across the longer dimension of the paper.

You can use the Escape function to change the orientation of the printer by passing GETSETPAPERORIENT as an argument. When you initially print text to the printer, Visual Basic will use the currently selected orientation. Sending the Escape function will not take effect until you perform a Printer.EndDoc. After you perform a Printer.EndDoc, output will print in the orientation that you have selected.

To determine if your printer supports landscape mode, do the following:

1. From the Windows 3.0 Program Manager, run the Control Panel.

2. From the Control Panel, select the Printers icon.

3. From the Printers dialog box, choose the Configure button.

4. The Configure dialog box will contain an option for landscape orientation if landscape is supported on your printer.

The following example demonstrates how to change the printer orientation to landscape. Please note that your printer must support landscape mode for these commands to have any effect.

1. Run Visual Basic, or from the File menu, choose New Project (ALT, F, N) if Visual Basic is already running. Form1 is created by default.

2. Add a command button (Command1) to Form1.

3. Add the following code to the global module GLOBAL.BAS:

```
Type OrientStructure
   Orientation As Long
   Pad As String * 16
End Type
' The following Declare statement must be on a single line:
Declare Function Escape% Lib "GDI" (ByVal hDc%, ByVal nEsc%,
ByVal nLen%, lpData As OrientStructure, lpOut As Any)
```

4. Add the following code to the Command1_Click event procedure of the Command1 button on FORM1:

```
Sub Command1_Click ()
   Const PORTRAIT = 1
   Const LANDSCAPE = 2
   Const GETSETPAPERORIENT = 30
   Const NULL = 0&
   Dim Orient As OrientStructure
  '* Start the printer
  Printer.Print ""
  '* Specify the orientation
  Orient.Orientation = LANDSCAPE
  '* Send escape sequence to change orientation
  x% = Escape(Printer.hDC, GETSETPAPERORIENT,
  Len(Orient), Orient, NULL)
  '* The EndDoc will now re-initialize the printer
  Printer.EndDoc
  Printer.Print "Should print in landscape mode"
  Printer.EndDoc
End Sub
```

# Q: How can I access the information in the Windows initialization files from within a Visual Basic application?

There are several Microsoft Windows API functions that can manipulate information within a Windows initialization file. GetProfileInt, GetPrivateProfileInt, GetProfileString, and GetPrivateProfileString allow a Microsoft Visual Basic for Windows program to retrieve information from a Windows initialization file based on an application name and key name. WritePrivateProfileString and WriteProfileString are used to create/update items within Windows initialization files.

Windows initialization files contain information that defines your Windows environment. Examples of Windows initialization files are WIN.INI and SYSTEM.INI, which are commonly found in the C:\WINDOWS subdirectory. Microsoft Windows and applications for Microsoft Windows can use the information stored in these files to configure themselves to meet your needs and preferences. For a description of initialization files, review the WIN.INI file that comes with Microsoft Windows.

An initialization file is composed of at least an application name and a key name. The contents of Windows initialization files have the following format:

```
[Application name]
keyname=value
```

There are four API function calls (GetProfileInt, GetPrivateProfileInt, GetProfileString, and GetPrivateProfileString) that you can use to retrieve information from these files. The particular function to call depends on whether you want to obtain string or numerical data.

The GetProfile family of API functions is used when you want to get information from the standard WIN.INI file that is used by Windows.

The WIN.INI file should be part of your Windows subdirectory (C:\WINDOWS). The GetPrivateProfile family of API functions is used to retrieve information from any initialization file that you specify.

The formal arguments accepted by these API functions are described farther below.

The WriteProfileString and WritePrivateProfileString functions write information to Windows initialization files. WriteProfileString is used to modify the Windows initialization file, WIN.INI.

WritePrivateProfileString is used to modify any initialization file that you specify. These functions search the initialization file for the key name under the application name. If there is no match, the function adds to the user profile a new string entry containing the key name and the key value specified. If the key name is found, it will replace the key value with the new value specified.

To declare these API functions within your program, include the following Declare statements in the global module or the General Declarations section of a Visual Basic for Windows form:

```
Declare Function GetProfileInt% Lib "Kernel"(ByVal lpAppName$,
  ByVal lpKeyName$, ByVal nDefault%)
Declare Function GetProfileString% Lib "Kernel" (ByVal lpAppName$,
  ByVal lpKeyName$, ByVal lpDefault$, ByVal lpReturnedString$,
  ByVal nSize%)
Declare Function WriteProfileString% Lib "Kernel"(ByVal lpAppName$,
  ByVal lpKeyName$, ByVal lpString$)
Declare Function GetPrivateProfileInt% Lib "Kernel"
  (ByVal lpAppName$, ByVal lpKeyName$, ByVal nDefault%,
  ByVal lpFileName$)
Declare Function GetPrivateProfileString% Lib "Kernel"
  (ByVal lpAppName$, ByVal lpKeyName$, ByVal lpDefault$,
  ByVal lpReturnedString$, ByVal nSize%, ByVal lpFileName$)
Declare Function WritePrivateProfileString% Lib "Kernel"
  (ByVal lpAppName$, ByVal lpKeyName$, ByVal lpString$,
  ByVal lpFileName$)
```

**note:** *Each Declare statement must be on a single line.*

The formal arguments to these functions are described as follows:

| Argument | Description |
| --- | --- |
| lpAppName$ | Name of a Windows application that appears in the initialization file. |
| lpKeyName$ | Key name that appears in the initialization file. |
| nDefault$ | Specifies the default value for the given key if the key cannot be found in the initialization file. |
| lpFileName$ | Points to a string that names the initialization file. If lpFileName does not contain a path to the file, Windows searches for the file in the Windows directory. |
| lpDefault$ | Specifies the default value for the given key if the key cannot be found in the initialization file. |
| lpReturnedString | Specifies the buffer that receives the character string. |

| Argument | Description |
|---|---|
| nSize% | Specifies the maximum number of characters (including the last null character) to be copied to the buffer. |
| lpString$ | Specifies the string that contains the new key value. |

Here are the steps necessary to create a Visual Basic for Windows sample program that uses GetPrivateProfileString to read from an initialization file that you create. The program, based on information in the initialization file you created, shells out to the Calculator program (CALC.EXE) that comes with Windows. The sample program demonstrates how to use GetPrivatePro-fileString to get information from any initialization file.

1. Create an initialization file from a text editor (for example, you can use the Notepad program supplied with Windows) and save the file under the name of NET.INI. Type in the following as the contents of the initialization file (NET.INI):

[NetPaths]
WordProcessor=C:\WINWORD\WINWORD.EXE
Calculator=C:\WINDOWS\CALC.EXE

**note:** *If CALC.EXE is not in the C:\WINDOWS subdirectory (as indicated after "Calculator=" above), replace C:\WINDOWS\CALC.EXE with the correct path.*

2. Save the initialization file (NET.INI) to the root directory of your hard drive (such as C:\) and exit the text editor.

3. Start Visual Basic for Windows.

4. Create a form called Form1.

5. Create a push button called Command1.

6. Within the Global Declaration section of Form1, add the following Windows API function declarations. Note that the Declare statement below must appear on a single line.

```
Declare Function GetPrivateProfileString% Lib "kernel"
    (ByVal lpAppName$, ByVal lpKeyName$,ByVal lpDefault$,
    ByVal lpReturnString$,ByVal nSize%, ByVal lpFileName$)
```

7. Within the (Command1) push button's click event, add the following code:

```
Sub Command1_Click ()
'* If an error occurs during SHELL statement then handle the error.
On Error GoTo FileError
'* Compare these to the NET.INI file that you created in step 1
'* above.
lpAppName$ = "NetPaths"
lpKeyName$ = "Calculator"
lpDefault$ = ""
lpReturnString$ = Space$(128)
Size% = Len(lpReturnString$)
'* This is the path and name the NET.INI file.
lpFileName$ = "c:\net.ini"
'* This call will cause the path to CALC.EXE (that is,
'* C:\WINDOWS\CALC.EXE) to be placed into lpReturnString$. The
'* return value (assigned to Valid%) represents the number of
'* characters read into lpReturnString$. Note that the
'* following assignment must be placed on one line.
Valid% = GetPrivateProfileString(lpAppName$, lpKeyName$,
lpDefault$, lpReturnString$,
Size%, lpFileName$)
'* Discard the trailing spaces and null character.
Path$ = Left$(lpReturnString$, Valid%)
'* Try to run CALC.EXE. If unable to run, FileError is called.
Succ% = Shell(Path$, 1)
Exit Sub
FileError:
MsgBox "Can't find file", 16, "Error lpReturnString"
Resume Next
End Sub
```

# Q: How can I create a bitmap with a transparent background in Visual Basic for Windows?

A transparent image shows the background behind it instead of the image itself. You can use an icon editor such as the IconWorks sample program provided with Visual Basic to create icons that contain transparent parts.

The following shows you how to make certain parts of a bitmap transparent. The six general steps required to create a transparent bitmap are as follows:

1. Store the area, or background, where the bitmap is going to be drawn.

2. Create a monochrome mask of the bitmap that identifies the transparent areas of the bitmap by using a white pixel to indicate transparent areas and a black pixel to indicate non-transparent areas of the bitmap.

3. Combine the pixels of the monochrome mask with the background bitmap using the And binary operator. The area of the background where the non-transparent portion of the bitmap will appear is made black.

4. Combine an inverted copy of the monochrome mask (step 2) with the source bitmap using the And binary operator. The transparent areas of the source bitmap will be made black.

5. Combine the modified background (step 3) with the modified source bitmap (step 4) using the Xor binary operator. The background will show through the transparent portions of the bitmap.

6. Copy the resulting bitmap to the background.

Here is some example code:

1. Run Visual Basic, or from the File menu, choose New Project (ALT, F, N) if Visual Basic is already running. Form1 is created by default.

2. Add the following controls to Form1 with the associated property values:

| Control | Name (or CtlName) | Property | Settings |
| --- | --- | --- | --- |
| Picture | pictSource | Picture | "WINDOWS\THATCH.BMP" |
| Picture | pictDest | Picture | "WINDOWS\ARCHES.BMP" |
| Command button | cmdCopy | Caption | "Copy" |

3. From the File menu, choose New Module (ALT, F, M). Module1 is created.

4. Add the following code to the cmdCopy_Click event procedure of Form1.

This code calls the TransparentBlt( ) function to copy a source bitmap to a destination (background) picture control. White (QBColor(15)) areas of the bitmap are made transparent against the background bitmap.

```
Sub cmdCopy_Click ()
Call TransparentBlt(pictDest, pictSource.Picture, 10, 10,_
QBColor(15))
End Sub
```

5. Add the following code to the General Declarations section of Module1. Enter each Declare as a single line:

```
Type bitmap
bmType As Integer
bmWidth As Integer
bmHeight As Integer
bmWidthBytes As Integer
bmPlanes As String * 1
bmBitsPixel As String * 1
bmBits As Long
End Type
Declare Function BitBlt Lib "GDI" (ByVal srchDC As Integer, ByVal_
srcX
As Integer, ByVal srcY As Integer, ByVal srcW As Integer, ByVal srcH
As Integer, ByVal desthDC As Integer, ByVal destX As Integer, ByVal
destY As Integer, ByVal op As Long) As Integer
Declare Function SetBkColor Lib "GDI" (ByVal hDC As Integer, ByVal
cColor As Long) As Long
Declare Function CreateCompatibleDC Lib "GDI" (ByVal hDC As Integer)
As Integer
Declare Function DeleteDC Lib "GDI" (ByVal hDC As Integer) As Integer
Declare Function CreateBitmap Lib "GDI" (ByVal nWidth As Integer,_
ByVal
nHeight As Integer, ByVal cbPlanes As Integer, ByVal cbBits As
Integer, lpvBits As Any) As Integer
Declare Function CreateCompatibleBitmap Lib "GDI" (ByVal hDC As_
Integer,
ByVal nWidth As Integer, ByVal nHeight As Integer) As Integer
Declare Function SelectObject Lib "GDI" (ByVal hDC As Integer, ByVal
hObject As Integer) As Integer
Declare Function DeleteObject Lib "GDI" (ByVal hObject As Integer) As
Integer
Declare Function GetObject Lib "GDI" (ByVal hObject As Integer, ByVal
```

```
nCount As Integer, bmp As Any) As Integer
Const SRCCOPY = &HCC0020
Const SRCAND = &H8800C6
Const SRCPAINT = &HEE0086
Const NOTSRCCOPY = &H330008
```

6. Add the following Sub procedure to the General Declarations section of Module1. TransparentBlt( ) accepts six parameters: a destination picture control (dest), a source bitmap to become transparent (srcBmp), the X,Y coordinates in pixels where you want to place the source bitmap on the destination (destX and destY), and the RGB value for the color you want to be transparent. TransparentBlt( ) copies the source bitmap to any X,Y location on the background making areas transparent.

```
Sub TransparentBlt (dest As Control, ByVal srcBmp As Integer, ByVal
destX As Integer, ByVal destY As Integer, ByVal TransColor As Long)
Const PIXEL = 3
Dim destScale As Integer
Dim srcDC As Integer     'source bitmap (color)
Dim saveDC As Integer    'backup copy of source bitmap
Dim maskDC As Integer    'mask bitmap (monochrome)
Dim invDC As Integer     'inverse of mask bitmap (monochrome)
Dim resultDC As Integer  'combination of source bitmap & background
Dim bmp As bitmap        'description of the source bitmap
Dim hResultBmp As Integer 'Bitmap combination of source & background
Dim hSaveBmp As Integer  'Bitmap stores backup copy of source bitmap
Dim hMaskBmp As Integer  'Bitmap stores mask (monochrome)
Dim hInvBmp As Integer   'Bitmap holds inverse of mask (monochrome)
Dim hPrevBmp As Integer  'Bitmap holds previous bitmap selected in DC
Dim hSrcPrevBmp As Integer  'Holds previous bitmap in source DC
Dim hSavePrevBmp As Integer 'Holds previous bitmap in saved DC
Dim hDestPrevBmp As Integer 'Holds previous bitmap in destination DC
Dim hMaskPrevBmp As Integer 'Holds previous bitmap in the mask DC
Dim hInvPrevBmp As Integer  'Holds previous bitmap in inverted mask_
DC
Dim OrigColor As Long  'Holds original background color from source_
DC
Dim Success As Integer 'Stores result of call to Windows API
If TypeOf dest Is PictureBox Then 'Ensure objects are picture boxes
  destScale = dest.ScaleMode 'Store ScaleMode to restore later
  dest.ScaleMode = PIXEL 'Set ScaleMode to pixels for Windows GDI
  'Retrieve bitmap to get width (bmp.bmWidth) & height (bmp.bmHeight)
```

```
Success = GetObject(srcBmp, Len(bmp), bmp)
srcDC = CreateCompatibleDC(dest.hDC) 'Create DC to hold stage
saveDC = CreateCompatibleDC(dest.hDC)'Create DC to hold stage
maskDC = CreateCompatibleDC(dest.hDC)'Create DC to hold stage
invDC = CreateCompatibleDC(dest.hDC) 'Create DC to hold stage
resultDC = CreateCompatibleDC(dest.hDC) 'Create DC to hold stage
'Create monochrome bitmaps for the mask-related bitmaps:
hMaskBmp = CreateBitmap(bmp.bmWidth, bmp.bmHeight, 1, 1, ByVal 0&)
hInvBmp = CreateBitmap(bmp.bmWidth, bmp.bmHeight, 1, 1, ByVal 0&)
'Create color bitmaps for final result & stored copy of source
hResultBmp = CreateCompatibleBitmap(dest.hDC, bmp.bmWidth,
bmp.bmHeight)
hSaveBmp = CreateCompatibleBitmap(dest.hDC, bmp.bmWidth,
bmp.bmHeight)
hSrcPrevBmp = SelectObject(srcDC, srcBmp)  'Select bitmap in DC
hSavePrevBmp = SelectObject(saveDC, hSaveBmp) 'Select bitmap in DC
hMaskPrevBmp = SelectObject(maskDC, hMaskBmp) 'Select bitmap in DC
hInvPrevBmp = SelectObject(invDC, hInvBmp) 'Select bitmap in DC
hDestPrevBmp = SelectObject(resultDC, hResultBmp) 'Select bitmap
Success = BitBlt(saveDC, 0, 0, bmp.bmWidth, bmp.bmHeight, srcDC,
0, 0, SRCCOPY) 'Make backup of source bitmap to restore later
'Create mask: set background color of source to transparent color.
OrigColor = SetBkColor(srcDC, TransColor)
Success = BitBlt(maskDC, 0, 0, bmp.bmWidth, bmp.bmHeight, srcDC,
0, 0, SRCCOPY)
TransColor = SetBkColor(srcDC, OrigColor)
'Create inverse of mask to AND w/ source & combine w/ background.
Success = BitBlt(invDC, 0, 0, bmp.bmWidth, bmp.bmHeight, maskDC,
0, 0, NOTSRCCOPY)
'Copy background bitmap to result & create final transparent bitmap
Success = BitBlt(resultDC, 0, 0, bmp.bmWidth, bmp.bmHeight,
dest.hDC, destX, destY, SRCCOPY)
'AND mask bitmap w/ result DC to punch hole in the background by
'painting black area for non-transparent portion of source bitmap.
Success = BitBlt(resultDC, 0, 0, bmp.bmWidth, bmp.bmHeight,
maskDC, 0, 0, SRCAND)
'AND inverse mask w/ source bitmap to turn off bits associated
'with transparent area of source bitmap by making it black.
Success = BitBlt(srcDC, 0, 0, bmp.bmWidth, bmp.bmHeight, invDC,
0, 0, SRCAND)
'XOR result w/ source bitmap to make background show through.
Success = BitBlt(resultDC, 0, 0, bmp.bmWidth, bmp.bmHeight,
srcDC, 0, 0, SRCPAINT)
Success = BitBlt(dest.hDC, destX, destY, bmp.bmWidth, bmp.bmHeight,
```

```
        resultDC, 0, 0, SRCCOPY) 'Display transparent bitmap on backgrnd
        Success = BitBlt(srcDC, 0, 0, bmp.bmWidth, bmp.bmHeight, saveDC,
        0, 0, SRCCOPY) 'Restore backup of bitmap.
        hPrevBmp = SelectObject(srcDC, hSrcPrevBmp) 'Select orig object
        hPrevBmp = SelectObject(saveDC, hSavePrevBmp) 'Select orig object
        hPrevBmp = SelectObject(resultDC, hDestPrevBmp) 'Select orig object
        hPrevBmp = SelectObject(maskDC, hMaskPrevBmp) 'Select orig object
        hPrevBmp = SelectObject(invDC, hInvPrevBmp) 'Select orig object
        Success = DeleteObject(hSaveBmp)'Deallocate system resources.
        Success = DeleteObject(hMaskBmp)'Deallocate system resources.
        Success = DeleteObject(hInvBmp) 'Deallocate system resources.
        Success = DeleteObject(hResultBmp) 'Deallocate system resources.
        Success = DeleteDC(srcDC) 'Deallocate system resources.
        Success = DeleteDC(saveDC)'Deallocate system resources.
        Success = DeleteDC(invDC) 'Deallocate system resources.
        Success = DeleteDC(maskDC)'Deallocate system resources.
        Success = DeleteDC(resultDC) 'Deallocate system resources.
        dest.ScaleMode = destScale 'Restore ScaleMode of destination.
    End If
End Sub
```

7. From the Run menu, choose Start (ALT, R, S) to run the program.

8. Click the Copy button. The thatched pattern in the first picture is copied onto the second picture (an image of arches), making the arches show through areas of the previously white thatched pattern.

---

## Q: How can I create a floating window—a window that always stays on top of every other window on the desktop?

You can create a floating window, such as that used for the Microsoft Windows version 3.1 Clock, by using the SetWindowPos Windows API call.

A floating (or topmost) window is a window that remains constantly above all other windows, even when it is not active. Examples of floating windows are the Find dialog box in WRITE.EXE, and CLOCK.EXE (when Always on Top is selected from the Control menu).

There are two methods to produce windows that "hover" or "float," one of which is possible in Visual Basic for Windows. This method is described below:

Call SetWindowPos, specifying an existing non-topmost window and HWND_TOPMOST as the value for the second parameter (hwndInsertAfter).

Use the following declarations:

```
Declare Function SetWindowPos Lib "user" (ByVal h%, ByVal hb%,
   ByVal x%, ByVal y%, ByVal cx%, ByVal cy%, ByVal f%) As Integer
' The above Declare statement must appear on one line.

Global Const SWP_NOMOVE = 2
Global Const SWP_NOSIZE = 1
Global Const FLAGS = SWP_NOMOVE Or SWP_NOSIZE
Global Const HWND_TOPMOST = -1
Global Const HWND_NOTOPMOST = -2
```

To set the form XXXX to TOPMOST, use the following code:

```
success% = SetWindowPos (XXXX.hWnd, HWND_TOPMOST, 0, 0, 0, 0, FLAGS)
REM success% <> 0 When Successful
```

To reset the form XXXX to NON-TOPMOST, use the following code:

```
success% = SetWindowPos (XXXX.hWnd, HWND_NOTOPMOST, 0, 0, 0, 0,_
FLAGS)
' success% <> 0 When Successful
```

**note:** *This attribute was introduced in Windows version 3.1, so remember to make a GetVersion() API call to determine whether the application is running under Windows version 3.1.*

## Q: Under Microsoft Visual Basic for Windows, how can I determine when a shelled process has terminated?

Executing the shell function in a Visual Basic for Windows program asynchronously starts another executable program and returns control back to the Visual Basic application. The shelled program continues to run indefinitely until the user closes it, not when your Visual Basic program terminates. However, your program can wait until the shelled program has finished by polling the return value of the Windows API function GetModuleUsage. The following text describes the method and provides a code example.

Using the Windows API function GetModuleUsage, your program can monitor the status of a shelled process. The return value from the Shell function can be used to call GetModuleUsage continuously within a loop to poll whether or not the shelled program has finished executing. If the Shell function is successful, the return value is the instance handle for the shelled program. This instance handle can be passed to GetModuleUsage, to determine the reference count for the module. When GetModuleUsage returns a value of 0 or less, the application has finished its execution.

Regardless of the WindowStyle used to shell the program, this algorithm works correctly. Additionally, this method does work under the following situations:

◆ Shelling to Windows programs

◆ Shelling to MS-DOS programs

◆ Shelling to applications that do not display a window

Here are the steps necessary to build a Visual Basic for Windows program that uses the Shell function to execute the Windows Notepad accessory. The program is an example of how to use the Windows API function Get-ModuleUsage to wait until a shelled process has terminated before resuming execution.

1. Run Visual Basic for Windows, or from the File menu, choose New Project (ALT, F, N) if Visual Basic for Windows is already running.

   Form1 is created by default.

2. Add the following code to the General Declarations section of Form1:

```
Declare Function GetModuleUsage% Lib "Kernel" (ByVal hModule%)
```

3. Add the following code to the Form_Click event procedure of Form1:

```
Sub Form_Click ()
 x% = Shell("notepad.exe") ' Modify path as needed.
 While GetModuleUsage(x%) > 0 ' Has Shelled program finished?
 z% = DoEvents()   ' If not, yield to Windows.
 Wend
```

```
MsgBox "Shelled application just terminated", 64
End Sub
```

4. From the Run menu, select Start (ALT, R, S) to run the program.

5. With the mouse, click on Form1. The Notepad application is shelled.

The MsgBox statement following the Shell function is not executed, as it would normally be without the While loop above it. The message box does not appear until Notepad is closed by choosing Exit from its File menu (ALT, F, X).

# Q: How can I use the LPSTR returned from an API function call to get the string data it points to?

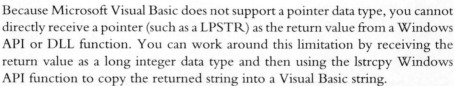

Because Microsoft Visual Basic does not support a pointer data type, you cannot directly receive a pointer (such as a LPSTR) as the return value from a Windows API or DLL function. You can work around this limitation by receiving the return value as a long integer data type and then using the lstrcpy Windows API function to copy the returned string into a Visual Basic string.

An LPSTR Windows API data type is actually a far pointer to a null-terminated string of characters. Because an LPSTR is a far pointer, it can be received as a 4-byte data type, such as a Visual Basic long integer. Using the Visual Basic "ByVal" keyword, you can pass the address stored in a Visual Basic long integer back to the Windows API lstrcpy routine to copy the characters at that address into a Visual Basic string variable. Because lstrcpy expects the target string to be long enough to hold the source string, you should pad any Visual Basic string passed to lstrcpy to have a size large enough to hold the source string before passing it to lstrcpy. Failure to allocate enough space in the Visual Basic string may result in an Unrecoverable Application Error or General Protection Fault when you call lstrcpy.

The following is an example program that demonstrates the use of lstrcpy to retrieve a LPSTR pointer returned from the Windows API GetDOSEnvironment routine. Note that the capability of the Windows API GetDOSEnvironment routine is already available through the Environ function built into Visual Basic; therefore, the following program mainly serves as an example of using lstrcpy.

```
'*** General declarations ***
Declare Function GetDosEnvironment Lib "Kernel" () As Long

' The following Declare statement must appear on one line.
Declare Function lstrcpy Lib "Kernel" (ByVal lpString1 As Any, ByVal
lpString2 As Any) As Long

'*** Form Click event code ***
Sub Form_Click()
 Dim lpStrAddress As Long,  DOSEnv$
 ' Allocate space to copy LPSTR into
 DOSEnv$ = Space$(4096)
 ' Get address of returned LPSTR into a long integer
 lpStrAddress = GetDOSEnvironment()
 ' Copy LPSTR into a Visual Basic string
 lpStrAddress = lstrcpy(DOSEnv$, lpStrAddress)
 ' Parse first entry in environment string and print
 DOSEnv$ = RTrim$(LTrim$(DOSEnv$, Len(DOSEnv$) - 1))
 Form1.Print DOSEnv$
End Sub
```

## Q: How can I create a scrollable viewport using Microsoft Visual Basic for Windows?

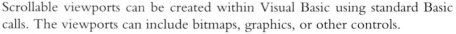

Scrollable viewports can be created within Visual Basic using standard Basic calls. The viewports can include bitmaps, graphics, or other controls.

To create a scrollable picture with clipping, you must have two picture controls. The first picture control is called the stationary parent picture control. Within the parent picture control, you need to create a movable child picture control. It is the child picture control that will be moved within the parent picture control. Moving the child picture within the parent picture control creates the clipping effect. During run time when you move the child picture, it will now be clipped by the boundaries of the parent picture.

To create these two picture controls, do the following:

1. Choose the picture box control from the Toolbox window in Visual Basic.

2. Draw a picture on the form. This is the parent picture.

3. Again choose the picture box control from the Toolbox window.

4. Draw the second picture on top of and within the boundaries of the first picture control. This is the child picture.

The sample application to follow shows how to create a scrollable bitmap within a viewport. Perform the preceding sequence to create a parent/child picture control. Add a horizontal scroll bar and a vertical scroll bar to the form.

Make sure that the path to your bitmap is correct. Several of the properties are set during run time, which could have been set during design time as well.

Moving the thumb of the two scroll bars will move the child picture within the parent picture. The handle (upper-left corner of the picture) to the child picture will be located either at (0,0) of the parent picture or to the left and/or right of the parent picture.

Since the clipping region is that of the parent picture, the child picture will appear to move across the parent picture viewport.

```
Sub Form_Load ()
Const PIXEL = 3
' Set design properties, included here for simplicity.
Form1.ScaleMode = PIXEL
Picture1.ScaleMode = PIXEL
Picture2.ScaleMode = PIXEL
' AutoSize is set to TRUE so that the boundaries of
' Picture2 are expanded to the size of the actual bitmap.
Picture2.AutoSize = TRUE
' Get rid of annoying borders.
Picture1.BorderStyle = NONE
Picture2.BorderStyle = NONE
' Load the picture that you want to display.
Picture2.Picture = LoadPicture("c:\win\party.bmp")
' Initialize location of both pictures.
Picture1.Move 0, 0, ScaleWidth - VScroll1.Width,_
        ScaleHeight - HScroll1.Height
Picture2.Move 0, 0
' Position the horizontal scroll bar.
HScroll1.Top = Picture1.Height
HScroll1.Left = 0
HScroll1.Width = Picture1.Width
' Position the vertical scroll bar.
VScroll1.Top = 0
VScroll1.Left = Picture1.Width
VScroll1.Height = Picture1.Height
' Set the Max value for the scroll bars.
HScroll1.Max = Picture2.Width - Picture1.Width
```

```
VScroll1.Max = Picture2.Height - Picture1.Height
' Determine if child picture will fill up screen.
' If so, then there is no need to use scroll bars.
VScroll1.Enabled = (Picture1.Height < Picture2.Height)
HScroll1.Enabled = (Picture1.Width < Picture2.Width)
End Sub

Sub HScroll1_Change ()
  ' Picture2.Left is set to the negative of the value because
  ' as you scroll the scroll bar to the right, the display
  ' should move to the Left, showing more of the right
  ' of the display, and vice-versa when scrolling to the
  ' left.
Picture2.Left = -HScroll1.Value
End Sub

Sub VScroll1_Change ()
  ' Picture2.Top is set to the negative of the value because
  ' as you scroll the scroll bar down, the display
  ' should move up, showing more of the bottom
  ' of the display, and vice-versa when scrolling up.
Picture2.Top = -VScroll1.Value
End Sub
```

## Q: How can I determine if a specific application is running under Windows?

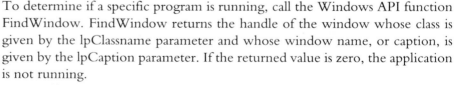

To determine if a specific program is running, call the Windows API function FindWindow. FindWindow returns the handle of the window whose class is given by the lpClassname parameter and whose window name, or caption, is given by the lpCaption parameter. If the returned value is zero, the application is not running.

By calling FindWindow with a combination of a specific program's class name and/or the title bar caption, your program can determine whether that specific program is running.

When an application is started from the Program Manager, it registers the class name of the form. The window class provides information about the name, attributes, and resources required by your form. All Visual Basic forms have a class name of "ThunderForm." You can determine the class name of an application by using SPY.EXE, which comes with the Microsoft Windows Software Development Kit (SDK) version 3.0 or 3.1.

If the window has a caption bar title, you can also use the title to locate the instance of the running application. This caption text is valid even when the application is minimized to an icon.

Because another instance of your Visual Basic program will have the same class name and may have the same title bar caption, you must use DDE to determine if another instance of your Visual Basic program is running. (This DDE technique is not shown here.)

The following example shows three ways to determine if the Windows Calculator is running. To create the program, do the following steps:

1. Run Visual Basic, or from the File menu, select New Project (ALT, F, N) if Visual Basic is already running. Form1 will be created by default.

2. Declare the Windows API function FindWindow in the Global-Declarations section of Form1. The variables are declared as "Any" because you can pass either a pointer to a string, or a NULL (or 0&) value. You are responsible for passing the correct variable type. Note that the Declare statement should be entered on just one line:

```
Declare Function FindWindow% Lib "user" (ByVal lpClassName As Any,_
ByVal lpCaption As Any)
```

3. Add the following code to the form's Click event. This example demonstrates how you can find the instance of the application with a combination of the class name and/or the window's caption. In this example, the application will find an instance of the Windows calculator (CALC.EXE).

```
Sub Form_Click ()

lpClassName$ = "SciCalc"
lpCaption$ = "Calculator"
Print "Handle = ";FindWindow(lpClassName$, 0&)
Print "Handle = ";FindWindow(0&, lpCaption$)
Print "Handle = ";FindWindow(lpClassName$,lpCaption$)
End Sub
```

4. Run this program with CALC.EXE running and without CALC.EXE running. If CALC.EXE is running, your application will print an arbitrary handle. If CALC.EXE is not running, your application will print zero as the handle.

Below are some class names of applications that are shipped with Windows:

| Class Name | Application |
| --- | --- |
| SciCalc | CALC.EXE |
| CalWndMain | CALENDAR.EXE |
| Cardfile | CARDFILE.EXE |
| Clipboard | CLIPBOARD.EXE |
| Clock | CLOCK.EXE |
| CtlPanelClass | CONTROL.EXE |
| XLMain | EXCEL.EXE |
| Session | MS-DOS.EXE |
| Notepad | NOTEPAD.EXE |
| PBPARENT | PBRUSH.EXE |
| Pif | PIFEDIT.EXE |
| PrintManager | PRINTMAN.EXE |
| Progman | PROGMAN.EXE (Windows Program Manager) |
| Recorder | RECORDER.EXE |
| Reversi | REVERSI.EXE |
| #32770 | SETUP.EXE |
| Solitaire | SOL.EXE |
| Terminal | TERMINAL.EXE |
| WFS_Frame | WINFILE.EXE |
| MW_WINHELP | WINHELP.EXE |
| #32770 | WINVER.EXE |
| OpusApp | WINWORD.EXE |
| MSWRITE_MENU | WRITE.EXE |

## Q: How can I use the data control in Microsoft Visual Basic for Windows to scroll up and down in a recordset?

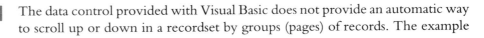

The data control provided with Visual Basic does not provide an automatic way to scroll up or down in a recordset by groups (pages) of records. The example in this section shows you how to use the MoveNext and MovePrevious methods to scroll up or down in a recordset by groups (pages) of records without displaying all the records.

Usually, when you use the MoveNext and MovePrevious methods to scroll up or down by a specified number of records, all the records are displayed as you move through them. This is undesirable behavior if you want a way to scroll through the recordset by pages.

In order to display only the record you have scrolled to, without displaying all the records in between, you need to use the Clone method to clone the data control's recordset.

Once you clone the recordset, you can use the MoveNext and MovePrevious methods to move to the desired record within the cloned recordset. Then set the Bookmark property of the original recordset to the Bookmark property of the cloned recordset. This makes the desired record the current record in the original recordset and causes the fields of this record to be displayed in the bound data controls.

Perform the following steps to create an example program that demonstrates how to scroll up and down by pages in a data control's recordset:

1. Start Visual Basic or from the File menu, choose New Project (ALT, F, N) if Visual Basic is already running. Form1 is created by default.

2. Add a data control (Data1) to Form1.

3. Add two text boxes (Text1 and Text2) to Form1.

4. Add two command buttons (Command1 and Command2) to Form1.

5. Using the following table as a guide, set the properties of the controls you added in steps 2, 3, and 4.

| Control Name | Property | New Value |
| --- | --- | --- |
| Command1 | Caption | "Page Up" |
| Command2 | Caption | "Page Down" |
| Data1 | DatabaseName | BIBLIO.MDB* |
| Data1 | RecordSource | Authors |
| Text1 | DataSource | Data1 |
| Text1 | DataField | AU_ID |
| Text2 | DataSource | Data1 |
| Text2 | DataField | Author |

\*Provide the full path to this file, which should be in the Visual Basic directory—usually C:\VB.

6. Add the following code to the General Declarations section of Form1:

```
Const PAGEUP = 1
Const PAGEDOWN = 2
Const Records_per_Page = 10
```

7. Add the following procedure to Form1:

```
Sub Page (RecSet As Dynaset, ByVal iDirection As Integer, ByVal
  Records As Integer)
Dim dsClone As Dynaset
Dim i As Integer
'Copy the visible recordset. This is necessary so that you can
'move through the clone recordset without displaying each record.
Set dsClone = RecSet.Clone()
'Set the current record of the cloned recordset to the current
'record of the visible recordset.
dsClone.Bookmark = RecSet.Bookmark
'Scroll up or down N number of records in the cloned recordset.
i = 1
Do While i <= Records And Not dsClone.EOF And Not dsClone.BOF
If iDirection = PAGEUP Then
dsClone.MovePrevious
Else
dsClone.MoveNext
End If
i = i + 1
Loop
'If the above loop caused a BOF or EOF condition, move to the
'beginning or end of the recordset as appropriate.
If dsClone.BOF And iDirection = PAGEUP Then
dsClone.MoveFirst
ElseIf dsClone.EOF And iDirection = PAGEDOWN Then
dsClone.MoveLast
End If
'Change the bookmark of the visible record set to the bookmark
'of the desired record. This makes the current record of the
'visible recordset match the record moved to in the cloned
'dynaset. The fields of the record are displayed in the data
'bound controls without displaying any intervening records.
```

```
RecSet.Bookmark = dsClone.Bookmark
End Sub
```

8. Add the following code to the Command1_Click event for Form1:

```
Sub Command1_Click ()
'Scroll up 10 records in the recordset associated with Data1
Page Data1.RecordSet, PAGEUP, Records_per_Page
End Sub
```

9. Add the following code to the Command2_Click event for Form1:

```
Sub Command2_Click ()
'Scroll down 10 records in the recordset associated with Data1
 Page Data1.RecordSet, PAGEDOWN, Records_per_Page
End Sub
```

10. From the Run menu, choose Start (ALT, R, S), or press F5 to run the program. Click the "Page Up" or "Page Down" button to scroll up or down in 10-record increments. Change the value of Records_per_Page to modify the pagesize.

# Q: I have VC++ and VBWIN Pro. Do I still need the Visual Control Pack?

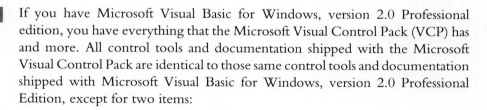

If you have Microsoft Visual Basic for Windows, version 2.0 Professional edition, you have everything that the Microsoft Visual Control Pack (VCP) has and more. All control tools and documentation shipped with the Microsoft Visual Control Pack are identical to those same control tools and documentation shipped with Microsoft Visual Basic for Windows, version 2.0 Professional Edition, except for two items:

1. A new copy of the MSCOMM.VBX Custom Control that works with Visual C++, version 1.0

2. Enhanced Control Development Kit (CDK) documentation, with helpful hints on creating Custom Controls for use with Microsoft Visual C++, version 1.0

The Microsoft Visual Control Pack is shipped with a newer MSCOMM.VBX Custom Control. This newer MSCOMM.VBX Custom Control was slightly enhanced to work with Microsoft Visual C++, version 1.0. It does not work any differently or any better that the old one when used in the Visual Basic for Windows, version 2.0 product.

If you have Visual C++, version 1.0 and currently own Microsoft Visual Basic for Windows, version 2.0 Professional Edition, you can get a free copy of the new MSCOMM.VBX Custom Control from Microsoft Visual Basic Product Support (206-646-5105).

The documentation for the CDK shipped with the VCP is a slightly enhanced version of the documentation for the CDK that was shipped with Microsoft Visual Basic for Windows, version 2.0 Professional Edition. This slightly enhanced version of the CDK documentation has some helpful hints on how to create Custom Controls for use with both Microsoft Visual Basic for Windows, version 2.0 and Microsoft Visual C++, version 1.0.

This slightly enhanced CDK documentation was also shipped as part of the April 1993 release of the Microsoft Developer Network (MSDN) CD.

**note:** *The new MSCOMM.VBX Custom Control and the enhanced CDK documentation are included in Microsoft Visual Basic for Windows, version 3.0 Professional Edition.*

## Q: I have multiple .DLL and .VBX files. Which ones should I use?

Because many Windows applications (and Windows itself) use .DLL and .VBX files (Custom Controls used by application created with Microsoft Visual Basic or Microsoft Visual C++), you may end up with multiple files with the same name in different directories.

This can be a problem when running various Windows applications, since a previously loaded application could be using a .DLL or .VBX file that is a later version of one required by another Windows application. You need to make sure that your applications are using the most recent version of a .DLL and/or .VBX file.

If you have multiple .DLL and/or .VBX files with the same name and in different directories, follow these steps:

1. Check the Data/Time stamp on each of these files.

2. Remove the older of these files, and retain the more recent copies.

3. Place the more recent copies of these files in your \WINDOWS\SYSTEM directory.

This will insure that your Windows application, and Windows itself, is using the most recent version of a given .DLL and/or .VBX file.

# Index

## G